THE
GREAT WAR

UNSEEN ARCHIVES

THE
GREAT WAR

UNSEEN ARCHIVES

Rare and unseen photographs and facsimile reports
The complete story of the First World War

———◆———

ROBERT HAMILTON

Photographs from the Daily Mail

ATLANTIC
PUBLISHING

Published by Atlantic Publishing in 2014

Atlantic Publishing
38 Copthorne Road, Croxley Green
Hertfordshire, WD3 4AQ, UK

Photographs and Newspaper facsimilies
© Daily Mail Archive, Associated Newspapers

Additional photographs © Getty Images:
144 bottom, 145 bottom, 149 bottom, 173 bottom, 174 bottom,
184 bottom, 253 top and bottom, 254 bottom, 256 bottom, 258 bottom,
259 bottom, 261 bottom, 308 , 363, 370 bottom, 375, 377, 378, 429.

ISBN 978-1-909242-33-3
(Also available in the USA from Welcome Rain: ISBN 978-1-56649-391-8)

Printed in China

Key to Maps

Military Units – Types

- ✉ Infantry
- ◩ Armoured
- ⌒ Airborne
- ⬚ Parachute
- • Artillery

Military Units – Size

XXXXX	Army Group	X	Brigade
XXXX	Army	III	Regiment
XXX	Corps	II	Battalion
XX	Division	I	Company

Military Movements

- → Attack
- ⇢ Retreat
- ✛ Aircraft
- ✳ Explosion
- ⊕ Airfield

Geographical Symbols

Buildings		Railway		Canal		Marsh/swamp
Urban area		River		Border		Rocks and beach
Road		Seasonal river		Bridge or pass		Woodland

The contemporary maps in this book were specially drawn for publication at
the time and were prepared from the official reports as they were published
on a daily basis. They give a perspective on how the public would have
followed the progress of the war. The colour maps drawn for this book are
from today's historical perspective. The key for these maps is shown above.

Acknowledgements:
Research: Alan Pinnock
Newspaper photography: Harry Chambers
Contemporary Maps: Malcolm Swanston
Editorial production: Alison Gauntlett
Chronology: Jane Benn
Design: John Dunne
Production: Cliff Salter

Thanks to:
The team at Associated Newspapers
without whose help this book would not
have been possible. Particular thanks to:
Alan Pinnock, Rachel Swanston, Ray Archer
and Jonathan Baines.
Thanks also to: Sarah Rickayzen,
Ruth Wiseman, Lyn Mellor, Josh Rickayzen
and Mel Cox.

Contents

Chapter One

1914

The Road to War

Chapter Two

1915

A Deepening Stalemate

Chapter Three

1916

Trench Warfare

Chapter Four

1917

A World War

The War to end all Wars

The First World War shaped the world we inhabit. It pitted the mightiest imperial powers against one another in a four-year-long struggle and left the map of Europe redrawn. Over 15 million lives were lost, the number of wounded dwarfing even that figure. Nor were the risks borne solely by those in uniform, for this was a "total war" where civilians also perished. Few families were left untouched.

An assassin's bullet provided the spark to a global conflagration without precedent, but war was in the air long before the heir to the Austro-Hungarian empire was struck down by a Serbian nationalist on 28 June 1914. Long-standing pacts and alliances had created two great power blocs, and an arms race had been ongoing since the early years of the new century. Once the Habsburg rulers, with German backing, decided to bring Serbia to heel over the outrage, the stage was set for a cataclysmic showdown. Kaiser Wilhelm II knew that Russia would not stand idly by while Serbia suffered, and that meant war with France, Russia's treaty ally. As party to a Triple Entente with France and Russia, Britain's position was less clear, but once the German army violated neutral Belgium, the die was cast. Britain, said Prime Minister Herbert Asquith, would not "sheath the sword" until that country was liberated, and "the military domination of Prussia is wholly and finally destroyed".

Patriotic fervour and thoughts of a short, glorious war soon vanished as the opposing armies became mired in a deadlocked struggle. Fighting took place as far afield as Africa, the Far East and the south Atlantic, but striking a knockout blow in the European theatre was the preoccupation of the rival strategists. It was easier said than done, for in trench warfare holding the line was one thing, attacking an entirely different proposition; the bloodbaths of the Somme and Ypres bore ample testament to that. New technologies, including aircraft, tanks, submarines and chemical weapons, expanded the field of martial combat, providing fresh challenges and opportunities; new avenues for sacrifice and heroism.

The Great War: Unseen Archives, provides a comprehensive narrative and pictorial guide to the conflict that was meant to be "the war to end all wars". The important battles, strategic decisions and turning points are described in detail, while contemporary maps show the terrain fought over inch by inch; the same maps pored over by a concerned public wondering how their loved ones were faring. Over 1,000 photographs tell their own graphic story of how the Great War played out in all its theatres, and a day-by-day chronology provides an instant reference point for assessing the course of the conflict through its key events. There are also over 500 contemporaneous newspaper articles showing how matters at the front were reported for home consumption. It is illuminating to compare the objective accounts with the sanitised offerings sanctioned by the Press Bureau. On 3 July 1916, two days after British forces sustained 60,000 casualties on the first day of the Somme offensive, *The Times* spoke of a "well planned advance, not marred by any vain and headlong rushes," adding, "the broad results so far are extremely favourable". Controlling the dissemination of information was deemed every bit as important as commanding a million-strong army. Soldiers' letters were rigorously scrutinised and censored,

putatively to prevent security breaches that might assist the enemy, but chiefly to ensure that the official line went unchallenged. Massaging the truth was a small price to pay for maintaining morale, a prime imperative in time of war.

The major figures – men such as Haig, Foch, Pershing, Hindenburg and Ludendorff – naturally take centre stage; but the cast for this human tragedy extends far beyond the senior commanders. The exploits of T E Lawrence, Edith Cavell and the Red Baron are recounted, along with lesser known examples of unstinting valour and service. Men such as Albert Ball and Billy Bishop, both prominent among the new breed of fighter aces. Men such as Walter Tull and Percy Jeeves, sporting stars who excelled in a very different arena from that they were used to. Men such as Wild Bill Donovan and Alvin York, American heroes whose remarkable stories were turned into Hollywood movies.

The unsung majority, of course, were the regulars, volunteers and conscripts who did their bit without fanfare or recognition. Many enlisted together and died together under the "Pals" scheme, quietly dropped as the repercussions on communities became grimly manifest. The Tommies dutifully accepted appalling conditions, some even finding a camaraderie and sense of purpose that may have been absent from their normal lives. There was resignation, with gallows humour a common coping strategy. "We're here because we're here because we're here," they sang ad nauseam, to the tune of Auld Lang Syne. Adversity spawned rich creativity. The poetry of Owen, Sassoon and their ilk is well known, but there was also a frontline newspaper, written by men of the ranks for their peers, which offered a poignant and often darkly funny perspective. In one edition an infantryman advertises his billet, a "cheap,

desirable residence" offering "good shooting". The trenches were a source of linguistic exchange as well as verminous infestation. "Lousy", "bumf" and "cushy" were some of the words that became part of everyday vocabulary. And of course, it was unwise to "put your head above the parapet", unless you had a particular wish to be "pushing up the daisies".

Anything that helped maintain spirits was encouraged, but threats to order could not be tolerated. The disciplinary code was severe, and took little account of nervous disorders. At home, the interrogation of those claiming exemption from conscription on grounds of conscience was also frequently intolerant. Men in civilian garb might be accosted in the street and handed a white feather by strangers who had no idea of their personal circumstances. One recipient was a Victoria Cross winner. Notwithstanding that faux pas, the contribution made on the home front was no less important, for this was a war of industrial production as well as frontline battles; a war in which Britain and Germany each sought to exert an economic stranglehold on the other. Women still striving for equal voting rights took on new workplace roles as the menfolk put on khaki. The spectre of a German victory required the mobilisation of all available resources.

The last combatants of World War One have passed on, joining the less fortunate "lost generation". But the legacy of this century-defining clash, a thread running through the rise of Nazism, the 1939-45 conflict and the Cold War, is still with us. This authoritative volume seeks to illuminate a momentous period in world history, whose ability to prompt impassioned debate and divide opinion is undiminished.

Chapter One

1914

The Road to War

Europe in 1914 was a continent of dynasties and power blocs. With the Ottoman Empire in terminal decline, there were five major players on the European stage: Great Britain, Russia, Austria-Hungary, Germany and France. George V, the second son of Edward VII, acceded to the British throne in 1910, continuing the Hanoverian line which dated back to 1714. Tsar Nicholas II, of the Romanov dynasty, ruled over the vast Russian Empire, as he had since 1894. The Habsburg Emperor Franz Josef I had presided over the Dual Monarchy of Austria-Hungary since 1867. Kaiser Wilhelm II headed the German Empire, having succeeded the Iron Chancellor, Otto von Bismarck, in 1888. Raymond Poincaré, the President of France, led the only republic among the continent's chief power brokers. The First World War would be ignited by an assassin's bullet in Sarajevo on 28 June 1914, but it was the relations between these five powers which held the key. Alliances and enmities that were forged long before that fateful day in the Bosnian capital were the difference between yet another local Balkan difficulty and a worldwide conflagration.

The German Empire was the youngest of Europe's great imperial powers, and its founding sowed the seeds for resentment which would be crystallised in the Great War. The new Reich was formed following a glorious victory in the Franco-Prussian War of 1870-71 when the Prussian Army, backed by Germany, had marched into Paris and exacted a heavy price for peace from the vanquished French: £200 million in reparations and the secession of the provinces Alsace and Lorraine.

France thus had good reason to despise and mistrust her neighbour, and over the next forty years Britain would come to be equally wary. For in that time Germany rapidly developed into a potent industrial and military power. The Kaiser, a neurotic megalomaniac who was invariably photographed in full military regalia, did little to assuage the concerns of countries which feared aggression. Wilhelm cast covetous eyes around him and the chief objects of his envy were Russia and Britain, the latter possessor of an empire on which the sun famously never set. The competitive friction which grew between these nations was not ameliorated by the fact that Kaiser Wilhelm, King George V and Tsar Nicholas II were first cousins. Familial ties would count for nothing when it came to choosing allies and underwriting the security of other sovereign states.

Alliances – and Anticipation

Suspicion and resentment were rife in the east of the continent, too. Austria-Hungary and Russia were hardly on more cordial terms, and once again the ill-feeling had grown over a number of years. At issue was the fact that Franz Josef's disparate empire included Slavs of the Balkan states, with whom Russia had a natural kinship. Relations between the Austro-Hungarian and Russian empires had been severely strained since the former's annexation of Bosnia and Herzegovina in October 1908. Russia wasn't prepared to go to war over the issue, however, much to the chagrin of another Balkan country with burning nationalistic ambitions, Serbia. Not only did the Serbs fear that their own land might also be swallowed up by Austria-Hungary, but their hopes for a pan-Slavic state was looking an increasingly distant prospect. Serbia realised it could not take on Franz Josef's mighty empire alone and was forced to accept the status quo. It was a climb-down, one which could only act as a recruiting sergeant for the Black Hand, the secret society committed to the formation of a greater Serbian state. The passion its members held for the cause, and the lengths they were prepared to go to in order to serve it, were encapsulated in the society's motto: "Unity or Death". This fanaticism was to be the spark for a continent that was waiting to explode.

The tensions across Europe in the early years of the twentieth century made national security a key issue. Isolation meant possible exposure and vulnerability; dependable allies were needed. Austria-Hungary and Germany had formed an alliance in 1879. They were joined by Italy, whose antipathy to France made that country's decision largely a negative one. Thus was created a powerful central European axis, a state of affairs which exercised the diplomatic minds in London, Paris and St Petersburg. France and Russia had formed a defensive Dual Alliance in 1893, leaving Britain to decide on its position.

European tinder-box

At the turn of the century there were those in the British government who favoured an accommodation with the continent's most powerful, and potentially most dangerous, opponent: Germany. Overtures were made but they came to nothing, so Britain turned to France. These traditional enemies had clashed as recently as 1898, almost going to war over a territorial dispute in Sudan. Relations thawed after Edward VII's state visit to Paris in May 1903. It was a triumphant charm offensive, and by the time the monarch left the French crowds were cheering "notre Roi". This smoothed the way for the diplomats to get to work, and on 8 April 1904 the two countries signed a historic agreement. The Entente Cordiale, as it came to be known, dealt primarily with outstanding issues between the two in distant corners of the globe. Significantly, it was a friendly understanding, not a formal alliance; neither country was under any obligation to support the other in time of war. But it was a watershed moment in terms of dividing the continent into two rival camps. And three years later, when Britain settled its long-standing differences with Russia, the battle lines were delineated more clearly still. The signing of the Anglo-Russian Convention in August 1907 paved the way for the Triple Entente, a formidable potential threat to the Triple Alliance of Austria-Hungary, Germany and Italy. Crucially, it also meant that if war did ensue, the countries of the Triple Alliance would have enemies on both eastern and western fronts.

Across Europe many tried to anticipate the flashpoint which would be the precursor to a wider conflict. Some eagerly awaited it. The continent had not seen war for forty years, denying states and individuals the opportunity to cover themselves in military glory, to test might and mettle. Those who felt it would be a relief for the waiting to end almost got their wish in 1911, when France and Germany clashed over their respective interests in Morocco. But although sabres were rattled, the Powers chose peace over escalation. Restraint was also shown in 1912-13, when two Balkan wars were fought. Then, on 28 June 1914, the tinder-box was ignited.

Archduke Franz Ferdinand, the 51-year-old nephew of Franz Josef and heir to the Habsburg throne, was well aware of the potential danger of his visit to Sarajevo. There had been previous assassination attempts by disaffected Bosnian Serbs, and for his well-publicised trip through the streets of the capital that June day he wore a jacket of a specially woven fabric that was thought to be bullet-proof. Franz Ferdinand had a reforming zeal for this part of the Austro-Hungarian Empire. Oppression of the Serb population would end under his leadership, but that was a future prospect; for now his intention was to win over the people – but to take suitable precautions just in case. Ironically, the Archduke's moderation

Right: **Germany's hopes for a short, victorious war were dashed after the invasion of northern France failed to sustain the momentum vital to the success of the Schlieffen Plan.**

helped to galvanise the Black Hand into action. If oppression had fanned the flames of Serbian nationalism, a more tolerant incumbent of the Austro-Hungarian throne might dampen the ardent desire of those committed to see a Greater Serbia established. From the moment the Archduke's visit to Sarajevo had been announced, the Black Hand had got to work in earnest.

Assassination in Sarajevo

In the event, the seven-strong assassination squad had fortune on their side. After a failed attempt to blow up the car carrying the Archduke and his consort Sophie, it seemed that the gang had lost their chance. But as one of their number, 19-year-old Gavrilo Princip, was pondering his next move, he was confronted by his target. The driver of the Archduke's car had taken a wrong turn, and Princip turned his 22-calibre Browning pistol on its occupants. Franz Ferdinand was struck in the neck; Sophie, who was pregnant with their fourth child, took a bullet to the stomach. Both were soon declared dead.

Austria-Hungary immediately decided that the trail of guilt led to Belgrade and determined to exact a high price from Serbia over the events in Sarajevo. The Habsburg Empire was outraged by the murders, but it wanted more than mere revenge; this was a perfect pretext to teach Serbia a lesson. If the Serbs were crushed and humbled, it would consolidate an empire that was in danger of becoming fractured.

With Russia, long-standing friend of the Serbs, waiting in the wings, Austria-Hungary sought assurances from its chief ally, Germany. The bellicose, unstable Kaiser sanctioned any action that Franz Josef's government saw fit to take against Serbia. He couldn't risk Austria-Hungary falling to a two-pronged attack, from Serbia in the south and Russia in the east. Moreover, Wilhelm may have calculated that if a European war was imminent, then it might as well be fought at a time of Germany's choosing. And Germany was ready now.

On 23 July the Austrian government issued an ultimatum to Serbia. Its very specific demands and the imposition of a forty-eight-hour time limit for a reply prompted Britain's Foreign Secretary, Sir Edward Grey, to remark that, if Serbia accepted, it would be "the greatest humiliation I have ever seen a country undergo". Yield Serbia did, but not to the letter of the demand, not to the point of threatening its very existence as an autonomous independent state. Austria-Hungary was spoiling for a fight; on 28 July war on Serbia was formally declared.

Russia initially tried to steer a narrow course, caught between a desire to support her Serb brothers whilst not antagonising Germany. Partial mobilisation – against Austria-Hungary alone was considered, but this proved unworkable. On 31 July Germany issued Russia with an ultimatum of its own: to cease mobilisation forthwith. No reply came and the following day Germany declared war on its eastern neighbour.

Alliances on the Eve of War
July 1914

Austro-German Alliance, 1879–1918

Triple Alliance, 1882–1915

Franco-Russian Alliance, 1894–1917

Triple Entente, 1907–1917

Varying independence and nationalist movements sponsored by Russia, 1879–1914

Sympathetic to Central Powers

Sympathetic to Entente Powers

Neutrality internationally guaranteed

Neutral

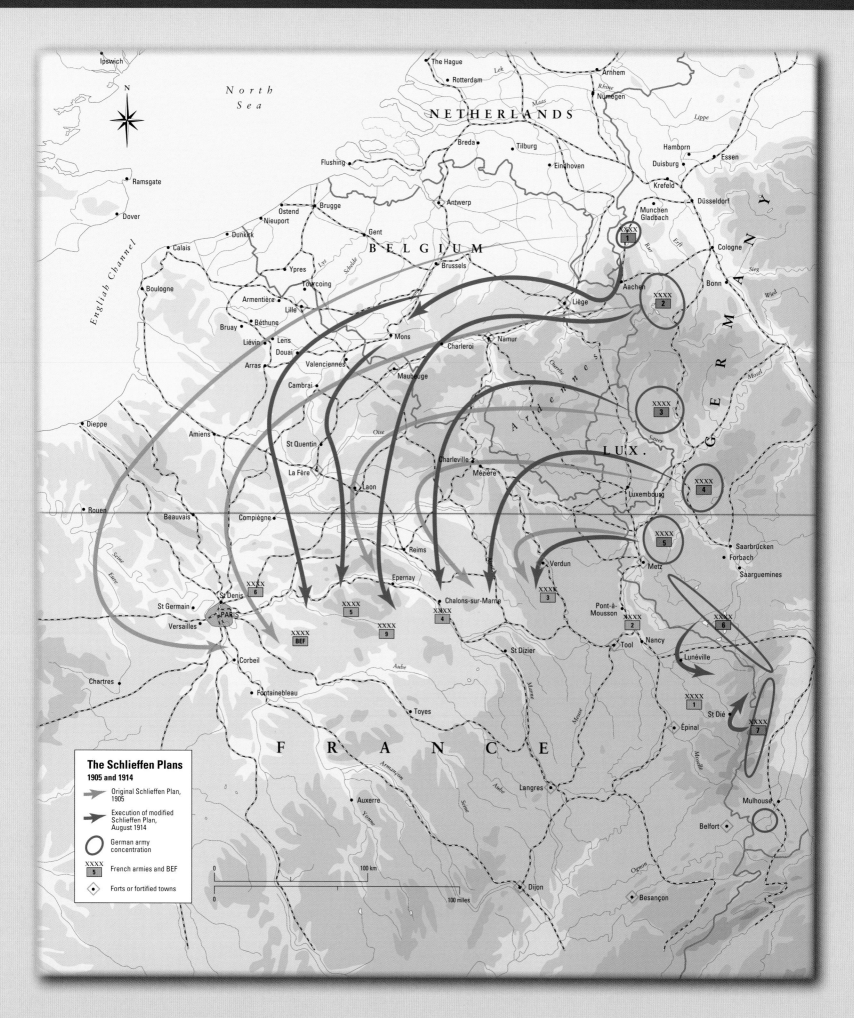

The Schlieffen Plans
1905 and 1914

→ Original Schlieffen Plan, 1905

➡ Execution of modified Schlieffen Plan, August 1914

◯ German army concentration

XXXX
5   French armies and BEF

◇ Forts or fortified towns

Top left: **Tsar Nicholas II with his wife Alix of Hesse and their five children in 1913.** It was Russia's decision to stand with Serbia against Austria-Hungary that led to Germany to declare war on its eastern neighbour on 1 August.

Top middle: **After Edward's death in 1910, his son George (right) became king.** George V, the Kaiser and Tsar Nicholas II of Russia were descendants of Queen Victoria and first cousins. They were on friendly terms although the unpredictable Wilhelm II dominated the family relationships.

Top right: **The Kaiser captured in 1905 in his customary full military regalia.** He ascended the German throne in 1888 and quickly cast aside the shrewd 'Iron Chancellor' Otto Von Bismarck. He replaced Bismarck's conservative foreign policy, which had emphasised diplomacy and an avoidance of conflict, with a rash and belligerent quest for glory.

Above left: **King Edward VII with his nephew Kaiser Wilhelm II of Germany (right), Princess Alice of Battenberg and Maria of Russia.** Edward was often referred to as the "uncle" of Europe as he was related to most of the European monarchs. His relationship with Wilhelm was often strained, with the English king preferring peace to aggression.

Above right: **President Woodrow Wilson is inaugurated as the 28th President of the United States of America in March 1913.** When war broke out the following year he immediately declared the country's neutrality.

Right: **Former US President Theodore Roosevelt with Wilhelm II on the Döberitz military training field in May 1910.** Roosevelt, who had won the Nobel Peace Prize in 1906 for his part in settling the Russo-Japanese War, reportedly found the German leader "vain as a peacock".

Right: A peaceful scene in Piccadilly Circus in 1900. At the time Britain was fighting in the Second Boer War and after its conclusion in 1902, changed her foreign policy to ensure she built up more solid relationships with her Allies, making pacts with France, Russia and Japan.

Below right: The funeral cortège of Queen Victoria enters Paddington Station in February 1901. She had reigned for sixty-three years and was succeeded by her son Edward VII.

Below far right: Edward VII's coronation celebrations in August 1902. During his brief reign he was very supportive of army and naval reforms but was also active in forming treaties between Britain, France and Russia.

Opposite above left: Stanley Spencer's airship was exhibited at the Ranelagh Air Show in 1903. In the same year the Zeppelin *LZ2* was launched; the forerunner of the Zeppelin airship used by Germany for reconnaissance work and bombing raids during World War I.

Opposite above middle: Shoppers in Regent Street in 1911. Around Europe tensions were starting to build with countries pledging loyalty to each other for protection.

Timeline of Events, 1870-1914, leading up to the declaration of war

1870 The Franco-Prussian War began signalling the rise of German military power and imperialism. It was provoked by German statesman Otto von Bismarck.

1871 The Treaty of Frankfurt was signed on 10 May after Paris was besieged and France capitulated. The treaty with Germany ended the Franco-Prussian War and led to the Unification of Germany. King Wilhelm I was proclaimed Kaiser and Otto van Bismarck became the first Chancellor of a united Germany.

1879 The Austro-German Alliance, also called the Dual Alliance, was a pact between Austria-Hungary and the German Empire in which the two powers pledged to help one another in case of an attack by Russia.

1881 The Three Emperors League was set up as an attempt to restore stability to Eastern Europe by linking Russia with the Dual Alliance of Austria-Hungary and Germany.

Austria-Hungary made an alliance with Serbia to prevent Russian aggression in Serbia with the Austro-Serbian Alliance of 1881.

1882 The Triple Alliance was established between Germany, Austria-Hungary and Italy.

The secret agreement was renewed periodically until the outbreak of World War I.

1888 After his father's untimely death, 29-year-old Crown Prince Wilhelm became ruler Kaiser Wilhelm II of Germany. Fifty-seven-year-old Frederick III had only reigned for 99 days.

1889 Beginning of the Anglo-German Naval Race which saw the build up of arms by both Britain and Germany.

1894 The Franco-Russian Alliance established a political and military pact between France and Russia. In the event of war, France wanted support against Germany, and Russia against Austria-Hungary.

26-year-old Nikolai Aleksandrovich Romanov was crowned Tsar Nicholas II of Russia after his father, Alexander III, died from liver disease.

1901 On 22 January, Great Britain's Queen Victoria, whose bloodline ran through most of the ruling houses of Europe, died. She was succeeded by her eldest son who became King Edward VII of Great Britain.

1902 Italy negotiated the Franco-Italian Agreement with France, a secret treaty under which Italy would remain neutral should Germany attack France.

Bulgaria allied itself with Russia in an attempt to ward off the possibility of Austro-Hungarian aggression in the Russo-Bulgarian Military Convention.

1904 The Entente Cordiale was agreed between France and Britain and signed on 8 April. The agreement resolved long-standing colonial disputes in North Africa and established a diplomatic understanding between the two countries.

1904 Japan issued a declaration of war to initiate the Russo-Japanese War. The conflict developed out of the rivalry between Russia and Japan for dominance in the Far East.

1905 On January 22 a group of peaceful demonstrators marched to present a petition to Tsar Nicholas II. Imperial forces opened fire on the demonstrators, killing and wounding hundreds. The "Bloody Sunday massacre" led to a series of strikes and riots which cost the Tsarist regime support among the workers and farmers.

Above far right: **Lord Haldane** (left) and Churchill in February 1912. Haldane was made Secretary of State for War in 1905 and engineered the Haldane Reforms, which established the British Expeditionary Force, the Territorial Force, the Imperial General Staff and the Officer Training Corps.

Below right: **A family begin their** holiday at Waterloo Station in May 1914. Only three months later, and ironically the day after August Bank Holiday, tensions in Europe reached their peak and Britain delivered its final ultimatum to Germany.

Below far right: **Lord and Lady** Churchill take a trip to Hendon. Appointed First Lord of the Admiralty in 1911, Churchill was a great believer in using aircraft in combat situations and was an advocate of modernisation. One of his first objectives in this new post was to instigate a programme to replace coal power with oil power in any new battleships built.

1905 The First Moroccan Crisis was sparked when Kaiser Wilhelm II arrived in Tangiers to declare his support for the sultan of Morocco, provoking the anger of France and Britain. The crisis worsened German relations with both France and the United Kingdom and led to a breakdown in trust between the major European powers.

1906 The arrival of Britain's first "dreadnought" class battleship, HMS *Dreadnought*, heralded a revolution in battleship design and represented a marked advance in naval technology.

1907 Signed on August 31, the Anglo-Russian Entente was an alliance in which Britain and Russia settled their colonial disputes in Persia, Afghanistan and Tibet. The agreement led to the formation of the Triple Entente.

1908 On October 6 Austria-Hungary announced its annexation of the dual provinces of Bosnia and Herzegovina in the Balkan region of Europe, formerly under the control of the Ottoman Empire.

1909 The annexation of Bosnia and Herzegovina changed the Russian perspective and led to the Raccogini Agreement, negotiated between Russia and Italy, which established a Russo-Italian commitment to the status quo in the Balkans.

1911 The Second Moroccan (Agadir) Crisis, was sparked by the deployment of French troops in Morocco. Germany reacted by sending the gunboat, Panther to the port of Agadir. The manoeuvres of Panther sparked hostility with the British who saw the gunboat's deployment as an attempt to establish a German naval base on Morocco's Atlantic coast.

1911 The Italo-Turkish war was started after Italy presented the Ottoman government with an ultimatum demanding that Italy be allowed to occupy Tripolitania and Cyrenacia.

1912 Britain and France drew up the Anglo-French Naval Convention, which promised British protection of France's coastline from German naval attack, and French defence of the Suez Canal.

The First Balkan War lasted from October 1912 until May 1913. The conflict began when Montenegro declared war on the Ottoman Empire. Serbia, Bulgaria and Greece soon followed suit, thus forming the Balkan League. The combined armies of the Balkan states overcame the Ottoman armies and achieved rapid success.

1913 The 28th President of the United States of America, Woodrow Wilson was privately sworn-in in the President's Room of the US Capitol on Sunday 4 March, with the public ceremonies a day later on Monday 5 March.

Albania's independence was recognized at an international summit of the six Great Powers at the Conference of London on 29 July following the successes of the Balkan League armies in the First Balkan War.

The Second Balkan War began when Serbia, Greece and Romania disagreed with Bulgaria over the spoils of the First Balkan War in Macedonia. Serbia and Greece formed an alliance against Bulgaria, and the war began in June when King Ferdinand of Bulgaria ordered his troops to attack Serbian and Greek forces in Macedonia.

After the Bulgarians were defeated in the Second Balkan War, The Treaty of Bucharest was signed on 10 August by the delegates of Bulgaria, Romania, Serbia, Montenegro and Greece. Under the terms of the treaty, Greece and Serbia divided up most of Macedonia between themselves, leaving Bulgaria with only a small part of the region.

Since the Ottoman Empire was not represented in the peace talks between Bulgaria and the other combatants, separate negotiations were held leading to The Treaty of Constantinople which was signed on 29 September at the Ottoman capital of Istanbul.

June/July 1914

28   The heir to the throne of the Austro-Hungarian Empire, the Archduke Franz Ferdinand and his wife were assassinated at Sarajevo by Serbian Nationalist Gavrilo Princip.

29   The Secretary of the Austro-Hungarian Legation at Belgrade sent a despatch to Vienna accusing Serbia of complicity in the assassination.

2   It was announced that the Kaiser would not attend the Archduke's funeral.

4   The funeral of Archduke Franz Ferdinand took place at Artstetten in Austria.

5   Kaiser Wilhelm II received a special envoy from the Austrian Emperor at Potsdam palace and promised full German support for Austria against Serbia.

7   Austria-Hungary convened a Council of Ministers, including Ministers for Foreign Affairs and War, the Chief of the General Staff and Naval Commander-in-Chief.

14   The Council of Austro-Hungarian Ministers finally determined on action against Serbia.

15   Hungarian Prime Minister Count Tisza made a statement in parliament concerning relations with Serbia insisting, "they must be cleared up".

17   Austria-Hungary reported that Serbia had called up 70,000 reservists and was preparing for war.

French politicians Raymond Poincaré and René Viviani left Paris to visit to Tsar Nicholas II in St Petersberg.

19   The Council of Austro-Hungarian Ministers approved the draft ultimatum to Serbia.

20   Austria-Hungary sent troops to the Serbian frontier.

21   Conferences were held at Ischl and Budapest to discuss Serbia.

The French Ambassador in Berlin, Jules Cambon, informed Paris of the first steps towards German mobilisation.

23   The Austro-Hungarian Government presented Serbia with an unconditional ultimatum demanding an answer within 48 hours.

24   The German Government submitted a note to Entente Governments approving the Austro-Hungarian ultimatum to Serbia.

The British Foreign Minister Sir Edward Grey initiated proposals for an international conference in order to avert war.

The Belgian Government declared that in the event of war Belgium would remain neutral.

25   The Serbian Government ordered a mobilisation of troops.

Austria-Hungary severed diplomatic relations with Serbia and began to mobilise its own forces.

The Serbian Government transferred from Belgrade to Nish.

Russia arranged for troops to be stationed on the Russo-Austrian frontier.

26   The Austro-Hungarian Government ordered partial mobilisation against Serbia.

The Montenegrin Government ordered mobilisation.

Kaiser Wilhelm II returned from the Baltic to Berlin.

Sir Edward Grey suggested a Conference of Ambassadors in London.

27   The French and Italian Governments accepted British proposals for an international conference.

The German High Seas Fleet was recalled from Norway to its war bases.

28   Emperor Franz Joseph of Austria-Hungary declared war on Serbia and Russia.

Russia began to mobilise her armed forces.

The German Government rejected British proposals for an international conference.

In his role as First Lord of the Admiralty Winston Churchill ordered the British Fleet to its war base at Scapa Flow.

29   The Russian Government ordered partial mobilisation against Austria.

Hostilities commenced between Austria-Hungary and Serbia: Belgrade was bombarded by Austrian artillery.

The German Government made proposals to secure British neutrality.

Churchill persuaded Asquith to authorize the "Warning Telegram" to all British naval stations warning that war was a possibility.

As part of extensive preparations German patrols crossed the French border.

30   The Tsar signed the order for the mobilisation of Russian army.

The British Government rejected German proposals for British neutrality. Prime Minister Herbert Asquith gave a speech in House of Commons.

The Australian Government placed the Australian Navy at the disposal of the British Admiralty.

31   Russia announced general mobilisation.

Austria-Hungary ordered general mobilisation including men up to 50 years old.

The German Government declared Kriegsgefahrsustand (imminent-danger-of-war) and sent an ultimatum to Russia to halt mobilization within 24 hours.

The Turkish Government ordered mobilisation.

The Belgian army was mobilised.

The London Stock Exchange was closed as the crisis escalated.

Top: The teenage princes, Edward, right, and Albert, with their sister Mary at Balmoral just before the outbreak of war. Prince Albert (later to become George VI) saw action at the great naval battle of Jutland and was mentioned in dispatches for his actions aboard HMS *Collingwood*. As the future heir to the throne Edward was not allowed to fight on the front line but visited the trenches whenever possible and was consequently awarded a Military Cross in 1916.

Above: King George V and Queen Mary with their French counterparts, President and Madame Poincaré.

DAILY MAIL JUNE 29, 1914

Murder of the Austrian heir and his wife

WE REGRET TO STATE that the Archduke Francis Ferdinand, the heir to the throne of Austria-Hungary, and his morganatic wife, the Duchess of Hohenberg, were assassinated yesterday.

The assassination took place at Sarajevo, the capital of Bosnia, which State, together with Herzegovina, was annexed by Austria-Hungary from Turkey in 1908. Bosnia, which is bounded on the south by Montenegro and Servia, has a large Slav population that is discontented with Austrian rule.

The Archduke had paid no heed to warnings to him not to go to Bosnia on account of the disturbed state of the province. Anti-Austrian demonstrations were made before his arrival at Sarajevo on Saturday. Two attempts were made to kill the Archduke and his wife at Sarajevo yesterday. The first failed; the second was only too successful.

A 21-year-old printer of Servian nationality living in Herzegovina threw a bomb at the Archduke's motor-car in the street. The Archduke deflected the bomb with his arm. It fell to the ground and exploded. The heir to the throne and his wife escaped, but a number of other people were injured, six of them seriously.

A little while later the Archduke and his wife were driving to see the victims of the bomb explosion, when a schoolboy aged 19, apparently also of Servian nationality, threw at them a bomb which, however, did not explode, and then fired at them with a Browning automatic pistol. Both were wounded and both died shortly afterwards.

The assassination of Archduke Franz Ferdinand in Bosnia's capital gave Austria-Hungary the excuse it needed to give Serbia a bloody nose.

Main image: Archduke Franz Ferdinand, heir presumptive to the Austria-Hungarian throne, and his family.

Bottom left: On 28 June, during a visit to Sarajevo, the Archduke and his wife Sophie arrive for a reception at the City Hall. An attempt to blow up their official car earlier in the day had failed.

Top left: A few hours later they leave the building. Gavrilo Princip, a member of the Serbian Black Hand, grasped an unexpected opportunity when the car took an unscheduled detour, shooting the couple and killing them instantly.

August 1914

1   The British Government ordered naval mobilisation.

The German Government ordered general mobilisation and declared war on Russia.

Hostilities commenced on the Polish frontier.

French military mobilisation was ordered.

Italy and Belgium announced their intention to remain neutral.

2   The German Government sent an ultimatum to Belgium demanding passage through Belgian territory.

German troops invaded Luxembourg.

Hostilities began on the French frontier near Belfort.

The British Government guaranteed naval protection of French coasts against German aggression in the English Channel.

3   The Belgian Government refused German demands. King Albert I of Belgium appealed to King George V for diplomatic intervention.

The British Government guaranteed armed support to Belgium should Germany violate Belgian neutrality.

Germany declared war on France.

The British Government ordered a general mobilisation of troops.

Grand Duke Nicholas was appointed Commander-in-Chief of the Russian armies.

4   The British Government sent an ultimatum to Germany to stand down from hostilities. A state of war was declared at 11.00 p.m. when they failed to comply.

Belgium severed diplomatic relations with Germany.

Germany declared war on Belgium.

German troops crossed the Belgian frontier and attacked Liège in the first battle action on the Western Front as the Battle and Siege of Liège began.

5   Montenegro declared war on Austria-Hungary .

The German minelayer Königin Luise was sunk as she attempted to lay mines off the British coast in the first German naval loss of the war.

6   Austria-Hungary declared war on Russia.

Serbia declared war on Germany.

Field-Marshal Earl Kitchener was appointed as Secretary of State for War in Great Britain.

The Royal Navy cruiser HMS Amphion was sunk by a German mine in the North Sea.

7   The city of Liège was occupied by German forces.

The first members of the British Expeditionary Force landed in France.

French troops invaded Alsace.

8   Montenegro severed diplomatic relations with Germany.

In the West African Campaign, British and French forces crossed the frontier of Togoland and occupied the capital city of Lome.

The Swiss Government mobilised and proclaimed a state of siege.

9   Montenegro declared war on Germany.

The cruiser HMS Birmingham sank the German submarine U-15 in the North Sea.

10 France severed diplomatic relations with Austria-Hungary.

11 The German warships Goeben and Breslau entered the Dardanelles.

Lord Kitchener began a recruiting campaign with his "Your King and Country Need You" poster, calling for men aged between 19 and 30 to enlist for Kitchener's New Army.

12 Great Britain declared war on Austria-Hungary .

13 Austrian forces crossed the River Drina and began the invasion of Serbia.

13 The first four squadrons of the Royal Flying Corps flew from Dover to France.

Fate of the Black Hand conspirators

Gavrilo Princip – the man who fired the shot that precipitated the march to war – was soon in police custody, his attempt to commit suicide thwarted. Already suffering from tuberculosis, Princip had been more than willing to strike a blow against Serbia's imperial oppressor, then end his own life. Now he would have to answer for his actions in a court of law. Nedjelko Cabrinovic was also in police hands. He, too, was terminally ill; he, too, had tried to take his own life after seeing the bomb he threw at the archduke's car miss its target. Both had been issued with cyanide capsules that failed to act.

Princip and Cabrinovic maintained their vow of silence in the face of severe interrogation. Suspicion that Serbia was behind the attack remained just that. The picture changed when a third conspirator, Danilo Ilic, was tracked down and arrested. Ilic's nerve failed him and he turned informer. One of the seven-strong gang evaded capture; the other six were tried and convicted in October 1914.

"We are not criminals," Cabrinovic told the court. "We are honest people. We wanted to do good and we shall die for our ideals." An equally defiant Princip welcomed his fate and martyrdom. "I suggest you nail me to a cross and burn me alive. My flaming body will be a torch to light my people on their path to freedom."

He was not to be granted his wish to go out in a blaze of glory, for the law of the land decreed that no person under the age of 20 could be given a death sentence. Princip was born in 1894, but as there was doubt as to whether he was 19 or 20 when he fired the fatal shots, the court handed down a 20-year jail sentence. Princip's illness meant he was never going to see out that term. He died in April 1918, a postman's son elevated to national hero for his sacrifice in advancing Serbian nationalism. Cabrinovic received the same sentence, but he, too, did not live to see the armistice.

Three of the remaining Black Hand confederates who were put on trial also received jail terms. The only member of the assassination squad to face the hangman's noose was 23-year-old Danilo Ilic, the man who had cooperated with the police in the hope of receiving more lenient treatment.

One of the seven-strong gang evaded capture; the other six were tried and convicted in October 1914.

A Strong Support

A Strong Support

The reviving, strength-giving power of OXO has received remarkable endorsement in the great war. It is invaluable for all who have to undergo exertion, either to promote fitness or to recuperate after fatigue.

OXO aids and increases nutrition; it stimulates and builds up strength to resist climatic changes; it is exactly suited to the needs of our men at the front, and in training, as well as for general use in the home.

OXO is made in a moment and, with bread or a few biscuits, sustains for hours.

A cup of OXO between meals is an efficient safeguard against Colds and Influenza.

Large numbers of the OXO staffs have joined His Majesty's Forces; wages at the rate of over £5,000 per annum are being paid to them or their dependents.

OXO

"ONLY BRITISH-MADE!"

Say all good Housewives, That's why they always buy

MAYPOLE MARGARINE

BRITISH-MADE from Choicest NUTS and MILK.

One Quality Only! 6D. A LB. The Very Best.

The Only Perfect Substitute for Butter.

Opposite: Crowds in Sarajevo try to attack the assassin Gavrilo Princip as police lead him away. The Serb nationalist then made a failed attempt to commit suicide but eventually died in prison four years later from tuberculosis.

Top: Britain's newly appointed Secretary of State for War Lord Kitchener (middle) with Lord Haldane (left), now the Lord Chancellor, outside the War Office.

Above right: In the weeks after the assassination tensions rapidly escalated, armies were mobilised, and on 4 August crowds gathered outside the War Office in Whitehall, London, waiting for news.

Above: Advertisers were quick to show support for the war effort.

DAILY MAIL JULY 25, 1914

European crisis

RUSSIA, APPARENTLY on the appeal of Servia, intervened yesterday in the crisis with Austria.

Causes of the Crisis.- The Austrian heir and his wife were murdered on June 28 at Sarajevo, capital of the Austrian province of Bosnia, by a Servian sympathiser. Servians are Slavs (i.e. of kin with Russians). Most of the Bosnians are Slavs. Pan-Servians dream of a 'Greater Servia' to include Austrian Slavs. Bulgaria is a Slav Czardom.

Austrian Demands. Austria has made 10 demands on Servia. The chief are:
1. A reply by 6 p.m. to-night.
2. Punishment of Servian accomplices in the assassinations at Sarajevo.
3. An end to 'Greater Servia' plots against Austria.
4. The publication in the front page of the Servian official journal to-day of an official apology for and condemnation of 'Greater Servia' dreams.

Count Berchtold, the Austrian Foreign Minister, to-day goes to Ischl, where the Emperor is, to await the Servian reply. If a satisfactory reply has not been given by 6 p.m. to-night the Austrian Minister in Belgrade, the Servian capital, has been ordered to leave Servia.

August 1914

14 The Russian Commander-in-Chief issued a proclamation promising autonomy to Poland.

15 The Japanese Government sent an ultimatum to Germany demanding evacuation of Tsingtau in Eastern China.

16 The last forts of Liège were captured by German forces.

17 The Serbs defeated the Austro-Hungarians at the Battle of the Cer (also known as the Battle of the Jadar River).

The Belgian Government transferred from Brussels to Antwerp.

19 The Battle of Cer ended.

French forces re-entered Mulhausen in the Alsace.

20 Brussels was evacuated as German forces occupied the city.

After the Battle of Gawaiten-Gumbinnen in Eastern Prussia the towns of Goldap and Lyck were occupied following the Russian victory.

Pope Pius X died in Rome.

21 The Battle of Charleroi between French and German troops was fought between the towns of Mons and Meuse.

German forces from German South-West Africa invaded British South Africa.

22 Austria-Hungary declared war on Belgium.

Part of the Battle of the Frontiers, the Battle of the Ardennes began.

23 The first major action for the British Expeditionary Force, the Battle of Mons began as a subsidiary of the Battle of the Frontiers, when the Allies fought with Germany on the French borders.

Germany severed diplomatic relations with Japan after Tsing-tau was blockaded by the Japanese.

Japan declared war on Germany.

24 The British Army retreated from Mons.

The Battle of the Ardennes ended with a German victory.

25 The fortified city of Namur was captured by German forces.

Mulhausen was again retaken by German forces and evacuated by the French.

The Austrian First Army defeated Russia at the First Battle of Krasnik.

Japan declared a "State of War" with Austria-Hungary.

26 The Belgian city of Louvain was burnt and looted by German troops.

At the Battle of Le Cateau the British Expeditionary Force suffered over 7000 casualties and was forced to retreat.

German and Russian forces clash in the Battle of Tannenberg

German forces in Togoland capitulated to the Allied forces and the town of Atakpame was occupied.

27 British Marines landed at Ostend accompanied by the Royal Naval Air Service.

Lille and Mezières were occupied by German forces.

Alexandre Millerand was appointed French Minister for War

28 In the Battle of Bight at Heligoland the German light cruisers *Köln*, *Mainz*, and *Ariadne* were sunk by the British Navy.

29 The First Battle of Guise (also known as the Battle of St Quentin) began when the French Fifth Army attacked the town of St Quentin in Northern France.

30 The First Battle of Guise ended with a tactical French victory.

Paris was bombed for the first time by German aircraft.

German Samoa was occupied by the New Zealand Expeditionary Force.

The Schlieffen Plan

On 3 August, a mere forty-eight hours after declaring war against Russia, Germany was also at war with Russia's ally, France. The Reich was far from idle during that period, however, for time was of the essence. Germany had long feared the prospect of war on both her eastern and western fronts and had contingency measures for just such an eventuality. The Schlieffen Plan, as it was called, involved a rapid strike to neutralise the threat from France, after which German forces could turn their full attention to Russia. Speed of action was critical to the plan's success. The full might of the German Army had to be in position on the eastern front before Russia was ready to fight. The geography of the latter country meant that there was a window of opportunity before it posed a threat to Germany. But it was a window which would soon be slammed shut. Accordingly, even before war was formally declared between Germany and France, German forces were on the march westwards.

Under the Schlieffen Plan, Germany aimed to attack France through Belgium, rather than directly across the border which the two countries shared. Not only was Belgium a neutral country, but both Germany and Great Britain were long-standing guarantors of that neutrality. The Kaiser was obviously quite prepared to disregard this commitment when faced with a greater prize. But what would Britain's stance be?

"England Expects . . . ."

Below: **The crowds around the War Office continued to gather. An ultimatum had been delivered to Germany earlier in the day and Britain finally declared a state of war on 4 August 1914, at 11pm.**

Above: **During the conflict the image of Britannia was frequently used for propaganda purposes to encourage feelings of patriotism and duty.**

Opposite above: **Scenes in Throgmorton Street, London, on the eve of the war.**

Opposite below: **Marble Arch in 1904. Many of the men in this photograph would eventually be destined for the front line.**

DAILY MAIL AUGUST 3, 1914

Great war begun by Germany

THE GERMAN GOVERNMENT declared war upon Russia at 7.30 on Saturday evening. There was still hope of peace when this action was taken. The Czar had pledged his word to the Kaiser that he would not mobilise or attack Austria while negotiations with her were in progress.

The German Army was active yesterday. It crossed the French frontier, without any declaration of war, at three distinct points. It invaded France at Longwy, 270 miles from London, close to the Luxemburg frontier; at Cirey, near Nancy; and at Delle, near Belfort.

German troops were last night in French territory.

Germany invades Belgium

Many powerful voices in Asquith's government were vehemently against Britain becoming sucked into a European conflict. Thorny domestic issues, notably the question of Home Rule for Ireland, provided a difficult enough agenda, and Britain was under no treaty obligation to take up arms. On 3 August the Belgian government rejected German demands to be allowed unhindered passage through their country. Albert, King of the Belgians, looked to Britain – and so did Germany. To the amazement of the German Chancellor, Theobald Bethmann-Hollweg, the Asquith government unequivocally chose to honour its commitment to Belgium. Germany's efforts to persuade Britain to stand aside while Belgium and France were invaded had come to nothing. The French were having grave doubts as to whether the Entente Cordiale would bring Britain to their aid; but in the event it was the violation of Belgium which dissolved almost all remaining opposition to war amongst the British Cabinet.

On 4 August it was Britain's turn to deliver an ultimatum, expiring at midnight that day. If German forces did not withdraw from Belgium, Britain would declare war. The deadline came and went. An incredulous Bethmann-Hollweg remarked: "Just for a scrap of paper Great Britain was going to make war on a kindred nation who desired nothing better than to be friends with her." If Germany had badly misjudged Britain, Sir Edward Grey was far more perceptive. While there was widespread euphoria among the peoples of all the belligerents in August 1914, Grey was in sombre mood: "The lamps are going out all over Europe; we shall not see them lit again in our lifetime."

> *"Just for a scrap of paper Great Britain was going to make war on a kindred nation who desired nothing better than to be friends with her."*

BRITISH ULTIMATUM TO GERMANY.

TO REPLY BY MIDNIGHT.

The Unsatisfactory Answers of Germany.

BELGIUM'S APPEAL.

In the House of Commons this afternoon Mr. Asquith announced the despatch by Britain of an ultimatum to Germany.

MR. ASQUITH SAID A TELEGRAM WAS SENT THIS MORNING BY SIR E. GREY TO THE BRITISH AMBASSADOR AT BERLIN INFORMING HIM OF THE

SUMMARY OF TO-DAY'S WAR NEWS.

It is reported, but not confirmed, that German and French warships have fought off Flamborough Head.

Germany is stated to have declared that if she considers it essential she will break through Belgian territory by force of arms.

German troops are said to have invaded Belgium.

A German company is reported to have reached Mars-la-Tour.

The British Government have been informed officially that German troops are in Belgium. At noon to-day the German Embassy issued a statement that no troops had crossed the frontier.

A correspondent says that Belgium may interrupt German communications by flooding the country on their invasion route.

The Commander-in-Chief of the French Army is on his way to the frontier.

The Cabinet sat from 11.30 to 1.35 p.m.

Lord Haldane is taking over Mr. Asquith's duties as Secretary of State for War till the Cabinet can find a way of relieving him.

It is reported that Lord Morley has resigned from the Cabinet. Mr. John Burns, it is said, also may re-

THE BULLYING OF BELGIUM.

Germany Prepared to Carry Through "Essential Measures" by Force of Arms.

AEROPLANE BOMBS.

FRENCH FRONTIER TOWN DAMAGED.

TURKEY THE LATEST POWER TO MOBILISE.

TO PAY?

DAILY MAIL AUGUST 3, 1914

British warning to Germany

WE UNDERSTAND that an intimation has been conveyed to the German Government to the effect that if a single German soldier is ordered to set foot on Belgian soil the British Navy will take instant action against Germany.

Germany has also seized a British liner at Kiel and a British collier at Brunsbuettel, near the canal.

The German Emperor officially ordered a mobilisation of the entire forces of Germany at 5.15 yesterday afternoon. Actually the German mobilization had been secretly begun three days ago, on July 31.

The French Government ordered the mobilisation of all its forces to begin at midnight of Saturday-Sunday. In seven or eight days the French armies, with a strength of at least 1,000,000 men, will be ready to fight on the frontier. Behind them will be other armies ready to give them all support.

Italy has intimated that she will not support Germany and Austria. Her treaty of alliance with them does not compel her to fight in a war of aggression. She was only bound to intervene if Germany and Austria were attacked without provocation. Italian neutrality will be maintained by a general mobilisation of the Italian forces.

BY THE KING.
A PROCLAMATION
REGARDING THE DEFENCE OF THE REALM.

GEORGE R.I.

WHEREAS by the law of Our Realm it is Our undoubted prerogative and the duty of all Our loyal subjects acting in Our behalf in times of imminent national danger to take all such measures as may be necessary for securing the public safety and the defence of Our Realm:

AND WHEREAS the present state of Public Affairs in Europe is such as to constitute an imminent national danger:

NOW, THEREFORE, WE strictly command and enjoin Our subjects to obey and conform to all instructions and regulations which may be issued by Us or Our Admiralty or Army Council, or any officer of Our Navy or Army, or any other person acting in Our behalf for securing the objects aforesaid, and not to hinder or obstruct, but to afford all assistance in their power to, any person acting in accordance with any such instructions or regulations or otherwise in the execution of any measures duly taken for securing those objects.

Given at Our Court at Buckingham Palace, this Fourth day of August, in the year of our Lord one thousand nine hundred and fourteen, and in the Fifth year of Our Reign.

GOD SAVE THE KING.

LONDON: Printed by EYRE AND SPOTTISWOODE, Ltd., Printers to the King's Most Excellent Majesty.

Opposite: **Crowds in Whitehall in patriotic spirit. In Westminster Prime Minister Herbert Asquith explained to a packed House of Commons that all negotiations to maintain peace with Germany had failed.**

Inset above and top: **On the outbreak of war Buckingham Palace issued a proclamation for the Defence of the Realm, which was read by the King of Arms from the steps of the Royal Exchange (top).**

Right: **Cheers and choruses of the National Anthem are heard outside Buckingham Palace all through the evening. Later that night the King and Queen, accompanied by Prince Edward and Princess Mary, make an appearance on the balcony to acknowledge and wave to the waiting crowds.**

Above right: **Lord Gordon Lennox leads the Second Grenadier Guards past Buckingham Palace soon after the outbreak of war. The country had prepared itself; the Grand Fleet was in its war station, and the Army mobilisation plans were fully in place.**

Many of the people in all the nations involved seem to have felt a kind of joy, even euphoria at this point. Sir Edward Grey was far more perceptive when he stated "The lamps are going out all over Europe; we shall not see them lit again in our lifetime".

READING THE WAR BULLETINS IN NEW YORK.

The "Times-square Debating Club" (see Page 4).

United !

England is mobilising her army to-day, and thanks to the statement made yesterday by Sir Edward Grey the whole world knows where our country stands and what her future action will be.

We stand pledged to guard the north and west coasts of France against hostile attack and to uphold the neutrality of Belgium with all the means in our power. Behind that pledge there will be found the authority of practically the whole nation whose confidence the Foreign Secretary unreservedly enjoys. True, there were protests during last night's debate in the House against the Government's decision, but they were voiced by little men whose crankiness is notorious, and Mr. Balfour did well to describe them as the dregs and lees of the debate. They have no significance, and not one of their authors would have the smallest chance of re-election if he appealed to his constituents.

Very different from the well-intentioned puerilities of the small if talkative peace-at-any-price section was Mr. Redmond's fine pronouncement on the attitude of the Irish Volunteers. The spectacle of these men standing shoulder to shoulder with their Ulster brethren in order to defend Ireland from invasion and permit the departure of the British troops elsewhere is one not only to raise enthusiasm in the breasts of Englishmen but very serious misgivings in those of our enemies, who have relied over-much on the supposed division of our forces at home.

Almost at the same moment comes Australia's splendid offer of 20,000 men to show that the Empire is behind us, and that wide as our dominions are our hearts beat together all the world over.

There is no longer any doubt of the ultimate issue, and grave as it is it will be faced by us as our fathers would have faced it, knowing our honour to be secure.

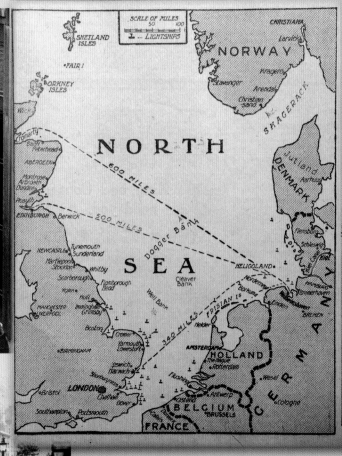

WHERE GERMANY IS INVADING FRANCE AND BELGIUM.

Opposite above: German Red Cross workers in Berlin receive flowers just before leaving for the front.

Opposite middle: Passers-by read the Royal proclamation posted on a building in Whitehall.

Opposite below: Crowds gathered around the Victoria Memorial outside the Palace cheer and sing through the night. Initially there seemed to be a sense of euphoria around the country.

Above: As the crowds in the capital began to disperse, patriotism was at its height and there was a general view that it would "all be over by Christmas".

Top: A workman removes the brass plate from the German Embassy. Hostile crowds had begun to gather outside on the day war was declared and the German ambassador Karl Max, Prince Lichnowsky, immediately returned to Germany. He had made valiant attempts to maintain peace between the two countries.

Above right: A map of the North Sea shows the position of Wilhelmshaven, the primary base for the German High Seas Fleet. The location of Dogger Bank and Heligoland, sites of two early sea battles of the conflict, can also be seen.

The Greatest Battle of All Time.

TWO MILLION

MEN.

French fortresses on the German frontier. They go into France—if they get there at all—by a side entrance. Then the nature of the Ardennes country heavily wooded as it is, largely discounts the assumed superiority of the French artillery by giving the troops shelter and concealment.
But there is disadvantages as well. To ... ammunition ... other supplies ... and complicates the sanitation and ...

At Sea.

HOW THEY SANK THE SUBMARINE.

Deadly Gunnery of H.M.S. Birmingham.

GERMAN WAR CHEST

"The People's Savings Will Be Taken First."

BERLIN, Wednesday.
The semi-official *Norddeutsche Allgemeine Zeitung* says:—

CAMERA SPY CAUGHT AT DOVER.

Sentry's Shot at Suspect Up a Telephone Pole.

[FROM OUR OWN CORRESPONDENT.]
Dover, Wednesday.

HELP THE QUEEN'S GUILD!

AN APPEAL TO OUR 40.000

Fighting begins – with German successes

The rival powers each anticipated a short, successful war. Bullish German troops posed next to road signs which read "To Paris"; equally bullish French troops did the same next to signs indicating the way to Berlin. This was hugely optimistic, if not flawed, thinking. Even if one of the protagonists succeeded in landing a heavy pre-emptive blow, it was never likely to result in capitulation. The reason was simple: this was a war of alliances. If, for example, France suffered grievously from a German onslaught under the Schlieffen Plan, she was hardly likely to yield as long as Britain and Russia stood by her side. And although Italy stood on the sidelines, refusing to take up arms with her Triple Alliance partners, Germany and Austria-Hungary also gained strength from the knowledge that they all stood together. In other words, the same alliances that had been triggered, domino-style, to bring Europe to war also militated against a quick victory for either side.

Even so, the Central Powers, as the German and Austro-Hungarian forces were known, received early encouragement. German forces swept through Belgium and the fortress town of Liège fell, a strategic victory that was vital to the success of the Schlieffen Plan. On 17 August the Belgian government removed from Brussels to Antwerp; three days later the capital was also in German hands. Reports of atrocities emerged, and it soon became clear that the German Army wanted more than mere subjugation; it intended to obliterate anything in its path and crush the spirit as well as succeed militarily. The sacking of the cathedral town of Louvain in the last days of August shocked the civilised world. The magnificent university library, with its many priceless books and manuscripts, was destroyed. The invading force claimed that shots had been fired against the army of the Reich, and many civilians paid the ultimate price. A month later Reims Cathedral suffered a terrible bombardment, despite the fact that a Red Cross flag flew from its tower.

The French, meanwhile, were putting their own plan into action. Led by Field-Marshal Joseph Joffre, French forces concentrated their efforts on an offensive through Lorraine, hoping to make inroads into German territory thereafter.

Although aware of the broad principles of the Schlieffen Plan, the French calculated that the Germans would overstretch themselves in attacking through the Low Countries, leaving a soft underbelly on the Franco-German border. It wasn't soft enough. The German army, swelled by the use of reservists, easily repulsed France's attack. From strong wooded positions, German machine guns cut down in droves French soldiers whose brightly coloured tunics reflected a tradition of attacking with élan, but also made inviting targets. Joffre soon had to rethink his strategy. If his men couldn't achieve a breakthrough, then the Germans must be prevented from doing so. Joffre duly redeployed large numbers to the west, where British forces were also now gathering.

The German army swept through Belgium quickly and Liege, the fortress town, fell.

WHERE THE GREAT BATTLE IS TAKING PLACE.

KEY
ALLIES +
GERMANS ✕

SCALE OF MILES

Top: Soldiers in the Russian Army prepare for battle. Germany declared war on Russia on 1 August and planned a swift defeat of France before Russia had a chance to mobilise its troops, thereby avoiding a war on two fronts. In the event, the Allies were able to stop the advance in the west while Russia mobilised far quicker than Germany anticipated.

Above: A graphic of the "probable fronts" of the opposing armies published on 25 August 1914.

Right: A band heads a column of troops through Berlin at the beginning of the war. Germany had mobilised its armies and under the Schlieffen Plan had already entered Belgium to march on their ultimate target: Paris.

Opposite right: By 17 August the Belgian government had left Brussels for the safety of Antwerp and only three days later the German army entered and occupied the country's capital.

Opposite left: A map published in August outlining Germany's territorial ambitions.

British Army engage the enemy at Mons

The British Expeditionary Force, consisting of some 50,000 troops and five cavalry brigades, crossed the Channel and was soon in the thick of the action.

By 20 August the German army had swept through Brussels and was close to making an incursion into French territory. It was on course to skirt to the west of Paris before turning to march on the capital and face French forces along the heavily defended Franco-German border. The clock was ticking. Russia had mobilised far more quickly than Germany's leadership anticipated; already the six-week window that Schlieffen had allowed for victory in the west appeared a gross miscalculation. And now, in the Belgian town of Mons, Germany's progress was impeded by the British Expeditionary Force, the latter's first taste of action since setting foot on Continental soil. The BEF, under Sir John French, were positioned to the left of their French allies. Before a shot was fired in anger, the expectation persisted that victory would soon be won. They had little idea of how large and formidable was the opponent heading south to meet them. The first bloody exchange at Mons revealed the hollowness of the assumption that the troops would be home by Christmas.

On the morning of Sunday 23 August German artillery opened up on the BEF's defensive line alongside the Mons-Condé canal. General von Kluck – the man assigned the key role of overseeing Germany's extreme right wing in the Reich's planned advance into France – then ordered an infantry attack. It put them in open ground and in the sights of British Enfield rifles. "The worst marksman could not miss," one rifleman recorded. "Such tactics amazed us."

Although von Kluck's army sustained the greater early losses as dug-in regulars fired off 15 rounds per minute, it was the Allies, faced by overwhelming odds, who were soon on retreat. News came through that French troops were on the back foot, making the British position more untenable and underlining the need to fall back. In the fog of the battlefield, one cavalry unit that had attempted to attack at nearby Elouges did not receive the order to withdraw. It was enveloped by German troops, one of the last cavalry charges before the Western Front combatants took to their trenches.

The retreat was briefly broken off at Le Cateau, where the rival forces engaged. The BEF's II Corps, under General Sir Horace Smith-Dorrien, struck a telling blow that held up the German pursuit long enough to provide valuable breathing space. In choosing to stand and fight Smith-Dorrien acted against orders, citing Field Service Regulations that granted leeway to the commander on the ground. Though he was initially congratulated for an engagement that allowed an orderly, unmolested retreat, there was bad blood between him and Sir John French, and Smith-Dorrien was removed from his post the following spring. His fortune contrasted with that of I Corps leader Sir Douglas Haig, who kept to the order when his men were not far from Smith-Dorrien's. His star was rising, promotion soon to come.

On the morning of Sunday 23 August German artillery opened up on the BEF's defensive line alongside the Mons-Condé canal.

Opposite below: **On 7 August the first batch of British troops disembarked in France. Within three weeks 120,000 members of the British Expeditionary Force were in Europe.**

Opposite above: **Allied troops in France. The German army came tantalisingly close to taking Paris in August 1914. Many fled the capital, fearing that its fall was imminent.**

Above: **Sailors and members of the Red Cross and Marine Light Infantry arrive in Ostend from Antwerp. They were preparing to defend the city from attack.**

Top: **British troops outside Mons. The training the British Expeditionary Force received put an emphasis on rapid marksmanship, with the soldiers able to fire accurately at a target fifteen times per minute. This skill was to prove very effective in later battles.**

2,000 BRITISH CASUALTIES.
(OFFICIAL).

TROOPS PRESSED BY THE ENEMY.

The nation would be prepared to make whatever sacrifice was required. Tributes were paid by Lord Kitchener to the Press, the civil community, the railway companies, and to the heroism of the Belgian defenders.

Canada, India, Australia, and New Zealand were all sending powerful contingents. The Territorials at home were nobly responding to the stern call of duty.

"In spite of hard

Over seventy battalions had already

NAMUR.

No German Report of Its Capture.

REUTER'S AGENCY IS INFORMED

INDICTMENT OF FIG GERMANY.

AN APPALLING OFFICIAL DOCUMENT.

MURDER AND RAPINE.

WAR ON WOMEN AND LITTLE CHILDREN.

"The Angels of Mons"

The retreat back across the border into France gave rise to one of the war's strangest episodes, reports of heavenly archers coming to aid of exhausted British Tommies as they fell back. The legend of the "Angels of Mons" was born.

If these astral visions sounded like a public relations stunt, putting a positive spin on a clear military reverse, it's because that's exactly what it was. Or at least that was the outcome, if not the intention. The man behind the supernatural tale of sky-riding bowmen raining arrows down on the enemy hordes was writer Arthur Machen. His florid and fanciful tale, based on the Mons retreat, appeared in the London *Evening News* a month after the battle took place. It included references to St George, invoking the spirit of Agincourt. The fact that it sat alongside news reports seemed to blur the line between fact and fiction. Many readers took the piece at face value, and it quickly became part of folklore, often retold, much embellished. Even the author's insistence that it was all the product of his imagination cut little ice with staunch believers. They preferred the word of soldiers who came forward to bear first-hand witness to the veracity of the story. To a God-fearing populace a military setback thus became a potent symbol that a higher authority was on the side of the Allies. It also brought comfort to many bereaved families to believe that their loss had been in pursuit of a rightful cause that had divine endorsement.

DAILY MAIL AUGUST 18, 1914

The British army in France

THE BRITISH Expeditionary Force is in France. This news, officially promulgated to-day, discloses the great secret. The military authorities have accomplished a thrilling feat. With perfect secrecy they have mobilised, assembled in British ports, and moved to France the largest army that ever left British shores. We may justly congratulate them on their energy and organisation. They have worked in silence with admirable efficiency.

This is not the first time that a British army has gathered on French soil. But it is the first time that British troops have entered France to aid her. The cause for which that gallant army marches today is the same as that for which its forefathers fought in 1814 and 1815. It has gone forth to defend the right, to protect the weak against lawless attack, to uphold the great cause of human freedom against the onslaught of military despotism. It stands, as the England of 1814 stood, for liberty against tyranny. And in that fight, however protracted, however terrible, it will not quail. He was a wise French soldier who said that England, when she had once taken hold, never let go. Through whatever suffering and sacrifices this army which she has sent forth with all her love and faith will carry her standard to victory.

The Russian Front

The Battle of Tannenberg

In accordance with the Schlieffen Plan, Germany began the war with the aim of delivering a speedy knockout blow to France, content to maintain a holding position on its eastern front. Russia, it was thought, was a lumbering giant that would be slow to mobilise. Berlin soon found that the window of opportunity before Russian troops gathered on its Prussian doorstep was a matter of days, not weeks.

For her part, Russia also had two adjacent enemies to contend with. Germany was the superior force, and there was the possibility of making significant gains while its attention was trained on Paris. On the other hand, Austria-Hungary was clearly the weaker foe, thus there was a case for striking further south. Russia could ill afford to divide its resources. Moreover, north-south transport links were poor, making it a cumbersome task to move men and equipment between those two points of attack. In the end, the decision was made to commit Russian forces on both fronts: into East Prussia in the north, and the Austro-Hungarian province of Galicia to the south. That division of manpower did not prove costly in the latter theatre, where Russia made early inroads into the Austro-Hungarian front line and scored a notable victory at Lemberg. But it was a different story as tsarist forces launched a two-pronged attack into East Prussia.

Early encounters

The Russian First Army, led by General Pavel Rennenkampf, took the direct westward line into enemy territory. General Alexander Samsonov's Second Army took a route to the south of the Masurian Lakes through Russian-controlled Poland, from where he would strike northward into East Prussia. The plan was for Rennenkampf to force the German army back, a retreat that would drive it into the gun-sights of Samsonov's men. The man charged with holding the line for Germany was General Maximilian von Prittwitz. His Eighth Army was at a numerical disadvantage, though the deficit was mitigated by superior armaments and training.

The early encounters went Rennenkampf and Russia's way. Prittwitz paid the price for failure, replaced by 66-year-old Paul von Hindenburg, brought out of retirement to deal with the looming crisis. Joining him as chief-of-staff was Erich Ludendorff, who

had distinguished himself during Germany's march through Belgium. They executed a plan that had in fact been drawn up before von Prittwitz's dismissal: to concentrate their resources on Samsonov's army, leaving the northern position lightly defended. Rennenkampf was cautious by nature, and he was even less inclined to take risks if it meant aiding Samsonov, for there was little love lost between the two men. Intercepted messages confirmed that the new German leadership had calculated correctly: Rennenkampf was ensconced in a hotel and would not be on the march any time soon.

Top left: **Russian troops march westwards.** Although they were poorly trained and lacked equipment, the Russian army had strength in numbers.

Top right: **Germany's infantry under the command of Paul von Hindenburg on the march in late August 1914.** At the end of August Russia and Germany clashed at the Battle of Tannenberg. Within two weeks the Germans had virtually destroyed the Russian Second Army, with nearly 80,000 Russians killed or wounded and over 90,000 taken prisoner.

Above: **The remnants of the Russian Second Army in full-scale retreat after their crushing defeat.**

Below: **Russian soldiers creep across no-man's-land to cut wires in front of German trenches.** Trench warfare was rare in the east because the front was so long.

Below left: **Tsar Nicholas II was to take command of Russia's war effort in 1915.** His failure to make any decisive improvements would become a major factor in provoking the Russian Revolution.

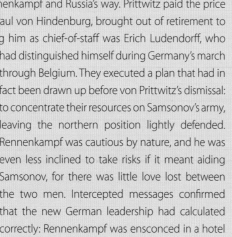

Russia's crushing defeat

The German Eighth Army marched on its diluted and overstretched Russian enemy. Samsonov's men were in no condition to fight, but he had been ordered to engage the enemy forces when it was thought they might be attempting to evacuate East Prussia altogether. They met in the last days of August near Tannenberg, where the "Russian steamroller" was halted in its tracks. Samsonov quickly realised that the position was hopeless. With his men corralled into an area of forest and no sign of assistance from the First Army, Samsonov turned his gun on himself. Over 90,000 prisoners were taken. Rennenkampf's forces were then swiftly rebuffed, their general soon relieved of his command. Hindenburg and Ludendorff, by contrast, were national heroes, the former eventually taking over as Germany's Chief of General Staff.

The Battle of the Masurian Lakes

Hindenberg and Ludendorff then turned their attention to the First Army, commanded by General Rennenkampf. The Battle of the Masurian Lakes began on 9 September 1914. The battle was not quite the disaster for the Russians that Tannenberg had been, but the First Army only escaped to fight another day because of Rennenkampf's decision to retreat.

To capitalize on Germany's successes, Austria-Hungary began an offensive in Galicia in September, but the ramshackle imperial army was unable to defeat the Russians who took the strategic fortress of Lemberg. Germany's new Chief of Staff, Erich von Falkenhayn, wanted to turn its attention back to the Western Front, but he had to reinforce Austria-Hungary in the east. As a result, a major redeployment of troops from the west to the east took place.

If the Battle of Tannenberg represented a crushing defeat for Russia and the Allies, it did succeed in one crucial regard. With the outcome hanging in the balance, Germany's high command had hastily redirected troops from west to east to forestall the possible catastrophic loss of East Prussia. That allowed the French army to strike back against a weakened enemy at the Marne in the first week of September, ending German hopes of a swift victory on the Western Front. The march on Paris was halted when the prized objective was tantalisingly close.

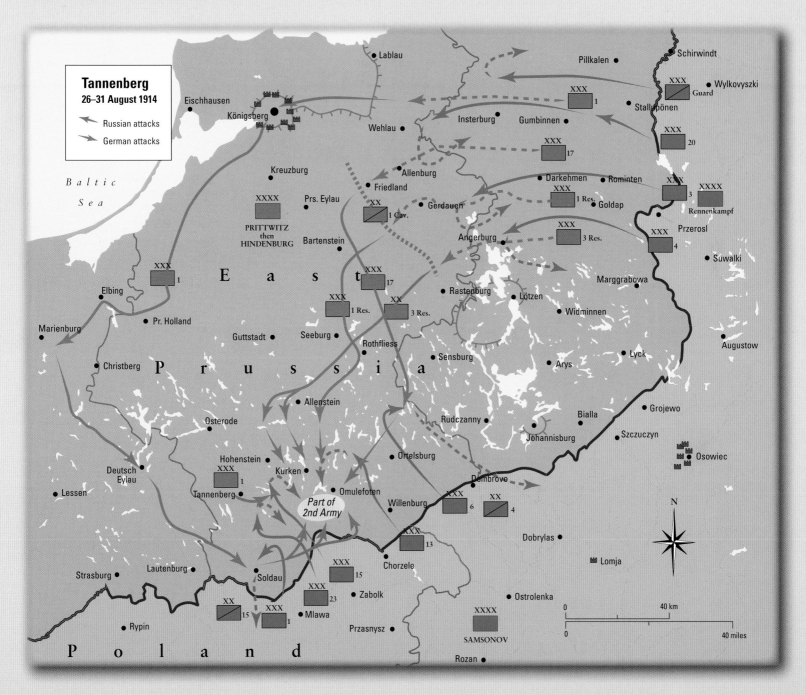

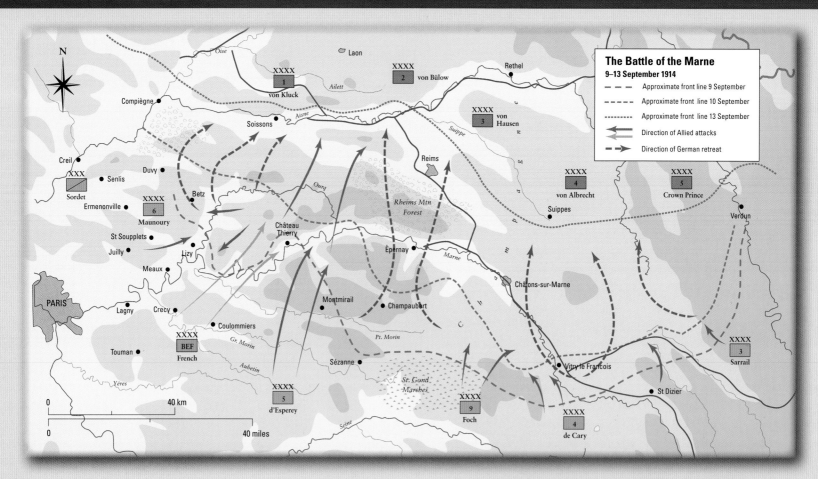

The Battle of the Marne
9–13 September 1914

- – – – Approximate front line 9 September
- – – – Approximate front line 10 September
- ······· Approximate front line 13 September
- ⟵ Direction of Allied attacks
- ⟶ Direction of German retreat

Schlieffen Plan fails

The Schlieffen Plan had started to unravel. The vast German front was supposed to pivot south and then push eastwards, taking in Paris before closing in on the main French contingent on the Franco-German border. But the German generals were struggling to reinforce the huge front their men were fighting on, and were further hampered by the fact that Belgian forces had blown up many key communication routes. The German line was being stretched too thinly and was manned by troops who were exhausted and under-resourced. The response was to close ranks, but this had adverse consequences. It meant that when the German right wing, under General von Kluck, swung south, the army was west of Paris; instead of sweeping through the capital, it now lay behind them, untouched.

The Battle of the Marne

Failing to march into Paris was a military as well as a psychological blow, for it meant that von Kluck's army was itself exposed, liable to attack from the rear. Joffre saw his chance and knew it was time to strike. Von Kluck was forced to turn west to face the threat of the French Sixth Army. During the Battle of the Marne, which began on 5 September, von Kluck's westward surge meant that his men had become dangerously isolated from the nearest German contingent, Field Marshal von Bulow's Second Army, which was now some 30 miles away. Fearing that this gap would be exploited by the Allies, the Germans opted for a tactical retreat. They withdrew to a strong position on high ground north of the River Aisne, with Allied forces in pursuit. Neither side could make further headway.

THE GERMANS' DESPERATE DASH TO PARIS.

GET THERE AT ALL COSTS.

WHAT DELAY MEANS TO THEM.

RUSSIA IN BERLIN IN A FORTNIGHT.

POSITION OF THE ALLIES TO-DAY.

OUR SPECIAL MILITARY CORRESPONDENT MAKES IT PLAIN TO-DAY THAT THIS WAR IS A WAR BY TIME-TABLE.

HE QUOTES THE OPINION OF A VERY HIGH AUTHORITY THAT IN A FORTNIGHT, OR LITTLE MORE, THE ADVANCE TROOPS OF THE RUSSIAN ARMY WOULD BE AT THE GATES OF BERLIN

THE GERMANS FEAR IT, AND THEY REALISE THAT THEIR ONLY HOPE IS TO SMASH FRANCE BEFORE THAT DAY, AND TURN THEIR TROOPS BACK TO FIGHT THE RUSSIANS

THE GERMAN SITUATION—JUDGED FROM THE ULTIMATE RESULT—IS HOPELESS.

THEIR TIME-TABLE MUST BEAT THEM.

MEANWHILE THEY ARE HACKING THEIR WAY, WITH THE DESPERATION OF DES-PAIRING MEN, TOWARDS PARIS.

THE MORE THEIR LINES ARE STRUNG OUT, THE MORE TOWNS THEY "OCCUPY." THE BETTER THEY THINK THEIR CHANCES OF GETTING FAVOURABLE TERMS WHEN PEACE IS IN VIEW.

HIGHLAND BRIGADE IN BATTLE.

British Bravery in Hot Fighting.

BIG GERMAN LOSS.

The Daily Mail correspondent telegraphs from Amsterdam under yesterday's date:—

The war correspondent of the *Telegraaf*, wiring on Monday from Ghent, says:

The most serious fight in Belgium took place near ——, where the German centre tried to cross the Meuse and became engaged in a very hot encounter with French troops, strongly supported by a brigade of Highlanders. The engagement took place between —— and ——.

Near —— the French and British troops had to withstand many furious attacks by German cavalry, but held their ground. Near —— the French and British drove back the Germans with heavy loss.

The Germans advanced in close formation, and having been forced to abandon their previous direction on ——, tried to push on to —— and ——.

[The Press Bureau passed the above after deleting the names of towns and adding that it did not accept responsibility for its accuracy.]

RAIDS REPULSED.

Germans Threaten British Lines of Communication.

Telegraphing from Paris at 8.30 last night, *The Daily Mail* correspondent sends the following message, which contains numerous excisions made by the Censor:—

The German cavalry corps which made a threatening raid against the English lines of communication from the direction . . . . has been successfully repulsed. It was in three columns, of which the strongest, after circling round . . . where they blew up the station, burnt the town hall, . . .

Then it proceeded . . . . arriving at 2 a.m., and there they dragged women and children from bed to make them walk in front of them as a shield against the French fire.

Finally on the road . . . . one column was ambushed by French artillery in a wood.

Opposite middle: **French soldiers behind a ditch waiting to engage the enemy at the Battle of the Marne in September 1914. The successful attack from the Allied forces halted Germany's march on Paris with their armies retreating to high ground north of the River Aisne.**

Opposite below: **Fallen soldiers after the Battle of the Marne.**

Top: **British marines in Ostend. Germany's advance through Belgium was punctuated by a series of atrocities. Execution and rape were used as part of a deliberate policy of "schrecklichkeit" – frightfulness. Despite all attempts by the Allies, Germany controlled most of Belgium by the end of September.**

September 1914

1 Lord Kitchener visited France for a meeting with the French War Minister about the deployment of the British Expeditionary Force.

2 The French government left Paris for Bordeaux.

3 Part of the series of engagements which made up the Battle of Galicia, the Battle of Rawa began between Austria-Hungary and Russia.

The torpedo gunboat HMS *Speedy* was sunk in the Humber Estuary by a German Mine.

Queen Mary started a "Work for Women" fund.

4 The German Government agreed to observe the "Declaration of London" – a code of laws relating to maritime warfare.

5 The British warship HMS *Pathfinder* was sunk by a submarine in the North Sea - the first ship ever to be sunk by a torpedo.

The First Battle of the Marne started along the Marne River near Paris.

8 Austrian forces began the second invasion of Serbia.

9 The First Battle of the Masurian Lakes began as the Germans pushed the Russian First Army back across the Eastern Front.

German politician Theobald von Bethmann Hollweg spelt out Germany's war aims.

11 The Russians defeated Austria-Hungary at the Battle of Rawa.

The Australian Expeditionary Force occupied the Bismarck Archipelago in German New Guinea.

12 The Battle of Marne effectively ended the month long German advance towards Paris when the Germans were defeated.

13 The Allied offensive against the German armies continued in the First Battle of the Aisne.

14 The First Battle of the Masurian Lakes resulted in a German victory when the Russian Army withdrew from East Prussia.

General Erich von Falkenhayn replaced Helmuth von Moltke as German Chief of Staff.

17 The Commander of the Russian Third Army, General Radko Dimitriev began the Siege of Przemyśl attacking the series of fortifications constructed by the Austro-Hungarian Empire.

18 General Von Hindenburg was appointed Commander-in-Chief of the newly formed Ninth German Army.

19 Reims Cathedral was bombarded by German incendiary shells.

20 The 2000 ton Third Class cruiser HMS *Pegasus* sank following a severe bombardment by the German cruiser *Königsberg* in Zanzibar harbour on the east coast of Africa.

21 Jaroslaw in Austrian Galicia was taken by Russian forces.

22 The First Battle of Picardy began as the French Tenth Army attempted to outflank German forces in the "Race to the Sea" – a series of battles that decided the location of the Western Front.

23 British warplanes bombed the Zeppelin sheds at Dusseldorf.

24 Péronne was captured by German forces.

25 One of the ongoing battles fought in the "Race to the Sea", the First Battle of Albert began when the French Tenth Army under the command of General de Castelnau attacked the German troops at Albert on the Western Front.

26 The First Battle of Picardy ended with neither side gaining the advantage.

27 The Siege of Antwerp began when the city's outlying forts were shelled by German guns.

28 Fighting was abandoned when the First Battle of the Aisne ended with no decisive winner.

German heavy siege guns shelled the outlying forts of Antwerp in Belgium.

29 The Battle of the Vistula, also known as the Battle of Warsaw, opened on the Eastern Front by the newly formed Ninth German Army against Russian forces.

30 The city waterworks were destroyed during the Siege of Antwerp.

Top: Writing home in the trenches. Using an age-old method of fighting, the first trenches of the conflict were dug under the orders of General Erich von Falkenhayen following the Battle of the Marne. After Germany's retreat from the Allies the General was determined they would not lose the land gained and ordered their construction to maintain their position. The Allies had no choice but to follow suit.

Above: British marines in Ostend.

Top right: The first German trenches along the bank of the River Aisne where the Kaiser's army were on the defensive. The Battle of the Marne marked the end of the Schlieffen Plan and although Paris was safe, the Germans had captured a large amount of territory in the north-east corner of France.

Middle right and right: Germans forces entered and swiftly took the town of Tirlement in Belgium. Guns shelled the buildings and the cavalry played at war by attacking the flying and panic-stricken populace, shooting and "sticking" them at random. A thousand refugees fled leaving everything behind.

Opposite: British soldiers clearly in a jovial mood as they head to the front. In a matter of months the British Expeditionary Force, the country's professional army, had been all but wiped out.

THE BRITISH DRIVE THE GERMANS BACK 10 MILES.

ENEMY RETIRING WITH SEVERE LOSSES.

ALLIES RESOLUTELY PUSHING HOME THE ATTACK.

OUR CASUALTIES SMALL

CAPTURE OF PRUSSIAN BATTALION.

GERMANS ENTER PARIS—AS PRISONERS.

The great battle in France is progressing admirably for the Allies.

The British have driven the Germans back ten miles after a stubborn resistance.

The Germans have suffered severely at all points.

Our casualties are small considering the fighting.

One German battalion (1,000 men), a machine gun company and several ammunition wagons have been captured by the British and French.

An Allied force, operating from Paris and the valley of the Ourcq, threatens the enemy with envelopment.

The direction of the German retreat will bring this Allied force in upon the enemy's rear.

In the centre heavy fighting has taken place, and the enemy has at one point been pressed back in the direction of Rheims.

Three hundred Germans have entered Paris—as prisoners.

General Joffre has telegraphed to Lord Kitchener his warm thanks for the constant and energetic support of the troops.

BRITISH FIGHTING ALL DAY.

"POSITION VERY SATISFACTORY."

OFFICIAL REPORTS LAST NIGHT.

PRESS BUREAU, Tuesday, 11.25 p.m.
The general position continues satisfactory.

The Allies are gaining ground on their left along the line of the Ourcq and of the Petit Morin; the British troops have here driven the enemy back ten miles.

Fighting has been in progress farther to the right along the line Montmirail—Le Petit Sompuis, neither side gaining the advantage.

Farther to the right again, from near Vitry-le-Francois to Sermaise les Bains, the enemy has been pressed back in the direction of Rheims.

In the vicinity of Lunéville an attempt of the Germans to advance has been repulsed.

11.50 p.m.
The pressure against the enemy continues all along the Allies' front.

The British force has been engaged all day.

The enemy opposed to it, after a stubborn resistance, retired, and is now crossing to the north of the Marne.

The 5th French Army has advanced with equal success and reports many captures.

THE GORDONS SURPRISED.

NARRATIVE OF A SURVIVOR.

HOW COLONEL GORDON DIED.

The following narrative of how the Gordon Highlanders suffered is apparently supported by the heavy list of officers' casualties published in yesterday's *Daily Mail*. It is clear, of course, that not the whole battalion but only a portion suffered. The account was submitted to the censor last Friday, but he refused to pass it for publication. Last night permission to publish was given, with the proviso that the Press Bureau accepts no responsibility for the accuracy of any of the statements made in it.

FROM OUR
GEOR

Incredible
appear, it
by Private
Gordon H
signalman
similar t
British V
Here l
The Gor
Sunday
day we
ing all
action
machi
which

At
was
quie
were
tren
cou
tre

GEN. JOFFRE TO LORD KITCHENER.

PRECIOUS BRITISH SUPPORT.

WHAT IT MEANS IN THE GREAT BATTLE.

M. Millorand, French Minister for War, Bordeaux, to Lord Kitchener.
Septembre 7.

Monsieur le Ministre et Cher Collègue,—Je suis heureux de vous transmettre le télégramme suivant que le Général Joffre me prie de vous faire parvenir:

Le Commandant-en-Chef des Armées Françaises exprime à Lord Kitchener ses chaleureux remerciments pour l'appui constant donné a nos Armées par les Forces Britanniques pendant tout le cours des opérations. En ce moment même cet appui très précieux et se manifeste d'une l'action actuelle.

THE DUPE OF GERMANY.

PANIC IN AUSTRIA.

BANKRUPT AND BROKEN EMPIRE.

FROM OUR SPECIAL CORRESPONDENT LATELY IN VIENNA.
MILAN, Sept. 3.

Panic rules to-day in Austria.

The great, unwieldy, bankrupt Empire, dragged reluctantly like a tame dog at the heels of Germany into a world-war, is in a state of desperate muddle and fear. Her armies, half-hearted at the first, openly mutinous, are beaten back at every point, by Russians to north and east by Serbs and Montenegrin mountaineers to the south. Austria is like her methods of war; her soldiers advance blundering in vast serried masses; they are mown down by

"CASH IS GOING TO COUNT."

MR. LLOYD GEORGE ON THE MONEY WEAPON.

The First Hundred Millions Our Enemies Can Stand, but the Last They Cannot, Thank God.

COST TO BRITAIN SO FAR £26,500,000.

In an inspiriting speech yesterday Mr. Lloyd George, replying to a deputation from the Association of Municipal Corporations, declared that in the war account much more than the present ...

... ed by Parliament's Treasury ... that roughly ... isbursed to ... ... the war has ... ... uarter millions a ... ... period, or at ... ... 0 a year. ... hundred millions ... ... million pounds. ... ... e in view of the ... ... uation should not ... ... as great as it was ...

... satisfactory. The ... ... ember 5 is only ...

WHERE THE ALLIES ARE PRESSING BACK THE GERMANS IN FRANCE.

KEY
ALLIES +
GERMANS +
FORTS +

The map shows the probable fronts of the opposing armies, but does not pretend to show the precise position of the troops.

Stalemate on both fronts

Battle of Ypres

As it was proving impossible for either side to breach the enemy line, both spread out laterally instead, a manoeuvre that was dubbed the "Race to the Sea". There was just one serious attempt to break the deadlock in this time, the month-long First Battle of Ypres. On 31 October the Germans held the initiative after breaking through at Gheluvelt, on the Menin-Ypres road. The Allies rallied but at great cost, particularly to the BEF, which was all but wiped out. The status quo was restored, and as winter set in the opposing armies dug in along a line which eventually stretched from the North sea to Switzerland. All thoughts of a swift victory evaporated; it was now a war of attrition.

There was stalemate, too, on the Eastern Front. With their forces concentrated in the west, the Germans were content with a short-term holding operation against the Russian army. The Austro-Hungarian forces, with their multi-ethnic make-up and indifferent leadership, were nowhere near as formidable as those of the Reich.

Below left: A mitrailleuse gun in use in a Russian front line trench in Poland. These out-dated weapons were developed in France during the 1860s and used in the Franco-Prussian War. After proving very cumbersome on the battlefield and with a lengthy loading time they were eventually replaced by the Maxim machine gun.

Opposite top: Inhabitants leaving Reims. The Germans had taken control of the city on 5 September but were forced to withdraw by Allied troops nine days later. Despite this they persistently bombarded the city over the course of the war.

Opposite middle: Refugees from Antwerp gather together what possessions they can after the town falls to the Germans on 9 October 1914. Over one million inhabitants fled to the Netherlands, Britain and France while tens of thousands of Belgian soldiers were interned for the duration of the war.

Opposite below right: Soldiers and transport from the 1st Middlesex dodging bursting shrapnel at Signy Signets on 8 September. Over one million French and British soldiers fought at the Battle of the Marne against nearly one and a half million German troops. The French brought in 6,000 additional infantry soldiers from the capital after commandeering 600 taxicabs. The Allies successful use of reconnaissance aircraft to aid fighting tactics helped force the German troops to withdraw.

Opposite below left: A map dating from 21 September showing the probable fronts of the opposing armies in the Eastern war area.

THE BATTLE OF THE AISNE.

BRITISH PRESSURE ON THE LEFT.

GERMANS GIVING WAY.

CALL FOR FRESH MEN.

PRESS BUREAU, Wednesday, 5.30 p.m.

The general position upon the Aisne continues to be favourable, and the enemy have delivered several counter-attacks, especially against the 1st Army Corps.

These have been repulsed, and the Germans have given way slowly before our troops and the French armies on our right and left.

The enemy's loss is very heavy and we have taken 200 prisoners.

FROM OUR OWN CORRESPONDENT.

PARIS, Wednesday.

An official communiqué issued this afternoon states:

During Monday and yesterday (Tuesday) the enemy's rearguards, pressed by the Allied forces, were obliged to make a stand and were reinforced by the bulk of the German armies.

The enemy is fighting a defensive battle all along the front, of which certain parts have been considerably strengthened.

This front is bounded by the district of Noyon, the plains to north of Vic-sur-Aisne and Soissons, the Massif of Laon, the heights to north and west of Rheims, and a line from the north of Ville-sur-Tourbe through the Argonne to a point north of Varenne—Varenne has been abandoned by the enemy—and thence to the Meuse in the direction of the Bois de Forges, north of Verdun.

During their retreat after the battle of the Marne the Germans abandoned numerous prisoners, whose ranks were swelled by a large number of stragglers hidden in woods. An exact estimate of these prisoners and captured material has not yet been made. For this reason the Minister of War, who is not desirous of giving incorrect figures, has withheld a detailed statement.

"Our Losses Enormous."

September 8.

We went forward again to the attack against an enemy perfectly entrenched. In spite of his artillery fire, which nothing could silence, we passed through the wood again. As soon as we reached the northern edge a perfectly insane fire opened on us, infantry and shell fire with redoubled intensity.

A magnificent spectacle lay before us; in the far background Lanbaree was in flames, and we saw the enemy retreating, beaten at last. The enemy withdrew from one wood to another, but shelled us furiously and scattered us with his machine guns. We got to the village at last, but were driven out of it again with heavy loss. Our losses were enormous. The 178th Regiment alone had 1,700 men wounded, besides those killed. It was hell itself. There were practically no officers left.

One word more about this artillery range; there were telephone wires everywhere.

It is thought that French officers hidden in trees were telephoning our exact situation in the woods.

September 9.

We marched to Œuvry. The enemy was apparently two kilometres in front of us. Where was our intelligence branch? Our artillery arrived half an hour too late unfortunately.

The French are indefatigable in digging trenches. We passed through a wood and lost touch altogether. We saw companies retiring, and we ourselves received the order to withdraw.

We passed through Lanbaree once more, where we found piles of bodies, and we billeted at Germinon. There was a rumour that the 1st Army had had some disastrous fighting. Our sappers prepared the bridge for demolition. We passed through Chalons-sur-Marne. I am terribly depressed; everybody thinks the situation is critical. The uncertainty is worst of all.

I think we advanced too quickly, and were worn out by marching too rapidly and fighting incessantly. So we must wait for the other armies. We went to Mourmelon le Petit, where we dug ourselves in thoroughly. Four of our aviators are said to have been brought down by the enemy.

REPULSE BY BRITISH WITH HEAVY LOSSES.

BATTLE TO CROSS THE AISNE.

BREATHLESS DUEL IN THE AIR.

A great battle is in progress on the Aisne.

The Germans have rallied and are holding a fortified position, which the British and French are attacking all along the line.

The German front runs from Noyon to a point north of Verdun and Metz.

The British have captured 200 prisoners and inflicted very heavy losses on the enemy.

The French report the capture of many stragglers and much material.

The German right flank is apparently "in the air."

The British submarine E 9 has safely returned from sinking the German cruiser Hela off Heligoland.

In the east the Russians have achieved a stupendous success, by far the greatest and most important yet obtained in this war.

They have driven the remainder of the Austrian armies into Jaroslav and Przemysl and cut their communications.

The Russian cavalry have seized Lisko, a point of great strategic importance on the railway through the Carpathians from Przemysl to Budapest.

General Delarey, one of the most famous of the Boer leaders, has been accidentally killed. This is a great blow, as he was to have held a command in the South African force operating against German South-West Africa.

WHERE RUSSIA IS FIGHTING THE AUSTRIANS AND GERMANS.

October 1914

1 The First Battle of Arras began when the French Army attempted to outflank the German Army and prevent its movement towards the English Channel during the "Race to the Sea".

2 Termonde in Belgium was taken by German forces at the same time as the Belgians retired across the River Nethe.

3 The British Admiralty started laying down a defensive mine-field in the North Sea between the Goodwins and Ostend.

4 The First Battle of Arras ended in a victory for the French defensive forces.

5 The Ottoman army officer and politician Essad Pasha returned to Albania where he was nominated head of a Provisional Government.

6 British troops disembarked at Ostend and Zeebrugge in order to work with the Belgian army.

7 The Belgian Government transferred from Antwerp to Ostend as the evacuation of Antwerp began.

8 The second British air raid on Germany took place as Zeppelin sheds at Cologne and Düsseldorf were attacked again.

9 The port of Antwerp was taken and British troops were forced to retreat to neutral Holland.

11 The Russian cruiser *Pallada* was torpedoed by a German submarine off Hangö in the Baltic Sea.

12 Ostend and Zeebrugge were evacuated by the Allies.

The Battle of Messines began between the river Douve and the Comines-Ypres canal as part of the "Race to the Sea" campaign.

13 The Battle of Armentières started and merged into the Battle of Messines to the north and the Battle of La Bassée to the south of the Western Front.

14 French and British troops occupied Ypres as the Belgian Government fled to France.

15 Ostend and Zeebrugge were occupied by German forces.

HMS *Hawke* was torpedoed by the German submarine *U-9*. The British warship quickly sank with the loss of her captain and the majority of the crew.

16 The British Indian Expeditionary Force sailed from Bombay to the Persian Gulf in preparation for the defence of Mesopotamia.

Another of the "Race to the Sea" conflicts, the Battle of Yser began between Nieuwpoort on the Belgian coast and the city of Diksmuide.

17 The Royal Navy sank four German destroyers off the Dutch coast.

18 The city of Roulers in north west Belgium was occupied by German forces following a fierce three day battle.

19 The First Battle of Ypres, also called the First Battle of Flanders, began as the German and Allied forces fought for the strategic town of Ypres in western Belgium.

20 The steam ship SS *Glitra* was the first British merchant vessel to be sunk by a German submarine.

21 The Battle of Langemarck, part of the wider First Battle of Ypres began as an encounter battle between British and German troops.

23 Advanced troops of the Indian Expeditionary Force arrived at the Bahrein Islands in the Persian Gulf.

24 The Battle of Langemarck ended and the focus of the fighting at Ypres moved south.

25 Chief of the Imperial General Staff, British army officer General Sir Charles Douglas died and was replaced by General Sir James Murray.

26 German forces began an unprovoked invasion of Angola in Portuguese West Africa.

27 The King George V-class battleship HMS *Audacious* was sunk by a German mine off the coast of Donegal, Ireland.

28 After a trial in Sarajevo, Gavrilo Princip was sentenced to 20 years' imprisonment. The Serbian nationalist escaped the death penalty because he was under 21 when he shot Archduke Ferdinand and the Duchess Sophie von Hohenberg.

29 Turkey entered the war and commenced hostilities against Russia when Turkish warships bombarded Odessa, Sevastopol and Theodosia.

30 Lord Fischer was appointed First Sea Lord in succession to Prince Louis of Battenberg who resigned due to hostility to his German ancestry.

31 Turkey attacked the Russian fleet in the Black Sea.

The French and Belgian forces secured the coastline of Belgium as the Battle of the Yser ended.

This page: German troops in the capital city of Brussels. After occupation the country was put under martial law; many civilians were executed by random shootings and over 100,000 workers were deported to Germany.

Opposite above: The ruins of Louvain. Over a five-day period the city was looted and burnt. Its university and library of ancient manuscripts were destroyed along with many other public buildings, as the Germans carried out a planned strategy of intimidation to gain the obedience of its inhabitants.

Opposite below: Kitchener (left) on his way to Westminster Abbey. He was convinced Britain's much-vaunted naval supremacy would count for little, as the outcome of the war would be decided on land.

THE DAILY MAIL, TUESDAY, NOVEMBER 17, 1914.

FIRST VICTORIA CROSSES OF THE WAR.

GLORIOUS DEEDS | NATIONAL MONUMENT | PRINCE OF WALES AT THE FRONT | KAISER'S PUZZLE IN RUSSIA. | MILLION A DAY WAR.

POSTMAN V.C.

HERO'S MODEST STORY OF DEED THAT WON FAME.

Sergeant John Hogan, of the 2nd Manchesters, who, as recorded yesterday, has with Second-Lieutenant Leach, of the same regiment, been awarded the Victoria Cross for recapturing some trenches from the Germans after two attempts by their comrades had failed, received the first intimation of his honour yesterday morning, when the matron of Macclesfield Infirmary, where he is recovering from shrapnel wounds to his face, showed him the official announcement in the newspapers.

Hogan modestly remarked, " I have done nothing to deserve the Victoria Cross." He was very reluctant to discuss the deed which had won him fame. " The Germans surprised us early on the morning of October 29 and drove us out of the trenches. The position was important, and after two unsuccessful attempts to retake the trenches Mr. Leach and I, at the head of ten men, crawled 100 yards amid an inferno of bullets, and then had a hand-to-hand fight with the occupants of the trenches. We killed eight of them, wounded two, and made sixteen prisoners."

Hogan, who is thirty years old, was a postman at Oldham until he rejoined his regiment as a reservist at the outbreak of the war.

What pleased him most about the honour was that his fiancée would be delighted. He is to be married before he returns to the front. As he put it, " It will do a bit of good to a certain young lady."

Second-Lieutenant Leach, who is twenty years old, was born in the Army, his father being a colour-sergeant in the King's Royal Lancasters. As a boy he lived in Manchester. Six or seven years ago his family removed, and young Leach eventually joined the Northampton Regiment. He went out to the war as a corporal, was soon promoted sergeant, and a few weeks ago received a commission and was then posted to the 2nd Manchesters.

25TH VICTORIA CROSS.

CLEARING ENEMY OUT OF OUR TRENCHES.

The 25th Victoria Cross awarded since the beginning of the war was announced in a supplement of the *London Gazette* on Saturday, as follows:—

To LIEUTENANT WALTER LORRAIN BRODIE, 2nd Battalion Highland Light Infantry.

For conspicuous gallantry near Becelaere on November 11 in clearing the enemy out of a portion of our trenches which they had succeeded in occupying. Heading the charge he bayoneted several of the enemy and thereby relieved a dangerous situation.

As a result of Lieutenant Brodie's promptitude 80 of the enemy were killed and 51 taken prisoners.

This Victoria Cross hero, who a few weeks ago was gazetted a captain, is the

LIEUT. W. L. BRODIE, V.C.

second native of Edinburgh to win the coveted honour, the other being Private George Wilson, who was selling papers in the streets there just before the war broke out. Captain Brodie is the son of a chartered accountant, and the other day was in Edinburgh spending a short and muchneeded furlough of five days.

PERSISTENT HERO.

WOUNDED MAN WHO WOULD GO BACK.

V.C. INSTEAD OF GOING TO HOSPITAL.

NORTH-EASTERN FRANCE, Wednesday.

I have been told the story of the incident which, with gallant conduct on all occasions, won for Sergeant Harlock, 113th Battery R.F.A., the Victoria Cross. I will try to give it in the words of a comrade.

" We were in action in an open field and it was hot, I can tell you—' Jack Johnsons ' and shrapnel. One shell burst right under Bombardier Harlock's gun and cut the trail in two, clean, and killed the Number One. Harlock got splinters in his right thigh. He went to the dressing station and the doctor dressed him and told him to get into the ambulance and go to the hospital.

" Well, Harlock goes outside, but he doesn't look for any ambulance, but comes back to the battery. Hang me! he hadn't been there five minutes before he got it in the back. Down he walked once more to the dressing station, and when he was dressed the doctor puts him in charge of an orderly. The pair set out, but Harlock pointed out to the orderly that the doctor seemed a bit ' narked,' and that there were plenty of men who wanted the orderly's attention more than he did, and if the orderly went back to the dressing station he (Harlock) could find his way all right.

" The orderly agreed about it, but says to Harlock, ' No jokes, mind, or you'll get me into trouble. You go straight to the hospital.' Harlock said ' Good morning,' but thought if he could walk to the hospital he could just as easily go back to the old 113th. So back he came again, and he hadn't been with us five minutes before he got some splinters in his arm. It was rotten luck, and he was afraid to go back to the doctor again, so he just stayed there till we went out of action in the evening.

" Some of our officers saw the doctor that night and told him about Harlock, and then they had him down and reprimanded him. But I think they had their tongues in their cheeks when they did it. Anyhow, he's promoted sergeant and got the V.C."—Central News.

First Victoria Crosses awarded

The Victoria Cross, the highest military honour awarded for gallantry in the face of the enemy, had been in existence since 1856. Over 600 VCs were awarded during the Great War, the first of which were given for valour shown by an officer and a private at Mons on 23 August 1914.

Lieutenant Maurice Dease and Private Sidney Godley were members of 4th Battalion The Royal Fusiliers, which came under heavy fire as it held the line at Nimy, just north of Mons. Dease was exposed to enemy shelling as he led the machine-gun unit on the canal bridge. He suffered multiple wounds in his effort to hold up the German advance, eventually succumbing to his injuries.

With the machine-gun crew all dead or incapacitated, Private Godley arrived on the scene and took charge of the weapon, providing cover for his retreating battalion. He, too, was hit, yet still managed to hurl the gun into the canal before staggering towards Nimy. Godley survived, but there would be no more heroics; he spent the next four years in a prisoner-of-war camp.

Opposite: A tobacconist in Poplar, London, is attacked during an anti-German riot. Before the start of the conflict thousands of German immigrants settled in Britain, with many concentrated around the capital. Riots in front of houses and businesses owned by Germans became commonplace around the country. They were often prompted by the violence German troops had reportedly inflicted on Belgian and French civilians.

The Defence of the Realm

The British Parliament wasted little time in passing legislation that curtailed individual freedoms in the interest of national security. The Defence of the Realm Act became law four days after war was declared, and was extended over time to impose further restrictions. These were not just widely accepted but welcomed as the country united at a time of national emergency. Measures that would have had civil libertarians frothing at the mouth in peacetime were generally recognised as a small price to pay if they helped defeat the enemy.

The powers were wide-ranging. Land and property, including factories and machinery, could be commandeered. Safeguarding the country's infrastructure was vital, and to that end trespassing on railway lines became a serious offence. Even loitering near bridges and viaducts carried risk of arrest. Binoculars could not be purchased without good reason, and restrictions were placed on any potential means of signalling, from kite-flying to carrier pigeon. Light pollution – a potential beacon to enemy aerial raiders – could also bring the long arm of the law down on an individual. A *Times* leader in October 1914 reflected police complaints that too much internal light was leaking out into the street and warned people to guard against illuminating potential target areas. Licensing hours were amended and beer watered down to keep drunkenness to a minimum and production levels up. There was even an order prohibiting people from buying a round or treating a friend to a drink, another move to put a brake on consumption. King George V entered into the spirit by banning alcohol in the royal household.

Controlling the exchange and dissemination of information was a key plank of the new legislation. That meant censorship both of personal correspondence and newspaper reports. In the month that the first shots were fired the Press Bureau was established to keep war reportage on a tight leash. Both sides recognised the value of propaganda. The British press carried casualty figures and battle reports intended to encourage, not alarm. Accounts of outrages perpetrated by enemy soldiers were fabricated, or at least massaged. "Today the German monster threatens the world with bloodshed, slavery and death" ran the titles of one propaganda film, the accompanying animation depicting a German-helmeted ogre. At the same time Germans were also being drip-fed similar scare stories. One had the French planning to contaminate their drinking water with deadly bacteria. It played well with the public to paint the enemy as a barbaric horde. The First World War was the first conflict in which propaganda was employed on a mass scale, and thus provided ample evidence to confirm that the truth indeed was an early casualty.

The transmission of information that might aid the enemy clearly fell foul of The Defence of the Realm Act (DORA), but disloyalty extended to criticism of how the war was being prosecuted. Any communication or publication that might engender disaffection or panic among the population was a breach of the law. Under the catch-all provisions of DORA people could be arrested without warrant, imprisoned without trial and dealt with by courts martial.

In the month that the first shots were fired the Press Bureau was established to keep war reportage on a tight leash. Both sides recognised the value of propaganda.

GERMANY'S TOURIST SPIES.

How They Paved the Way in Flanders.

For the past few years the Isle of Wight in particular and many other English seaside places have become increasingly popular summer resorts for German visitors. How they may be presumed to have spent some of their time on our shores can not much longer be in doubt in light of the confessions, now appearing in the German Press, that the holidays of these "tourists" along the Belgian coast have been passed in gathering local data of military and naval use to Germany. Following is a quotation from a recent article in the semi-offical "Cologne Gazette" with regard to operations on the Yser :—

"The territory in which we are now fighting is well known to us through the numerous visits paid to it by countless German tourists. One knows exactly how many canals and sluices and dikes there are, and where they are, and just how they are affected by sudden rainfalls."

THURSDAY, NOVEMBER 12, 1914.

THE FIGHT FOR CALAIS.

NEED OF MORE MEN.

The Germans are able to claim to-day a gain of ground in the battle for Calais, the first to their credit for many weeks. They have retaken Dixmude, the little town in the marshes about which a terrific conflict has surged for weeks. If their own report can be trusted—and it is to some extent borne out by the tone of the French communiqué—they have also advanced slightly in the neighbourhood of Ypres. The public will not exaggerate the nature of these successes, transient as it will hope they may prove. The advance is very small and scarcely measurable even on the large-scale map which we publish to-day. But it is an advance. And it is an advance in a quarter where, until lately, the Allies had been making progress. It is to be explained by two facts—the arrival of German reinforcements and of more German heavy artillery. If we are to beat back the enemy we too must be in a position to pour in men. Victory in the desperate and bloody struggle now proceeding depends ultimately on our recruiting.

The King's Speech yesterday proclaimed in noble terms the resolution of the Empire to secure "at whatever sacrifice the triumph of our arms." If that triumph is to be attained speedily, or, indeed, to be attained at all, more men must be forthcoming. All the available evidence points to the existence in Germany of reserves which are still unexhausted. Germany is throwing into the war the whole energy of her people and her Government. Unless Great Britain displays equal or greater energy it may go hard with the Allied cause. Yet the very people who prevented this country from arming before the war came and altogether misjudged the character of German policy are now assuring this country that it is doing quite well enough. No doubt a large number of men have been raised—we have to-day nearly 1,800,000 men under arms. But all the good judges, from Lord Kitchener downwards, are agreed that this figure is not sufficient. Until such judges

He did his duty. Will YOU do YOURS?

Follow me!

YOUR COUNTRY NEEDS YOU

Above left: Lord Kitchener was selected as Secretary of State for War the day after the conflict was declared. Kitchener had been the hero of the campaign to win back the Sudan in 1898, after which he commanded troops in the Boer War, then became Commander-in-Chief in India, reorganising the Indian Army.

Top right: Kitchener inspects the troops at Aldershot. He accurately predicted that it would be a long and bloody war and was responsible for the huge recruitment campaign to build up the British Army.

Left: This iconic image of Kitchener was used on a September 1914 recruiting poster, designed by Alfred Leete. It was widely distributed, even covering the base of Nelson's Column.

Above insets: Different slogans and messages were used to recruit troops. By May 1915 1,700,000 men had enlisted voluntarily.

Opposite top and middle: The wholehearted response to the call for recruits at the Central London Recruiting Depot on the first day of the war. With the widely held conviction that it would be all over by Christmas, nearly 300,000 men volunteered to join up and fight by the end of the month.

Opposite below: Lance-Corporal Edward Dwyer, a recipient of the Victoria Cross, gives a rallying speech before a large crowd in Trafalgar Square.

"YOUR COUNTRY NEEDS YOU"

THE SLUMP IN RECRUITING.

Why the Men Do Not Come Forward.

RECRUITERS' VIEWS.

Unintelligent Censorship of News Blamed.

"Another 100,000 men urgently wanted for Lord Kitchener's new Army," say the Government. And side by side with the appeal comes the statement that recruiting is not satisfactory.

The *Evening News* can fully confirm that regretable announcement. Exhaustive inquiries made both in London and the provinces afford irrefutable evidence that recruiting has dwindled to insignificant proportions.

What are the reasons given by the men who know, the recruiting officers themselves, for this subsidence of the martial spirit so general six weeks ago? Summarised they may be given as follow :—

(1) The obvious hint of " No more men wanted " given when the standard of physical requirements was raised at the height of the recruiting boom.

(2) Suppression of all war news which might stimulate the imagination of young men and rouse enthusiasm for the Army.

(3) The unintelligent censoring of stories from the fighting line.

MR. ASQUITH'S PROMISE TO THE NATIONS.

We shall never sheathe the sword, which we have not lightly drawn—

Until Belgium recovers in full measure all and more than all that she has sacrificed;

Until France is adequately secured against the menace of aggression;

Until the rights of the smaller nationalities of Europe are placed upon an unassailable foundation.

Until the military domination of Prussia is wholly and finally destroyed.

—*Mr.* ASQUITH *at the Guildhall.*

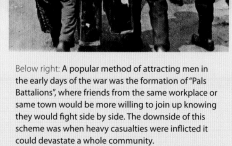

Top: Recruits drilling in Regent's Park. Men would initially be sent to a regimental depot to receive their kit and basic training. This was followed by a period at the main training camp, where they would join a battalion.

Left: "Kitchener's Army" leaving Temple Gardens. By the time conscription was introduced in 1916 nearly two and a half million men had volunteered.

Bottom left: A doctor carries out examinations of recruits for the British army. Initially applicants had to be between the ages of 19 and 30 and be medically fit to fight abroad.

Above right: New members of Kitchener's army leave the recruiting depot after enlisting.

Below right: A popular method of attracting men in the early days of the war was the formation of "Pals Battalions", where friends from the same workplace or same town would be more willing to join up knowing they would fight side by side. The downside of this scheme was when heavy casualties were inflicted it could devastate a whole community.

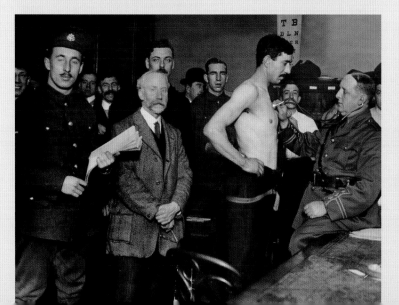

A popular method of attracting men in the early days of the war was the formation of "Pals Battalions" where friends from the same workplace or same town would be more willing to join up knowing they would fight side by side.

Above: A group of children accompanies some new recruits. As the casualty figures escalated so age and height restrictions for volunteers were increasingly relaxed.

Middle: Troops at Waterloo Station preparing to leave for the front. Britain's decision to maintain only a small professional army created huge problems. When men enlisted in droves there wasn't enough equipment to go round, or personnel to train them. Broomsticks often replaced rifles during exercises.

Right: Lance-Corporal Charles Jarvis, awarded the Victoria Cross for his part in demolishing a bridge under enemy fire in Belgium, is pictured at Woodford Green recruiting station using his celebrity status to encourage civilians to enlist.

G. R.

Your
King & Country
need another
100,000 Men.

IN the present grave national emergency another 100,000 men are needed at once to rally round the Flag and add to the ranks of our New Armies.

Terms of Service
(Extension of Age Limit).

Age on enlistment 19 to 38. Ex-Soldiers up to 45. Minimum height 5 ft. 4 ins. except for ex-soldiers and those units for which special standards are authorised. Must be medically fit. General Service for the War.

Men enlisting for the duration of the War will be able to claim their discharge, with all convenient speed, at the conclusion of the War.

Pay at Army Rates.

Married men or Widowers with Children will be accepted, and if at the time of enlistment a recruit signs the necessary form, Separation Allowance under Army conditions is issuable at once to the wife and in certain circumstances to other dependents.

Pamphlet with full details from any Post Office.

How to Join.

Men wishing to Join should apply in person at any Military Barrack or at any Recruiting Office. The address of the latter can be obtained from Post Offices or Labour Exchanges.

God Save the King.

Horsepower at the Western Front

The British Expeditionary Force regulars were primed and ready for action as soon as war was declared. British boots were on the ground within a matter of days. Ensuring sufficient British hooves for the task in hand was potentially a thornier problem. There were motor vehicles at the army's disposal, though not nearly enough for the massive logistical undertaking facing its leaders. Light railways would also play a part in supplying the front. But horsepower was still vital, both for carrying hussars and lancers into battle, and for pulling wagons that contained materials essential for the waging of war.

At the outbreak of war there were some 25,000 horses at the army's disposal. Four times that number were needed immediately, and in a requisitioning sweep of the country the target was quickly met. Farms, stables and all manner of businesses had to give up their animals at a time of national need. Horses and mules were taken to do work they might in some cases be used to, but in circumstances to which they certainly were not accustomed.

Those horses assigned to one of the new cavalry regiments were sent to remount centres for a necessarily brief period of training. Then came the matter of transporting the animals to France, an experience many found stressful. Some had to be forced up gangways, others winched aboard. For those discomforted by the process it was the merest taste of much more extreme conditions they would face when pressed into service on the other side of the Channel.

Farms, stables and all manner of businesses had to give up their animals at a time of national need.

This page: Packhorses, cavalry and motor machine guns march to their rendezvous on what used to be a German road. During the conflict it soon became obvious that the days of the cavalry charge were over and horses and mules were primarily used as a means of transport. Many were requisitioned from farms and stables in Britain and taken out to the Front, where they were often subjected to gruelling conditions.

Opposite: Soldiers seemingly at a loss as to how to free a horse and its load stuck fast in the glutinous earth.

THE CARE OF THE WAR-HORSE AND THE STORY OF THE GUN

A procession of convalescent war-horses being exercised at an Army Veterinary Corps Camp at a British base. "The wonderful skill with which the wounded horses are treated," writes Mr. Beach Thomas, "is only equalled by the extraordinary care taken of them on the battlefield and on the march by the soldiers. The result is that where the Germans reckon the life of a draught-horse on active service to be twenty days, one particular British charge of 1,000 had only lost 8 dead and 45 sick and wounded after two months and a half."

A slow-moving column of horse-drawn wagons made an open target, and enemy shells rained down on known transport routes.

Within a matter of days a cavalry charge against the advancing German army in Belgium illustrated that frontal assaults in the face of modern weaponry could be very costly. As a war of movement rapidly turned into a war of entrenchment, the cavalry dismounted and joined the infantry; the role of horses became chiefly beasts of burden, bearers of field guns, supplies and the injured. A slow-moving column of horse-drawn wagons made an open target, and enemy shells rained down on known transport routes. One such, near Ypres, was under constant observation and regularly bombarded. Horses and men alike had to take their chance negotiating "Hellfire Corner", said to be the most dangerous stretch of road on earth. Artillery and bullets were by no means the only threat. Disease and exposure accounted for many equine deaths, and the mud of Flanders was so treacherous in places that a false step could see an animal irretrievably stuck. In such cases a bullet was sometimes the pragmatic solution, the kindest end.

In the final months of the war, when Germany's spring offensive of 1918 foundered and the tide turned decisively in the Allies' favour, the cavalry at last was able to play its part in pressing home the advantage. This was a war that straddled the old and the new: lance-wielding horsemen sharing the battlefield with tanks, while the earliest dogfights took place in the skies above.

A constant supply of horses had been needed during the hostilities, many sourced from America in the latter stages of the conflict. With the armistice came a very different problem: hundreds of thousands of animals, only a fraction of which was required by the army for peacetime duty. Some were repatriated. Many were sold and put to work in France and Belgium, where at least the toil was unaccompanied by exploding shells and shrapnel wounds. The unluckiest had a grimmer fate, killed and butchered to provide much needed food for a war-ravaged continent.

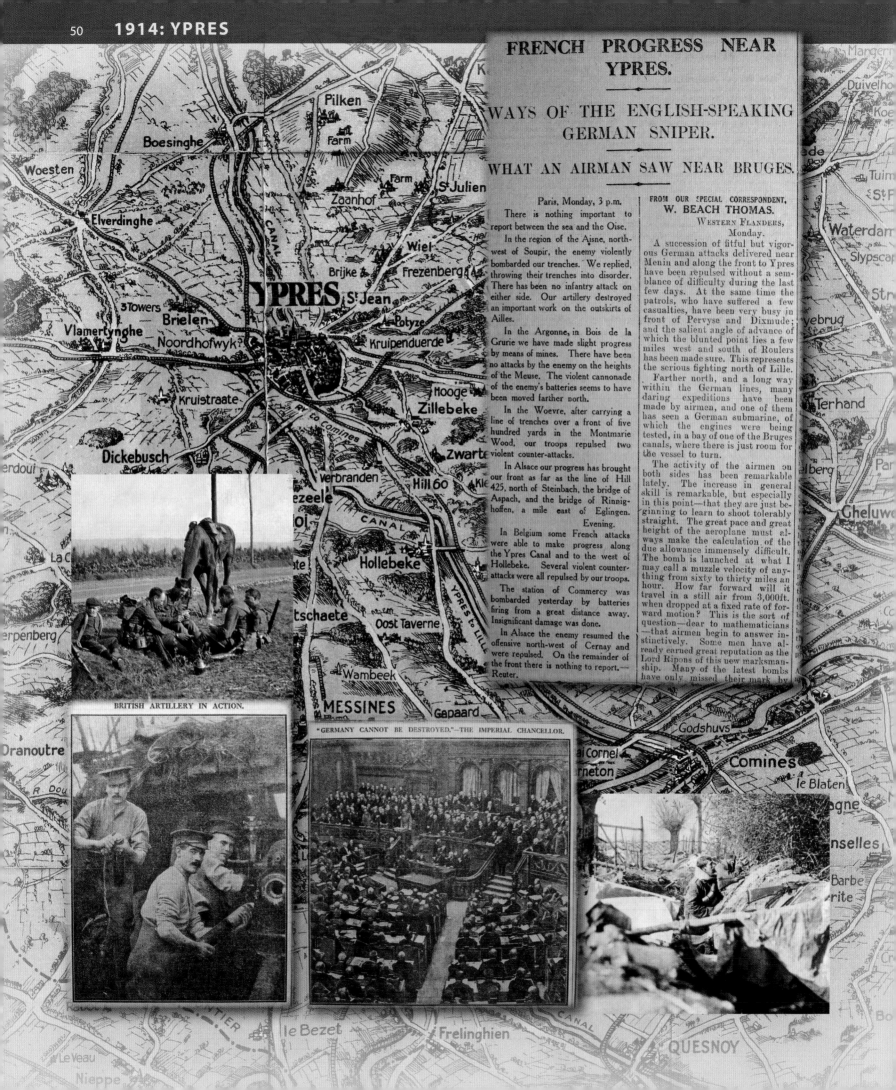

BRITISH ARTILLERY IN ACTION.

"GERMANY CANNOT BE DESTROYED."—THE IMPERIAL CHANCELLOR.

FRENCH PROGRESS NEAR YPRES.

WAYS OF THE ENGLISH-SPEAKING GERMAN SNIPER.

WHAT AN AIRMAN SAW NEAR BRUGES.

Paris, Monday, 3 p.m.

There is nothing important to report between the sea and the Oise.

In the region of the Aisne, north-west of Soupir, the enemy violently bombarded our trenches. We replied, throwing their trenches into disorder. There has been no infantry attack on either side. Our artillery destroyed an important work on the outskirts of Ailles.

In the Argonne, in Bois de la Grurie we have made slight progress by means of mines. There have been no attacks by the enemy on the heights of the Meuse. The violent cannonade of the enemy's batteries seems to have been moved farther north.

In the Woevre, after carrying a line of trenches over a front of five hundred yards in the Montmarie Wood, our troops repulsed two violent counter-attacks.

In Alsace our progress has brought our front as far as the line of Hill 425, north of Steinbach, the bridge of Aspach, and the bridge of Rinnighoffen, a mile east of Eglingen.

Evening.

In Belgium some French attacks were able to make progress along the Ypres Canal and to the west of Hollebeke. Several violent counter-attacks were all repulsed by our troops.

The station of Commercy was bombarded yesterday by batteries firing from a great distance away. Insignificant damage was done.

In Alsace the enemy resumed the offensive north-west of Cernay and were repulsed. On the remainder of the front there is nothing to report.—Reuter.

FROM OUR SPECIAL CORRESPONDENT.
W. BEACH THOMAS.

WESTERN FLANDERS,
Monday.

A succession of fitful but vigorous German attacks delivered near Menin and along the front to Ypres have been repulsed without a semblance of difficulty during the last few days. At the same time the patrols, who have suffered a few casualties, have been very busy in front of Pervyse and Dixmude; and the salient angle of advance of which the blunted point lies a few miles west and south of Roulers has been made sure. This represents the serious fighting north of Lille.

Farther north, and a long way within the German lines, many daring expeditions have been made by airmen, and one of them has seen a German submarine, of which the engines were being tested, in a bay of one of the Bruges canals, where there is just room for the vessel to turn.

The activity of the airmen on both sides has been remarkable lately. The increase in general skill is remarkable, but especially in this point—that they are just beginning to learn to shoot tolerably straight. The great pace and great height of the aeroplane must always make the calculation of the due allowance immensely difficult. The bomb is launched at what I may call a muzzle velocity of anything from sixty to thirty miles an hour. How far forward will it travel in a still air from 3,000ft. when dropped at a fixed rate of forward motion? This is the sort of question—dear to mathematicians—that airmen begin to answer instinctively. Some men have already earned great reputation as the Lord Ripons of this new marksmanship. Many of the latest bombs have only missed their mark by

Turkey sides with the Central Powers

The lustre of Hindenburg's triumph for the Central Powers was tarnished by events further south. The Austro-Hungarian forces, which had invaded Serbia in the first days of the war, had their early gains snatched away from them. The aged King Peter, determined to lead from the front, galvanized the dispirited Serbs and near-defeat was turned into a stunning victory. By mid-December a largely peasant army had driven the Austro-Hungarian army back across the Danube.

Germany's ally fared little better against the Russians, suffering a heavy defeat at the Battle of Lemberg. Such reverses would prompt one German general to remark that being bound to Austria-Hungary was like being "shackled to a corpse". Even so, as 1914 drew to a close the knockout blow proved as elusive in the east as it had in the west. Neither side had the manpower or tactical supremacy to gain a decisive edge; neither side was so weak or tactically inept to invite failure.

The balance was tilted somewhat when Turkey joined the fray in early November. The Turks sided with the Central Powers, hoping to arrest the decline of the Ottoman Empire by joining forces with the winning side. Russia's Black Sea coast came under attack, and Britain, France and Russia all declared war on a new foe. Although it gave the Allies yet another front on which to fight, Turkey's intervention was still not of an order which would tip the balance in favour of a swift victory. By the end of the year – by which time the conflict was supposed to be over – early optimism gave way to the grim reality of a long, drawn-out struggle.

Many people had believed that the war would be over by Christmas 1914, but this was far from being the case. On Christmas Day the opposing forces in the forward trenches on the Western Front put their enmity to one side and exchanged pleasantries in no-man's-land. It was, however, only a temporary respite from the fighting. Germany's Schlieffen Plan for a swift advance into France had ground to a near halt and, by the end of 1914, some German commanders felt that, with the failure of the Plan, Germany would be unable to secure ultimate victory.

The Turks sided with the Central Powers, hoping to arrest the decline of the Ottoman Empire by joining forces with the winning side.

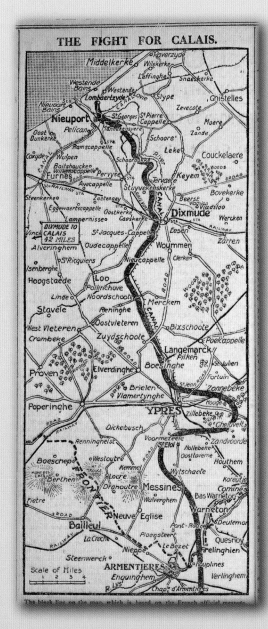

THE FIGHT FOR CALAIS.

Opposite above left: **The Honourable Artillery Company fought in the First Battle of Ypres, which became the final part of the "Race to the Sea".**

Opposite right: **Allied trenches at Wytschaete during the First Battle of Ypres. Little did they know they were destined to return three years later to fight on the same battlefield during the Battle of Messines.**

Opposite middle: **The historic scene in the Reichstag on 2 December when Herr Bethmann-Hollweg made a violent attack on Britain for her part in the war and the sum of £250,000,000 was voted for war purposes with only one dissenting voice.**

Above: **British sappers at work. The men responsible for engineering, construction and demolition work made a crucial contribution to the war effort.**

Left: **The approximate battleground between Nieuport and Armentières according to French sources on 12 November.**

WEDNESDAY, NOVEMBER 25, 1914.

GUNS AND BAYONETS AND THE PRICE OF VICTORY.

THE POINT   RIGHT PARRY (Low)   RIGHT PARRY (High)   THROW POINT   BUTT STROKE   ON GUARD

"A brilliant bayonet charge." Many times during the past few weeks these words have appeared in print, and on every occasion the British bayonet has utterly routed the German masses. Here is a series of photographs which illustrate the different thrusts and positions employed by our troops at the front on those rare occasions in the present war when a bayonet charge can be made.

DAILY MAIL OCTOBER 16, 1914

The arrival of the Canadians

PLYMOUTH HAS BEEN the scene of many memorable incidents in British history, but never of a more stirring and significant one than when yesterday the transports bearing the Canadian troops dropped anchor in its harbour. They received a west-country welcome that was local in form but absolutely national in the spirit behind it. What Plymouth was privileged to witness was something more than the arrival of so many thousands of hardy natural soldiers; it was a living picture of the Empire in action; it was the scattering of all the illusions of Imperial disintegration with which the Germans have bemused themselves; it was a spectacle, hardly to be paralleled since the Crusades, of free and self-governing communities voluntarily embracing a cause that passionately appeals to their hearts and consciences.

LONDON SCOTTISH IN A HARD FIGHT.

GLORIOUS SUCCESS AT A HEAVY PRICE.

REPEATED BAYONET CHARGES.

FROM OUR SPECIAL CORRESPONDENT.

NORTH OF FRANCE.

The full story of the first action in which the London Scottish have taken part since they have been in France has just reached me.

It forms a page of mingled heroism and tragedy. This fine corps, one of the "crack" regiments of Territorials, has won its spurs, and has earned undying fame for the whole Force which it typified—but it has paid the price.

The regiment marched out nearly 1,200 strong.... The only Germans who got to close quarters with the London Scottish lie stretched on the bloody field of Messines, bayoneted.

For several weeks the London Scottish, scattered in various ports and bases of France, endured the tedium of "fatigue" duty. They guarded prisoners, they mounted sentry at docks and military stores, they acted as military police, they daily performed the sad duty of furnishing the escort which paid the last military honours to the brave dead who were borne from the hospital to the grave.

TO BATTLE.

.... the call to action sounded. The scattered detachments were collected. The regiment found itself an entity again. A brief time was spent in drilling. .... it was despatched in motor-omnibuses and again it made a short stay. .... the motor-omnibuses were marshalled once more and the regiment was taken direct to .... in the direct path of a strong German force which was determined to force a way through the British lines.

.... the London Scottish moved into action. They were supporting the —— Cavalry Brigade, the men of which, dismounted, were lining the trenches to repel fierce German assaults which had been launched against the British position.

The task before the London Scottish was to occupy a ridge crowned with wide-stretching beet fields, and as they advanced across the open they came full into range of shrapnel fire from the German artillery posted a couple of miles away. There was practically no cover. .... They advanced by short sprints, and fell prone, flattening themselves against the ground. ... The fire of the German artillerymen was murderously accurate. Many fell before, as one of them sorrowfully admitted, they had ever set eyes on a German.

The battalion pushed on in face of the fearful fire ploughing their ranks. The advancing Germans met them. A few moments of desperate work with the bayonet followed and then the German ranks broke and fled.

The London Scottish had endured and they had won, heavy though the price had been.

Two farmhouses were occupied as temporary hospitals and filled with stretcher cases. The Germans shelled the houses and at great peril the wounded had to be removed.

Opposite above right: Wounded soldiers arriving at Ostend, having failed to prevent the fall of Antwerp. Germany occupied the town until its liberation at the end of the war.

Opposite above left: Scenes in a German prison camp during the typhus epidemic in November 1914. Germany had been inundated with prisoners from the very start of the war and had very little suitable accommodation. Overcrowding and poor hygiene led to frequent outbreaks of disease. Here prisoners carry coffins to the graveyard outside the camp.

Opposite below: General Sam Hughes greets and inspects Canadian troops. Britain's Empire contributed considerable numbers of soldiers to the Allies' fighting force. Australia sent more than 400,000 men, Canadian forces numbered in excess of 625,000, India sent nearly one and a half million and New Zealand over 125,000.

Top right: Canadian troops enjoy a break from duty, if not mud. The Daily Mail greeted their arrival in Plymouth in October 1914 with the following words: "For all that Canada has done in this war, for her splendid troops, for her gifts, for her instinctive comprehension of the stake that is on the table, and above all for the spirit in which she has asserted her right to take a hand in the game, the British people are profoundly grateful. Never was the assistance she has so lavishly offered more welcome and never was it more needed."

Middle right: Belgian soldiers at the start of the Ypres campaign. As the winter conditions began to set in, the need for warm clothing was evident. The Belgian army had been severely depleted by this stage with the total manpower available down to 80,000.

Right: By the close of the year stalemate had set in on the Western Front. The military leaders on both sides would find that an entrenched army was a formidable obstacle.

The war at sea

The naval arms race between Britain and Germany had been a feature of the prewar period, yet the first 20 months of the conflict saw only limited attempts to test their relative strength on the high seas. Britain's Grand Fleet maintained a clear numerical advantage, not least in terms of the mightiest weapon afloat: the dreadnought. So great was the advance in both offensive and defensive capability of HMS *Dreadnought* when it was launched in 1906 that it gave its name to an entire class. First Sea Lord Admiral Sir John Fisher had overseen the introduction of the "all-big-gun" ship that rendered all other designs obsolete. With its array of 12-inch guns, 11-inch armour, rangefinder accuracy to over 6,000 yards and Parsons steam turbine engine, *Dreadnought* had immense firepower and could make 21 knots. From her position of strength, Britain was content to keep the Kaiser's High Seas Fleet penned in, to close down supply routes and choke off Germany's much needed import lifeline. The latter needed to level the odds before it could risk breaking the blockade or contemplating a large-scale engagement.

The Royal Navy drew first blood when the rival forces met in the Battle of Heligoland Bight, fought in late August 1914. Germany responded with a series of autumn attacks on Britain's east coast. By hitting towns such as Scarborough, Whitby and Yarmouth, the raiders kept well south of Scapa Flow and Rosyth, home to the main body of the Grand Fleet. As was the case with the Zeppelin attacks, these raids were not costly in terms of casualties or damage to property, but they tweaked the nose of the country whose naval superiority had been unchallenged for a century. If those assaults irked Britain's political and military leaders, then an encounter off the South American coast on 1 November 1914 caused major consternation.

Von Spee targets The Fleet

The thorn in Allied flesh was the East Asiatic Cruiser Squadron led by Admiral Graf von Spee, operating out of the Chinese port of Tsingtao. When Japan joined the Allies on 23 August and Tsingtao's fall was imminent, von Spee put to sea, determined to inflict as much damage as possible on enemy shipping. He allowed one of his squadron, *Emden*, to head for the Indian Ocean, where its captain ran a highly effective lone-wolf operation before finally meeting his nemesis. Von Spee, meanwhile, led the rest of his ships to the Chilean coast, where he scored a decisive victory over the British force patrolling those waters. Losses in the Battle of Coronel included the flagship of the defeated commander, Admiral Sir Christopher Cradock.

Von Spee next targeted the Falkland Islands, which he assumed would be lightly defended. He arrived in time to meet much stiffer opposition, for the Admiralty had moved quickly to avenge the Coronel debacle. Cradock's ships had been of an older design; now von Spee had to deal with a task force led by battlecruisers *Invincible* and *Inflexible*, which Fisher ordered post-haste to the South Atlantic. They were faster and better armed, thus the Battle of the Falkland Islands, which took place on 8 December, was almost a foregone conclusion. Von Spee and two serving sons were among the 2,000 hands that went down as *Scharnhorst*, *Gneisenau*, *Leipzig* and *Nürnberg* were dispatched. Only one German ship escaped, and that was accounted for early in the new year.

Opposite top, opposite bottom and this page top: The Grand Fleet, pictured shortly before war was declared. It was widely believed that Britain still reigned supreme on the seas, although more than a century had passed since the battle of Trafalgar. At the beginning of the war most of the Navy's larger ships were stationed at Scapa Flow or Rosyth in Scotland with smaller ships grouped around the British coast. It would be almost two years before Admiral Sir John Jellicoe was able to test his ships against the German navy in the one significant maritime battle of the war at Jutland.

Bottom: At Heligoland Bight, the first naval skirmish of the war, the German light cruiser SMS *Mainz* was hit by a torpedo and gunfire and the crew forced to abandon ship. 89 of the crew, including the captain, were killed but the British successfully rescued 348 men.

Middle: Only an hour after being hit, the SMS *Mainz* rolls and begins to sink. One of the survivors was the son of Admiral Alfred von Tirpitz, the architect of the German Fleet. Churchill personally sent a message to him via the US Embassy in Berlin to reassure him that his son had been saved.

Opposite upper middle: SMS *Emden* had successfully captured or sunk thirty Allied warships and merchant vessels before the Allies sent sixty ships to hunt her down. The Australian light cruiser HMAS *Sydney* finally caught her while she was docked.

Opposite lower middle and opposite bottom left: The *Emden* raised anchor and a battle between the ships then ensued. Eventually the *Emden* was deliberately beached on North Keeling Island when the captain realised she was sinking. The landing party managed to escape but those still on board, including the captain Karl von Mulller, were captured and imprisoned in Malta.

The Royal Navy drew first blood when the rival forces met in the Battle of Heligoland Bight, fought in late August 1914.

GERMANS BOMBARD THREE ENGLISH TOWNS:

BOMBARDMENT OF SCARBOROUGH.

DAMAGE TO CHURCHES, AN HOTEL, AND PRIVATE HOUSES.

46 PERSONS KILLED AND 66 WOUNDED.

WHITBY & HARTLEPOOL SHELLED.

The war has been brought to our shores in no uncertain manner. At the breakfast hour yesterday German warships vigorously shelled the Hartlepools, Scarborough, and Whitby, the last two being entirely unfortified towns.

Unfortunately there has been loss of life. The names of 10 dead at Scarborough are issued by the police, but there are also some wounded. A considerable proportion of these are after the Germans' own heart—women and children. At West Hartlepool 7 soldiers were killed and 14 wounded, and 22 civilians are among the dead and 50 wounded. The material damage is nearly all to private property. At Scarborough three churches, hotels, and many private houses were wrecked or damaged. Seventeen people were killed. At Whitby, sad to relate, the ruins of the famous old abbey were still further laid low. Two people were killed and two wounded.

The patrol ships engaged the Germans on the spot and a patrolling squadron went in pursuit, but the enemy escaped at full speed in the mist. But the splendid outstanding fact is that England is cool and ready for the enemy.

SCARBOROUGH'S VICTIMS.

"MURDER" VERDICT URGED BY JURY.

"THE ENEMY WILL KNOW ALL ABOUT THIS."

The inquest on the seventeen Scarborough victims—eight women, four children, and five men—of the German raid on Wednesday, was held yesterday at Scarborough.

The coroner, Mr. George Taylor, said they were assembled to inquire into the circumstances of a tragedy such as had been unknown in that town for a thousand years. It had resulted from a bombardment of Scarborough by the ships of an enemy who were conducting war contrary to all the rules of civilised nations. It was an attack on an unfortified and defenceless town.

It might be that this method of conducting warfare was intended to terrorise the inhabitants of English towns, and at the same time to inspire confidence in the minds of the German people. A great deal was heard about German "Kultur," but he thought this nation was not disposed to imitate it. A similar visitation to our coast might be made again unless the British Fleet should be in a position to defend it, but our Fleet had a great deal to do, and a duty to discharge much more vital and important than that of meeting occasional attacks on defenceless populations.

FOUR ENEMY SHIPS.

Chief Petty Officer Arthur Dean, chief officer of the coastguard at Scarborough, said he was in his house at breakfast when the first gun from the German ships went off at 8.5 a.m. on Wednesday. "I walked out of my door and saw the walls of the castle tumbling down. I stayed outside about two minutes, and then saw two large cruisers in sight from behind the castle towards South Bay. They opened fire with all their guns on the starboard side. They kept up an incessant fire. After-

SCENE OF THE GERMAN RAID.

Contour map of the coast from Hartlepool to Scarborough of Scarborough.

RAID DIARY.

SCARBOROUGH.
Railway guard walking along foreshore heard shell burst. Counted a dozen altogether. Churches, hotels, and other buildings seriously damaged.

thirty shells fall. 2 killed wounded.

HARTLEPOOL.
War Office announces at 1.5 p.m.: "German ships engaged

ing I was getting up as usual to go to business. The morning was very hazy, and there was a dense fog over the sea. My house is close to the railway station, just on the turning facing the railway. I was on the landing outside my room when I was startled by a terrific crash, which at the moment I mistook for a violent thunderstorm.

"I found immediately afterwards on going to the window that a shell, the first of the bombardment, had fallen and burst in a place called Falsgrave. This was some little distance away from my house, but I saw from the window dense smoke and a fierce light like the reflection of the sun.

"Almost immediately afterwards I heard a second terrific report, and then following that many others in various parts of the town. The second shell that followed, which I was able quite easily to identify, fell in Prospect-road. That was the shell which I am convinced killed Mrs. Merryweather. Her husband keeps the post office at the corner of Prospect-road.

"At this moment shells seemed to be pouring in all over the place, and the noise was frightful. The firing of the shells was immediately followed by the explosions in the town. Looking from my window at that time there was a vivid picture of destruction. The roads, streets, and pavements were covered with broken glass, bricks, stones, and shattered masonry, and there was a stifling smell of explosives.

SEEKING SAFETY.

Daily Mail

THE PAPER THAT PERSISTENTLY FOREWARNED THE PUBLIC ABOUT THE WAR.

THURSDAY, DECEMBER 17, 1914

WHAT WAS THEIR OBJECT?

Yesterday for the first time in two centuries British towns were shelled by a foreign foe and British blood spilt on British soil. What was the German object in attacking unfortified coast and a commercial harbour?

The first motive was to throw a sop to their hatred of England. Held back from Calais, checked in Poland, with Turkey staggering under redoubtable blows, and Austria dismayed, German militarism felt something must be achieved against its most detested foe.

The second motive was to take the revenge the German public demanded for the destruction of Admiral von Spee's

---

DAILY MAIL   DECEMBER 17, 1914

Germans bombard three English towns

THE WAR HAS been brought to our shores in no uncertain manner. At the breakfast hour yesterday German warships vigorously shelled the Hartlepools, Scarborough, and Whitby, the last two being entirely unfortified towns.

Unfortunately there has been loss of life. The names of 17 dead at Scarborough are issued by the police but there are also some wounded. A considerable proportion of these are after the German's own heart –women and children. At West Hartlepool, 7 soldiers were killed and 14 wounded, and 22 civilians are among the dead and 50 wounded. The material damage is nearly all to private property. At Scarborough three churches, hotels, and many private houses were wrecked or damaged. At Whitby, sad to relate, the ruins of the famous old abbey were still further laid low. Two people were killed and two wounded.

The patrol ships engaged the Germans on the spot and a patrolling squadron went in pursuit, but the enemy escaped at full speed in the mist. But the splendid outstanding fact is that England is cool and ready for the enemy.

What was their object?

Yesterday for the first time in two centuries British towns were shelled by a foreign foe and British blood spilt on British soil. What was the German object in attacking unfortified coast resorts and a commercial harbour?

The first motive was to throw a sop to their hatred of England. Held back from Calais, checked in Poland, with Turkey staggering under redoubtable blows, and Austria dismayed, German militarism felt something must be achieved against its most detested foe.

The second motive was to take

the revenge the German public has demanded for the annihilation of Admiral von Spee's squadron in the South Atlantic.

The third motive was to proclaim, especially to neutral countries, that German ships could move in the North Sea.

The fourth motive was the vain hope of creating panic so that troops might be kept here who would otherwise be sent to the Continent.

The fifth motive, and the most important, was to force the British Admiralty to keep a larger force than hitherto in the narrower part of the North Sea where that force would be liable to constant mine and submarine attacks from the Germans.

There will be no panic

Neither the British Admiralty nor the British public will fall into the snare. There will be no panic. There is rather a sense of stern content and satisfaction that the issue has at last been made clear. The war has come home to the nation and the nation is ready.

The Germans show no respect for the laws of the war. We must defend our homes against their methods. We must recognize that in this age of mines, submarines, and aircraft the conditions of war have changed. Our Scarboroughs and Hartlepools must have adequate defence. The nation is not taken aback. The German belief that a show of force on the coast and half a dozen bombs from a Zeppelin can demoralise the British people is a pitiful delusion. What the nation realizes from yesterday's events is that new and sterner efforts must be made to win, that more aid must be sent to our Allies, and that the preoccupation of every man and every woman must be to crush for ever the tyranny of German militarism.

Opposite: On 16 December 1914 the German High Fleet set out to bomb Scarborough, Whitby and Hartlepool. Scarborough, the first target, was subjected to ninety minutes of shelling, with the castle, the Grand Hotel and various properties and churches hit.

The two battleships responsible, SMS *Derfflinger* and *Vonn der Tann*, then turned their attention to Whitby where the abbey (middle left) and local houses provided ideal targets. The attacks caused great resentment towards the High Fleet and anger at the British navy for failing to protect the coastline.

Meanwhile three other ships, including SMS *Blücher*, had concentrated on the more important target of Hartlepool with its factories and docks. Although there were attempts to defend the town, 300 houses along with factories, churches and the railway, were struck when the town was hit by 1150 shells, which killed 86 civilians and injured over 400 more.

November 1914

1 Great Britain broke off diplomatic relations with Turkey.

German forces captured Messines, south of Ypres.

In naval action at the Battle of Coronel, HMS *Good Hope* and HMS *Monmouth* were sunk by a German cruiser squadron commanded by Admiral von Spee.

2 Russia declared war on Turkey.

3 British and French naval fleets bombarded forts at entrances to the Dardenelles.

In the first major event of the war in Africa, the Battle of Tanga began when the British Indian Expeditionary Force attempted to invade German East Africa.

4 The German cruiser SMS *Yorck* was accidentally sunk by German mines near Wilhelmshaven in the North Sea.

5 Great Britain and France formally declared war on Turkey because of the help given to the German attack on Russia.

Great Britain annexed Cyprus.

6 Turkey severed diplomatic relations with Belgium.

7 Tsingtau in China fell to Japanese forces who took over 2000 prisoners.

9 At the Battle of Cocos in the Indian Ocean, the German cruiser *Emden* ran aground to avoid sinking after being severely damaged by the Australian cruiser HMAS *Sydney*.

11 The Battle of Łódź began between German and Russian forces in severe winter conditions on the Eastern Front.

13 The South African forces of General Botha crushed the rebel commandos of General Christian de Wet at Mushroom Valley in the Orange Free State.

14 Field Marshal Earl Roberts died in France whilst visiting Indian troops.

15 The Battle of Cracow began.

16 The first elements of the Indian Expeditionary Force landed in Egypt.

The Prince of Wales became aide-de-camp to Sir John French.

17 Chancellor David Lloyd George announced his first War Budget.

18 SMS *Breslau* and SMS *Goeben* were engaged in combat with the Russian Black Sea Fleet off the Crimean coast. SMS *Goeben* was damaged after the Russians attempted to intercept the German battleships.

20 The British Admiralty announced an extension to the North Sea mine-fields.

21 British airmen raided a Zeppelin factory at Friedrichshafen.

22 The First Battle of Ypres ended the Race to the Sea. The Germans were prevented from reaching Calais and Dunkirk.

23 The Portuguese Government announced its intention to cooperate with Great Britain.

24 A Royal Warrant increased the pay of subordinate Army officers.

25 Three German divisions were surrounded by General Rennenkampf's Russian Army in the Battle of Łódź.

26 Over 700 sailors died when an internal explosion ripped apart HMS *Bulwark* in the harbour at Sheerness in Kent.

27 General Paul von Hindenburg was promoted to Field Marshal.

Reims town and its cathedral were badly damaged by German bombardment on the Western Front.

28 The Germans suffered a bad defeat by the Russians near Brzezany in Poland.

29 King Edward VII left England to visit the army in France.

30 The Battle of Lowicz-Sanniki began on the Eastern Front.

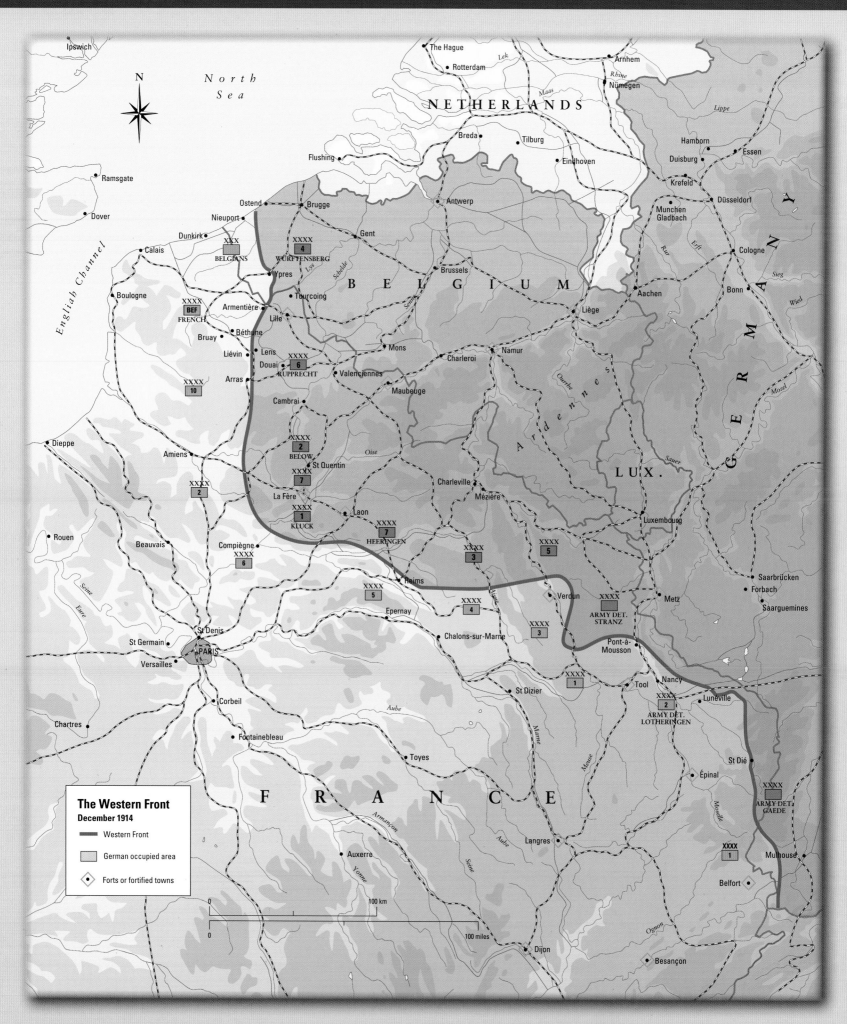

N
North
Sea

English Channel

NETHERLANDS

BELGIUM

LUX.

GERMANY

FRANCE

Ipswich
Ramsgate
Dover
Calais
Dunkirk
Boulogne
Dieppe
Rouen
Beauvais
Chartres
St Germain
Versailles
St Denis
PARIS
Corbeil
Fontainebleau
Amiens
Compiègne
Beauvais
Ostend
Nieuport
Brugge
Ypres
Tourcoing
Armentière
Lille
Béthune
Bruay
Liévin
Douai
Lens
Arras
Cambrai
St Quentin
La Fère
Laon
Reims
Epernay
Chalons-sur-Marne
Toyes
Auxerre
Langres
St Dizier
Dijon
Besançon
Belfort
Mulhouse
St Dié
Épinal
Lunéville
Nancy
Tool
Metz
Forbach
Saarguemines
Saarbrücken
Pont-à-Mousson
Verdun
Mézière
Charleville
Maubeuge
Valenciennes
Mons
Charleroi
Namur
Brussels
Gent
Antwerp
Liège
Aachen
Bonn
Cologne
Krefeld
Düsseldorf
Munchen Gladbach
Duisburg
Hamborn
Essen
Nümegen
Arnhem
The Hague
Rotterdam
Breda
Tilburg
Eindhoven
Flushing
Luxembourg

The Hague

Lek
Rhine
Maas
Rur
Erft
Sieg
Wied
Lippe
Mosel
Schelde
Semre
Lys
Oise
Aisne
Meuse
Marne
Aube
Seine
Eure
Yonne
Armançon
Ognon
Moselle
Sauer
Ourthe
Ardennes

XXX BELGIANS
XXXX 4 WÜRFTENBERG
XXXX BEF FRENCH
XXXX 6 RUPPRECHT
XXXX 10
XXXX 2 BELOW
XXXX 7
XXXX 1 KLUCK
XXXX 7 HEERINGEN
XXXX 2
XXXX 6
XXXX 5
XXXX 4
XXXX 3
XXXX 3
XXXX 5
XXXX 1
XXXX 1
XXXX 2 ARMY DET. LOTHERINGEN
XXXX ARMY DET. STRANZ
XXXX ARMY DET. GAEDE
XXXX 1

The Western Front
December 1914

Western Front
German occupied area
Forts or fortified towns

0   100 km

0   100 miles

Top and middle: **Men of the new Royal Naval Division, holding defensive positions in Antwerp. King Albert I of Belgium had ordered the town to be garrisoned and after a request from Belgium the BEF provided additional troops to protect the town from German attack. Eventually the king evacuated the town to Ostend.**

Bottom: **German dead awaiting burial outside the French trenches at La Bassée in late October. German troops had captured the town in autumn 1914.**

December 1914

1 The first units of Australian and New Zealand Expeditionary Forces arrived at Suez in Egypt.

The Battle of Limanova-Lapanov began between the Austro-Hungarians and the Russian Army near Kraków in Poland.

2 Austrian forces crossed the Danube and occupied Belgrade.

4 Fighting began at Qurna in Mesopotamia between British and Turkish forces.

The Portuguese Expeditionary Force left Lisbon for service in Angola.

5 French airmen carried out the first Entente bombing of a city when they dropped bombs on air sheds at Freiburg-in-Breisgau in Germany.

8 In the Battle of the Falklands a Royal Navy task force destroyed Von Spee's German cruiser squadron.

9 The town of Qurna was occupied by British forces after the Turks surrendered.

10 Field Marshal von der Goltz left Germany to take command of the Turkish Army.

11 Portuguese President Bernardino Luís Machado Guimarães resigned.

12 Naval officer and politician Victor Hugo de Azevedo Coutinho succeeded Guimarães as President of Portugal.

13 The British submarine B-11 sunk the Turkish battleship Messoudieh in the Dardanelles.

15 A German airship was sighted off the East coast of England – the first appearance of a hostile aircraft in Britain.

16 On the East coast of England Whitby, Scarborough and Hartlepool were shelled by a German battle cruiser fleet.

17 The Turkish offensive began in the Caucasus.

18 Britain proclaimed Egypt as a Protectorate.

19 Britain proclaimed Prince Hussein Kemal Pasha as Sultan of Egypt after his nephew Khedive Abbas Hilmi was deposed.

20 The First Battle of Champagne began between the French and German armies.

21 The first air raid took place in Britain when the German aircraft dropped bombs in the sea near Dover.

22 Admiral Sir George Astley Callaghan was appointed Commander-in-Chief, The Nore.

23 Captain Piper, the commanding officer of SMS Yorck, was court-martialled and sentenced to two years' imprisonment for the loss of his ship through negligence.

24 The second German air raid resulted in the first aerial bomb being dropped on English soil near Dover.

25 In some sectors of the Western Front, an unofficial Christmas truce was observed between German and British forces.

The Cuxhaven Raid took place when British ship-based aircraft mounted an attack on the German naval forces at Cuxhaven in Germany.

29 At the Battle of Sarikamish in the Caucasus Campaign, the Russians began an assault against the Turks.

30 The English trawler Ivy struck a mine and sank in the North Sea with the loss of all five crew.

Christmas truce 1914

The first Christmas of the war was bitingly cold. With the freezing temperatures came the grim reality that the opposing lines along the Western Front were there for the long haul. As far as the generals were concerned, Christmas was a day like any other. British soldiers did receive a "Princess Mary Box" – a seasonal gift of tobacco and chocolate, its name taken from King George V's daughter, who had set up the fund and whose image was depicted on the brass container in which the presents were shipped. But apart from that small token of festive cheer it should have been warring business as usual.

Gifts had also reached the German lines, courtesy of the Kaiser. They included Christmas trees, the decoration of which was a long-standing tradition in that country, one that had arrived in England with Queen Charlotte, the German wife of George III, and was popularised in the Victorian era. When British soldiers first saw these twinkling lights across the divide on Christmas Eve it was thought it might be a prelude to an attack. But the guns had fallen silent and the strains of "Stille Nacht" – "Silent Night" – floated across no-man's-land. The penny then dropped. The British responded with a carol of their own, and a bout of competitive singing ensued, replacing the swapping of gunfire and trading of shells. The two camps applauded each other's efforts, and soon heads were raised above the parapets, confident that for now at least it was not in danger of taking a bullet.

The two camps applauded each other's efforts, and soon heads were raised above the parapets, confident that for now at least it was not in danger of taking a bullet.

CHRISTMAS IN THE TRENCHES.

GREAT PREPARATIONS IN FRANCE.

AN INFORMAL TRUCE EXPECTED.

FROM OUR SPECIAL CORRESPONDENT.
GEORGE C. CURNOCK.

Paris, Wednesday.

More than 3,000,000 French soldiers will spend their Christmas Day in the trenches, camps, and barracks of France, far from their children and homes. The roads to the trenches are filled to-day with wagons taking great stores of good and comforting gifts to these brave fellows.

One at least will receive with his Christmas parcel a little letter which I read yesterday. When he gets it I hope he will pass it down the trench. I am sure it will bring a smile, and perhaps a tear, to the face of these impressionable men in the blue coats and red trousers who are holding the line to-morrow.

Here is this charming little letter written by René Pierre Fredet: "I hope that the soldiers will put their shoes in the trenches, and that le Petit Jésus will fill them, for we are quite ready to give our share of good things in order that they may be well filled."

It was no copy-book sentiment which made little René Pierre write his letter, but the genuine expression of a thought which is filling the hearts of millions of children in France to-day. There is not a child in France who would not give up his Christmas gifts to make the soldiers in the trenches happier.

CHRISTMAS AT THE FRONT.

British soldiers gathering mistletoe in the fighting area, where it grows so profusely.

CHRISTMAS IN THE GERMAN LINES.

A German field postal section sorting out parcels sent from the Fatherland for distribution among the men in the fighting line.

Below: On Christmas Eve, British soldiers noticed Christmas lights appearing in the German trenches and the following morning they heard cries of "Happy Christmas". The British responded with similar good wishes in German, giving rise to an informal armistice. Slowly both sides emerged from the trenches and met in no-man's-land to exchange pleasantries and gifts. The ceasefire also gave both sides a chance to collect and bury their fallen comrades.

Opposite above: During the truce the Northumberland Hussars 7th Division and German officers and their men met on the Bridoux-Rouges Bancs Sector.

Opposite middle: An opportunity for a member of the machine gun corps to kiss a French farm girl under the mistletoe.

Opposite below: Royal Scots Fusiliers dug in at La Bouteillerie during the winter of 1914. As the Germans were entrenched on enemy soil the onus was on the Entente Powers to find a way of removing them. Almost all military leaders at the time believed that offensives would bring reward, albeit possibly at great cost. But the costs were invariably high and the rewards modest.

On Christmas morning British and German soldiers along the 500-mile Western Front took the unofficial ceasefire a step further, venturing out into the pock-marked, corpse-strewn ground that separated them. Among them was Captain Charles Stockwell of the Fifth Welsh Fusiliers, who recalled that "a German officer appeared and walked out into the middle of no-man's-land, so I moved out to meet him amidst the cheers of both sides." He seemed, said Stockwell, "a very decent fellow".

Others followed their lead. There were handshakes, exchanges of food and other small tokens. There were conversations, perhaps with the aid of a translator. If language was a barrier, gesture sufficed. Football could be wordlessly enjoyed and impromptu games were organised, with helmets for goalposts. As well as allowing a brief moment of human fellowship during the season of goodwill, the truce also gave the men the chance to bury fallen comrades. They joined together to recite the 23rd Psalm – "The Lord is My Shepherd". Makeshift altars were constructed to celebrate Mass.

On the morning of 26 December, the truce came to an end in most places. Shots were fired into the air to signal that hostilities were being resumed. To categorise the festive respite as the humble ranks cocking a snook at authority was a misreading of events. Some NCOs and officers warmly embraced the ceasefire, though there were commanders on both sides who deplored the fraternisation and ordered that no such friendly relations be established again. General Horace Smith-Dorrien, commander of II Corps, was one who fulminated over the perceived cosying up to the enemy. "To finish this war quickly," he instructed, "we must keep up the fighting spirit and do all we can to discourage friendly intercourse."

And indeed there was no cessation on the scale of the Christmas 1914 truce. But nor was it the last example of amity temporarily replacing enmity. Covert messages were occasionally passed between the rival lines, arranging brief lulls in the fighting. Other missives might warn apologetically that they would have to resume firing as top brass were in the vicinity. These cessations were born of a live-and-let-live code for which there was plenty of historical precedent. To some members of the officer class this was deemed subverting the warring process, a practice to be stamped out whenever it occurred. To those who laid their weapons aside it was a mutually beneficial moment of shared interest and common humanity.

CHRISTMAS TREES IN GERMAN TRENCHES.

TROOPS FEAST WHILE BELGIANS FAST.

FROM OUR SPECIAL CORRESPONDENT, JAMES DUNN.

ROTTERDAM, Friday.

Sentiment and shrapnel mingled in the German trenches this Christmastide. From correspondents at Sluis, Maastricht, Bergen-op-Zoom, and Sas van Gent I have received reports stating that great Christmas celebrations have taken place in the trenches, at the depots, and along the frontier. The enemy made merry in obedience to the military order, for notices were issued several days ago that the troops must do their best to enjoy Yuletide.

Hundreds of thousands of parcels arrived from Germany containing knitted articles, sweets, cakes, and tobacco. In addition the poor Belgian peasantry were bled to assist the German Christmas. Huge levies of wine and cigars were made in Ghent and Bruges, and the Belgian people were even asked to make Christmas cakes for the German soldiers. The Belgians in reply asked where the flour was to come from as they had eaten nothing but black bread for a long time, and even that was scarce.

While the German soldiers were feasting, drinking, and roaring wine songs the unfortunate Belgians were glad to have a Christmas dinner of half a loaf. Meat or vegetables are unknown, while butter and cheese are rare luxuries.

Chapter Two

1915

A Deepening Stalemate

On Christmas Day 1914 the opposing forces in the advanced western trenches put their enmity in abeyance and exchanged pleasantries in no-man's-land. It was but a temporary respite. The new year brought fresh initiatives to try and break the impasse. Perhaps technology held the key. Aircraft, tanks, flame-throwers and poison gas would all be deployed, but these were still in their infancy; there remained the widespread belief that victory would go to the side which possessed the mightier battering ram of men and shells.

By the end of 1914 some German commanders felt that, with the failure of the Schlieffen Plan, Germany could not secure victory. One of the Entente powers would have to be removed from the equation. General Erich von Falkenhayn, Germany's new Chief-of-Staff, favoured a fresh onslaught on the Western Front. The British Expeditionary Force had been wiped out and Britain was replacing them with volunteers rather than conscripts. It would be some time before "Kitchener's Army" was ready for battle, and Falkenhayn realised this was a window of opportunity. However, Austria-Hungary needed reinforcing, and if the Central Powers wanted to pick off one of her enemies, Russia was the natural target. A huge redeployment of troops from west to east thus took place. Russia had done well enough against the ramshackle forces of Germany's ally; how would she fare against the awesome military machine of the Reich itself?

Russians in retreat

The territorial gains in the east were some of the most spectacular of the entire conflict. At the start of the year the Russians held a line some nine hundred miles long, stretching from the Carpathians to the East Prussian Frontier. Yet, they would soon be in full-scale retreat. Lemberg and Przemysyl, such recent glorious triumphs for the Russian army, were both reclaimed by the Central Powers in June. The Allies were stunned but not surprised when Warsaw fell on 4 August. The only crumb of comfort in London and Paris was to applaud a well-executed tactical retreat. Reviewing the first year of the conflict on 15 September 1915, War Secretary Lord Kitchener told the House of Lords:

"The success of this great rearguard action has been rendered possible by the really splendid fighting qualities of the Russian soldier, who in every case where actual conflict has taken place has shown himself infinitely superior to his adversary. It is these fighting qualities of the men of the Russian Army which have empowered her able generals and competent staff to carry out the immensely difficult operation of retirement of a whole line over some hundred to two hundred miles, without allowing the enemy to break through at any point or by surrounding their forces, to bring about the tactical position which might involve the surrender of a considerable portion of the Russian Army."

This was a charitable view based on political expediency rather than military reality. The truth was that the ill-equipped Russian forces were in disarray, and their ability to live to fight another day had more to do with Falkenhayn's reluctance to press home his advantage than any shrewd manoeuvring on the part of the retreating ranks. Tsar Nicholas certainly saw little merit in his army's performance. He sacked his Commander-in-Chief, Grand Duke Nicholas, and took personal control of his forces in the field. More significant perhaps, was that, although the Russians were on the back foot, they were not cowed into submission. German hopes for an early armistice in the east were dashed.

Heavy casualties

On the Western Front it was a year of heavy casualties for little gain. While Kitchener's recruits were undergoing a rapid programme of military training, the Allied trenches in France and Belgium were largely manned by the French. The National Register Bill, introduced in July 1915, required every man and woman between the ages of 15 and 65 to submit personal details, but the question of undertaking national service remained a polite enquiry; Britain would hold out against conscription for another year.

Germany's redeployment of eight divisions to the Eastern Front meant a significant weakening of the Reich's forces in the Western theatre. But Germany had a new weapon to compensate for the lack of manpower. Gas was first used by the Central Powers in the east at the beginning of the year and by April Britain and France also had to contend with this new threat, described by Sir John French as "a cynical and barbarous disregard of the well-known usages of civilized war and a flagrant defiance of the Hague Convention."

It was on 22 April, the start of the Second Battle of Ypres, that the western Allies were first confronted with a thick yellow asphyxiating gas cloud. There was chaos in the Allied line, but the Germans were naturally wary of following up too quickly and exposing themselves to the chlorine's deadly effects. Using makeshift respirators of handkerchiefs soaked in water or urine, the Allies rallied. By the end of the battle, on 25 May, the stalemate remained.

The Allies, meanwhile, planned offensives of their own. On 10 March they made their first serious attempt to break the enemy line, at Neuve Chapelle. The village was successfully wrested from German hands, although Sir John French's report made grim reading: 12,000 men either killed, wounded or missing for a gain of three hundred yards on a front of half a mile.

The Battle of Neuve Chapelle and the Second Battle of Ypres exposed a dire shortage in Britain's munitions production. Demand far outstripped supply and when this reached the public domain it precipitated a political crisis. In May the Liberal government was replaced by a coalition. Asquith retained the premiership, while Lloyd George was moved from Chancellor of the Exchequer to a new department, the Ministry of Munitions.

Aerial bombardment

The war was also being waged at sea and in the air. Zeppelins had bombed Paris in the early days of the conflict, and on 19 January 1915 British civilians had to face an aerial bombardment for the first time. Parts of the Norfolk coastline were the first to come under attack, with further raids on the south-east and North Sea coast in the following months. Fatalities were few but the fact that they were almost all non-combatants added a new dimension to the conflict. It was called "frightfulness" at the time; terror tactics in modern parlance. This new strategy on the part of the Central Powers was more about damaging morale than inflicting huge casualties. It was a policy that was also soon in evidence on the high seas.

On 18 February 1915 Germany declared the waters around Great Britain and Ireland a war region. This did not mean that the German fleet had to emerge from the safety of Kiel in order to prosecute the war. Instead, using submarines and mines, Germany blockaded the waters around the British Isles. The Allies were employing a similar tactic, putting to good use the fact that control of the North Sea provided a natural blockade of the German fleet. Both sides were wary, the Allies of the U-boat threat, and the Germans of committing themselves to a sea battle against the superior numbers of the British fleet. This shadow-boxing could bring no quick reward. And the perceived inactivity of the mighty Royal Navy earned it scornful comments from many in the trenches. The Germans tried to increase the effectiveness of their blockade by announcing that commercial shipping would be attacked without warning. Winston Churchill, First Lord of the Admiralty, speaking in the House of Commons, condemned Germany's new terror threat as "open piracy and murder on the high seas".

On 7 May the Cunard liner *Lusitania* was sunk a few miles off the Irish coast with the loss of over 1000 lives. The German embassy in Washington had issued a statement a week earlier announcing that the vessel was a potential target but few took the threat seriously enough to cancel their trip. The US government responded to the loss of 128 American lives only with strong words, but the sinking of the *Lusitania* generated powerful anti-German feelings across the Atlantic and would be the first step along the way to the USA's entry into the war. These same feelings would also be widespread in Britain, where animosity often spilled over into violence. Shops with German connections, real or imagined, were attacked by angry mobs. Prince Louis of Battenberg had already resigned as First Sea Lord, faced with prejudice against his Germanic origins. The same sentiments would lead the royal family to adopt the name of Windsor.

Gallipoli

When war broke out the Allies' naval strength had been regarded as a vital factor in the forthcoming struggle. The first six months had shown little evidence of that supremacy, but in early 1915 an Anglo-French task force was deployed in the Mediterranean with the aim of changing all that. The plan was to attack Turkey through the Dardanelles, the narrow waterway from the open sea which led all the way to Constantinople. If that city could be taken there was every chance of forcing a passage through to their Russian allies, a major strategic coup.

In February the forts at the entrance to the Straits were bombarded by a fleet led by Vice-Admiral Sackville Carden. Progress up the Straits was slow and on 18 March three battleships were lost to mines. It was decided that the success of the campaign depended on the deployment of land forces. On 25 April British and French troops, together with soldiers from the Australia and New Zealand Army Corps, landed on the Gallipoli Peninsula. Everything was against Sir Ian Hamilton's men: the weather was bad, the terrain difficult and the enemy forces strongly positioned. John Masefield, the future Poet Laureate, commanded a hospital boat off Gallipoli and offered this insight to those who wished to picture the scene:

"Imagine the hills entrenched, the landing mined, the beaches tangled with barbed wire, ranged by howitzers and swept by machine guns, and themselves three thousand miles from home, going out before dawn, with rifles, packs and water bottles, to pass the mines under shell-fire, cut through the wire under machine-gun fire, clamber up the hills under fire of all arms, by the glare of shell bursts, in the withering and crashing tumult of modern war, and then to dig themselves in in a waterless and burning hill while a more numerous enemy charges them with the bayonet.

"And let them imagine themselves enduring this night after night, day after day, without rest or solace, nor respite from the peril of death, seeing their friends killed and their position imperilled, getting their food, their munitions, even their drink from the jaws of death, and their breath from the taint of death. Let them imagine themselves driven mad by heat and toil and thirst by day, shaken by frost at midnight, weakened by disease and broken by pestilence, yet rising on the word with a shout and going forward to die in exultation in a cause foredoomed and almost hopeless."

Opposite: **Troops going ashore from HMS** *Implacable* **during the Dardanelles campaign.**

Hopeless it proved. With the Allies pinned down, a fresh landing at Suvla was carried out in August but this was quickly nullified. By November it was clear that retreat was the only option. Churchill, one of the chief advocates of the campaign, had spoken of being just "a few miles from victory", but those few miles remained a far-distant prospect. Sir Charles Munro replaced Hamilton, and he was charged with leading the evacuation. Churchill resigned. The withdrawal at least was a spectacular success. It was effected between December 1915 and January the following year with barely a casualty, although the entire campaign had cost the Allies more than 250,000 men. Turkey's success in preventing the Allies from gaining access to the Black Sea and linking up with the Russian Army was that country's most significant contribution to the Central Powers' war effort.

Haig takes command

The autumn of 1915 saw Joffre planning yet another offensive on the Western Front. Driving the enemy from French soil was the over-arching concern in spite of the harsh experience of the spring offensive. Joffre clung to the hope that throwing yet more manpower and weaponry at the German line might bring the desired outcome. It didn't. British troops, however, fared better in the advance in Artois and Champagne. Sir Douglas Haig's First Army took Loos, and this time it was the German soldiers who had to contend with a gas attack, the first time that British forces had used this instrument of war. Lack of reserves prevented the attack from bearing fruit and the German forces were able to rally. Sir John French was blamed for keeping the reserves too far from the action, an error of judgment which would see him replaced by Haig as Commander-in-Chief of the British Expeditionary Force in December.

As the year drew to a close the Central Powers were in the ascendancy. Britain suffered a major blow in Mesopotamia, where her interests had become vulnerable targets since Turkey's entry into the war. In September a force led by General Charles Townshend took Kut-el-Amara but an attempt to push on to Baghdad proved to be a hopeless undertaking. As with Gallipoli, a bold offensive turned into full-scale retreat. Townshend's exhausted men struggled back to Kut. Though they held out for 143 days on paltry rations – just a little flour and horsemeat by the end – the outcome was inevitable. The surrender would finally come in April 1916, with some 13,000 men taken prisoner by the Turks.

The German advance

By the year's end the great German advance in the east had yielded remarkable territorial gains: Ukraine, Lithuania, modern-day Poland and parts of Belarus. Nor were they finished yet. In the autumn Austro-Hungarian forces mounted yet another assault on Serbia, this time with German support. For the Serbs it meant another attack from the north-west, but now the country faced a further difficulty, from the east. Bulgaria threw in her lot with the Central Powers in October. Ferdinand, Bulgaria's ruler, had been seduced by offers of parts of Serbian land, a bribe which played well with a country that had been forced to cede territory to Serbia during the Balkan wars. The addition of Bulgaria's weight to the attack on Serbia was crucial. When Anglo-French forces tried to help their Balkan ally by entering the country via Greece, Bulgarian troops blocked their way. Serbia was on her own.

Belgrade was quickly overrun and the Serbs were forced into a full-scale evacuation of the country, through the harsh mountain regions of Montenegro and Albania. Thousands perished on the flight to the Adriatic coast, from where the survivors were taken to Corfu in Allied ships.

Despite the considerable successes the Central Powers enjoyed in 1915 they had not achieved their great aim: to force one of the Entente Powers to the negotiating table. And by now the Allies had been bolstered by the addition of Italy to their ranks, the former Triple Alliance member switching sides in May 1915. The new year would bring a fresh attempt to break the deadlock: the long-awaited major sea battle between the naval superpowers, Britain and Germany.

SPECIAL PICTURES OF THE WAR IN AFRICA.

SERIOUS RUSSIAN RETREAT IN EAST PRUSSIA.

CZAR AT THE FRONT: CLIMAX OF ATTACKS FOR WARSAW.

A GRIM BIRTHDAY PRESENT FOR THE KAISER.

1915 begins: Stalemate at Soissons

Christmas 1914 came and went, and it was becoming all too apparent that this was a war for the long haul. The strategists set their sights for the new year. The British blockade was in place, but there was no telling how long strangulation of the German economy would take. Not soon was the answer, for in the short term Germany countered the loss of international trade by gearing its considerable domestic production to the war effort. On the campaigning front, leaders on both sides considered the great "East v West" question. Churchill was in the former camp, arch-proponent for an attack on the Central Powers' perceived Achilles' heel: Turkey. Russia was promised Constantinople in a post-victory Ottoman carve-up, which strengthened the resolve of Britain's eastern ally. It also ensured German peace overtures to the Tsar were resisted. Germany's chief of staff Erich von Falkenhayn knew one Entente power had to be eliminated, and with the failure of the Schlieffen Plan he looked eastwards. There was no immediate prospect of success in the west – his preferred option – and he also recognised the pressing need to shore up his brittle Austrian ally. France's chief concern was a German-held salient whose nose, around Soissons, was uncomfortably close to Paris. 1915 saw repeated Anglo-French attempts to punch a hole in the enemy line, efforts which merely confirmed the primacy of defence over attack. Here lay the great conundrum: the Western Front was clearly the principal theatre, but with its increasingly elaborate defences it was also the most difficult nut to crack; in Kitchener's words, "a fortress which cannot be taken by assault".

The Western Front was clearly the principal theatre, but with its increasingly elaborate defences it was also the most difficult nut to crack.

Left: Troops try to keep warm as they face the daily challenges of fighting on the Western Front. On average a soldier would spend about eight days on the front line, with clear plans in place for rotating the men.

Opposite left: A Belgian sentinel keeps watch. From 1915 countries began to issue troops with steel helmets to prevent injuries caused by shrapnel from exploding artillery shells on the front line.

Opposite middle and right: British soldiers on their way to the front. The conviction remained that throwing increasing numbers of men into the fray would bring the desired victory.

GREAT GERMAN AIR RAID OVER DUNKIRK.

FIERCE FIGHTING.

MORE GERMAN TRENCHES SEIZED.

IMPORTANT FRENCH CAPTURE ON THE AISNE.

161st DAY OF THE WAR.
90th DAY OF BATTLE FOR CALAIS.

The Aisne region is again a centre of interest. The French report says that to the north-west of Soissons two more lines of German trenches have been taken [...] 182, thus accomplishing the mission of the [...] known, the French [...] great disadvantage [...]

FRENCH OFFICIAL.

Paris, Monday, 3 p.m.

From the sea to the Lys there has been intermittent cannonading of slight intensity. In the region of Ypres our artillery effectively returned the fire of the enemy and succeeded in making very good practice on the German trenches.

AIR SQUADRON'S ATTACK.

50 GERMAN BOMBS ON DUNKIRK.

TWO MACHINES BROUGHT DOWN.

We print to-day a full account of the great German air raid on Dunkirk on Sunday, which was briefly reported in our later editions yesterday.

FROM OUR SPECIAL CORRESPONDENT.
G. WARD PRICE.

NORTHERN FRANCE,
Monday.

The biggest air raid of the whole war was carried out by the Germans against Dunkirk yesterday.

Fourteen armoured Aviatik biplanes [...] over [...] 30 p.m. [...] from [...] church [...] white [...] on the [...] the ap[...] the s[...] body o[...] the war [...] he ma[...] side s[...] aircra[...] the [...] [...] this [...]

were ranging on them with shrapnel, and all round the German fliers the white puffs were bursting. One of the biplanes turned back, and as the sun glinted on the steel sides the few people who had not taken shelter in their cellars raised a cheer, for they thought it was on fire.

However, more and more of the airmen came, not all at once but succeeding each other, while the [...]

U.S. VIEWS OF SIR E. GREY'S REPLY.

GENERALLY FAVOURABLE RECEPTION.

OUTBURST BY A NEWSPAPER.

FROM OUR OWN CORRESPONDENT.

NEW YORK, Monday.

Sir Edward Grey's preliminary reply to the American Note is now public property. The Washington correspondents who were received at the State Department yesterday have no official comment to communicate, except that "high [...] to reply [...] covery o[...] ocement [...] icials, [...] declar[...] will n[...] conside[...] regarded [...] esitation [...] nt of the [...] ined in the [...] notes, the [...] author [...] It [...]

that the British and American positions will be found to be not so far apart.

"Meanwhile it is pleasant to note that Great Britain volunteers to permit the renewal of rubber exports to the United States —an exhibition of comity in a field not covered by the present contraband negotiations."

The *New York Press* says:

"All fair-minded Americans will admit [...]

STIFF PROBLEM FOR THE TURKS.

PERIL OF FRESH TROOPS BY SEA.

GENERAL'S PATHETIC SURRENDER.

FROM OUR SPECIAL CORRESPONDENT.
H. HAMILTON FYFE.

PETROGRAD, Monday.

The part which the Black Sea Fleet is taking in the operations against the Turks is commented upon by the newspapers this morning as being capable of having a valuable influence on the campaign.

It seems that the transport which was sunk after the Russian ships had asserted [...] k Sea by driving [...] muidieh was the [...] tantinople after [...] the disaster to [...] response to an [...] troops. If the [...] blockade Trebi[...] ing of reinforce[...] nition, the task [...] be made much [...] d from Constan[...] tion. It would [...] ds of Asia Minor [...] e for the trans[...] rest garrison to [...] distance is 370 [...] rres, for she [...] ally the 24th [...] Dardanelles 35th [...]

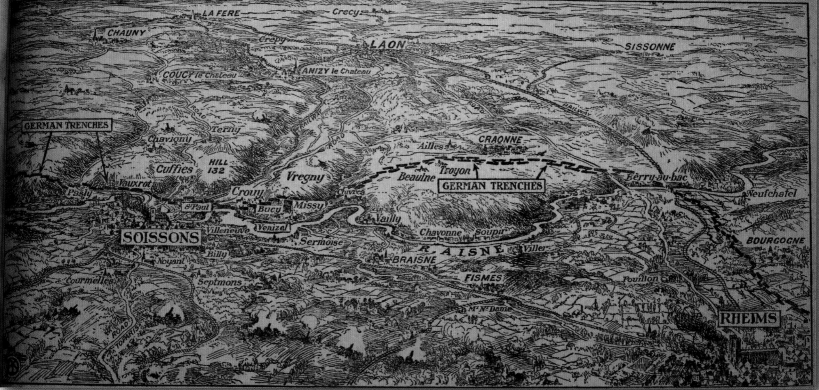

PICTURE MAP OF THE VALLEY OF THE AISNE, SHOWING THE LINE OF GERMAN TRENCHES FROM SOISSONS TO RHEIMS.

January 1915

1 The Royal Navy battleship HMS *Formidable* was sunk by a German submarine in the English Channel.

2 Royal Navy cruiser HMS *Fox* participated in a raid on Dar-es-Salaam in Tanganyika.

3 Belgium's Cardinal Desire Joseph Mercier was detained in his Malines Palace following the publication of open letters criticising German occupation forces.

4 The London Stock Exchange reopened.

6 Lord Kitchener reviewed the military situation in the House of Lords.

8 The Battle of Soissons began when French forces attacked German troops near Soissons in northern France.

9 The Germans shelled the cathedral and launched a counterattack at Soissons.

10 16 German aeroplanes tried to cross the English Channel. Bad weather thwarted the attempt and they bombed Dunkirk instead.

11 French forces made progress against German counter-attacks in the Battle of Soissons.

12 British forces landed on Mafia Island and captured its German garrison in German East Africa.

13 The British War Council instructed the Admiralty to prepare for a naval expedition in the Dardanelles.

14 The Battle of Soissons ended after the Germans launched a successful counter-attack against the French on the north bank of the River Aisne near Soissons.

15 The first of four French boats to be lost in the Dardanelles in 1915, the French submarine *Saphir* was sunk in the Dardanelles Narrows.

17 The Battle of Sarikamish ended when Russian troops defeated the Turks who suffered major casualties.

18 German forces mounted an attack against British-held Jasin in German East Africa.

19 The first successful Zeppelin raid took place on British soil when two aircraft bombed Great Yarmouth and King's Lynn.

21 Lieut-General Adolf Wild von Hohenborn replaced Erich von Falkenhayn as German Minister of War.

23 Heavy fighting continued in the Argonne and Alsace on the Western Front.

24 The Battle of Dogger Bank began in the North Sea between squadrons of the British Grand Fleet and the German High Seas Fleet.

25 Lieut-General Sir William Robertson was appointed Chief of the General Staff to the British Expeditionary Force.

26 Turkish troops began their advance through the Sinai desert to attack the Suez Canal.

27 Lieut-General Sir R. C. Maxwell was appointed Quartermaster General to the British Expeditionary Force.

28 The American merchant ship *William P. Frye* was sunk in the South Atlantic Ocean by a German cruiser whilst on its way to England with a cargo of wheat.

29 The Walney Island Coast Battery at Barrow-in-Furness was shelled by a German submarine.

30 British merchant ships were advised by the British Admiralty to fly neutral ensigns in British waters.

31 The Germans fired tear gas shells at the Russians in the Battle of Bolimów near Warsaw.

EXCLUSIVE PICTURES FROM THE BATTLEFIELD AT SOISSONS.

FRIDAY, JANUARY 23, 1915.

FIRST PHOTOGRAPHS OF THE GREAT NORTH SEA BATTLE.
THE BRITISH FLAGSHIP RACING INTO ACTION.

Admiral Hipper turned tail, abandoning the stricken Blücher, which sank with the loss of over 900 German lives.

Battle in the North Sea

Though the British fleet enjoyed superiority over its German counterpart, there was a wariness to commit to a large-scale engagement. Blockade was seen as the safer option, but there were skirmishes in which honours were shared. The Royal Navy had the better of the Battle of Heligo Bight in August 1914, while U-boats claimed their first scalps and surface raiders shelled Britain's east coast. On 24 January 1915 the navies squared up again in the North Sea. German codebooks had fallen into British hands, giving the Royal Navy forewarning of Admiral Hipper's plans for a scouting mission in the Dogger Bank sector. His target was fishing vessels thought to be reporting ship movements to the Admiralty, but instead he faced a battlecruiser squadron commanded by Sir David Beatty. Hipper turned tail, abandoning the stricken cruiser *Blücher*, which sank with the loss of over 900 lives. Though Beatty's flagship was disabled, it was a clear victory for the Grand Fleet, and but for communications problems could have been even more emphatic.

Left: SMS *Blücher*, an armoured cruiser from the German fleet had shelled the town of Hartlepool in December 1914. During the attack the British coastal battery successfully hit the ship six times but inflicted very little damage although six of the crew were killed. At the Battle of Dogger Bank the *Blücher* soon became the victim and after constant shelling, a fire broke out on board and the cruiser began to list.

Below: After a subsequent torpedo attack and further bombardment the crippled ship finally capsized with the loss of 900 men. British attempts to save the crew were thwarted by the sudden overhead presence of a Zeppelin and a

German seaplane; both thought the doomed cruiser was a British battleship and bombed the destroyers coming to her aid. Despite this, 234 men were rescued including Erdmann, the Captain at Sea.

Opposite: A vigilant British soldier keeps watch from the trenches, well protected by sandbags. The trenches created by the German army were generally more elaborate and much deeper than Allied constructions. One captured on the Somme in 1916 had been fitted out with electricity, ventilation and toilets and, bizarrely, was decorated with wallpaper.

Here the world sees for the first time the most dramatic moment of history's first Battle of Dreadnoughts. The wounded and broken Bluecher lies dying, and hundreds of her crew are seen facing death. Some of them against their will are slipping into the sea; some are jumping in. For near them is a British warship—the cruiser from which the photograph was taken—and they know that although German aircraft fly somewhere overhead dropping bombs upon the rescuers the humane work of rescue will still go on. On the starboard side of the capsizing German leviathan a score of miniature dramas reach a climax. The bow of the sinking ship is to the right of the spectator. The Bluecher turned over in one slow, even movement; then, when she was upside down, she floated for ten minutes with a number of the crew walking her bottom. One man, it will be seen, has clambered down to the bilge-keel, from which the water is pouring in sheets. Others are sliding down towards the water; one has taken a jump into the sea, and in the water several heads appear as

black dots. Some of the men on the side have stripped and are wearing only swimming jackets. The dense black group astern is perhaps the line of officers, linked arm in arm, who were seen there as the warship sank. White smoke pours from the hull amidships; dense black smoke from her forward. Great fires rage on board her. The wreck of the tripod foremast is seen to the right, foreshortened, and just below it and to the left of it a 6-in. gun. Abaft that is a turret with two 8.2-in. guns clearly outlined against the skyline. Neither funnel shows, but the mainmast appears strangely foreshortened and very dimly seen through the smoke abaft the second turret with its pair of 8.2-in. guns. Between the two turrets is another 6-in. gun. The lower edge of the armour belt runs as a black line for the whole length of the side. It shows no hit. Of the booms which carry the torpedo netting one forward has had the fastening shot away and is hanging, the others are in their usual place.

Photographic reproductions of the above wonderful picture may be obtained on written application to "Bluecher Picture Dept.," "The Daily Mail," Carmelite House, London, E.C. Reprints, 12 inches by 10, will be sent post free for 2s. 6d., and larger reproductions, 15 inches by 12, for 3s. 6d.

Copyright in the United States of America and Canada by the International News Service.] Printed and Published by the ASSOCIATED NEWSPAPERS, LIMITED, at "Daily Mail" Buildings, London and Manchester, Thursday, February 18, 1915.

"The First Blitz"

In October 1899 aviation pioneer Baden Baden-Powell – brother of the famous scout movement founder – wrote to *The Times* to highlight the importance of Count Ferdinand von Zeppelin's aluminium-framed, gas-filled "aerial steamship", which he had seen under construction. This aeronautical marvel, as large as an ocean-going liner and capable of achieving speeds of 22 mph, posed a political question for Britain, said Baden-Powell, for future wars would be decided in the skies. He exhorted that "we in England may not be long in following in the lead of our energetic cousins in making a bold and unsparing attempt to conquer this element".

Others clearly shared Baden-Powell's vision for the conduct of future warfare. In that same year the Hague Convention prohibited the dropping of explosives from balloons or any other flying machine. It was just one example of peacetime attempts to establish rules of engagement that fell by the wayside once countries took up arms.

Baden-Powell was prescient regarding the role of aircraft in conflict, though wide of the mark regarding the impact they would make in the conflagration that ignited 15 years after his letter appeared in *The Times*. That said, the cigar-shaped behemoths whose development was avidly reported in the British press did play a significant role in the Great War. They did not wreak major damage or inflict heavy casualties; but they did bring terror to the skies over Britain, and induced panic in its civilian population.

Bombing accuracy compromised

The raids began on 19 January 1915, when two airships appeared in the night skies over East Anglia. The timing was not accidental. The Kaiser had been reluctant to sanction such bombing missions, knowing that it would be impossible to target military installations and leave residential areas unscathed. The Zeppelin's chief advantage was its ability to maintain altitudes that effectively put it beyond the range of ground weapons or fighter aircraft – initially, at least. From such heights bombing accuracy was inevitably compromised. The Kaiser had hoped his army would crush all before it, and this scattergun aerial bombardment would not be needed. Only when Christmas came and went and the ground war was deadlocked was the decision made to rain explosives on British soil. The order was to avoid civilian areas, and in particular the palaces of royalty to whom the Kaiser was related. That was a forlorn hope, soon abandoned. It was now a war of attrition, where denting morale and hitting the enemy's industrial base were as important as trying to punch a hole in the Western Front.

Zeppelins had the better of things in the early days of the "First Blitz", as the raids came to be known. Defences were not potent enough and the airships roamed the night skies largely unhindered. But they were not inviolable. Adverse weather could spell disaster for these giants, and even if atmospheric conditions were favourable there were two glaring weaknesses. One was lack of speed and manoeuvrability: airships were ponderously slow compared with fighter aircraft. The other was the very substance that kept them aloft: hydrogen. Zeppelins contained vast envelopes of this highly flammable gas. If these could be breached and the hydrogen ignited, the vessel would descend in a fireball. For those who manned them this was their greatest fear. For those trying to defend British territory it was the Achilles' heel they were keen to exploit.

Above: The Zeppelin *L2* just pulling away on its maiden flight in January 1906. She was the largest Zeppelin ever built, measuring 160 metres in length, with double spotlights, four 80 hp engines and the capacity to hold a crew of 38. During the flight she was forced to make an emergency landing and was subsequently destroyed by a storm that raged that night.

Below right: Policemen and civilians hold up the remains of German incendiary bombs after a Zeppelin raid. These tin containers were usually filled with kerosene and oil and wrapped in tar-covered rope.

Opposite: Bomb damage left in Bury St Edmunds after the April 1915 Zeppelin attack. During the course of the conflict Germany conducted over fifty bombing raids on England. Beginning with attacks on King's Lynn and Great Yarmouth in January 1915, the terrifying airships appeared without warning, inflicting fear and panic in the civilian population.

They did not wreak major damage or inflict heavy casualties; but they did bring terror to the skies over Britain, and induced panic in its civilian population.

ZEPPELIN RAID ON ENGLAND LAST NIGHT

AIRSHIP ATTACK ON YARMOUTH, SHERINGHAM, AND KING'S LYNN.

THREE PERSONS KILLED BY BOMBS.

PRIVATE HOUSES AND SHOPS DAMAGED.

ZEPPELIN REPORTED OVER SANDRINGHAM.

AIRSHIPS SEEN GOING HOME OVER DUTCH ISLANDS.

A Zeppelin raid took place over England last night.

Three airships were first reported from Amsterdam.

The first bombs were dropped at Yarmouth between eight and nine o'clock, and the last that had been heard of them up to the time of going to press was that one passed over Hunstanton at 11 p.m.

Besides Yarmouth, where two persons were killed and one wounded, Sheringham and King's Lynn were also attacked. At Sheringham no one was killed, but at King's Lynn a boy lost his life and his parents were injured. The Central News says bombs were dropped at Sandringham, but other reports deny this.

The King and Queen returned to London from Sandringham yesterday afternoon. The news of his Majesty's intended return was published in yesterday's *Daily Mail*, but no doubt the latest news the Germans had when the air raid started was that the Royal Family were at Sandringham.

Three airships were reported this morning to be returning along the Dutch coast.

CALM OF THE PEOPLE.

FROM OUR SPECIAL CORRESPONDENT.
PERCY W. D. IZZARD.

A ZEPPELIN LANDING AFTER A FLIGHT.

MAN AND WOMAN KILLED.

YARMOUTH STREETS CLEARED BY SOLDIERS.

NARRATIVES BY RESIDENTS.

TOWN PLUNGED IN DARKNESS.

FROM OUR OWN CORRESPONDENT.
GREAT YARMOUTH,
Tuesday Night.

broken down by the concussion and many windows shattered.

NEAR SANDRINGHAM.

LAD KILLED AT KING'S LYNN.

FROM OUR SPECIAL CORRESPONDENT.
IPSWICH,
Wednesday Morning.

Many reports have reached me that bombs were dropped on Sandringham. The latest reports, however, show that although Sandringham was possibly in the area covered by the Zeppelins, well ...

way. Great assistance was rendered by the police authorities, by the National Guard, and by the Worcestershire Yeomanry."

KILLED IN BED.

Another account says the boy victim was named Goat, aged 17. He was in bed when the bomb crashed through the roof and killed him.

The Central News says King's Lynn correspondent telephones ...

HOW THEY STARTED.

REPORTS FROM DUTCH AND DANISH COASTS.

FROM OUR OWN CORRESPONDENT.
AMSTERDAM, Tuesday.

From information which I have received to-day from my correspondents ...

WHAT WAS SEEN AT SHERINGHAM.

SEARCHLIGHTS FLASHED TO THE EARTH.

UNEXPLODED BOMB PICKED UP.

FROM OUR OWN CORRESPONDENT.
SHERINGHAM, Tuesday Night.

A resident at Sheringham said: "It was about 8.30 that the Zeppelins came to Sheringham. I believe there were two. I certainly saw one myself.

"It was flying along at a great height. I was unable to judge the distance, but I should say not less than 3,000ft. It was a wonderful and awe-inspiring spectacle. The Zeppelin, like a great cigar, lay dim and dark against the blackness of the sky, but its outlines were unmistakable. The Zeppelin was fitted with searchlights, which now and again were flashed below, casting a weird ray of light on the dark town and countryside.

"Then came the crash of bombs. So far as is known four were dropped on Sheringham. One went through a house, another dropped on waste ground ..."

February 1915

1   A Turkish attack on El Qantara on the Suez Canal was repulsed by fire from British ships.

Russian forces counter-attacked against a German advance in continued fighting at Bolimów.

2   Forward elements of Turkish forces reached the Suez Canal.

3   Turkish troops attacked El Firdan and crossed the Suez Canal but were beaten back by Indian and Gurkha troops along with French ships.

Three of the conspirators involved in the killing of Archduke Franz Ferdinand and his wife were hanged by Austrian authorities.

4   The commander of the German High Seas Fleet publicly declared a war zone around the British Isles and announced that all merchant ships would be sunk without warning when a submarine blockade of Britain begins on 18 February.

5   The British, French and Russian Governments agreed to pool their financial resources.

6   British ocean liner RMS *Lusitania* arrived at Liverpool flying the flag of the United States.

7   The Second Battle of the Masurian Lakes, also known as the Winter Battle of the Masurian Lakes, began between German and Russian forces.

9   After being stationed at Salisbury Plain in England, units of the 1st Canadian Division embarked for France.

11 US President Woodrow Wilson warned Germany that attacks on US ships breached US neutrality whilst simultaneously protesting to Great Britain about the misuse of the American flag on British ships.

12 French troops began an offensive in Champagne on the Western Front.

14 German troops captured British trenches near St Eloi on the Western Front.

15 Allied governments suggested to Greece that it should intervene in support of Serbia and promised military support at the port of Salonika.

The sepoys of the Indian 5th Light Infantry mutinied against the British in Singapore.

16 The British Government decided to send the 29th Division to Gallipoli.

17 Two German Zeppelins were forced down by high winds in north-west Denmark.

18 The German submarine blockade of Britain came into force.

French forces made slight gains near Verdun, in Artois, Champagne and Vosges.

19 The Allied naval bombardment of the Dardanelles and Gallipoli began.

The Norwegian ship SS *Belridge* was torpedoed by a German submarine near Folkestone in Kent – the first victim of the German blockade.

20 The British Government issued orders for the deployment at Gallipoli of Australian and New Zealand troops who were in Egypt.

22 The Second Battle of the Masurian Lakes ended in a German victory with the Russians suffering heavy losses.

23 The Royal Marines landed at the island of Lemnos in the Aegean Sea.

24 The First British Territorial Division left England for France.

25 British ships resumed their bombardment of the Dardanelles forts.

26 Germans troops employed liquid fire for the first time against French troops in the Verdun Sector.

27 The Russians recaptured Przasnysz during the First Battle of Przasnysz in Poland.

28 The troops of the Princess Patricia's Canadian Light Infantry staged the first trench raid of the war near Ypres, Belgium.

Zeppelins raid Britain's East Coast

On the night of Tuesday, 19 January 1915, the first Zeppelin raiding party brought a new threat to the residents of England's east coast towns. Great Yarmouth and King's Lynn bore the brunt, taking direct hits that resulted in four fatalities. Yarmouth shoemaker Samuel Smith and spinster Martha Taylor were the first civilian air-raid victims, while the youngest casualty was 14-year-old Percy Goate, killed when a bomb struck the family home in King's Lynn. Percy's mother gave the following account at the inquest: "We were all upstairs for bed, me and my husband, with baby and Percy, when we heard a buzzing noise. My husband put out the light. I saw a bomb fall from the sky and strike the pillow where Percy was lying. I tried to wake him but he was dead, and then the house fell in." Medical reports suggested that shock had been a factor in his death, and in that of the fourth victim, 26-year-old Alice Gazely. Zeppelin raids had more to do with "frightfulness" – seeking to terrify and instil panic – than damaging property or claiming lives.

How the airships came to England.

Top: The remains of the Zeppelin *LZ3*, the airship responsible for the bombs dropped over Great Yarmouth in January 1915, lie wrecked on the Island of Fanoe in Denmark. On its final mission two of the engines failed and the commander Hans Fritz was forced to land, immediately setting fire to the ship and all its papers. The crew survived but were kept prisoners in Odense for the remainder of the war.

Above: Mr Galloway, superintendent of the Ipswich fire brigade, holds the culprit that exploded, causing a building to be burnt out.

Above right: Three of the bombs dropped over the Tyne by Zeppelins.

Right: Civilians in the streets watch for signs of a Zeppelin attack.

Opposite: Quartermaster Sergeant Rabjohn with his wife and daughter Mary after an air raid on Colchester in February 1915. At this stage there were no formal air raid shelter facilities – taking refuge in cellars or underneath furniture was the only protection for civilians. Five hundred people had been killed in air raids by the end of the conflict.

Poison gas

World War One was a battle between metallurgists, engineers and chemists as much as front-line troops. The years leading up to the conflict had seen a raft of technological breakthroughs offering industrial-age solutions to battlefield problems. Aircraft, submarines, tanks, machine guns, flamethrowers, high explosives – all were developed and deployed as the war leaders sought to gain the upper hand in a struggle where the knockout blow proved difficult to land. Perhaps the least spectacular of the new breed of weaponry was the gas shell: one more dense cloud floating above a bleak, denuded landscape that had already seen countless palls of smoking ruin. But here was an insidious attacker, a treacherous fog that assaulted eyes, ears and skin. Among the most poignant images of the war are those showing lines of soldiers blinded in a gas attack, each clutching the shoulder of the man in front as they shuffle to safety. The age of chemical warfare was upon us.

The concept was not new. The weapons potential of chlorine was mooted, but not acted upon, as early as the American Civil War. A generation later, at the 1899 Hague Convention, concerns that a belligerent would take that step were specifically addressed. The signatories, which included Germany, Britain and France, agreed to prohibit projectiles "the sole object of which is the diffusion of asphyxiating or deleterious gases". All three developed chemical agents such as tear gas, which, if not lethal, were certainly an irritant that could have a debilitating effect. The French fired the first tear gas grenades in the early weeks of the conflict, and the rival laboratories were soon busy in their own arms race, leaving others to worry about the flouting of international law.

First use at the
Second Battle of Ypres

In Fritz Haber Germany had one of the world's most eminent chemists, a future Nobel Prize winner whose work in the synthetic production of nitrates secured for his country a ready supply of fertiliser and explosives. Haber was also a key figure in the development of chlorine and phosgene, which attacked the lungs and could bring agonising death to the unprotected. Germany tried out chlorine in its Eastern operation early in 1915, but it was during the opening salvo of the Second Battle of Ypres in April where the experiment gained its first real results. The indications were encouraging, for the wind-driven agent induced widespread panic among defenceless French troops. A correspondent wrote to *The Times* after witnessing "the excruciating tortures and distress caused by the devilish gas", imploring British scientists to produce their own version of this new, deadly weapon. The Allies indeed responded in kind, even though "barbarous" was the epithet commonly applied to its unilateral use. A British attack at Loos in September 1915 was preceded by the release of 5,000 chlorine cylinders. They were termed an "accessory"; nomenclature was clearly important when so much vitriol was directed at Germany earlier in the year. By 1917 mustard gas had been introduced, a blister agent affecting the skin as well as internal organs. It was rarely lethal unless exposure level was high, but could incapacitate most painfully.

Top and above left: **Infantry in the trenches protect themselves from the dangers of poison gas. During the first major German chlorine gas attacks in April 1915, the only means of defence for soldiers were pieces of material soaked in their own urine, which neutralised the poison. British authorities swiftly responded by issuing cotton pads that could be dipped in bicarbonate of soda.**

Above: **Gas clouds from exploding shells creep along the ground near the Canadian lines on the Western Front. Chlorine gas was greenish in colour and had a distinctive smell which was at least easy to detect.**

Opposite: **The French were the first to use gas during the conflict after firing grenades filled with tear gas in August 1914. However, the quantity in each canister was so small it went unnoticed by the enemy and stocks soon ran out.**

DAILY MAIL 7 MAY 1915

A British Officer's Account of a Visit to Victims of Gassing

"THEIR FACES, ARMS, AND HANDS were of a shiny grey-black colour, with mouths open and bead-glazed eyes, all swaying slightly backwards and forwards trying to get breath. It was the most appalling sight, all these poor black faces, struggling, struggling for life, what with the groaning and noise of the efforts for breath. There is practically nothing to be done for them except to give them salt and water to try to make them sick. The effect the gas has is to fill the lungs with a watery, frothy matter which gradually increases and rises till it fills up the whole lungs and comes up to the mouth; then they die. It is suffocation; slow drowning taking in some cases one or two days."

The years leading up to the conflict had seen a raft of technological breakthroughs offering industrial-age solutions to battlefield problems.

March 1915

1   Great Britain and France announced a total blockade of merchant shipping to and from Germany.

2   The British naval bombardment of the forts resumed in the Dardanelles.

4   The French Government decided to send an Expeditionary Force to the Dardanelles whilst Turkish defenders drove off British landing parties at the entrance to the Narrows.

5   The Greek Government offered naval and military support for operations at the Dardanelles.

    British naval forces began the bombardment of the strategic city of Smyrna on the Aegean coast.

6   Prime Minister Eleftherios Venizelos resigned after a disagreement with King Constantine of Greece about the country's role in the war.

7   The Greek Government asked for an explanation of the British occupation at Lemnos.

9   The British Government explained that it was a military necessity to attack Lemnos.

    The British bombardment of Smyrna ended.

10 The British army attacked at the start of the Battle of Neuve Chapelle, giving support to the much larger French offensive in Champagne.

    Dimitrios Gounaris replaced Eleftherios Venizelos as Prime Minister of Greece.

11 The armed merchant cruiser HMS *Bayano* was torpedoed and sunk by German submarine *U-27*.

12 General Sir Ian Hamilton was appointed to command the Allied Mediterranean Expeditionary Force in order to gain control of the Dardanelles straits.

14 The German cruiser SMS *Dresden* was scuttled by her crew after it was attacked by British warships off the coast of Chile.

15 The Royal navy cruiser HMS *Amethyst* was damaged by field artillery whilst on minesweeping duties in the Dardanelles.

17 Following his appointment earlier in the month, General Sir Ian Hamilton took up his position as Commander-in-Chief of the Allied Mediterranean Expeditionary Force.

18 The Allied naval attack of the Dardanelles forts was repelled by the defending Turks. British battleships HMS *Irresistible* and HMS *Ocean* and the French battleship *Bouvet* were all sunk in the battle.

20 The British Government guaranteed that Greece would have Lemnos after the war.

21 In the first German airship raid on Paris two Zeppelins dropped high explosives and bombs on the capital city.

22 The Siege of Przemyśl ended when the Russians captured the fortress at the strategically important city.

23 Originally built as a tramp steamer, HMS *Manica* was the first kite balloon ship to be commissioned by the Admiralty.

25 The German military commander General Liman von Sanders was appointed to command the Turkish forces at Gallipoli.

28 The first American casualty of war was killed when the cargo-passenger ship Falaba was torpedoed by the German submarine *U-28*.

29 The British and United States Governments agreed that rubber would not be exported except to Great Britain.

30 South African forces occupied Aus in German South West Africa.

31 The city of Libau on the Baltic Sea was shelled by the Germans.

"The men came tumbling from the front line. I've never seen men so terror-stricken, they were tearing at their throats and their eyes were glaring out. Blood was streaming from those who were wounded and they were tumbling over one another. Those who fell couldn't get up because of the panic of the men following them, and eventually they were piled up two or three high in this trench. One chap had his hand blown off and his wrist was fumbling around, tearing at his throat."

Private William Quinton, Bedfordshire Regiment

Poison gas as an offensive weapon had drawbacks. The first was atmospheric conditions. Wind direction and strength was an obvious issue, as British soldiers found to their cost in the Loos attack. Over 2,000 men were laid low by chlorine that did not drift uniformly towards the German trenches. An unlucky few were killed. Freezing temperatures could also nullify the effect of a gas attack. Then there was the matter of dispersal. Scientists gave much thought to producing a gas cloud that could saturate the target area to the required level. Heavier-than-air phosgene lingered longer, and was also considerably more potent than chlorine.

The morality of gas warfare

The second impediment was that defence was soon to hand: the simple expedient of using masks. A water-soaked cloth offered a measure of protection against chlorine, and the ammonia in urine provided a chemical barrier. One soldier described how he was taking no chance with a doused handkerchief; he submerged his head in a bucket of urine to minimise his personal risk. Masks with rather more sophisticated filtration were developed, for horses as well as men. The box respirator, introduced by the British in 1916, was particularly effective. Meanwhile, the morality question hung in the air like the noxious vapour itself. Responding to a Red Cross statement condemning the use of gas, Germany defended it as a weapon that sought to disable the enemy and was thus no worse than any other. Knowing that the French had developed gas shells before the war, the military hierarchy would have been "irresponsible" to stand idly by. This unapologetic line was articulated in February 1918, just before Germany launched its final bid for outright victory. The tenor was pugnacious, suggesting that if the Entente was sympathetic to the Red Cross appeal, it had nothing to do with humanitarian concerns. "Only that party which feels itself to be inferior in its employment will readily decide to abandon it. For the weaker party, therefore, this propaganda against the use of stupefying gas will be a welcome means of attempting to strike an effective weapon out of the stronger party's hand."

"The father of chemical warfare"

In the final reckoning, gas played a minor role as an instrument of war. Even in that first serious deployment, by the Germans at Ypres in 1915 against unwary Allied ranks, it failed to break the Western Front stalemate. Canadians held the line and rudimentary protection was rushed to the sector. For the victims of a gas attack, however, drowning in their own bodily fluids was an unspeakably horrific end. The terror quotient of gas was greater than the number of lives it claimed or damaged.

The horror was too much for Fritz Haber's wife, a fellow chemist who committed suicide over research that Haber saw as his patriotic duty. His attempts to extract gold from sea water to help meet Germany's postwar reparations payments were somewhat less successful, but his pioneering work in fertiliser production – described as plucking "bread from air" – was a boon to mankind, worthy alone of elevating its author to national-hero status. That was not to be his fate. Under Hitler Germany turned its back on the man sometimes called "the father of chemical warfare", his Jewish faith counting against him more than his efforts on behalf of his country. A decade after his death in 1934, Haber's work on the production of pesticide gases was adapted for use in Nazi concentration camps, where the death toll dwarfed the losses of the earlier conflict and victims included members of his own family.

Top: **British Red Cross nurses** working on the front line are given gas masks in case of attack.

Middle: **Troops sound the alarm** during a poison gas attack.

Above left and right: **By July** the "smoke helmet" had been designed by Major Cluny MacPherson, a doctor working with the Newfoundland Regiment. A simple flannel bag soaked in chemicals covering the entire head, with eyeholes and a breathing tube, became the world's first gas mask and was rapidly adopted by the British army.

Opposite above: **French** artillerymen wearing "the cagoule" anti-asphyxiation mask prepare to load a field gun.

Opposite below: **A demonstration** of the different types of gas masks available. The use of chlorine was soon followed by phosgene – more deadly and much more difficult to see, with its effects taking 24 hours or more to manifest themselves. Troops were issued with a PH gas helmet to help combat the effects, but despite this around 85,000 deaths were caused by phosgene poisoning during the conflict.

WHAT 350 MASSED GUNS DID AT NEUVE CHAPELLE

Wonderful as was the heroism of the British troops at Neuve Chapelle, the village recaptured by us from the Germans, the victory was made possible only by the massing of 350 guns which spoke at once on a front of barely 2,000 yards. Above are the ruins of the village of Neuve Chapelle after the terrible bombardment.

The Battle of Neuve Chapelle

The battle began on 10 March 1915. By this time, a huge influx of troops from Britain had to some extent relieved the French situation in Flanders and enabled a continuous British line stretching from Langemarck to Givenchy. The ultimate aim of the battle was to cause a rupture in the German lines which would then be exploited with a rush on Aubers Ridge and possibly even Lille, a major enemy communications centre. A simultaneous French assault on Vimy Ridge was also planned although the situation in Champagne soon led to this particular part of the operation being postponed. This was to be the first time that aerial photography was to play a prominent part in a major battle with the entire German line being mapped from the air.

The Battle of Neuve Chapelle was the first planned British offensive of the conflict. Although they managed to capture the village of Neuve Chapelle itself the offensive was eventually abandoned after the British registered over 11,000 casualties. Just over two kilometres of land had been regained.

SCENE OF THE BATTLE OF NEUVE CHAPELLE.

OUR 350 GUNS AT NEUVE CHAPELLE.

FOE'S TRENCHES REDUCED TO PULP.

SIR J. FRENCH'S ORDER.

A bombardier of the Royal Marine Artillery wrote the following letter during the bombardment of Neuve Chapelle while observing shell fire. The following Army Order is the one to which the writer refers:

The attack which we are about to undertake is of the first importance to the Allied cause. The Army and the nation are watching the result, and Sir John French is confident that every individual in the IV. Corps will do his duty and inflict a crushing defeat on the German VII. Corps which is opposed to us.

H. RAWLINSON, Lieut.-General.

This is very much active service now. I am writing this letter in a quaint little French town during a terrific battle.

I am stuck up here with an officer and we are observing for our heavy gun. We arrived overnight. Even now, as I write, the shells are bursting perilously near.

Well, as I told you, our troops are advancing, and this promises to be one of the biggest engagements of the war. Our General, Sir John French, sent us all a message of encouragement last night (which I enclose, and which please keep for me).

It is rather misty at present, and we can't see the results of our shot very clearly. I must knock off for a minute, as they are just about to fire again.

Now we can see better, and the last shot has set fire to the railway station in the town we are bombarding.

Just received news that our infantry has captured their first line of trenches. Next shot coming.

The guns are making a terrible noise now, and it is a wonderful sight.

We now hear that Neuve Chapelle has been captured by our troops, and from here we can see our shells bursting in the enemies' lines. We seem fairly immune now—no shells have come over for a long time.

There is now a large cloud of smoke in the direction our big shells have been dropping, and we must have set fire to another large building. The town will soon be untenable for the Germans. It is sad to think of the number of innocent people that must be killed and injured, but it cannot be helped—it is the fortune of war.

We have the Canadians and Indian troops working at our point of the line. Fine fellows they are, and very eager to get at close quarters with the "Huns." We hear terrible tales of the enemy's doings when they were in possession of this town a few months ago. What they couldn't take with them they destroyed, and the wanton damage they did is enormous. I expect you will hear full particulars of this engagement before I shall, but probably it will last some days. Anyhow we are about to fire again, so I will close.

A GERMAN FRONT LINE TRENCH AFTER THE BATTLE OF NEUVE CHAPELLE

"The bombardment lasted three-quarters of an hour," said a combatant, describing the Battle of Neuve Chapelle in yesterday's "Daily Mail." "Then a whistle blew, and our men came swarming out of the trenches, officers in front carrying rifles and bayonets. They ran across the 'No-Man's-Land' of 200 yards which divided the trenches, raked all the time by German machine guns." Here is a German front-line trench after the British had stormed it.

THE CHEERING CANADIANS AND THE VICTORS OF NEUVE CHAPELLE

"I should like to mention that the Canadian division showed their mettle and have received the warm commendation of Sir John French for the high spirit and bravery with which they have performed their part." (Lord Kitchener in the House of Lords.) The photograph shows Canadian cavalry cheering the King as he rode their mounted ranks after the inspection held at Salisbury Plain immediately before the Canadians left for the front.

BRAVERY OF TWO GERMANS
Officers Serve Machine Guns to the Last.

The Germans left alive in the trenches, half demented with fright, surrounded by a welter of dead and dying men, mostly surrendered. The Berkshires were opposed with the utmost gallantry by two German officers, who had remained alone in a trench serving a machine gun. But the lads from Berkshire made their way into that trench and bayoneted the Germans where they stood, fighting to the last. The Lincolns, against desperate resistance, eventually occupied their section of trench and then waited for the Irishmen and the Rifle Brigade to come and take the village ahead of them.

Meanwhile the second 39th Garhwalis on the right had taken their trenches with a rush and were away towards the village and the Biez Wood. Things had moved so fast that by the time the troops were ready to advance against the village the artillery had not finished its work. So, while the Lincolns and the Berks assembled the prisoners who were trooping out of the trenches in all directions, the infantry on whom devolved the honour of capturing the village waited.

One saw them standing out in the open.

FRENCH, BRITISH AND BELGIAN BATTLE FRONTS COMPARED.

Below and opposite below: **Haig** gave the British artillery four tasks – destroy the German wire and front-line trenches, protect the flanks, form a barrier behind the German front trenches to isolate them from reinforcements and neutralise the German artillery and machine-guns.

LIKE AN EARTHQUAKE.
Hardly a Stone Left Standing in the Village

The village was a sight that the men say they will never forget. It looked as if an earthquake had struck it. The published photographs do not give any idea of the indescribable mass of ruins to which our guns reduced it. The chaos is so utter that the very line of the streets is all but obliterated. Once upon a time Neuve Chapelle must have been a pretty little place, as villages in these parts go, with a nice clean church (whence it probably got its na...), some neat villas in the main street with gaudy shutters, half a dozen estaminets, a red-brick brewery, and on the outskirts a little old white château. Now hardly stone remains upon stone.

It was indeed a scene of desolation into which the Rifle Brigade—the first regiment to enter the village, I believe—raced headlong. Of the church only the bare shell remained, the interior lost to view beneath a gigantic mound of débris. The little churchyard was devastated, the very dead plucked from their graves, broken coffins and ancient bones scattered about amid the fresher dead, the slain of that morning—grey-green forms asprawl athwart the tombs. Of all that once fair village but two things remained intact—two great crucifixes reared aloft, one in the churchyard, the other over against the château. From the cross that is the emblem of our faith the figure of Christ, yet intact though all pitted with bullet marks, looked down in mute agony on the slaying in the village.

The din and confusion were indescribable. Through the thick pall of shell-smoke Germans were seen on all sides, some emerging half dazed from cellars and dug-outs, their hands above their heads, others dodging round the shattered houses, others firing from the windows, from behind carts, even from behind the overturned tombstones. Machine guns were firing from the houses on the outskirts, rapping out their nerve-racking note above the noise of the rifles.

GLORIOUS STORY
OF
NEUVE CHAPELLE
PRODIGIES OF BRAVERY.
GERMAN ARMY NOT INVINCIBLE.
"WE BROKE THE LINE."
REGULARS CHEER TERRITORIALS.

We have received the following description of the Battle of Neuve Chapelle, which is the first full and independent account of the engagement:—

For many reasons the brilliant British success at Neuve Chapelle is one of the most interesting engagements of the war. For the first time the British Army has broken the German line and struck the Germans a blow which they will remember to the end of their lives.

The importance of our success does not, however, lie so much in the capture of the German trenches along a front of two miles, the killing of some 6,000 Germans, and the taking of 2,000 prisoners. It is the revelation of the fact that the much-vaunted German Army machine, on which the whole attention of a mighty nation has been lavished for four decades, is not invincible.

Neuve Chapelle has above all things shown the British soldier that in him the German has met his master and that, given proper artillery support, the offensive can be taken against the German line, strong though it is, with every chance of success.

When the German official history of the war comes to be written it will be seen how close we were to turning this brilliantly fought engagement into a victory which would have exercised a decisive influence on the rest of the campaign. The issue at stake after the capture of Neuve Chapelle on the morning of March 10 was great enough to justify far greater losses than those we sustained in the magnificently executed attempt to push forward the advantage already gained.

If we were prevented, mainly by unfavourable weather conditions, from benefiting to the full by our success, we held the ground we had won, despite repeated and desperate counter-attacks by fresh German troops hastily thrown into the field.

We were pioneers at Neuve Chapelle. Imbued with the fighting spirit of our fathers, our Army, after months of inaction, was the first to put to the test the lessons learned during the long winter in the trenches. Like all pioneers, we had to pay the price; but the lives so freely, so gallantly given will not have been laid down in vain.

There had been a gain of some three hundred yards on a front just half a mile in length – but it had cost the Allies 12,000 men either killed, wounded or missing.

Munitions

The regulars of the British Expeditionary Force were cut down at an alarming rate in the early months of war. Along with the need to address the manpower issue, the government faced a worrying shortfall in the supply of munitions. By spring 1915 the crisis was such that daily quotas for the number of rounds issued had to be imposed. Lloyd George, given responsibility for dealing with the shell shortage, was appointed munitions minister in the new Asquith-led coalition. It fell to him to mobilise the nation's resources and increase capacity. That meant taking on recalcitrant trade unionists more accustomed to capping output and resisting "dilution" – using unskilled labour in automated processes. Skilled male workers were exempted from active service, but to keep that number to a minimum women were employed in factory roles usually the preserve of men. By the end of the war almost one million women were employed in munitions work.

Above right: **During the "Shell Crisis" of 1915, it was widely believed there was a shortage of artillery shells getting to the front line. This lack of ammunition for the troops and the failed naval attack on the Dardanelles was blamed on the Liberal government; after a Cabinet split Prime Minister Asquith formed a coalition with the Conservative party to strengthen his position. David Lloyd George was appointed to the newly created post of Minister of Munitions and swiftly resolved the issues.**

Opposite above and below: **Workers busily producing large shells at two munitions factories in France. One located in Le Creusot (below) and the other in Champagne-sur-Seine (above).**

Right: **Chinese labourers at work in a French munitions factory. During the conflict the French government pioneered a scheme to allow Chinese men to fill non-military roles and help solve the shortage of labourers created by men leaving their jobs for the front. Britain joined the scheme but trade union pressure prevented them from working on the home front. Instead they were sent to France where they supported the troops by digging trenches and building roads and railways amongst many other necessary tasks.**

Below: **Munitions workers turning 12-inch shells for naval guns. The Munitions of War Act, passed in 1915 to resolve the Shell Crisis, brought private companies under the control of the Minister of Munitions. Working hours and conditions were regulated and it became very difficult for employees to resign, although there were much tighter health and safety procedures. Across the Commonwealth countries, factories and supplies came under the Imperial Munitions Board to guarantee the supplies needed.**

By the end of the war almost one million women were employed in munitions work.

DAILY MAIL JUNE 15, 1915

Our shell shortage – a French opinion

THE LACK OF SHELLS and ammunition, says the Temps to-night, is the principal reason why Great Britain does not defend a larger line in France. The revelation of this shortage has caused some surprise in France.

How is it that a great industrial country like England, whose territory remains inviolate, has been unable to furnish its Army with the munitions which it needs? The fact is that the manufacture of war material, especially field artillery and shells, is a special industry demanding minute and precise attention. Representative English industries such as sheet iron, rails, and locomotives do not require the work of great precision which, on the contrary, is indispensable to most of the important French industries. It was, therefore, more difficult for England to find workmen capable of learning to turn out war material.

But England is tenacious, and every month her sword will weigh more heavily in the balance.

Changing roles for women

In Edwardian England women were struggling to break the shackles of historic gender roles. That they were disadvantaged politically was clear: excluded from the democratic process. But there were also limitations on employment opportunities. Though there were around six million women active in the labour market in 1914, there was clear demarcation between jobs deemed suitable for the sexes. Middle-class women in employment invariably became housewives once they married, while domestic service was the single largest trade among working-class girls.

For many women, securing voting rights was the issue from which all improvements flowed. The Reform Acts of the 19th century had enfranchised men; women now demanded that their voice also be heard when it came to electing those who sought to govern. The suffrage campaign gained momentum following the formation of the Women's Social and Political Union in 1903. Peaceful protest gave way to militant action, including arson and bombing. At the 1913 Derby, one of the highlights of the sporting and social calendar, Emily Davison became a martyr to the cause when she threw herself in front of the king's horse. A few months before the assassination in Sarajevo, Sylvia Pankhurst – daughter of WSPU founder Emmeline – was jailed for an act of civil disobedience, her attempt to go on hunger strike stymied by force-feeding. That sat uncomfortably with Herbert Asquith's Liberal administration, but far from yielding to suffragette demands, the government responded by passing a law under which those in custody whose health gave cause for concern could be released – then rearrested once they had recovered. The "Cat and Mouse Act", as it was known, showed that the corridors of power were holding firm. Agitators would face the full force of the law if they chose to stray beyond the boundaries of peaceful protest.

The Board of Trade issued a clarion call, inviting women to register for paid employment.

Releasing men for the military

The picture changed dramatically once hostilities ensued. The WSPU suspended its campaign and swung behind the war effort. Initially, women's contribution lay in volunteering for hospital duty, fundraising and providing creature comforts for servicemen with their knitting needles or by collecting cigarettes and books. But as the casualty toll mounted and conscription finally introduced, they were needed to take on all manner of traditional men's roles, from factory work to tilling the soil. As early as March 1915 the Board of Trade issued a clarion call, inviting women to register for paid employment, and informing employers that they could release men for military service safe in the knowledge that women would bridge the gap. If they took skilled jobs, the work was broken down into tasks suitable for the untrained. This "dilution", along with concerns that women might undermine their male counterparts by doing the same work for less money, raised concerns among trades unions. In a compact with the government reached in spring 1915, union leaders accepted that the exigencies of war required some working practices to be relaxed.

Left: A female railway porter. By the end of the war the number of women taking on this type of unskilled employment in stations had increased ten-fold.

Below: Women at a Regent's Park garden party raise funds for blind soldiers. Throughout the country, women were encouraged to aid the war effort in different ways. While many took to the factories, some joined official voluntary organisations such as the Red Cross or the Voluntary Aid Detachment, while others encouraged fund raising and the sale of war bonds.

Bottom and opposite bottom: During the conflict the number of women employed in munitions factories, familiarly known as the "Munitionettes", increased from just over 200,000 to nearly one million. Women were needed to cover the jobs left by men fighting on the front, and helping out with arms productions gave them a sense of supporting their men folk on the frontline. An added incentive was the pay: although on average half a man's wage, it was far more than they originally received in traditional women's roles before the war.

Above: Female fire fighters line up ready for work. This sector was on duty at a munitions factory where twenty-four women covered three shifts over a 24-hour period.

Below left: The South Metropolitan Gas Company employed female meter girls.

Below right: A woman confidently controls the trains in Birmingham. The first railway jobs offered to women were level crossing gatekeepers. These roles could be fitted around a family and appealed to widows with young children as a rent-free home was often included.

April 1915

1   French pilot Roland Garros shot down a German aircraft with a forward-firing machine gun bringing in the era of the dogfight.

3   Britain completed the construction of an anti-submarine net barrage across the Straits of Dover.

4   Russian forces captured the village of Cisna and reached Sztropko in the Carpathians.

5   The United States demanded reparation for the sinking of their merchant ship *William P. Frye* in January 1915.

   The French army began a broad offensive from Meuse to Moselle on the Western front.

6   French forces attacked the Germans east of Verdun in the Battle of the Woëvre.

8   The Turkish government commenced mass deportation and massacre of Armenians.

9   An assassination attempt failed on the life of the sultan of Egypt, Hussein Kamel.

10   French troops continued their advance between the Meuse and the Moselle.

11   The German battleship *Kronprinz Wilhelm* was interned at Newport News in south eastern Virginia.

12   British and Indian forces attacked Ottoman troops in Mesopotamia at the beginning of the Battle of Shaiba, southwest of Basra.

   The Greek Government rejected the Allied offer of Smyrna to Greece – made to entice the Hellenic Republic to join operations at Gallipoli.

14   The Battle of Shaiba ended when the British successfully defended the city of Basra.

   The Germans accused the French of employing poison gas at Verdun.

15   The Belgian town of Ostend was bombed by Allied aircraft.

16   Turkish forces occupied the city of Urmia in northern Persia.

   The British transport ship SS *Manitou* was attacked by the Turkish torpedo-destroyer *Demir Hissar*.

17   Heavy fighting at Hill 60 near Ypres resulted in British forces regaining possession of the strategically significant area of high ground.

   The German-commanded vessel Demir Hissar was intercepted south of the Greek island of Chios by British destroyer HMS *Minerva* and forced to run aground.

18   Fighting continued on Hill 60 with an unsuccessful German counter-attack.

20   Armed Turks attacked Armenians in Van but they were repulsed. Outside the city, all Armenian owned property was destroyed and the Turks laid siege.

22   The Second Battle of Ypres began with the Battle of Gravenstafel Ridge which marked the first time that Germany used poison gas on a large scale on the Western Front.

23   The British Government declared a blockade of the Cameroons.

24   The Battle of Julien began as a counter-attack by the Allied troops to try to regain ground lost to the Germans after the Battle of Gravenstafel Ridge in the Second Battle of Ypres.

25   The Gallipoli Campaign started when Allied troops landed on the peninsula in the Ottoman Empire.

26   The Treaty of London – a secret pact between the Triple Entente and Italy – was signed in London by Great Britain, France, Russia and Italy in order to win the support of Italy against its former allies in exchange for substantial gains of territory.

27   The British submarine *E14* took part in an operation in the Sea of Marmora where she sank the Turkish gunboat *Nurel Bahr*.

28   The first Allied advance was repelled at the First Battle of Krithia during the Gallipoli Campaign.

29   German Zeppelin *LZ-38* bombed Ipswich and Bury St Edmunds in Suffolk.

30   German forces occupied Shavli in the Baltic Provinces.

The dangers of munitions work

Sectors where women were a rarity, such as transport, agriculture and engineering, suddenly had a considerable female presence. Auxiliary arms of all three services were eventually formed, allowing women to follow the menfolk into uniform. Shell production alone gave employment to almost one million women. There were obvious dangers in handling explosives, and detonations during the production process claimed a number of lives. In January 1919 a massive explosion in a London munitions factory killed 11 women in a death toll of 69. There was also the more insidious danger posed by the chemicals and fumes. Early symptoms of increased toxicity levels in the body were similar to the common cold and doubtless widely ignored. Headaches and rotting teeth were also common complaints. "Munitionettes" also became accustomed to the yellowing of the skin that gave them the "canaries" tag. Heavy, and sometimes hazardous, work provided a bond between those making sacrifices at the front and those supporting the war effort at home. And if the wage women drew rarely matched that of their male counterparts, it usually represented a sizeable increase on their prewar income, providing a level of economic independence many had never enjoyed.

Women whose horizons had been widened were more inclined to smoke, drink, sport shorter hemlines and venture out unescorted.

Just 8 million enfranchised

Demobilisation brought a different problem as returning heroes needed to be accommodated in the labour market. As early as December 1918 the president of the Women's Industrial League, Lady Rhondda, voiced her fears that those of her sex would be expected to "resume the condition of helots…hewers of wood, provided they do not use an edged tool; drawers of water, provided they do not fit the pipe to the pump". Old employment patterns were largely re-established, but old attitudes were less easily readopted. Women whose horizons had been widened were more inclined to smoke, drink, sport shorter hemlines, venture out unescorted and even use the odd bit of industrial language. Many of those who had made a vital contribution were still denied a say in the running of the country, however. While Asquith conceded that women had "worked out their own salvation" and earned the right to vote, only those over 30 who fulfilled certain property criteria were on the electoral roll in the December 1918 general election. Eight million were enfranchised, but it would be another decade before the right was extended to 21-year-old women and parity with men achieved.

This page: **Traditionally male roles such as newspaper printing and driving steam tractors were given to women.**

Opposite above left: **Female workers in a munitions factory guide the shells down from the overhead cranes.**

Opposite top right and middle right: **Coal was frequently delivered by women.**

Opposite below right: **The "Tar Women" spraying the roads in Westminster.**

Opposite middle left and below left: **Many women opted to work in the forestry industry. Some of these services were part of the Women's Land Army, working under the Board of Agriculture, while others were part of the Women's Forestry Corps controlled by the Board of Trade.**

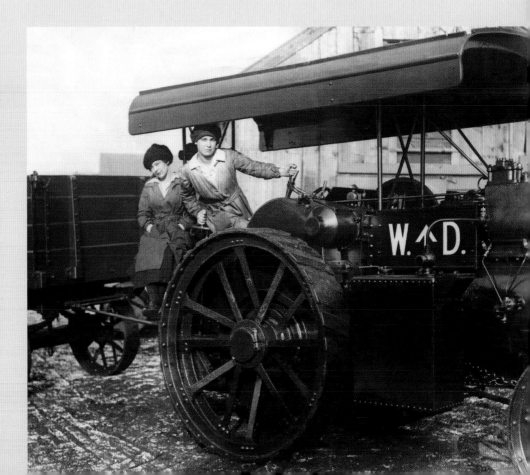

Second Battle of Ypres

The beginning of April 1915 saw Sir John French and his generals absorbing the lessons of Neuve Chapelle, which had delivered considerably less than it promised. Renewed offensives were hamstrung by a lack of ammunition, and in any event the Western Front now had to share the focus of British effort with the Gallipoli campaign, which was about to get underway. Plans for the next coordinated Anglo-French attack were still in the making when the enemy took the initiative.

On 22 April, German guns pounded the Allied line, waiting for a change of wind direction that would allow them to play their latest trump card. The prevailing conditions turned in their favour at 5.00 pm, and the infantry advanced behind a curtain of chlorine gas that wreaked choking, spluttering havoc on those it enveloped. The natural inclination to cower was the worst possible course of action against a heavier-than-air gas. Standing tall offered the best chance of escaping its insidious clutches. Another counterintuitive outcome was that some who fled the scene – as many French colonial troops did - remained enshrouded, while those who stood their ground saw the gas pass through.

Within minutes the chlorine had claimed over 5,000 Allied lives. Langemarck and Pilckem were soon in German hands. The familiar image of crocodiles of blinded soldiers, each with an arm on the shoulder of the man in front, shuffling to the infirmaries, was born. That there was disarray in the assailed, defenceless ranks was understandable, yet there were also examples of great heroism; men who refused to take a backward step until overcome by the noxious fumes. The saviour that day was the lack of foresight on the part of the German commanders, who did not have reserves in hand to exploit the breach. Had it been planned as a line-breaking assault rather than an experimental exercise to see what gas shells could do; had the wind been favourable on the morning of the 22nd, when the whole day lay ahead to capitalise on the opening created; and had the advancing Germans been less reticent about pursuing their own deadly cloud, things might have turned out very differently. As it was, Britain's 2nd Army, led by General Smith-Dorrien, rallied and countered, and the immediate crisis passed. The Germans tried again, Canadian troops bearing the brunt. Allied reserves were rushed forward. Smith-Dorrien advocated withdrawing to a shortened, more defendable position, and in answer received a dismissal notice from Sir John French, who had been distrustful of him since the Battle of Le Cateau. His replacement, Sir Herbert Plumer, recommended virtually the same action as his predecessor and was answered in the affirmative. The withdrawal took place at the beginning of May.

Germans call a halt

Fighting continued for three more weeks, at places such as Frezenburg and Bellwaerde. Meanwhile, the Allies took advantage of rudimentary gas masks, in some cases nothing more than urine or water-soaked handkerchiefs, rendering the chlorine onslaught less effective than it had been on day one. The Germans finally called a halt to what was their only significant Western Front offensive of the year on 25 May. Ypres remained in Allied hands, albeit with the loss of important high ground in the sector. Falkenhayn's primary focus was Russia at this point. The Ypres attack had been undertaken in large part to create a semblance of activity in the west, and to give the new chemical weapon a more substantial trial after a faltering test in freezing temperatures on the Russian front in January. He now turned his attention eastwards once more, having secured a more favourable strategic position at the Salient and with a casualty toll comfortably in his favour. The instigators of the Second Battle of Ypres were thus left with crumbs of comfort to mitigate the overall failure of the scheme.

HILL 60 BECOMES A SECOND YPRES BATTLE.

SECOND BATTLE OF YPRES.

FRONT EXTENDING ON BOTH WINGS

HILL 60 COUNTER - ATTACKS DEFINITELY FAIL.

GERMAN LOSSES GREATER THAN THOUGHT.

262nd DAY OF THE WAR.

The German attacks on Hill 60 are still being violently pressed, and the engagement is developing into a second battle of Ypres. The fighting is extending on either wing, and the famous German 17in. howitzers have come into action.

LANDING AT ENOS.

Our Sofia correspondent in an important message, dated Tuesday, states that Bulgarian witnesses saw Enos bombarded by the Allied Fleet and that fugitives from Enos reported a landing of British troops there. This is supported by the German wireless message that the German warships, after a most dangerous encounter with the Turkish fleet, had a brush.

LATE WAR NEWS.

FRENCH OFFICIAL.

PARIS, Thursday, 11 p.m.

Near Langemarck, to the north of Ypres, the British troops repulsed two attacks. At Hill 60, near Zwartelen, the German counter-attacks, whose violence seems explicable by the desire to repair a defeat that has been denied by the official communiques of the Imperial General Staff, have definitively failed.

The losses of the enemy are higher than the figures indicated yesterday.

In the sector of Rheims there was an artillery duel.

In the Argonne. At Bagatelle a German attack of no great importance was repulsed.

RUSH UP HILL 60.

"THE MEN FOLLOWED SPLENDIDLY."

GRAPHIC ACCOUNT.

The Liverpool *Daily Post* to-day publishes the following letter from a Liverpool officer to his father in Liverpool regarding the desperate fighting for Hill 60:—

ALLIES LAND IN TURKEY.

TROOPS AT ENOS, IN THE AEGEAN.

ATTACK ON THE PORT.

FROM OUR OWN CORRESPONDENT.

SOFIA, Tuesday.

HUGE U.S. EXPORTS TO NEUTRALS.

NEARLY DOUBLED.

IMPORTS FROM US HARDLY AFFECTED.

FROM OUR OWN CORRESPONDENT.

NEW YORK, Thursday.

THE STORY THAT GOT RECRUITS.

LORD DERBY'S TRIBUTE.

CORRESPONDENTS WANTED

LORD KITCHENER AND RECRUITING.

GRATIFYING RESULTS.

MR. ASQUITH'S PLEDGE TO OFFICERS.

PENSIONS ON TEMPORARY RANK SCALE.

There was natural reluctance to advance into territory where noxious gas had caused such mayhem.

Below: At Ypres 168 tons of chlorine gas was released over a 4-mile line. Nearly 6,000 French and colonial troops were killed instantly with many more blinded and 2,000 captured as prisoners of war. With the gas rapidly filling the trenches, many more were forced into the open and directly into the line of German fire. Although this created a gap in the Allied defence, the German commanders failed to exploit the advantage and Canadian forces were able to hold the line for several days.

Opposite below left: The King's (Liverpool Regiment) facing a charge by German troops during the initial day's fighting at the Second Battle of Ypres, where the Germans released clouds of chlorine gas for the first time.

Opposite below right: Canadians move a gun into position at Ypres, 22 April 1915.

The language of war

Any evaluation of the cultural impact of the 1914-18 conflict immediately brings to mind the poetry of Owen, Sassoon and their ilk, the artwork of Paul Nash and literary works such as Robert Graves' *Goodbye To All That*. But the war also had a lasting influence on the English language; understandably so as it brought together men from different classes and continents, creating a melting pot in which words and phrases were exchanged and invented. Vocabulary that had once been particular to an area entered the mainstream. Stress, discomfort and boredom were the instruments of linguistic creativity and cross-fertilisation. The currency of the trench was banter, slang, nicknames, jargon, jokes and swearing. Anyone who called his cold, damp, infested dugout "The Ritz" had a sense of irony, while there were plenty of euphemisms for subjects no one wanted to discuss in stark terms: fear and death. Much better to talk about "getting the wind up" and "copping it". Or having "gone west". Or "pushing up daisies".

Expressions such as the "Jack Johnson" – a shell packing the punch of the reigning heavyweight champion when war broke out – may have been of the moment. Many others were repatriated, for this was a civilian army and after demobilisation men took the vocabulary of the front line back to their old lives. There these expressions became as entrenched as the men themselves had been, enriching everyday discourse. "Lousy" and "crummy" came into widespread use as a term for inferiority from their adjectival roots describing lice-ridden trench life. Information handed down from official sources was "eyewash" or "bumf" – bumfodder; from high-level communiqué to toilet paper at a single creative stroke. Men might "grouse" about conditions and articulate how "fed up" they were. To take their mind off things when they had time away from the front soldiers might go on a "binge" and get "blotto". A parcel from home always raised spirits, and if it was a mate's bounty he might "whack" it round. A fair share on civvy street thus became "getting your whack". If there were no spoils to divide, perhaps "scrounging" might bear fruit. In the forward line they might fire off a rapid "snapshot", perhaps through a "loophole" opening in the defensive banking. It was clearly unwise to "raise one's head above the parapet". If the shot went astray, or indeed if anything was a failure, then it was a bit of a "washout". Despite the trench camaraderie, there was always the risk of having possessions "knocked off", and doubtless the perpetrators hoped they wouldn't be "rumbled". There was even a word for not knowing a word: "thingumajig" became a useful catch-all when an expression wouldn't come readily to mind.

Rubbing shoulders with people from other parts of the globe brought an international dimension to the evolutionary process. "Souvenir" ousted "keepsake" when it came to mementos. The French word "dégommé" – applied to those relieved of command – gave us "degummed" and thence "come unstuck" for any action ending in failure. The Arabic "buckshee" was appropriated, as were the Hindi-derived "cushy", "chit" and good old "Blighty" itself. There was even linguistic trading with the enemy: "strafe" comes from the German verb "to punish".

Some of these words originated during the 1914-18 period, others pre-dated it. But the war was the vehicle through which a new vocabulary was disseminated far and wide and became embedded as the guns fell silent.

The Arabic "buckshee" was appropriated, as were the Hindi-derived "cushy", "chit" and good old "Blighty" itself.

Left: Despite the trench camaraderie, there was always the risk of having possessions "knocked off", and doubtless the perpetrators hoped they wouldn't be "rumbled".

Below: Scottish troops at the entrance to their hut. To take their mind off things when they had time away from the front, soldiers might go on a "binge" and get "blotto".

The Wipers Times

The great strides made in education during the 19th century meant that the men who fought in the First World War were a largely literate force of regulars, volunteers and conscripts. There were keen writers as well as avid readers, and the idea of getting a soldier's perspective into print held enormous appeal. A number of trench publications sprang up, the most famous of which was *The Wipers Times*. The very title – a corruption of Ypres that was easier on the English-speaking tongue – and its punning sub-head "Salient News" was an indication of the wit and inventiveness it brought to the coverage of the conflict. In offering the thoughts, reflections and insights of battle-zone infantry it had an immediacy that other journals separated from the action by time and space could not match. From its first edition on 12 February 1916, *The Wipers Times* showed a rich humorous vein that bore witness to the humble Tommy's indomitable spirit.

Advertised in the first number was a "cheap, desirable residence" offering "good shooting" and was available at a bargain price as "owner going abroad". Elsewhere the question of street noise was addressed, a problem that prompted residents to complain "that their rest is seriously interfered with". The piece concluded on a hopeful note: "We should like to see the nuisance put a stop to immediately."

The adventures of "Herlock Shomes"

Censorship was obviously an issue. Circulation of any material that might harm the war effort would not have been tolerated, and the matter was neatly addressed in the opening editorial, written by the paper's founder Captain F J Roberts of 12th Battalion Sherwood Foresters. "There is much that we would like to say…but the shadow of censorship enveloping us causes us to refer to the war, which we hear is taking place in Europe, in a cautious manner." Roberts went on to apologise for anything in the 12-page publication that might fall below an expected standard: "Any little shortcomings in production," he wrote, "must be excused on the grounds of inexperience and the fact that pieces of metal of various sizes had punctured our press." He was truthful on both counts. Roberts had a flair for journalism but no formal training, and the press on which the paper was printed had been stumbled upon in a bombed-out Ypres building a few weeks earlier.

Issue No.1 also contained the first instalment of a "Herlock Shomes" adventure, and the first of many poetic offerings, including this pithy piece of verse:

The world wasn't made in a day,
And Eve didn't ride on a 'bus,
But most of the world's in a sandbag,
The rest of it's plastered on us.

Right: **Gilbert Frankau** was commissioned into the 9th Battalion of the East Surrey Regiment from the start of the war. He regular contributed his poetry to the *Wipers Times* and became a popular novelist after he was invalided out in early 1918.

Far right: **The delight on this** Tommy's face is evident as he collects a pile of letters and parcels from home. By 1917, 19,000 mailbags were crossing the Channel each day, sent from a vast purpose-built sorting office in Regent's Park covering five acres. Letters were censored as the government were worried about sensitive information being leaked.

Apart from jokey pieces bearing a "Belary Helloc" or "Cockles Tumley" by-line, the contributors remained anonymous. One unnamed poet put his stamp on Gray's Elegy, opening with: "A six-inch tolls the knell of parting day". Others went the nursery rhyme route with lines such as: "Bah, bah, Quarter, have you any rum?" and "Little Jack Horner at Hell Fire Corner". An early edition aimed to boost circulation by offering readers an insurance scheme – with a catch. "In the event of death caused by a submarine, anywhere in the Wipers district, your next of kin will be entitled to claim 11s 7d if you had at the time of death one of our coupons fully signed and bearing name of Newsagent." Death and its financial implications hilariously intertwined for men who might meet their end at any moment, though not from a torpedo. Another advertisement offers velveteen corduroy breeches at 9s 11d – what any fashionable soldier going over the top ought to be wearing.

And so it goes on. A correspondent rails about the road being in a state of disrepair, interfering with his morning constitutional; a Situations Wanted column seeks a platoon commander, the stipulation "Applicant must be offensive" a clear sideswipe at the HQ directive regarding maintaining an offensive spirit; and in a glossary of army terms we are informed that "trench" takes its name "from the trenchant remarks from those inhabiting them".

The Wipers Times, together with other journals conceived, written, published and distributed in the thick of so much devastation, captures the mood, spirit and experience of the front-line soldier like no other historical record.

Another advertisement offers velveteen corduroy breeches at 9s 11d – what any fashionable soldier going over the top ought to be wearing.

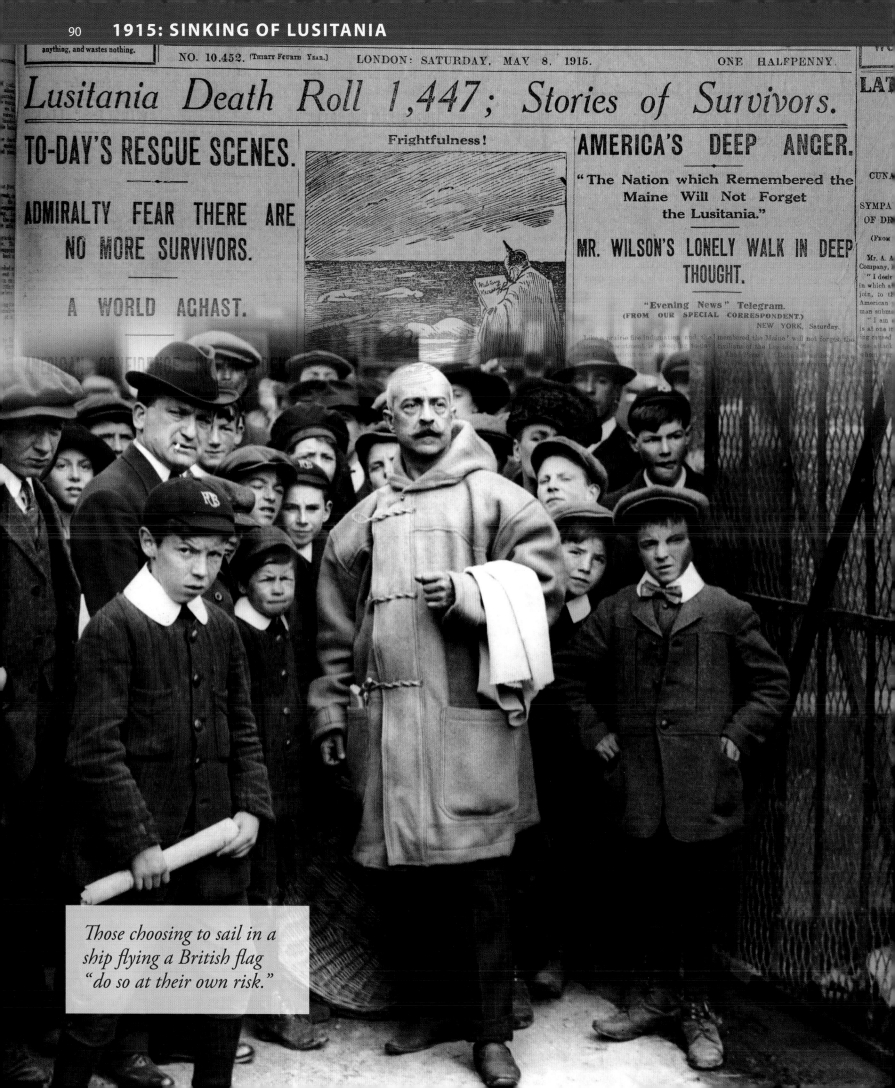

anything, and wastes nothing.

NO. 10,452. [Thirty Fourth Year.]   LONDON: SATURDAY, MAY 8, 1915.   ONE HALFPENNY.

Lusitania Death Roll 1,447; Stories of Survivors.

TO-DAY'S RESCUE SCENES.

ADMIRALTY FEAR THERE ARE NO MORE SURVIVORS.

A WORLD AGHAST.

Frightfulness!

AMERICA'S DEEP ANGER.

"The Nation which Remembered the Maine Will Not Forget the Lusitania."

MR. WILSON'S LONELY WALK IN DEEP THOUGHT.

"Evening News" Telegram.
(FROM OUR SPECIAL CORRESPONDENT.)
NEW YORK, Saturday.

Those choosing to sail in a ship flying a British flag "do so at their own risk."

War of words follows Lusitania outrage

Germany was a relative latecomer to submarine technology, its U1 craft not launched until 1906. The German navy had barely 20 operational "Untersee" boats at the outbreak of war – far fewer than the Allies – but in design and capability they were highly advanced. Notice was served in September 1914, when U21 torpedoed a British cruiser to record the first submarine kill in battle, and days later three more Allied ships fell victim to a single U-boat sweep inside an hour. On 4 February 1915 the threat increased significantly as Germany declared the waters around Britain to be a war zone. Attack from an unknown, unseen assailant prompted one Admiralty man to describe these stealthy assassins as "underhand and damned unEnglish". Doubtless there were old salts who viewed submarine attacks per se as despicable, even on military targets. When a U-boat sank the pride of the Cunard merchant fleet on 7 May 1915, the backlash was as extreme as might have been expected.

Even before the *Lusitania* left New York on 1 May on her week-long, Liverpool-bound voyage, there was disquiet in the air. Printed in the American press, right next to her sailing schedule, was a German Embassy warning that such vessels were "liable to destruction" as they entered British waters. Those choosing to sail in a ship flying a British flag, it added, "do so at their own risk." Some took the threat more seriously than others. A key point in *Lusitania*'s favour was that she was not just the last word in luxury but could cruise at 24 knots, and thus thought to be far too quick through the water for a lumbering U-boat to target. The top speed was curtailed somewhat as some of her massive boilers were shut down in the interest of economy; but she was still fleet enough to outpace any submarine. Whether speed would be her saviour, or her passenger liner status, *Lusitania* was heading straight towards a German undersea raider patrolling the waters off Ireland's southern coast.

This page: **Scenes at the Cunard London office as friends and relatives read the latest lists of those missing and the fortunate survivors.** On 1 May, 1915 the British liner RMS *Lusitania* sailed from New York, destined for Liverpool. Six days later a German U-boat torpedoed the ship just off the coast of southern Ireland. This, combined with a resulting internal explosion, led to her sinking within 20 minutes, with the loss of almost 1,200 lives.

Opposite: **One of the lucky 764 survivors from the *Lusitania* arrives home.** The ship sank so quickly there was only enough time to launch some of the lifeboats, even though there were sufficient for everyone on board. The disaster caused outrage on both sides of the Atlantic and although Britain urged the United States to enter the conflict, President Wilson maintained neutrality for another two years.

PASSENGERS ON THE LUSITANIA.

MISS MARTHA ALLAN.   LADY MACKWORTH.   LADY ALLAN.

Although two years would pass before the US joined the fray, the sinking of the Lusitania was an important staging post on the way to that April 1917 declaration.

Frightfulness!

LUSITANIA

Here is an adaptation of a "Falaba" cartoon which appeared in *The Brooklyn Daily Eagle* when that ship was sunk some days ago. For "Falaba" one may now read "Lusitania."

Lusitania: America's condemnation

U20 made two kills while *Lusitania* was in mid-Atlantic. The Admiralty was well aware of the situation, but did not advise a change of course, merely issuing a standard U-boat alert. The liner's captain, William Turner, did alter course, however, seeking a landmark to get his bearing in heavy fog. On the afternoon of 7 May, with visibility improved and the Irish coastline on the port horizon, she was struck on the starboard bow by one of U20's torpedoes. A mere 18 minutes later – a fraction of the time it had taken *Titanic* to sink three years earlier – *Lusitania* disappeared beneath the waves. Of the 1,900 passengers and crew, 1,200 lost their lives. The casualty list included 128 American citizens.

Both sides sought to manage the fall-out from one of the greatest maritime disasters on record. To the Allies it was an act of egregious infamy that deserved unmitigated condemnation and contempt. At least, that was the line for public consumption. Privately, it was hoped an event such as this would stir America into action. Germany's leaders, meanwhile, looked to lend legitimacy to the episode by highlighting the speed with which *Lusitania* sank. A single torpedo should not have mortally wounded the 800-foot giant, certainly not in such a time frame. Reports of a second explosion hard on the heels of the first led Germany to claim – correctly – that the ship had been carrying munitions. The Admiralty preferred to foster the idea of a multiple torpedo strike, and that was what the subsequent Board of Trade inquiry concluded. The official line may have played fast and loose with the facts, but political expediency dictated that here was a stick with which to beat the enemy in the propaganda war. As Lord Mersey, who headed the inquiry, put it: "The *Lusitania* case was a damned, dirty business!"

A single torpedo strike

There was predictable outrage in America. The pressure on Woodrow Wilson's administration was ratcheted up a few notches, and Germany scaled back its U-boat operation to avoid further provocation. Although two years would pass before the US joined the fray, the sinking of the *Lusitania* was an important staging post on the way to that April 1917 declaration. Winston Churchill himself acknowledged as much when, years later, he wrote: "The poor babies who perished in the ocean struck a blow at German power more deadly than could have been achieved by the sacrifice of 100,000 fighting men."

So what did send *Lusitania* to the watery depths 11 miles off the southern Irish coast in less than 20 minutes? It is now accepted that there was but a single torpedo strike, though expeditions to the wreck have ruled out the munitions cargo as the source of the second blast. One theory suggests that coal dust may have ignited, another has one or more of the boilers exploding. A century on, it remains a catastrophe where the effects are more easily described than the cause.

U 21 SANK THE LUSITANIA.

Kaiser Decorates the Chief Murderer.

"PATHFINDER" ECHO.

"EVENING NEWS" TELEGRAM.
(FROM OUR SPECIAL CORRESPONDENT.)
ELSINORE (Denmark),, Wednesday.

The Kaiser has conferred upon the commander of Submarine U 21, Captain-Lieutenant Hersing, the Order Pour le Merite, in recognition of Hersing's "gallant act" in torpedoing the Lusitania.

∗∗∗ The fact that the U 21's commander has received the highest German decoration has been announced; but this is the first definite statement that it was conferred for the sinking of the Lusitania. The only other man upon whom the Order has been bestowed who is not either a Prince or a general was the submarine captain Weddigen, a German national hero.

It was the U 21 that sank the Pathfinder in the early days of the war. We have the authority of Herr Olton von Gottberg, a German writer, who saw this inscription on a torpedo-tube: "Through a shot from this tube on September 5, 1914, the captain sank the English cruiser Pathfinder."

For this feat Hersing received the Iron Cross—and many offers of marriage from patriotic Fräulein.

He has (again according to Herr Olton von Gottberg) sunk a number of merchant vessels in the Irish Sea.

BERLIN'S VIEW OF AMERICA.

U.S.A. Only Too Glad To Be Compensated in Cash.

AMSTERDAM, Saturday.

The first news of the sinking of the Lusitania, which was made known in Berlin early this morning, caused mixed amazement and enthusiasm.

The newspaper comments run on ordinary lines, with praise for the pluck and daring of the submarine.

Hundreds of telegrams have been sent to Admiral von Tirpitz congratulating him.

The sinking of the Lusitania is considered the German answer to the destruction of the German squadron under Admiral von Spee.

The papers say nothing so far about the consequences. Some hint that if American lives had been lost America would only be too glad to be compensated in cash.

The Copenhagen correspondent of the same news agency says:—

I have received a telegram from Berlin stating that the papers have printed in colossal type the news of the sinking of the Lusitania.

The torpedo is regarded as a new triumph for Germany's naval policy.

The general impression is that England "has got what she deserves."

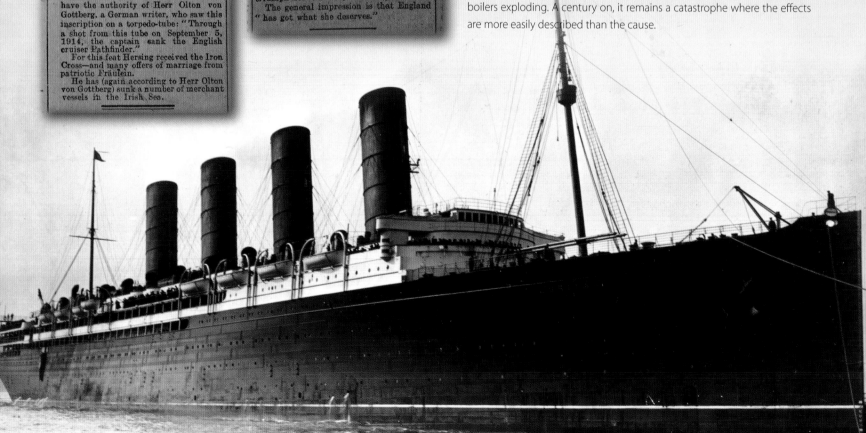

German airships return to bomb the East Coast

Zeppelin attacks on Britain resumed in April 1915, three months after the first airship bombs had fallen. Coastal areas from the Home Counties to Tyneside were targeted. In the early hours of Monday, 10 May, 60-year-old Agnes Whitwell sustained fatal burns when an incendiary bomb crashed through the bedroom ceiling of her Southend home. At the end of the month London came under attack for the first time. The dockland area was the primary objective, but most of the ordnance fell on residential property, killing seven. Defences gradually improved, and Zeppelin raids dwindled as they became increasingly vulnerable to ground and air fire.

Top left: Damage caused by a Zeppelin raid on Spital Road, Maldon, Essex, on 15 April 1915. The commander of the Zeppelin *L6* airship, Captain Oberleutnant Freiherr von Buttlar, later admitted he had no idea where he and his crew were and which town they bombed.

Above left, middle and right: In May 1915 the Bull and George hotel in Ramsgate, Kent, was the victim of a Zeppelin *LZ38* piloted by Hauptmann Erich Linnarz. Two people in the hotel later died of their injuries. By now civilians were starting to seek out proper forms of shelter and in Ramsgate tunnels and caves in the chalk cliffs were used.

Left: Linnarz was back for the raid on Southend later in the month. Five planes from the Royal Naval Air Service gave chase but he had already begun the journey home before they could gain enough height to launch an attack. A total of seventy bombs were dropped with three people killed. The *LZ38* was also responsible for the first bomb attack on London at the end of May. On this occasion ninety bombs and thirty grenades were released over several areas including Hoxton, Stoke Newington and Whitechapel, killing seven and injuring thirty-five civilians. The Allies were able to retaliate the following month when the airship was bombed and destroyed at its hangar in Evere, Belgium.

Gallipoli

Britain's standing army was small in comparison to her major allies. Until "Kitchener's Army" of recruits were battlefield ready, that would remain the case. To make matters worse, the bloody encounters of the first few months of war, not least the First Battle of Ypres, all but wiped out the BEF regulars – Britain's professional soldiers. At that same time the Central Powers were bolstered by Turkey's entry into the fray, opening up yet another front on which Russia was expected to fight. Britain's beleaguered eastern ally was sorely in need of assistance. No great help in terms of manpower could be offered, but the chance for Britain to play her trump card – naval strength – had much to recommend it. With the Western Front deadlocked, perhaps the breakthrough could be achieved in the east?

Britain's war leaders were split on the issue. Among the "Easterners" in the War Council was First Lord of the Admiralty Winston Churchill, the plan's chief architect. By "forcing the Dardanelles" – the narrow straits that led to Constantinople and thence to the Black Sea – it was hoped that the Ottoman

threat would be neutralised; that pressure on Russia would be relieved and a supply line to that country opened up; and that criticism over Britain's contribution to the war effort would be rebutted. There was a further carrot: in the event of a successful outcome the undeclared Balkan states might side with the Allies, keen to align themselves with the victors.

The Admiralty was well aware of the problems associated with the enterprise. The terrain stacked the cards in favour of defence, and some senior Allied figures favoured a combined land-and-sea attack. Troops, it was argued, needed gunship support, while the navy needed soldiers on the ground to take out key defensive positions. For the two services acting in tandem the operation was demanding enough; for one of them acting alone it was risky in the extreme.

Above left: **On 25 April landings were made at six separate beaches on the Galipoli peninsula.**

Above right: **Cutters, destroyers and transport ships were used before the troops transferred to smaller craft.**

Right: **The Lancashire Fusiliers carry supplies onto W beach. After landing the Lancashires successfully battled their way through the barbed wire entanglements and reached the cliffs but the regiment lost over half its numbers, with six men later awarded the Victoria Cross in what became known as the "6 VCs before Breakfast". The beach was to become the main British base at Helles for the remainder of the campaign.**

Britain's war leaders were split on the issue. Among the "Easterners" in the War Council was First Lord of the Admiralty Winston Churchill, the plan's chief architect.

Churchill's Dardanelles timetable

An Anglo-French task force reached the mouth of the straits in mid-February 1915. France had wanted to delay, but Churchill, spoiling to get the fleet into action, refused to budge on the timetable. The French felt they had no alternative but to assist, and not simply out of duty to an ally. Here were two colonial powers whose interests in the region might overlap when the war was over, thus France was not about to sit on the sidelines while the British navy, given a fair wind, sailed to the heart of the Ottoman Empire.

The wind was anything but fair. After bombarding the outermost fort defences, the fleet entered the strait on 18 March. It was a disastrous day for the Allies, six ships lost to Turkish mines and guns. The attack was called off. Turkish leader Enver Pasha crowed that history would paint him as the man who had shown that the British fleet did not rule the high seas.

War Minister Lord Kitchener had sanctioned the Dardanelles assault as the vessels were outdated and it did not mean taking the eye off the ball – the Western Front. If it succeeded the gains were considerable; if not, the losses modest. But instead of accepting defeat Kitchener approved an escalation of the operation: committing an initial 70,000 ground troops. He sanctioned the release of the 29th Division, which had been bound for the Western Front. They were joined by French troops and ANZACS – men from the Australian and New Zealand Army Corps – who had been stationed in Egypt. Now at last it would be a joint land-and-sea attack, which increased the chances of success. And with it the risks.

Instead of accepting defeat Kitchener approved an escalation of the operation: committing an initial 70,000 ground troops.

Below: A map of the area, published by the *Daily Mail* in 1915, clearly shows Churchill's intentions. By forcing an entry through the Dardanelles, he hoped to set up a sea route into the Sea of Marmara, through the Bosphorus and into the Black Sea so that ships and supplies could sail directly to Russia.

Turkish defence holds

A three-pronged invasion was launched on 25 April 1915. The 29th Division landed at various points around Cape Helles on the tip of the Gallipoli peninsula. The ANZACS put to shore further north along the Aegean coast. French troops landed on the Asiatic side of the strait as a distraction. British fortunes were mixed, success in some places, the sea turning blood-red in others. Meanwhile the ANZACS, who landed a mile from the intended spot, found themselves in a cove surrounded by steep cliffs. There were heavy losses, and as the operation proceeded any minor advances came at a considerable cost.

The Allies couldn't break through the Turkish defence, the Turks couldn't drive the Allies back into the sea. The armies dug in, a stalemate that mirrored the scene in France and Flanders. When a fresh injection of troops in August failed to break the deadlock, withdrawal became the clear if unpalatable option. Sir Charles Monro took charge of the operation in the autumn and endorsed that view, leading Churchill to waspishly observe: "He came, he saw, he capitulated." Churchill had by then lost credibility, however, and the retreat began in December. That, at least, went remarkably well, scarcely a single casualty added to the toll by the time the evacuation was completed in January 1916.

Gallipoli was a disastrous chapter for the Allies. The battling qualities of the enemy had been underestimated. Leadership on the ground was abject. Maps were said to be no better than tourist guides. Disease accounted for as many lives as shellfire. Someone had to be held accountable and the failure was laid squarely at the door of Churchill, who left the Admiralty with his reputation badly tarnished.

The Anzacs, who landed a mile from the intended spot, found themselves in a cove surrounded by steep cliffs.

Right: **Australian troops leaving Mudros Bay on the Greek island of Lemnos, the advanced base for the operations.**

Above and above right: **Vessels head towards Suvla Bay on 6 August, ready to embark on a fresh attack.**

Top right: **Seaplanes were used by the Allies for reconnaissance work. As long as the seas were calm, underwater mines could be seen from a height of over 3,000 feet.**

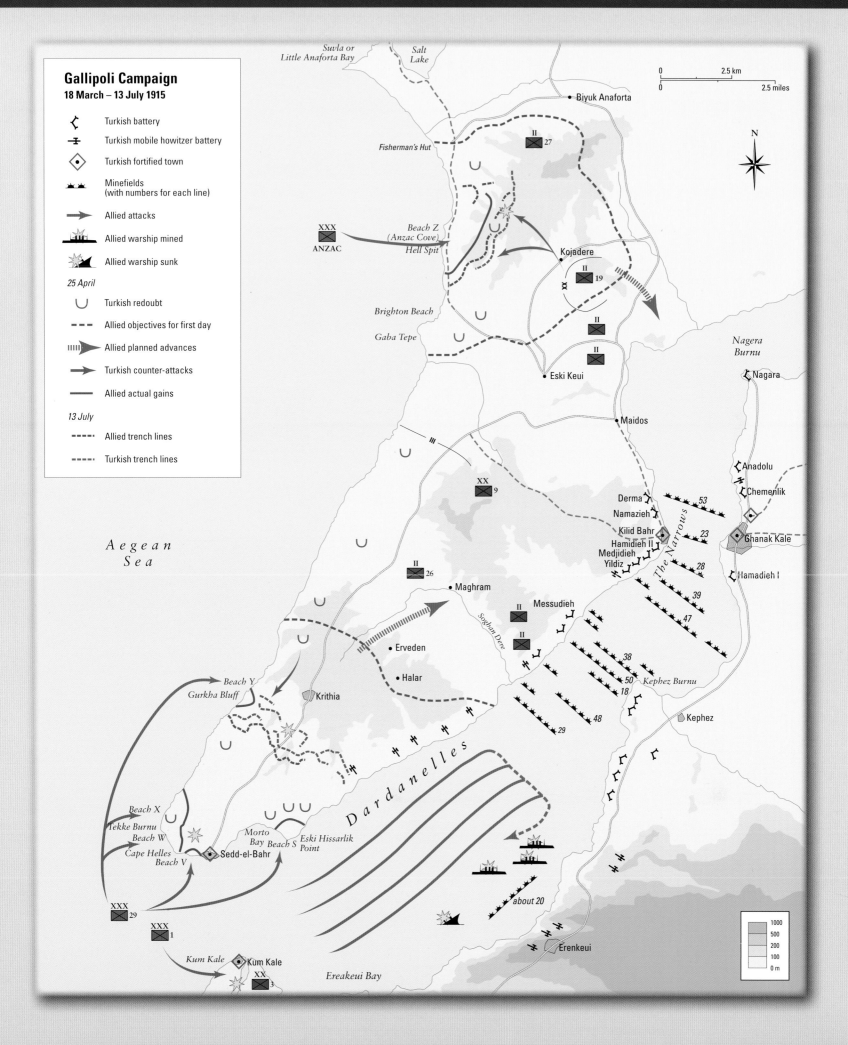

Gallipoli Campaign
18 March – 13 July 1915

⌐	Turkish battery
⊤	Turkish mobile howitzer battery
◇	Turkish fortified town
✶✶✶	Minefields (with numbers for each line)
➤	Allied attacks
✸	Allied warship mined
✸	Allied warship sunk

25 April

∪	Turkish redoubt
- - -	Allied objectives for first day
⫸	Allied planned advances
➤	Turkish counter-attacks
——	Allied actual gains

13 July

- - -	Allied trench lines
- - -	Turkish trench lines

Suvla or
Little Anaforta Bay

Salt
Lake

• Biyuk Anaforta

Fisherman's Hut

Beach Z
(Anzac Cove)
Hell Spit

XXX
ANZAC

Kojadere

Brighton Beach

Gaba Tepe

• Eski Keui

Nagera
Burnu

⌐ Nagara

Maidos

⌐ Anadolu
⌐ Chemenlik

XX
9

Derma
Namazieh
Kilid Bahr
Hamidieh II
Medjidieh
Yildiz

53

23

◇ Ghanak Kale

28

Hamadieh I

II
26

• Maghram

Messudieh

39

47

Aegean
Sea

Soghan Dere

• Erveden

• Halar

38

50

18

Kephez Burnu

48

29

• Kephez

Beach Y
Gurkha Bluff

Krithia

Beach X

Tekke Burnu
Beach W

Cape Helles
Beach V

Morto
Bay Beach S
Eski Hissarlik
Point

Sedd-el-Bahr

Dardanelles

The Narrows

about 20

XXX
29

XXX
1

Kum Kale • Kum Kale

XX
3

Ereakeui Bay

• Erenkeui

1000	
500	
200	
100	
0 m	

Above: Lord Kitchener visits the troops. Although still a very popular public figure, a combination of the Shell Crisis and his decision to support Churchill over the planned Dardanelles Campaign seriously undermined his position in the Cabinet.

Above right and below left: Survivors from HMS *Triumph* are ferried to safety. On 25 May the battleship had spotted the German submarine U-boat *U-21* near Gaba Tepe and opened fire, but was hit by a torpedo on her starboard side, causing an explosion. The ship immediately began to list but fortunately the destroyer HMS *Chelmer* was able to evacuate most of the crew to safety.

Right: Life on board the transport ships was cramped, with troops filling every available space.

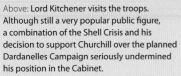

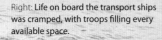

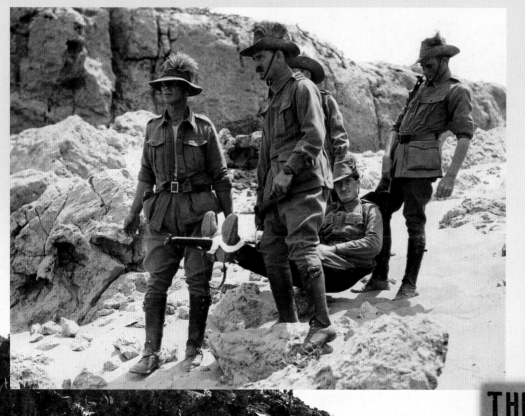

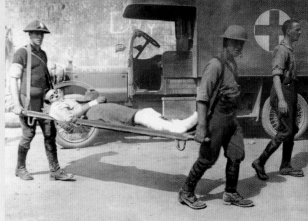

Left and above: Australia's ambulance men carry wounded soldiers to safety. During the course of the campaign over 11,000 Anzacs were killed, with another 25,000 wounded.

Below: Australians on the beach surrounded by supplies. On 24 May a brief truce was declared to allow both sides to retrieve and bury their dead.

THE PENINSULA ONE GREAT FORTRESS.

ALLIED TROOPS OUTNUMBERED BY TWO TO ONE.

MACHINE GUNS ALL-IMPORTANT.

"The Army of Sir Ian Hamilton, the Fleet of Admiral de Robeck, are separated only by a few miles from a victory such as this war has not yet seen."—*Mr. Winston Churchill at Dundee, June 5.*

TWO important messages from the Dardanelles will help the country to correct its early misapprehensions on the campaign there.

Lack of information led everyone to believe that the Allied Fleets would quickly smash the forts and batteries of the Turks to powder and open the way to Constantinople.

To-day the nation understands that the Straits and Gallipoli can not be won from the water alone, and that the operation is a great war in itself—the most complex in history and one of terrible severity.

As Mr. Churchill has said, "only by a few miles" are we separated from victory, but every square yard of those miles is a natural defence, enormously strengthened by all the instruments of destruction.

Reuter's correspondent and Mr. Granville Fortescue of the "Daily Telegraph," de-

scribing the obstacles, make us feel proud of the troops who face them with such splendid bravery, and Sir Ian Hamilton's latest report of an advance of a thousand yards on the left shows that their almost superhuman courage is not fruitless.

The messages of the two correspondents tell us that:—

The enemy has two soldiers to our one.

He has trenches loopholed at every yard, and

A great supply of machine guns, grenades and cricket ball bombs, and howitzers.

He enfilades us from the Asiatic shore.

Every ravine is a field of obstacles, every ridge a fort.

Mines abound in the water, guns are along the shore.

All Turkey is an armed camp, and the soldiers are training grimly and have the kind of fighting job that suits them.

Naval gunfire is accurate, but disappointing in its results.

Gallipoli is, in fact, "one great fortress."

TURKISH GRIP ON GALLIPOLI.

250,000 Well-Entrenched Men With German Officers.

"EVENING NEWS" TELEGRAM.
(FROM OUR SPECIAL CORRESPONDENT.)
ATHENS, Tuesday.

The Turks in the Gallipoli Peninsula now have 250,000 men, perfectly entrenched in strong positions, with at least one German officer per unit.

The fighting consists of a series of attacks and counter-attacks. During the day the Allies' attack is assisted by the warships, whose shells search the enemy's positions, inflicting great losses; but at night, when the ships are unable to fire lest they hit our own troops, the Turks counter-attack vigorously in dense mass, after the German system.

Owing to these tactics the Turkish losses are enormous. They are estimated up till the end of last week at 100,000, including many German officers.

The prisoners say that the fire of the warships produces terrible effects, making the Peninsula a sheet of flame.

KEY MAP SHOWING POSITION

TURKEY IN EUROPE

TURKEY IN ASIA

Scale of Miles

REFERENCE

Principal Roads thus
Principal Forts thus
Heights in feet
The Letters against the Forts are those referred to in the Admiralty despatches

In the 'Dardanelles.

A British soldier warming up his dinner in a rest camp. An official photograph circulated on behalf of the Press Bureau by C.N.

It took only a modest number of Turkish soldiers with machine guns on high ground to derail the Allies' plan almost before it got underway.

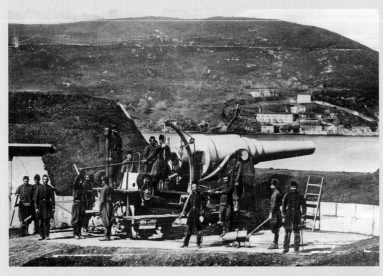

Top left: After the landings in April the troops had no alternative but to remain on or close to the beaches. The Allies' invasion seemed to quickly run out of momentum, giving the Turks the opportunity to reorganise their troops and bring in reinforcements.

Upper middle left: A marine landing party sparks mild interest from the locals. Ironically one group of soldiers walked straight into Krithia village without any opposition but had no orders to use this to their advantage and eventually retreated to the beach.

Lower middle left: A battery at the entrance to the waterway.

Bottom left: Crosses made by Australian troops at Gallipoli – for themselves. On the wood the men carved their names and the words "Killed in Action". They left the date to be filled in later. Wherever the soldiers went they took their crosses with them.

Above: The scene from an officer's dugout on the cliffs near Cape Helles showing a splash made by one of the Turkish shells which fell perilously near a steamer at anchor.

Opposite above: HMS *Cornwallis* fires at the Turks as troops retreat from the beaches at the close of the Gallipoli campaign.

Opposite below: A map published in 1915 gives readers a "bird's eye" view of the Dardanelles.

Main image: British soldiers leave the transport in a trawler to land on the Gallipoli peninsula. This was the first batch to set off from this particular transport, and the sailors and troops that remained aboard gave them a hearty send off, while cheer after cheer came from the battleships as they went past.

Right: Troops disembark from a transporter (opposite above) ready to head for the shore.

Below right: Allied troops in the ravines. The blistering heat and poor sanitation led to a huge population of flies. This, combined with the number of rapidly decomposing unburied bodies, led to an outbreak of dysentery in the trenches, which further debilitated the exhausted soldiers.

Opposite below: The Lancashire Fusilliers prepare to go ashore at Cape Helles.

THE DARDANELLES.

German-led Turks Attack Stubbornly.

ALLIES' PROGRESS.

"EVENING NEWS" TELEGRAM.

(FROM OUR SPECIAL CORRESPONDENT.)
ATHENS, Thursday.

The troops of the Allied landing expedition have completely foiled all efforts to impede their progress, although the Turks, being reinforced, have at*acked with great stubbornness, and are led by German officers.

The Allies are steadily continuing their landing successfully, despite the opposition.

The late desperate fighting on the Gallipoli peninsula cost much loss to both sides, but especially to the enemy, whose wounded, who were conveyed to Constantinople, run into thousands.

The more severely wounded on the British side are taken to hospital ships at Moudros, while the slightly wounded are sent to Egypt.

Mitylene telegrams report the continued bombardment of the Smyrna forts by the British fleet, and further allied action is daily expected.

THROUGH TURKISH EYES.

AMSTERDAM, Friday.

The following official communiqué has been received from Constantinople:—

During yesterday's (Wednesday) attacks against the enemy's left wing at Avi Burnu we destroyed one of the enemy's battalions. A portion of the very strong fortifications was captured, together with over a hundred rifles and one machine gun.

Our operations against Sedd el Bœhr yesterday evening caused heavy losses to the English. We captured three machine guns and a quantity of munitions. Altogether we captured ten machine guns.—Central News.

May 1915

1   The Battle of Gorlice-Tarnów began when German troops broke through Russian lines in Galicia.

    The American tanker *Gulflight* was torpedoed without warning off the Scilly Islands by the German submarine *U-30*.

2   The Turks attacked French and British forces in the First Battle of Krithia in the Dardanelles.

3   The Triple Alliance was denounced by Italy.

4   The Battle of Julien ended when British forces were withdrawn from forward positions to take up new defensive lines to the east of Ypres.

5   Hill 60 was captured by the Germans during the Second Battle of Ypres.

6   The Second Battle of Krithia began, continuing the Allied attempts to advance on the Helles battlefield during the Gallipoli Campaign.

7   The British ocean liner RMS *Lusitania* was torpedoed and sunk off the south-west coast of Ireland by the German submarine *U20*. 1198 citizens were killed including more than 100 US citizens – creating a diplomatic crisis between Germany and the USA.

    Japan presented an ultimatum to China demanding territorial concessions.

8   The second British-French assault on Turkish defences near Krithia failed and brought the the Second Battle of Krithia to an end.

9   The short-lived Battle of Aubers Ridge began a British offensive against German forces on the Western Front. The battle was a disaster for the British army as, despite suffering heavy losses, no ground was won and no tactical advantage gained.

    The city of Libau was occupied by the Germans.

10 The German Zeppelin *LZ-38* bombed Southend in Essex.

11 German forces evacuated Shavli in the Baltic Provinces.

12 A Turkish destroyer torpedoed and sank the British battleship HMS *Goliath* in Morto Bay off Cape Helles at the south-westernmost tip of the Gallipoli peninsula.

13 South African forces captured and occupied Windhoek, the capital of German South West Africa.

14 The British War Council met for the final time.

Prime Minister and dictator of Portugal, General Joaquim Pimenta de Castro was overthrown by a politico-military uprising which also led to the resignation of President Manuel de Arriaga.

15 José de Castro took over as Prime Minister of Portugal after the deposition of General Joaquim Pimenta de Castro.

    The British army attack in the Artois region of France in the beginning of the Battle of Festubert.

17 The German Zeppelin *LZ-38* carried out further attacks on Dover and Ramsgate.

19 Russian forces captured Van in Armenia during the Battle of Van.

21 The Russian Expeditionary Force landed at Enzeli en route to Persia.

22 British troops advanced towards La Quinque Rue in the Battle of Festubert.

23 The Italian government ordered mobilisation and declared war on Austria.

    The British submarine *E11* sank a gunboat and other small craft in the Sea of Marmora.

24 The Battle of Bellewaarde Ridge began with German artillery bombardment on British troops during the Second Battle of Ypres.

25 The "Shell Crisis", precipitated by a shortage of artillery shells on the front lines, resulted in the formation of a coalition government between Prime Minister Herbert Asquith and Tory leader Andrew Bonar Law.

26 A British naval battle squadron gathered at Malta before joining the Italian fleet in the Adriatic.

    The German Zeppelin *LZ-38* bombed Southend again.

27 First Lord of the Admiralty, Winston Churchill was demoted to Chancellor of the Duchy of Lancaster as he was held responsible for the unsuccessful Dardanelles and Gallipoli campaigns.

28 Sir Henry Bradwardine Jackson was appointed First Sea Lord of the Admiralty following Admiral Lord Fisher's surprise resignation.

31 The first Zeppelin raid on London took place.

    British and Indian troops broke through the Turkish lines at Qurna, north of Basra.

OUR BIG

Below: The Dardanelles campaign was conceived as an alternative to the stalemate that had set in on the Western Front. In fact it too became synonymous with deadlock and heavy losses. Churchill, one of the chief proponents of the campaign, resigned when the decision to withdraw was taken.

JOB IN GALLIPOLI.

TO FLATTEN HIM OUT.

The Allies couldn't break through the Turkish defence, the Turks couldn't drive the Allies back into the sea. The armies dug in, a stalemate that mirrored the scene in France and Flanders.

DARDANELLES LOSSES.

3,798 in June : Total Figures 42,434.

In the Commons this afternoon Mr. Asquith announced the total British casualties in the Dardanelles (naval and military) to the end of June as follows:—

	Killed.	Wounded.	Missing.	Totals.
Officers:—	541	1,257	135	1,933
Other Ranks:—	7,543	25,557	7,401	40,501
Aggregate			=	42,434

*** The total up to the end of May was 38,636. The losses in June were therefore 3,798.

ITALIANS INVADE AUSTRIA.

The Italian Front

As a Triple Alliance member since 1882, Italy might have been expected to swing behind the Central Powers as the battle lines were drawn post-Sarajevo. But Germany and Austria's treaty ally stayed her hand, keen to see where allegiance would bring the greatest advantage. Discussions took place with each of the warring parties, effectively a bidding war for Italy's sons. The country's opportunistic prime minister, Antonio Salandra, drove an unwilling parliament into backing the Entente, believing that victory would come sooner rather than later and swathes of Austrian-held territory with a sizeable Italian population would meet her avowed expansionist aspirations. Those gains were spelt out in April 1915, when a secret agreement was reached in the Treaty of London. Behind closed doors Salandra drove a hard bargain, informed by "sacro egoismo" self-interest that the Entente accepted as the price of welcoming a new ally into the fold. Italy joined the combatant ranks a month later, initially declaring only against her Habsburg neighbour. Berlin blithely announced that it was "uninjured by the defection of the third ally and her desertion to the enemies' camp". It could scarcely have said anything other, and yet those dismissive words had the ring of prophecy, for Italy's contribution to the Allied effort was marginal at best. Modest achievements, however, came at an exorbitant cost.

Under the command of General Luigi Cadorna, the Italian army embarked upon a lengthy, bitter struggle with Austrian forces in the inhospitable Alpine terrain that separated the two countries. Cadorna ruled with a rod of iron, a man who sacked underlings by the dozen and trained his gun on any foot soldier he felt had not acquitted himself well enough in the field. He was not averse to employing the ancient Roman practice of decimation: singling out every 10th man from an underperforming entity for disciplinary treatment.

Salandra believed that victory would come sooner rather than later and swathes of Austrian-held territory with a sizeable Italian population would meet her avowed expansionist aspirations.

Below: The frontier line between Italy and Austria. On the right is the King of Italy. On the left the Duke of Abruzzi, commander of the navy.

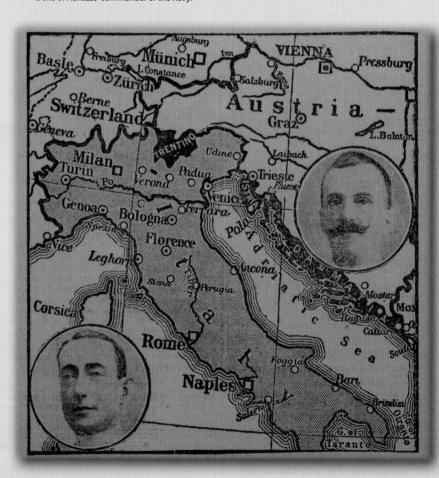

THE MARCH ON TRIESTE.

ITALIANS WITHIN 16 MILES.

ANOTHER GAIN.

RUSSIA'S "COMPLETE" VICTORY.

'20,000 GERMAN LOSSES.'

Our Special Correspondent at Rome reports that in their advance from Monfalcone, the Italians have now taken the heights and, beyond them, a navigable canal and the docks and naval yards of Porto Rosega.

They are now within sixteen miles of waiting Trieste. The road and the railway run along the foreshore of the gulf; and Italian warships proved in the bombardment of Monfalcone that they could operate in these waters to support the land forces.

At Monte Nero, beyond the middle Isonzo, the Italians have sent advance parties to spurs cleared by artillery, and have found the bodies of some of the defenders and many rifles and quick-firing guns.

ITALIANS PRESS ON.

Another Gain on the Road to Trieste.

NAVAL YARDS SEIZED.

"EVENING NEWS" TELEGRAM.
(FROM OUR SPECIAL CORRESPONDENT.)
ROME, Friday.

The capture of Monfalcone has been followed by that of Porto Rosega and the navigable canal lying between the two towns.

All the shipyards are in Italian hands. The vessels there recently included a small cruiser, which was being built for China.

It is believed that most of the ships were blown up by the retiring Austrians.

** Porto Rosega is an Austrian establishment at the head of the Gulf of Trieste. It lies some three miles south of Monfalcone.

TO-DAY'S OFFICIAL.

Gradisca Firmly Held By Our Ally.

ROME, Friday evening.
The following communiqué is issued this evening:—

ITALY.

To-day was marked by some progress in certain parts of our front. Our reconnoitring force pushed beyond Monte Nero, and found among the rocks which had been battered for the last few days by our guns and rifles, over forty enemy dead, and the remnants of many rifles and quick-firing guns.

The information of prisoners agrees in stating that enemy forces over six battalions strong, with quickfiring guns endeavoured to take our troops in the rear in the Monte Nero region. This surrounding movement, however, was unsuccessful thanks to the stout resistance and rapid manoeuvring of the Bersaglieri and the Alpini.

The town of Gradisca, which has been held for some days by our troops,

June 1915

1 French troops captured the trenches at Souchez, north of Arras on the Western Front.

2 The British Government announced a blockade of the coast of Asia Minor.

3 Przemyśl was retaken by Austro-German forces.

San Marino declared war on Austria-Hungary.

4 The Third and final Battle of Krithia began at Gallipoli as the Allies attempted to push inland from their beach-heads.

5 The First Franco-British ministerial conference was held at Calais in order to coordinate war policy and strategy.

6 Zeppelin L9 bombed Hull on the east coast of England causing considerable damage.

7 The German airship LZ37 was destroyed in the air near Ghent in Belgium by Lieut Warneford of the Royal Naval Air Service – the first time an airship was successfully shot down by an aeroplane.

8 William Jennings Bryan resigned as United States Secretary of State in disagreement with President Wilson's policy towards Germany.

9 Italian forces captured the town of Monfalcone along the Isonzo front.

10 Allied forces captured Garua in the Cameroons.

12 German troops attacked north of Shavli and at Mosciska in Galicia.

13 Greek statesman Eleftherios Venizelos won in the Greek elections. His party of Venizelists won 193 out of 316 seats.

15 The Zeppelin L10 was involved in an unsuccessful bombing raid on the north-east coast of Britain.

16 British troops advanced in Bellewarde, a small hamlet north of Hooge and east of Ypres in Belgium.

17 The Russian evacuation of Lemberg began as Austrian forces pushed forward in Galicia.

18 The Second Battle of Artois ended in stalemate in the final Allied offensive of Spring 1915.

19 South African forces began an advance on Otavifontein in German Southwest Africa.

20 The Royal Naval cruiser HMS Roxburgh was damaged by a torpedo from German U boat U-38.

21 British troops reached the Euphrates in Mesopotamia, and re-occupied Aden.

22 Austro-Hungarian forces recaptured the city of Lemberg from the Russians.

23 The First Battle of the Isonzo began when Italian troops attacked the Austro-Hungarian army on the Italian Front.

24 Robert Lansing was appointed Secretary of State in the USA following the resignation of William Jennings Bryan earlier in the month.

25 The German press published an official statement addressing the German use of poison gas at the start of the Second Battle of Ypres two months earlier.

26 Montenegrin forces captured San Giovanni di Medua in Albania.

28 The Battle of Gully Ravine began at Cape Helles on the Gallipoli peninsula between Indian and British troops and the Ottoman army.

29 A bill was introduced in Britain for the creation of a National Register.

30 The Royal Navy destroyer HMS Lightning sank after striking mines off the Kent coast of England.

Football in the trenches

As the 1914-15 season drew to a close it was clear that football could not continue. The decision to suspend the League and Cup competition came as no surprise, and the global conflict brought forth the heroic side of the footballing fraternity. Nobility was shown in the famous Christmas Day truce of 1914, when German and British soldiers played an impromptu game in no-man's-land. And even at the height of battle football was often used as a morale booster. Members of some regiments invoked the names of their beloved clubs as they advanced, and even dribbled balls onto the battlefield. Back in England, regional football replaced the traditional competitions between 1915 and 1918. These were low-key affairs and fixtures were organised so as not to interfere with the war effort. After Armistice Day on 11 November 1918 the appetite of both clubs and supporters to reinstate the official programme was huge. There was even talk of getting a truncated FA Cup competition off the ground immediately. In the end the authorities decided in favour of starting afresh the following season, and 1919-20 thus became the first postwar campaign.

Below: The 1915 FA Cup Final was a subdued affair held at Old Trafford on a damp afternoon before a crowd of only 50,000; many were servicemen displaying signs of the injuries sustained in battle. Sheffield United won the match against Chelsea 3-0 but this was to be the last cup final played until 1920 following the suspension of the Football League and the FA Cup.

FOOTBALLERS' DUTY TO THE ARMY.

To the Editor of The Daily Mail.

Sir,—I was surprised to find in The Daily Mail a statement from Colonel Grantham that only 122 professional footballers had joined the Footballers' Battalion.

Now in the country there are probably 4,000 or 5,000 professional footballers who, because of their calling, must be young men in the prime of life. The majority of them are single, and it is sad to think that only 122 have joined the battalion specially formed for them.

One who has officiated often in Southern League football and has frequently gone into the players' dressing-rooms, can easily imagine what a fine battalion 1,000 footballers would be—"hard as nails and fit as fiddles."

I see arrangements are already being tentatively made to continue football next year. There are two ways to stop it absolutely: (1) For the War Office to take over all professional grounds and utilise them as drill grounds; (2) for the present referees and linesmen to refuse to officiate in further matches after this season until the war is over. I intend to refuse.   LINESMAN.

FOOTBALL TO STOP.

NO MORE PROFESSIONALISM TILL WAR OVER.

The Football Association have decided that no Cup-tie or League football matches shall be played next season until the war is over. A statement to this effect was made by Mr. Charles Crump, the senior vice-president of the Football Association, in presenting the cup and medals to the winners of the Amateur Cup at New Cross.

A resolution to this effect will be adopted probably at the council meeting to be held on the eve of the Cup Final at Manchester on Friday. At the last council meeting on March 29 the Football Association passed a resolution giving itself power to suspend the game either sectionally or entirely if it thought desirable.

Mr. F. J. Wall, secretary of the Football Association, said that no agreements would be entered into for next season. A very large number of players are now engaged on Government contracts and munitions of war.

OUR CASUALTIES.

The Premier Announces Total as 330,995.

4,499 OFFICERS KILLED.

How the Roll of Honour Has Grown.

Mr. Asquith, in a statement issued to-day, announces the total of the British casualties as—

330,995.

They may be sub-divided as follows:—

	Officers.	Men.
Killed - - -	4,499	64,814
Wounded -	8,517	188,977
Missing - -	1,412	62,776

The figures are thus classified:—

Military.
(Up to July 18).

	Officers.	Men.
Killed	4,000	57,384
Wounded	8,430	188,190
Missing	1,383	62,502
	13,813	308,076
Total, 321,889		

Naval.
(Up to July 20.)

	Officers.	Men.
Killed	499	7,430
Wounded	87	787
Missing	29	274
	615	8,491
Total, 9,106.		

The military casualties are made up as follows:—

FRANCE.

	OFFICERS.	MEN.
KILLED	3,288	48,372
WOUNDED	6,803	156,308
MISSING	1,163	50,969
	11,254	255,649
Total, 266,903.		

DARDANELLES.

	OFFICERS.	MEN.
KILLED	567	7,567
WOUNDED	1,379	28,635
MISSING	198	10,892
	2,144	47,094
Total, 49,238.		

[These figures include casualties to the Naval Division.]

OTHER THEATRES.

	OFFICERS.	MEN.
KILLED	145	1,445
WOUNDED	248	3,247
MISSING	22	641
	475	5,333
Total, 5,748.		

[These figures exclude casualties in German South-West Africa.]

Previous official announcements have given the British casualties at various dates as follows:—

Up to August 25	2,000
Up to October 31	57,000
Up to February 4	104,000
Up to April 11	139,347
Up to May 31	271,616

The casualties in other wars fall into insignificance before these figures. In the whole of the Franco-German war of 1870-71 the German losses were 28,000 killed and 101,000 wounded.

In the Boer War our losses in the field were 5,744 killed and 22,829 wounded. To these were added 16,168 who died of disease or wounds.

The British losses in the Crimea were 20,526; but of these only 12 per cent. died in battle.

600,000 lives were lost in the American Civil War.

In connection with the figures issued to-day, it should, of course, be remembered that about 60 per cent. of the wounded return to duty.

LIFE-SAVING STEEL HELMETS.

300,000 FRENCH WEARING THEM ALREADY.

PARIS, Monday.

The *Intransigeant* states that 300,000 steel helmets for the French soldiers at the front have already been distributed. They are being supplied at the rate of 25,000 daily.

Specimen helmets have been received in Paris after undergoing a fusillade. They all bear marks of bullets which would have killed soldiers wearing the regulation képi. A small device, which is hardly visible, distinguishes the different corps; for instance, a hand grenade for infantry, a hunting horn for chasseurs, an anchor for Colonial infantry, and crossed guns for artillery.—Exchange.

**The Daily Mail was the first to call attention to the importance of armour in modern trench warfare. As we pointed out, a very large proportion of the wounds received in France are in the head. Various patterns of helmets and breastplates have been described and illustrated in our columns during the past few weeks.

Above: Dead soldiers lie abandoned in the trenches. At times unofficial truces were organised to allow the dead and wounded to be collected from no-man's-land. On these occasions stretcher bearers showing the Red Cross flag would recover the men, sometimes swapping the enemy dead for their own troops.

Opposite top: The map-diagram shows the Russian territory held by the Germans (coloured black), the population of this territory as compared with the population of Russia and the dates and rough direction of the five attacks on Warsaw which led to its capture. Inset is a portrait of Leopold of Bavaria whose army captured the city.

Opposite below: A Zouave sentry at watch on the French front. The Zouave light infantry regiments in the French Army originated in Algeria and their men were easily identified by their traditional uniform of baggy trousers, oriental headgear and short jackets.

July 1915

1 The Battle of Otavi was fought between South African and German forces in German South West Africa. The final battle of the South-West Africa Campaign ended with a decisive South African victory.

2 The British government formed the Ministry of Munitions and passed the Munitions of War Act which required compulsory arbitration of labour disputes and banned strikes and lockouts.

3 The Germans continued their advance into Poland along the Eastern Front.

5 Fierce fighting continued between French and German troops at Souchez, Arras and on the Meuse.

6 British and French ministers held the first Allied war conference at Calais.

7 The First Battle of Isonzo ended with a victory for the Austro-Hungarians.

The Italian armoured cruiser Amalfi was torpedoed and sunk in the Adriatic by the Austro-Hungarian submarine U-26.

9 German troops in South-West Africa surrendered to General Botha's South African forces at Tsumeb, 370 km north of Windhoek.

11 The German cruiser SMS Königsberg was destroyed and sunk in the Rufiji river in German East Africa by British river monitors.

12 The German Government announced its intention to take control of the coal industry.

13 A new Austro-German offensive began on the Eastern Front.

14 The Canadian Prime Minister Sir Robert Borden attended his first meeting of the British Cabinet.

15 The National Registration Act became law in Great Britain.

16 The Battle of Krasnostav began.

17 Bulgaria signed a secret alliance with Germany, Austria and Turkey.

18 Following the conclusion of the First Battle of Isonzo earlier in the month, the Second Battle of Isonzo began on the Italian Front with heavier artillery support against the Austro-Hungarian army.

20 The Battle of La Linge began between French and German forces near the Vosges mountains of Alsace.

21 The Russian town of Ivangorod was invaded by Austro-German forces.

22 British forces captured Bukoba on Victoria Nyanza in German East Africa.

23 Austrian warships bombarded Ortona and the Tremiti Islands in the Adriatic Sea.

24 Rozan and Pultulsk in North Poland were captured by German forces.

25 The American steamer Leelanaw was torpedoed off the Scottish coast.

26 Italian troops landed on and occupied Pelagosa Island in the middle of the Adriatic.

28 Germans forces crossed the Vistula between Warsaw and Ivangorod.

29 The East Persia Cordon was established in order to protect British interests and prevent enemy infiltration from Persia into Afghanistan.

30 German troops used flame throwers for the first time against the British lines at Hooge in Belgium.

The Pope sent an appeal for peace to belligerent Governments.

31 The Battle of Strelcze was fought on the Eastern Front.

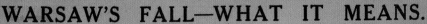

August 1915

1   The Galata bridge in Constantinople harbour was destroyed by British submarines.

3   The Second Battle of Isonzo ended with no strategic result as both sides ran out of artillery ammunition.

    Russian forces evacuated Van in Armenia.

4   Russian troops evacuated Warsaw but took up defensive positions on the north side of the Vistula River.

5   After the Russian withdrawal the Germans occupied Warsaw in Poland.

6   The Battle of Sari Bair (also known as the August Offensive) began – the last and unsuccessful attempt by the British to seize the Gallipoli peninsula from the Ottoman Empire.

7   Heavy fighting continued in the Battle of Sari Bair. British troops were supported by New Zealand and Australian troops.

8   The Turkish battleship *Barbaros Hayreddin* was sunk by the British submarine *E11* in the Dardanelles.

9   British troops recaptured the trenches at Hooge.

10 A surprise Turkish counterattack from Sari Bair on Gallipoli forced the Allies to withdraw.

    The German Zeppelin *L12* was damaged by aircraft fire during a raid on Dover in the English Channel.

12 A British torpedo carrying seaplane took off from HMS *Ben-my-Chree* and sank a Turkish supply ship in the Sea of Marmara.

    A British advance at Suvla towards the Tekke Tepe Hills was repulsed by the Turks in the Gallipoli Campaign.

13 The passenger ship HMT *Royal Edward* was torpedoed and sunk by the German submarine *UB-14* in the Aegean Sea.

15 The National Register was taken in Britain.

16 Lowca and Harrington near Whitehaven in Cumberland were shelled by a German submarine.

17 The city of Kovno on the Eastern Front fell to Austro-German forces.

19 The German battle cruiser SMS *Moltke* was torpedoed by British submarine *E1* in the Gulf of Riga.

20 British airmen destroyed a German submarine off Ostend, Belgium.

21 The Battle of Scimitar Hill in the Gallipoli Campaign, which ended in another strategic failure, was the final British offensive in the Dardanelles.

    Italy declared war on Turkey.

22 Ossowietz in northern Poland was stormed by German forces.

23 British warships bombarded German positions at Zeebrugge and Knocke on the Belgian coast.

25 German occupying forces established a Polish government in Warsaw. General Hans Hartwig von Beseler was named Governor General.

26 German forces occupied the fort of Olita on Niemen and captured Byelostok and Brest-Litovsk in Poland.

27 Johann Heinrich von Bernstorff notified Secretary of State Robert Lansing that, "full satisfaction" would be given to the United States for the sinking of the ocean liner SS *Arabic* on 19 August.

29 A combined British, Anzac and Gurkha force failed to take Hill 60 at Suvla.

30 The British Government agreed that the Allies could guarantee eventual freedom and self-determination of Bosnia, Herzegovina, South Dalmatia, Slavonia and Croatia, provided Serbia agreed.

SOME OF THE FALLEN.

MEN WE LOVED.

GAPS IN A CIRCLE OF FRIENDS.

By HAL MORTON.

On this anniversary let me look back and pay tribute to those men who went out, brave-hearted and great of soul, never to return. Before me are the names of eight brave men and good friends. They are names known outside the intimate circles of family and friendship, and, with one or two exceptions, their owners had lain down the pen, put aside the brush, and left the playing field at the call of the drum.

Rupert Brooke.

First, for several reasons, among those whose spirits are not dead must we place the young Adonais, Rupert Brooke, sub-lieutenant of the Royal Naval Division, who died from sunstroke at Lemnos. He was a young poet of genius, and therefore he had more to give than most men. He has gone down into silence taking his songs with him—the young poet is the only one of us who may carry riches

beyond the grave. As soon as war broke out there came into the verse of Rupert Brooke a fiery idealism, in which, it may be said, he forged his own sword. No man went into battle with a higher mind. Patriotism, not the flag-waving vagaries of the popular bard, but the deep love of English earth and the memory of all things English and good, came to him:—

> God! I will pack and take a train
> And get me to England once again!
> For England's the one place I know
> Where men with splendid hearts may go.

Dear, splendid heart, what is it possible to say? Those who knew you in the old days can imagine your scorn at the thought of anyone mourning the songs that might have been yours. You lived for your ideals and you died for them: it has made you a greater poet.

R. W. Poulton Palmer.

FRIDAY, APRIL 16, 1915.

139,000 BRITISH CASUALTIES.

CHIEFLY WHY.

Since the Cabinet in general and the War Office in particular forbid the publication of any but optimistic war news, the nation can only obtain a glimmering of the facts by meditating on the rapidly growing casualty lists.

In the new kind of warfare with which the world is confronted it is obvious that the death roll must be higher than in such campaigns as that fought in South Africa fifteen years ago. The nation is prepared to pay the price, even when it weeps for the best and noblest of its sons. They did not murmur at the lot of sacrifice, and the nation will not murmur in so far as that sacrifice is necessary and inevitable. But it may justly observe that while its late Minister of War was busy cutting down the British artillery the Germans were steadily increasing theirs and providing heavy howitzers without stint.

Modern war, as Sir John French has intimated in no hesitating terms, is mainly a matter of shells and guns to fire those shells from. We entered upon this war without sufficient artillery, and, while the artillery has since been increased, the Government do not seem to have awakened quickly enough to the fact that this is a shell war. On certain occasions during this struggle the French Army has fired 200,000 shells in a single day. Despite this fact, which must have been known, the necessity of ordering shells in sufficient numbers does not appear to have been recognised at the earliest possible date. In short, the Government did not see that war was coming. When war came they did not see that shells would be wanted in such quantities. The mistake which they made by under-estimating the need of shells they are now repeating by under-estimating the need of men. Ours is at present the ignoble position of holding only 31 miles in the firing line. Our French comrades are fighting furiously along a front of 543 miles. If we are to play a worthy part we shall require such an increase in our strength as can be supplied and maintained only by compulsory

---

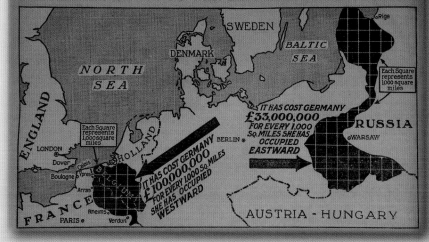

THE COST OF GERMANY'S WAR EXPLAINED FOR EVERYBODY.

SECOND YEAR OF WAR BEGUN TO-DAY.

WARSAW FRONT STILL INTACT.

RUSSIANS FALL BACK IN EXTREME NO

SANGUINAR[...] NA[...]

[A]USTRIANS CAPTUR[...]

MACKENSEN [...]

[...]DAY of 2nd YEAR of W[...]
[...]espite extremely desperate
[...]uinary battles on the N[...]
[...]denburg can claim only a s[...]
[...]nce near Lomja. Macken[...]
[...]ces in the south has agai[...]
[...] war h[...]

SIR E. GREY TO U.S.

NO REAL DIFFERENCES.

FRIENDLY ANSWER.

BLOCKADE EXPLAINED.

An important correspondence between
Sir Edward Grey and the American Am-
[...] Page, is [...]
[...] document [...]
[...] are by S[...]
[...] there is n[...]
[...] Britain [...]
[...] practise [...]
[...] il with th[...]

[...]n point[...]
[...] oblige[...]
[...] even wh[...]
[...]tral sh[...]
[...] of the s[...]
[...]d rules[...]
[...] her has[...]
[...] sunk ne[...]
[...]how far[...]
[...]y neut[...]
[...]ts have [...]
[...] neithe[...]
[...]rman a[...]
[...]ranth[...]
[...]itish G[...]
[...]rough[...]

LIQUID-FIRE SHELL

A GERMAN WEAPON AT HOOGE.

MORE TERRIFYING THAN EFFECTIVE.

FROM OUR SPECIAL CORRESPONDENT.

THE KING TO HIS WELSH GUARDS.

COL[...]

The
colou[...]
Guard[...]
ham P[...]
ing da[...]
upon t[...]

With[...]
and Si[...]
George[...]
toria w[...]
a cons[...]
civilian[...]

The[...]
the Bis[...]
Welsh [...]
Father[...]
y Botel[...]
the re[...]

The[...]
subalte[...]
leading[...]
His o[...]
subalte[...]
Immed[...]
rolling [...]
territo[...]

SP[...]

Not [...]
King [...]
sent to[...]
few [...]
The [...]

AUSTRALASIANS' ASSAULT.

AUGUST 4.

THE KING'S JOURNE[Y] TO ST. PAUL'S.

EMPIRE'S VOW.

TO-DAY'S WORLD-WID[E] MEETINGS.

In every corner of the Empire
[...] nation will pledge its faith to-day in
[...] justice of the cause of the Allies and [...]
[...] for peace with honour. In every te[...]
and village the following resolution [...]
be put:—

"That on the anniversary of the decl[a]-
[...]tion of a righteous war this mee[...]
records its inflexible determinatio[...]
[...] continue to a victorious end the stru[...]
[...] in maintenance of those ideals of lib[...]
and justice which are the common [...]
sacred cause of the Allies."

The two great events in London to-[...]

The King at St. Paul's ... ... N[...]
Mr. Balfour at London Opera House 8 [...]
The Central Committee of Nati[...]
[...] Patriotic Organisations, 62, Cha[...]
[...], S.W., has linked up the bi[...]
[...]untry places with the great cities[...]
[...]roughout the day, always with a fa[...]
[...] trumpets on the call to prayer[...]

A YEAR AGO TO-DAY.

Tuesday, August 4, 1914.

To-day a year ago we declared war on Germany. Our demand for assurances that
the neutrality of Belgium would be respected had been summarily rejected, and at
eleven o'clock—midnight by Berlin time—
the inevitable consequences followed.

On the same day the German Chancellor
in the Reichstag admitted that German
troops had entered Belgium "in contradic-
tion to the rules of international law," and
he palliated this self-confessed "wrong" by
the doctrine that "necessity knows no law."
In conversation with the British Ambassador he declared that Great Britain was
going to war "just for a word, 'neutrality,'" "just for a scrap of paper."

Lord Morley and Mr. Burns resigned from
the Cabinet.

Sir John Jellicoe and Sir John French
were appointed to their commands.

LAST AUGUST 4 ALL THESE
PEOPLE WERE WATCHING
CRICKET AT THE OVAL.

SINCE THEN 2,500 TIMES THIS
NUMBER OF PEOPLE HAVE
BEEN KILLED IN THE WAR.

GERMANY'S IMPORTANT GAINS

A NEUTRAL VIEW.

[The following appears in the "New York World."]

Germany has not only kept most of the gains she made at the
beginning of the war, but has succeeded in preventing her enemies
from invading the Fatherland. With the exception of a small
portion of Alsace at the extreme south of the western battle line
there are no foreign foes on German soil.

While Austria is not yet entirely clear of Russians on her Galician
border, and the Italians have made slight inroads on her southern
frontier, the loss of territory sustained by the Dual Alliance is insignificant,
and of no real economic moment.

The gains Germany has made, on the other hand, are of the utmost importance from an economic standpoint.

By conquering Belgium and the north-eastern portion of France,
Germany has obtained possession of nearly two-thirds of the total
ore deposits of Europe, and an even greater proportion of the
steel mills and machine shops and factories that can be used for
the manufacture of war supplies and equipment.

Likewise Germany is in possession of the great textile centres of France,
and in Lille, Roubaix and Tourcoing has more than three-quarters
of the textile factories of France within her grasp.

Besides, the great coalfields of Belgium and mines of Flanders and Artois
further add to the economic advantages she has derived from the
bold advance she made at the very beginning of the war.

Below: British and German casualties occupy a crater recently
made by a mine. While many in the foreground lay waiting for
help, the British soldiers are ordered to continue the advance.

THE DAILY MAIL, TUESDAY, OCTOBER 12, 1915.

NEARLY 8000 GERMAN DEAD LEFT AT LOOS.

BRITISH BEAT OFF GERMANS.

"VERY SEVERE" ENEMY REVERSE.

OVER 7,000 GERMAN DEAD.

Not a Man Got Within 40 Yards.

OUR LOSSES LIGHT.

LATE WAR NEWS.

MARKED FRENCH PROGRESS.

GROUND GAINED IN ARTOIS.

GERMAN WORK TAKEN IN CHAMPAGNE.

FRENCH OFFICIAL.

Paris, Monday, 11 p.m.
We have made very marked progress in the wood to the west of the Souchez-Angres road in the valley of Souchez and to the east of the redoubt in the Bois de Givenchy. We have also gained ground on the plateau towards La Folie. About prisoners, the Guard re-...made from...

NEW SERBIAN BATTLES.

ENEMY ATTACK ON WESTERN RIVER FRONT.

FIERCE RESISTANCE TO SOUTHERN ADVANCE

MORE BRITISH AT SALONICA.

LATE WAR NEWS.

SERBIAN OFFICIAL.

ALLIES' BALKAN DIPLOMACY.

EXPECTED STATEMENT

RUSSIA'S NEW HOME MINISTER.

TO ATTACK GERMAN INFLUENCES.

SYMPATHY TOWARDS WORKERS.

FROM OUR SPECIAL CORRESPONDENT
H. HAMILTON FYFE.

Petrograd, Sunday.
Following the reception of a number of Russian journalists, M. Kyosteff, the new Minister of the Interior, was good enough to receive me this morning. He is a man who makes a very favourable impression...

THE CENSOR.

PASSING ON THE BLAME.

SIR JOHN SIMON'S EXCUSE.

It's the Fighting Departments.

Lord Selborne's attack on the "mischievous stupidity" of the censorship has drawn his colleague, Sir John Simon, who is responsible for the Press Bureau, to write a letter "to a correspondent" in his defence.

Top: The road to Loos and a captured German trench can be seen in this official photograph taken after a recent attack.

Above: A deserted street immediately after the battle. The British Army deployed chlorine gas for the first time, using it with great success in some areas whereas in others, adverse conditions blew the gas back towards its own troops, poisoning over 2,000. There were pockets of success – Loos was captured and some divisions were able to move on towards Lens. However, a lack of ammunition and reserves meant the Allies were eventually forced to retreat.

Right: The scene of the British advance near Lens, south of La Bassée Canal.

The Battle of Loos

In summer 1915 the Allies made plans for an autumn offensive in northern France, the "Big Push" that would herald a return to a war of movement. Russia was also urging a pressure-relieving attack in the west. It was to take place at Loos, led by First Army commander Sir Douglas Haig, with BEF overlord Sir John French retaining control of the reserve. Haig's 75,000-strong contingent gave him a 6:1 advantage, but the enemy were strongly entrenched in an industrial landscape dotted with mineworks and slagheaps. A shell shortage was a further impediment, to circumvent which chlorine was used when battle commenced on 25 September, the first British deployment of poison gas. Requests for a larger time window had been denied, and unfavourable wind conditions did rebound on Allied infantry. The breadth of front also diluted the effectiveness of the artillery bombardment. Haig and French were on differing wavelengths regarding positioning of the reserve, kept too far back to exploit gains that included the taking of Loos itself. The battle dragged on until early November, by which time the Allied casualty toll stood at 60,000. French's replacement by Haig as Commander in Chief of British forces was a direct consequence of this latest costly failure.

The battle dragged on until early November, by which time the Allied casualty toll stood at 60,000.

Left: By the time the skirmish was over the small mining town of Loos had been completely destroyed; not a single building or tree survived the poundings.

Below: British soldiers return from front-line duty after the battle. Sir John French was criticised for his handling of reserves in the attack, and in December 1915, was replaced as Commander-in-Chief of the British Expeditionary Force by Sir Douglas Haig. It was the first battle in which Kitchener's Army played a major part.

NEW GALLIPOLI LANDING.

"CONSIDERABLE PROGRESS."

AUSTRALASIANS' MAGNIFICENT FEAT.

STRONG POSITIONS CAPTURED AFTER FIERCE FIGHTING.

SIR IAN HAMILTON'S REPORT.

Tuesday.

Fighting at several points on the Gallipoli Peninsula has taken place during the last few days. Substantial progress has been made.

In the southern zone 200 yards on a front of 300 yards has been ... ield in spite of determined ... heavy loss to the enemy. ... zone have been beaten off. ... een made and their whole- ... t assistance.

... the name is formed from ... a footing on the Chunuk ... also been gained and a ... successful storming of ... y's losses have been con- ... night under cover of a

... cessfully effected and

with 1 Nordenfeldt gun, 2 ... mber of bombs ... unition, and ...

OUR E 7 SUNK.

LOSS OFF DARDANELLES.

3 OFFICERS AND 25 MEN PRISONERS.

ADMIRALTY, Thursday.

The enemy claims to have sunk Submarine E 7 (Lieutenant-Commander Archibald D. Cochrane, R.N.) off the Dardanelles and to have taken 3 officers and 25 men of the crew prisoners.

As no news has been received from this submarine since September 4 it must be presumed that this report is correct.

GALLIPOLI LOSSES 87,630.

41,000 IN A MONTH.

Mr. Tennant stated in the House of Commons yesterday that the Dardanelles casualties up to August 21 were:

	Officers.	Men.
Killed	1,130	16,478
Wounded	2,371	59,257
Missing	373	8,021
Totals	3,874	83,756
Grand Total	87,630	

On July 27 Mr. Asquith stated that the losses up to July 18 were 46,622.

Therefore, in 34 days we have lost 41,008 men, within 5,000 of the losses in the previous three months of the campaign. The whole of the British casualties in this period were 60,093.

In the casualty lists last night there were 25 officers (4 dead) and 2,319 men (506 dead). Of these, 2,039 men (430 dead) were from the Dardanelles.

20,000 AUSTRALIAN LOSSES.

FROM OUR OWN CORRESPONDENT.

SYDNEY, Thursday.

Official reports show that the Australian casualties in Gallipoli during the four months have been over 20,000, including 4,000 killed.

Second strike at Suvla Bay

By August 1915 the Gallipoli campaign had become as deadlocked as France and Flanders. Total casualties for the opposing armies already exceeded 100,000, and as soaring temperatures brought flies and disease, that figure could only rise. From the British perspective, the Dardanelles was a considerable drain on resources, not the avenue to success that had been hoped. The War Council sanctioned the deployment of five new divisions, giving Sir Ian Hamilton one final chance to break the Turkish line and keep alive hopes of taking Constantinople. On 6 August the latest landing force disembarked at Suvla Bay, on the northern fringe of the peninsula. Ill-trained soldiers and poor leadership meant that the ANZACs on their right bore the main burden of a bitter, unrewarding battle for the Sari Bair heights. Stalemate returned, and in October General Monro, Hamilton's replacement, saw no option but to withdraw. Kitchener endorsed that view and evacuation plans were drawn up.

The War Council sanctioned the deployment of five new divisions, giving Sir Ian Hamilton one final chance to break the Turkish line.

Below: The office of the commandant at Suvla Bay in September 1915. Sir Ian Hamilton's plan to attack and take the Sari Bair ridge and the high ground on Chunuk Bair and Hill 971 ultimately failed, after the mountainous terrain and poor co-ordination by the military leaders thwarted Allied troops.

THE WEARY MARCH OF THE WOUNDED MEN.

OUR NEW LANDING IN GALLIPOLI.

OUTFLANKING FORCE AT SUVLA BAY.

TURKISH REPORTS.

Constantinople news in the German wireless last night reveals that one of the new British landings in Gallipoli took place in Suvla Bay, at the northern corner of the west coast and about three miles north of the area occupied by the Australasian force.

The statement says:

BERLIN, Friday.

Reliable reports from Constantinople state that the latest landing operations of the French and British are relatively

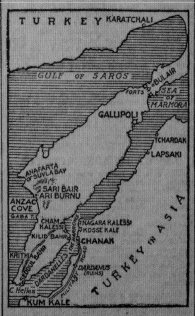

unimportant and their official reports unreliable and partly untrue.

At Karatchali (Thrace coast) 350 men tried to land but were repulsed, leaving twenty dead.

In Anafarta (Suvla) Bay 1,500 British landed and attempted to outflank the Turkish positions at Ari Burnu. They were repulsed without making any progress.—Wireless Press.

Top left: A group of Turkish prisoners taken at the Suvla Bay landings, destined for Egypt or Lemnos for the duration of the conflict. British commanders had underestimated the fighting ability of the Turkish Army; their commander Mustafa Kemal was able to anticipate Allied attacks. He used the country's high ground to great advantage so his troops could ambush the Allied troops on the beaches below, bombarding them with ammunition. After the war, he became the first president of Turkey taking the name Atatürk.

Top middle: Sergeant MacMillan of the Australian Imperial Guards organises musical entertainment while keeping watch for the Turkish soldiers, who are barely 30 metres away.

Top right: British troops occupy the Dardanelles Forts. The August Offensive proved to be the last major confrontation between the two sides and the frontlines remained unchanged for several months afterwards.

Above: Injured soldiers preparing to board a hospital ship.

Below: Shrapnel Valley was often referred to as Death Valley by the troops and was the main path from the beach to the Anzac front. It consequently received constant shelling from the Turks based high up in the hills, so traverses were built into the sides enabling men to dash from one to the other and take cover.

THE LANDING.

ARMY'S SECRET SAIL TO SUVLA BAY.

ASHORE ON PITCH-BLACK NIGHT.

TURKS' GUNS AT DAWN.

OUR UNWAVERING LINE.

By E. ASHMEAD-BARTLETT.

DARDANELLES, Aug. 8.

The arrival of the promised reinforcements from England has at length enabled Sir Ian Hamilton to undertake a flanking movement on a grand scale for the purpose of forcing the Turks to abandon their positions.

The plans of the Commander-in-Chief were kept a profound secret, and no one outside of certain officers on the General Staff and the corps commanders had any real knowledge of his intentions until after the expedition sailed on the night of August 6.

It was hoped to take the enemy completely by surprise and to obtain a firm foothold on the shore before he could bring up his reinforcements. In this it would seem as if we have been successful, for two divisions were yesterday put ashore almost without opposition. The enemy probably had accurate knowledge of the arrival of large reinforcements, for it is almost impossible to keep movements of troops unknown in the Near East, and his airmen have frequently flown over our camps. He knew, therefore, we were preparing to strike, but on the vital point as to where the blow would fall he seems to have been entirely ignorant.

On August 6 the final preparations were at length complete, and the main movement was preceded by a general bombardment of the Turkish trenches round Achi Baba, and in the afternoon a division made a successful attack, car-

The black patches indicate approximately the territory occupied by our forces in the Gallipoli Peninsula.

rying several lines of Turkish trenches. This movement was, however, really in the nature of a feint to hold the enemy round the mountain and to frighten him from moving troops to reinforce his other positions.

Opposite above: Troops haul one of the big guns onto the beach.

Opposite below: These Australians gave quaint names to their dugouts with "Splinter Villa" chosen on this occasion. In the closing months of the campaign, reports revealed the throwing of gifts between the two sides across no-man's-land – the Turks sending dates and sweets with the Allies throwing cigarettes and tins of beef in return.

Top: Troops and a gun are towed aboard a raft at Suvla Bay in the Dardanelles. While the stalemate persisted summer turned to winter and

troops had rain and snow to contend with. A heavy rainstorm in late November flooded the trenches with many soldiers drowned. Snow followed in December giving rise to severe cases of frostbite and soldiers dying from exposure.

Above left: Marines on guard duty. Withdrawal from the campaign was discussed in October but Hamilton didn't want to damage the reputation of the British. That month he was replaced by Sir Charles Monro who recommended evacuation to Kitchener when he visited the trenches the following month.

Above right: Transporting food up to the trenches. Kitchener took Monro's recommendation to the commanders of the various sectors. By now Bulgaria had allied with the Central Powers, establishing a land route between Germany and the Ottoman Empire which guaranteed a constant supply of weapons and ammunition to the Turks. They all agreed and Kitchener appealed to the British Cabinet.

Below: The British Cabinet finally ordered the evacuation of Suvla and Anzac Cove on 7 December. The Allies employed many tricks to cover their escape. These included Heath Robinson-like contraptions which would fire weapons, giving the impression that positions were still manned, allowing 40,000 troops to leave in broad daylight undetected by the Turkish or German leaders. A garrison was kept at Helles until 28 December when it was decided to evacuate these troops too.

FIRST WAR EDITION. No. 6,123. THE DAILY MAIL, THURSDAY, AUGUST 12, 1915.

FURTHER GAINS IN GALLIPOLI.

AUSTRALASIANS' GREAT DASH.	U BOAT SUNK.	GERMAN ARMED SHIP BLOWN UP.	LATE WAR NEWS.	MYSTERY HUSBAND.	COTTON AND DEATH.
THEIR AREA IN GALLIPOLI NEARLY	ITALIAN SUCCESS. — GERMANS DISAPPOINTED AT SUBMARINE RESULTS. — CANDID NAVAL EXPERT.	MEETING WITH OUR CRUISERS. — SELF-DESTRUCTION BEFORE	GERMAN LOSSES AT KOVNO. 3 BATTALIONS ALMOST ANNIHILATED.	WIFE WHO DOUBTS HIS IDENTITY. — PUZZLED RELATIVES. — SOLDIER'S STRANGE RETURN.	STRONG SPEECH BY SIR W. RAMSAY. — VIGOROUS LETTER BY LORD C. BERESFORD.

THE VALLEY OF DEATH AT GALLIPOLI.

TUESDAY, AUGUST 10, 1915.

SPLINTER VILLA

September 1915

1   The German Government accepted the United States' demands for limitation of submarine activity.

2   On the Eastern Front German forces captured Grodno and attacked Vilna .

3   The Second Battle of the Isonzo ended with an Austro-Hungarian victory over Italian forces.

4   The British passenger ship Hesperian was torpedoed by German submarine *U-20* near Fastnet off the Irish coast.

5   Tsar Nicholas II took personal control of Russia's armies at the military headquarters in Mogilev (Mahilyow) in Eastern Belarus.

6   US newspapers published secret documents reporting that Austrian Ambassador Dr Konstantin Dumba was involved in a scheme to sabotage the American munitions industry.

7   Russian troops began a counter-offensive on the Sereth River at Tarnopol in Galicia.

8   Two Zeppelins successfully attacked London, dropping bombs on the docks of the capital city.

9   American Secretary of State Robert Lansing requested that the Austro-Hungarian government recall its ambassador Dr Konstantin Dumba as his presence was no longer acceptable.

10 Four Allied warships rescued more than 4,000 Armenians from Musa Dagh in Armenia and took them to Port Said in Egypt where they remained in Allied refugee camps until the end of the war.

12 The three-masted Norwegian sailing ship *Bien* was sunk in the North Sea by German submarine *U-6*.

13 Following another Zeppelin raid on London, Admiral Sir Percy Scott was tasked by the First Lord of the Admiralty Arthur Balfour to establish the London Air Defence Area to defend England's capital city from the increasing threat of air attack.

15 German submarine *U-6* was attacked and sunk by British submarine HMS *E16* off Stavanger in Norway.

16 German troops captured Pinsk in Belarus on the Eastern Front.

18 German forces capture Vilna (now Vilnius) but suffered heavy casualties.

19 The Gorlice–Tarnów Offensive ended when the Russian lines collapsed and the Russian troops retreated.

21 The Bulgarian government ordered a partial mobilisation of its forces.

    Greek Premier Eleftherios Venizelos asked for a guarantee of 150,000 British and French troops as a condition of Greece's intervention in the war.

22 French airmen dropped bombs on the Royal Palace at Stuttgart in Germany.

23 The Greek Government ordered precautionary mobilisation as a "measure of elementary prudence" in view of Bulgarian actions.

24 The French and British Governments informed the Greeks that they would be prepared to send the troops requested.

25 The Great Allied Offensive focused on Loos and Champagne when the British 1st Army, commanded by General Douglas Haig, attacked German positions at the start of the Battle of Loos.

26 General Sir Archibald James Murray was appointed Chief of the Imperial General Staff, replacing Sir James Wolfe-Murray who had resigned the previous day.

27 Greek premier Venizelos obtained the secret consent of King Constantine I to the proposed Allied expedition to Salonika.

28 Austrian Ambassador Dr Dumba was recalled from the United States.

    The Greek Government refused the Allied offer of troops.

29 French troops attacked in Champagne and progressed towards Tahure on the Western Front.

30 Lord Derby assumed responsibility for recruiting in Britain.

Left: A map showing the position of Bulgaria on the German road to Constantinople and the main railway through Serbia and Bulgaria.

Below: Troops in the market in Nish. On 6 October Serbia was invaded on two fronts by Germany, Austria-Hungary and Bulgaria, who had recently sided with the Central Powers. Germany was keen to conquer the country to establish a rail link down to the Ottoman Empire. British troops called in to assist Serbia arrived too late and the army with many civilians retreated to Albania. The town of Nish was occupied until October 1918.

Opposite above: Serbian prisoners on their way to "lunch" during a brief stop at a railway station.

Opposite middle: Lady Louise Paget, wife of the diplomat Sir Ralph Paget, established a military hospital in Skopje, Serbia, during the First Balkan War, when her husband was Minister to Serbia. After the First World War broke out the hospital continued to operate although she was forced to return home to recuperate temporarily in 1915 when she contracted typhoid.

Opposite below: Romanian soldiers on parade in 1915. Lord Kitchener, keen for the nation to join the Allies, sent a military attaché to court them. After his visit, Lieutenant-Colonel Christopher Thomson warned Whitehall that the country was ill-prepared for fighting on two fronts and would be a liability. However, his advice was ignored and a Military Convention signed the following August, with the Allies promising to give Romania the territory of Transylvania in the event of a victory.

Belgrade fell on 9 October, while Serbs made their arduous escape westward through Albania to the Adriatic coast.

Germans shell strategic Serbia

Austria-Hungary knew that once the Russian Bear had been roused, its chance to punish Serbia for the assassination of Archduke Franz Ferdinand might be lost. Austrian leader Franz Conrad saw a window of opportunity while Russia mobilised and concentrated his forces against the country deemed culpable for Sarajevo. The fighting was brutal, but dogged Serbian resistance saw Austrian forces expelled from the country by Christmas. Ten months later it was a different story. A renewed assault in autumn 1915 included a threat from Serbia's eastern neighbour, Bulgaria having thrown in its lot with the Central Powers under the dangling carrot of territorial gain. German might was also ranged against the beleaguered Serbs, whose own appeal for assistance foundered when Allied forces failed to make progress after landing at the Greek port of Salonika. Belgrade fell on 9 October, while Serbs – army and civilians together – made their arduous escape westward through Albania to the Adriatic coast, and thence by Allied ships to refugee camps on Corfu. Thousands perished in the march across treacherous mountainous terrain in appalling weather. One hundred and fifty thousand made it to the island, many of those soon joining the Allied force in Salonika, driven by the desire to liberate their homeland.

LATEST WAR EDITION.   THE DAILY MAIL, MONDAY, NOVEMBER 8, 1915.   5

ENEMY'S ADVANCE OVER SERBIA'S DEAD.

BULGARS IN NISH.

SERBIANS CAME TO THE LAST

GERMA

MON

of the Allies from Kuprulu, in the south.

M. Lautard left Prishtina for Uskub, but on arriving at Ferizovitch the authorities forbade him to

LORD KITCHENER.

SHORT VISIT TO THE EAST.

DOOR SHUT ON RUNAWAYS.

NO PASSAGES IN CUNARD LINERS.

REFUSAL.

STRANDED.

CORRESPONDENT.

RAID ON A LONDON NEWSPAPER.

SEIZURE OF THE "GLOBE" PLANT AND TYPE.

A MILITARY WARRANT.

Press Bureau, Saturday, 5.50 p.m.

This afternoon Chief Inspector Fowler, with other police officers, acting under the authority of Major-General Sir Francis Lloyd, K.C.B., as competent military authority, entered the premises of the Globe newspaper, occupied

OUR BLOCKADE.

NEW U.S. NOTE.

GROUNDS OF PROTEST.

SEARCH OF SEIZED SHIPS.

CHAMPIONING THE "RIGHTS OF NEUTRALS."

THREE WEEKS OF THE WAR IN SERBIA.

The battle line three weeks ago.   The battle line to-day.

The shaded section in each map indicates approximately the enemy gains in Serbia then and now.

Thousands of Serbs perished in the march across treacherous mountainous terrain in appalling weather.

Top left: A Serbian man lies dead and abandoned. By the end of the conflict Serbia had lost 60 per cent of its male population through army and civilian deaths.

Above left: By the middle of 1915 all of Russian Poland, Lithuania and most of Latvia had been invaded by Germany. Many of the occupants either fled or were ordered out of the area by the German Army.

Above: The shaded areas in the maps indicate approximately the gains made by the Central Powers in Serbia over a three-week period to mid November.

Left and opposite: Soldiers from the Russian Army in the Carpathians. In September 1915 Tsar Nicholas II assumed control of the fighting on the Eastern Front but this had little impact. Men were being sent to the front with very little training and were often unarmed. The supply of weapons and ammunition was poor and it was assumed men would find something to fight with once they reached the battlefields.

Opposite above: The vast areas where German forces were fighting in Europe.

Edith Cavell

Heroine and inspiration

At the outbreak of war Edith Cavell was working in Brussels; a trained, dedicated nurse using her skills to improve health care in her adopted land. Scarcely a year later this worthy but obscure figure was dead, the victim of an outrage that shocked the world and shaped public opinion. Cavell's name was invoked to boost recruitment in her native country and, like the sinking of the *Lusitania*, her tragic story played no small part in weakening America's neutral stance.

Edith Cavell was born in the Norfolk village of Swardeston on 4 December 1867. She was a clergyman's daughter, her upbringing instilling in her a sense of duty and service. She never married or had children, and looked to her own resources to make her way in the world. With fewer avenues open to her than a man of similar education and accomplishments, she initially turned to governess work before finding her vocation in nursing. Edith was 30 by the time she made the career switch, but made up for lost time through assiduous study. Working at various London hospitals she accepted nothing less than best practice, and was equally keen to pass on her knowledge and skills to young nurses. To that end she accepted an offer to head a training school in Brussels in 1907. Belgium was well behind Britain in terms of nursing standards and the esteem in which that profession was held. Under Edith's leadership the school flourished and standards were driven up. Once one goal was met she set another, and plans to expand the school were in hand when war was declared in August 1914. At the time she was on holiday at the family home in Norfolk, but returned to Belgium immediately, knowing that her expertise would be needed. The school operated under a Red Cross banner. She cared nothing for a casualty's allegiance; wounds were her sole concern, not the uniform.

Secret police swoop to arrest Cavell

The conflict was still in its early days when Cavell, as well as treating the injuries of Allied soldiers, began helping secure them safe passage out of the country. From November 1914 to July 1915 some 200 men evaded capture thanks to a clandestine operation in which Cavell played a key role; where codes, passwords and subterfuge replaced the normal tools of her trade. The school came under observation. There were searches and close shaves. She knew it was only a matter of time before her luck ran out, and on 5 August the German secret police swooped to arrest Edith, along with over 30 others suspected of resistance activity.

Her interrogation and trial were little more than a farce. Questioning was conducted via translators and she had no way of knowing whether the German confession she signed was an accurate representation of her words. Her captors were not interested in the fact that she ministered to anyone in need, nor that she was simply helping men avoid being shot. The prosecution asserted that this Englishwoman was aiding enemy soldiers, hastening their return to the battlefield where they could kill the brave sons of the Fatherland. She deserved a traitor's punishment: a capital sentence befitting a heinous crime.

Outrage as Cavell is executed

Cavell accepted her fate with equanimity and stoicism. "Nothing matters when one comes to the last hour but a clear conscience before God," she wrote. She was executed by firing squad on 12 October 1915 and buried without ceremony in an unmarked grave. But as news of the outrage reached England, it quickly became clear that the decision to make an example of her backfired as men signed up in droves. "Remember Edith Cavell!" the cry went up from recruiting sergeants, her photograph having as galvanising an effect as the famous Kitchener poster.

Six months after the Armistice, in May 1919, Edith Cavell's body was brought home. At the family's request she was interred at Norwich Cathedral, but her selfless heroism was marked at a Westminster Abbey service en route to her final resting place. Numerous awards, tributes and honours were bestowed upon her, the most famous of which is Sir George Frampton's monument in St Martin's Place, close to Trafalgar Square. As well as a statue of Cavell it depicts a mother comforting a child: the strong taking care of the weak. It was a symbol of the humanity that the woman who inspired it demonstrated, even when her own life was at risk. "Humanity" is etched into one of the monument's four faces, along with Devotion, Fortitude and Sacrifice. Also inscribed are words written by Cavell on the eve of her death: "Patriotism is not enough. I must have no hatred or bitterness for anyone."

THE MARTYRDOM

OF

NURSE CAVELL.

FULL STORY OF GERMAN DECEIT AND TREACHERY.

TOLD BY THE AMERICAN MINISTER.

"SHE WAS HAPPY TO DIE FOR HER COUNTRY."

ALL THE DOCUMENTS.

Nurse Edith Cavell was condemned and shot by the Germans in Brussels for aiding English and Belgians to escape from Prussian cruelty.

She had lived in Brussels for nine years. A trained English nurse, she went there to found a nurses' training home. She and her pupils were known in Germany. When the Hun trampled on Belgium she tended the pillow of the wounded, Belgian and German alike.

But an Englishwoman first, when she saw the chance to help the hapless victims and her fellow-countrymen to cross the frontier, she took it. She admitted it. She was arrested and calmly told what she had done. But for her own words there was no evidence to convict her.

She was kept in a cell. She had no opportunity of defence. The charge and the depositions were kept secret by the Germans from the only man who could help her, the American Minister in Brussels. He used superhuman efforts to reach her, but the German heart was stone.

She was tried in secret. The American Minister, pleading for reprieve, was assured by the Germans that he should be told the moment she was sentenced. He was never informed. But he learned by chance that, while they were uttering these false promises, she was already doomed. In short, afraid that time and pity might prevail, the Germans secretly hurried on the crime.

From his sick bed the Minister wrote one last heart-breaking cry for pity. She was shot in the dark ere the ink was dry. She was "happy to die for her country," she had said a few hours before.

And the man who conceived, and—by his refusal to answer the final appeal—executed, this crime against humanity is Baron von Bissing, fit subject of his Kaiser.

LATE WAR NEWS.

ZEPPELIN BOMBS ON LONDON.

Top: A policeman inspects the remains of 33 Leslie Park Road.

Above left: A five-Zeppelin raid set off on 13 October with the intention of bombing London. One of the bombers veered off target making the town of Croydon the next unwitting victim. In Edridge Road, a mother and daughter were thrown onto the street from their bed while next door a roof collapsed,

Above middle left: Three boys from the same family were killed when Beech House Road was hit.

Above middle right: The remains of 69-73 Stretton Road. The airship responsible for these attacks on Croydon was the Zeppelin Z14, under the command of Commander Böcker. A total of nine people were killed and fifteen injured.

Above: The Z15 was the only airship to succeed in hitting the capital. The South Western Bank in the City was bombed along with other locations at Charing Cross, Holborn and Aldgate.

Opposite: Edith Cavell during her early years as a governess.

October 1915

2 The Greek Premier Eleftherios Venizelos asked the British and French to land troops at Salonika as soon as possible.

3 Germans recaptured part of Hohenzollern Redoubt on the Western Front.

4 The Entente Powers sent an ultimatum to Bulgaria.

5 Russia notified Bulgaria that diplomatic relations were at an end.

  The political crisis in Greece continued to grow as King Constantine refused to support the policy of Venizelos who then resigned again.

6 Serbia was invaded by Germany, Austria-Hungary and Bulgaria.

  King Constantine of Greece assured Britain that his country would remain neutral, but nonetheless Greek mobilisation and Allied disembarkation at Salonika began.

7 Austro-Hungarian and German forces attacked across the Danube into Serbia.

8 The new Greek Government, with Alexandros Thrasivoulou Zaimis as the new Premier, confirmed their policy of armed neutrality.

9 Belgrade was captured by Austrian forces.

  Wumbiagas, in the Cameroons, was captured by British forces.

10 The Greek Government rejected the Serbian plea for help against invasion.

11 Bulgarian forces began hostilities against Serbia.

12 Following a court-martial, British nurse Edith Cavell was executed by German firing squad for helping POWs escape from Belgium to Holland.

13 A sustained Zeppelin airship raid on London and the Eastern counties resulted in over 200 casualties.

  French Foreign Minister Theophile Delcassé resigned and was temporarily succeeded by René Viviani.

14 Bulgaria joined the Central Powers, declaring war on Serbia and invading Macedonia.

15 Great Britain and Montenegro declared a state of war with Bulgaria.

  The Romanian Government refused assistance for Serbia.

16 France declared war on Bulgaria.

  Allied forces began a naval blockade of the Aegean coast of Bulgaria.

17 The British Government offered Cyprus to Greece in return for supporting Serbia against Bulgaria.

18 The Third Battle of the Isonzo began between Italian and Austrian-Hungarian forces along the Soča River in western Slovenia.

19 Italy and Russia declared war on Bulgaria.

20 The Greek Government rejected Britain's offer of Cyprus.

21 Allied naval squadrons bombarded Dedeagatch in Bulgaria.

  Bulgarian forces captured the city of Veles in Serbia.

22 Bulgarian forces captured the cities of Kumanovo and Uskub on the Southern Front.

23 The German armoured cruiser Prinz Adalbert was sunk by the British submarine E8 in the Baltic.

24 La Courtine in Champagne was captured by French forces.

  Venice was bombed by Austrian aircraft.

27 William Morris Hughes replaced Andrew Fisher as Prime Minister of Australia.

28 British battle cruiser HMS Argyll ran aground and was wrecked on Bell Rock off the east coast of Scotland.

  General Sir Charles Munro took command of the Mediterranean Expeditionary Force.

29 French Premier René Viviani and Minister for War Alexandre Millerand both resigned.

30 Aristide Briand succeeded Viviani as Prime Minister of France.

THE DAILY MAIL, WEDNESDAY, DECEMBER 29, 1915.

COMPULSION AT LAST!

SINGLE MEN FIRST.

MR. ASQUITH'S PLEDGE TO BE CARRIED OUT AT ONCE.

COMPULS IMME

ANOTHER CA

VERY FEW

SINGLE MEN FIRST.

"THE DAILY MAIL" CAMPAIGN.

SEVEN MONTHS' HISTORY.

ecision of the Cabinet to fulfil delay the pledge that single men compelled to join the colours before ried men who have enlisted are sets the seal of success upon a which has been conducted for aths in the columns of The Daily

KHAKI ARMLET.

THE MARK OF THE WILLING MAN.

THREE CLASSES TO WEAR IT.

HOW IT AFFECTS YOU.

War Office, Saturday.

The Secretary for War has decided to issue khaki armlets, bearing the Royal Crown, to the following classes of men:—

1. Men who enlist and are placed in groups awaiting a call to join the colours.
2. Men who offer themselves for enlistment and are found to be medically unfit.
3. Men who have been invalided out of the Service with good character, or have been discharged "not likely to become efficient" on medical grounds.

There will be a distinctive mark for each of the three classes. The armlets are in process of manufacture. Notice will be given when they can be issued, together with instructions as to issue.

WHAT IT MEANS.

THE WILLING AND THE UNWILLING.

The official announcement given above fulfils the suggestion made first in The Daily Mail on July 30. It means that the nation is divided practically into the willing and the unwilling.

If you have enlisted and are awaiting your call you will wear your armlet and everybody will know that you are as much a recruit as if you were in khaki.

If you have offered and been found medically unfit your armlet will prove your willingness and protect you from badgering.

If you have left the Army for good reason you will be equally unassailable.

VOSGES GAIN.

GERMAN TRENCHES CARRIED.

OUR MONITORS SHELL THE COAST.

FROM OUR SPECIAL CORRESPONDENT.

Rotterdam, Tuesday.

Great activity prevails on the western front. British monitors have bombarded the Belgian coast between Ostend and Westende.

The troops are fighting under great difficulties owing to floods and storms, but heavy artillery actions, mine explosions

SERBIANS' NEED.

A CALL TO BRITAIN.

FROM OUR OWN CORRESPONDENT.

Paris, Tuesday.

"What the Serbian Army needs most at present is bread," was what Dr. Vesnitch, the Serbian Minister in Paris, told me to-day in the course of a conversation on the situation of King Peter's forces in the mountains of Albania.

"We had four armies at the beginning of the campaign," the Minister said. "Now they exist only in scattered remnants. In the course of the most terrible retreat history has ever known they were forced to blow the breeches out of their

"DAILY MAIL" FREE INSURANCE FOR 1916.

FULL PROTECTION AGAINST ACCIDENTS WHILE TRAVELLING.

HOW TO QUALIFY.

SIX £1,000 CLAIMS PAID.

Since The Daily Mail Free Insurance Scheme was first offered to our readers on January 1, 1914, 295 claims for benefits have been settled, including six death claims of £1,000 each.

At the end of the first year's working of the scheme it was found possible to extend the list of "travel accidents" covered to include "holiday accidents," such as death from drowning while boating or bathing, and accidents so private motor-cars and private horse-drawn

BIG GUNS FOR SALONICA.

50 MILES OF DEFENCE.

CHANGING TONE IN GREECE.

MISUNDERSTANDINGS EXPLAINED.

The Allied defences round Salonica extend for 50 miles. One of our special correspondents at Athens reports that sixty 12in. guns have been landed.

FROM OUR SPECIAL CORRESPONDENT, W. H. CRAWFURD PRICE.

Athens, Monday, 9.45 p.m.

At a moment when, as I telegraphed yesterday, it is impossible to foretell the effect which would be created upon public opinion by the violation of Hellenic soil

Below: Lord Kitchener makes his great recruiting speech at the Guildhall in July 1915. (Left to right in front row): Sir Edward Carson; Lord Kitchener; Colonel Sir Charles Wakefield; the Lord Mayor of London, Sir Charles Johnston; the Bishop of London, Arthur Winnington-Ingram; Churchill and Mrs Churchill. Kitchener's declaration that "Men, materials and money are the immediate necessities" was followed up with a poster showing quotes from the speech (opposite below).

THERE IS STILL A PLACE IN THE LINE FOR YOU

THIS SPACE IS RESERVED FOR A FIT MAN

Will you fill it?

BRITAIN·NEEDS YOU·AT·ONCE

AT THE FRONT!

Every fit Briton should join our brave men at the Front

ENLIST NOW.

TAKE UP THE SWORD OF JUSTICE

This page: Recruitment posters were produced throughout the war. They sent out a variety of messages using patriotism, guilt and glory among many other themes.

We're both needed to serve the Guns!

FILL UP THE RANKS! PILE UP THE MUNITIONS!

LORD KITCHENER SAYS:-

'MEN, MATERIALS & MONEY ARE THE IMMEDIATE NECESSITIES. ......

DOES THE CALL OF DUTY FIND NO RESPONSE IN YOU UNTIL REINFORCED — LET US RATHER SAY SUPERSEDED — BY THE CALL OF COMPULSION?'

Lord Kitchener Speaking at Guildhall, July 9th 1915

ENLIST TO-DAY.

Conscription legislation passed

By the end of 1915 Britain faced an acute manpower shortage for frontline duty. For 17 months the country had relied on its standing army, reservists and volunteers, augmented by colonial forces. Attrition rates meant recruitment had to be stepped up, and throughout 1915 there was much discussion about whether that should be achieved by statutory means. In July the Government passed the National Registration Act, which required those aged 15-65 to provide personal details and thus gave the political leaders a picture of the untapped potential. It then made one final attempt to harness that resource by voluntary means via a recruitment scheme instituted by Lord Derby. Men could enlist or "attest" – agree to serve if called upon at a later date. When the scheme closed in mid-December, it became apparent that vast swathes of the target population were still doggedly refusing to do what many considered their patriotic duty. In particular there were large numbers of unmarried men showing reluctance to come forward. Compulsion was anathema to most Liberals, but in January 1916 the Military Service Act was passed, requiring all single men aged 18-41 to attest if they had not already done so. Four months later the net was widened to include married men, and the age parameters were increased in a succession of amendments. Ireland was initially excluded from the legislation, a decision regarded by Unionist MPs as "an insult and humiliation to the loyal and patriotic population of that country". But Irish Nationalists had already come out vociferously against conscription, and the Government opted for discretion. By spring 1918 the manpower situation was so serious that political sensitivities had to be laid aside. Ireland was incorporated into the conscription legislation in April of that year, but as the tide turned in the Allies' favour enforcement was unnecessary.

Tribunals for concience issues

The Act allowed exemptions to be granted, for example to those medically unfit or employed in reserved occupations. Appeals could also be made on conscience grounds – if military service clashed with religious beliefs or personal moral compass. Tribunals were established to consider the merits of such cases, to determine the sincerity or otherwise of appellants' claims. It's doubtful that much time was given over to the pianist who pleaded that he had to practise daily to maintain the required standard. The position of conscientious objectors, on the other hand, provoked much heated debate. Many thought they were shirkers who ought to be given short shrift. Some came to the same conclusion by different means, arguing that anyone who accepted the benefits offered by society – benefits that included liberty which was ultimately underpinned by force – had a responsibility to act when that society was threatened. "He takes the goods but does not give the price," as one who espoused that view put it. "He should give up all the wealth and enjoyment procured for him by the fighting of others, or else fight."

Above: **Although levels of volunteers remained high during 1914, by 1915 numbers were beginning to fall, especially after the Gallipoli campaign. The government was reluctant to implement conscription and so used recruitment drives, propaganda and the "Derby Scheme" instead. Lord Derby's plan asked men between the ages of 18 and 41 to attest their willingness to serve, on the understanding that all single men would be called up before the youngest married volunteers. They were then given a grey armband with a red crown to prove their commitment.**

Opposite: **Attested men hand in their armlets at White City. By the time the scheme closed in December 1915, more than one million single men had still failed to enlist. The British government responded by following the example of every other major combatant and introduced conscription.**

Below: **The Military Service Bill was passed in January 1916 and called up all men between the ages of 18 and 41 but excluded married men, those widowed with children or men in reserved occupations. Under the new legislation, those originally deeemed medically unfit could be re-examined.**

Above: **"Father, I've heard you say you are opposed to compulsion in any form. I don't want to do any lessons today. I can please myself, can't I?"**

The Times did not go that far, but in a leader column that appeared shortly after conscription was introduced the distinction was made between those with a valid objection to taking life and anyone who refused to dig trenches, act as stretcher-bearers or serve in a similar capacity. The latter, it fulminated, "is a parasite and deserves to be treated as a pariah". Life was difficult enough for conscientious objectors in non-combatant roles – or the "No-Courage Corps", as it was dubbed by detractors. Many distinguished themselves without firing a shot. Those who stuck to the "absolutist" line – refusing to engage in any form of military service – had a much tougher time. Consider the following exchange between an Ebbw Vale colliery worker and his tribunal interrogator:

Q. Would you object to serving in the Royal Army Medical Corps?

A. Yes. It would not be proper in accordance with my convictions to heal the wounds of one man in order that he may inflict wounds on another.

Q. Do you consider that the four million men now with the Army are heathens or wholly indifferent to the teachings of the Bible?

A. I hold no brief for any other man's conscience.

Q. If you had a mother and someone attempted to kill her, what would you do?

A. I would place myself between the aggressor and the object of the assault.

Q. But suppose he had a revolver and you placed yourself between them?

A. I would not sacrifice my principles.

Q. You enjoy a scrap?

A. I don't think that point arises and does not embrace the taking of life.

This kind of fencing was typical, the tribunal seeking to test the robustness of the appellant's plea, while in some cases the latter might have had coaching on how to deflect such questions. If appeals were denied – and they usually were – men were forced to join the ranks, risking disciplinary action if they failed to appear or refused to obey an order. Thousands were imprisoned, with numerous reports of ill-treatment.

The Government made one final attempt to harness untapped potential by voluntary means via a recruitment scheme.

November 1915

2 British Prime Minister Herbert Asquith declared Serbian independence to be an essential object of the war.

3 The first meeting of the newly constituted British War Committee was held.

The Third Battle of the Isonzo ended in a victory for Austro-Hungarian forces.

4 Lord Kitchener set sail for Gallipoli with the objective of gaining firsthand knowledge of the situation.

General Sir Charles Munro was given command of the British Salonika Force. Sir William Birdwood took command of the Mediterranean Expeditionary Force at Gallipoli.

5 Bulgarian forces captured Nish in Serbia following 3 days of fighting.

Kitchener left London on a visit to the Near East.

6 The French offensive against the invading German army, the Second Battle of Champagne, ended in a stalemate.

7 The German cruiser SMS *Undine* was sunk by the British submarine *E19* in the Baltic.

8 The Italian passenger steamer SS *Ancona* was sunk by an Austrian submarine off the coast of Tunisia, while sailing under the Austrian flag.

10 The Fourth battle of the Isonzo began as Austrian forces continued to resist the Italian bid to cross the River Isonzo.

11 Prime Minister Herbert Asquith announced the composition of a new British War Cabinet; Winston Churchill resigned from the Government.

14 The North African Senussi order began hostilities against the British when they attacked an Egyptian post at Sollum.

15 Representatives of the Central Powers left Teheran as Russian forces advanced.

16 Bulgarian forces captured the Babuna Pass and Prilep in southern Serbia.

17 An Anglo-French conference was held in Paris to discuss aid to Serbia and the situation at Gallipoli.

British steam ship SS *Anglia*, which had been requisitioned for use as a hospital ship, hit a mine and sank in the English Channel.

18 In Britain new restrictions were imposed on the opening hours of London's clubs.

20 King Constantine of Greece and his Government assured Lord Kitchener that Greece would never attack Allied troops.

22 The Battle of Ctesiphon began as Turkish troops halted the British advance on Baghdad.

23 The British Western Frontier Force began military operations against the Senussi.

The Allied Powers sent a Note to the Greek Government demanding non-interference with Allied troops and guaranteeing the eventual restoration of occupied Greek territory.

24 The Greek Government accepted the Allied demands of the previous day.

Field Marshal von der Goltz took command of Turkish forces in Mesopotamia.

25 The Battle of Ctesiphon ended with a strategic victory for the Ottoman Empire when the British retreated to the city of Kut-al-Amara.

29 Afonso Augusto da Costa succeeded José de Castro as Portuguese Prime Minister.

30 The Pact of London was formally signed by Great Britain, France, Russia, Japan and Italy: each country declared it would not make separate peace.

WOUNDED WARRIORS & THE CALL FOR MEN.

Philosopher convicted for circulating subversive material

For some prominent figures, including parliamentarians and intellectuals, coercing men to take up arms was intolerable. Crusading left-wing journalist Archibald Fenner Brockway was a leading light in forming the No-Conscription Fellowship, whose agenda – despite its name – went beyond campaigning against compulsory military service. Most were pacifists, a stance that brought Brockway a collection of white feathers as indignant women – no doubt with their own menfolk in uniform – discounted principle and saw only cowardice. Publishing anti-conscription material and refusing the call-up himself earned Brockway a jail term.

Among the NCF supporters was the distinguished philosopher and mathematician Bertrand Russell. "War does not determine who is right, only who is left," said Russell, whose grandfather had served the country as a Liberal prime minister. In 1916 the NCF published a leaflet entitled *Two Years' Hard Labour for Refusing to Disobey the Dictates of Conscience*. It highlighted the case of a teacher who had been placed on non-combatant duty and adopted a stance of passive resistance towards authority, for which he was court-martialled. When some of those distributing the leaflet were arrested, Russell came forward to assert his authorship. He was charged under the Defence of the Realm Act and fined £100 for circulating material "likely to prejudice the recruiting and discipline of His Majesty's Forces". Dismissal from his lecturing post at Cambridge University swiftly followed.

Below: At the beginning of the war men needed to be 5 feet 6 inches tall, with a minimum chest measurement of 36 inches. However, as the need to encourage more volunteers increased, the height requirement was lowered and the age limit raised from 30 to 40. Even "Bantam" battalions were created where men were between 5 feet and 5 feet 3 inches.

Opposite above: Enlisted recruits on the march in October 1915. Even the introduction of conscription the following year did not harness the numbers hoped for. Many were employed in essential war work and others were not healthy enough to pass the fitness test.

Opposite below: A map shows the Allies' perspective of The Great War after 17 months.

" War does not determine who is right, only who is left" — Bertrand Russell

GREAT RUSH TO ENLIST.

2 A.M. RECRUITING

BESIEGED TOWN HALLS.

POLICE CONTROL CROWD.

PREMIER AND MARRIED MEN'S HOMES.

Recruiting took a real spring forward yesterday, and especially last night. Men released from business thronged to recruiting stations that were already overflowing.

Doctors and officials toiled in many instances until long past midnight. Everywhere men who could not possibly be attested promised cheerfully to return this morning. All realise that the recruiting officials have been ready for weeks, and that now the great rush has come every nerve must and will be strained to cope with it.

MR. ASQUITH'S PLEDGE TO THE MARRIED.

As Given to Lord Derby on November 19.

"Married men are not to be called up until young unmarried men have been. If these young men do not come forward voluntarily Mr. Asquith will either release the married men from their pledge or introduce a Bill into Parliament to compel the young men to serve, which, if passed, would mean that the married men would be held to their enlistment. If, on the other hand, Parliament did not pass such a Bill, the married men would be automatically released from their engagement to serve."

It was explained that by "the young men" was meant "the vast majority of young men" (1) not engaged in munition work, or (2) not indispensable for civil employment, or (3) with reasons considered satisfactory by the local tribunals exempting them; and the pledge added:—

"If there remains a considerable number of young men not engaged in these pursuits who could perfectly be spared for military service they should be compelled to serve."

The "Fetch-Me's" Last Chance.

Lord Derby at the Mansion House on October 19 said:— "Speaking only as man to man, this is the last effort on behalf of voluntary service."

The group enlisting was finally closed this week.

THE MARCH OF THE SINGLE MEN.

THE RECRUITING RUSH.—Handing out railway passes after a batch of recruits had been attested in London on Saturday. The "single men first" assurance induced many married men to join under the "group system."

SPLENDID CANADA !—A typical volunteer from the "Land of the Maple Leaf." Incidentally, this man is the tenth crack shot for his company.

NOT WAITING TO BE FETCHED.—The Premier's declaration that all unmarried men must serve had the effect of stimulating recruiting in London on Saturday. No appeals from Jack Johnson were needed.

PLENTY OF ELIGIBLE RECRUITS—BUT WHY JACK JOHNSON?

PRINCIPAL EVENTS OF THE GREAT WAR IN 1915 TOLD IN A MAP.

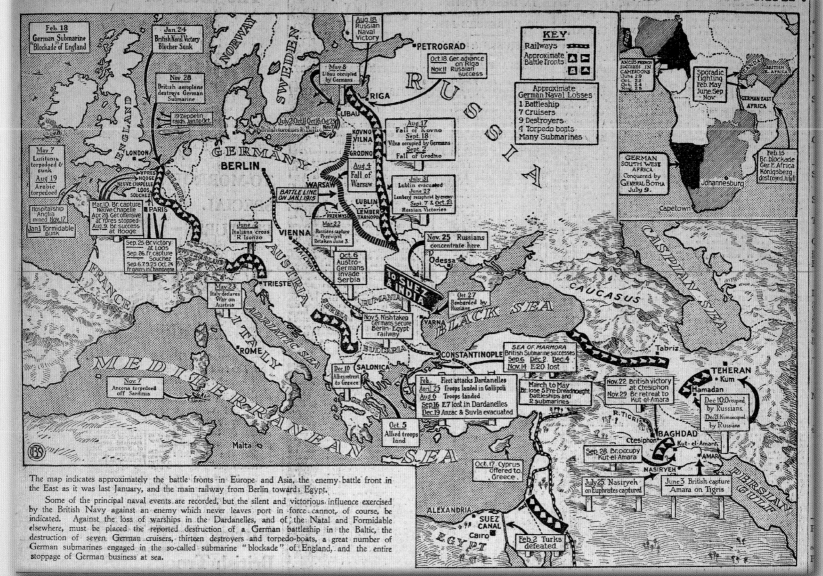

The map indicates approximately the battle fronts in Europe and Asia, the enemy battle front in the East as it was last January, and the main railway from Berlin towards Egypt.

Some of the principal naval events are recorded, but the silent and victorious influence exercised by the British Navy against an enemy which never leaves port in force cannot, of course, be indicated. Against the loss of warships in the Dardanelles, and of the Natal and Formidable elsewhere, must be placed the reported destruction of a German battleship in the Baltic, the destruction of seven German cruisers, thirteen destroyers and torpedo-boats, a great number of German submarines engaged in the so-called submarine "blockade" of England, and the entire stoppage of German business at sea.

"The Form which finds Servants."

FRIDAY, DECEMBER 24, 1915.

REGISTER TO-DAY.

THE CHRISTMAS SPIRIT IN WAR-TIME.

THE "FLUFFIES' AT THE ZOO.—Fur-coated Highlanders on Christmas leave from the trenches visit the Zoological Gardens. Their girl hostesses—a party of Palladium girls—have nicknamed them the "Fluffies." ["Daily Mail" Photograph.

THE "FLUFFIES" AT THE ZOO.—"Ye don't go to billets from the firing line in this style, ye ken." The "Jocks" enjoy the novelty of a bath-chair ride round the gardens before going off to lunch. ["Daily Mail." Photograph.

THE YULE LOG (Flanders type)

PICTURES OF THE SECOND WAR-TIME CHRISTMAS.

THE CHRISTMAS TOAST.—British and French soldiers fraternising in France drink to the Allied Armies.

THE CHILDREN'S CHRISTMAS.—Some of the little guests at the Children's children at the Savoy Hotel.

THE YULETIDE CONCERT.—British Red Cross nurses sing and play a "Tommy" to help him to enjoy his Christmas.

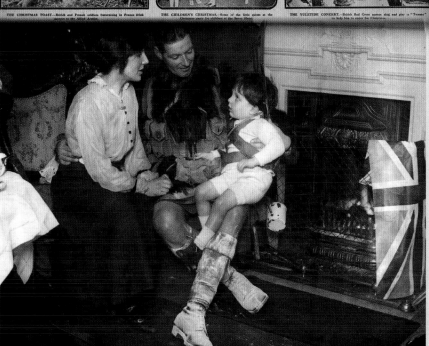

Above left: Cheery troops make their way back to Britain on Christmas Eve, looking forward to spending the festive season with their families.

Above: A battle-worn soldier stops to purchase toys for his children on his arrival back in London.

Left: Daddy arrives home safely. This soldier has been fighting at Loos and still has chalk on his uniform.

SIR DOUGLAS HAIG SUCCEEDS SIR JOHN FRENCH.

| SIR J. FRENCH TO COMMAND AT | FIGHT IN WESTERN EGYPT. ENCOUNTER WITH 1,200 | WARNING NOTE BY LORD DERBY. | 200,000 ALLIES AT SALONICA. GERMANIC SUBJECTS | HUN TRADING TO STOP. SIR JOHN SIMON'S PROMISE | OUR LOAN IN THE U.S. MESSRS. J. P. MORGAN |

THE HUN AS HE IS.—Some German soldiers who were made prisoners when the British captured the trench in which they are photographed. The large saw held by the man in the foreground is used for cutting barbed wire. Some of the men are holding hand grenades. ["*Daily Mail*" Photograph.]

Above: Sorting the mail which carries festive greetings from home. The Royal Mail played a vital part during the conflict being the only means of communication for troops and their families. It boosted morale and sent many reassuring messages back to worried families.

Top left: Christmas over and it is time for this soldier to report back for duty. By the time troops were fully equipped, their kit and provisions weighed approximately 30 kilograms.

Top right: Some men were not so lucky and spent Christmas interned at one of the many prisoner of war camps.

Below: Families line the platform at Waterloo to wave goodbye to their loved ones returning to the Western Front. The year ended with David Lloyd George taking over from Asquith as Prime Minister of the coalition government and becoming head of a much smaller War Cabinet with greater power over decisions.

December 1915

1 Italy announced her adherence to the Pact of London.

2 Bulgarian forces captured Monastir in Serbia.

3 Following the retreat from their defeat at Ctesiphon in November, British forces reached Kut al Amara.

4 The American anti-war peace expedition of Henry Ford set sail for Europe on the Oscar II.

5 The French submarine *Fresnel* was sunk by Austrian destroyers off the coast of northern Albania.

6 The Allied War Council held a military conference in Paris.

7 The Siege of Kut began when the Ottoman Army besieged the British-Indian garrison in the town of Kut al Amara in Mesopotamia.

President Woodrow Wilson delivered a war message to Congress denouncing anti-American plotters.

8 British forces at Anzac Cove and Suvla in Gallipoli were ordered to evacuate.

In Flanders Fields was published in *Punch* magazine. It was written by Canadian medical officer John McRae after presiding over the funeral of a friend and fellow soldier earlier in the year.

10 German attachés Captain Boy-Ed and Captain Papen were recalled from the USA by their Government.

11 General and politician Yuan Shikai accepted the title of Emperor of China.

12 Greece conceded Allied demands regarding Salonika.

13 The Affair of the Wadi Senab concluded two days of action fought in Egypt's western desert between the Senussi and British and Indian forces.

14 Hamadan in western Persia was occupied by Russian troops.

15 Field Marshal Sir John French resigned as Commander-in-Chief of British forces on the Western Front and was replaced by Sir Douglas Haig.

17 German light cruiser SMS *Bremen* sunk in the Baltic after striking a Russian naval mine.

18 US President Woodrow Wilson married Edith Galt at her home in Washington.

19 The Allies started the preliminary evacuation of Gallipoli.

20 The evacuation of 83,000 troops from Suvla Bay and Anzac Cove in Gallipoli was completed.

21 The Japanese passenger steamer *Yasaka Maru* was torpedoed and sunk by a German U-boat near Port Said in the Mediterranean Sea.

23 British naval operations began on Lake Tanganyika.

24 The French passenger steamer *Ville De La Ciotat* was torpedoed in the Mediterranean Sea by German submarine *U-34*.

26 The British government entered into a treaty with Ibn Sa'ud, the Emir of Nejd, accepting protectorate status and agreeing to make war against Ibn Rashid, who was being supported by the Turks.

28 British and Indian forces at Cape Helles were ordered to evacuate Gallipoli.

29 Draft rules were approved for the Inter-Allied War Council.

30 P&O passenger liner SS *Persia* was torpedoed and sunk without warning by German U-Boat commander Max Valentiner.

Chapter Three

1916
Trench warfare

1916 in brief

Despite the reverses of 1915 the Allies went into the new year with renewed optimism. Kitchener's recruits would soon be ready for battle and the munitions crisis had largely been overcome. But the question of turning these advantages into military success remained. The Central Powers were adept at redeploying from one battle zone to another as the need arose, and the Allies now determined to implement an obvious counter-measure. At a meeting at Chantilly in December 1915 it was decided that new offensives on the main fronts had to be better co-ordinated. Concerted attacks would stretch the enemy's forces, hopefully to breaking point.

Germany's plan for the new year also involved a major fresh assault in the west. 1915 had seen the Central Powers assume mastery of the Eastern Front and Falkenhayn now proposed to repeat the trick in France. He was astute enough to realise that France and Britain could not be overrun, nor did they need to be. Falkenhayn believed that there were strategic targets in France, well within reach of his army, that would bring the desired outcome. If one of these could be taken, or merely threatened, the patriotism and pride of the French would demand nothing less than total commitment – even total sacrifice – to prevent what in cold, detached terms would be a modest territorial loss. The historic city of Verdun, situated on the River Meuse, was identified as the place where the French would willingly bleed to death. And when that happened, Falkenhayn concluded, Britain too would be mortally wounded. The Reich's troops received a seductive exhortation: that their efforts in the forthcoming struggle at Verdun would result in peace being signed in that city. With such high stakes it was little wonder that the siege of Verdun was called Operation Gericht (Judgment).

The Battle of Verdun

The Germans stole a march by launching their offensive first. The Battle of Verdun began on 21 February 1916. Twelve hundred guns, including the famous 42-centimetre Big Bertha, launched one of the fiercest bombardments of the entire war. In previous battles artillery was the precursor to an infantry advance; at Verdun Falkenhayn envisioned a huge bombardment concentrated on a mere eight-mile front as the key to victory.

On the fourth day the Germans took Fort Douaumont, the largest of the city's famous defensive strongholds. As predicted, the French refused to cede a city that was a symbol of national pride, regardless of the fact that it was of no great strategic value. The German trap was sprung. But the French were not content merely to become cannon fodder to a hopeless cause. Under General Pétain, who assumed command of the city's defences, they would fight fire with fire.

Pétain was a general of the modern school, recognising that noble sacrifice with élan – the traditional French way – had at times to become subservient to technology. His own artillery began inflicting heavy casualties on the German ranks. With lines of communication badly damaged, Pétain also made sure that one key road to the south of the city remained open. The "Voie Sacrée" or "Sacred Way", as it became known, would be remembered for the ceaseless snake of trucks carrying fresh troops and supplies to the front, bringing exhausted and shell-shocked men in the opposite direction for well-deserved rest and recuperation. Pétain, the man who would be reviled as a collaborator in World War II, became a national hero for the part he played in helping to save Verdun. The battle raged until June. Unsurprisingly, there was by now some wavering among the Reich's hierarchy. A victory that was expected within days had failed to materialise after four months. With a decision on Verdun in the balance, news came through of a major Russian offensive in the east. General Alexei Brusilov's rout of the Austro-Hungarian army forced Falkenhayn into a large-scale redeployment to that theatre. No sooner was this done than British forces began their own offensive on the River Somme. Falkenhayn had missed his chance and the action at Verdun was scaled down. During the remainder of the year the French regained all the territory they had lost. The aggregate death toll was about 700,000, with French losses marginally the greater. Yet again it was carnage on a monumental scale for no discernible benefit. Even so, President Poincaré proudly declared Verdun an "inviolate citadel" defended by men who had "sowed and watered with their blood the crop which rises today". The Verdun campaign cost Falkenhayn his job, and he was replaced as Chief-of-Staff by Hindenburg in August.

Somme Offensive

France played a supporting role as the Allies now launched their own offensive on the Somme. A huge week-long artillery bombardment was a prelude to an attack by front-line troops on 1 July. As with the German army in February, optimism was great among Allied troops who sang: "We beat 'em on the Marne, we beat 'em on the Aisne, we gave them hell at Neuve Chapelle and here we are again". However, the artillery attack had not done its work, proving ineffectual against the heavily entrenched enemy. Worse, it gave the Germans prior warning of the imminent assault. The infantry attacked in close ranks and were easy prey for the German Maxim machine guns. By nightfall the casualty figure stood at 57,000, the worst day in British military history. The more tactically astute French made some gains but overall it was a black day for the Allies.

Haig was undeterred by the losses. Although never as bad again, the overall verdict of the Somme offensive made grim reading. Positions Haig had hoped to secure on the first day were still in German hands in mid-November. Allied casualties exceeded 600,000, with German losses up to half a million. The campaign had seen British tanks deployed for the first time, but these did not make the impact that had been hoped for. By the end of the year a decisive breakthrough on the Western Front remained as elusive as ever.

1916 saw the death of the man whose recruitment campaign had seen more than two million British men enlist since the outbreak of hostilities. Lord Kitchener was aboard HMS *Hampshire* bound for Russia when the ship was sunk off the Orkneys. Despite his efforts the rate at which men were volunteering had slowed by the start of 1916. The Government responded by introducing the Military Service Bill on 5 January. Single men aged 18-41 would now be conscripted. Asquith wanted the sons of widows to be exempted, but this quickly fell by the wayside. The exigencies of war – and the huge losses on the Western Front in particular – meant that before the year was out married men up to the age of 41 were also being called up.

In addition to Britain's new conscripts, the Allied ranks were swelled in August 1916 by a new ally, Romania. It was hoped that King Ferdinand's decision to join the Entente Powers might tip the balance in their favour in the Balkans,

but that quickly proved to be wide of the mark. "The moment has come to liberate our brothers in Transylvania from the Hungarian yoke," said the King, but on 5 December Bucharest fell almost without a struggle. If recruiting; allies or conscripts made no tangible difference in 1916, what of the long-awaited battle for supremacy on the high seas?

The naval battle

For nearly two years the British and German fleets had avoided full-scale confrontation. Despite the furious efforts of the Reich leading up to war it was the British navy which had more ships and greater firepower. The mighty Dreadnought, whose turbine engines could propel it to 21 knots and whose 12 inch guns had a ten-mile range, was a formidable fighting machine. However, the first Dreadnought had appeared in 1906 and Germany had had a decade in which to respond in kind. Moreover, the Royal Navy hadn't been tested in battle since the days of Nelson and was led by Admiral Sir John Jellicoe, a cautious man who had grown up in the age of steam.

Wary of German mines and torpedoes, the British fleet had been executing a distant blockade policy. Based at Scapa Flow, Jellicoe's ships had a natural stranglehold on the North Sea and the German fleet remained tied up in harbour for long periods. In January 1916 the new commander of Germany's High Seas Fleet, Admiral Reinhard Scheer, masterminded a plan to neutralise Britain's naval superiority. Scheer knew that to prevent his country from being slowly starved of resources, he had to attack. His plan was to split up the enemy fleet, thus increasing his chances of victory. Raids on Britain's east coast were carried out, forcing Jellicoe to deploy a battle-cruiser squadron south to Rosyth. Phase one of Scheer's scheme had been accomplished. Phase two was to lure the battle cruisers into the open sea by parading a few of his own ships off the Norwegian coast. The battle-cruiser squadron, led by Sir David Beatty, duly obliged. Lying in wait not far from the German outriders was the entire High Seas Fleet. Unbeknown to Scheer, however, British intelligence had cracked the German naval code. Scheer had hoped to overpower the battle-cruiser squadron and escape before the main British fleet could reach the scene. But, thanks to the code-breakers Jellicoe was already steaming into action.

The Battle of Jutland

Beatty's squadron engaged the enemy at around 4pm on 31 May 1916. He was soon faced with two major reverses as both the *Indefatigable* and *Queen Mary* exploded and sank within twenty minutes of each other. Only two of *Indefatigable's* 1,019-strong crew survived, and 1,286 men lost their lives on the *Queen Mary*. A bewildered Beatty famously commented: "There seems to be something wrong with our bloody ships today." Later investigation would suggest that the way in which the cordite was stored was the Achilles heel of a powerful fighting machine.

Not only was German gunnery having the better of the exchange but Scheer was closing in fast. When Beatty sighted the main body of the German Fleet he turned his battle-cruisers north towards Jellicoe and the Grand Fleet. It was now Britain's turn to try and lure the enemy into a trap.

When the battle lines were drawn it was Jellicoe who held a huge tactical advantage. By the time the two fleets engaged his ships were arranged broadside across the German line, a manoeuvre known as "crossing the T". The German fleet came under heavy bombardment and, despite the loss of the *Invincible* in yet another spectacular explosion, Jellicoe seemed assured of success. Scheer's answer was to effect a brilliant 180-degree turn, his ships disappearing into the smoke and confusion. Jellicoe, ever mindful of exposing himself to torpedo fire, was reluctant to follow, but soon discovered that he didn't need to. For inexplicably, Scheer's forces performed a second about-face manoeuvre and headed directly back towards the British line. Jellicoe was in a dilemma: to engage carried the prize of an outright victory, but with German torpedoes now within range there was a considerable risk of further losses. He chose discretion and retreated. By the next morning the German fleet had slipped away. The Battle of Jutland – or Skagerrak, as the Germans called it – was over.

Germany hailed it as a great victory, and with some justification since Britain's losses were substantially higher. Fourteen ships of the Grand Fleet had been sunk, while Scheer had lost eleven vessels. Over 6,000 British sailors lost their lives; Germany's casualties were less than half that number. There was certainly disappointment in Britain both at governmental level and in the population at large. On the other hand, Germany never threatened Britain's mastery of the seas again. Scheer advised the Kaiser that maritime strategy should now focus on the deployment of U-boats, not surface ships.

A protracted conflict

Both on land and at sea, 1916 had been as indecisive as its predecessor. By the end of the year each of the protagonists faced a new threat: destabilisation from within. War weariness set in. The privations of a protracted conflict meant that the euphoria of August 1914 was now a distant memory. Each country sought to quell unrest within its own borders while actively encouraging it within those of its enemies. Britain's greatest crisis came at Easter, when Sinn Fein members took over Dublin's Post Office. The uprising was brutally put down and the rebel leaders were executed. Meanwhile in the Middle East Britain was actively trying to foment revolution in pursuance of its war aims. The Arabs of the Hijaz were moved to rise up against the Ottoman Empire on British promises of post-conflict independence. T. E. Lawrence, who played a prominent part in the guerrilla war that the Arabs began to wage, knew from the start that Britain had no intention of honouring its pledge. The seeds of mutiny and revolution were sown in 1916; the following year would witness a dramatic harvest of these pent-up feelings which would affect the course of the war.

With the strain showing and disaffection growing, the desire for a settlement naturally gathered momentum. On 12 December 1916 Germany sued for peace. But the note that was passed to the Allies spoke of the "indestructible strength" of the Central Powers and stated that "a continuation of the war cannot break their resisting power". Unsurprisingly, such language was hardly seen as magnanimous among the Entente Powers. Lloyd George, who had replaced Asquith as prime minister in December 1916, gave a trenchant reply. It was a "sham proposal" and entering into discussions on the basis of its contents "would be putting our heads in the noose with the rope end in the hands of the Germans". All sides may have been eager to end hostilities, but not at any price.

January 1916

1   Under the command of Canadian General Charles Macpherson Dobell, British forces captured Yaunde in the Cameroons.

2   The P&O British cargo ship SS *Geelong* sank in the Mediterranean Sea following a collision with a British steamer. She was on a voyage from Sydney via Port Said to Gibraltar and London with a general cargo which included tea and lead.

4   A relief force started out from Ali Al-Gharbi to save the besieged defenders of Ku-al-Amara.

6   The Battle of Sheikh Sa'ad began along the banks of the Tigris River between the Anglo-Indian Tigris Corps and the Ottoman Sixth Army.

5   An Inter-Allied Conference was held in Rome.

7   British forces captured the forward Turkish positions at Sheikh Sa'ad.

8   Under the command of Lieutenant General Sir Fenton John Aylmer the Battle of Sheikh Sa'ad ended – the first in a series of assaults by the Tigris Corps to attempt to break through the Ottoman lines to relieve the besieged garrison at Kut-al-Amara.

9   The Allied evacuation of Helles marked the end of the Gallipoli Campaign which resulted in an Allied defeat and an overwhelming victory for the Ottoman Empire.

10   General Sir Archibald Murray succeeded Sir Charles Munro as Commander of the Mediterranean Expeditionary Force.

11   Corfu was occupied by Allied troops.

Russian forces began an offensive into Armenia.

12   An Armistice was drawn up between Montenegro and Austria.

13   The Battle of Wadi took place. The conflict was an unsuccessful attempt by Lieutenant General Sir Fenton John Aylmer to relieve beleaguered forces under siege by the Ottoman Army at Kut-al-Amara.

14   Lieutenant General Sir Percy Lake was appointed as Commander-in-Chief in Mesopotamia, replacing Sir John Nixon.

16   French General Maurice-Paul-Emmanuel Sarrail assumed command of all Allied forces in Salonika.

17   Montenegro surrendered to the Central Powers.

20   The Armistice between Montenegro and Austria ceased as negotiations broke down.

21   As part of the attempt to relieve Kut al Amara, a British assault against Turkish positions was launched at the Battle of Hanna and was once again repulsed.

23   Austro-Hungarian forces captured Scutari on the Southern Front.

British forces attacked Senussi tribesmen at Halazin near the Mediterranean seaport of Mersa Matruh.

24   German officer Reinhard Scheer was promoted to Admiral and given control of the High Seas Fleet.

25   The personal envoy of US President Wilson, Edward House, met with German officials in Berlin on a mission for peace.

26   A communiqué was sent from Sir Charles Townshend to the Kut Garrison in order to boost the flagging morale of his garrison troops.

27   The Military Service Act 1916 was passed by the British Parliament to introduce conscription. The law required that all unmarried men and widowers 18-41 years of age without dependants should make themselves available for national service.

28   Louis Dembitz Brandeis was controversially nominated by President Wilson to become a member of the US Supreme Court.

29   Paris was bombed by German Zeppelins.

31   East Anglia and the Midlands were bombed in a raid by several German airships.

Evacuation of Gallipoli

In eight long months on the Gallipoli peninsula the Allies learned from bitter experience the difficulties of attacking a determined Turkish army that commanded the heights. The same difficulties applied to any planned withdrawal: how to remove the entire task force from beaches that were overlooked. Surely ground and air-based enemy spotters would soon realise what was afoot, and give the Allies as hostile a sending-off as the reception had been? The massive undertaking was to be completed at Anzac and Suvla Bay by 20 December 1915, and unsurprisingly the details were kept top secret. Withdrawing under the cloak of darkness was the easy part; more difficult was fooling the watching Turks that the thinning numbers represented business as usual. A variety of ruses was employed to create the illusion. Troop-laden boats were ostentatiously shown heading towards the shore, suggesting reinforcement, not exodus. The same troops, and plenty more besides, went in the opposite direction at night. Periods with little or no shellfire were introduced, so that a spell of inactivity did not raise suspicions. Games of cricket were organised; Britain and her Empire at play – hardly the thing if a disappearing act was in the offing. Burning candles were used to set off fireworks. And as the final act played out, unmanned rifles were set to fire by ingenious Heath Robinsonesque means. An enemy taking pot shots was a sure sign of a live threat, and that's how it was perceived. The noise of army boots on the move, by contrast, was a giveaway, and measures were taken to muffle the marching columns as they made for the embarkation points. As a final flourish in the quest to confuse, three huge mines were laid, timed to explode at two-minute intervals.

PHOTOGRAPHS FROM GALLIPOLI.

The field telephone plays an important part in modern warfare. Telephonists at work in a Gallipoli dug-out.
["Daily Mail" Photograph.

The rugged nature of the country at the Gallipoli Peninsula makes it exceedingly difficult for the transport of big guns. Here artillerymen are seen hauling a gun into position up a steep hill. ["Daily Mail" Photograph.

"THY WILL BE DONE."—The lonely grave on the slopes of Gaba Tepe of Gunner George Cuthbertson, of the Royal Garrison Artillery. The headstone bears the inscription "Thy will be done!" ["Daily Mail" Photograph.

GALLIPOLI ENTIRELY EVACUATED.

OUR LAST MAN LEAVES GALLIPOLI.

SOUTHERN FRONT EVACUATED.

ONE WOUNDED.

8 MONTHS' HEROISM.
GLORIOUS BUT VAIN.
NAVY'S FINE PART.

The Navy, which effects the transport and movement of troops by sea, has achieved another brilliant feat in withdrawing the whole British force from the dismal peninsula of Gallipoli with a

...LOST.

H.M.S. KING EDWARD VII. SUNK.
BATTLESHIP MINED.
ABANDONED IN HEAVY SEA.

DEATH OF LORD BURNHAM.
A GREAT JOURNALIST.

We deeply regret to announce that Lord Burnham died early yesterday morning at his London residence, Norfolk-street, W. He had been ill for some time.

The King and Queen have telegraphed to Colonel the Hon. H. Lawson, expressing...

TWO BIG BATTLES.
RUSSIANS REPULSE GREAT ATTACK.
ONSLAUGHT ON THE MONTENEGRINS.

The Russians lost but retook Czernowicz, a town on the Styr, in Volhynia. They gave up some ground to Galicia and stopped a heavy attack on the...

ANTI-COMPULSIONISTS' BAD TIMES.
LABOUR LEADERS HECKLED.

MR. J. H. THOMAS'S "IF."

AND FOR

Withdrawing under the cloak of darkness was the easy part; more difficult was fooling the watching Turks.

Right: On 7 January the Turks attacked the British troops at Gully Spur without success. That night, during the cover of a naval bombardment, the remaining British soldiers headed towards the makeshift piers to board their boats. The last men evacuated the Gallipoli peninsula at 4 am on 9 January 1916.

Far right: Once all the trenches were abandoned, the ammunition, equipment and supplies that could not be transported were blown up before departure. Redundant vehicles had their wheels destroyed.

Below: In the operation led by Sir John de Robeck over 35,000 troops, nearly 4,700 horses, 127 guns, 328 vehicles and 1,600 tons of equipment were safely removed.

Opposite: During the evacuation those in command had no alternative but to leave hundreds of mules behind. These were slaughtered to stop the Turks using them.

UNDOING THE DARDANELLES BLUNDER.

SUVLA AND ANZAC EVACUATED.

GREAT ARMY WITHDRAWN WITHOUT TURKS KNOWING.

MOVE TO ANOTHER SPHERE.

CASUALTIES INSIGNIFICANT: FINE NAVAL SUPPORT

YPRES HEAVILY SHELLED.

VIGOROUS BRITISH REPLY.

44 AIR FIGHTS.

BIG FRENCH BOMBARDMENT

BRITISH OFFICIAL.

GENERAL HEADQUARTERS, FRANCE, Monday, 9.3 p.m.

To-day, opposite the southern portion and centre of our line, we bombarded several portions of the enemy's trenches.

Hostile artillery heavily shelled Ypres

GREEK KING'S CHANGED MIND.

LIGHTNING EFFECT OF ALLIES' DECISION.

BERLIN BLUFF FAILS.

NEW GREEK MOVE ON FRONTIER.

BRUSH WITH BULGARS.

Greek troops are reported to have occupied Doiran Metaxas and Ghevgeli. Hostile

the blockade was raised next day. The whole of Athens rejoiced. The King himself said he was inconceivably relieved to be rid of an intolerable anxiety; he could now sleep again, though, he added, the future was not without its dangers. Therefore, the whole situation altered within twenty-four hours the most marked factor being the change in the King's attitude.

COAL £5 A TON.

The great point is, What caused this and will the factors that caused it endure? In the first instance the blockade had great effect. Wheat ships were everywhere stopped, coal was £5 a ton, and there were only 10,000 tons at the Piraeus. Greece was cut off from other countries. It was impossible even to communicate directly with the United States, cable facilities being refused. But it is only just to say that perhaps a more powerful factor is the growing dislike of Germany. This

"TOO LATE."

MR. LLOYD GEORGE WARNS THE GOVERNMENT AND LABOUR.

THE SHELL SCANDAL IN MAY.

Germans' 250,000 a Day : British 2,500 a Day.

"You can only talk of over-ordering when we have as much as the enemy."

LATEST WAR EDITION.   THE DAILY MAIL, WEDNESDAY, DECEMBER 22, 1915.   5

ONLY 3 CASUALTIES IN SUVLA WITHDRAWAL.

MR. ASQUITH'S APPEAL TO SINGLE MEN.

ANOTHER "COMPULSION" DEBATE.

3 A.M. GAS ATTACK.

ALERT BRITISH GUNNERS.

RARE DAY FOR THE AIRMEN

FROM OUR SPECIAL CORRESPONDENT

SUVLA BAY.

3 MEN WOUNDED— 6 GUNS LEFT.

TURKS' VERSION.

"FIRE" IN FOG.

Yesterday, as reported by us left

WARNED OFF THE SEAS.

GERMAN SHIPPING PLOT.

ATTEMPT TO SELL BOATS IN NEUTRAL PORTS.

FROM OUR OWN CORRESPONDENT

New York, Monday

LATE WAR NEWS.

RUSSIAN SUCCESS IN PERSIA.

KUM TAKEN AFTER A BIG BATTLE.

ENEMY'S COMPLETE DEFEAT.

SERBIANS' LAST ATTACK.

TRYING TO JOIN THE ALLIES.

BREACH MADE BUT CLOSED.

KATCHANIK BATTLE

THE ARMISTICE: WONDERFUL PHOTOGRAPH FROM ANZAC.

Right: A picture taken by a wounded Anzac on 'Lone Pine' Plateau during an armistice to allow the Turks to remove their dead and wounded. On the left is a Turk holding aloft the white flag of truce.

Above: The four men who claim to have been the last to leave the inhospitable shores of the Gallipoli Peninsula when the evacuation took place.

The great escape

The deceptions worked brilliantly. Of the massive explosions that covered the 20 December withdrawal, Anzac commander General William Birdwood wrote: "The result was wonderful, in that the whole of the Turks, evidently anticipating a big attack, lined their trenches, and for about an hour continued to fire away as fast as they could possibly load; meanwhile our men were well down on their way to the beach in comfort."

All that was left for the Turks to discover, after the Allied horse had bolted, were the carcases of animals that could not be accommodated in the evacuation. Other supplies were ditched in the sea or smashed; every effort was made to ensure the enemy would not profit from the Allied departure. A jubilant Birdwood reported: "I never…dared to hope that we could possibly meet with the success we did."

The slickly executed exit from Anzac Cove and Suvla left only the Cape Helles contingent seeing in the new year on the peninsula. The last of those left on 8 January. With the closing of the chapter, the final bill could now be reckoned. Almost half a million Allied troops had been committed to the campaign; nearly 10 per cent of those did not return, killed in battle or lost to disease. The overall casualty count was considerably higher. Turkey threw as many men into the defence of its homeland and had an even higher death toll.

A stunningly successful evacuation could not mask the fact that Gallipoli was an ignominious defeat for the Allies. As the war rolled on in other theatres, Gallipoli became the subject of a Royal Commission; so abject a failure had to come under the microscope. Sir Ian Hamilton, campaign commander until he was effectively sacked in October 1915, was judged the chief scapegoat. Lord Kitchener's death – drowned when HMS *Hampshire* was sunk off the Orkneys in June 1916 – removed him from the firing line. Lack of resources was also highlighted as a major factor. The Commission found that for the undertaking to succeed, a greater concentration of men and matériel was required, at the expense of Western Front activity. "This condition," it said, "was never fulfilled."

This page: The remaining troops march along the Valley of Death to make their way towards the beaches.

Opposite: As HMS *Cornwallis* sails away at 5 am, the last view of the peninsula shows the burning remains of the stores left behind. Although figures vary, some 50,000 Allied troops were killed and another 123,000 wounded during the campaign, with many more succumbing to severe illnesses such as dysentery and typhoid. There are now 31 Commonwealth War Grave Commission cemeteries in Gallipoli.

SUVLA BAY.

3 MEN WOUNDED — 6 GUNS LEFT.

TURKS' VERSION.

OUR "ESCAPE" IN FOG.

Mr. Asquith stated yesterday, as reported fully elsewhere, that we left behind at Suvla a relatively small quantity of stores and six guns, which were destroyed. We had only three men wounded.

FROM OUR SPECIAL CORRESPONDENT, JAMES DUNN.

ROTTERDAM, Tuesday.

The German papers this morning are boasting of a "great Turkish victory" in Gallipoli by the withdrawal of the British troops. The *Vossische Zeitung* declares that "the military reverse is the rightful punishment for the incredible light-heartedness with which the campaign was begun without careful preparation."

The *Rotterdam Nieuwsblad* says: "This is the end of an unfruitful campaign." The *Nieuw Rotterdamsche Courant*, commenting on the Turkish jubilation, says: "The British report is probably the true one, for the Turks have not succeeded in fulfilling their boast of driving the enemy into the sea. The British had chosen their time well." The paper describes the whole British campaign as a "pitiful failure, the lead being in such bad hands that they failed to occupy heights farther inland. The Turks received shells from Germany and made the position impossible. It is a great success for the Turks, who are able to concentrate on another front.'¹

TURKISH REPORT.

TALE OF GREAT ATTACK BY US AT SEDDUL BAHR.

Turkish Official. AMSTERDAM, Tues.

The Turkish official report for yesterday says: "On Saturday night and Sunday morning our troops, after a heavy artillery preparation, began an offensive movement against the enemy's positions near Anafarta (Suvla) and Ari Burnu (Anzac). In order to hold up this movement, the enemy in the afternoon undertook an attack in full force at Seddul Bahr, which completely failed.

"The enemy was forced to the conclusion that our attack in the north was bound to succeed, and during Sunday night he hastily embarked part of his forces. Nevertheless, despite a thick fog, the enemy could not hinder his pursuit by our troops during his retirement.

"The latest reports to-day state that our troops so thoroughly cleared Anafarta and Ari Burnu of the enemy that not a single enemy soldier remained behind there. Our troops advanced to the coast and took very great booty in munitions, tents, and guns. We shot down an enemy aeroplane, which fell into the sea, and took the pilot and observer prisoners.

"The enemy attack at Seddul Bahr on Sunday took the following course:—He for a time kept up a vigorous fire on our positions from his land guns of all calibres and from monitors and cruisers. Then he successively attacked our right wing, centre, and left wing with all his forces, but our troops checked the attacks and drove the enemy back to his original positions with enormous losses."

The Agence Milli of Constantinople gives a similar account of the British withdrawal, transforming it in the same way into a brilliant Turkish victory. It says: "Since Sunday there has been fierce fighting in all sectors of the Dardanelles front. The enemy at Anafarta and Ari Burnu has been beaten and is in full flight. Our troops have reached the sea near Ari Burnu. The booty is immeasurably great. A thick fog permitted the enemy to escape without leaving behind a great number of prisoners."—Reuter.

AMSTERDAM, Tuesday.

ZEPPELIN RAID ON ENGLAND LAST NIGHT.

RAID BY SIX ZEPPELINS.

BOMBS ON EASTERN, NORTH EASTERN AND MIDLAND COUNTIES.

NO CONSIDERABLE DAMAGE YET REPORTED.

WAR OFFICE, Tuesday, 1.40 a.m.

A Zeppelin raid by 6 or 7 airships took place last night over the Eastern, North-Eastern, and Midland Counties.

A number of bombs were dropped, but up to the present no considerable damage has been reported.

A further statement will be issued as soon as practicable.

Dvinsk Liveliness : The Russians signal a violent German artillery fire west of Dvinsk and a recrudescence of activity in the Riga region.

Western Front : There is a bill in

TURKS CUT OFF IN ARMENIA.

UNOFFICIAL REPORT.

VIOLENT GERMAN FIRE NEAR DVINSK.

The Germans have begun vigorous artillery actions west of Dvinsk and Riga. An unofficial report from Petrograd says that the Turks in Armenia, at Erzerum and Melazghert, are cut off from the rest of the army, but the Russian Headquarters statement seems to indicate that the present operations have been concluded, the chief result being that our Ally's troops can now winter in a more favourable district.

FROM OUR SPECIAL CORRESPONDENT.
ATHENS, Sunday.

I learn from a very reliable source that the Russian action at Erzerum has already had the effect of withdrawing the Turkish 1st Army Corps eastward. This corps had been intended to reinforce the Turks in Mesopotamia ; but it is probable that over a fortnight must elapse before the Turkish relief forces can reach Erzerum.

PETROGRAD, Monday.

It is announced that, following on the Russian success in the Caucasus, the Turkish troops operating on the left wing are at present shut up in the region of the fortress of Erzerum and almost entirely deprived of freedom of movement, as they cannot pass in front of the forts. At the same time, the Turkish forces in Erzerum and Melazghert are completely cut off from the rest of the army.—Reuter.

Russian Official. PETROGRAD, Monday.

Caucasus Front : The operations extending over a fortnight on the Turkish front were carried out according to plan and have

FRESH ATTEMPT ON PARIS.

ONE BOMB OVER 2 CWT.

BETHMANN'S TRICK.

BRITAIN THE ONLY PEACE OBSTACLE.

BUELOW'S MANŒUVRES ADMITTED.

"ANY SACRIFICE TO BEAT ENGLAND."

The following statement attributed to the German Chancellor is clearly another clumsy German effort to sow discord among the Allies by attempting to shew that only England stands in the way of peace :—

FROM OUR OWN CORRESPONDENT.
NEW YORK, Monday.

Dr. von Bethmann-Hollweg, the German Imperial Chancellor, recently called into conference the leaders of the various party groups in the Reichstag and gave for their edification a "frank outline of the situation" as it appeared to him and presumably to the German military authorities.

His observations are now reproduced for the benefit of the American people in the *Deutsches Journal* by the managing editor, Gustav Schweppendick, who has been acting as Berlin correspondent of the *New York American*. The *Deutsches Journal* is a daily newspaper published in New York by Mr. Hearst. Mr. Schweppendick states that the views of the Chancellor were communicated to him by one of the party leaders present at the conference.

Dr. von Bethmann-Hollweg devoted the burden

FIGHTING IN WEST.

SOMME BATTLE CEASES.

4 EXPLOSIONS IN ENEMY LINES.

FRENCH LONG-RANGE BOMBARDMENT.

FROM OUR SPECIAL CORRESPONDENT.
JAMES DUNN.

ROTTERDAM, Monday.

The activity on the western front has temporarily stopped owing to misty weather. The situation from Nieuport, on the coast, to Arras is one of extreme tension, the enemy's attacks south of Arras having sent a thrill of excitement along the entire front.

Behind the German lines rumour follows rumour almost hourly. It is not too much to say that the Germans expect attacks daily, and the men are kept on duty for long hours in the trenches, the reserves sleeping when and where they can.

French Official. PARIS, Mon., 11 p.m.

In Belgium our heavy artillery directed an effective fire upon the enemy works at the Steenstrate bridge (north of Ypres). The abutment of the bridge on the eastern bank was damaged.

To the south of Eoye (at the bend in the line) our trench guns wrecked the German works in the district of Fresnières.

North of St. Mihiel our long-range guns bombarded the enemy cantonments of Combes, roads of Hattes and St. Maurice.

HUN CAMP TUNNEL.

BATHROOM DIGGING TO A MOUTH ORGAN.

DONINGTON MEN'S WORK AT MAIDENHEAD.

Further daring attempts by German officer prisoners at Philberds, Maidenhead, Berks, to escape were investigated by a military court at the Holyport Prison yesterday. The president was Lieutenant-Colonel Chase.

There were two indictments against Lieutenant Otto Thelen, of the German Army Flying Corps, and Lieutenant Hans Keilhack, of the German Navy, for attempting to escape from the internment camp and in doing so damaging property belonging to the King.

The prisoners, who were defended, had been previously convicted for escaping by tunnelling from Donington Hall. They tunnelled fifty yards and were caught at sea.

The case for the prosecution was that on January 17 Sergeant-Major Johnson, R.E., went with Foreman Headlong to the bathroom at the camp, the door of which was fastened. Headlong forced the door, and immediately a man stepped out clothed in a dressing gown. The sergeant-major entered and found that the floor-boards had been taken up and that excavation work was in hand. In the hole made candles, a spade, and iron bars were found, and in the recess was a box containing clothes and a biscuit tin.

The accused were afterwards removed to a hut, and on January 26 Captain and Adjutant Armstrong got a Boy Scout to crawl underneath the hut, and later he obtained a chisel and recovered some

BY THE MAN WHO DINED WITH THE KAISER

SUBMARINE SECRETS.

GERMANS SUSPICIOUS OF TURKS.

DR. LEDERA.

SPIES AND SPYING.

FALSE BIRTH CERTIFICATE.

I REACH SAFETY.

BY THE DAILY MAIL CORRESPONDENT WHO DINED WITH THE KAISER

This will be a chapter on spies and on submarines.

One of the axioms of those employed in secret service work for a newspaper should be to seek material by staying at the best hotel in any city in which he is making investigations. Big fish swim in large lakes. Furthermore, the visitors at large hotels

This page: Two men pick through the remains of 12-14 King's Street in Wednesbury. On 31 January 1916 Germany sent nine airships to attack Liverpool but, as was often the case, poor navigation and bad weather changed their target and instead bombs hailed over the West Midlands. The Smith family lived at number 14 and all three children and their father were killed. Only their mother survived because she had left the house to investigate the noise outside, thinking there was an explosion at the nearby factory.

Zeppelins expand their reach

January 1916 marked the anniversary of the first major Zeppelin raids on Britain. *The Times* chose this moment to report on the work of the Anti-Aircraft Corps, the solicitors, accountants, architects and the like who combined their regular jobs with manning the stations, keeping watch for aerial raiders. For a basic pay of 4s 2d per day these men typically worked a 12-hour shift, which included rest periods, but at the sounding of the alarm they were required "to be at their respective posts, with the gun cleared for action, within 30 seconds". The correspondence page of the same newspaper was also full of heated debate on how to negate the airship menace; a debate sparked by Sir Arthur Conan Doyle's contention that "we can tolerate no more outrages upon our civilian population, and that any further raids will be followed by immediate reprisals". The celebrated author's advocacy of tit-for-tat raids on German civilian targets divided opinion.

At the end of the month the British mainland received its latest Zeppelin visit, and Paris was also hit. The French capital recorded some 260 deaths from airship-launched ordnance, around half the number of fatalities Britain suffered over 57 separate raids. 1916 was a turning point, however. The Royal Flying Corps assumed responsibility for home defence at a time when explosive and incendiary bullets were being developed. The days of aerial incursions being carried out with impunity were numbered.

"We can tolerate no more outrages upon our civilian population, and that any further raids will be followed by immediate reprisals".

Top: Two houses in Union Street, Tipton were completely destroyed. In one, three adults and two children from the same family died. In all 14 people across the town perished and the gas main set alight.

Above left: At 107-111 Shobnall Street, Burton-on-Trent, a woman and two children were killed. A total of 61 civilians died and over 100 were injured in the attacks.

Above right: A house in Eridge Road Croydon was destroyed in October 1915.

Left: Workmen's dwellings demolished by the raiders in February 1916. By now the Army was starting to assume control of the British ground defences, developing more effective anti-aircraft guns and using searchlights, initially manned by the police force.

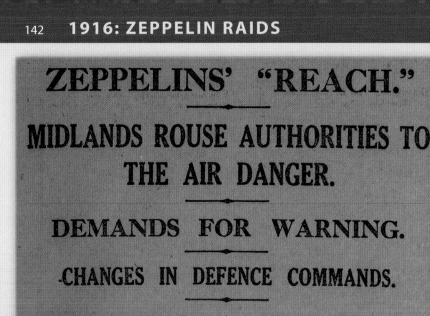

ZEPPELINS' "REACH."

MIDLANDS ROUSE AUTHORITIES TO THE AIR DANGER.

DEMANDS FOR WARNING.

CHANGES IN DEFENCE COMMANDS.

Western Guns Active: Excellent results gained by the Allies' heavy guns in France and Flanders were

AIR DEFENCES.

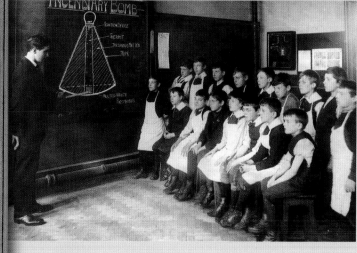

THE DISTANCE WHICH ZEPPELINS CAN COVER.

Top: Boys in a technical class at school in Bradford have a lesson on the construction of a Zeppelin incendiary bomb.

Above left: A row of four houses is left partially demolished.

Above middle: Edinburgh was attacked in early April and although the raid only lasted a few minutes, sixteen were killed and thirty injured, with one bomb falling on the Grasmarket in front of the White Hart hotel. Some people were hurt after running out into the street to watch.

Left: Baytree Road in Brixton was bombed on the night of 23-24 September 1916. Twelve airships headed for the capital; not all found the right location but in total 371 bombs were dropped killing 40 and injuring a further 130.

Far left: A newspaper article reveals the range of a Zeppelin's flying capabilities.

Below left: This British Coastal Class airship, built in 1916, was shot down by German seaplanes on 21 April 1917.

Opposite page and above: Houses in Lowestoft hit by battle cruisers in the Lowestoft raid of April 1916. The German High Fleet set sail on 24 April with a plan to attack the coastal ports of Lowestoft and Great Yarmouth while also enticing the British fleet to put to sea where they intended to open fire. The following day German vessels shelled Lowestoft, wrecking 200 houses in the space of ten minutes. Fortunately, poor visibility thwarted the attack on Yarmouth and the attempts to destroy the Grand Fleet failed.

Left: A chart showing the approximate limit of operations for Zeppelins from the bases at Brussels and Heligoland. Depending on the number of bombs carried the Zeppelin range is between 500 and 600 miles.

LOWESTOFT BOMBARDMENT, APRIL 25TH 1916, PRIVATE HOUSE, ESPLANADE

BOMBARDMENT OF LOWESTOFT APRIL 25TH 1916, CLEVELAND AS SOUTH SIDE

BOMBARDMENT OF LOWESTOFT, APRIL 25TH 1916.
LONDON ROAD SOUTH.

February 1916

1 The Norwegian Government prohibited all foreign submarines from using their territorial waters.

2 Boris Vladimirovich Stürmer replaced Ivan Longinovich Goremykin as Prime Minister of Russia.

8 The British Government requested naval assistance from Japan.

The French armoured cruiser *Admiral Charner* was torpedoed and sunk by a German U-boat near Beirut.

9 A combined British-Belgian naval force sank the German gunboat *Hedwig von Wissmann* during the Battle for Lake Tanganyika.

10 The Military Service Act became operational in Britain.

The German Government advised the United States that all defensively armed merchant ships would be considered as belligerents from 1 March onwards.

11 The light cruiser HMS *Arethusa* struck a mine and sank off Felixstowe on the east coast of Britain.

12 Russian forces began an attack on the Turkish city of Erzurum during the Erzurum Offensive.

14 The Allied powers issued a guarantee of eventual independence and indemnification of Belgium.

15 An agreement was reached between the British Government and Bakhtiari chieftains for co-operation in protection of Persian oilfields.

16 After days of fighting in deep snow and intense cold, Russian forces captured Erzurum from the Ottoman Army.

The War Office took over responsibility for the air defence of London and the rest of Britain from the Admiralty.

17 The last German forces left southern Cameroons for internment in Spanish territory.

18 The final remaining German post in Mora surrendered to British and French troops in the West African Campaign in Cameroon.

19 Brigadier General Tighe was succeeded by Lieutenant General Jan Smuts in command of British forces in East Africa.

21 The longest battle of the war, the Battle of Verdun, began with a German offensive on hilly terrain north of the city of Verdun-sur-Meuse in north-eastern France.

22 French troops counterattacked at Verdun. The Germans captured Haumont Wood but the French held Brabant on the Meuse.

23 The Portuguese Government seized German steamers in the River Tagus.

24 Germans breached the French line at Verdun but were unable to gain an advantage.

25 German forces captured the key French position at Fort Douamon on the approaches to Verdun.

26 The British Western Frontier Force defeated the Senussi in action at Agagiya in western Egypt.

27 Austrian forces captured Durazzo from Italian troops.

28 The nucleus of a long-range British bomber squadron was formed to attack German industrial centres.

29 Converted ocean liner SS *Alcantara* was sunk in action against German armed merchant cruiser SMS *Greif* in the North Sea.

The deception game

Well over 100 German agents are known to have operated in Britain during the war. Sixty-five were uncovered and brought to book, some of those suffering the same fate as Carl Hans Lody, whose court case had been headline news in

autumn 1914. Public exposure of those engaged in subversive activity was beneficial as a reassuring demonstration that the intelligence service was on top of the espionage threat. On the other hand, as an MI5 report noted, success was by no means measured simply by the number of arrests. A valuable contribution was also made "by hampering the enemy's intelligence service, and causing it to lose money, labour, and, most precious of all, time, in overcoming the obstacles placed in its way". That said, spies rounded up clandestinely offered the potential to spread disinformation. One of those was Karl Müller, whose arrest in February 1915 did not stop him from continuing to "correspond" with his Antwerp-based spymasters. For months British intelligence staff sent bogus reports purporting to be from Müller, information credible enough to be swallowed by the enemy. The deception even continued once the press embargo was lifted and Müller's name appeared in print. On 5 June the outcome of his trial, held in camera, was published: a guilty verdict and death sentence, carried out later that month. Belatedly, the penny dropped in Antwerp. When reports from Müller continued from beyond the grave, these were readily accepted by German intelligence bosses, believing they were one step ahead of their British counterparts. They did not appear to grasp that since late February their man's correspondence had been written by a different hand. It was all part of a high-stakes game: who was fooling whom?

A double agent was an obvious boon to the intelligence service. There was less chance of a slip-up if the spy himself made contact with his controllers. It was a dicey business, though, and it was not always certain where loyalties lay. Robert Rosenthal offered to switch his allegiance when he was uncovered in 1915, but the authorities were unconvinced and he met his death in July that year. There were doubts over any such offer made in extremis, or when the highest bidder secured an individual's services. One whom British intelligence did place faith in, and reaped the rewards for doing so, operated under the codename Como. He supplied the Germans with copious amounts of disinformation, and was even asked by his supposed employers to investigate

the whereabouts of other German agents with whom contact had ceased. A number of fifth columnists, once in the country, chose neither to work for the Fatherland nor render their services to the other side.

The recruitment of Harish Chandra as a double agent provided evidence of Germany's attempts to use agitation and subversion as a means of undermining the enemy. India was viewed in Berlin as fertile ground for an insurrectionary harvest. A jihad, as called for by Ottoman Turkey, would have been disastrous for Britain, whose army contained a significant number of Indian Muslims. Chandra was part of a revolutionary movement, attempting to subvert the loyalty of Indian POWs held in Germany when he was arrested in October 1915 and persuaded to switch sides. Information he supplied confirmed that there was little support for the kind of holy war Germany sought to foment. A 1916 report on the situation advised that Britain should not discourage such efforts for they consumed German resources with no prospect of achieving their objective. The failure to stir anti-Raj resentment did not prevent Berlin from offering support to any uprising that might destabilise an enemy state, from Irish Republicanism to Russian revolutionaries. MI5, for its part, kept a close eye on any potential enemy within. The anti-conscription movement and pacifists were closely monitored, as were left-wing activists. Attempts to spread sedition fell on stony ground.

Probably the most famous espionage agent of the period was exotic dancer Mata Hari, the stage name of Margarethe Zelle. Dutch by birth, she cast herself as having Oriental blood on the strength of a period living in Java during a short-lived marriage, lending mystique to her risqué theatrical performance. She had a string of lovers, dispensing her favours to high-ranking French and German officials. Mata Hari appeared on MI5's radar, suspected of being in the pay of the Germans, but after being questioned on two separate occasions there was deemed insufficient evidence to act. The French, it seemed, sought to capitalise on her connections with the enemy, only to then suspect that she was working as a double agent. Some accounts have her attending the German spy school in Antwerp. Hard facts are few, but what is certain is that Mata Hari's luck ran out in Paris in February 1917. The French intelligence authorities arrested her and extracted a confession, which ultimately led to a firing squad in October that year. Rejecting the proffered blindfold, she blew a kiss to her executioners. *The Times* report of her death said "she was proved to have communicated important information" to the enemy. A British official who examined her file after the sentence was carried out was not so sure. Lieutenant Colonel Pakenham concluded that her espionage activities, like her stage act, traded heavily on fantasy. He believed Mata Hari revelled in the role of femme fatale, courting both sides but providing little of substance to either. The evidence against her was certainly flimsy, and it has even been suggested that the French used this headline-grabbing trial to take the spotlight off worrying news from the battle front, where the failed Nivelle Offensive brought mutiny to the ranks. It seems the best known spy of the era, a woman whose name has become synonymous with espionage and intrigue, peddled low-grade intelligence at best, for which she paid with her life.

Lieutenant Colonel Pakenham believed Mata Hari revelled in the role of femme fatale, courting both sides but providing little of substance to either.

Fallen cricketer's name lives on in literature

The battlefields of World War One are strewn with the remains of those who might have achieved greatness in every conceivable field of endeavour. One member of that lost generation was cricketer Percy Jeeves, whose name might have raised few flickers of recognition beyond familial ties and *Wisden* aficionados had he not been immortalised by a literary giant.

Percy Jeeves' roots were in Yorkshire, but it was in the Midlands where he carved his reputation on the green sward with bat and ball. Spotted by a Warwickshire club official holidaying in the Dales, Jeeves signed for the county after impressing in trials in spring 1912. He had just two seasons in the first class game – 50 matches in total – but in that time emerged as a bright England prospect. In May 1913 his sharp medium pace brought him eight Leicestershire wickets, including three in five balls without a run being scored. He notched an aggregate 69 runs in the same match, proving his worth as a more than useful lower order batsman. That month he also claimed the prize wicket of Surrey's Jack Hobbs, the country's foremost batsman known simply as "The Master". He ended the season as Warwickshire's top wicket-taker with 106, taken at barely 20 runs apiece. Only a handful of men in the county game took more wickets at a lower cost that year.

When war broke out, Percy Jeeves swapped cricket whites for khaki, joining a pals' battalion that became the 15th Royal Warwickshires. His Western Front service began in November 1915 and ended eight months later at the Somme, during a night raid on High Wood on 22 July. Defence was particularly favoured here, a fact underlined by the severe casualties sustained by the Royal Warwickshires and the 1st Royal West Kents, who also played a prominent role in the attack. Exactly what befell 28-year-old Percy Jeeves that night is unknown. His body was never recovered, but his name is recorded for posterity at Thiepval, and also lives on in the pages of one of P G Wodehouse's greatest comic creations. Wodehouse, a cricket enthusiast, had seen Jeeves in action and, as well as being taken with his prowess on the field, thought the Warwickshire all-rounder's name perfect for the character of his gentleman's gentleman, the eloquent, ever-resourceful manservant to foppish, upper-crust Bertie Wooster. Reginald Jeeves made his first appearance shortly before Percy's death, but over the following decades it was the ingenious valet who most readily sprang to mind at the mention of that surname, while the fine sportsman who inspired his creator became something of a forgotten hero. In 1919 *The Times* recorded that Warwickshire was "one of the most unfortunate counties" in terms of the talent it had lost to the battlefield. That was in no small part down to the absence of Percy Jeeves from the postwar side.

Opposite above left: Carl Hans Lody was executed by firing squad at the Tower of London soon after the war began.

Opposite below left: A British intelligence sergeant examines a civilian's papers.

Opposite below right: Mata Hari was arrested in February 1917 and accused of spying for Germany and causing the deaths of at least 50,000 soldiers. After being found guilty, she was executed by firing squad in October that year.

Right: Percy Jeeves played 50 matches for Warwickshire before joining up in 1914.

Below: Convalescing soldiers watch a ladies cricket match at Hurlingham in July 1917.

The Warwickshire all-rounder's name was perfect for the character of his gentleman's gentleman, the eloquent, ever-resourceful manservant to foppish, upper-crust Bertie Wooster.

THE DAILY MAIL, THURSDAY, FEBRUARY 24, 1916.

HUGE GERMAN ATTEMPT TO BREAK IN NEAR THE FORTRESS OF VERDUN.

LATE WAR NEWS.   THE ONLY PEACE.   MOEWE AGAIN.   Mrs. LYTTELTON'S   HEAVY SNOW THIS   LORD DERBY'S
GREAT BATTLE RAGING NEAR   MR. ASQUITH EXPOSES   ENGLISH PRIZE SENT TO   GERMAN MAID.   MORNING.   TASKS.

Battle of Verdun

Over Christmas 1915 Germany's Chief of General Staff Erich von Falkenhayn weighed his options for the new year. Where was the Allies' weak point? Russia, certainly; but on the Eastern Front he hoped political instability might do his work for him. If Russia was torn apart by internal strife, it would save him from having to strike eastwards, with all the resource implications that such a campaign would entail. For now Falkenhayn hoped his Austrian ally could hold the line while he looked elsewhere for a breakthrough. Italy was briefly considered as a target but quickly dismissed; overcoming such a junior partner among the Allies could not influence the outcome. That left Britain and France, and the latter, he was convinced, was the more vulnerable. While Britain was strengthening under "Kitchener's Army" of recruits, France was reeling from heavy losses sustained in 1915. Approaching "breaking point", as he put it in a December letter to the Kaiser. And yet the events of the past year had shown that in trench warfare it was easier to defend than attack, even for beleaguered French troops. Thus he would not feed wave upon wave of German infantry into the gun-sights of the enemy. Instead he would launch an onslaught on a carefully chosen French position; one that had no great military significance but possessed such powerful historical and cultural resonance that France would defend it to the last drop of blood. Such a place was Verdun.

Verdun stripped of defences

Situated some 140 miles east of Paris on the banks of the River Meuse, Verdun was a garrison town surrounded by a ring of hill-fortresses, 21 in total. Its natural defences were such that France's Commander-in-Chief, Joseph Joffre, had deemed an attack extremely unlikely; so unlikely that hundreds of guns had been removed for deployment in parts of the field where the need was more urgent. Dissenting voices were ignored. The decision to strip Verdun of most of its armaments gained credibility after the fall of Liège and Namur, fortress towns that had fallen to the German army alarmingly swiftly in the march through Belgium. Such defences, some argued, were ineffective in the face of modern artillery.

Opposite top left: **Fort Douaumont, the largest of Verdun's famous fortresses, fell to the Germans almost instantly. This famous landmark was manned by a skeleton force of 56 elderly gunners who could offer no meaningful defence.**

Opposite top middle: **The damage caused to Verdun after the initial bombardment. On the right, the medieval towers of the Port Chausée built in 1380, still stand proudly protecting the city.**

Opposite top right: **The Germans launched their first attack on 21 February, bombarding the French soldiers with 140,000 troops and 1,200 artillery guns with a further 168 planes on hand. In contrast the Allies only had 30,000 men in position. The German guns stretched along an eight-mile line and within four days rapidly captured 10,000 French prisoners.**

Opposite below left: **French grenade throwers at work in the trenches.**

Opposite below middle: **Kaiser Wilhelm and his son Wilhelm, the Crown Prince (right), meet German troops at the start of the Verdun offensive. The attack was part of a plan devised by the German Chief-of-Staff Erich von Falkenhayn who wanted to "bleed France white" by launching an attack on the Verdun area.**

Opposite below right: **Wire frames protect the troops in the trenches from grenade attacks.**

Below: **Brown stars on a map of the Verdun region mark the location of some of the forts surrounding the city.**

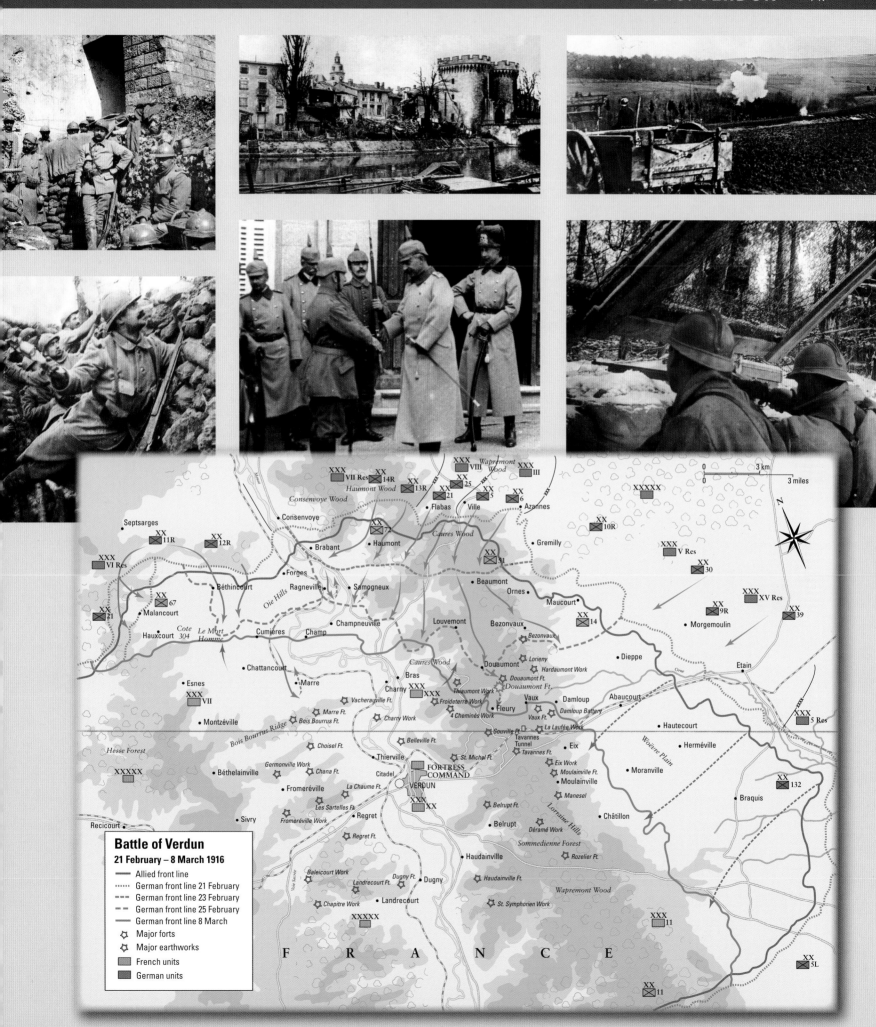

Battle of Verdun
21 February – 8 March 1916

—— Allied front line
········· German front line 21 February
- - - German front line 23 February
– – German front line 25 February
—— German front line 8 March
✧ Major forts
✧ Major earthworks
French units
German units

Operation "Judgement"

Falkenhayn knew nothing of the firepower he would face at Verdun. Nor would it have signified much, for his objective was not to win a great victory and hoist the German flag in the town centre. His game was to attack without reaching the goal. To inflict casualties, drain resources, weaken resolve. France could be brought to her knees over Verdun, and if that was achieved it was merely a matter of time before Britain was crushed.

Operation Gericht – "Judgement" – was launched on 21 February 1916. Bad weather had caused a week's delay, and belatedly Verdun was reinforced as Joffre realised an attack was imminent. Over 1,000 guns – including 420mm "Big Berthas" – pounded an eight-mile stretch of the French line, which was soon on the retreat. German infantry followed up, flamethrowers becoming part of the battlefield lexicon. Fort Douaumont, the most famous bastion in Verdun's defensive ring, was taken with ease on 25 February. The indignity staring France's leaders in the face called for prompt action. The loss of the town, as Falkenhayn had anticipated, was unthinkable, and to forestall that eventuality Joffre turned to General Philippe Pétain, a strategist whose star had risen dramatically since the war's beginning. "Ils ne passeront pas" was his watchword: "They shall not pass".

The very appointment of 60-year-old Pétain – a man whose reputation as a master of the defensive preceded him – had a marked effect on the spirits of the French troops. Pétain resolved to launch a counter-offensive and retake lost ground. He also recognised that maintaining a supply line to Verdun was crucial, and the order went out to keep the road south to Bar le Duc serviceable for the stream of trucks that used it night and day. This vital artery – "La Voie Sacrée" or "Sacred Way", as it became known – provided Pétain with the tools to strike back.

More German infantry for renewed offensive

As the French artillery opened up, Falkenhayn's plan began to go awry. From the outset there had been a communication problem with Crown Prince Wilhelm, the Kaiser's son who commanded the 5th Army. "Little Willie" did not seem to appreciate the subtlety of the scheme: to attack without pressing home the advantage. Now, in the light of French retaliation, he wanted to mount an assault on a much wider front as a means of taking Verdun, which he considered a great prize. France's losses thus far had been significantly greater than Germany's – Falkenhayn's plan had been working. Yet to the outside world, and even to his own general, it appeared that a siege had been rebuffed, a symbolic outpost gloriously saved. The architect redrew his plan. More German infantry were thrown into the fray in a renewed offensive, this time on both sides of the Meuse: the very antithesis of the original conceit. The casualty figures edged towards parity.

Below left: French soldiers send information by wireless to headquarters. After Marconi's work at the beginning of the century, ground forces frequently used wireless telegraphy during the conflict, although it was perilous work.

Bottom left: French soldiers had precious little rest in 1916. As continual reinforcements were needed,

a total of 259 out of the 330 infantry regiments in France were brought to fight at Verdun. However, as Crown Prince Wilhelm, in charge of the 5th Army, renewed his attacks on the French troops, Pétain was able to organise counter-attacks to slow down the German advance.

Below: French troops defend their position. For the first time the German soldiers used

flamethrowers to help them advance the eight miles they needed to capture Verdun. These incendiary devices emitted a jet of flames that could stretch for 20 yards and enormous clouds of smoke.

Opposite: French troops under shellfire during the Battle.

Allies relieve the pressure

Following the promotion of Pétain, General Robert Nivelle took over as Verdun's defender, another commander with steely resolve and a glowing reputation. He couldn't prevent the fall of Fort Vaux, but in the summer Germany wavered in its intent and the offensive stalled. The Russian steamroller cut a swathe through Galicia, leading Falkenhayn to deploy forces eastwards. Then, in the last week of June the British bombardment that was the prelude to the "Big Push" on the Somme began. France's long-awaited wish for her allies to strike and relieve the pressure on Verdun had been realised. The crisis point had passed, and as the Somme became the focal point of Western-Front action in the second half of the year, the battle wound down with Forts Douaumont and Vaux back in French hands. Verdun had been held at enormous cost, French casualties estimated at 400,000. Unusually, the losses of the attacking army were smaller, but not significantly so.

Falkenhayn paid the inevitable price for failure, sacked long before the battle ground to a halt. It has been suggested that his original intention may indeed have been to capture Verdun, the whole idea that it was a scheme to break the will of the French superimposed at a later date to gloss over events that patently did not go his or Germany's way. No documentation pre-dating the battle supports the stated aims outlined years later in Falkenhayn's memoirs. Those recollections may be an accurate reflection of his thinking during the Christmas 1915 period. They may not. Whether the objective was territorial gain or to "bleed France white", neither was achieved.

VIOLENT FIGHTING FOR VERDUN.

FORGES VILLAGE ENTERED BY GERMANS.

ENEMY REPULSE AT GOOSE HILL.

LIQUID FIRE ATTACK IN CHAMPAGNE.

16th DAY of VERDUN BATTLE.

The enemy has been unable to advance at the key position of Douaumont (4½ miles from Verdun), but there has been heavy infantry fighting to the west of the Meuse, where the Germans succeeded in entering the village of Forges. From Goose Hill they were repulsed.

The Germans have up to date engaged about twenty divisions, or 300,000 men, in the assaults. They have suffered losses which Lord Northcliffe estimates at 100,000, and have expended an immense quantity of ammunition without even producing any psychological result. Such an unsuccessful assault on a formidable position will not procure the right "atmosphere" for floating their new loan. They must therefore fight on and continue their efforts to reach Verdun.

The extension of the battle is to be expected as the enemy's total force on the French front is estimated at 118 divisions, or 1,800,000 men. It is just possible that this tremendous blow at Verdun is intended to attract the French reserves there and open a path for a terrific German attack elsewhere. If so, the strategy has failed. Nothing can prevent the enemy from concentrating an enormous number of heavy guns against some point of the French line and then suddenly opening a crushing fire. But as this plan has been tried so far without result at Verdun, it is not likely to succeed elsewhere.

If the Germans persist in such attacks,

LATE WAR NEWS.

FRENCH OFFICIAL.

PARIS, Monday, 11 p.m.

In Champagne the Germans launched an attack accompanied by jets of liquid fire upon our positions between Mont Tetu and Maisons de Champagne.

On our right the enemy, stopped by our curtain fire, was not able to leave his trenches. On the left, in the vicinity of Maisons de Champagne, he succeeded in penetrating into a small advanced work.

In the Argonne we exploded in the region of Courtes Chausses a mine which destroyed a German post and caused an enormous crater, of which we are organising the southern lip.

Between the Haute Chevauchée and Hill 285, after having exploded two mines, the enemy, following up the explosion, gained a footing at some points in our first line. A fight ensued, in the course of which we ejected the enemy from our trench and we captured one side of the crater. Our artillery has been very active in all parts of this sector.

West of the Meuse, after a violent bombardment which lasted all the morning on the front between Béthincourt and the Meuse, the Germans launched a strong attack against Forges, situated on our advanced line. During a very violent encounter they succeeded in carrying the village. Several attempts to debouch upon the Goose Hill were stopped short by our counter-attacks, which drove back the enemy into Forges.

To the east of the Meuse there was inter-

IRON STAND BY FRENCH AGAINST NEW GERMAN ONSLAUGHT.

GREAT FRENCH RESISTANCE.

GERMAN MASS ASSAULTS ON VERDUN HEIGHTS.

DOUAUMONT VILLAGE ENTERED AFTER GREAT LOSSES.

FRENCH REGAIN

BATTLE FOR KEY POSITION.

FRENCH BAYONETS TELL.

4 GERMAN ONSLAUGHTS.

FURIOUS STRUGGLE IN THE VILLAGE.

FROM OUR OWN CORRESPONDENT.
Paris, Friday.

attack, pushed well home with cold steel, drove the Germans helter-skelter back to Les Chambrettes and the Haudromont ravines.

Smarting under their repeated checks, the Germans resumed their shattering artillery fire, ploughing up the ground in all directions and reducing the rocks to powder with thousands of monster shells. Dusk had fallen when, on an order from the Crown Prince, a fourth advance was made against the sadly battered plateau of Douaumont. The troops who had been fighting all day had been withdrawn, and it was fresh Prussian brigades which now must into action.

SEAPLANE RAIDER WRECKED.

BABY-KILLERS' FATE.

1 OBSERVER DROWNED, THE OTHER CAPTURED.

ADMIRALTY, Friday.

V.C.'s SACRIFICE.

BODY THROWN ON LIVE BOMB.

COMRADES' LIVES SAVED.

FIGHT OF THE CLAN MACTAVISH

FIRST FULL ACCOUNT

CAPTAIN'S "BLUFF"

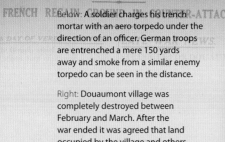

Below: A soldier charges his trench mortar with an aero torpedo under the direction of an officer. German troops are entrenched a mere 150 yards away and smoke from a similar enemy torpedo can be seen in the distance.

Right: Douaumont village was completely destroyed between February and March. After the war ended it was agreed that land occupied by the village and others similarly obliterated, would not be adopted by another commune, but remain preserved as villages "that had died for France".

Opposite above right: A striking image of a ravine on the Meuse heights in March 1916 shows the destruction wrought by tons of high explosives hurled at the French positions, honeycombing the ground with shell-holes.

Opposite bottom and opposite above left: French infantrymen on duty in trenches. The Germans continued their slow advance and captured Le Mort Homme Hill (Dead Man's Hill) on 29 May.

The greatest battle

DAILY MAIL   FEBRUARY 29, 1916

"The greatest battle of the greatest war" – for so the Germans already describe it – sways to and fro on the hills north of Verdun and seems steadily to extend. The Germans are attacking in enormous force and with the utmost fury. The incomparable French are maintaining the defence with that tenacious coolness and readiness to riposte which distinguish their modern army. There is as yet no sign of any decision and there is a good deal to suggest that the conflict is only in its first stage.

It has been suggested that the Germans are mad in attacking at one of the strongest points of the French line. The German staff, however, has every reason to be anxious to impress neutrals whose decision is believed to hang in the balance by dealing a terrific blow at the French. It has always held that any fortress and any position can be taken provided the necessary sacrifices are made.

The preliminary methods have been the same at Verdun as against the Russians on the Dunajetz – but with this immense difference, that at Verdun the French are well prepared, have numerous lines of defence behind their advanced positions, and are abundantly munitioned. Their most dangerous difficulties are that some new form of attack may be attempted by the enemy, whether by aircraft or by gas. The German bombardment is described as being of a fury which has never been approached before. That gives some measure of its violence. In the culminating point of Mackensen's assault on the Dunajetz 700,000 shells were discharged by the enemy in four hours, while, in addition, many new and devilish devices were employed in the shape of liquid fire, asphyxiating gas, and aircraft dropping asphyxiating bombs. The artillery fire in the present battle, we are told, is changing the very appearance of the country. But the monster guns are not this time all on Germany's side; the French are well equipped with rivals of the monster 17in. Kruppe.

Fort Douaumont lost

Fort Douaumont was a key plank in the defensive ring surrounding Verdun. Erected on a site well over 1,000 feet high, it held a commanding position, and concrete-reinforced walls posed a formidable obstacle to any would-be assailant. The fort had been strengthened in the 1880s, in the wake of defeat in the Franco-Prussian War. Douaumont was the jewel in the defensive crown, meant to secure the area from future attack. Fully manned, it accommodated over 600 soldiers, but by the time the German assault on Verdun was launched a skeleton garrison of only one-tenth that number occupied the fort. The fall of Belgium's fortress towns had cast doubts over their effectiveness in halting the enemy. Modern explosives, it was thought, rendered them redundant. That loss of faith was reflected in the removal of most of Douaumont's big guns as well as its manpower. German forces took possession on 25 February, a mere four days after the opening salvo. That they did so with relative ease struck a crushing psychological as well as military blow to a people for whom Fort Douaumont was a symbol of resistance, a structure invested with enormous national pride.

March 1916

1 Germany began an extended submarine campaign using a strategy of trying to lure the British Royal Navy's Grand Fleet into U-boat traps.

2 Russian forces captured Bitlis from the Turks in Armenia.

4 The German raider SMS *Möewe* returned to a heroes welcome in Bremen, Germany following a series of successful attacks on British ships in the Atlantic.

5 A combined British-South African Colonial force began an offensive towards Mount Kilimanjaro in East Africa.

7 Newton Diehl Baker was appointed US Secretary of State.

8 Another British attempt to relieve the besieged force at Kut-al-Amara was defeated on the Dujaila Redoubt.

9 The Fifth Battle of the Isonzo began when the Italians launched another offensive on the Isonzo River.

The German Government declared war on Portugal over the seizure of German ships in Lisbon.

10 British forces captured Taveta in East Africa.

11 The Battle for Latema Nek began in the Latema-Reata between Germany and British-South African forces in British East Africa.

12 The action at Latema Nek ended with an Allied victory.

An Allied conference at Chantilly discussed the forthcoming summer offensive on the Somme.

13 New Moshi in East Africa was occupied by British forces.

14 British forces reoccupied Sollum on the Egyptian coast.

15 Austria-Hungary followed Germany and declared war on Portugal.

16 General Pierre Auguste Roques succeeded Joseph Gallieni as French Minister of War.

At the Battle of Verdun the Germans successive attacks on Vaux were repulsed.

18 The Lake Naroch Offensive began when Russian forces attacked the Germans at Lake Naroch on the Eastern Front.

20 French politician Baron Denys Cochin was appointed Under-Secretary of State for foreign policy matters responsible for dealing with the blockade of Germany.

21 German forces retreated from the Kilimanjaro area after they were defeated at Nahe.

22 Yuan Shikai formally abandoned monarchism and relinquished the throne of China.

24 The passenger ship SS *Sussex* was torpedoed by a German U-boat in the English Channel.

26 Russian forces continued the attack at Lake Naroch without success.

27 Russian commanders suspended their offensive at Lake Naroch.

28 An Inter-Allied conference in Paris resulted in a declaration of unity on military, economic and diplomatic affairs between Belgium, France, Great Britain, Italy, Japan, Portugal, Russia and Serbia.

29 General Alexei Andreyevich Polivanov resigned as Russian War Minister and was succeeded by General Dmitry Savelich Shuvaev.

30 The Russian hospital ship *Portugal* was sunk by a torpedo from the German submarine *U-33* in the Black Sea.

31 A German airship raid targeted the East coast of England; the Zeppelin was subsequently shot down by gunfire in the Thames Estuary.

W GERMAN ASSAULT WITH 28,000 MEN BEFORE VERDUN.

| RECRUITING CRISIS. | FRENCH AIR ATTACKS. | THE COMMAND OF THE SEA. | U-BOAT CAPTURED. | GEN. TOWNSHEND TO THE KING. | TRICK ELECTION. |

HEAVAL IN THE CABINET.

VENTS OF YESTERDAY.

NS, BUT ANYTHING MAY HAPPEN TO-DAY.

WAR.
VERDUN.
KUT.
RRESPONDENT

TO-DAY'S STATEMENT.

QUESTIONS IN THE HOUSE.

OR PARLIAMENTARY REPRESENTATIVE
or Commons, M
s, by raise

FRENCH AIR ATTACKS.

HITS ON A GERMAN SHIP.

NEW VERDUN ASSAULT.

SMALL ENEMY GAIN AT GREAT COST.

FRENCH OFFICIAL

PARIS, Monday Afternoon.

Last night one of our air squadrons of nine machines, despite a heavy mist, carried out important bombing operations. Twelve bombs were dropped on Conflans way station, 16 on factories at Rom
s on Arnaville railway station, and
the railway at Pagny and Aza-sur-

THE COMMAND OF THE SEA.

3 MORE SHIPS SUNK.

Three ships were reported sunk yesterday, one British and two Norwegian. The vessels are:

Harrovian, 4,309 tons, British, owned by Messrs. J. Mathias and Sons, managing owners for the Cambrian Steam Navigation Co., Ltd. She was unarmed. The captain and seventeen of the crew have been landed, but the remainder of the crew in another boat are not yet accounted for.

Glendon, 1,917 tons, Norwegian, sunk by gunfire.

Papelera, Norwegian, 1,591 tons. Crew rescued by another Norwegian steamer.

Captain Selley and the crew of twenty-four men of the Cardonia, torpedoed on Sunday, were landed yesterday. The men, who were given very little time to escape, took to the boats and were picked up by a
steamer.

RULE THE NAVY.

U-BOAT CAPTURED.

OFFICER AND CREW THAT SANK THE SUSSEX.

PRESIDENT WILSON'S FINAL WORD.

HIS FOOT DOWN.

The French have captured the submarine, her commander and crew which torpedoed the Sussex. The capture was made off Havre on April 5.

Documentary evidence has been obtained of the crime.

. The above throws a strange light on the German Note to the United States explaining that the commander sketched the vessel he sank, which he was certain was a minelayer of the Arabis class.

From SYDNEY BROOKS.

New York, Monday.

The United States has survived so
may crises that the present one finds the
the country recovered by

GEN. TOWNSHEND TO THE KING.

"OUR SHEET-ANCHOR."

Mr. Malcolm asked the Prime Minister in Parliament yesterday if he would communicate General Townshend's reply to the King's telegram of admiration of his defence of Kut.

Mr. Asquith said the King had permitted him to communicate the following telegram from Sir Percy Lake:—

February 17, 1916.

General Townshend has asked me to request you to make the following communication to the King-Emperor:—

It is hard for me to express by words how profoundly touched and inspirited all ranks of my command have been by his Majesty's personal message. On their behalf and my own I desire to express to his Majesty that the experience and knowledge we have gained of his sympathy will be our sheet-anchor in this defence.

(Cheers.)

[It is worthy of note that the King's telegram to General Townshend, dated February 14, was not given to the public till April 1 and General Townshend's reply yesterday, two months after it was despatched.]

THE BAGHDAD ORDER.

TRICK ELECTION.

THE DUMMY GUN AND "WAIT AND SEE."

MR. KENNEDY JONES'S PROTEST.

WIMBLEDON TO-MORROW.

If the Coalition politicians do not accept the theory that to win a war it is necessary to concentrate superior forces at the decisive point, they practise it when there is an election to be won.

In Wimbledon, which polls to-morrow, Mr. Kennedy Jones's vigorous attack becomes daily more menacing. The Coalition has massed all its reserves of men and munitions. Hundreds of professional speakers belonging to the two party organisations have been hurried to the constituency, and yesterday they were at every cross-road denouncing the Independent candidate for inflicting on the electorate the trouble and turmoil of a contested election.

The humorous side of this chorus of denunciation is that the party truce has been making lean times for professional political speakers. So Mr. Kennedy Jones in compelling Sir Stuart Coats and the Coalition to a contest has been a friend in need to the hordes of Coalition orators.

THREE DAYS' CLASH.

GERMANS GAIN AND LOSE SECOND LINE.

A TERRIBLE FIELD.

ONLY 300 YARDS' ADVANCE.

From W. L. McALPIN.

PARIS, Monday.

Since Friday morning twelve score German heavy guns have been battering the French positions west and north of Dead Man Hill, and Cumières, to the east of the hill. Having succeeded in making an advance on the west and north, the enemy batteries of 6in. and 8in. guns are now hurling their 100lb. shells at Cumières and the southern slopes of Dead Man Hill.

The position on Friday—the 89th day of the battle of Verdun—when the Germans initiated this latest attack, may for the sake of convenience be divided into three main sectors: that of Avocourt to Hill 304 on the west, that of Dead Man Hill and Cumières in the centre, and from Haudromont to Vaux on the east. Each of these sectors measures roughly three miles in length, and they have all been the scene of the most terrible carnage since Saturday morning.

The result may be summed up thus: In the Avocourt sector the French, after withstanding the German onslaught on Saturday, counter-attacked with desperate violence yesterday morning and drove the Germans back at several points. In the central sector the Germans on Saturday secured a footing on Dead Man Hill, on whose summit stood the cross which gave this eminence its sinister name.

FRENCH DASH AT VERDUN.

240 PRISONERS IN A SURPRISE RAID.

French Official.   PARIS, Thurs., 11 p.m.

In the Argonne we cannonaded the enemy's communication roads and the Malancourt Wood.

West of the Meuse there was great artillery activity at Hill 304 and at Avocourt. Launching an attack in the Dead Man region, we chased the enemy from those parts of trench occupied by him on April 10.

East of the Meuse a violent bombardment at Douaumont and Vaux; some artillery in the Woevre.

On the rest of the front the day was calm.
3 p.m.

Throughout the night our second line on the left bank of the Meuse was bombarded.

Towards the end of the day our troops sharply attacked the German positions north-west of the pond at Vaux (right of the Meuse and north-east of Verdun). We occupied some sections of trench from which we ejected the enemy, and we also seized a fortified redoubt.

We inflicted serious losses on the enemy and took prisoners 10 officers, 16 non-commissioned officers, and 214 men, also capturing several machine guns and a quantity of material.

German Official.   Thursday.

To the east of Tracy le Mont a quantity of gas directed by the enemy last night against our trenches only spread in the trenches of the French themselves.

In the Meuse sector the enemy directed lively artillery fire against the positions we captured from him on the eastern bank of the river. In the Caillette Wood (south-east of Douaumont) the enemy's preparatory artillery fire developed towards the evening into a stormy attack. In a salient corner the attack reached into our trenches; otherwise it was repulsed with heavy sanguinary losses to the French. A few prisoners were also taken.

In the Woevre plain and on the hill to the south-east of Verdun the artillery battle is being continued with the greatest violence on both sides. There was no infantry activity.—Wireless Press.

Defending Fort Vaux

Erich von Falkenhayn, Germany's supreme commander and architect of the Verdun attack, reasoned that the French would go to any lengths to defend that historic city. The aim was not conquest but to consume French manpower in such numbers that capitulation would follow; Britain's "best sword" would be knocked from her hand. Though the plan foundered, the dogged defence of Fort Vaux demonstrated that the underlying logic was sound. Situated on the northeastern side of Verdun, not far from Douaumont, Fort Vaux was subjected to a massive bombardment on 1 June, up to 2,000 shells an hour raining upon its edifice. Major Raynal's garrison put up heroic resistance as the fighting moved to the fort's corridors and galleries. They faced flamethrowers and gas as well as the usual range of weaponry. Carrier pigeons bore desperate messages requesting assistance until they, along with the rest of the garrison's supplies, ran out. Surrender came on 7 June, when the men had been reduced to licking moisture from the walls and drinking their own urine.

Right: A German soldier operates a trench periscope. After French troops surrendered Fort Vaux the Crown Prince congratulated fort commander Major Raynal for his determined efforts and presented him with his own sword as a mark of honour.

Below: Troops press a heavy howitzer into action.

Opposite: In October the French launched their first offensive. Fort Douaumont was eventually re-captured and the following month Fort Vaux successfully taken after it was evacuated by the German Army.

LAST SHOT FIRED IN DUBLIN ON 8th DAY OF RISING.

'DUBLIN AT LAST SAFE.

REBELS ALL YIELD AND PRISONERS SENT TO ENGLAND.

ENNISCORTHY GIVES IN AFTER AN ATTEMPT TO PARLEY.

ROUND-UP IN THE COUNTRY.

From FIELD-MARSHAL VISCOUNT FRENCH,
Commanding-in-Chief, Home Forces.
Monday, 7 p.m.

All rebels in Dublin have surrendered and the city is reported to be quite safe.

Rebels in country districts are surrendering to mobile columns. There were 1,000 prisoners in Dublin yesterday, of whom 489 were sent to England last night.

It is reported from Queenstown that hopes were entertained that arms would be handed in to-day in the city of Cork.

During Sunday night the rebels at Enniscorthy (Wexford, in the south-east) made an offer to surrender their leaders and arms on condition that the rank and file were allowed to return to their homes. They were informed that the only terms that could be entertained were unconditional, and these terms were accepted by them at 6 a.m. It has been reported at a later date that the rebels are now surrendering to-day on these terms.

A column composed of soldiers and Royal Irish Constabulary captured seven prisoners in the neighbourhood of Ferns (north of Enniscorthy) to-day.

Wicklow, Arklow, Dunlavin, Bagenalstown, Wexford, New Ross, Counties Cork, Clare, Limerick, and Kerry are generally quiet. The whole of Ulster is reported quiet.

Monday, 1 p.m.

LATE WAR NEWS.

THE LAST SHOT.

SCORES OF DEAD IN DUBLIN P.O.

TOTTERING WALL PANIC.

CONSCIENCE-STRICKEN LOOTER.

BY OUR SPECIAL CORRESPONDENT,
Attached to Mr. Birrell's Party.
BY STEAMER AND TELEPHONE.
DUBLIN, Monday Night.

There was a slight engagement with the rebels in a house this morning near Westland-row. They called themselves the "Die hards," and offered a stubborn resistance, but were soon overcome.

One or two snipers were busy in the city up till noon, but the last shot was fired about 3 p.m., when a persistent rebel on the roof of a house near the docks was killed by some soldier marksmen who had been watching him for several hours.

Large crowds paraded Sackville-street to-day to see the ruins, which are still smouldering.

This morning there was a panic among the considerable crowd inside the General Post Office because a large wall threatened to fall. Several people were injured in the rush to get out.

SCORES OF DEAD IN P.O.

Scores of dead bodies of rebels lie in the ruined building and late this afternoon numerous of the horses that were killed

20th BIRTHDAY
OF
"The Daily Mail."

SPECIAL NUMBER
ON
THURSDAY, MAY 4,
CONTAINING THE
Story of 'The Daily Mail'
BY
LORD NORTHCLIFFE.

As there will be a great demand for this Special Number, an order should be given at once to a Newsagent.

FIGHT WITH U BOAT.

BRITISH COLLIER'S PLUCKY CREW.

News has been received in South Shields of a fight in the North Sea between the British collier Wandle (559 tons), armed for defence, and a German submarine.

RUSSIAN PUSH N.E. OF BAGHDAD.

TURKS THROWN BACK & GUNS CAPTURED.

RUSSIAN OFFICIAL.
PETROGRAD, Monday.

Towards Diarbekir (Upper Tigris) our Cossacks energetically drove back the Turks westward.

In the direction of Baghdad we threw back westward an important enemy detachment and captured a portion of his artillery and a number of ammunition wagons.—Reuter.

[The Russians were recently reported to have reached a point about 100 miles north-east of Baghdad.]

NEXT BATTLE IN ARMENIA.
PARIS, Monday.

A message from Tiflis to the *Journal* states that after the fall of Trebizond the principal centre of operations has moved southwards.

TURKISH CHIVALRY.

GENERAL TOWNSHEND KEEPS HIS SWORD.

MONTH'S FRENCH AIR GAINS.

31 HUNS DOWN TO THEIR 6

"UNDOUBTED ADVANTAGE."

French Official.   PARIS, Monday Night.

Our guns in Belgium wrecked trenches opposite Steenstraate and Boesinghe. A mine duel at the Dead Girl (Argonne). We occupied the southern lip of a crater made by one of our mines.

DEAD MAN FAILURES.

GERMANS AGAIN SUFFER ENORMOUS LOSSES.

French Official.   PARIS, Mon. Aftn.

COMPULSION.

THE ONLY FAIR WAY

MR. ASQUITH'S DECISION TO-DAY.

GROUP MEN'S QUANDARY.

BY OUR POLITICAL CORRESPONDENT.

Mr. Asquith will explain to the House of Commons to-day how the Government propose to get out of the mess into which the House landed them last week.

SERVICE FOR ALL.

Opposite: In May, immediately after the rebellion, a series of courts martial was held with fifteen men sentenced to death including Patrick Pearse and Tom Clarke. They were shot over a ten-day period in the execution yard at Kilmainham Jail in Dublin.

Opposite right: Roger Casement (above) made an unsuccessful appeal against his conviction and death sentence. James Connolly (below) was executed by a British firing squad because of his leadership role in the Easter Rising of 1916.

Below: The Royal Naval gunboat HMY *Helga* bombarded Sackville Street during the uprising causing serious damage to several buildings. It was renamed O'Connell Street in 1924 after Daniel O'Connell, a prominent nationalist leader of the nineteenth century. His statue can be seen at the lower end of the street by O'Connell Bridge.

Easter Rising 1916

As the storm clouds of war gathered, it seemed that one battle, at least, had run its course. The issue of Irish Home Rule, which had loomed large on the British political landscape for decades, appeared finally to be resolved. A bill was passed in 1912, but subject to a delay at the behest of the House of Lords. It was the Upper Chamber that had brought down the previous Home Rule Bill, but the recent Parliament Act established the primacy of the Commons, and the dissenting voices in the Lords could now merely defer implementation, their power of veto ended. That delay had profound implications. Britain was now embroiled in a Continental conflict; Ireland would have to wait for its limited measure of self-government to be enacted.

Unionists, in their Ulster stronghold, were violently opposed to the proposed change of constitutional status. With "Home Rule is Rome Rule" as their watchword, the Ulster Volunteer Force formed in 1913 to resist the imposition of the reviled legislation, by armed means if necessary. Westminster politicians thought this was the likely trouble spot, but there was discontent, too, in nationalist circles. Irish Parliamentary Party leader John Redmond was sanguine enough about the delay, for the principle of autonomy had been established, its enshrinement in law guaranteed. As the British army mobilised, Redmond pledged the support of the Irish Volunteers, a pro-Home Rule militia formed to counter the UVF threat. To Redmond and most of his supporters, Germany was the common enemy, Belgium a small Catholic country in an hour of need. The Volunteers signed up in droves to fight alongside loyalist Ulster regiments whose allegiance to the Crown was a given. But not all. To some nationalists among the Irish Volunteers, taking up arms in support of King and Country was too much to swallow. If this was the quid pro quo for Home Rule, it was a deal that could not be tolerated. In any event, Home Rule fell short of full independence; Ireland would still have to defer to Westminster in a number of areas. Far from marching to war to liberate faraway lands, this disaffected group of ardent separatists thought it the perfect time to strike a blow for Irish freedom. As the saying went: England's difficulty is Ireland's opportunity.

An enemy's enemy

The group rallied under Tom Clarke, who had spent over a decade in British jails for bomb outrages on the mainland. At Clarke's Dublin tobacconist's shop, he and a cadre of like-minded individuals – among them Patrick Pearse and Sean MacDermott – thrashed out a plan to liberate their country. They were joined by James Connolly, a left-wing radical and trade union leader who had formed his own Citizen Army. Connolly was bent on advancing the cause of independence as part of a grand design for establishing a workers' republic. Their plan involved seizing a number of strategic positions around the city, from which they could repel the inevitable retaliatory strike. The rebellion was set for Easter 1916.

A few days before the Easter Sunday operation was due to begin, a German submarine arrived off the coast of Co. Kerry. It carried Sir Roger Casement, former diplomat and fervent nationalist, who had acted as intermediary in seeking Berlin's help in the enterprise. He began his mission as soon as war was declared, and the early omens were positive. "If Ireland will do her duty, rest assured Germany will do hers towards us, our cause and our whole future," he wrote to nationalist colleagues in December 1914. There was talk of raising an Irish Brigade from POWs, perhaps fighting alongside sons of the Fatherland released from other duties. Whatever the German High Command knew of Irish history, it was clear that Britain had an insurrectionary element on its western frontier, a rebellion worth exploiting. In the case of an enemy's enemy, there was always room for fellowship.

Whatever the German High Command knew of Irish history, it was clear that Britain had an insurrectionary element on its western frontier.

DEATH SENTENCE ON CASEMENT.

UNMOVED PRISONER.

ANTI-ENGLAND TIRADE.

AN APPEAL.

At half-past four yesterday afternoon the jury in the High Court found Sir Roger Casement guilty of high treason, and he was sentenced to death by the Lord Chief Justice.

The scene was a solemn one. The prisoner stood up, tall and gaunt, by the rail of the dock, with a heavy roll of manuscript in his hands. Behind the three judges, with the bright sunlight playing on the vivid scarlet of their robes, stood three attendants, each with a black cap in his grasp. The Clerk called for silence, and at the announcement of Guilty from the foreman of the jury the three attendants placed three black caps upon the heads of the three judges—a triple act of gruesomeness which caused a shudder to run through the court.

The Lord Chief Justice sentenced the prisoner to be hanged. He made no speech. Slowly, and in commanding and resonant periods, he delivered the solemn phrases of death formed from time immemorial by the English law—that and no more. Sir Roger, still the courtly gentleman, entirely unruffled, bowed low to the stroke of the law and, with dragging footsteps, turned and disappeared behind the heavy green curtains. The historic trial was over at last. Between the pronouncement of the ver-

Insufficient German support

The plan suffered its first setback as a ship carrying an arms cache was intercepted by British warships. Casement, whose name was already known to British intelligence, was also soon in custody. Ironically, he had been disappointed with the level of German support and was on his way to urge abandonment of a scheme he thought doomed to fail. With the arrest of the man assumed to be the ringleader, the authorities adopted a relaxed view as the holiday weekend approached. The other Irish Volunteer conspirators on their radar could be arrested at leisure. The plotters, meanwhile, had a last-minute scare as the Volunteers' chief of staff Eoin MacNeill learned of the planned insurgency, which he was vehemently against. Caught between the desire to derail an uprising he thought to be pure folly and betraying his own, MacNeill placed an advertisement in the local Sunday newspaper instructing Volunteers not to participate in any action that day. A crisis meeting was held: it was decided that the operation would be launched 24 hours later, Easter Monday.

Reinforcements from the mainland

Occupation of the target sites around Dublin was successfully accomplished. The rebel leaders made for the General Post Office on O'Connell Street, from whose steps Patrick Pearse proclaimed the birth of the Irish Republic. "Ireland, through us, summons her children to her flag and strikes for her freedom," he declaimed, before helping man the barricades of rebel headquarters. There were some 2,500 British troops stationed in Dublin, and reinforcements were soon on the way from the mainland. In general, they were well received by the townsfolk; the rebels were on the receiving end of much hostile abuse from compatriots who thought their action ill-conceived. Dubliners who had family members fighting in France and Flanders scorned this unwanted dislocation to their lives and city.

The net tightened as the week wore on. The shelling intensified, the GPO building went up in flames, the rebellion crumbled. After the surrender, signed by Pearse on Saturday, 29 April, the heavy hand of the state bore down mercilessly on the insurgents. The fortunate were the rank and file who faced incarceration, jeered by a largely unsympathetic populace as they marched towards internment. Courts martial awaited the ringleaders, and retributive justice followed swiftly. Tom Clarke and Patrick Pearse were among the first to be shot, and it is said that had the killing stopped there, the public might have found such exemplary punishments acceptable. But they went on over a 10-day period. In total 15 men were executed, not including Casement, who was convicted of treason and hanged at Pentonville Prison in August. James Connolly was the last to face the firing squad. Wounded in the fighting and unable to stand, he met his end tied to a chair.

Irish Parliamentary Party loses ground

Many Irishmen who had been against the rebellion were swayed by the brutal punishment meted out. Those with nationalist sympathies who had condemned the action deplored further the price exacted by the British authorities. Grudging admiration for the rebels turned to firebrand support after they were martyred. Attitudes hardened under a martial-law regime that lasted for several months. The moderate Irish Parliamentary Party (IPP) rapidly lost ground to those espousing more militant nationalism. Politically, the big winner was Sinn Féin, a non-violent organisation that had taken no part in the Rising but whose name appeared in the newspapers as convenient journalistic shorthand for the episode. During the week-long struggle *The Times* referred to a "Sinn Fein conspiracy" in which the Germans had finally managed to get their "dupes" to carry out an "insane" armed uprising, something they had long angled for. Sinn Féin became the repository for the bitterness and frustration that pervaded the country in the aftermath of Easter 1916. The following year, Eamon de Valera – the highest-ranking survivor of the Rising – became party leader, ushering in the next chapter of the republican movement. Home Rule, once regarded as a great prize, was now considered a derisory offer, a tawdry compromise. Sinn Féin swept the nationalist vote at the IPP's expense in the December 1918 general election on a platform of seceding from the United Kingdom and establishing an assembly in Dublin. A renewal of the 1916 declaration of independence followed, and Britain was plunged into an internal war that was still raging long after the Armistice with Germany was signed.

Many Irishmen who had been against the rebellion were swayed by the brutal punishment meted out.

George Bernard Shaw on the Easter Rising:

Sir, – You say that "so far as the leaders are concerned no voice has been raised in this country against the infliction of the punishment which has so speedily overtaken them". As the Government shot the prisoners first and told the public about it afterwards, there was no opportunity for effective protest. But it must not be assumed that those who merely shrugged their shoulders when it was useless to remonstrate accept for one moment the view that what happened was the execution of a gang of criminals.

My own view – which I should not intrude on you had you not concluded that it does not exist – is that the men who were shot in cold blood after their capture or surrender were prisoners of war, and that it was, therefore, entirely incorrect to slaughter them. The relation of Ireland to Dublin Castle is in this respect precisely that of the Balkan States to Turkey, of Belgium or the city of Lille to the Kaiser, and of the United States to Great Britain.

Until Dublin Castle is superseded by a National Parliament and Ireland voluntarily incorporated with the British Empire, as Canada, Australasia and South Africa have been incorporated, an Irishman resorting to arms to achieve the independence of his country is doing only what Englishmen will do if it be their misfortune to be invaded and conquered by the Germans in the course of the present war.

Further, such an Irishman is as much in order morally in accepting assistance from the Germans in his struggle with England as England is in accepting the assistance of Russia in her struggle with Germany. The fact that he knows his enemies will not respect his rights if they catch him, and that he must therefore fight with a rope round his neck, increases his risk, but adds in the same measure to his glory in the eyes of his compatriots and of the disinterested admirers of patriotism throughout the world.

Below: **Scenes of devastation in Sackville Street where the General Post Office was located. The rebels had chosen the GPO to be their military command centre but were forced to surrender after shells fired at the building led to the outbreak of several fires.**

Above and Below right: **Newspaper photographs show Liberty Hall, the political base established by James Connolly, before and after it was shelled by the British authorities.**

Opposite below: **Two published photographs detail how the events unfolded.**

Siege in Mesopotamia

If the Western Front quickly became the key theatre for British forces, the strategic importance of the Middle East was also recognised from the outset. Protecting the Suez Canal, Britain's gateway to India and the Antipodes, was vital, as was securing her oil interests in Persia. Defending those assets was thus the immediate concern, and troops were dispatched to both quarters to safeguard them. In both cases, once the defensive mission had been accomplished, the scope to attack came into play.

The first Turkish assault on Suez came in February 1915 and was swiftly repulsed. The invading army endured a daunting journey across the Sinai Desert before they could fire a shot in anger, and found Britain's historic presence in Egypt, suitably reinforced, too tough a nut to crack. Further to the east, across the Arabian Peninsula, the struggle proved more equal. The Anglo-Indian force deployed to the Persian Gulf soon took possession of Basra, ensuring that the oilfields driving the new mechanised world were safe from enemy interference. What then? The desired long view was to incite the Arab population to rise up against an Ottoman overlord whose treatment of the indigenous people was far from benign. In the meantime the British-Indian army had in its sights advance into Turkish-held Mesopotamia – modern-day Iraq.

Townshend retreats to Kut

In overall command of the Allied force from spring 1915 was General Sir John Nixon, who dispatched Major-General Sir Charles Townshend into enemy territory along the Tigris, one of the rivers that gave Mesopotamia its name. There were sweeping early gains, and on 28 September Townshend took Kut-Al-Amara, a town bounded by a loop in the river. The supply line was worryingly overstretched, but under instruction from Nixon he pressed on towards the prized objective of Baghdad, only to be halted within 20 miles of that city. The battle that ended the advance, at Ctesiphon in late November, had no clear outcome, yet

Townshend – now 500 miles from his supply base – was concerned for the state of his men. Both armies sustained heavy casualties at Ctesiphon. Townshend believed the logistical situation favoured the enemy: it was considerably easier for Turkish commander Nur-Ud-Din to call up reinforcements and supplies. In fact Townshend's opponent was also contemplating withdrawal, a decision soon reversed as the weakened state of the Allied force became apparent. Having saved Baghdad, the Turkish army went on the attack, while Townshend fought rearguard actions in the retreat to Kut-Al-Amara, some 80 miles distant. This ignominious withdrawal and the events that followed would go down as one of the sorriest chapters in British military history.

Below: In early January 1916 General Aylmer was despatched with his troops up the Tigris in the first attempt to break the siege of Kut. They found their way blocked at Sheik Sa'ad and after three days of fighting successfully captured the area. However, there were 4,500 casualties out of a fighting force of just over 13,000 and they failed to have any impact on the beleaguered troops trapped at Kut.

Bottom: Forces on the ground try to assist Townshend and his men. In addition, attempts were made to drop supplies from the air to feed the starving soldiers.

Opposite below: Turks heading down the River Tigris from Diarbekir on rafts to reinforce the troops surrounding Kut.

Opposite top: Indian soldiers in Mesopotamia answer the roll call before going into the trenches.

GEN. TOWNSHEND'S PLIGHT.

TURKS AND HIS POSITION.

It is now a long time since any communication from General Townshend at Kut was published. Yesterday was the 141st day of the siege by the Turks of his sorely tried force. For the latest news of the condition of the garrison we have to rely on the Turkish official report of Thursday last, which said:

The position of the enemy invested at Kut-el-Amara is becoming very critical. The enemy commander, in order to avoid food difficulties, recently made the population evacuate the town. He is expecting aeroplanes to drop small bags of flour.

On Sunday the Turks stated that there was no change at Kut. Yesterday's Constantinople report had not come to hand late last night.

The last considerable attempt of the relief force to carry the Turkish position astride the river at Sanna-i-Yat, 13 miles north-east of Kut, took place on Sunday, when a brigade penetrated to the third line but was unable to maintain the ground gained. On Tuesday General Lake reported that there was no change. Since then nothing official has been published.

TURKS CLAIM BOAT CAPTURE.

AMSTERDAM, Wednesday.

According to a Constantinople telegram, an official report despatched on April 13, which arrived to-day, says: "On the night of April 12 we captured an enemy vessel travelling from Felchis in the direction of Kut-el-Amara. The captain and some of the crew were either killed or wounded. On board we found a great quantity of war material, provisions, and some machine guns."—Reuter.

Having saved Baghdad, the Turkish army went on the attack, while Townshend fought rearguard actions in the retreat to Kut-Al-Amara.

SIEGE OF GEN. TOWNSHEND'S FORCE.

ENOUGH SUPPLIES AT KUT.

RELIEF COLUMN STILL STOPPED.

INDIA OFFICE, Monday, 9.15 p.m.
Further telegrams received from Sir Percy Lake (the Commander-in-Chief in Mesopotamia) report that an armistice was concluded for a few hours on Saturday for the removal of the wounded and the burial of the dead.

During the last forty-eight hours the Tigris had risen 7ft. at Kut and 2½ft. at Amara, and prevented all movements of troops by land.

General Townshend reports that he has sufficient supplies. His troops have not been further engaged.

Ferocious Turkish onslaught

The Allied troops who reached Kut on 3 December were in anything but peak fighting condition. Townshend had large numbers of sick and wounded to deal with, and even the healthy were exhausted. Basra was still some 400 miles away, and the decision was made to fortify the town and await relief, initially estimated to arrive within two months. On that timescale Townshend felt no urgent need to cut rations.

The enemy was soon at the door, a ferocious Turkish onslaught over the Christmas period successfully rebuffed. Crude "jam-pot" bombs – simple receptacles crammed with nails and explosive – helped eke out ammunition stocks. Then, as weeks turned into months, food became a major issue. Sporadic air drops were a sticking-plaster solution to a situation growing more desperate by the day. Horsemeat was added to the menu and eventually became the staple; tediously repetitive to the British, rejected completely by the Indian infantry, some of whom deserted. Even the slaughter of thousands of animals couldn't prevent daily rations dropping to a meagre few ounces of meat.

Opposite: Sepoys (Indian infantry) fire at the Turks through the loophole of a sandbagged trench. Despite the eventual surrender of Kut and the humiliation of another defeat, the politicians were undaunted and ordered further advances in Mesopotamia. They focused for the rest of the year on improving road and rail links and the passage of supplies as well as establishing hospitals to guarantee more success in future campaigns.

Right: After his capture General Townshend spent the remainder of the war in relative luxury in a house on Prinkipo Island near Istanbul; a marked contrast to the thousands of Allied troops who did not survive captivity, due to disease or brutality from their Ottoman captors.

Below: An illustration of the battlefield in Mesopotamia, published on 24 April, shows the Turkish fortified positions on the River Tigris near Kut-el-Amara. The places where the British Relief Force was fighting are shown approximately.

Of the 13,000-strong garrison that became POWs, one-third would not survive the long forced march to internment or brutal prison camp regime.

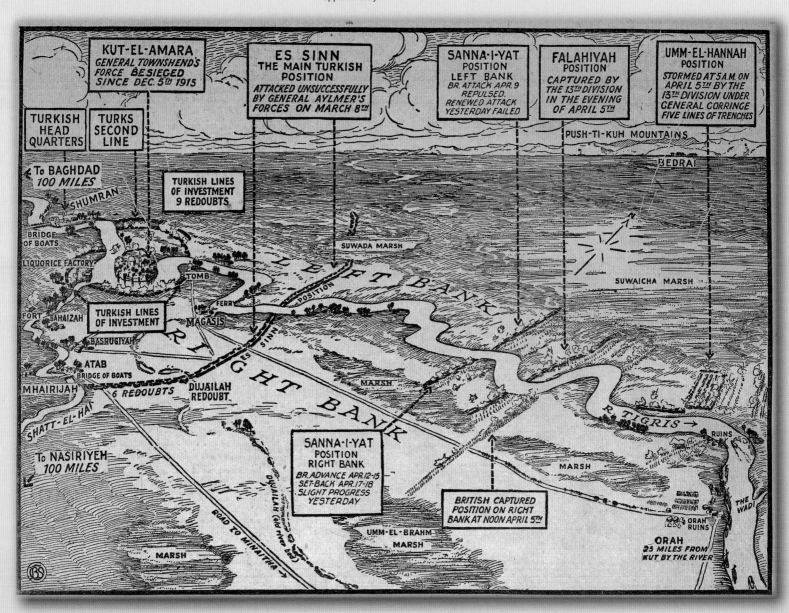

Townshend's unconditional surrender at Kut

Every attempt to relieve Kut failed. Those missions cost 23,000 lives, almost double the size of the garrison they were trying to help. With no military rescue forthcoming, financial inducements were offered. The Turks preferred unconditional surrender to a six-figure bribe, and on 29 April 1916 the 147-day siege ended on those humiliating terms. Before yielding the town Townshend ordered the destruction of anything useful to the victors. One ordeal was over, another about to begin. Of the 13,000-strong garrison that became POWs, one-third would not survive the long forced march to internment or brutal prison camp regime. Townshend himself was more fortunate. He sat out the war in comfortable surroundings, escaping privation and suffering, though not the sharp pen of historians. Following hard on the heels of the disastrous Gallipoli campaign, the Allies had again suffered a crushing defeat at the hands of the Ottoman army.

TOWNSHEND'S LAST MESSAGES.

"I CANNOT HOLD ON."

4OZ. OF FLOUR DAILY.

FIND OF HIDDEN GRAIN.

From EDMUND CANDLER,

MESOPOTAMIA, Wednesday, May 3.

The last communications from General Townshend were received by wireless on April 29 at 11.40 a.m. One said:

"Have destroyed my guns and most of my munitions are being destroyed, and officers have gone to Khalil (the Turkish Commander-in-Chief), who is at Madug, to say am ready to surrender. I must have some food here, and cannot hold on any more. Khalil has been told to-day, and a deputation of officers has gone in a launch to bring some food from the Julnar, the ship sent (by the relief force) night April 24 to carry supplies to garrison Kut."

The next stated:

"I have hoisted the white flag over Kut fort and town, and the guards will be taken over by a Turkish regiment which is approaching. I shall shortly destroy wireless. The troops go at 2 p.m. to camp near Shamran" (? Sherhan, on the Tigris, 48 miles north-west of Kut).

A prearranged signal from the wireless indicated at 1 p.m. that General Townshend's last message had gone through.

On the same day the Turkish General Khalil Bey Pasha received our parlementaires. He was anxious, he said, that the garrison should be well rationed, and that General Townshend especially, for whom he expressed the most profound admiration, should receive every possible comfort after the privations he had endured so gallantly.

He welcomed a proposal to send them (the garrison) stores, and regretted that the supplies at his command were not more plentiful.

Two barges loaded with a day and a half's iron rations left our camp yesterday.

TOWNSHEND FOR THE CAPITAL.

Negotiations with regard to the exchange of prisoners of war were so far satisfactory that a hospital ship, together with another ship of ours and two big barges laden with food and canteen stores, have been admitted to Kut, and are now on their way down stream with 177 sick and wounded.

SLIGHT GAIN BY TOWNSHEND RELIEF FORCE.

TURKS FORCED BACK SOUTH OF THE TIGRIS.

ADVANCE OVER BIG INUNDATIONS.

HEAVY FIRE ON ENEMY FLOODED OUT OF TRENCHES.

621st DAY OF THE WAR.
68th DAY OF BATTLE OF VERDUN.
129th DAY OF SIEGE OF KUT.

WAR OFFICE, Friday, 2.25 p.m.

General Lake reports that on Wednesday afternoon our forces on the right (south) bank of the Tigris forced back the enemy's advanced lines [before the Sanna-i-Yat position, about 13 miles north-east of Kut] over a distance varying from 1½ to 3 miles. In order to do so they had to cross an inundated belt, intersected by deep cuts from 500 to 1,200 yards wide, extending from the Tigris to the Umm-el-Brahm marsh.

On the left (north) bank the water from the marshes was driven by the north-west gale into some of the enemy's trenches at Sanna-i-Yat. The enemy were heavily punished as they took refuge from the flood in new position.

Turkish Official. Friday.

LATE WAR NEWS.

AUSTRIANS DRAW BACK.

RUSSIAN ATTACK IN GALICIA SPREADING.

Russian Official. PETROGRAD, Friday.

In the region of Trzibouchovtze, south-east of Buczacz (near the Dniester, on the southern front) we repulsed an enemy attack.

In the region of the mouth of the Strypa our troops carried the height called the

SURRENDER OF TOWNSHEND.

9,000 MEN BEATEN BY HUNGER AT KUT.

WAR OFFICE, Saturday.

After a resistance protracted for 143 days [until Saturday] and conducted with a gallantry and fortitude that will be for ever memorable, General Townshend has been compelled by the final exhaustion of his supplies to surrender.

Before doing so he destroyed his guns and munitions.

The force under him consists of 2,970 British troops of all ranks and services and some 6,000 Indian troops and their followers.

AMSTERDAM, Saturday.

A Constantinople official telegram received here via Berlin says: "The Vice Commander-in-Chief of the Turkish Army announces that the British garrison of Kut-el-Amara, 13,300 strong, under General Townshend, has surrendered unconditionally."—Reuter.

AMSTERDAM, Sunday.

The German papers attribute the Turkish success to the preparations of the late Marshal von der Goltz. The *Vossische Zeitung* considers that the fall of Kut is the heaviest blow ever struck at Great Britain, and other papers write in a similar vein.—Reuter.

Stalemate at Salonika

Bulgaria's decision to throw in its lot with the Central Powers in October 1915 gave Serbia another adjacent foe, this time on its eastern border. It had been a self-interested decision: the Central Powers were in the ascendant, and promises of Serbian territory might be delivered at little cost. The Serbs' appeal for help was promptly answered with the landing of an Anglo-French force at the Greek port Salonika in early October. This Allied gathering, which swelled to tens of thousands of troops, turned into "a wild goose affair" in the words of Herbert Asquith, Britain's prime minister when the first wave set foot on the Aegean shore. No effective relief reached the Serbians, who were routed and forced to embark on an arduous trek through Montenegro and Albania to the Adriatic coast, losing thousands along the way. It left the Salonika brigade largely kicking its heels. They were branded "gardeners", for clashes with Bulgaria were few and far between. The option of mass withdrawal receded, not least because of political sensibilities surrounding a certain French general. Maurice Sarrail was well connected but no great commander, and it was found expedient to assign him to this Hellenic backwater. Having been put in command of the

Allied force, he was not about to brand it a white elephant; and, again for political reasons, Britain could not contemplate pulling out unilaterally. As with Gallipoli, which lay across the sea 200 miles to the east, disease laid low men in their thousands; unlike the Dardanelles campaign, the troops involved had no determined enemy harassing them. Not until September 1918 – by which time Sarrail had been replaced by General d'Esperey – did the Allies strike a telling blow against the Bulgarian army, which laid down arms before the month was out. The Allied force stationed in Greece was much maligned for its contribution – or lack thereof – to the cause. Winston Churchill, at least, gave them their due, but there was faint praise in his observation that "it was upon this much abused front that the final collapse of the Central Empires first began".

Opposite below: After an urgent request for help the Allies landed at Salonika in October 1915 but it was too late; Serbian troops had retreated through Montenegro and into Albania, along with thousands of civilians.

Opposite above: Just one of the heavy weapons used by the French Army is brought ashore.

Top: French and British troops were tasked with the backbreaking job of digging roads to help defend the area. The existing dirt tracks were expanded and developed while the engineers also mapped out new routes.

Above left: On 5 May 1916 the Zeppelin LZ85 was brought down by HMS *Agamemnon* forcing it to crash land onto the Vardar marshes. Captain Scherzer (right), first officer of the airship, immediately ordered the 12-man crew to set fire to the vessel. They then attempted to escape but were swiftly captured and held prisoner.

Middle left: Afterwards the frame was retrieved and transported by barge to the harbour, where French mechanics rebuilt the structure next to the White Tower as a fitting trophy and a warning to the enemy.

Bottom left: A party of British marines on their way to the Greek customs office in Salonika.

Above right: A forward observation officer at work in the trenches. Due to the lack of activity the troops became known as the "Gardeners of Salonika".

Bottom right: Anti-aircraft defences spot hostile aircraft.

"It was upon this much abused front that the final collapse of the Central Empires first began". Winston Churchill

OPERATIONS ON THE WHOLE SALONICA FRONT.

| MACEDONIA LIVENS UP. | MUNITIONS FACTORY EXPLOSION. | OUR NEW PROSPECT FROM THE RIDGE. | SMUTS' MARCH ON A HUN CAPITAL. | MR. HOLZAPFEL. | REAL WAR FILM |

ERATIONS ON THE ENTIRE FRONT." | SERIOUS LOSS OF LIFE IN YORKSHIRE. | EXCELLENT BASES FOR ATTACK. | NEARING DAR-ES-SALAAM | M.P. ASKED TO POST-PONE HIS QUESTIONS. | THE SOMME BATT AS IT IS.

QUEL TO BULGARIAN MOVES. | | | WARSHIPS HELPING. | | GRIM AND GLORIOU

ERMAN ATTACKS FAIL ON SOMME RIDGE. | SHALLOW HUN LINES. | | | EFFECT UPON THE PUB

Top far left: The daily "Quinine Parade" gave every man serving in Salonika five grains as a precaution against malaria. Despite this there were constant outbreaks with the worst affected evacuated from the area when possible. Statistics later revealed that there were over 162,000 British hospital admissions between 1916 and 1918 due to malaria, in contrast to approximately 24,000 reported casualties.

Top left: During the early part of the occupation of Salonika, the Allies spent most of their time training, and also building a bastion eight miles north of the city. They used so much barbed wire it was eventually nicknamed the "Birdcage".

Middle far left: Venzelist volunteers, supporters of the Greek Prime Minister Eleftherios Venizelos, march through the streets of Salonika. They wanted Greece to join the Allies but King Constantine I, brother-in-law to Kaiser Wilhelm, kept the country's neutrality until his abdication in 1917. His son Alexander took the crown but Venizelos and his rival government seized control, declaring war against the Central Powers in June 1917.

Middle left: Hospitals away from the fighting often took the form of tented villages. Most of the patients were suffering from malaria, dysentery and black water fever rather than conflict injuries.

Bottom: In a French aviation camp near Salonika each tent is surrounded by flowerbeds, which are tended by soldiers in their leisure hours. Some are planted into sayings such as "Glory to our eternal France' and quotations from poetry.

Opposite page: Doctors and nurses pose outside the dugouts used to protect them during aerial bombardment.

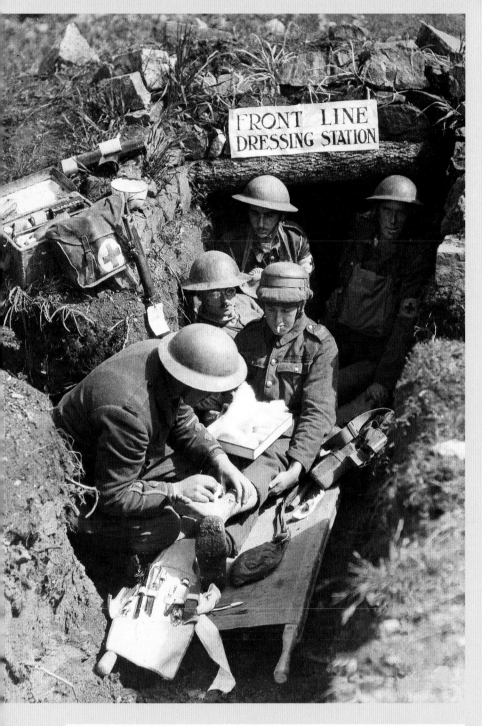

FRONT LINE DRESSING STATION

May 1916

1 The leaders of the rebellion in Ireland surrendered to British forces.

Reichstag member Karl Liebknecht was arrested following a pacifist demonstration.

3 Patrick Pearse and two other Irish rebel leaders were executed by a British firing squad.

German forces began an artillery bombardment of Hill 304, northwest of Verdun.

4 The German Government pledged to the United States that they would not attack merchant ships without warning.

5 The German airship *LZ85* was downed by British guns at Salonika.

German forces gained a foothold on Hill 304 at Verdun.

7 The verdict of the Court Martial was communicated to Irish rebel, Seán Heuston, that he had been sentenced to death and was to be shot at dawn the following morning.

8 White Star steamship SS *Cymric* was torpedoed and sunk by the German submarine *U-20* in the Atlantic Ocean.

9 The British and French Governments concluded the Sykes-Picot agreement regarding the eventual partition of Asia Minor. The agreement took its name from its negotiators, Sir Mark Sykes of Britain and François Georges-Picot of France.

10 Lord Wimborne resigned as Lord-Lieutenant of Ireland.

11 A German attack west of Vaux Pond was repulsed during the Battle of Verdun.

12 Irish republican and socialist leader James Connolly was executed by a British firing squad because of his role in the Easter Rising.

14 An Austrian offensive against Italy began with an artillery barrage in the province of Trentino.

15 In northern Mesopotamia Russian forces occupied Rowanduz.

The Allies began a blockade of the Hejaz coast to assist the Arab revolt under Sharif Hussein bin Ali, Emir of Mecca.

16 The House of Commons passed an extension to the Military Service Act bringing married men into the scope for conscription.

Austrian forces captured the Italian trenches at Soglio d'Aspio.

17 Earl Curzon of Kedleston was appointed as President of the Air Board in Great Britain.

18 Austrian forces captured Zugna Torta and Linz from Italy.

19 The Austrian offensive stalled in the Trentino when Italian troops held Monte Pasubio but the Italians then retreated from Monte Toraro and Monte Campolon.

20 German forces attacked Le Mort Homme and captured the summit of Hill 295 at Verdun.

21 Adolf Tortilowicz von Batocki-Friebe was appointed president of the newly created German food control board.

22 French forces launched an assault and gained a foothold in Fort Douaumont at Verdun.

23 British troops occupied the capital city of El Fasher in Darfur.

25 The Second Military Service Bill became law in Great Britain.

26 German and Bulgarian forces occupied Fort Rupel on the Greek border with Macedonia.

27 US President Wilson proposed a "universal association of nations" to settle future disputes.

28 German forces bombarded the British line between La Bassee Canal and Arras on the Western Front.

29 The first Despatch of Field Marshal Sir Douglas Haig, Commander in Chief of the British Armies in France and Flanders, was printed in the London Gazette. It covered the fighting at the Bluff, St Eloi and other actions of early 1916.

31 The Battle of Jutland began between Britain's Grand Fleet and Germany's Hochseeflotte in the North Sea.

HEAVY LOSSES IN NAVAL BATTLE.

GREAT BATTLE OFF DANISH COAST.

6 BRITISH CRUISERS SUNK.

GERMAN BATTLESHIP AND BATTLE CRUISER BLOWN UP.

ANOTHER BELIEVED SUNK AND 2 CRUISERS DAMAGED.

HUN LIGHT CRUISER AND 6 DESTROYERS
LOST AND 8 BRITISH DESTROYERS

NARRATIVE BY EYE-WITNESS.

BRITISH PURSUIT.

SIX ZEPPELINS.

FROM OUR OWN CORRESPONDENT.
COPENHAGEN, Friday.

A German destroyer was to-day sighted from the northern Lingvig lighthouse in a sinking condition and heavily damaged on her decks. She was being towed by another destroyer.

A German destroyer flotilla consisting of twelve vessels to-day passed the Little Belt (east Danish coast) for Kiel, returning from the North Sea battle.

The Zeppelin L 24, which with five other Zeppelins and several seaplanes took part in the battle, returned three times for ...

THE CLIMAX OF THE FIGHTING.

BETWEEN 6 AND 8 P.M.

FROM OUR OWN CORRESPONDENT.
CHRISTIANIA, Thursday, 7.10 o'clock.

From many parts of Jaederen (the south-west coast province of Norway) from Hvittingsö to Hiterö, a violent cannonade at sea is reported. It began at about 4 p.m. yesterday (Wednesday). The firing was at first relatively weak, but it increased steadily until between six and eight o'clock it reached its maximum. It ceased at about ten o'clock.

From no part of the Norwegian coast could the battle be seen and no steamer has yet arrived at a Norwegian port which was near the fighting, but the light westerly breeze clearly brought the sound of guns of many calibres up to the largest. Thousands of ...

GERMAN JOY.

DELIRIOUS PRESS.

"OUR SUPERIORITY."

NEWS ON THURSDAY.

From CHARLES TOWER,
HOOK OF HOLLAND, Friday, 7.43 p.m.

All Germany is beflagged to-day owing to the claims of "a complete victory in the greatest sea fight of modern times."

The German papers are crazy with delight. Captain Persius says in the *Tageblatt*:

Our whole High Seas Fleet, without any aid from coast batteries, has delivered a victorious blow against the most powerful Navy in the world. All Germany gratefully thanks admirals, officers, and men.

Count Reventlow, in the ...

THE LOST SHIPS

AND GALLANT CREWS.

By Our Naval Correspondent,
H. W. WILSON.

There will be deep sorrow throughout Great Britain to-day at the loss of so many gallant officers and men who have died like heroes in the discharge of duty.

THE QUEEN MARY
was a battle-cruiser of 27,000 tons, the last, but for the Tiger, built before the war. She was laid down at Jarrow in 1910, launched in 1912, and completed at the end of 1913. The Germans claimed to have sunk her earlier in the war. She had turbine engines of about 78,000-horse power, driving her at a speed of 28½ knots. She had special defence against mines and torpedoes and a very elaborate system of compartments.

Her armament consisted of eight 13.5in. guns carried in four huge armoured turrets so disposed that all eight guns fired on either broadside and four of them ahead or astern.

GERMAN ATTACK ON BRITISH.

TOTAL REPULSE NEAR YPRES.

FIGHTING STILL GOING ON

BRITISH OFFICIAL.
FRANCE, Friday, 10.25 p.m.
Sharp fighting has taken place to-day in the Ypres salient on a front of approximately 3,000 yards (1¾ miles) between Hooge and the Ypres-Comines railway.

Following on the artillery activity this neighbourhood reported in yesterday's intense and sustained bombardment, at ... a.m., which extended not only over front mentioned above but also over area behind.

This was followed about midday ...

Battle of Jutland

In January 1916 Germany's High Seas Fleet had a new commander. Admiral Reinhard von Scheer was more aggressive than his predecessor, but knew a full-scale meeting with a superior force was out of the question. He needed to pick his fight carefully, and by spring had formulated a plan to dent the Royal Navy's advantage and pierce the blockade that had bitten hard in his homeland. It involved sending a battlecruiser squadron under Admiral Franz von Hipper into the North Sea, hoping to draw Britain's Rosyth-based battlecruisers into open water. Following Hipper at a discreet distance would be the main body of the High Seas Fleet: the British ships would be led straight into a trap from which, once sprung, there would be no escape. Battlecruisers possessed the firepower of a battleship but with greater speed, achieved through a diminution in armoury. With Britain's battlecruiser stock depleted, it would go a long way towards levelling the fighting capacity of the two navies, and a large-scale battle could be contemplated.

The Royal Navy set a trap

Unbeknown to the German commander, the British Admiralty knew what he was up to, thanks to the enemy codebooks it had obtained. Britain's battlecruisers would indeed appear to take the bait, but the Grand Fleet, led by Sir John Jellicoe, would be just over the horizon. The Royal Navy had set a trap of its own, and on the afternoon of 31 May 1916, the opposing commanders prepared to land a heavy blow to the other's maritime capability. To the German navy the battleground was Skagerrak; the British called it the Battle of Jutland.

The first shots were fired at around 2.30 pm. In the opening phase, Hipper's ships met the British battlecruiser squadron under the command of Sir David Beatty. The latter took the pursuer role, seeming to be falling into the German trap as Hipper steered him towards the waiting High Seas Fleet. Britain took heavy early casualties as both *Indefatigable* and *Queen Mary* blew up after being hit. "The guns went up in the air like matchsticks," said one eyewitness to the sinking of *Indefatigable*, whose disappearance beneath the waves could be counted in seconds rather than minutes. There were just two survivors from a complement of over a thousand. A third battlecruiser, *Indomitable*, later suffered the same fate. Precision German gunnery had exposed the unwise practice of stockpiling shells near the guns in the quest to maintain a rapid firing rate. Beatty, whose flagship *Lion* was also hit, uttered his famous assessment: "There seems to be something wrong with our bloody ships today."

Ferocious bombardment

Beatty now took the role of the pursued, leading the High Seas Fleet north towards Jellicoe's ships. The latter, from his position aboard flagship *Iron Duke*, had a formidable task force, spearheaded by 24 dreadnoughts. But he was hindered by communications problems and struggling to grasp where exactly the enemy ships were. Potentially the most fatal misconception was that the High Seas Fleet had not yet left port.

At around 6.30 Jellicoe moved his battleships from column formation into a single line. The High Seas Fleet was heading straight towards it, Scheer's entire horizon filled with enemy warships threatening a full broadside. Whether by calculation, intuition or good fortune, Jellicoe had "crossed the T" – naval parlance for positioning his ships in relation to the enemy to form that letter-shape, and thereby gaining a major tactical advantage.

Facing a ferocious bombardment, Scheer executed a co-ordinated 180° turn for his entire contingent. Jellicoe tried to cover the withdrawal, but also vacillated as he feared a torpedo attack; hesitation that would attract much criticism.

Fighting continued as Scheer executed a second turn, then sent his battlecruisers straight at the enemy in a potential suicide run to cover his and the main fleet's back. The ever cautious Jellicoe stayed his hand, content to try and cut off the German retreat in fading light. Under cover of night the German ships melted away, steaming back to port as dawn broke and Jellicoe looked to finish the job. He had not "lost the war in an afternoon", as Churchill feared could have been the case if things had gone badly awry. But nor had he won a clear victory. Beatty would succeed him as Grand Fleet commander before the year was out.

Germany was first out of the blocks in issuing a favourable view of the battle. "Our High Seas Fleet," the official communiqué crowed, "encountered on May 31 the main part of the English fighting fleet, which was considerably superior to our own forces. During the afternoon a series of engagements developed between Skagerrak and Horn Reef, which were successful for us and which continued the whole of the night." The British response was more guarded, and *The Times* concluded: "It is clear that we have suffered the heaviest damage at sea we have met during the war."

The Times concluded: "It is clear that we have suffered the heaviest damage at sea we have met during the war."

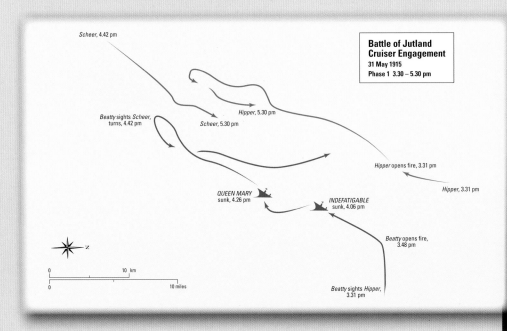

Opposite page: At the start of the conflict Britain's Royal Navy and the vessels of the Grand Fleet were the most powerful in the world.

This page: Two veterans from the Battle of Jutland. The British Admiralty Intelligence Department obtained copies of the German Navy secret signal books from the Russians, after a German cruiser was sunk in the Balkans. This enabled British experts to decipher some of the wireless messages they successfully intercepted. Through this and other means the Admiralty discovered the High Fleet's plans to set sail on 30 May 1916.

Submarine attacks intensify

In numerical terms Germany had certainly come out on top. Britain lost twice the tonnage and twice the manpower. And yet events proved that Scheer had scored only a pyrrhic victory. Two days after issuing its solemn 3 June leader, The Times gave a more upbeat – and prescient – evaluation. "Our hold on the sea is unshaken, the discipline and spirit of our sailors have never stood higher, and Sir John Jellicoe was again ready to put to sea on the evening of June 2. When will the Germans be ready to meet him?" Or as an American correspondent put it: "The German fleet has assaulted its jailer, but is still in jail."

And incarcerated it remained, apart from a tentative sortie three months after Jutland. Scheer lost faith in the ability of Germany's surface fleet as an instrument of winning the war. Beneath the waves, however, there was a trump card still to play. The U-boat was a mighty strike weapon, and its impact would be even greater if it were given a freer hand. Since Germany's February 1915 declaration that the waters around Britain were a war zone, all shipping had run the risk of attack. Now, in the months following the Battle of Jutland, submarine attacks intensified, and in February 1917 Germany adopted a stance of unrestricted warfare that gave U-boat commanders carte blanche to tighten the economic noose. By April a quarter of ships leaving British ports were failing to return.

Britain had employed various means to counter the U-boat threat. Hydrophones were used to detect their presence, depth charges deployed. Disguised "Q-ships" – which looked like defenceless merchant vessels but were in fact heavily armed – sought to lure submarines to the surface. These had only limited success. David Lloyd George, who entered 10 Downing Street in December 1916, called the sea "the jugular vein of Allied vitality", and a fatal haemorrhage was a distinct possibility unless an answer could be found. He pressed for the introduction of convoys, against the advice of some Admiralty men, including Jellicoe. The results were immediate. Allied losses fell dramatically, the U-boat threat neutralised just as American patience finally ran out and Germany added another powerful combatant to its list of enemies.

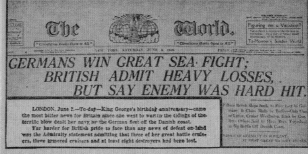

Top: The Allies outnumbered the High Fleet both in terms of numbers and the superiority of its vessels, speed and ammunition power. However, the Germans had the advantage with more accurate guns, more effective shells and thicker armour. Added to this communication between British vessels was poor, they used an over sensitive propellant and their magazine protection was limited.

Above: Men gather on Fleet Street to read news of the latest sea battles.

Below: The British lost three battle ships; HMS *Indefatigable,* HMS *Queen Mary* and HMS *Invincible* along with three armoured cruisers and eight destroyers. The Germans lost eleven vessels including one battle cruiser.

Left: Sir John Jellicoe, commander of the Grand Fleet at Jutland.

"The German fleet has assaulted its jailer, but is still in jail."

By April a quarter of ships leaving British ports were failing to return.

DAILY MAIL JUNE 3, 1916

Great battle off Danish coast

On the afternoon of Wednesday, May 31, a naval engagement took place off the coast of Jutland (Denmark.) The British ships on which the brunt of the fighting fell were the battle-cruiser fleet, and some cruisers and light cruisers, supported by four fast battleships. Among these the losses were heavy.

The German battle fleet, aided by low visibility, avoided prolonged action with our main forces, and soon after these appeared on the scene the enemy returned to port, though not before receiving severe damage from our battleships.

6 British cruisers sunk

The battle-cruisers Queen Mary, Indefatigable, Invincible, and the cruisers Defence and Black Prince were sunk. The Warrior was disabled, and after being towed for some time had to be abandoned by her crew. It is also known that the destroyers Tipperary, Turbulent, Fortune, Sparrowhawk, and Ardent were lost and six others are not yet accounted for. No British battle-ships or light cruisers were sunk.

German battleship and battle cruiser blown up

The enemy's losses were serious. At least one battle-cruiser was destroyed, and one severely damaged; one battleship reported sunk by our destroyers during a night attack; two light cruisers were disabled and probably sunk.

The exact number of enemy destroyers disposed of during the action cannot be ascertained with any certainty, but it must have been large.

Top left: News of the Battle of Jutland initially came through German wireless broadcasts and due to the rumours circulating, some sailors returned home to find their death had been reported to relatives. Britain lost about 6,000 seamen compared with 2,500 German losses.

Top right: HMS *Lion* served as Vice Admiral Beatty's flagship at the Battle of Jutland. During the exchanges she suffered a serious propellant fire that could have destroyed the ship had it not been for the bravery of Royal Marine Major Francis Harvey, the turret commander, who posthumously received the Victoria Cross for having ordered the magazine flooded.

Above left: An officer in charge of a naval search party makes inquiries into the character of a sailing ship.

Above right: The busy scenes at a naval recruiting office in London after news of the battle emerged. Manpower in the Royal Navy rose from 250,000 to 450,000 by the end of the conflict.

NORTH SEA HEROES; KILLED AND WOUNDED IN THE GREAT FIGHT.

Commander H. L. L. Fennell, lost in H.M.S. Queen Mary.

Lieutenant E. T. Donnell, killed in the destroyer Shark.

Lieut. Commander John S. Wilson, H.M.S. Indefatigable, killed.

Engineer Sub-Lieut. E. Champness, Queen Mary, killed.

Captain A. L. Cay, H.M.S. Invincible, killed.

Lieut. T. Flemming, H.M.S. Invincible, killed.

Lieut. W. Halliley, H.M.S. Nomad, killed.

Lieut. R. Gow, H.M.S. Defence, killed.

Lieut. R. E. Blyth, died of wounds.

Capt. C. Prowse, Queen Mary, killed.

Fleet-Paymaster John A. Place, killed.

Commander A. F. Coplestone-Boughey, H.M.S. Defence, killed.

Rev. C. A. Walton, St. Peter's, Clapham (Chaplain), killed.

Engineer Commander H. T. Mezzon, H.M.S. Defence, killed.

Midshipman H. Durrant, Queen Mary, severely injured.

Lieutenant C. R. Abercrombie, H.M.S. Defence, killed.

16-year-old hero of Jutland wins Victoria Cross

It was, according to one commentator, "one of the bravest acts of devotion to duty which the whole record of this war has given to us". The hero in question, John Travers Cornwell, was barely 16 years old when he made the ultimate sacrifice, giving his story a poignancy that touched the entire nation.

Essex-born Jack Cornwell was serving on the cruiser HMS *Chester* in the humble rank of Boy Ist Class when the tragedy that immortalised him occurred during the Battle of Jutland. A sight-setter on the ship's forward 5.5-inch gun, he was grievously wounded when the emplacement took a direct hit early in the action. With his crewmates lying dead or wounded around him, Cornwell remained dutifully at his post awaiting orders in the face of further heavy shelling. His race, of course, was run, and although he made it to a mainland hospital, his injuries were not survivable.

Cornwell was initially given a low-key funeral, but on 29 July he was reinterred with much pomp and ceremony. His gun-carriage borne, flag-draped coffin suggested the passing of a great statesman or military leader, such was the effect his story had when circulated at home. Cornwell's tender years meant he that he could receive a Bronze Star from his connection with the Boy Scout movement, as well as becoming the Royal Navy's youngest Victoria Cross recipient. Later, the Scouts introduced the Cornwell Badge, given for distinguished service, while his school in Walton Road was renamed in his honour. His heroics were also captured for posterity, noted artist Frank Salisbury commissioned to capture the scene on the *Chester*, where Jack valiantly stuck to his unserviceable guns.

Top right: Boy First Class J T Cornwell J/42563 after he was posted to HMS *Lancaster*, moored at Chatham, Kent.

Top far right: After his death the Admiralty commissioned Frank Salisbury to paint a picture of Cornwell at his gun, using Jack's brother Ernest as a model. It now hangs in St Paul's Church at HMS *Raleigh*, the naval training base in Cornwall.

Middle right: The gun manned by Cornwell on HMS *Chester* was taken to the Imperial War Museum in March 1936 and is still on display today, along with his medals, donated to the museum in 1968.

Right: Jack's mother Alice reads his citation alongside her three other children (l to r) George, Ernest and Lily.

Below right: Alice at a civic reception in honour of her son.

"One of the bravest acts of devotion to duty which the whole record of this war has given to us".

Lord Kitchener lost at sea

"We deeply regret to announce that Lord Kitchener has been drowned off the Orkneys in the sinking, by a mine or torpedo, of the cruiser *Hampshire*, in which he was travelling to Russia with a party on a special mission." This was the news that dominated *The Times*' edition of 7 June 1916. The Thunderer paid tribute to the hero of Omdurman and Khartoum, a man "who has so long been a popular idol". To John Bull he was "Britain's greatest soldier". The King instructed that Army officers wear mourning for a week. But even in the midst of the eulogising, there were hints that Kitchener's solitary approach and inability to delegate were a serious handicap, given the complexities of modern warfare. Already 64 when appointed War Secretary, Kitchener was schooled in Victorian-era soldiering, though must be credited with an early recognition that the issue would not be settled quickly. The recruitment drive he led swelled the ranks opportunely; in the pre-conscription period, "Kitchener's army" was vital to the country's defence. But his national-hero status among the populace did not extend to the corridors of Westminster. His aloofness and intransigence did not sit well with cabinet colleagues, and the antipathy was mutual. Before his untimely death he was becoming a marginalised figure, his reputation badly dented by the munitions crisis and his support for the disastrous Dardanelles campaign. Margot Asquith, wife of the Coalition leader, delivered a memorably stinging appraisal of the first member of the military to be handed the War Secretary brief: "If he was not a great man, he was a great poster."

LORD KITCHENER DROWNED

H.M.S. HAMPSHIRE SUNK WITH HIS STAFF AND A CREW OF 650.

GOING TO RUSSIA AT THE CZAR'S REQUEST.

MUNITIONS ADVISER AMONG THE LOST.

FROM ADMIRAL SIR JOHN JELLICOE,
Commander-in-Chief of the Grand Fleet.
Tuesday, 10.30 a.m.

I have to report with deep regret that his Majesty's ship Hampshire (Captain Herbert J. Savill, R.N.), with Lord Kitchener and his staff on board, was sunk last night about 8 p.m. to the west of the Orkneys, either by a mine or torpedo.

Four boats were seen by observers on shore to leave the ship. The wind was north-north-west and heavy seas were running.

Patrol vessels and destroyers at once proceeded to the spot and a party was sent along the coast to search, but only some bodies and a capsized boat have been found up to the present.

As the whole shore has been searched from the seaward I greatly fear that there is little hope of there being any survivors. No report has yet been received from the search party on shore.

H.M.S. Hampshire was on her way to Russia.

Lord Kitchener, on the invitation of his Imperial Majesty the Czar, had left England on a visit to Russia, accompanied by Mr. O'Beirne, Sir Frederick Donaldson, and Brigadier-General Ellershaw, and, at the request of his Majesty's Government, was to have taken the opportunity of discussing important military and financial questions.

WAR OFFICE, Tuesday.

Top: Lord Kitchener followed by Sir William Robertson, leaves the Hotel Crillion after the Allied conference in Paris. The countries had agreed on a British attack on the Western Front to try to relieve the war of attrition raging at Verdun.

Above far left: In 1914 Kitchener was created 1st Earl Kitchener of Khartoum.

Left: Kitchener disembarks from the *Iron Duke* in June 1916.

He was on his way to join HMS *Hampshire* to travel to Russia on a diplomatic mission. Lloyd George was due to accompany him but in the event remained at home.

Above left: An official salute as he boards the *Hampshire*. On 5 June Kitchener and the majority of the crew lost their lives when the ship sank just west of the Orkney Islands. His body was never recovered.

THE LAST MAN TO SEE LORD KITCHENER.

SURVIVORS' SPECIAL NARRATIVES.

WAITING CALMLY, HE WENT DOWN WITH THE SHIP.

BY OUR SPECIAL CORRESPONDENT.

How Lord Kitchener died was described to me by Leading Seaman Rogerson, a survivor from H.M.S. Hampshire, whose home is at Hertford.

"Of those who left the ship and have survived," said Rogerson, "I was the one who saw Lord Kitchener last. He went down with the ship. He did not leave her.

"I saw Captain Savill help his boat's crew to clear away his galley. At the same time the captain was calling to Lord Kitchener to come to the boat, but owing to the noise made by the wind and sea Lord Kitchener could not hear him, I think.

"When the explosion occurred Lord Kitchener walked calmly from the captain's cabin, went up the ladder, and on to the quarter-deck. There I saw him walking quite collectedly, talking to two of the officers. All three were wearing khaki and had no overcoats on. In fact, they were dressed as they were when they came on board. Lord Kitchener calmly watched the preparations for abandoning the ship, which were going on in quite a steady and orderly way.

"The crew just went to their stations and obeyed orders, and did their best to get out the boats, but that was impossible. Owing to the rough weather no boats could be lowered. Those that were got out were smashed up at once. No boats left the ship. What the people on shore thought to be boats leaving were the rafts. Men did get into the boats as these lay in their cradles, thinking that as the ship went under them the boats would float. But the ship sank by the head, and when she went she turned a somersault forward, carrying down with her all the boats and those in them.

"I do not think Lord Kitchener got into a boat. When I sprang to a raft he was still on the starboard side of the quarter-deck talking with his officers. From the little time that elapsed between my leaving the ship and her sinking I feel certain that Lord Kitchener went down with her and was on the deck at the time she sank. Of the civilian members of his suite I saw nothing.

Camouflage
Smoke and mirrors

Attempting to deceive the enemy is as old as martial engagement. The story of the Trojan horse is but one early example of commanders seeking advantage by creating illusion, and the art of deception moved on several notches in the First World War. The use of camouflage was one important innovation – "throwing dust in the enemy's eyes" was one contemporary definition. Khaki had been used to kit out British infantry since the mid-19th century, when improvements in rifle technology meant it was important to reduce visibility even at 1,000 yards from the enemy. But colour-matching to the environment was a relatively new idea in terms of military application. Observations in the animal kingdom showed the value of being able to blend into the background, and since this was a subject dealing with colour, tone, pattern and texture, it is perhaps understandable that artists were at the forefront of camouflage development.

"Thousands of camoufleurs"

Lucien Victor Guirand de Scevola, a respected portrait painter serving in the French army, was one of the first to experiment with painted canvases draped over gun emplacements. He was soon put in charge of the first dedicated camouflage unit in history, overseeing the work of thousands of "camoufleurs" as his ideas went into mass production in 1915. That same year the bright red trousers sported by French poilus were abandoned in favour of a more muted shade of blue. Similarly, America would swap the green tunic that had a long history at home for British khaki.

Royal Academician Solomon Joseph Solomon, who began the war as a private in the United Arts Rifles, was among the leading lights as Britain also investigated methods for making men and equipment less visible. As aerial reconnaissance increased, these pioneers recognised that mere covering with appropriately painted sheeting was not enough. Concealment of a three-dimensional object meant particular attention had to be paid to tell-tale shadows. Since the upper surface of solid objects appears lighter and the lower surface darker, throwing them into relief, efforts were made to neutralise these effects. By countershading the upper surfaces and counter-lightening those beneath, it was possible to nullify the effects of natural illumination, to create the illusion of a flat rather than solid object. What animals such as zebras and many species of fish achieve in their natural coloration, the camouflage pioneers sought to achieve by sleight-of-hand.

Painted screens

Observation posts were vital to intelligence-gathering, and many were established with visual trickery. A fabricated horse carcass made a useful place of concealment, as did dummy trees just large enough to hold an observer. Groups of lifesize infantry figures were sometimes painted on wood, so-called "Chinese attacks" whose aim was to confuse the enemy and draw fire when they were held aloft, perhaps revealing a sniper's position. A painted canvas screen might be used to show the continuation of a road that was in fact no longer there.

In the naval war, a number of ruses de guerre were employed. A vessel's outline might be altered by the addition of dummy funnels, or, in the case of Q-ships, benign appearance masked a very different reality. These merchantmen were wolves in sheep's clothing, decked out with concealed weaponry if an unsuspecting U-boat came too close. The deception was enhanced by apparent abandonment of the vessel when threatened by an enemy submarine. These "panic parties" suggested feeble submission, but on board there remained gunners ready to open fire, the white ensign hoisted in place of neutral colours just prior to the attack.

Top: **Two Allied soldiers wear camouflage clothing to go over the top in daylight.**

Right: **As a French naval gun roars into action on the Western Front, its camouflaged shelter can be seen on the right.**

Below far left: **British engineers camouflage a barbed wire trap in July 1918. French painter Lucien-Victor Guirand de Scévola led the camouflage industry in France and he invented the painted canvas netting used to hide gun positions and equipment. Its extensive use saw 7 million square yards produced by the end of the war.**

Below left: **Faked British trenches are set up to fool the enemy.**

Right: **A maze of trenches camouflaged to blend in with the surrounding landscape.**

"Razzle-dazzle" at sea

Q-ships were decoy vessels, but thoughts also turned to the issue of disguising sea-going craft. Somewhat counterintuitively, the answer lay in painting hulls in bold, geometric patterns, the kind of stark imagery that might be found in the Vorticist and Cubist art movements. However, it was noted marine artist Norman Wilkinson who became the chief architect of "dazzle" camouflage, a term derived from the Americanism "razzle-dazzle", meaning "to confuse". Designs that seemed to attract attention in fact tricked the eye, for this was an example of disruptive patterning, also common in the natural world. These patterns had the optical effect of breaking up what was in reality a continuous surface, and blurring the outline. Wilkinson quickly concluded that concealment was impossible in open water. "It will be obvious to anyone with sea experience," he wrote, "that from the low view of a submarine's periscope a surface vessel is seen almost entirely against a background of sky. The deep shadows cast by boat and promenade decks cannot be eliminated by paint." The aim, therefore, was to mask the direction of travel, in particular from U-boat commanders. As Wilkinson himself put it, the main objective was "the elimination of normal hull shapes and rectangles such as bridge ends by violently contrasting patterns in order to disguise the speed and course of the vessel attacked". He might also have referred to a discernible psychological effect his ideas produced, since crews working these ships certainly believed themselves more secure than those manning vessels decked out in uniform, more conspicuous livery. Both merchantmen and some warships were given the dazzle-painted makeover.

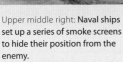

Above: A camouflaged street in France where over 500 soldiers are billeted.

Above middle: A disguised German trap into which three horses and a limber have plunged.

Bottom: The gunboat HMS *Kildangan* sports its dazzle camouflage. Each ship had its own unique pattern.

Top right: A German machine gunner lies under the protection of a camouflage tent.

Above right: This notice board positioned behind a hedge of camouflage gives a warning to the army drivers. A cautious Tommy lies prone on the ground beside it.

Upper middle right: Naval ships set up a series of smoke screens to hide their position from the enemy.

Lower middle right and bottom right: Camouflaged office of the Chief of Staff, 26th Division. These concealed headquarters housed American officers only a few miles from the front line.

BOTHA ADDS TO THE EMPIRE.

GERMAN S.W. AFRICAN ARMY SURRENDERS.

322,450 SQUARE MILES WON.

AN ULTIMATUM TO THE DOOMED FORCES.

PRETORIA, Friday.

It is officially announced that General Botha has accepted the surrender of the entire German forces in South-West Africa.

Hostilities have now ceased.

The whole of the citizen army will be brought back to the Union as quickly as possible.—Reuter.

CAPETOWN, Friday.

The German forces surrendered absolutely unconditionally.

General Botha presented an ultimatum to the commander, which expired at tea-time yesterday.—Reuter.

THE CONQUERED COLONY.

GENERAL BOTHA.

LORD KITCHENER AT THE GUILDHALL

Big Cheering Crowds Greet the War Minister.

Lord Kitchener opened at the ancient Guildhall to-day a three weeks' recruiting campaign for the City battalions.

With him on the platform were several other Cabinet Ministers, and in the hall were gathered the heads of the Corporation and of scores of great businesses in the famous Square Mile.

Lord Kitchener's drive was a triumphal progress. Along which his carriage drove in Queen-street and King-street the people were massed six deep.

BIG EXPLOSIONS AT HOUNSLOW.

Houses Three Miles From Powder Factory Shaken.

Early to-day two extremely violent explosions occurred at Messrs. Curtis and Harvey's powder factory at Hanworth, near Hounslow. The big explosions were followed by three or four smaller ones, and huge columns of smoke were plainly visible for miles round.

The workpeople, numbering several hundreds, however, resumed after breakfast when the explosions occurred. The extent of the damage is not yet known.

THE GOVERNMENT AND COMPULSION.

"OUR HANDS ARE ABSOLUTELY FREE," SAYS MR. LONG.

In the Commons on Monday Mr. Asquith was asked if he were able to assure the House, with respect to the National Registration Bill, that no such thing as the introduction of forced labour or conscription was contemplated.

Mr. ASQUITH replied:

"No such action as is referred to in the question is contemplated."

Mr. WALTER LONG told a deputation to-day:

"Let me say quite frankly that the Prime Minister would be the last man in this country to say anything in face of the situation in which we find ourselves which would prevent the Government adopting compulsory service to-morrow if they believed it to be right or necessary in order to bring the war to an end.

"Our hands are absolutely free."

Criticisms of the National Registration Bill were dealt with to-day by Mr. Walter Long, addressing at the Local Government Board representatives of municipalities and Urban District and Rural Councils throughout the country.

Some criticed the Bill, said Mr. Long, because they thought it was the forerunner of something else; others because they thought it foolish.

On the latter, men who were content to indulge in sneers at the expense of those who were working for their country, he had no breath to waste. He was content to leave them to the judgment of their fellow countrymen.

To the more serious critics who objected to national registration because they saw in it the first step to some form of compulsory service he wished to say that there was a great deal of criticism in the public mind upon the need of the Government.

cleared away many of the difficulties, and the position was more satisfactory.

A census four years old was practically useless for the purpose for which the register was required. He pledged his word that once the Government had the necessary information they would do their utmost to make practical use of it for the great purpose they all had in view—the termination of the war as rapidly as possible.

"NOT THE TIME FOR CRITICISM."

In earlier passages Mr. Long referred to the formation of the Coalition Government.

This was not the time, he said, to sit and criticise, or find fault, or to dwell on errors. Their duty to-day was paramount: it was to grapple with the present and to be ready for the future.

The policy of the late Government had been severely criticised. Criticism had been mainly in the direction of want of economically and wisely directed use of the services of the nation. If he had to find excuses for the late Government, he could do so in part.

War in Africa

When battle lines were drawn the British War Cabinet divided between "easterners" and "westerners", depending where they believed the focus of attention should lie. There was no "southerner" camp. Apart from guaranteeing British interests in Egypt, and in particular ensuring the Suez gateway remained open, Africa was inevitably something of a sideshow. That continent did see its share of fighting, however, for colonial rapaciousness meant the main belligerents had extensive territory spread across all its corners, often in close proximity. And it was in the African theatre that arguably Germany's greatest general waged war; a man who defied overwhelming odds and who conceded defeat only after news of the armistice filtered through.

Hundreds of thousands of Africans were pressed into service on behalf of their imperial masters, portering duties alone requiring vast manpower resources. Pack animals that might have been used in other theatres fell prey to disease, and it was African muscle that took up the slack. There was precious little reward for their effort or sacrifice. Decades would elapse between Woodrow Wilson's espousal of self-determination in his Fourteen Points and the "wind of change" blowing through a continent that wanted to shape its own destiny.

The scramble for imperial gains and enhanced prestige in resource-rich Africa had left Germany in control of four geographical areas. None was a military stronghold, but apart from the smallest – Togoland in the west, which fell swiftly to the Allies – they presented varying levels of threat and resistance. Cameroon, or Kamerun as it was to the German overlord, was a much larger territory, and though the capital, Douala, was soon in Allied hands, fighting moved into the interior and final victory was not achieved until February 1916. German South West Africa – present-day Namibia – shared a border with South Africa, the British dominion where memories of the Boer War were raw enough for allegiance to be divided. Some Afrikaners were only too happy to throw

in their lot with Germany if it meant striking back at a former enemy that had used concentration camps as a means of suppression. Prime Minister Louis Botha, himself a battle-hardened war veteran, pledged his loyalty to Britain, keen to repay the country that had granted self-government in 1910. He also had designs on absorbing Germany's neighbouring territory into an expanded South Africa as a dividend of victory. Botha, assisted by his defence minister and close political ally Jan Smuts – another warrior-statesman – quashed the internal rebellion before organising a successful cross-border invasion.

Lettow-Vorbeck: Germany's undefeated commander

The longest campaign took place in German East Africa, whose borders equate roughly to those of Tanzania. The Allies had a substantial numerical advantage over an enemy force that stood at less than 20,000, the majority of those askari tribesmen. That they failed to corner this small army, inflict a telling defeat or compel it to capitulate was in large measure down to the leadership of its brilliant commander, Paul von Lettow-Vorbeck. A career soldier, he had served in Africa before the war and gained priceless experience of bush fighting. Even so, with his seaborne supply route cut off, hostile territory on all sides and a 2,500-mile border to consider, von Lettow should have been more vulnerable than he proved to be. Recognising that outright victory was unattainable, he made his objective occupying as large an enemy force as possible. Accepting the caveat that his efforts were but a fleabite in the Entente's global strength, von Lettow did his disruptive best with great ingenuity, not simply in terms of tactical decision-making but in catering for his army's needs from the available resources, effectively living off the land.

Hundreds of thousands of Africans were pressed into service on behalf of their imperial masters.

Opposite: **The Cape Field Artillery marches along Adderley Street in Cape Town, after their return from German South West Africa. They are on their way to the City Hall, to be congratulated by the Mayor on their success in bringing the former German colony under British control.**

Far left: **British nurses at a military hospital in Nairobi in British East Africa**

Left: **Dr. Heinrich Albert Schnee (left) with Lieutenant Colonel Paul von Lettow-Vorbeck in Berlin. They were responsible for the political and military administration of German East Africa until the colony was lost after World War I.**

Heavy losses at Tanga

The first engagement, in November 1914, gave an indication of the task facing the Allies. An Anglo-Indian force landing at the port of Tanga soon found itself having to re-embark, having sustained heavy losses. Defeat was made worse by the fact that the retreating army left behind armaments that helped von Lettow keep an effective fighting force in the field. General Aitken, leader of the Allied force, did not have the best-trained soldiers at his disposal, but that did not exculpate him for presiding over a bruising encounter.

Von Lettow was largely unhindered in the months following the Tanga clash. With action in Cameroon and South West Africa ongoing, it was deemed prudent to play a waiting game. Needless to say, none of the warring parties entertained the thought of transferring men wholesale from the key European battlegrounds in pursuit of a minor victory on African soil. In spring 1916 the German commander faced a sterner test as General Smuts – now freed from duties closer to home – took up cudgels in a combined operation that also saw Belgian and Portuguese forces attacking from their own colonial outposts. Von Lettow knew when to strike, and when to melt away, crisscrossing borders when the need arose. The

months passed and he continued to elude and wrong-foot his opponents, ever mindful of the need to avoid the direct confrontation that Smuts, for his part, tried to orchestrate. Time and again he appropriated vital supplies from the Allies, and if on occasion he rode his luck in acquiring them, that was no bad trait in a commander, as Napoleon famously noted. A degree of ineptitude on the part of his would-be captors was also a factor in keeping the German army on the loose.

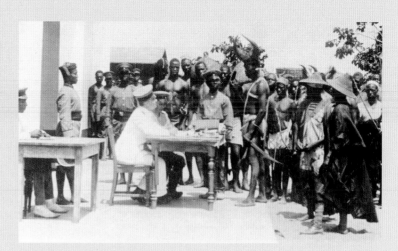

Above right: Togolese men in traditional dress are recruited into the army in German-controlled Togoland at the start of the conflict.

Below right: In German East Africa an estimated 12,000 local men, often referred to as askaris, were recruited to serve under German command. Von Lettow-Vorbeck's intention was to aid German victory by tying up British forces with a conflict in the colony.

Bottom: Men hung by the Germans in German East Africa were discovered when Dar-es-Salaam surrendered to the British.

Opposite above: To gain control of Lake Tanganyika from the Germans, the rather eccentric Lieutenant Commander Geoffrey Spicer-Simpson was put in command of two British armed motor boats sent over from England at the end of 1915. After 10,000 miles at sea they arrived at Cape Town and were then transported 3,175 miles to the lake, using a combination of rail, road and river.

Opposite below: The Allies successfully regained control of Lake Tanganyika by mid 1916. To return home the troops marched for thirteen days through the forests of northern Rhodesia where they were constantly welcomed by villagers bringing gifts. At River Lukuroo, local people met them with 150 canoes and took them as far as Lake Bangwelo to help them on their journey to N'Dolo in the Belgian Congo.

Paul von Lettow-Vorbeck's exploits made him a national hero. A recipient of the Prussian Order of Merit and the Iron Cross.

Guerrilla warfare

Von Lettow's guerrilla operation would be pored over by students of military history, used as an exemplar in lecture rooms full of budding army commanders. They noted the formidable obstacles he faced. Ammunition stocks became a pressing problem, while the hardships of operating in unforgiving tropical conditions were immense. Disease and malnutrition claimed countless lives. As one British officer wrote: "It is Africa and the climate we are really fighting, not the Germans." Still von Lettow kept on, until news of the armistice came through and he was able give up the struggle, the only German commander to remain undefeated in battle. When he surrendered to the British in Northern Rhodesia two weeks after hostilities had officially ceased, he led a unit of barely 1,000 men.

Paul von Lettow-Vorbeck's exploits made him a national hero. A recipient of the Prussian Order of Merit and Iron Cross, he was given a rapturous reception when he paraded through the streets of Berlin on horseback in 1919. Less typically, he was also highly regarded by those who fought against him, both for his military capabilities and the dignified manner and civility with which he bore himself. There existed not simply an absence of animosity, but respect and admiration between the former foes. In 1929 von Lettow was an honoured guest at a reunion for those who took part in the East Africa campaign, cheered to the rafters when Smuts introduced their old adversary. Referring to von Lettow's eel-like slipperiness, which he preserved by leading his men across vast swathes of inhospitable terrain, Smuts elicited much laughter when he observed: "I do not know whether he is a greater general or greater traveller." Years later, he also provided financial support to an impecunious von Lettow, who also has the distinction of having a Jurassic-era creature era named after him. When bones of the extinct animal were discovered in Tanzania in 1919, it was given the name dysalotosaurus lettowvorbecki – "uncatchable lizard".

June 1916

1 The only large-scale naval engagement of the war, the Battle of Jutland ended with a tactically inconclusive result. While the Royal Navy suffered more losses, the battle effectively ended any threat from the German High Seas Fleet, and British dominance of the North Sea was maintained.

2 The Battle of Mount Sorrel took place at Ypres when German forces attempted to capture the high ground around Ypres.

  German forces stormed Fort Vaux in the Battle of Verdun.

3 The National Defense Act authorised a five-year expansion of the US Army.

  The Allied Commander in Thessaloniki ordered all Greek officials out of the town, effectively imposing martial law.

4 The Russian Brusilov Offensive began on the Eastern Front.

5 TE Lawrence helped the Emir of Mecca in the Arab revolt against Turkish rule in Hejaz.

  HMS *Hampshire* struck a mine off the Orkneys and sank with the loss of nearly all the crew, and Great Britain's war minister, Lord Kitchener.

6 The Arab attack on Medina was repulsed by the Turkish garrison.

  President Yuan Shikai of China died and was succeeded by Li Yuanhong.

7 French troops at Fort Vaux surrendered to the Germans.

8 Voluntary enlistment in Britain was replaced by compulsion when the Second Compulsory Service Act came into operation.

  British forces occupied Bismarckburg and Belgian troops occupied Usumbura in German East Africa.

9 Arab forces captured the city of Jeddah in Arabia.

  German forces attacked Kondoa Irangi in German East Africa.

10 The New Zealand Government passed the Compulsory Service Bill.

11 The Battle of the Strypa began during the Brusilov Offensive.

12 Zaleszczyki in Galicia was taken by Russian forces.

13 The Battle of Mount Sorrel ended when British and Canadian troops secured the line near Ypres.

14 French politician Étienne Clémentel presided over the Allied Economic Conference in Paris.

15 Paolo Boselli was appointed Italian Prime Minister, following the collapse of the Salandra Government.

16 Italian forces began a counter-offensive against Austrian troops in the Trentino.

17 French defenders repulsed German attacks on Le Mort Homme at Verdun.

18 German flying ace and pioneer Max Immelmann was shot down and killed during aerial combat with a British squadron.

19 British and South African troops marched into Handeni in German East Africa.

21 The Entente Governments sent a Note to King Constantine demanding Greek demobilisation and a change of Government.

22 Alexandros Zaimis replaced Stephanos Skouloudis as Prime Minister of Greece.

23 German forces attacked and captured Fort Thiaumont at Verdun.

24 Massive preparatory bombardment to destroy German defences began at the Somme.

26 The trial of Roger Casement for high treason began.

27 The Emir of Mecca issued his Proclamation of Independence from Turkey.

28 The Italian cavalry reached Pedescala, north-east of Asiago on the Southern Front.

29 Roger Casement was found guilty of high treason and sentenced to death.

30 The Battle of the Strypa ended.

BIG BRITISH ATTACK AT YPRES.

LATE WAR NEWS.

CANADIAN DASH AT YPRES.

RECAPTURE OF LOST POSITIONS.

1,500 YARDS OF TRENCH.

SUCCESSFUL AUSTRALIAN RAID.

GERMANS SLIGHTLY NEARER VERDUN.

DAY OF THE WAR.
DAY OF BATTLE OF VERDUN.
DAY OF THIRD BATTLE OF YPRES.
DAY OF RUSSIAN OFFENSIVE.

Ypres: The Canadians by a splendid
yesterday morning regained all
second south-east of

BRITISH OFFICIAL.
FRANCE, Tuesday, 11.18 p.m.

At 1.30 this morning Canadian troops
made gallant and successful assaults
south-east of Zillebeke (south-east of
Ypres).

Their objective was our old positions

WAR AFTER THE WAR

MR. HUGHES & GERMAN TRADE VAMPIRE.

FROM OUR OWN CORRESPONDENT.
PARIS, Tuesday.

Sixty delegates, representing the eight
Allied Powers, will meet in secret at ten
o'clock to-morrow morning under the presi-
dency of M. Briand, the French Premier, at
the Quai d'Orsay for the first sitting of the
Allied International Economic Conference.
At the succeeding sittings M. Clémentel,
Minister of Commerce, will take the chair.

The members met this afternoon at the
Ministry of Commerce and agreed on a
working programme which will regulate
their sessions. Eight different programmes
are to be submitted for discussion. Questions as widely apart as freights and
aniline dyes, coal and frozen mutton, munitions and a tariff wall against Nuremberg
toys have a place on the agenda paper.
After the first plenary sitting the Conference will split into Committees charged
with drafting reports on special questions
to be submitted later to the whole Conference.

In French diplomatic and political circles
it is reported that Mr. Hughes, the Aus-

GREAT RUSSIAN STRIDES.

RAPID ADVANCE ON KOVEL.

DNIESTER FORTRESS CAPTURED.

From HAMILTON FYFE.
PETROGRAD, Monday.

There is good reason to believe that
Czernovitz has either been occupied by
the Russians or is on the point of being
occupied.

In the great victory gained at Dobro-
novtse (14 miles north-east of Czernovitz) General Letchitsky drove the
enemy from the only positions upon which
the town could be defended. The rout
of the Austrians here was one of the
most complete during a week of glorious
successes. Attacking both from the
east and north the Russians threw them
into utter confusion and thousands gave
themselves up, having lost all their officers. Many units were surrendered by

BUKOVINA TRIUMPH.

WHOLE ARMY CORPS CAPTURED.

Russian Official. PETROGRAD, Tues.

In view of the fact that the Austro-
Hungarian and Austro-German troops have at
many places withdrawn out of reach of the
blows of our southern armies, the number
of prisoners given in yesterday's communiqué shows for the moment but little increase, the total now being about 1,700 officers and 114,000 men.

It is confirmed that the troops of
General Letchitsky (in the Bukovina)
since the beginning of the operations have
captured

3 commanders of regiments.
754 other officers.
37,832 soldiers the whole army

DUBLIN MYSTERY

SERGEANT ACQUITTED

HIS SUSPICION OF AN OFFICER.

Company Quartermaster-Sergeant Rob-
Flood, 5th Batt. Royal Dublin Fusilie
was yester day found not guilty by a gen
court-martial on a charge of having m
dered at Guinness's Brewery on April
Lieutenant A. Lucas, 2nd King Edwar
Horse, and William John Rice, an employ
of the brewery company.

Captain E. Toler, Inniskilling Fusilie
said that Mr. Lucas was in the uniform
his regiment. He had a strong "Yanke
accent and was able to pass anywhere a
"Yankee." When he went out on inte
gence work he was in mufti.

Sergeant Flood, in evidence, said that
joined the battalion in London in 1899
had been a non-commissioned officer
fourteen years. On the day on which
took up duty in the brewery he noticed
one of the offices a small box of ammuniti
A civilian was there and the witness qu
tioned him about it, getting no repl
box which turned to Captain Mac

OUR YPRES GUNS' TRIUMPH.

PREPARATION DONE IN AN HOUR.

From W. BEACH THOMAS.
BRITISH HEADQUARTERS, FRANCE,
Wednesday.

The charge of the Canadian infantry,
who recovered "at the first intention"
their trenches at Ypres bore some likeness to a famous charge made within a
mile or two of this spot by the Guards
in 1914. Only to-day the hazel coppices
are thinner, the scattered oaks sparser,
and no pheasants fled cackling with the
flying Germans.

Though expected on both sides, the
attack was sudden and startling. From
the depth of a night dark and rainy and
cold our artillery broke out with the
suddenness of an eruption, and it could
be seen from afar, for there are few vantage points in Europe more salient than
the abrupt hills which stand up like
artificial heaps from the Flanders plain.
The concentration of fire was probably
greater than the German of the week
before; but the period was shorter. In
less than an hour the work was done.

KILLING BOMBARDMENT.

Those of us who saw the Canadians,
the wounded as well as the hale, come
back from that killing bombardment last
week perceived then, even in the eyes of
men blurred by toil and want of sleep, a
determined zest for a quick revenge. The
opportunity did not come at once; but
when it came it came quickly. It is one
of the most astonishing things in this
amazing war that such an advance as these
men pushed home in the small hours of
Tuesday morning met with few difficulties
and was far less costly than many almost
negative fights of which little is heard.

Spring on The Western Front

At a conference of Allied leaders at Chantilly in late 1915 the strategy for the new year was thrashed out. They settled upon a major summer offensive on all fronts, the partners acting in concert to forestall the possibility of German troops being speedily reassigned according to need. The Gallipoli evacuation freed up manpower, and British strength would be further bolstered as the latest cohorts of battle-ready troops were deployed during the spring. Meanwhile, Germany's chief of staff Erich von Falkenhayn remained intent on defeating Britain by prising her chief weapon – France – from her grasp. Russia, bruised from the battering received in 1915, was deemed no immediate threat; a holding operation in the east would suffice, allowing Falkenhayn to focus his efforts on his attempt to "bleed France white" at Verdun.

If these were the main objectives of the rival strategists going into 1916, they were not the only action hotspots on the Western Front in the year's early months. Diversionary attacks were needed to keep the enemy guessing, and on 14 February, a week before laying siege to Verdun, the Germans went on the offensive in the quest for a key vantage point at Ypres. Occupation of this unprepossessing hill on the bank of the Ypres-Comines canal – known as the Bluff – was of vital importance to the Allies if the salient was to be held. Fall it did, however, prompting an immediate retaliatory assault that returned the Bluff into its former hands.

Battle at St Eloi

Even as plans to retake the Bluff were being made, preparations were also underway for an Allied strike at St Eloi, a village lying some three miles south of Ypres. Here again there was a patch of raised ground – known as the Mound – this time held by the Germans and a nagging concern to the Allies overlooked. Shelling and surface mines had already created a lunar landscape at St Eloi, and the British were ready to add a few more craters with some sizeable underground explosions. A network of tunnels had been dug, some stretching to the German line, others terminating in no-man's-land. Just after 4 am on 27 March, the mines were detonated, the artillery opened up and troops poured over the top. The infantry were now wrestling for control of seven enormous craters, the largest 50 feet deep. The lower lying of these were soon filling with water in atrocious weather. For inexperienced Canadian troops caught up in the morass, it was a brutal baptism. There were nightmarish communication problems; accurate intelligence was at a premium. At times it was hard to know who held what. The struggle for this pitted wasteland raged until mid-April, the position at the winding down of the Battle of St Eloi materially unaltered from that which prevailed at the outset. This perceived fiasco prompted an inquiry and calls for heads to roll among the Canadian generals leading the operation. For political reasons, recriminations were limited to a shuffling of the hierarchy. Haig observed that keeping "a couple of incompetent commanders" was a small price to pay for Allied harmony.

Opposite: The jubilant Northumberland Fusiliers after their victory at St Eloi, just south of Ypres. Assisted by the Royal Fusiliers, they took the front and second line German trenches along a stretch of 600 yards, capturing many prisoners. Men, wearing the recently issued Brodie helmets wave their trophies of war found in the captured trenches.

Above: The battleground near Ypres.

Below: German soldiers show relief after their capture by the Northumberland Fusiliers at St Eloi.

Vimy Ridge in German hands

By the beginning of May, the German army had been pounding Verdun for over two months. British troops were arriving in numbers in the run-up to the big summer push, greeted with much relief by Joffre as they took over from the French 10th Army in Artois. The poilus departed to shore up Verdun, leaving Haig overseeing a British sector expanded by over 10 miles, now stretching from Ypres to the Somme. In the middle of that serpentine line stood Vimy, where there had been little fighting since the French suffered large losses attempting to capture the high ground the previous autumn. Germany's command of Vimy Ridge had thus gone unchallenged for some months, but the arrival of fresh British forces ended what appeared a cosy example of live-and-let-live inactivity. In fact, the Germans had been hard at work on tunnelling operations, and the Royal Engineers were immediately sent into action to counter that threat. A feverish underground battle took place as rival tunnellers vied to undermine the enemy's position. British sappers had the better of things, and the Germans were also concerned by the build-up of enemy troops. They decided to revert to surface warfare, and on 21 May launched a massive bombardment as a prelude to an attack. It was a notable success, yielding Allied ground and a favourable balance sheet in terms of casualties. There was an attempted British counter, but with the bigger picture of the Somme in mind, the decision was taken not to expend further time, manpower and shells on regaining the lost territory. For now Vimy Ridge remained firmly in German hands.

Top: Anzacs march past General Joffre.

Above left: British troops arrive in France in 1916. At its peak there were over two million troops fighting on the Western Front and by the end of the conflict just under 5.5 million men had fought there at some stage.

Middle left: A French captive military balloon or "sausage" as it was called by the troops, is prepared for flight. The balloons, tethered by a wire, enabled troops to gain height to observe German positions and manoeuvres, especially on very flat landscapes.

Below left: A vigilant German mans an outpost.

Bottom: The Germans launched a tactical attack on Mount Sorrel on 2 June in an attempt to take an important observation post and also to lure French and British troops away from Verdun.

The position at the winding down of the Battle of St Eloi was materially unaltered from that which prevailed at the outset.

Above left: The heavy guns used during the conflict were often placed on substantial mountings and had water-cooling mechanisms. They were able to sustain long-range automatic fire with deadly accuracy. However, they were very heavy and difficult to move and hence needed a large crew to operate them.

Below left: German troops crouch in the trenches ready to launch hand grenades at British troops. By 1916 German troops were using the new Model 24 grenade, often referred to as the stick grenade or "potato masher", due to its distinctive appearance. They could be thrown 30 to 40 yards and used a friction igniter to light a five-second fuse.

Above right: A Belgian soldier masked against a gas attack. In total 267,000 Belgian soldiers served during the conflict. From this fighting force 14,000 were killed and 54,000 injured.

Below right: Three styles of British uniform: officer's garb on the left, private's on the right, while a member of a Scottish regiment sports the kilted version.

Bottom: Members of the Northumberland Fusiliers return after their success at St Eloi. Between them they carry their trophies; one man has an eagle emblem on his helmet while another sports a German greatcoat.

RUSSIANS ROLLING BACK THE AUSTRIAN ARMY.

AUSTRIAN FRONT BROKEN FOR 100 MILES.

RUSSIANS TAKE 14,000 MORE PRISONERS.

ADVANCE ON ALL SOUTHERN LINE.

GERMAN FLANK EXPOSED AND IN DANGER.

BRITISH SHIP'S DASH.

1 000 MILES IN BALTIC.

GERMANS ELUDED.

FROM OUR OWN CORRESPONDENT.
COPENHAGEN, Friday.
The British steamer Dunrobin (3,617 tons, Newcastle) succeeded this afternoon in passing through the ... in her way

GEN. JOFFRE IN LONDON.

WAR COUNCIL AND VISIT TO THE KING.

HUN LIQUID FIRE ATTACKS FAIL.

OUR HEAVY GUNS ACTIVE.

ENEMY BOMBARDED AT MANY POINTS.

British Official. FRANCE, Fri., 11.5 p.m.
Last night a party belonging to the Gloucester Regiment entered the enemy's trenches south of Neuve Chapelle, and after successfully attacking also ...

GREECE CLIMBING DOWN.

ARMY DEMOBILISATION.

From J. M. N. JEFFRIES.
ATHENS, Thursday, 10.20 p.m.
M. Skouloudis, the Premier, has announced in the Chamber the demobilisation of the Greek Army. The action, he ...

THE HAMPSHIRE ON FIRE.

EXPLOSION AN HOUR AFTER SAILING.

BOATS SMASHED ON ROCKS.

WEDNESDAY, JUNE 14, 1916.

SPLENDID RUSSIANS.

The Russians are nobly maintaining the splendid record of daily achievement which has marked their present offensive. Yesterday's news shows that they are advancing very fast west of Lutsk. Farther south, they are now west of the Strypa, that little river in Galicia which has become so famous; and along the banks of which an almost continuous battle has raged for so many weary months. Their success at this point is the more striking because it has been gained against a German general, Count von Bothmer, who commands in his army at least two German divisions.

It is not to be supposed that the Russians can continue to capture the pick of the Austrian Army by the ten thousand. Their enemy is well supplied with munitions and has considerable reserves, while the difficulty of maintaining the supplies of the Russian forces as they advance through a country which has been devastated, where the roads and railways will almost certainly have been destroyed, must be very great. But our gallant Allies have already worked marvels, and the German Staff may to-day be regretting its costly campaign against Verdun and the "strafing" expedition against Italy, to both of which it is reported that Hindenburg was bitterly opposed.

The Brusilov Offensive

The first 18 months of war had left the Russian army reeling from the blows inflicted by its German counterpart. A lumbering, inefficient war machine cost Russia dear, with a casualty toll already running into millions. From Germany's perspective, after the failure to deliver an early war-winning strike in the west in 1914, Falkenhayn had looked eastward the following year. By 1916 he was confident enough in the damage his army had wreaked on tsarist forces to refocus on the west, executing his plan to "bleed France white" at Verdun. As the battle for the ancient fortress city ground on, Joffre was desperate for a relieving offensive to begin, in accordance with agreed Allied strategy. Haig vacillated, fearing his Kitchener recruits were not yet ready. In late May he was still expressing his concerns regarding "a collection of divisions untrained for the field" to an exasperated Joffre. Within a matter of days France's Commander-in-Chief had cheerier news. For on 4 June, almost a month before Haig relented and the first British troops went over the top at the Somme, a revived Russian army struck powerfully in the east.

The architect of a four-month Eastern campaign that delivered rich, if impermanent, returns was General Alexei Brusilov. He was the recently appointed commander of the front's southwest sector, facing an Austro-Hungarian enemy across Galicia and the Carpathian Mountains. Unlike Haig, who was keen to secure as much preparation time as possible, Brusilov actually brought forward his plans on learning of a successful Austrian attack on the Italian front in mid-May. In doing so he departed from the original scheme – a coordinated Russian attack along the Eastern Front – clearly frustrated at the north-based generals' dragging of their feet. Shock and surprise were to be Brusilov's weapons. The element of surprise was all too often surrendered as artillery bombardments signalled intent. The astute Brusilov would not go down that road, making sure that all preliminary operations were conducted under a cloak of secrecy. The "shock" element came in the deployment of troops that would deliver lightning strikes, punching holes in the enemy line through which the main body would pour. Moreover, those ruptures would be spread far and wide, creating confusion and preventing the enemy from reinforcing the line effectively.

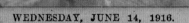

Above: Russian troops prepare torpedoes in the trenches. By 1916 improvements in industrial output and an increase in imports meant that the Russian Army had sufficient equipment to mobilise again.

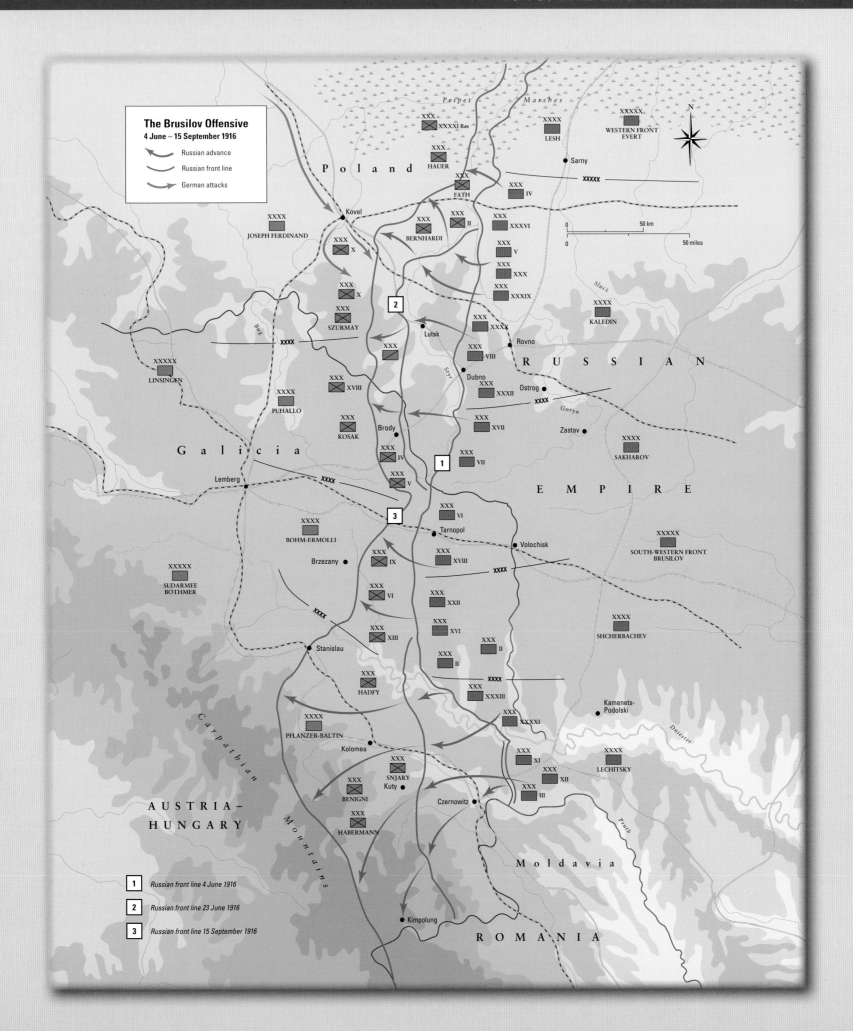

The Brusilov Offensive
4 June – 15 September 1916

↷ Russian advance
⌒ Russian front line
→ German attacks

Poland

Pripet Marshes

XXX
XXXXI Res

XXXX
LESH

XXXXX
WESTERN FRONT
EVERT

N

XXX
HAUER

● Sarny

XXX
FATH

XXX
IV

XXXXX

Kovel

XXXX
JOSEPH FERDINAND

XXX
X

XXX
BERNHARDI

XXX
II

XXXX
XXXVI

50 km

50 miles

XXX
X

XXX
V

XXX
XXX

XXX
XXXIX

XXX
SZURMAY

XXX

XXX
XXXX

Lutsk ●

XXX

XXXX
KALEDIN

Bug

XXXX

Sluce

XXXX
LINSINGEN

XXX
XVIII

Dubno ●

XXX
VIII

Styr

Rovno ●

R U S S I A N

XXXX
PUHALLO

Ostrog ●

XXX
XXXII

XXXX

Goryn

XXX
KOSAK

Brody ●

XXX
IV

XXX
XVII

Zastav ●

XXXX
SAKHAROV

Galicia

XXX
V

XXX
VII

1

Lemberg ●

XXXX

E M P I R E

XXXX
BOHM-ERMOLLI

XXX
VI

3

Tarnopol ●

XXX
XVIII

Volochisk ●

XXXXX
SOUTH-WESTERN FRONT
BRUSILOV

Brzezany ●

XXX
IX

XXX
XXXX

XXXXX
SUDARMEE
BOTHMER

XXX
VI

XXX
XXII

XXX
XVI

XXXX
SHCHERBACHEV

XXX
XIII

XXX
II

Stanislau ●

XXX
II

XXXX

XXX
HADFY

XXX
XXXIII

● Kamenets-
Podolski

XXXX
PFLANZER-BALTIN

XXX
XXXXI

Dniester

Kolomea ●

XXX
XI

XXXX
LECHITSKY

A U S T R I A –
HUNGARY

Carpathian

XXX
SNJARY

Kuty ●

XXX
XII

XXX
BENIGNI

Czernowitz ●

XXX
III

Mountains

XXX
HABERMANN

M o l d a v i a

Prut

1 Russian front line 4 June 1916

2 Russian front line 23 June 1916

3 Russian front line 15 September 1916

Kimpolung ●

R O M A N I A

ITALIAN AND RUSSIAN SUCCESSES.

KE 8,000 PRISONERS. | **KNOCKING OUT THE HUN GUNS.** | **BRITISH OUTSIDE GUILLEMONT.** | **MR. A. HENDERSON.** | **DEAR LIVING.**

IDGEHEAD CAPTURED. | OUR EAGLE-EYED AIRMEN | ADVANCE FROM THE SOUTH-WEST. | HIS POSITION IN THE MINISTRY. | £1 WORTH ONLY 12s. TO BUY FOOD.

RUSSIAN VICTORY | From W. BEACH THOMAS. | | By OUR POLITICAL CORRESPONDENT. | A Government calculation is published to-day that the war has increased the cost of

One million more Russian casualties

Initially, the results were staggering; Russia's finest hour of the war in terms of territorial gain and enemy killed or captured. Austria's military chief, Franz Conrad, was forced to rein in his assault on Italy. The Allied plan to dilute the forces of the Central Powers gained further traction when Russian forces in the northern sector belatedly opened up. German troops soon halted that advance, as they had a poorly conceived and executed attack in March, but at a cost of tying down valuable resources. Meanwhile, in the south Brusilov's onward march carried on into September, by which time his men had taken a 60-mile-deep bite into enemy ground. As was so often the case, seizing territory and holding it were two different things. Rapid advances meant stretched supply lines, and exhaustion if reserves were not readily available. Success brought a natural headiness and desire to continue when discretion was the wisest course, particularly as the Habsburg line was now stiffened by German manpower. Such was the fate of Brusilov's Offensive. He had taken Austria-Hungary to the brink in what was the Entente's most significant success to date. He had also helped convince Romania – the last undeclared Balkan state – to side with Allies. That coup was the final nail in Falkenhayn's coffin; from August 1916 Hindenburg and Ludendorff were helming the war effort. But on the debit side, the newcomer to the Entente fold offered barely a fleabite and was quickly squashed, despite Russian support. Bucharest fell on 6 December. And the ground so spectacularly won by Brusilov changed hands yet again in the closing months of the year, leaving the retreating troops in anything but peak fighting condition. The offensive had taken an immense physical toll – over one million added to Russia's casualty register – with psychological damage to match. The mood of disenchantment soon infected the entire country.

As was so often the case, seizing territory and holding it were two different things. Rapid advances meant stretched supply lines, and exhaustion.

Opposite below: German soldiers fasten their rations of bread to their knapsacks on the Eastern Front in Prussia.

Opposite: The Habsburg line was now stiffened by German troops. More than two million German men would meet their deaths before the war was over.

Above: France's General Balfourier talks to English and Russian officers while flanked by Serbian and Japanese military leaders.

Below: A field kitchen in Russia, with all its fires going.

GREAT SOMME ADVANCE.

M. VENIZELOS' MOVE. LATE WAR NEWS.   'SILK' STOCKINGS.

The Somme

In November 1916 the Allies' major offensive of the year wound down. A *Times* correspondent said of the five-month Somme campaign that it had been "not one battle but 50 battles, and 50 victories". That 100 per cent approval rating, understandable when a white hot war was being waged and managing the national mood was a serious business, plummeted when the grim facts became public knowledge. The Somme became synonymous with industrial-scale blood-letting, wastefulness of human life for marginal gain. It also put under the microscope the reputations of those who formulated the plan and cleaved to it with unbending faith even as the death toll soared.

No one dared pass on the information that the bombardment had not had the desired effect.

The Big Push

The Allies went into 1916 intent on stretching Germany's resources to breaking point. Russia and Italy would play their part in a co-ordinated attack, while the focal point of the Western Front offensive would be an Anglo-French assault on a 25-mile stretch of the enemy line astride the River Somme. For Sir Douglas Haig, who replaced Sir John French as BEF commander in December 1915, the "Big Push" offered the chance to wrest the initiative, to end the stalemate and return to a war of movement. The shell shortage had been addressed, and "Kitchener's Army" was being readied. After an artillery bombardment the like of which had never been seen, those recruits would stroll through the enemy line unhindered. "You will meet nothing but dead and wounded Germans," said General Sir Henry Rawlinson, commander of the newly formed Fourth Army and the man charged with implementing the plan. His confident prediction didn't stop him from having ambulance trains ready to take heavy casualties.

Haig's timing

The fact that Verdun was under siege from late February made little difference to the Allied operation, except with regard to the timing. By early summer the beleaguered French needed the Somme attack to begin sooner rather than later in order to relieve the pressure on their historic fortress town. For Haig there was a balance to be struck between coming to the aid of an alliance partner and not pressing the New Army into service too soon. Late June gave due weight to both considerations. When the attack was launched, France could commit only five divisions; Britain would be very much the senior partner.

Above: **The calm before the storm.** Two infantrymen share a quiet moment on the eve of the Somme offensive.

Opposite above: **A column of the East Yorkshire Regiment march into action along a peaceful country lane. Many of those fighting on the Somme were Kitchener's recruits and this was to be their first taste of the battlefield.**

Opposite middle: **This new recruit, believed to be Private Joseph Bailey from the Sheffield Pals, became one of the first soldiers to be killed in the offensive. Eight battalions went "over the top" on the first day with the three Pals battalions suffering the heaviest casualty rate.**

Opposite below: **Lancashire Fusiliers fix their bayonets prior to assault. By the start of the Somme offensive one million manganese steel helmets were delivered to the front line. Weighing two pounds each, they were designed to withstand shrapnel travelling at 750 feet per second.**

The bombardment begins

The week-long bombardment began on 24 June. Even as the first of over a million shells pounded the German line, the plan began to unravel. The infantry upon whose heads the bombardment rained incessantly went to ground. And in the chalky subsoil of the battlezone the Germans dug very deep, over 30 feet in places. While they were safely ensconced in their bunkers, shrapnel shells exploded harmlessly above. Many were duds. Crucially, only a fraction of the ordnance had the explosive power to penetrate to the depths where the subterranean army had taken refuge. Add in the fact that those million and a half shells were spread over a vast area and the picture became even worse for Haig and Rawlinson. The former did not take criticism well; no one dared pass on the information that the bombardment had not had the desired effect. Thus on 30 June 1916, the eve of battle, Haig noted in his diary: "The wire has never been so well cut, nor the artillery preparation so thorough".

German infantry prepared

The guns at last fell silent on the morning of 1 July. With a final destructive flourish, huge mines that had been laid beneath the enemy line were exploded. The effect of these was chiefly the same as the other shells: churning up the same ground, launching the same barbed wire into air until gravity delivered it back to earth. As it came to rest for the final time, the German infantry needed no clearer signal that the Allies were on the march. They emerged from the underground sanctuaries to set up their machine gun emplacements in plenty of time to greet the advance.

The German infantry emerged from the underground sanctuaries to set up their machine gun emplacements in plenty of time to greet the advance.

Whistles blown at 7.30 am

In the British forward trenches whistles were blown at 7.30 am to signal the start of the attack. Some in the first wave that went over the top kicked footballs ahead of them, as if to blithely suggest that this would be the extent of their day's shooting. The men who struck out into no-man's-land were encumbered with kit weighing up to 70lb – heavy enough for a footslog over open ground; an enormous burden when the bullets began flying. Some wore reflective material on their backs to ensure that any supporting artillery fire went well over their heads. But it was the shellfire in front of them that did the damage. In their thousands soldiers of the new citizen army were cut to pieces, every fallen body exposing those behind to deadly fire. Where gaps in the barbed wire had been opened up, these attracted both oncoming soldiers and the attention of German machine-gunners. The laudable idea of encouraging men from the same community to join up together rebounded as some "Pals' battalions" sustained heavy losses, leaving entire communities bereft. Still the troops ventured forth towards the enemy, at walking pace and in orderly lines as instructed. It was "as though they were going to the theatre", said one German soldier of the sedate advance.

Creeping barrage

Communications were difficult, but it became clear that the cavalry ranks waiting to consolidate a glorious infantry breakthrough would not be needed. There had been some gains: the German line breached to a depth of a mile in places, a couple of target villages taken. The use of a "creeping barrage" – where foot-soldiers advanced behind a moving curtain of shellfire – reaped dividends where it was efficiently employed. To the south the French made encouraging progress, attaining all set targets. Their artillery bombardment was concentrated on a narrower front, and the German line facing them was more lightly defended. These were bright spots in a day that ended with almost half of the 120,000 troops deployed on the casualty list. Nearly 20,000 lay dead, for the capture of less than three square miles. It was the darkest day in the annals of British military history, but the generals were not about to allow such details to throw them off a course that had been months in the plotting.

DAILY MAIL   JULY 3, 1916

The first day's gains

A great battle had been fought. Another is being fought, and many more have yet to be fought. It will probably be called in England the Battle of Montauban and in France the Battle of the Somme. But, whatever we call it, or however we judge it, we must think of it as a battle of many battles, not to be likened in duration or extent, or perhaps intention, to such affairs as Neuve Chapelle or Loos.

It is and for many days will continue to be siege warfare, in which a small territorial gain may be a great strategical gain; and the price we must pay is to be judged by another measure than miles or furlongs or booty.

We are laying siege not to a place but to the German army – that great engine which had at last mounted to its final perfection and utter lust of dominion.

In the first battle, which I saw open with incredible artillery fury at 6 o'clock this morning, we have beaten the Germans by greater dash in the infantry and vastly superior weight in munitions. I may, perhaps, claim to be in some position to estimate methods and results. I watched the night bombardments, both German and British. I saw at close quarters the hurricane of the morning bombardment, which heralded that first gay, impetuous, and irresistible leap from the trenches, many of which I had visited earlier, knowing what was to come.

Above: **For the first time the British commanders planned to use the tactic of the "creeping barrage"; a line of artillery fire moving forward just ahead of the advancing infantrymen.**

Below: **The Northumberland Fusiliers were one of the first regiments to go over the top at La Boiselle. The village was an important strategic target and successfully fell to the Allies on 6 July.**

Opposite above: **A series of mines prepared by the Royal Engineers were designed to destroy German defences and provide cover for the advancing Allies at the start of the offensive. The majority were blown up at 7.28am on the first day of the Battle but failed to make any significant impact as German commanders had moved troops to the safety of their deep dug-outs.**

Opposite middle and below: **Within a matter of days the millions of pounds of explosives used on the battlefields resulted in complete desolation with casualties littering the landscape.**

CRATER CAUSED BY EXPLOSION OF A MINE JUST BEFORE THE ASSAULT

ORIGINAL BRITISH FRONT LINE

GOMMECOURT.

BRITISH FAILURE THAT WON THE DAY.

MARCH THROUGH A DEATH ZONE.

MAIN GERMAN FORCE PINNED DOWN.

MR. BEACH THOMAS IN FRICOURT.

Mr. Beach Thomas describes below first his visit to Fricourt and then the most glorious feat of the battle, the British attack at Gommecourt against the Germans' heaviest mass, an attack that failed at the spot but made possible success elsewhere.

From W. BEACH THOMAS.

PRESS CAMP, FRANCE,
Monday.

This morning, the third day of the battle, I was able to penetrate into Fricourt village itself and move up close to the edge of the wood some 500 yards behind our infantry, just at the time when they completed their brilliant attack across the base of the German wedge left at this place by the fighting of the first day.

Midland and Northern troops, attacking, the one from the north, the others from the south, joined hands just before noon at the base of the German wedge and put the finishing touch on a singularly well-executed manœuvre.

The regiments to the south, moving from the direction of the newly conquered village of Mametz, soon cleared the wood in front of them—just behind Fricourt Wood proper. The others were held up for a little while by a machine gun hidden in the edge of a copse. The fire of this gun could be heard rattling in little angry bouts whenever a group of men showed themselves; and apparently it could not be exactly located. But the check was a short one. The gun was outflanked, our troops made their way both across the open ground and down trenches into the scarified wood and were soon in touch with the other party. The German promontory was cut right across at the base and every man behind the cut was in our hands.

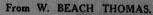

Nearly 20,000 lay dead, for the capture of less than three square miles.

The Battle of Albert

The Somme Offensive can be split into a number of distinct phases, the first of which spanned the costly opening day and ran through to 13 July. The Battle of Albert, as it was known, revealed the hollow optimism of the plan to penetrate a German line crushed under the weight of the ferocious preliminary bombardment. The artillery – and heavy guns in particular – was spread too thinly, there were too many duds and insufficient high-explosive shells to inflict the kind of damage Haig hoped for. Skeleton sentry crews faced the hit-and-miss onslaught; the main body of the German army was insulated in deep dugouts awaiting the call. The French, learning hard lessons from Verdun, adopted more flexible tactics instead of advancing in rigid lines and presenting an inviting daylight target. They made headway in the south, helped by the fact that the enemy had not anticipated a concerted strike in this area. There were also gains in the southern sector of the British front, around Fricourt and Mametz, which Haig sought to exploit in the period 2-13 July. By the end of the Battle of Albert, the British had in their sights the German second line at Bazentine Ridge, Haig having recalibrated the objective as a "wearing-out" assault – a precursor to a renewed late-summer attack – rather than a swift, decisive breakthrough.

Opposite below: After seven days of fighting, Trônes Wood was captured on 14 July by British troops commanded by Lieutenant-Colonel Maxwell. It was at some cost; there were just under 4,000 casualties and only tree stumps, barbed wire and bodies remained.

Opposite left: The battle line from Arras to the Somme as it was when the offensive started. Arrows indicate the main line of advance. The British line ends near the Somme while the French line continues south.

Opposite right: The southern part of the battleground. The space between the dotted line and the black line represents the ground gained by the Allies. Figures indicate height in metres. The inset map shows the line from Lille to Peronne.

Right: The combination of shell craters and heavy rain produced difficult terrain for men, animals and motor vehicles, including the latest battlefield weapon: the tank.

Below: Due to the high casualty rate in the first phase of the war the majority of the British fighting force were now volunteers from Kitchener's Recruits and the Territorial Army. Retired soldiers and inexperienced men gained senior positions swiftly, reducing the levels of competence.

The Battle of Albert revealed the hollow optimism of the plan to penetrate the German line.

The Somme battleground

The decision to make the sector east of Amiens astride the River Somme the point of the Allied offensive in summer 1916 was driven by the fact that this was where the British and French armies rubbed shoulders. In its original conception, the French were to lead the charge. The bloodbath of Verdun changed all that: the poilus would play a supporting role; Britain, for the first time, was to be the senior partner in a joint operation. And not before time, as far as many of France's high-ranking figures were concerned.

This area of Picardy had been relatively quiet, for there were no important strategic targets in sight. Joffre, the plan's original architect, was simply out to inflict casualties on a scale the enemy could not withstand. When Haig took the reins, the scheme developed into an attack on a 14-mile front, between Serre in the north and Maricourt in the south. There was to be a diversionary raid at Gommecourt, just above Serre, while the French Sixth Army would attack on either side of the river on a further eight-mile front. The breadth of the offensive was meant to counter the problem of flanking fire that bedevilled narrow-front assaults, but had the disastrous corollary of diluting the artillery barrage. Haig wanted to puncture the German line, with two cavalry divisions ready to exploit holes created by the gunners and infantry. The failure to entertain the prospect that the enemy might have dug deep into the chalk, negating the effects of the bombardment, set up a battle that was brutally attritional. Falkenhayn's directive that every inch of lost territory should be retaken immediately ensured that it ground on. The battle evolved into a piecemeal struggle, though Haig never abandoned hopes that these would lead, incrementally, to a dramatic outcome. Almost 100 small-scale attacks were launched in the two-month period from mid-July, delivering less than three square miles into Allied hands. The desperate need for good news prompted the BEF commander-in-chief, under fire from his political masters, to throw the newly arrived tanks into action in mid-September. When the offensive was finally brought to a halt, the Allies had penetrated seven miles at most. French gains came at a fraction of that cost. Estimates of German casualties vary, but were high enough for Ludendorff to comment that his army "had been fought to a standstill".

Left: A wounded soldier is helped to safety by a comrade. On the first day of the Somme the British suffered just under 60,000 casualties with 90 per cent of these claimed by German Maxim machine guns.

Above: French troops on the march following their defeat of the German Second Army after an attack from both sides of the Somme.

Below: The "Big Push" at a glance. This pictorial map shows the territory over which the Allies had advanced since 1 July. The thick black line to the left represents the Allied front before the advance, while the thick broken line to the right is the new front. The numerous captured villages are circled. Each dotted square represents 9 square miles.

Opposite: German casualties lie abandoned in a trench taken by the Allies.

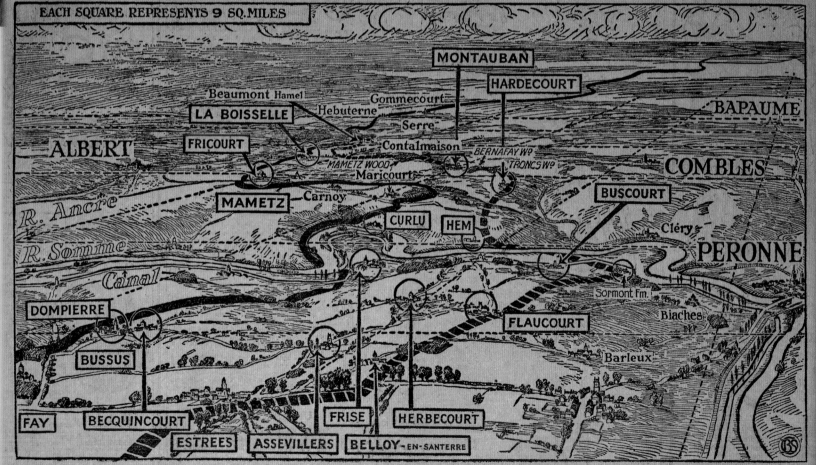

BIRD'S-EYE VIEW OF THE SOMME BATTLE GROUND.

EACH SQUARE REPRESENTS 9 SQ.MILES

BRITISH STRUGGLE IN A WIRED WOOD.

GERMAN GAIN AFTER FIVE REPULSES, BUT LOSS AT OTHER POINTS.

FRENCH STORM HILL BY PERONNE.

707th DAY OF THE WAR.
11th DAY OF ANGLO-FRENCH OFFENSIVE.

Somme Battle : After five repulses the Germans got a slight gain in the Trones Wood, a little over a mile east of Montauban. The British made progress in the Mametz Wood, east of Ovillers, and near Contalmaison (2½ miles east-north-east of Albert), where 3 guns and several hundred prisoners were taken. A wonderful despatch from Mr. Beach Thomas describes the epic struggle at this point. South of the Somme the French have brilliantly carried a height which dominates Péronne and is less than a mile from it. Since Sunday's reports they have captured over 1,000 prisoners.

Péronne is an important junction where three lines meet, one from Montauban, a second from Chaulnes, and a third from St. Quentin and the north. The first two are under the fire of the Allied artillery.

FRENCH RUSH A HEIGHT.

POSITION THAT DOMINATES THE RIVER.

French Official. Paris, Monday Night:

North of the Somme a quiet day. South of the river some progress during the day in the region between Biaches and Barleux and near the latter village. In the outskirts of Biaches we carried a small fort, where an enemy detachment still held out. We took 113 prisoners, including 10 officers.

South-east of Biaches by a brilliant attack we carried Hill 97 (1,500 yards south-west of Péronne), which dominates the river and had been strongly held. We also took the Maisonnette Farm on the summit and rushed a copse north of the farm. Parties of the enemy still remain in a redoubt near the extremity of the copse.

VIOLENT VERDUN FIRE.

North of Verdun the enemy artillery, vigorously countered by our guns, shelled with great violence the regions of Froide—

July 1916

1 The Battle of the Somme began on the Western Front. The opening day of the battle was the worst single day's fighting in British military history with casualties of nearly 60,000 British troops.

2 The Battle of Erzincan began between Russian and Turkish troops.

3 The Russian and Japanese Governments concluded a treaty regarding future policy in the Far East.

4 Heavy thunderstorms impeded progress at the Somme as British troops continued their advance in La Boiselle.

5 British and Indian troops entered Tanga on the Indian Ocean in German East Africa.

7 David Lloyd George succeeded the late Lord Kitchener as British Secretary of State for War.

9 The British liberal politician Edwin Samuel Montagu was appointed Minister of Munitions in Great Britain.

10 The Italian destroyer *Impetuoso* was torpedoed and sunk by a German U-boat in the Adriatic Sea.

11 A German submarine shelled Seaham harbour in County Durham.

12 British forces succeeded in clearing Mametz Wood, four and a half kilometres past the German lines on the Somme.

13 British troops temporarily pierced the German line at Bezantin Ridge on the Somme.

14 The Battle of Bazentin Ridge began, launching the second phase of the Somme Offensive.

British troops occupied the German port of Mwanza in German East Africa.

15 A subsidiary attack of the Somme Offensive, the Battle of Delville Wood began when South African troops attempted to clear the woods of German forces.

17 The Battle of Bazentin Ridge ended in a tactical British victory.

18 The British Government ratified a treaty with Ibn Saud, the Emir of Nejd.

19 The Battle of Fromelles was a combined operation by British and Australian troops to divert attention from the Battle of the Somme.

20 The Battle of Fromelles ended with a decisive German victory.

22 Sergei Sazonov resigned as Russian Foreign Minister and was succeeded by Boris Stürmer.

23 The two week struggle for the French village of Pozières and the surrounding ridge, the Battle of Pozières Ridge began.

25 Russian forces captured Erzingian in Armenia which was then evacuated without further fighting.

27 British naval Captain Charles Fryatt was executed by the Germans after he was court-martialled following his unsuccessful attempt to ram and sink a German U-Boat.

28 British troops captured Delville Wood and Longueval village and progressed towards Pozières.

29 The German Government rejected Britain's offer to permit sea passage of humanitarian foodstuffs going to Poland from the United States.

30 The first combined Franco-British aerial operations took place on the Western Front.

The Black Tom Island munitions plant in New Jersey was destroyed by an explosion. It was suspected to be the work of German saboteurs.

31 The British Prime Minister denounced the execution of Captain Fryatt in the House of Commons.

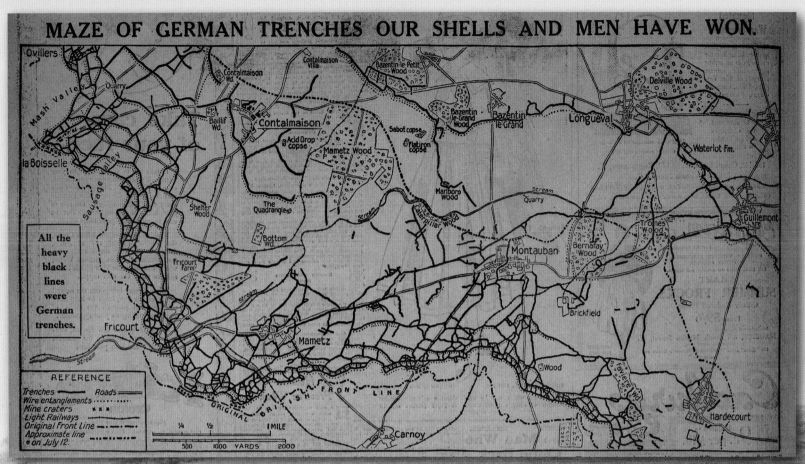

MAZE OF GERMAN TRENCHES OUR SHELLS AND MEN HAVE WON.

All the heavy black lines were German trenches.

REFERENCE

Trenches ——— Roads ———
Wire entanglements ·········
Mine craters ✶✶✶
Light Railways —·—·—
Original Front Line — — —
Approximate line —··—··—
on July 12.

¼ ½ 1 MILE
500 1000 YARDS 2000

Opposite: Men of the Royal Warwickshire Regiment enjoy a well-earned sleep in the open after their part in the Battle of Albert.

Top left: A procession of big guns makes its way to the Front. 250,000 shells were fired on the first day of the Somme and the bombardment could be heard on Hampstead Heath, London, 300 miles away.

Middle left: French poilus bring in a badly wounded soldier. French troops originally fought in their traditional red pill-box hats, blue frock-coats and red pantaloons. However, a new blue uniform was swiftly introduced as the red was dangerously visible on the battlefield. In 1915, they also brought in their own version of the steel helmet – the Adrian helmet.

Below: The first batch of British prisoners taken by the Germans after the Somme Offensive began. In 1915 Germany established a series of internment camps, although officers were housed in separate, smaller buildings.

3 VILLAGES CAPTURED.

BRITISH CARRY 2½ MILES OF SECOND GERMAN DEFENCES.

COUNTER-ATTACKS CRUSHED.

WEST KENTS HOLD OUT 48 HOURS AND WIN.

BRITISH OFFICIAL.

FRANCE, Friday.

10.4 A.M.—This morning at dawn I attacked the enemy's second system of defence. Our troops have broken into the hostile positions on a front of four miles and have captured several strongly defended localities. Heavy fighting continues.

9.17 P.M.—It is now possible to give further details of the action begun at daybreak this morning. Having driven the enemy back step by step to his second system of defence, the period 11th to 12th July (Tuesday and Wednesday) was mainly spent by our troops in bombarding these formidable positions and in other necessary preparations for a further advance.

This morning, after an intensive bombardment, the assault was launched at 3.25 a.m. The enemy was driven from his trenches on the whole front of attack and many prisoners fell into our hands.

Fierce fighting has continued all day, as the result of which we have steadily increased our gains and are now in possession of the enemy's second positions from Bazentin-le-Petit village to Longueval village (both inclusive) and the whole of Trônes Wood.

In Trônes Wood we relieved a party of the Royal West Kent Regiment, who, separated from our own troops in the recent fighting and surrounded by the Germans, had gallantly held out in the northern end of the wood for forty-eight hours.

Two determined counter-attacks on our new positions were completely crushed by our fire. Later in the day, after a fierce counter-attack, the Germans succeeded in recapturing the village of Bazentin-le-Petit, but were at once driven out again by our infantry, and the whole village is once more in our hands.

HAND-TO-HAND IN OVILLERS.

WEEK'S STRUGGLE IN A DUST HEAP.

MR. BEACH THOMAS'S DESPATCH.

From W. BEACH THOMAS.

WITH THE BRITISH ARMY IN THE FIELD, Thursday.

In Ovillers, on the left of our advance, our troops have fought a hand-to-hand fight for a week and more, gaining ground without a set-back, though all the time till to-day the progress was measured by yards, or at most by chains. Twenty-tw yards here may mean a mile elsewhere.

Ovillers is a village with a church in the middle and many good solid houses close together. Nevertheless, Ovillers has seen no street fighting, no house-to-house fighting, for the place of these things is no more seen. To-day it would trouble you to find the church or any street or any house. The village has vanished more completely than Neuville St. Vaast or Souchez, through which the old padre walked without recognising the place of his life habitation. I speak the bare fact.

Yet neither is the substitute for houses a mere dusty knoll, for, like other town-

The battle of Bazentin Ridge

General Rawlinson commanded the attack on Germany's second position at Bazentine Ridge on 14 July, an assault that brought welcome news for the Allies a fortnight after the devastating losses incurred on day one of the Somme battle. The bombardment that preceded the advance was more concentrated than 1 July and more effective, not least because of a well executed creeping barrage. Rawlinson's decision to gather the men in no-man's-land under cover of darkness – a plan Haig thought ill-advised – proved inspired, allowing a dawn raid that caught the Germans off guard. Keeping the pre-advance barrage to a five-minute burst helped maintain the element of surprise. In a matter of hours the British were in possession of a 6,000-yard stretch of the enemy's second line between Bazentin le Petit and Longueval. The strategically important High Wood appeared to be within their grasp, but the initiative was lost in a delay while the cavalry were brought up. The arrival of German reserves ensured that the struggle for High Wood and the neighbouring Delville Wood would rage for several weeks.

Australian casualties alone exceeded 5,000, Germany's losses a mere fraction of that.

Battle of Fromelles

The Battle of Fromelles marked the first significant action involving Anzac troops on the Western Front. It was a diversionary attack, intended to occupy the German line 45 miles north of the Somme. The target was an imposing salient known as Sugar Loaf, from where the Germans could oversee the ground across which the attack would come. A seven-hour bombardment opened up on 19 July, achieving little apart from alerting the enemy to what was afoot. The defending machine-gunners had a field day, a grisly confirmation of one British staff officer's prediction that the assault would result in "a bloody holocaust". British soldiers attacking the other side of the salient fared no better than their Aussie comrades. The sole encouraging note was struck when Anzacs managed to occupy part of the forward trench, but without support that foothold was soon lost. The Fromelles battle was over inside 24 hours. Australian casualties alone exceeded 5,000, Germany's losses a mere fraction of that.

Below: **Troops outside their dugouts near Bazentin-le-Petit after the village and neighbouring Bazentin-le-Grand were taken.**

Opposite: **A platoon of the Worcestershire regiment in good spirits marches to the front line.**

THE DAILY MAIL, THURSDAY, JULY 20, 1916.

GERMANS REGAIN SOME OF THEIR LOST GROUND.

HEAVY ATTACKS ON THE BRITISH.	RUSSIA'S WATCH FOR WEAK POINTS.	THE PUSH FROM OVILLERS.	ENGLISHWOMAN IN A BERLIN CELL.	BRITISH NAMES.	WAR ELECTION
GROUND LOST BUT MOSTLY REGAINED.	VOLHYNIA GUNS ACTIVE.	GERMAN GAS SHELLS.	A "RETALIATION" EXCUSE.	THE CASE OF THE STOCK EXCHANGE.	REBUFF TO CABINET.
GUNS SCATTER GERMANS GATHERING FOR ASSAULT.	From HAMILTON FYFE.	From W. BEACH THOMAS.			THE HOUSE DEMANDS LEADERSHIP
					VOTES FOR SOLDIERS PLEA.

BROTHERS KILLED.

LORD ST. DAVIDS LOSES HIS SECOND SON.

Lord St. Davids has received news that his only surviving son and heir, Captain Roland Philipps, Royal Fusiliers, was killed in action on July 7. Captain Philipps, who was wounded in March this year, was awarded the Military Cross in April.

Lord St. Davids' elder son, Captain Colwyn Philipps, Royal Horse Guards, was killed in May last year and there is now no heir to the title.

Lieutenant Harry L. Cholmeley, Border Regiment, who was killed on July 1, aged 23, was the youngest son of Mr. L. C. Cholmeley, of Messrs. Frere, Cholmeley, and Co., of Lincoln's Inn-fields. One brother, Second-Lieutenant H. V. Cholmeley, Grenadier Guards, was killed on April 7, and the only surviving brother, Captain G. H. Cholmeley, London Regiment, was wounded on July 1.

Lieutenant P. Neill Fraser, North Staffordshire Regiment, killed, was a brother of Miss M. Neill Fraser, the Scottish golfer, who died of typhus last year in Serbia, where she was one of the Scottish nurses.

Captain A. N. S. Jackson, of the King's Royal Rifles, the famous Oxford runner who in the Olympic Games at Stockholm in 1912 established a record (3min. 56 4-5sec.) for the 1,500 metres (937 yards), was wounded in the recent fighting

FAMILY'S SACRIFICE.

TWO BROTHERS KILLED, THIRD BROKEN IN INTERNMENT.

SIR. T. EDEN'S RETURN.

Sir Timothy Eden, who has just returned to Windlestone Hall, Durham, after being interned in Germany since the beginning of the war, is confined to bed, but is progressing favourably. He was released because of ill-health.

Sir Timothy, who is 23, was completing his education in Germany when the war broke out. His father, Sir William Eden, who had the famous lawsuit with Whistler over Lady Eden's portrait, died in February last year, and as the eldest son, Lieutenant John Eden, 12th Lancers, was killed in action in October 1914, the present baronet succeeded to the title while a prisoner. Midshipman William Nicholas Eden, another brother, who was just 16, went down in the Jutland battle in the Indefatigable. Sir William's only daughter is Lady Brooke, wife of Brigadier-General Lord Brooke; Lieutenant Robert Anthony Eden, the heir presumptive, is in France.

HEAVY ATTACKS ON THE BRITISH.

GROUND LOST BUT MOSTLY REGAINED.

GUNS SCATTER GERMANS GATHERING FOR ASSAULT.

BRITISH OFFICIAL.

FRANCE, Wednesday.

2.10 P.M.—The enemy's attack last night, the beginning of which has already been reported, was directed against our new positions to the east of Bazentin village. Very large German reinforcements had been collected for this attack.

After an intense artillery fire the first assault was delivered in dense masses about 5.30 p.m. Fighting continued all night, and was particularly violent in Delville Wood [on the right of the four miles of the second German line in our hands].

After suffering very heavy losses the enemy recaptured a portion of Delville Wood, and also obtained a footing in the northern outskirts of Longueval [adjoining the south-western edge of the wood]. The struggle in these areas is still violent.

Elsewhere his attack, including three separate assaults on Waterlot Farm (south-east of Delville Wood), completely broke down under our fire.

On the rest of our front no event of importance has occurred.

9.30 P.M.—North of the Somme heavy fighting is still in progress in Longueval village and Delville Wood. In both these places we have already regained most of the ground lost last night.

South of Delville Wood this afternoon we dispersed with our fire a large body of Germans massing to attack Waterlot Farm from the direction of Guillemont [south-east of the farm].

Battle of Delville Wood

Two weeks' fighting left the Allies with a reasonable grip on the village of Longueval, through which the German Second Line ran. The next target was the adjacent forested area, 3,000 South African troops in the vanguard of an attack that opened up on 15 July. Delville Wood was soon rechristened "Devil's Wood" by the men who fought there, for it was a hell-hole of chaos, confusion and blood-letting. Haig had the cavalry on stand-by, thinking this could be their moment at last. That optimism evaporated as the opposing forces fought bitterly over ground reduced to matchwood. At the height of the battle seven shells rained down on the same benighted patch of earth every second. The South African brigade was reduced to a quarter of its strength when relief came. An attack on 27 July put the Allies in command, but repeated German counters added to the aggregate toll. Delville Wood was eventually secured in the first week of September, though it would change hands again, more than once, before the guns fell silent.

This page: **The strategically important Delville Wood was soon renamed "Devil's Wood" by British soldiers. At the height of the battle, German shells rained down at a rate of 400 a minute, resulting in almost total deforestation.**

Opposite middle: **Troops use the camouflage of a smokescreen to launch another attack.**

Opposite above and below: **Delville Wood marked the first major involvement on the Western Front of the South African First Infantry Brigade, under the command of Brigadier-General Henry Lukin. After a ferocious six-day battle only 750 of the 3,000-strong South African force survived to see relief troops arrive. Despite their losses the South African troops managed to hold onto the wood.**

Delville Wood was eventually secured in the first week of September, though it would change hands more than once before the guns fell silent.

GROUND WON IN POZIÈRES.

AUSTRALIANS IN CONTINUOUS FIGHTING.

VERY HEAVY GERMAN LOSSES.

MR. LLOYD GEORGE ON OUR GREAT RESOURCES IN MEN.

MANY MORE BIG GUNS AND SHELLS WANTED.

BRITISH OFFICIAL.

FRANCE, Monday.

12.6 P.M.—Apart from continuous heavy shelling by both sides a night of comparative calm followed the severe fighting of yesterday.

Yesterday, between High Wood [the Foureaux Wood] and Guillemont the repeated counter-attacks of the enemy gained for him no advantage, and very heavy casualties were inflicted by our artillery and machine-gun fire. We have gained some ground near High Wood and in the direction of Guillemont.

In the neighbourhood of Pozières our troops have secured important advantages, in spite of the stubborn defence of the enemy, and a large portion of the village is now in our hands.

In this neighbourhood we have captured 2 guns and 60 more prisoners.

9.43 P.M.—Fighting has continued in the village of Pozières, where the number of prisoners taken by the Australian troops has reached a total of 6 officers and 145 other ranks.

In other parts of the battle-front there has been considerable artillery activity on both sides.

Between the Ancre and the sea nothing of importance has occurred.

721st DAY OF THE WAR.
25th DAY OF ANGLO-FRENCH OFFENSIVE.

Battle of the Somme: The fighting shows no diminution in fury, though it has now reached its 25th day. With the exception of the Battle of Verdun, which has lasted for five months, this is the severest struggle in this war of fearful and prolonged encounters, and it has been glorious to British arms.

The first ten days of infantry fighting, from July 1 to 10, witnessed our capture of the enemy's whole first system of defences on a front of 14,000 yards and to a depth of 2,000 yards. On July 11 and 12 the enemy's second line was severely bombarded. Our troops then attacked it, in the second phase of the battle, on a front of four miles, and by the 14th had broken into it at several points. By the 15th they had reached Foureaux, or High Wood, which is of great tactical importance, because it commands the neighbouring country.

FRENCH TAKE A BATTERY.

60 MACHINE GUNS CAPTURED SINCE THURSDAY.

French Official. PARIS, Monday Night.
South of the Somme in a small operation we captured this morning an enemy battery south of Estrées.

Since Thursday last we have taken on the Somme front more than 60 German machine guns.

Afternoon.
On the Somme front the night was quiet. The weather continues bad.

MR. LLOYD GEORGE'S REVIEW

GENERALS MORE THAN SATISFIED.

Mr. Lloyd George, speaking in the House of Commons last night as Secretary for War, said the question of making the best use of

Above left: The pipes and drums of the Black Watch played to the troops after the initial capture of Longueval.

Above right: Troops take advantage of the water collected in shell-holes to have an early morning wash.

Below: A well-earned breakfast for members of the Black Watch.

Opposite above: The Labour batallion build a road over captured ground. During 1916, the recruitment of men to maintain roads, railways and provide a network of support to the troops gradually became more formalised, using conscientious objectors or those not medically fit for battle.

Opposite middle: An officer receives information by wireless and gives the order to open fire. At the beginning of the war the Government took control of part of the Marconi Company; operators were swiftly trained when commanders realised the advantages of delivering messages by wireless.

Opposite below: With the increasing use of trench warfare and the introduction of the tank, cavalry troops were used less and less. The last major cavalry charge took place on High Wood at the start of the Somme campaign. They successfully forced some Germans to surrender but at the cost of 100 men and 130 horses.

DAY OF AIR RAIDS BEHIND GERMAN LINES.

BRITISH PILOTS BLOW UP A TRAIN AND FIRE A SHELL DEPOT.

FRENCH REPEL ALL ATTACKS.

SERIOUS ENEMY LOSSES AND NO GAIN.

728th DAY OF THE WAR.
32nd DAY OF ANGLO-FRENCH OFFENSIVE

Battle of the Somme : Our troops have held all the ground gained and have made a slight advance at some points. The French have repulsed a series of terrific counter-attacks by the enemy north of the Somme, and have inflicted serious losses. Our Allies held all their new ground.

To-day's casualty lists contain the names of 273 officers and 3,793 men.

Russian Front : The battle continues furiously in Volhynia. The Russians have crossed the Stokhod east of Kovel on a front of 19 miles at least and have captured a whole Hungarian regiment (if at full strength, 3,200 men) at one point, and at another about 1,000 men. Berlin alleges that our Allies have been driven back on the Lower Stokhod and have lost 1,900 prisoners. If so, the Germans on the Lower Stokhod are now

BRITISH OFFICIAL.

10.15 P.M.—There has been no infantry fighting on the British front to-day and no incident of importance has occurred.

The Royal Flying Corps have carried out several bombing raids and dropped 7 tons of bombs on the enemy's communications and billets.

In one case a train was blown up; in another an ammunition depot was set on fire and a hostile aeroplane on the ground was destroyed.

There were many aerial combats and several enemy machines were driven to the ground in a damaged condition. Three of our machines are missing.

1.40 P.M.—Last night was spent in improving the positions gained yesterday, and there were no further de-

The shading indicates the ground gained between Thiepval and Peronne since July 1. Yesterday afternoon the French reported violent fighting near Monacu Farm and Hem, while the British were active north of Bazentin.

placed in an awkward position and cannot profit by their success.

Great interest centres on the vast operations now in progress in Galicia,

velopments of the situation. As a result of local encounters we advanced our posts at some points on the plateau north of Bazentin-le-Petit (east-south-east of Pozières).

Opposite top left: **The Royal Garrison Artillery in action firing two 8-inch Howitzers in the Fricourt-Mametz Valley. The Allies used over 400 heavy guns at the Somme, one for every 60 yards of the Front on which the attack took place.**

Opposite top right: **Troops remain in the safety of their trench as they wait for the order to advance.**

Opposite middle left: **A group of soldiers load a heavy trench mortar, more commonly known as a "flying pig" among the British troops. These tubes were ideally suited for trench conditions; missiles were fired straight into the air and fell down over the enemy.**

Opposite below: **Gordon Highlanders on the march with a wounded German soldier on a makeshift stretcher.**

Below: **A sentry from the Worcestershire Regiment keeps watch at Ovillers. The sandbags filled with earth offered protection against enemy rifle fire, while the loophole provided a good vantage point.**

August 1916

2   The Italian Dreadnought *Leonardo da Vinci* sank in Taranto harbour in Southern Italy after an internal explosion caused her to capsize.

3   The Irish Nationalist Roger Casement was hanged at Pentonville Prison for his involvement in the Easter Rising in Dublin earlier in the year.

     The Battle of Romani began. The unsuccessful attempt by the German led Ottoman force to seize control of the Suez Canal was the last ground attack on the critical waterway during the war.

5   The advance of the main body of British forces began through the Nguru Hills during the East Africa Campaign.

6   The Sixth Battle of the Isonzo was launched against a combined German-Austro-Hungarian force. Also known as the Battle of Gorizia it was the most successful Italian offensive along the Isonzo River in North Eastern Italy during the war.

8   The Portuguese Government accepted the participation of Portugal in the war and extended military co-operation to the Europe.

9   Italian Chief-of-Staff Luigi Cadorna led his forces to take Gorizia and establish a bridgehead across the Isonzo River during the Sixth Battle of the Isonzo.

10   After its initial success the Brusilov Offensive came to an end with the loss of about 500,000 Russian and 375,000 Austrian lives.

11   The German colonial district of Mpwapwa in German East Africa was occupied by British forces.

12   Italian troops landed at Salonika in Greece to join Allied forces.

15   A British air attack and naval bombardment was launched on Bagamoyo on the German East African coast. The Germans were overrun and the German garrison taken.

     During the Caucasus Campaign the Armenian towns of Mush and Bitlis were re-occupied by Turkish forces.

17   Luigi Cadorna had succeeded in moving forward 5km along a 20km-front and ended the offensive in the Sixth Battle of the Isonzo.

The Treaty of Bucharest of 1916 was signed between Romania and the Entente Powers. The treaty stipulated the conditions under which Romania agreed to join the war on the side of the Entente.

18   A combined British-French offensive was launched on the German held village of Guillemont with three British corps attacking the village while the French attacked the nearby village of Maurepas.

19   Two town-class light cruisers, HMS *Falmouth* and HMS *Nottingham* were sunk by U-boats.

22   The Morogoro Region of Kilosa in Tanganyika (now Tanzania) was captured by British forces.

23   The German blockade-breaking cargo submarine Deutschland returned to Bremerhaven in Germany.

24   In another engagement between the Russian Caucasus army and their Ottoman counterparts, Mush and Bitlis were again taken by Russian forces.

25   Russian forces cross the Danube into the Dobrudja to assist Romanian forces.

26   Under General Smuts, the city of Morogoro in Tanganika was taken by British forces.

27   Following the Treaty of Bucharest, the Romanian Government ordered mobilisation of their armies and crossed the border of the Austro-Hungarian Empire into the much-contested province of Transylvania.

28   Germany declared war on Romania and Italy declared war on Germany.

29   Brasov in Transylvania was occupied by Romanian forces.

     Field-Marshal von Hindenburg succeeded General von Falkenhayn as Chief of the General Staff of the German Field Armies with General von Ludendorff as Chief Quartermaster-General.

30   The National Schism, caused by the disagreement on foreign policy between King Constantine I of Greece and revolutionary Eleftherios Venizelos, led to the Venizelist revolt in Salonika.

Battle of Pozières

Pozières, a village lying on the Albert-Bapaume road, was one of the opening-day battle objectives that failed to materialise. On 23 July, three weeks after it was meant to have fallen, Australian troops led the fight to capture the ridge upon which Pozières stood, part of the German Second Line. These Anzacs barely had time to draw breath after arriving at the front before they were hurled into the fray, and took heavy losses during the two weeks it took to complete the operation. Both village and ridge were in Allied hands by 7 August, but efforts to push on towards Mouquet Farm – opening the way to Thiepval – met stern German resistance. The casualty count stood at 23,000, a toll said to have left the Aussies with a deep distrust of Mother Country commanders. As one private put it: "Without doubt Pozières was the heaviest, bloodiest, rottenest stunt that ever the Australians were caught up in."

The casualty count stood at 23,000, a toll said to have left the Aussies with a deep distrust of Mother Country commanders.

Top: A German shell bursts close to an advanced dressing station.

Middle: Groups of soldiers watch British shells explode in and around the village of Pozières.

Bottom: By the time the battle was over, the village of Pozières was completely destroyed. Buildings were reduced to rubble and the Australians had suffered 23,000 casualties. Unlike some French villages that suffered a similar fate and were left as memorial sites, Pozières was rebuilt and the Australian flag always flies overhead as a memorial to these men.

Top: Two British soldiers are buried on the battlefield while the Padre reads the solemn words of the burial service.

Middle: The bodies of dead German soldiers lie scattered on the battlefield.

Right: Highlanders at the front line march to the accompaniment of bagpipes.

GROUND WON IN POZIÈRES.

AUSTRALIANS IN CONTINUOUS FIGHTING.

VERY HEAVY GERMAN LOSSES.

MR. LLOYD GEORGE ON OUR GREAT RESOURCES IN MEN.

MANY MORE BIG GUNS AND SHELLS WANTED.

BRITISH OFFICIAL.

FRANCE, Monday.

12.6 P.M.—Apart from continuous heavy shelling by both sides a night of comparative calm followed the severe fighting of yesterday.

Yesterday, between High Wood [the Foureaux Wood] and Guillemont the repeated counter-attacks of the enemy gained for him no advantage, and very heavy casualties were inflicted by our artillery and machine-gun fire. We have gained some ground near High Wood and in the direction of Guillemont.

In the neighbourhood of Pozières our troops have secured important advantages, in spite of the stubborn defence of the enemy, and a large portion of the village is now in our hands.

In this neighbourhood we have captured 2 guns and 60 more prisoners.

9.43 P.M.—Fighting has continued in the village of Pozières, where the number of prisoners taken by the Australian troops has reached a total of 6 officers and 145 other ranks.

In other parts of the battle-front there has been considerable artillery activity on both sides.

Between the Ancre and the sea nothing of importance has occurred.

721st DAY OF THE WAR.
25th DAY OF ANGLO-FRENCH OFFENSIVE.

Battle of the Somme: The fighting shows no diminution in fury, though it has now reached its 25th day. With the exception of the Battle of Verdun, which has lasted for five months, this is the severest struggle in this war of fearful and prolonged encounters, and it has been glorious to British arms.

The first ten days of infantry fighting, from July 1 to 10, witnessed our capture of the enemy's whole first system of defences on a front of 14,000 yards and to a depth of 2,000 yards. On July 11 and 12 the enemy's second line was severely bombarded. Our troops then attacked it, in the second phase of the battle, on a front of four miles, and by the 14th had broken into it at several points. By the 15th they had reached Foureaux, or High Wood, which is of great tactical importance, because it commands the neighbouring country.

The fight for Foureaux Wood has been carried on in face of a growing concentration of German artillery. None the less, in the third phase of the battle which is now in progress our troops have greatly extended the gap in the German second system of defences and reached the third line, beyond which open country is reported by the airmen.

FRENCH TAKE A BATTERY.

60 MACHINE GUNS CAPTURED SINCE THURSDAY.

French Official. PARIS, Monday Night.

South of the Somme in a small operation we captured this morning an enemy battery south of Estrées.

Since Thursday last we have taken on the Somme front more than 60 German machine guns.

Afternoon.

On the Somme front the night was quiet. The weather continues bad.

MR. LLOYD GEORGE'S REVIEW

GENERALS MORE THAN SATISFIED.

Mr. Lloyd George, speaking in the House of Commons last night as Secretary for War, said the question of making the best use of the man-power of the nation was under searching review at the present moment, and there was no doubt a decision would have to be taken in regard to it in a very short time. There was no doubt at all that our resources in this direction were infinitely greater than they appeared to be on paper, and it was just as well that the enemy should know it. To what extent

THURSDAY, AUGUST 24, 1916.

THE KING ON THE SOMME BATTLEFIELDS—HISTORIC PHOTOGRAPHS.

Right and opposite: King George V, a keen supporter of the troops, visited the Western Front several times, and on one occasion broke his pelvis when a horse rolled on top of him. He had previously served in the Royal Navy but was forced to end his service when he became second in line to the throne following the death of his older brother Albert in 1892.

DAILY MAIL · AUGUST 16, 1916

The King on the Somme battlefield

The King returned yesterday from another visit to the front. The following is the General Order to the Army in France which his Majesty sent to General Sir Douglas Haig:-

Officers, N.C.O.s, and men.

It has been a great pleasure and satisfaction to me to be with my Armies during the past week. I have been able to judge for myself of their splendid condition for war and of the spirit of cheerful confidence which animates all ranks, united in loyal co-operation to their Chiefs and to one another.

Since my last visit to the front there has been almost uninterrupted fighting on parts of our line. The offensive recently begun has since been resolutely maintained by day and by night. I have had opportunities of visiting some of the scenes of the later desperate struggles, and of appreciating to a slight extent the demands made upon your courage and physical endurance in order to assail and capture positions prepared during the past two years and stoutly defended to the last.

I have realized not only the splendid work which has been done in immediate touch with the enemy – in the air, under ground, as well as on the ground – but also the vast organizations behind the fighting line, honourable alike to the genius of the initiators and to the heart and hand of the workers. Everywhere there is proof that all, men and women, are playing their part, and I rejoice to think their noble efforts are being heartily seconded by all classes at home.

The happy relations maintained by my Armies and those of our French Allies were equally noticeable between my troops and the inhabitants of the districts in which they are quartered, and from whom they have received a cordial welcome ever since their first arrival in France.

Do not think that I and your fellow countrymen forget the heavy sacrifices which the Armies have made and the bravery and endurance they have displayed during the past two years of bitter conflict. These sacrifices have not been in vain; the arms of the Allies will never be laid down until our cause has triumphed.

I return home more than ever proud of you. May God guide you to Victory.

George R.I.

Tragic downside of "Pals" scheme

Between the annihilation of the BEF professionals in the opening months of the war and the introduction of conscription in 1916, Britain relied on volunteers to maintain its army strength. War Secretary Lord Kitchener had led the drive to raise a New Army and fronted the famous poster campaign, urging the nation's menfolk that duty beckoned in this hour of desperate need. Lord Derby was also a prime mover in a staggeringly successful recruitment process that quickly exceeded its initial 100,000 target. For many patriotic fervour and the desire to fight for a just cause on behalf of king and country was enough. But the chance to serve with those they lived amongst or worked alongside added a spur of camaraderie to the devotional incentive. As Lord Derby put it when he addressed the men of Merseyside on 28 August 1914: "This should be a battalion of pals, a battalion in which friends from the same office will fight shoulder to shoulder for the honour of Britain and the credit of Liverpool". The rate of enlistment was such that Liverpool soon had enough men to furnish four battalions, and the idea was not slow in catching on across the land. All manner of groups – from sportsmen to stockbrokers to school alumni – or simply men from the same community, grasped the opportunity to head into battle shoulder to shoulder. The make-up of these units made for immediate cohesion. They marched to the step of a shared connection; a common bond to match the common purpose. But this well-intentioned idea was to have tragic consequences for some towns and villages. Where a policy of dispersal across the regiments might have spread the casualty count, concentration of men from the same area also concentrated the losses if a pals' battalion happened to find itself in the thick of fierce fighting. Among the hardest hit were the Accrington Pals, who suffered grievously on the first day of the Somme battle.

The Accrington Pals

Accrington and its neighbouring districts had been quick to answer the call, one of the smallest urban areas to muster a 1,000-strong battalion. Those who formed the 11th Battalion of the East Lancashire Regiment had a considerable wait before they were able to show their mettle. There was a lengthy period of training, and when they finally headed overseas in December 1915, it was to Egypt, part of an Allied force ready to counter any threat to the Suez Canal. By February 1916 concerns over an imminent Turkish attack had subsided and the 11th East Lancashires were redeployed to the Western Front, where plans were being laid for a large-scale summer offensive. They were anything but battle hardened, and now were heading for a baptism of fire unparalleled in British military history.

The Accrington Pals had by now been subsumed within the 94th Brigade, 31st Division, made up of similar units from across the Lancashire-Yorkshire region. They arrived at the front line at around 3.00 am on 1 July, having undertaken an exhausting six-mile march from their rearward position, a trek begun the previous evening. It was hardly the best preparation for a battle due to begin four hours later, but that didn't matter – as long as this was the walkover everyone expected. Anything less and they faced a daunting task: taking the hilltop fortress at Serre. Defences here would have taxed the most astute generals and crack troops. The Pals lacked nothing in spirit but were ill prepared to wrest this formidable redoubt from the German army's 169th Infantry Regiment.

Virtually every Accrington household was affected in some way, the grim news met with a blanket drawing down of blinds.

Top: **William Young, a private in the East Lancashire Regiment, was awarded the Victoria Cross after rescuing his sergeant in December 1915. He was shot twice and eventually died of his wounds.**

Above: **Fellow Victoria Cross recipient Alfred Smith also served with the East Lancashires. He lost his life in Gallipoli when he dropped a grenade by accident and covered it with his body to avoid injury to others.**

Bottom: **The 11th Battalion of the East Lancashire Regiment, known as the Accrington Pals, was one of the worst hit on the first day of the Somme. Out of a force of around 700 men, 585 were reported dead or injured in one day.**

"Mown down like meadow grass"

Seven hundred and twenty went over the top that morning. Like all the others, they walked into no-man's-land heavily laden with kit. Like all the others, they anticipated an unhindered advance. And like all the others, they quickly found that the week-long artillery bombardment had not killed or incapacitated the enemy ranks. The dug-in German machine-gunners emerged from their sanctuaries, and the Pals were "mown down like meadow grass", in the words of one observer. To make matters worse, the preliminary shelling had been as ineffective in smashing the barbed wire as it had been in neutralising the living, breathing defence. Those who survived long enough made for the gaps, clustering in the enemy's sights. Some actually made it to the German trenches, as did some of their 94th Brigade comrades from the Sheffield Battalion to their left. There were reports that a few reached the village of Serre itself. Brigadier-General Hubert Rees, who was in temporary command of the 94th, reported: "Not a man wavered, broke the ranks or attempted to go back." He added: "I have never seen, indeed could never have imagined such a magnificent display of gallantry, discipline and determination." But the situation was hopeless, not least because the men of the 13th and 14th York and Lancaster Regiment – the 1st and 2nd Barnsley Pals that formed the second wave – were also cut to pieces. Without reinforcements, the shattered remains of the Accrington battalion had no option but to scramble back to their own trench haven. In less than an hour the toll of killed, wounded or missing stood at 584. Just 136 of the 720 who set out escaped unscathed.

Virtually every Accrington household was affected in some way, the grim news met with a blanket drawing down of blinds and incessant tolling of the church bells. It was a scene repeated in towns and cities across the land, places such as Bradford and Grimsby. For weeks the Barnsley Chronicle printed lists of the town's fallen heroes. Communities had their hearts ripped out. The most unfortunate parents might have lost more than one son. Widows and their orphaned children were left to pick up the pieces. It was too great a burden to bear, as the authorities now appreciated. The idea of "pals" marching into battle together was quietly shelved as the calamitous downside of close-knit comradeship revealed itself on the opening day of the Somme battle.

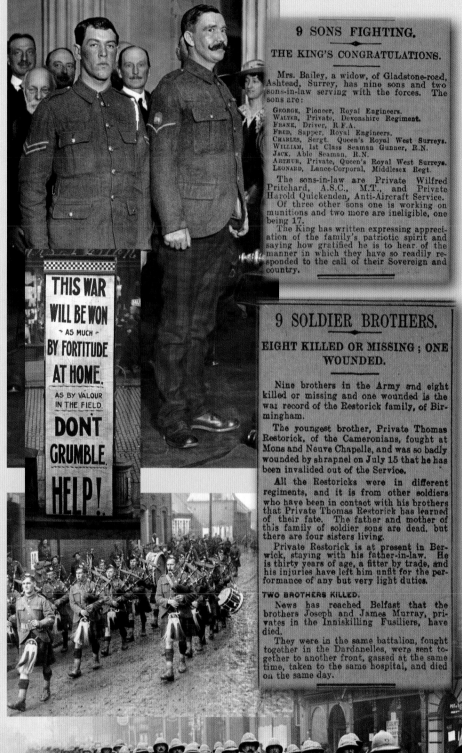

9 SONS FIGHTING.

THE KING'S CONGRATULATIONS.

Mrs. Bailey, a widow, of Gladstone-road, Ashtead, Surrey, has nine sons and two sons-in-law serving with the forces. The sons are:

GEORGE, Pioneer, Royal Engineers.
WALTER, Private, Devonshire Regiment.
FRANK, Driver, R.F.A.
FRED, Sapper, Royal Engineers.
CHARLES, Sergt. Queen's Royal West Surreys.
WILLIAM, 1st Class Seaman Gunner, R.N.
JACK, Able Seaman, R.N.
ARTHUR, Private, Queen's Royal West Surreys.
LEONARD, Lance-Corporal, Middlesex Regt.

The sons-in-law are Private Wilfred Pritchard, A.S.C., M.T., and Private Harold Quickenden, Anti-Aircraft Service.

Of three other sons one is working on munitions and two more are ineligible, one being 17.

The King has written expressing appreciation of the family's patriotic spirit and saying how gratified he is to hear of the manner in which they have so readily responded to the call of their Sovereign and country.

9 SOLDIER BROTHERS.

EIGHT KILLED OR MISSING; ONE WOUNDED.

Nine brothers in the Army and eight killed or missing and one wounded is the war record of the Restorick family, of Birmingham.

The youngest brother, Private Thomas Restorick, of the Cameronians, fought at Mons and Neuve Chapelle, and was so badly wounded by shrapnel on July 15 that he has been invalided out of the Service.

All the Restoricks were in different regiments, and it is from other soldiers who have been in contact with his brothers that Private Thomas Restorick has learned of their fate. The father and mother of this family of soldier sons are dead, but there are four sisters living.

Private Restorick is at present in Berwick, staying with his father-in-law. He is thirty years of age, a fitter by trade, and his injuries have left him unfit for the performance of any but very light duties.

TWO BROTHERS KILLED.

News has reached Belfast that the brothers Joseph and James Murray, privates in the Inniskilling Fusiliers, have died.

They were in the same battalion, fought together in the Dardanelles, were sent together to another front, gassed at the same time, taken to the same hospital, and died on the same day.

THIS WAR WILL BE WON – AS MUCH – BY FORTITUDE AT HOME. AS BY VALOUR IN THE FIELD. DON'T GRUMBLE. HELP!

Top: **Spencer John Bent**, a drummer in the 1st Battalion of the East Lancashire Regiment, was 23 years old when he won the VC. Bent had distinguished himself on several occasions – bringing ammunition and food to the trenches while under heavy fire and venturing into no-man's-land to rescue wounded men who were lying exposed to enemy fire. He survived the war and died on 3 May 1977.

Middle: **The band of a Highland regiment** pipes its way through a newly captured village.

Middle inset: **The National War Aims Committee** displays a poster in Coventry. This organisation was set up to focus on promoting patriotism at home by issuing posters, pamphlets and films as well as organising rallies.

Right: **Members of the Legion of Frontiersmen**, who were attached to the Royal Fusiliers, parade through the streets. This paramilitary group was set up in 1905 with the aim of fostering patriotism and preparing citizens for war.

"This should be a battalion of pals, a battalion in which friends from the same office will fight shoulder to shoulder".

Life in the trenches

When the war of movement ground to a halt and the armies dug in, commanders and foot soldiers both faced alien conditions. For the leaders it was a question of how to break the stalemate. For the infantry it was a matter of dealing with the privation and daily grind of trench life. Even for those fortunate enough to dodge a bullet or shell there was much hardship. As the months turned into years waiting for a breakthrough, the men had to endure considerable physical discomfort, while the psychological pressures told on some more than others.

The distance between the opposing lines varied along the front, no-man's-land reduced to a few metres in some places. Soldiers lived in constant fear of shellfire and snipers. Significant casualties were inflicted on men ensconced in trenches and rudimentary dugouts that offered little protection against shrapnel or the elements. Yet there were also long periods of non-engagement, time given over to routine maintenance and inspections, eating and ablutions, rest and recuperation. There was monotony as well as mayhem. At dawn and dusk – the commonest time for attacks to be launched – the men were ordered to "stand to" and placed on high alert. A "mad minute" of rapid fire might ensue. Most were then stood down, unless on fatigues or sentry duty.

Linked networks

The forward or fire trenches were divided into bays. Long straight runs were avoided to mitigate the effects of any explosion, or enemy fire if the line was breached. The trenches were around two metres deep and built up above ground level at both front and rear to give added protection. The parapet was on the enemy side, while the raised earthworks at the back of the trench was called the parados. By standing on a fire step some 18 inches off the ground men could shoot over the top of the parapet, or through a "loophole". Behind these advanced positions were the support and reserve trenches, the entire network linked by communications trenches that facilitated the movement of men and provisions, invariably under cover of darkness. There were also shallower sap trenches stretching into no-man's-land, from which enemy activity might be observed at closer quarters. The whole was a maze of thoroughfares, which were given names such as Oxford Street and Lovers Lane.

In terms of calorie intake the soldier did not fare too badly, but there was little variety in the rations. Corned beef – or bully beef – was a staple, along with bread and biscuits, tea and jam. Cigarettes at least were plentiful, and many whiled away the hours chain-smoking. There was also a daily tot of rum, dispensed by one of the NCOs.

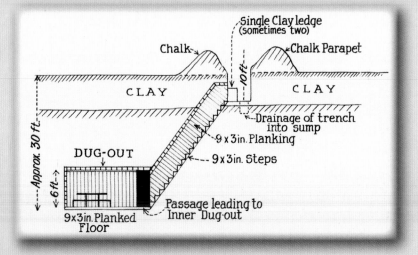

Top: A sketched plan of a German dug-out – found at Fricourt and drawn by a British officer – clearly shows how well-designed and deep they were.

Above: Soldiers quietly wait for the Padre inside a trench church which has been dug out from the side of a parapet by the poilus.

Right: Much of the time in the trenches could be spent playing the waiting game. In between battles officers drew up rotas to ensure a balance of duties, sleep and rest time, but this inevitably led to boredom as soldiers waited for orders.

Opposite: Trench foot, caused by wet, cold conditions was common. This began to improve in 1915 when soldiers were ordered to change their socks twice a day and were supplied with whale oil to repel the moisture.

Health hazards

The concentration of so many men in such a confined space inevitably presented a sanitation problem. Notwithstanding the efforts of those assigned to latrine duties and attempts to disinfect the area where men lived cheek by jowl using chloride of lime, open sewers and decaying corpses created a terrible stench. They also brought rats in droves. As one veteran recalled: "The knowledge that the gigantic trench rats had grown fat through feeding on the dead bodies in no-man's-land made the soldiers hate them more fiercely than almost anything else." The reviled creatures spread infection and bred in such numbers that taking pot shots at them had little effect on the population. Lice, nits and ticks were no less of an infestation problem. Men ran candle flames over their clothing to rid it of unwanted guests. Eggs were difficult to dislodge from the seams, however, and body heat provided ideal incubation conditions. Lice were not just an irritation; they also caused trench fever, a debilitating illness necessitating a lengthy period of convalescence. It took time for doctors to discover how that disease was transmitted; frostbite and exposure were easier to diagnose, and trench foot also had a simpler causal connection. Protracted submersion in cold water and mud made the lower limbs liable to fungal infection that in the most severe cases could turn gangrenous and require amputation. The duckboards laid down on the trench floor were intended to provide a firm, dry footing above ground, but in heavy rain they did not always give adequate protection. Bitter winter temperatures and broiling summer heat brought different health hazards, before the enemy had fired a shot.

Lice caused trench fever, a debilitating illness necessitating a lengthy period of convalescence.

Camaraderie in the Trenches

Troops manned the various trenches on a rotation basis. After a few days on the forward line they would usually be withdrawn to the support and reserve trenches, and if there was no urgent situation, a short period of rest further from the front brought welcome respite. Here, understandably, they let off steam in predictable ways, including alcoholic binges and visiting brothels. Venereal disease in the ranks was no small problem.

Any misfortune that rendered a soldier unfit for duty, be it from shell or infirmity, meant an incremental depletion in frontline resources. Medical staff were under pressure to patch up the problem – physical or psychological – and return men to the fray. Soldiers, for their part, came to realise that a non-life-threatening condition had its compensations. "Blighty wound" entered the army lexicon for injuries that could result in a man being invalided home. Officers were on the lookout for any suspicious injury that might have been self-inflicted, an offence that carried severe disciplinary penalties.

If there was a crumb of comfort in the infantryman's lot, it came from the knowledge that adversity was a collective experience. Hardship forged deep bonds of friendship and a strong sense of camaraderie. Trench life was hellish, but at least it was a shared hell.

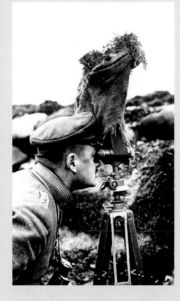

Opposite above: For four years the Belgian Army successfully guarded the Allied sector between Nieuwpoort and Ypres but did not have the military strength to assist in any major offensives.

Opposite below: Snug holes built into the sides of an Allied trench provide a welcome resting spot for weary soldiers.

Above left: While German officers pore over maps and plans in a hillside trench, several soldiers write letters home. Meanwhile, the sentinel posted on the edge of a ridge closely watches the opposite hill and intervening valley for any sign of attack.

Above middle: A German trench periscope doubles as a field glass.

Above right: Allied troops load a trench mortar.

Below main image: Men of the London Rifle Brigade wait for orders.

Below inset: Infantry in the trenches prepare for a gas attack. A mix of phosgene and chlorine was often used on the Somme, with the chlorine providing the vapour to carry the phosgene. This combination became known as "White Star" after the markings painted on the shells.

Hardship forged deep bonds of friendship. Trench life was hellish, but at least it was a shared hell.

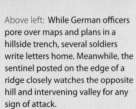

The Somme
July – September 1916

- - - - - Front line on 1 July
– – – – Front line on 14 July
———— Front line on 15 September
→ British attacks
→ French attacks
→ German attacks

• Serre

XX 52

XXX

• Miraumont

• Warlencourt

XX 185

• Bapaume

• Beaumont Hamel

XX 29

Hamel

• Beaucourt

• Le Sars

XXXX
2
BELOW

XX 36

XXX

• Courcellette

• Gueadecourt

• Le Transloy

XX 49   XXX 32

XXX
14 Res.
STEIN

• Thiepval

XX 26 Res.

• Martinpuich

• Flers

• Morval

• Sailly-Saillisel

XXX   XX 8

• Pozieres

• Bozentin-le-Petit

• Ginchy

• Aveluy

XX 19

• Ovillers

• La Boisselle

• Combles

• Rancourt

XXX 3

XX 34

• Montauban

• Hardecourt

• Mourepas

XX 12

• Bouchovesnes

• Albert

XXX 21   • Fricourt

• Mametz

XX 17

XX 7   XX 18   • Corgoy   XX 30   • Maricourt

XXX 20

XXX 8

XX 9

XX 39

XX 11

• Olery

• St Quentin

XXXXX   XXX

XXX 20   XXX

• Bray

• Frise

XXXX
4
RAWLINSON

BRITISH
XXXXX
FRENCH

XX

XX 2 Col.

→

Perrone

XXX 1 Col.

XX 3 Col.

• Florcourt

XX 121

• Dompierre

XX 4 Col.

• Barleux

XXXX
6
FAYOLLE

• Provorl

XXX

XX

• Foucaucourt

XXX 35

• Fresnes

• Vermandovillers

• Abraincourt

XXX 17

• Lihons

• Epenoncourt

XXXX

• Chaulmes

N

XX

• Rosieres

XXX 30

0   5 km
0   5 miles

Main picture: A soldier
from the Cheshire
Regiment is posted on
look out duty while
his comrades rest in a
captured German trench
in Ovillers-la-Boiselle.

Opposite right: Reporting
progress on 30 August.

DELVILLE WOOD TRIUMPH.

12 HOURS' UNBROKEN FIGHTING.

MACHINE-GUN HEROISM.

TWO SMALL GAINS.

Bad weather has prevented any considerable British operation on the Somme. One or two small gains have been made, in which prisoners have been taken.

From W. BEACH THOMAS.

WITH THE BRITISH ARMY IN THE FIELD, Monday.

Delville Wood—for ever famous as Devil's Wood in the annals of many regiments—is now wholly within our lines, and we have had four days for the investigation of its every corner. I wonder whether it is understood how clever and courageous a feat of arms was the final capture, the sequel to a five weeks' struggle. The state of the wood is, of course, indescribable and is best left undescribed. Much of the fight is as little describable, because it consisted for a while of an artillery storm and nothing else. After very heavy fire the enemy, probably by accident, opened one of his very intensest bombardments with 8in. shells and the 5.9 just about the time fixed for the attack, and neighbouring troops who started later than those within the wood bore this for an hour while waiting for their chance to "go over." They were highly tested and highly triumphed.

Conscription increased

Until January 1916 Britain shunned coercion as a means of prosecuting the war. For 17 months, Regulars, Territorials and Reservists, augmented by Kitchener's volunteers, made up Britain's fighting force. Every effort was made to put persuasion before compulsion. Within weeks of the War Secretary's famous recruitment drive, the age limit was raised to 35, and the response was such that the machinery by which men were adopted into uniform struggled to cope. In spring 1915 the pinch-point was munitions, not men, regardless of the fact that the BEF had been all but wiped out. But as the "shell scandal" was addressed, not least by the use of female labour, the military manpower issue became a growing concern. In February 1915 the monthly enlistment figure dropped to under 100,000 for the first time, a decline replicated throughout the year. In September it barely nudged above 70,000. One reason for this was that the call for volunteers had been a victim of its own success. The number of men swapping civilian occupations for khaki put labour at a premium. That in turn meant wage levels were high, and those reaping the economic benefit had to weigh that sacrifice against service to the Crown. In many cases this was the exact opposite of the situation pertaining in August 1914, when men might have joined up because life in uniform seemed to offer so much more than their current lot.

With recruitment numbers remaining stubbornly below par in 1915, a National Register was taken in August to give an idea of the untapped resources. It revealed that five million men fell within the age parameters for military service. Over two million of those were unmarried, and even discounting those in starred occupations – around one-third – it still identified over a million single men as potential recruits. There was a final appeal to get as many of these into uniform as possible in an autumn 1915 drive headed by Lord Derby. When that failed to produce the desired results, the government bowed to the inevitable. On 27 January 1916 the Military Service Act brought single men aged 18-41 into the conscription net, Britain joining the other major belligerents in making soldiering a matter of statutory obligation. Over 250 MPs either voted against the bill or abstained, an indication of the queasiness many felt over the issue. Ireland was too hot a political potato to be covered by the legislation, and exemptions were also possible in the rest of the home countries, for key workers, the medically unfit, those with dependants whose absence would cause "serious hardship", and on grounds of conscience. The latter group posed a particular difficulty. Most conscientious objectors made a heartfelt, principled stand, but there were undoubtedly some who hitched themselves to that wagon for less noble reasons.

MUNITIONS YOUNG MEN TO GO.

ALL UNSKILLED UNDER 30.

HOME SERVICE MEN AS SUBSTITUTES.

Under pressure from the recruiting authorities managers of controlled firms are now prepared to release all fit unskilled men under the age of 30.

This will automatically send to the Army many useful recruits. It will leave at the same time a gap which must be filled. To do this the substitution scheme outlined in *The Daily Mail* yesterday has been framed. In the first instance the large number of men suitable for munition work now in home service units will be used as substitutes.

No man will be used against his wish. If found medically fit for the work he will be given his choice of employment—in the Army at Army rates, or in munition works at the special rates arranged under the substitution scheme.

Men liable for service but not actually in the Army will be enrolled under this scheme by local tribunals to whom they apply for exemption, or by permission of a local recruiting officer if already passed for service but not actually called up.

Conscientious objectors ordered by tribunals to do work of national importance are to be dealt with in future under this scheme. No man fit for active service or for garrison duty abroad will be employed as a substitute.

There were 750,000 exemption applications in the first six months following the passing of the Military Service Act. Tribunals were set up to hear such cases and became increasingly stringent over time. Even those who convinced their interrogators of the moral or religious imperative that made it unconscionable for them to bear arms were expected to fulfil non-combatant roles. Stretcher-bearing and food preparation were two obvious avenues, but a Non-Combatant Corps was also formed; an attempt on the authorities' part, perhaps, to keep those with pacifist leanings together rather than risk having those views disseminated throughout the ranks. There were around 16,000 COs in World War One, of which some 1,500 took the absolutist position of refusing to do anything in support of the war effort. Men whose pleas the tribunal rejected were deemed to have enlisted, and thus made them liable to court martial and imprisonment. Thirty-four received death sentences, though all were commuted. There were a number of instances where absolutists appeared before several courts martial, a cycle of non-cooperation followed by a period of incarceration. Disenfranchisement was an added sanction. Conscientious objectors were liable to have the right to vote removed as well as having to endure widespread contempt and opprobrium.

Single men who attested under the Derby Scheme were drafted into the army alongside the first conscript wave in spring 1916. Still the figures disappointed, and in early April the first of the married volunteers were summoned to the Colours. A month later saw the Military Service Act amended to make all married men up to the age of 41 liable to the call-up. The final widening of the net came in April 1918 when the upper age limit was extended to 51. It also extended conscription to Ireland, though events made it unnecessary for that incendiary amendment to the legislation to be invoked.

Opposite above left: **Estreham Road in Streatham, London, was the victim of a Zeppelin attack in late September.**

Opposite above middle: **Holy Trinity Church in Hull was hit in June 1915. The remnants of the windows were used to make a new stained glass window for the south transept.**

Opposite above right: **Workmen begin the clean-up operation after another attack.**

Opposite bottom: **In May 1916 a second Military Service Act was passed, extending conscription to married men. The first groups who responded to the call are pictured marching down Whitehall.**

Above left: **Another London terrace is shattered during a raid.**

Above right: **German officers are taken to the Donington Hall prison camp in Leicestershire. In 1915 German pilot Gunter Plüschow had made a successful escape from the camp. He reached London and hid in the British Museum at nights before boarding a ferry to the Netherlands, from where he made his way back to his native country.**

Left: **A British provincial town is combed for men who might be avoiding military service.**

ZEPPELIN FALLS IN FLAMES NEAR LONDON.

DESTROYED NEAR | HOW SHE FELL. | NEW SOMME OFFENSIVE | ZEPPELIN SUNDAY. | GR

The man who tamed the Zeppelin threat

By summer 1916, airship raids over Britain's east coast had been ongoing for 18 months, visiting death and destruction upon the civilian population. They were not a daily occurrence – the aggregate death toll for all these incursions was under 600 – but the psychological impact was considerable. Defences were rudimentary. Mesh netting was placed over some public buildings, and people were cautioned to remain indoors in the event of an attack, advice that backfired tragically when properties took a direct hit.

Germany engaged in total war

Germany's new weapon had dominion over the skies, much to the satisfaction of the campaign's orchestrator-in-chief, Commander Peter Strasser. He believed in this technological wonder lay the key to the Fatherland's victory. Germany was engaged in total war, and as such Strasser was a firm advocate of schrecklichkeit – "frightfulness" in British journalese. "Let terror be Germany's salvation," Strasser declared, as the raids became ever bigger and bolder. Surely it was but a matter of time before the enemy was cowed into submission?

Yielding to the menace of the world's first long-range bomber was far from the thoughts of those overseeing the mainland's defences. There were two strands to that armoury: anti-aircraft batteries and fighter planes fitted with machine-guns. Unfortunately, both had limitations. The altitude airships could reach neutralised the threat of ground weaponry, and Zeppelins also appeared to be impervious to close-range firing. When pilots peppered the skin, it was found they merely left pinpricks that did nothing other than allow a little of the hydrogen to seep harmlessly into the atmosphere. It is no exaggeration to say that Strassers's headaches were less to do with Britain's countermeasures, more

about overcoming other obstacles. Altitude sickness was one, until oxygen was routinely used during sorties. Navigation was another. Flying high above dense cloud was good for security, not so helpful for accurate bombing. A separate manned capsule dangling far below the mother ship helped in this regard, the occupant of the former relaying observations made from his umbilical vantage point. Then, of course, there was the ever-present danger of adverse weather.

Britain ready to strike back

The boffins seeking to counter the Zeppelin threat knew that a vast envelope filled with a highly flammable gas ought to make an inviting target. Getting the hydrogen to ignite was the problem. Incendiary bullets were thought to be the answer, but these, too, met with little success when they were tried out. Lack of oxygen to aid the combustion process was identified as the issue. An ingenious solution was soon devised: using a combination of explosive and incendiary bullets in the magazine; one to rip great holes in the envelope and allow sufficient oxygen into the mix, the other to provide the spark for this volatile cocktail. By September 1916, Britain was ready to strike back.

Left: On 23 September the Zeppelin *L32* set out for a bombing raid on London. After dropping its load on Purfleet it had turned for home when Frederick Sowrey of the Royal Flying Corps fired incendiary ammunition at the ship, which caught fire and immediately fell to the ground in Great Burstead, Essex, killing all 22 crew. As word spread, Londoners flocked to the site by train, car and bicycle, jamming the roads and fighting for space in the railway carriages, in order to view the wreckage.

Above: The blaze was so fierce even the framework disappeared.

Opposite above: Lieutenant William Leefe Robinson (middle) of the Royal Flying Corps was the first British pilot to shoot down a German airship during the conflict. He targeted the *SL-11* as it flew over the village of Cuffley in Hertfordshire.

Opposite below: Despite the rain, onlookers descended on the village to view the wreck of the airship.

Celebrated airman

A substantial cash prize was on offer to the first man to down one of these aerial raiders. Lieutenant William Leefe Robinson needed no added incentive to contribute to the war effort. Born in India on 14 July 1895, this Sandhurst graduate had joined the Worcestershire Regiment and seemed destined to make his mark in the army. But he transferred to the Royal Flying Corps early in 1915, operating as an observer while undergoing pilot training, which he completed in September that year. Twelve months later, when he had just turned 21, Robinson was the most celebrated airman in the land.

The action that inscribed his name into the history books took place on the night of Saturday, 2 September 1916. A 16-strong German raiding party carrying over 30 tons of explosives set a course for London, the largest airship attack of the conflict. Lieutenant Robinson, of 39 Squadron, had already taken to the skies, on a routine patrol in a BE 2c reconnaissance aircraft equipped with the latest incendiary and explosive bullets in its magazine. At around 2.00 am, high above the Hertfordshire village of Cuffley, he had one of the raiders, *SL-11*, in his sights. Robinson made two runs, strafing the craft's fabric covering, seemingly to no avail. With his remaining ammunition drum he targeted a single section of the hull, and *SL-11* was soon crashing earthwards ablaze, its fiery end witnessed by a cheering throng on the ground.

These cigar-shaped giants with their relatively large ordnance payload brought terror to the skies over Britain.

Leefe Robinson earns a place in history

If not quite an end to the airship threat – Germany soon introduced a new generation of vessels that could climb to 20,000 feet – it was undoubtedly a significant moment in the battle over British air space. Momentous, too, for Robinson, who was awarded the Victoria Cross within days and soon promoted to captain. He was also a celebrity. In a letter to his parents he told how "babies, flowers and hats have been named after me, also poems and prose have been dedicated to me – oh, it's too much!"

Though he survived the war, Robinson's story had an unfortunate end. In April 1917 he was brought down over France in a dogfight with the crack squadron headed by Manfred von Richthofen – the Red Baron. He saw out the rest of the conflict as a POW, where his fame and exploits counted against him. Repeated escape attempts brought further rough treatment from his captors, who "harried and badgered and bullied him every way possible", according to one witness. His ordeal left him in a weakened state, and when he was finally repatriated in December 1918, he was struck down by influenza. William Leefe Robinson died on 31 December 1918, barely a fortnight after returning home. He left behind a fiancée who had already lost her first husband to the war. His VC, the first to be awarded for an act of valour on – or, at least, over – British territory, gives him a place in perpetuity in the annals of military history.

V.C. FOR THE "ZEPPELIN" DESTROYER.

"I ONLY DID MY JOB."

There is not much chance of Lieutenant Robinson, V.C., being reckless. His deprecatory "I only did my job," is the plain, self-made portrait of this modest, quiet hero, who has laughingly said that, short of a marriage ceremony, he cannot conceive of anything more unnerving to man than the congratulations of this week. His reputation among his men is solely that of an officer so keen on his "job" that he often works in the sheds with them like a mechanic. He is utterly sincere when he is abashed and nervous at the fame and glory that have come to him for only doing his "job."

For the rest he is radiantly youthful and happy and ingenuous, a young hero with the pleasantest, most musical of voices, a wonderfully slim and lithe figure, a great and rather surprised gratitude to all who express their infinite gratitude to him—and part of this sketch of him is that when he issued from Windsor Castle he had hidden his Victoria Cross in its leather case in his pocket.

There were barely 50 Zeppelin raids in total, the aggregate casualty toll far less than the first morning of the Somme offensive.

Top: Lieutenant William Leefe Robinson was awarded a Victoria Cross for his actions. Pieces of the wrecked airship were sold to raise money for the Red Cross to aid wounded soldiers.

Above and below: The funeral of the crew of the *SL-11* airship took place at Potters Bar cemetery. The coffins of the sixteen victims were placed in one large grave with a separate space for the commander. Last rites were observed and men of the Royal Flying Corps lowered the coffins as the "Last Post" was played.

THE RAIDERS' FUNERAL.

ARMY CHAPLAIN TO ASSIST AT BURIAL TO-DAY.

The bodies of the crew of the German airship destroyed in London on Sunday morning are to be buried this afternoon at three o'clock at Potter's Bar Cemetery and not, as was stated yesterday, at Cheshunt. The officiating clergy will be the vicar of Potter's Bar, the Rev. G. R. P. Preston, the vicar of South Mimms, the Rev. Allen Hay, and an Army chaplain to be nominated by the War Office.

The sixteen coffins, which now ...e in the little iron chapel at Cuffley, will be taken to the cemetery about two o'clock in one of the Air Service motor vehicles usually used for transporting aeroplanes. The whole funeral service will take place in the cemetery.

One large grave, 25ft. long and 7ft. wide, has been made for the crew, and a separate grave has been dug for the remains of the commander. The graves were dug by one man and two women.

Letters of protest against the military funeral will be found in the opposite page.

From HAROLD ASHTON.

An "observer's" tale of the great fight in the air should rank as an epic among the thrilling tales of the war.

Before Lieutenant Robinson ran into the airship he destroyed he had already been up in the air two hours hawking for victims. Though he was hampered by a dense drift of earth fog when he started, he rose undaunted. He was soon drenched by fog, but he kept on until he got clear of the bank and found calm, cold air above.

A little before two o'clock, after coming down a few hundred feet, he rose again in wide and ever-widening circles, taking as a centre of his spirals the flickering ribbon of light which cut into the sullen patches of grey cloud through which an occasional star shone. The first glimpse of the raider was obtained at a height variously estimated as from 10,000ft. to 12,000ft. She came ·osing out of a smudge of cloud like an Ouse chub from the shadows of a mud bank, prowling for food.

Instantly she was spotted—and the grand aerial entertainment began. At this moment the airman was 8,000ft. up, climbing so rapidly that his machine was "almost standing on her tail." Apparently the airship had not yet seen him. She was manœuvring swiftly and changing her altitude to dodge the pyrotechnic doses that were peppering her from below. Our airman himself was in very much the same predicament. He was in almost a direct line of the fire from the friendly guns below. He could only trust to his own speed and the beneficent grace of the little cherub who sits up aloft. Presently, at 2.10 a.m., within a few seconds, according to the "observer's" timing, the airship sighted the aeroplane, and swerved suddenly to starboard as she was attacked.

HORNET V. HIPPOPOTAMUS.

The hornet worried the hippopotamus. Already the great beast was burning astern and there was trouble in her aft gondola. Shrapnel from the anti-aircraft guns below was still bursting around. The airman's planes were "holed" and straining as he tossed and danced into his seemingly erratic but actually well-considered evolutions. With friend and foe to deal with, you would think he had his hands full. So he had: but he kept a cool head through it all.

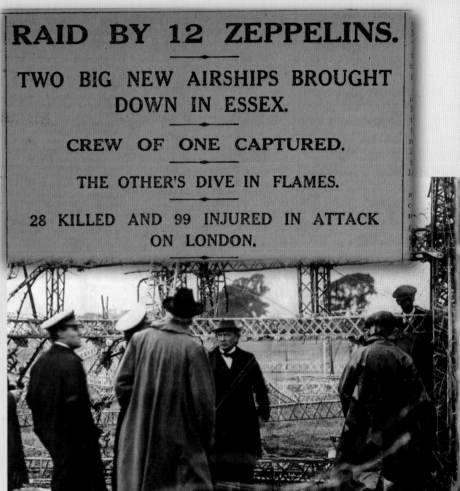

RAID BY 12 ZEPPELINS.

TWO BIG NEW AIRSHIPS BROUGHT DOWN IN ESSEX.

CREW OF ONE CAPTURED.

THE OTHER'S DIVE IN FLAMES.

28 KILLED AND 99 INJURED IN ATTACK ON LONDON.

Above: After the *L32* hit the ground in Great Burstead, local villagers gathered to view the remains.

Bottom: A second Zeppelin, the *L33*, was also damaged by anti-aircraft fire and was forced to land on farmland at Little Wigborough, Essex. The crew was able to escape before it caught fire.

Below left: Special Constable Edgar Nicholas went to investigate and intercepted the crew walking along the road. He made an arrest and,

with the help of colleagues, handed the prisoners over to the military authorities.

Below middle: The gondola of the *L33* was closely guarded after the crash so military personnel could study its manufacture and design. Some of the information gathered was used in future airship design.

Right: Lloyd George and Balfour (back to the camera) visit the airship wreck.

Below right: On 1 October a letter appeared in the *New York Times* from Kaptitan Heinrich Mathy stating that he would "smash London". On the same day, this much-feared German flying ace set off, along with ten other airships, but was picked out by searchlights over Potters Bar, Hertfordshire. The airship was attacked by Wulstan Tempest from the Royal Flying Corps and caught fire in the air. All were killed with many, including Mathy, electing to jump rather than burn to death.

Battle of Guillemont

Guillemont, which faced the British right flank and lay just behind the Second German Line, was the subject of repeated Allied assaults. Haig identified this village and its environs as a key target, for it would protect the French left, paving the way for a future joint attack. On 23 July men of the Manchester Regiment made encouraging but unsustainable gains. A week later it was Liverpool Pals who bore the brunt of an unsuccessful attack, carried out in thick fog. Poor visibility aided the defenders, who were able to fire randomly in the direction of the advance. 8 August witnessed yet another catastrophic failure, leaving Haig in fulminating mood, with Fourth Army commander Sir Henry Rawlinson firmly in his sights. "The only conclusion that can be drawn from the repeated failure of attacks on Guillemont is that something is wanting in the methods employed." He ordered that the next effort should be on a broader front – a clear sideswipe at Rawlinson's piecemeal approach – and of such magnitude as to "to beat down all opposition". It took place on 3 September, when German resistance finally crumbled and Guillemont fell to the Allies.

"The only conclusion that can be drawn from the repeated failure of attacks on Guillemont is that something is wanting in the methods employed."

Opposite top: Welsh Guards resting in the trenches at Guillemont.

Opposite middle and opposite below: Infantry exposed to enemy fire on the open ground of the battlefield. The area around Guillemont was a maze of German underground tunnels and dug-outs, adding to the dangers faced by Allied troops.

Above: An armoured motor-car and an ambulance pull-in alongside rows of stretchers.

Right: British gunners watch German prisoners being escorted away.

German prisoners

The first prisoners of war, on both sides, were interned aliens. In Britain the Aliens Restriction Act was passed in August 1914, requiring foreign nationals to register with the authorities. Civilians with Germanic roots, especially those with tell-tale names, fell victim to a torrent of anti-German sentiment as "spy mania" broke out. Richard Noschke was one who found himself on the receiving end. He had married an English girl in the 1890s, lived and worked in the country for 25 years and spoke accent-free English. He fitted the bill perfectly as "much more British in sentiment than German", as one MP described the body of German expatriates steeped in the culture of their adopted land. Yet Noschke found himself ostracised and then incarcerated, embittered by the attitude of former friends and colleagues.

To these numbers were soon added uniformed POWs. Camps were hastily set up, or existing buildings converted, to contain those arriving from France. Alexandra Palace was one of the more famous buildings commandeered for the purpose, though there were eventually 600 of varying sizes dotted around the country, housing a population that ran to a peak of around 115,000. Some 25,000 of those were civilian internees, the remainder combatants who had served in the German army. Frith Hill, near Frimley, Surrey, was one such camp. *The Times'* edition of 29 September 1914 described the scene there, reporting on wounded hordes whose injuries came at the hands of the British infantry whose fire was "most deadly in its accuracy". The prisoners were said to have praised the medical attention they received from their captors, which was, apparently, superior to the German ambulance work in the field; they were also "grateful for cigarettes given them by civilian onlookers". Contrast that picture of contentment with a poster depicting a German nurse pouring water onto the ground before a captured, wounded Tommy desperate for a drink. Another poster urged men to enlist in order to fight those who "have stripped and insulted British prisoners and have shot some in cold blood". In Germany there were similar scare stories regarding maltreatment of captured troops in an attempt to spur recruitment to the Fatherland's cause. Inevitably, both sides actively engaged in the propaganda war. Under the Hague Conventions of 1899 and 1907, the way in which POWs were to be treated had been enshrined in international law. Doubtless there were instances when all combatants fell well short of the prescribed standards of dignity and decency.

Being penned in behind barbed wire had varying psychological effects on the detainees. Some POWs felt a sense of emasculation and shame, while others accepted sitting out the war with rather more phlegmatic resignation. Remaining out of the firing line, even if compelled to do non-military-related work on behalf of the enemy, was a relief to certain individuals, anathema to others. Negotiations between the belligerents regarding prisoner exchanges were conducted throughout the war, in advance of the mass deportation that occurred afterwards. That was a sizeable undertaking, not completed on Britain's part until 1920.

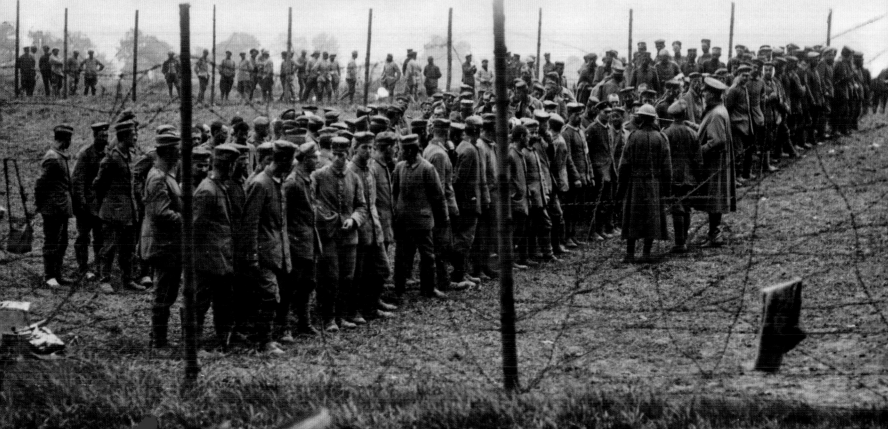

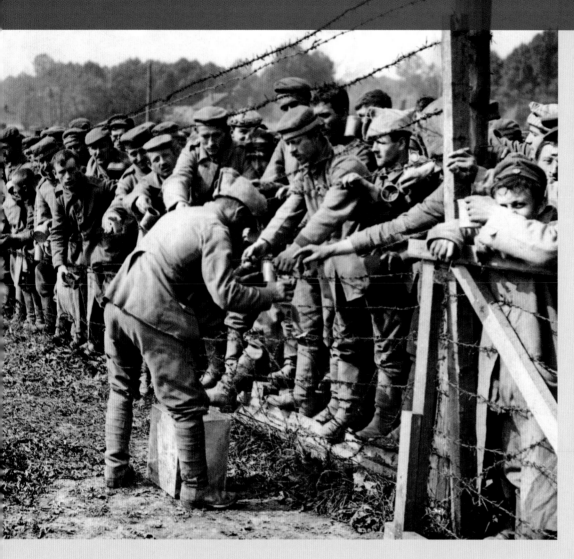

Opposite above: **A German colonel, major and an adjutant captured near St Pierre Divion.**

Opposite below: **Prisoners at Carnoy await instructions from British officers.**

Above left: **German prisoners eagerly hold out their cups for water.**

Top right and above right: **Between July and October 1916 the French took some 40,000 prisoners on the Somme, while the British captured approximately 30,000 men.**

Right: **Large numbers of prisoners behind French lines wait for transportation to an internment camp.**

Below: **A long, straggling line of captives leaves the battlefield.**

GREAT FRENCH DASH ON SOMME.

HALF-HOUR'S WONDERFUL WORK.

GERMAN FIRST LINE ON 4-MILE FRONT CARRIED.

OUR DARING AIRMEN.

GERMAN GIBES AT THEIR OWN.

From W. BEACH THOMAS.

WITH THE BRITISH ARMY IN THE FIELD, Monday.

The recent fighting has taught us m...
through many different channels, of
enemy's mental as well as materi...
sources. We now know in some deta...
what his troops think of our attac...

BULGAR RETREAT BEFORE ALLIES.

TWO MILES OF TRENCHES TAKEN.

RUSSO-RUMANIAN STROKES.

MOUNTAIN STORMED.

DANUBE ISLET FORT OCCUPIED.

GERMANY DAY BY DAY.

BOAST ABOUT HOLLAND.

By FREDERIC WILLIAM WILE.

WITH

A

LIFE

Battle of Ginchy

The Allies had hoped to take Ginchy in the same sweeping advance that finally wrested Guillemont from Germany's grasp on 3 September. The villages were a short distance apart, Ginchy lying just to the northeast, but such was Falkenhayn's determination to hold every inch of ground at all cost that no objective was going to be easily secured. The attack on Ginchy was renewed six days after Guillemont fell, the 16th (Irish) Division leading the charge. It was successful, as was the rebuffing of the inevitable German counter that soon followed, but as ever the price had been steep. Over 4,000 casualties were added to the Somme account by the time Ginchy was taken. Haig was buoyed by the success, however, entertaining hopes of a mid-September breakthrough in which his beloved cavalry might finally be pressed into service.

Above right: The battlefield grave of an unknown British soldier in Ginchy is marked by his cap and rifle.

Right: A desolate image shows French and German trenches extending close to each other with German dead lying on the small patch of no-man's-land in between.

Below: The Battle of the Somme evolved into a piecemeal struggle, though Haig never abandoned hopes that small gains would lead, incrementally, to a dramatic outcome.

Opposite above: A British officer watches as German trenches near Leuze Wood are shelled. Troops soon renamed it "Lousy Woods".

Opposite below: Australian troops quickly captured the village of Mont St Quentin at the beginning of September. Commander John Monash had ordered them to "scream like bushrangers" as they attacked.

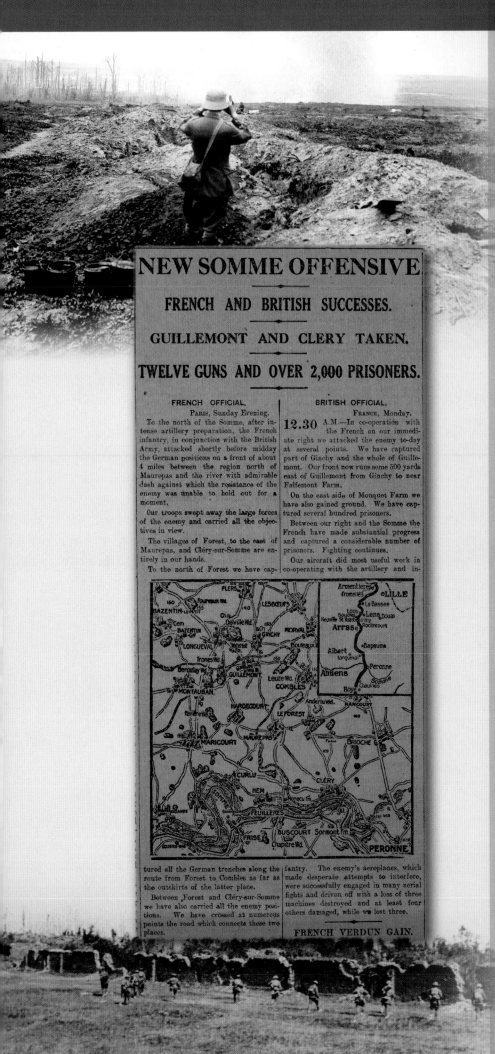

NEW SOMME OFFENSIVE

FRENCH AND BRITISH SUCCESSES.

GUILLEMONT AND CLERY TAKEN.

TWELVE GUNS AND OVER 2,000 PRISONERS.

FRENCH OFFICIAL.

PARIS, Sunday Evening.

To the north of the Somme, after intense artillery preparation, the French infantry, in conjunction with the British Army, attacked shortly before midday the German positions on a front of about 4 miles between the region north of Maurepas and the river with admirable dash against which the resistance of the enemy was unable to hold out for a moment.

Our troops swept away the large forces of the enemy and carried all the objectives in view.

The villages of Forest, to the east of Maurepas, and Cléry-sur-Somme are entirely in our hands.

To the north of Forest we have captured all the German trenches along the route from Forest to Combles as far as the outskirts of the latter place.

Between Forest and Cléry-sur-Somme we have also carried all the enemy positions. We have crossed at numerous points the road which connects these two places.

BRITISH OFFICIAL.

FRANCE, Monday.

12.30 A.M.—In co-operation with the French on our immediate right we attacked the enemy to-day at several points. We have captured part of Ginchy and the whole of Guillemont. Our front now runs some 500 yards east of Guillemont from Ginchy to near Falfemont Farm.

On the east side of Mouquet Farm we have also gained ground. We have captured several hundred prisoners.

Between our right and the Somme the French have made substantial progress and captured a considerable number of prisoners. Fighting continues.

Our aircraft did most useful work in co-operating with the artillery and infantry. The enemy's aeroplanes, which made desperate attempts to interfere, were successfully engaged in many aerial fights and driven off with a loss of three machines destroyed and at least four others damaged, while we lost three.

FRENCH VERDUN GAIN.

September 1916

1 Bulgaria declared war on Romania.

The British and Russian Governments concluded the "Sykes-Picot" agreement for the eventual partition of Asia Minor.

2 Fourteen Zeppelins raided England dropping bombs from Gravesend, east of London, to Peterborough. One Zeppelin, *Schutte-Lanz S.L. 11*, was shot down over London by a British airplane.

3 The British advanced at Guillemont and the French captured Foret; at the same time the Battle of Delville Wood ended with a tactical victory for the Allies.

4 Dar-es-Salaam in German East Africa was surrendered to British forces.

5 British troops captured Leuze Wood during the Battle of Guillemont.

6 The Battle of Guillemont ended.

7 The Battle of Kisaki took place between German and South African forces near the town of Kisaki during the East African campaign.

8 The Battle of Kisaki ended in a German victory.

9 In the intermediate phase of the Battle of the Somme, British troops captured the German held village of Ginchy, a strategically important post at the Battle of Ginchy.

10 French and Serbian forces broke out of Thessaloniki, advancing north on the Macedonian Front.

11 Greek Prime Minister Alexandros Zaimis tendered his resignation.

12 The Battle of Kajmakcalan began in the foothills of Mount Kajmakcalan on the Macedonian Front between Serbian and Bulgarian soldiers.

14 Italian and Austro-Hungarian forces again fought each other along the Isonzo River as the Seventh Battle of the Isonzo began.

15 The Battle of Flers-Courcelette saw the first deployment of British armoured tanks when the British Fourth Army launched a large scale offensive on the Somme. The battle signified the start of the third stage of the Somme Offensive.

16 Nikolaos Kalogeropoulos replaced Alexandros Zaimis as Prime Minister of Greece.

18 The Seventh Battle of the Izonzo ended. Italian troops under the command of Field Marshall Luigi Cadorna succeeded in wearing away at Austro-Hungarian resources, both in terms of manpower and in crucial artillery availability.

19 Belgian forces captured Tabora, the capital city of German East Africa.

Allied forces began a naval blockade of the Greek Macedonian Coast between the Rivers Struma and River Mesta.

20 The Brusilov Offensive ended with a decisive Russian victory.

22 The Battle of Flers-Courcelette ended; the strategic objective of a breakthrough had not been achieved although tactical gains had been made with the capture of the villages of Martinpuich, Courcelette and Flers.

23 Twelve Zeppelins bombed London and the English East Coast. Two of the invading aircraft were brought down.

24 French aircraft bombed the Krupp munitions works at Essen in Germany.

25 The Battle of Morval began with an attack by the British Fourth Army on the German held villages of Morval, Gueudecourt and Lesboeufs .

26 The Battle of Thiepval Ridge began with the aim of building on the Fourth Army attack at Morval 24 hours earlier.

28 The Battles of Morval and Thiepval Ridge both ended with victories for Allied forces.

29 Eleftherios Venizelos and Admiral Condouriotis announced the formation of a new Greek Provisional Government in Crete, in opposition to government in Athens.

30 Serbian forces captured the eastern and western peaks of Mount Kajmakcalan as the the Battle of Kajmakcalan came to an end.

Battle of Flers-Courcelette

The mid-September phase of the Somme battle was buttressed by the arrival of the tank. Not the 1,000 Haig had pressed for; just 32 of these armour-plated, tractor-driven vehicles were ready for action on the morning of 15 September, which opened up on a six-mile front. There was a school of thought that the tank should have been held back until available in much greater numbers, but the need to see what they could do on the battlefield was pressing. "This is a vital battle," wrote one of HQ's top brass, "and we should be in error to throw away anything that might increase our chance of success." There was early encouragement in the centre as the new Allied weapon played a part in the capture of Flers. Resistance was relatively light as this early objective was secured and the original German Second Line pierced. Some enemy troops fled in the face of the metal monster, others surrendered. Meanwhile, at Courcelette in the west, the Canadians were in occupation of the village by the end of the day, though at significant cost. Martinpuich, another German stronghold, also fell. But overall, despite the acquisitions and greatest territorial gain since 1 July, Haig was no nearer the major breach in the German line he had hoped for.

Top: A wounded soldier receives a welcome helping hand.

Right: An ammunition truck struggles to cope with the lunar-type landscape.

Below: The Wiltshire Regiment cross a piece of open ground.

Opposite above left: Canadians escort German prisoners down a communication trench near Courcelette. They were only too eager to cry "Kamerad" to protect themselves.

Opposite above right: Members of a Highland regiment on their way to the trenches.

Opposite below: Canadians go over the top, but this time the advance is aided by the appearance of tanks on the battlefield for the first time. This new armoured monster terrified many German soldiers.

Opposite top: A graphic published on 15 August showing the terrain of the battlefield and the original front line just south of Fricourt.

"This is a vital battle and we should be in error to throw away anything that might increase our chance of success."

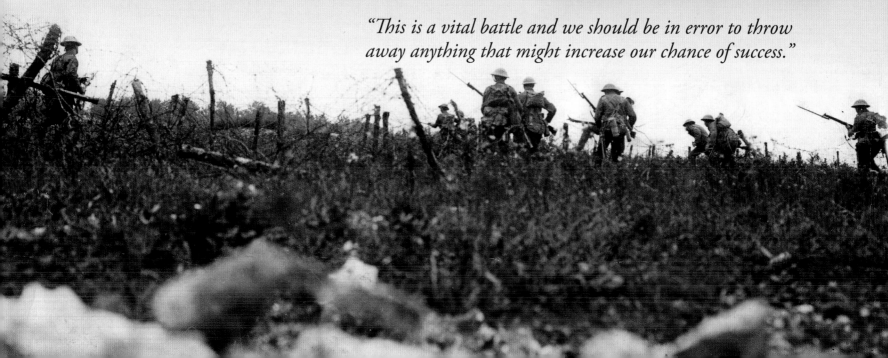

THE RIDGE WHICH THE BRITISH HAVE HAD TO CLIMB.

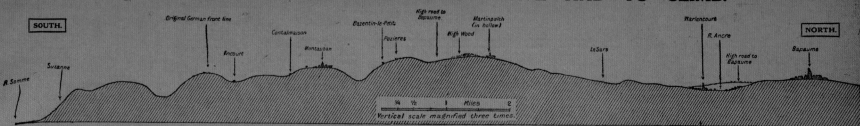

SOUTH.   NORTH.

Vertical scale magnified three times.

CANADIANS ON THE SOMME—THE PUSH OF THE BIG GUN.

PICK-AXES FORWARD.—These sturdy Canadians, carrying pick-axes, are seen going forward to consolidate and organise some of our recent gains of ground on the Somme. [Canadian Official Photograph.

TOWARDS BAPAUME!—A big artillery unit in the colossal struggle on the Somme. Such guns are doing their routine work of smashing the German receding positions, prefatory to the fine advance of the Allies' waves of infantry. [French Official.

"ZEPPELIN STRAFER" AT MACHINE-GUN PRACTICE.—Flight-Lieutenant Brandon, D.S.O., one of the R.F.C. officers recently decorated for gallantry in the air, trying a machine gun. ["Daily Mail" Photograph.

Tanks fail to tilt balance at the Somme

Aside from the fact that the initial artillery bombardment failed to wreak the anticipated devastation on the German positions, from the outset there were strategic fault lines in the Somme offensive. Haig saw it as an opportunity for a major breakthrough, while Rawlinson favoured setting limited objectives and consolidation: a "bite and hold" approach. As the battle wore on, the aim seemed to drift between the two. There were opportunities to penetrate the enemy ranks in a way that would have gladdened Haig's heart, but when they weren't capitalised upon it became politic to present limited gains as delivering attritional body blows to the enemy.

Those brighter moments included an audacious dawn attack on 14 July that caught the Germans off guard. A month later, the British deployed their new secret weapon, christened from the "water tank" cover name assigned when it was under wraps. The brainchild of one Colonel Ernest Swinton, it was Churchill at the Admiralty who took up cudgels on behalf of this armoured attack vehicle that ran on caterpillar tracks. Exactly one year before the tank first appeared on the battlefield it had been a wooden model. Fifty had been built by the time of the 15 September attack at Flers; fewer than Haig expected, but he was keen to see if they could make a difference in an offensive that was already six weeks old. They couldn't. Tanks that made it through to confront the enemy did create panic and confusion, but this was infant technology and early models were unreliable, prone to becoming bogged down and not as impervious to shellfire as might have been expected. One tank commander lost his bearings and fired on his own line. It was clearly a military innovation that had much promise, though unleashed, perhaps, too soon. Certainly tanks did not swing the Somme offensive dramatically in the Allies' favour; their day would come the following year.

It was clearly a military innovation that had much promise, though unleashed, perhaps, too soon.

Opposite top and opposite middle right: The first official photographs of tanks going into action at the Battle of Flers-Courcelette were released after the new weapon was taken off the secrets list. The British Mark I "male" tank carried two Hotchkiss 6-pounder guns and four machine guns. It had a tail wheel designed to provide balance, but after proving to be ineffective this was abandoned in later models.

Opposite below right: Six French tanks take part in an organised attack on German lines. The French had been developing their own tank models at the same time as the British, but whereas Britain had opted to join all its expertise together to produce the Mark I, several independent companies had designed and made the French models.

Opposite bottom: Tanks were manned by three drivers, a subaltern and four gunners, including an NCO. The noise, exhaust fumes and heat were intense and crew members were often sick or unwell even after very short journeys.

Above: The C24 was a "female" tank going by the name of *Clan Cameron*. Its commander was Captain Harold Cole who was awarded the MBE after the end of the war.

Below and right: Infantrymen wait in the safety of the trenches as a tank moves in on the attack.

Battle of Morval

Morval had been one of the immediate targets of the Allied attack launched on 15 September. Haig's scheme was to push through reinforcements – including cavalry – and establish a flank guard along a line connecting Morval with Bapaume; forces that would assail the enemy from the side and rear while the frontal assault continued. By the time the Battle of Morval opened on 25 September, the objectives were more modest, the kind of "bite-and-hold" operation favoured by Rawlinson. In particular, the advance would remain within the compass of covering artillery. Driving forward behind a creeping barrage, the infantry enjoyed a resounding success, quickly taking possession of Lesboeufs – another missed target from 10 days earlier – as well as Morval itself. The Germans yielded Combles to the French the following day, at the end of which Gueudecourt was also in Allied hands. It was an impressive two days' work, but the cautious, measured approach also provided the Germans with breathing space in which to regroup and form a fresh defensive line.

Below: **Reserves move up to support the advance on Morval. Poor weather had caused the attack to be postponed by a few days and the heavy rain and fog grounded aircraft and affected artillery observation, while infantrymen floundered in the mud.**

Opposite above: **Motor lorries filled with Allied troops pass through a Somme village. The British Army began the war with just over 500 vehicles and by the end possessed 22,000 trucks.**

Opposite below: **Once the signal is given troops leave their trenches at Morval. A shell can be seen exploding in the distance.**

Driving forward behind a creeping barrage, the infantry enjoyed a resounding success.

Battle of Thiepval

Twenty-four hours after the attack on Morval was launched, General Gough's Reserve Army began its assault on Thiepval. Pounded since the opening day – when it was meant to have fallen – Thiepval had proved resilient. While the buildings were heavily battle scarred, there were plenty of cellars that German machine-gunners put to good use. Four divisions, two of them Canadian, attacked on a 6,000-yard front, which extended eastwards to Courcelette. Tanks were again deployed, and to good effect as German strongpoints in Thiepval itself offered dogged resistance. The village was cleared by the morning of the 27th, and Gough's men also established a significant foothold on the ridge running from Thiepval to Courcelette.

Above left: British soldiers watch for the enemy. Thiepval marked the first major battle for the Reserve Army under the command of Lieutenant-General Sir Hubert Gough.

Above right: New Zealanders carry their kit as they move up to the trenches. The country had already introduced military conscription in 1909 and had been the first Dominion to send troops to assist the Allies. A total of 120,000 men saw active service during the conflict.

Top right: German prisoners are led out from a trench in Thiepval. The village was taken by the Allies on 27 September.

Below: A German trench captured during the battle.

Opposite above: Exhausted soldiers enjoy a brief respite leaning against a shattered wooden barrier.

Opposite below: Soldiers watch for signs of any further enemy activity.

October 1916

1 The Battle of Le Transloy was the final offensive mounted by the British Fourth Army during the Battle of the Somme.

4 The troop transport ship RMS *Franconia* was torpedoed and sunk by the German submarine *U-47* in the Mediterranean Sea.

5 The Battle of the Cerna Bend began in Macedonia between the Bulgarian and Entente armies.

6 Serbian troops attacked Bulgarian troops near the villages of Dobroveni and Skochivir on the Macedonian Front, but were counter-attacked and pushed back. The Bulgarians took the village of Brod.

7 In the Battle of Brasov the city was recaptured by Austro-Hungarian forces.

8 Under the command of Kapitänleutnant Hans Rose the German submarine *U-53* sank five merchant ships off the coast of Rhode Island, USA.

9 The Eighth Battle of the Isonzo began and continued the Italian attempts to extend the bridgehead established at Gorizia.

Eleftherios Venizelos arrived in Thessaloniki to establish a pro-Allies provisional Government and to raise an army.

10 Allied Governments sent an ultimatum to the Greek Government demanding surrender of the Greek naval fleet.

Spyridon Lambros replaced Nikolaos Kalogeropoulos as Prime Minister of Greece.

11 The Greek Government acceded to the Allied demands.

12 The Eighth Battle of the Isonzo ended with little territorial change and heavy Italian casualties.

13 The Norwegian Government prohibited belligerent submarines from using her territorial waters.

14 The Transylvanian frontier into Romania was crossed by German troops.

15 Anti-Entente demonstrations were held in Athens.

16 On the Western Front French troops gained a foothold in Sailly at the Battle of Morval.

17 During the Senussi Campaign the Allied Western Frontier Force moved to attack the enemy Senussi troops at the Affairs in the Dakhla Oasis.

18 General Henry Rawlinson mounted further attacks against the Germans at Gueudecourt during the Battle of Le Transloy.

19 French forces began a new offensive to capture Fort Douaumont at Verdun.

21 Austrian President Count Karl von Stürgkh was assassinated by Friedrich Adler, son of the founder of Austria's Social Democratic Party.

22 Constanza in Dobrudja was captured by German and Bulgarian forces on the Eastern Front.

23 The British minesweeper HMS *Genista* was sunk by a German U-boat off the west coast of Ireland.

24 French forces opened the First Offensive Battle of Verdun and recaptured Fort Douaumont.

26 The naval engagement, the Battle of Dover Strait took place when the German Empire launched flotillas of U-boats in order to disrupt the Dover Barrage and destroy all Allied shipping in the Strait.

27 By the time the Battle of Dover Strait ended the British had lost one destroyer, one troopship and several drifters while the Germans suffered only minor damage to a single torpedo boat.

28 Ernst von Korber was appointed Austrian President following the assassination of Count Karl von Stürgkh earlier in the month.

29 The Sherif of Mecca was proclaimed King of the Arabs.

30 Hermann von Stein succeeded Adolf Wild von Hohenborn as German Minister for War.

31 The Ninth Battle of the Isonzo was launched – the third of three short-lived offensives fought on the Isonzo front in the autumn of 1916. The battle started with an attack on Vrtojba and the northern and central areas of the Karst Plateau.

Below: The Canadian Infantry march to the front line in October 1916. Over 600,000 Canadians took part in the war with 170,000 wounded and 60,000 losing their lives. To recognise the significant part they played, the country was accorded its own representative at the Paris Peace Conference and signed the treaties as a separate nation, although it remained part of the British Empire.

Battle of Transloy Ridge

Allied successes in the second half of September left Haig in upbeat mood, determined to build on the gains already made as the Somme offensive entered its fourth month. He envisaged driving through Bapaume and even reaching Cambrai a further 15 miles to the northeast. Standing in his way was the new German front line, which ran along the ridge at Le Transloy. Further trenches were being constructed beyond, giving a formidably deep defence mirroring that which the Allies faced on 1 July. It was highly ambitious to say the least, and conducted in deteriorating weather. This phase of the Somme battle, undertaken by Rawlinson's Fourth Army, commenced on 1 October. The capture of Le Sars on 7 October was something of a false dawn. Resistance was ferocious, casualties heavy, gains strictly limited. Poor visibility hampered aerial support, and at ground level it was difficult to pinpoint German positions with accuracy. Haig was in a cleft stick. The situation might have called for discretion, but he was determined not to provide the enemy with the latitude that might allow him to recover and strengthen. The battle ended after a failed attack on 5 November, in which Rawlinson had little faith but which Haig insisted go ahead.

Top: **Two Canadian official kinema operators film a battle on the horizon. On the right a photographer is at work, while two artillery observers are busy alongside them. At the start of the war Lord Kitchener banned British journalists from directly reporting on the war and instead appointed Colonel Ernest Swinton to write reports that were vetted by Kitchener before being sent to the newspapers.**

Above left and right: **A light-hearted moment as soldiers optimistically suggest that the wreckage of a Hansom cab might make it to the seat of government.**

Left: **Shell holes soon become useful observation posts.**

Opposite top right: **A panoramic view of the remains of the village of Dompierre.**

Opposite above left: **Despite the shell bursting nearby, members of the Red Cross carry the wounded across no-man's-land.**

Opposie middle right: **The steel helmet and gas mask were also introduced into the Dutch Army. Although the country remained neutral throughout the conflict, the Army was mobilised at all times.**

Opposite below: **An all-too-familiar scene on the British Western Front showing the everyday aspects of war. Beside a broken railway a dozen crosses mark soldiers' graves, shell cases are strewn about and a transport wagon is heading to the front line.**

The capture of Le Sars on 7 October was something of a false dawn. Resistance was ferocious.

Battle of Ancre

As the Somme offensive rolled into November, Haig wanted one last flourish ahead of the mid-month Allied conference at Chantilly; a fresh prize he could trumpet before the weather rendered further action impossible. It would be both fillip and spur to the Allies if he could attend the meeting "on top of the capture of Beaumont Hamel for instance, and 3,000 German prisoners". As for the War Committee, now openly expressing reservations about the achievements thus far and the wisdom of continuing, any good news would be welcome. Gough's Fifth Army was tasked with delivering the bounty, and to that end attacked along the banks of the Ancre on 13 November. The fact that there had been little movement on this stretch of front was advantageous, for there were not the logistics problems that bedevilled those parts of the line that had advanced across treacherous terrain since 1 July. The battle was in full cry when Haig went to Chantilly, and already there were gains that met his aspirations. By the time the operation wound down on 19 November, Beaumont Hamel, Beaucourt and St Pierre Divion were all in Allied hands. A fourth target, Serre, had not been secured. What sounded like an impressive strike rate had to be set in the context of the original plan, which had all four villages as day-one objectives. Haig's end-of-term report struck a positive note: Germany was not broken, but the four-and-a-half-month offensive had "placed beyond doubt" the ability of the Allies to prevail in the great struggle.

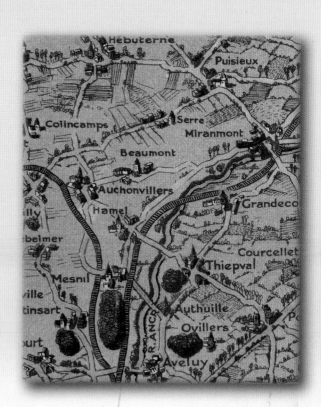

Germany was not broken, but the four-and-a-half-month offensive had "placed beyond doubt" the ability of the Allies to prevail in the great struggle.

Opposite: Injured men from the Middlesex Regiment are wheeled to makeshift hospitals to receive treatment.

Above: A morning stroll in Picardy along a road covered in thick, soup-like mud. By November the weather had further deteriorated but Haig was intent on one more attack before the end of the year.

Right: A Belgian trench mortar gunner waits for the signal to fire.

Below: The village of Bucquoy, destroyed in the Battle of Ancre, lies in ruins.

November 1916

1 French forces recaptured Fort Vaux near Verdun.

4 The Ninth Battle of the Isonzo ended with a limited Italian advance. 1916 had seen five Isonzo operations on top of four undertaken the previous year.

5 Germany and Austria declared an "Independent State of Poland".

Although the Battle of Le Transloy officially ended on 18 Nov, a final attack was made without success. The battle ended with no significant gain along the Transloy Ridge.

6 In the Sudan operations against the ex-Sultan of Darfur resulted in his defeat and death near the frontier of Wadai at the Affair of Gyuba.

7 Woodrow Wilson was re-elected as President of the United States of America.

8 The American Steamer Columbian was sunk by German submarine U-49 near Cape Finisterre.

9 An aerial battle took place between British and German aeroplanes near Bapaume in northern France.

11 The Battle of the Ancre Heights ended with a British victory over German forces.

12 British forces occupied Shiraz in Persia.

13 In the final significant phase of the Battle of the Somme, the Battle of the Ancre saw a renewal of the Allied offensive; British troops finally captured Beaumont Hamel.

15 An Inter-Allied conference was held in Paris to discuss ways to counter German mobilisation of Belgians and Poles.

16 The Battle of Târgu-Jiu began in Romania.

17 Germans broke through the Romanian front at the Battle of Târgu-Jiu in the Jiu Valley.

18 After four-and-a-half months of fighting the Battle of the Somme ended with enormous losses on both sides. Allied forces had pushed back the German line but the offensive cost more than 1 million casualties.

19 French and Serbian forces captured Monastir in Serbia.

The Entente Governments presented another ultimatum to King Konstantinos of Greece demanding that all representatives of the Central Powers be expelled.

20 German diplomat Gottlieb von Jagow resigned as German Foreign Minister.

21 German forces occupied Craiova in Romania on the Eastern Front.

The British Hospital Ship HMHS Britannic sank after hitting a German mine in the Aegean Sea.

Emperor Franz Joseph I of Austria died and was succeeded by his great-nephew Charles I.

22 German and Austrian forces captured Orsova in Hungary.

23 The British hospital ship Braemar Castle was damaged after hitting a mine in the Aegean Sea.

The Provisional Greek Government at Salonika declared war on Bulgaria and Germany.

24 Boris Stürmer resigned as Russian Premier and Foreign Minister was succeeded by Alexander Trepov as Premier.

26 A German naval raid took place on Lowestoft on the east coast of England during which the naval trawler HMT Narval was sunk.

27 Two Zeppelins were shot down during a German airship raid on Hartlepool and Great Yarmouth on the east coast of England.

28 The first German daylight aeroplane raid on London took place. The Germans hoped that by making raids on London and the South East, the British Air Force would be forced into protecting the home front rather than attacking the German Air Force.

29 David Beatty was appointed to replace Admiral Sir John Jellicoe as Commander of the Grand Fleet.

30 Allied forces began disembarking at Piraeus in Greece.

"Sham" peace proposal

As general disaffection grew, and the strain of the conflict became more and more apparent, the desire for an end to the war naturally gathered momentum. Germany actually sued for peace on 12 December 1916, but the note that was passed to the Allies was somewhat unusually worded, given its aim. It spoke of the "indestructible strength" of the Central Powers and stated that "a continuation of the war cannot break their resisting power". Perhaps not surprisingly, such language did not have the intended effect; not even the most generous of the Entente Powers could see this as being in any way conciliatory. Lloyd George, who had replaced Asquith as Britain's Prime Minister in December 1916, responded accordingly. It was a "sham proposal", he said, and entering into discussions on the basis of its contents "would be putting our heads in the noose with the rope end in the hands of the Germans". Though all sides may have been eager to end hostilities, they were not willing to do so at any price.

BETHMANN'S FURY.

"ENGLAND'S MONSTROUS AIMS."

The following statement by the German Chancellor is nothing but the old and hopeless German trick of attempting to divide the Allies.

FROM OUR OWN CORRESPONDENT.

NEW YORK, Sunday.

The *New York World* to-day publishes a nebulous statement, sanctioned by Herr Bethmann Hollweg, the German Chancellor, and edited by Herr Zimmermann, the Foreign Under-Secretary, purporting to give the "objectives" of Germany. Primarily the statement is a tirade against Great Britain. All the Allies, it says, are fighting for conquest, but "the most monstrous of all are England's aims—she is bent on crushing Germany wholly and wiping her from the face of the earth."

In whining tones the Chancellor proceeds: "England is too fiendishly clever and her aims are too gigantic to reduce them to words. By every foul means this 'friend of little peoples' is seeking to force them into fighting against us. For their good? let me ask. Or is it the time-honoured tradition of England to have others pull the chestnuts out of the fire for her?"

Bottom and opposite above: The desolation of the Ancre Valley can be seen from these panoramic views taken from Hamel, looking toward Miramount.

Below: British troops receive dinner rations from field kitchens in the Ancre area.

Opposite below: Troops walk alongside the River Ancre. The battle marked the end of the Somme offensive during which six miles were gained along a 16-mile front.

BRITISH AND FRENCH ADVANCE ON SOMME.

SEIZED BY BRITISH.	REICHSTAG SHUT DOWN.	TO WHOM IT MAY CONCERN.	BETHMANN'S FURY.	GREEK KING AGAIN.	TEN IN
ADVANCE ON FRONT OF 4½ MILES.	LEVY EN MASSE STEPS.		"ENGLAND'S MONSTROUS AIMS."	STILL PLAYING WITH THE ALLIES.	THE WO
OF SAILLISEL TAKEN.	NO DISCUSSION.	TAKE NOTICE.			ALI
E WOOD ENTERED AND 522 PRISONERS.	From CHARLES TOWER.			From J. M. N. JEFFRIES.	VAGARIES

SEIZED BY BRITISH.

ADVANCE ON FRONT OF 4½ MILES.

OF SAILLISEL TAKEN.

E WOOD ENTERED AND 522 PRISONERS.

: 95th DAY.

From SIR DOUGLAS HAIG.

FRANCE, Sunday Night.

in yesterday

Today we attacked at several points

REICHSTAG SHUT DOWN.

LEVY EN MASSE STEPS.

NO DISCUSSION.

From CHARLES TOWER.

AMSTERDAM, Sunday.

Late on Friday night the German Government, or rather the new German triumvirate—Hindenburg, Ludendorff, and Gröner—decided to muzzle the Reichstag for the whole winter to prevent public discussion of the extreme measures now to be taken.

The announcement made to the

TO WHOM IT MAY CONCERN.

TAKE NOTICE.

The following figures, the only certified record of an actual daily net sale exceeding—or even approaching—a million copies published by any daily newspaper, should suggest to the Hide-the-Truth Press that even in their own commercial interests they are unwise to mislead the Public

BETHMANN'S FURY.

"ENGLAND'S MONSTROUS AIMS."

FROM OUR OWN CORRESPONDENT.

NEW YORK, Sunday.

The *New York World* to-day publishes a nebulous statement, sanctioned by Herr Bethmann Hollweg, the German Chancellor, and edited by Herr Zimmermann, the Foreign Under-Secretary, purporting to give the "objectives" of Germany. Primarily the statement is a tirade against Great Britain. All the Allies, it says, are fighting for conquest, but "the most monstrous of all are England's aims—she is bent on crushing Germany wholly and

GREEK KING AGAIN.

STILL PLAYING WITH THE ALLIES.

From J. M. N. JEFFRIES.

ATHENS, Saturday Night.

Greece is confronted by another crisis to-day with the presentation of Admiral du Fournet's Note demanding the cession of destroyers, torpedo craft, and other light vessels of the Greek Fleet for service as coast guards and for protection against German submarines.

The Government, after a long Cabinet Council, over which the King presided, refused.

It was not a very categorical reply and is possibly intended to give the Cabinet time for consultation with Germany

TEN IN

THE WO

ALI

VAGARIES

By D. T

Mr. Curti for ten mo German w hatred of E

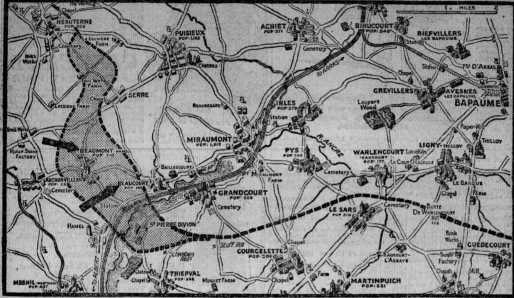

MORE GERMAN FORTS STORMED.

BRITISH CAPTURE BEAUCOURT

BEAUMONT CAVES "AS BIG AS BUCKINGHAM PALACE."

ADVANCE SOUTH OF BAPAUME

From GENERAL SIR DOUGLAS HAIG.

FRANCE, Tuesday, 10.50 a.m.

We have stormed the heavily fortified village of Beaumont-Hamel [west of the Ancre and north-west of Thiepval] and have advanced to the outskirts of Beaucourt-sur-Ancre [a mile and a quarter east of Beaumont-Hamel].

The number of prisoners is increasing, and considerably over 4,000 have passed through the collecting stations since yesterday morning. Fighting continues.

3.40 p.m.

The village of Beaucourt-sur-Ancre is in our hands.

Prisoners reported up to date number considerably over 5,000 and more are coming in.

To-day a successful local advance was made east of the Butte de Warlencourt (i.e., south of Bapaume). Practically all our objectives were gained and some 80 prisoners were taken in this area.

See the very large map in the Back Page.

Opposite top left: Most of Beaumont Hamel, including the railway station, was destroyed.

Opposite top right: A memorial to the German soldiers who fell when Beaumont Hamel was captured by the Allies.

Opposite middle right: Troops climb aboard the remains of a railway wagon destroyed by shellfire at Beaucourt.

Opposite middle left: The front line north and south of Ancre, 15 November, showing the recent gains that include the fortress village of Beaumont-Hamel.

Opposite bottom: The site of Beaumont Hamel's church is reduced to rubble. The 51st Highland Division took the village on 13 November 1916, one of the Allies' final successes before Haig closed down the Somme offensive.

Top: Troops negotiate frozen ponds of muddy water in December 1916. The weather caused military operations to be temporarily suspended and men concentrated on survival in the freezing, wet conditions.

Left: Tommies on their way to the trenches pass through St Pol. They smile broadly at the camera knowing the photograph will be sent back to England.

Below: Two maps suggesting why Germany is now keen for peace. The first shows the territory Germany occupied in 1914, the second illustrates the extent of the German Empire at the end of 1916.

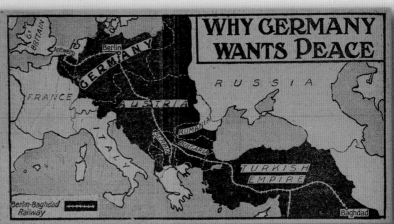

WHY GERMANY WANTED WAR

WHY GERMANY WANTS PEACE

The Somme: one million casualties

The village of Thiepval, taken on 25 September, had been a day-one objective. Other scraps of territory changed hands more than once, and always at a heavy human cost. Germany's determination to retake every inch of high ground conceded meant their losses, too, mounted. Haig was not about to blink, pressing on resolutely until the taking of Beaumont Hamel during the battle's final action allowed him to wind down the operation on a positive note. There should have been little cause for back-slapping as this had been another 1 July target.

As winter set in and stock was taken, it was self-evident that the blunt instrument of attrition rather than the rapier of penetration best characterised the 141 days of attack and counter. Having both objectives hovering over the battlefield was a boon to Haig, for although his grand design had not materialised, he could lay claim to seriously weakening the enemy's manpower, matériel and morale.

A century on, the cost-benefit analysis of the Somme campaign continues unabated. Seven miles was the maximum extent of the Allies' territorial gain. Early in the new year the German army would willingly concede ground as they withdrew to the Hindenburg Line, shortening the front and conserving vital resources. And so the battle would be reckoned not in terms of a sweeping territorial success but how much damage had been inflicted upon the enemy. There were over a million casualties in total, shared in roughly equal measure. The grim statistics would forever taint Haig's reputation in the eyes of many, the Somme regularly invoked as an exemplar of crass leadership and prodigal futility. Apologists point to the mighty blow that was dealt the Kaiser's army, and that the Allies were left firmly on the front foot at the dawn of the new year. As one officer of the Reich put it, the Somme was "the muddy grave of the German field army".

The Somme was "the muddy grave of the German field army".

Above: A build-up of traffic on the muddy roads around the Somme. The graves of German soldiers can be seen on the right.

Below left: Stretcher-bearers transport a Canadian infantryman to safety. Many conscientious objectors volunteered for this dangerous non-combat job where the casualty rate was high.

Below right: Canadians back from the trenches are given coffee at the canteen.

Opposite above: The battle ground north of the Somme showing successive stages of the British advance from 1 July, as recounted from General Haig's despatch. The broken line at the top and right indicates the Front at the end of the 1916.

Opposite below right and left: British troops trudge along the wet road that skirts swamps, shattered trees and broken buildings and vehicles. The cost of the Somme offensive was nearly 624,000 Allied casualties and a further 146,000 killed or missing.

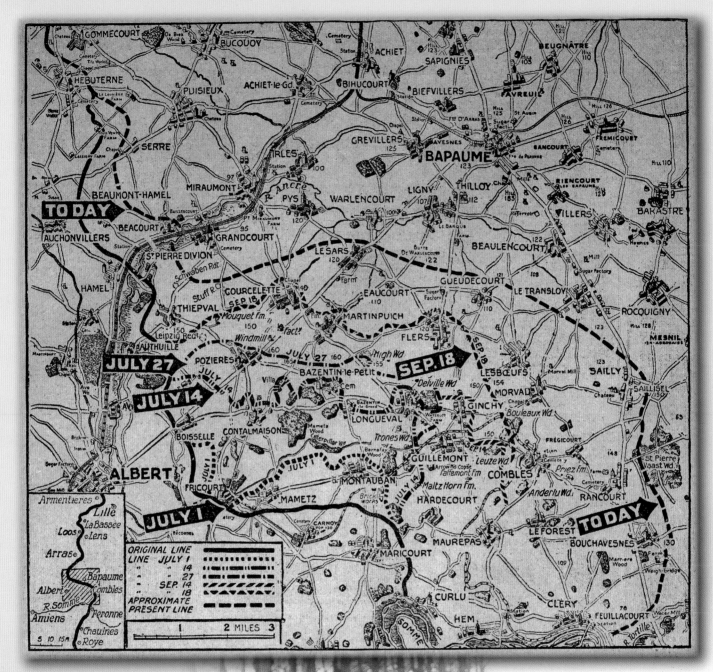

Above: Australian troops make their way to the trenches in December 1916.

Above right: A borrowed stove provides warmth and a much-needed cup of tea.

Below: Seven miles was the maximum extent of the Allies' territorial gain in the Somme campaign.

Opposite above: French troops stand outside the now rather battered-looking Fort Douaumont, retaken from the Germans on 24 October. During the preliminary bombardment the French had fired over 855,000 shells.

Opposite middle: British and French officers take refreshments on the front at Trouville.

Opposite below left: A lane captured by the French contains the remains of a German dugout while the body of an abandoned German infantryman lies in the foreground.

Opposite below right: French soldiers come straight from the trenches to be awarded British decorations.

GREAT FRENCH VICTORY AT VERDUN.

| STORM VERDUN TRESSES. | TIGRIS MOVE. BRITISH OFFENSIVE | MEATLESS DAY. THURSDAYS FIXED. | PLEA FOR IRELAND. MAJOR REDMOND AND | STRIKERS' LAST CHANCE. | ORDE TROOPS |

FRENCH STORM VERDUN FORTRESSES.

FULL SUCCESS WITH SMALL LOSS.

ADVANCE OF TWO MILES.

REPLY TO THE PEACE TRICK.

FRENCH OFFICIAL REPORT,

PARIS, Friday Night.

'After artillery preparation lasting several days we attacked the enemy north of Douaumont, between the Meuse and the Woevre [i.e., on the whole line north and north-east of Verdun], on a front of over 6 miles.

The attack was launched at 10 a.m. The enemy front was everywhere pierced to a depth of about 2 miles. Besides numerous trenches we captured the villages of Vacherauville and Louvemont, the Chambrettes farms [2 miles north of Douaumont], and the Hardaumont and Bezonvaux works.

We made a large number of prisoners, whose exact number has not yet been counted. Seven thousand five hundred prisoners, including 200 officers, have already passed through the collecting stations.

We took or destroyed numerous guns, including heavy and field pieces and trench guns, in addition to a great quantity of material.

Notwithstanding the unfavourable weather our air service took a

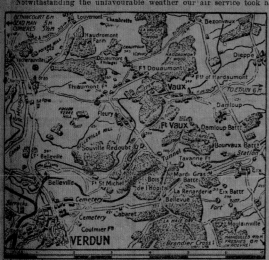

brilliant part in the fighting. Our success is complete. The troops are displaying the greatest enthusiasm. Our losses are slight.

THE ITALIAN BIG PUSH DOING WELL.

Italian army stalemate

Under the command of General Luigi Cadorna, the Italian army targeted the port of Trieste, the pursuit of which required crossing the Isonzo river and defeating an enemy that commanded the high ground. By the end of 1916, this had been the scene of nine indecisive battles, the Italian army bearing the greater brunt of the casualty toll. Meanwhile, the Austrian attack on the Trentino in May that year might have reaped greater dividends had its leaders not been forced to redeploy troops to meet a fresh Russian assault. Italian pleas for the Brusilov Offensive to begin as a matter of urgency were answered, providing timely relief.

"CONQUERING THE ALPS"—ITALY'S DIFFICULTIES SHOWN IN PICTURES.

ANOTHER ADVANCE BY THE ITALIANS.

3,498 MORE PRISONERS.

CARSO WOODS AND CAVES CLEARED.

SPLENDID AID TO RUMANIA.

Important new successes have been won by the Italians on the Carso, north-west of Trieste. Another 3,498 prisoners have been captured, bringing the total to over 8,200.

The battle is still raging and our Allies are bombarding the ground on their right flank, possibly in preparation for an advance along the coast road and railway to Trieste, 12½ miles distant.

No more effective aid could be given to Rumania than by this splendid attack which Count Cadorna is delivering with such vigour and skill.

4,731 PRISONERS TAKEN BY ITALIANS.

GORIZIA HEIGHTS STORMED.

SUBSTANTIAL GAINS ON CARSO.

20 GUNS AMONG BOOTY.

The Italians have made another magnificent push, east of Gorizia and on the Carso, and have captured from the Austrians positions of the greatest importance 14 miles from Trieste.

They have taken 132 officers, 4,599 rank and file, two 4in. weapons, and 18 field guns.

GREAT ITALIAN CAVALRY CHASE FROM GORIZIA.

URSUIT FROM GORIZIA. | RAPID RUSSIAN ADVANCE. | POZIÈRES BATTLE. | U-LINER'S CAPTAIN. WIFE AN ENGLISHWOMAN | WAR DEBT EQUALS OUR INCOME. McKENNA HOPEFUL. | THE QUEEN IN TH FIGHTERS' STREETS TOUCHING SCENES A HACKNEY.

Opposite above: General Luigi Cadorna was Chief of Staff of the Italian Army during the conflict. He was dismissed in 1917 but later reappointed as the Italian representative to the Allied Supreme War Council set up in Versailles.

Opposite below: Conditions in the winter of 1916-17 were very severe for the troops. In Germany the supply of potatoes had completely run out and civilians were forced to eat turnips, normally regarded as cattle food, leading to the re-naming of the time as the "turnip winter". A general shortage of food impacted on people's health and it is believed about 750,000 German people died during the winter through a combination of influenza and starvation.

Opposite right: Newspaper cuttings from early November 1916.

Left: Luigi Cadorna visiting Alpine veterans from Monte Nero with Generals Armando Diaz, Mario Nicolis di Robilant, Tedeschi e Montanari at Kobarid.

Below: Generals Luigi Cadorna and Carlo Porro in San Martino del Carso, Italy, 1916.

Salonika and the struggle for Monastir

The combined Allied force stationed at Salonika encountered a host of problems that hampered its long awaited offensive in 1916. Logistics were difficult, while malaria laid many low, adding to the woes faced by the senior commander in Macedonia, General Maurice Sarrail. Since setting foot on Greek soil in early October 1915 in a forlorn bid to aid the Serbs, the Allies had done little to justify their presence. Bulgaria had control of the mountainous region that separated the two, and there was no heavy artillery to dislodge them. Little wonder the Germans called it a vast internment camp. Falkenhayn was content to have this large enemy contingent corralled and impotent. There was no pressing need to go on the attack, which might prod neutral Greece into action on the Entente side. The Allies certainly wooed their host ardently, but ruler King Constantine's pro-German sympathies, cemented in familial ties with the Kaiser, provided an effective counterweight to those voices urging that the suitor should be accepted. The Gallipoli debacle hardly helped the Allies' efforts to persuade Greece off the fence.

By August 1916, Sarrail was finally ready to go on the attack with his 300,000-strong army. News arrived from Bucharest that Rumania would join the Allies if the multinational Macedonian force engaged the Bulgarians. Rumanian prime minister Ion Bratianu wanted guarantees that his country would not have to fight on two major fronts; that Bulgaria would have its hands full in the south, allowing Rumanian troops to focus their attention on their northern Austro-Hungarian neighbour.

The Bulgars wrong-footed Sarrail by launching their own offensive on both flanks while the ink was still drying on the agreement bringing Rumania into the war. The Serbs manning the outpost around Florina bore the initial brunt. The town was assailed, and the jubilant advancing army entertained thoughts of overrunning Salonika itself inside a week. To the east, the French were faring no better. The Bulgarians, flushed with their early success, found it was not to be all plain sailing as they hammered away at regrouped Serbian positions around Lake Ostrovo in late August.

Sarrail's planned counteroffensive targeted the town of Monastir in the west. If it could be taken, a route to Serbia was opened up, and also a path to Bulgarian heartlands. Accordingly, attacks in the east were simply to pin down enemy forces there – which were bolstered by German units – preventing them from switching manpower to the chief battleground.

The struggle for Monastir opened on 12 September. Florina, some 14 miles distant, was retaken with relative ease, but the drive towards the main target was slow and painful. With mountains rising on each side, and entrenched Bulgars standing in their way, the senior commander, Cordonnier, was minded to be cautious and await reinforcement. Sarrail would have none of it. The word from headquarters was clear: Cordonnier had numerical advantage and should press on forthwith. "Success is scarcely likely and would certainly prove costly," Cordonnier advised, but the attack would begin on schedule on 30 September if Sarrail insisted. The first frontal attack was in fact launched on 6 October, with results that vindicated Cordonnier's stance. A second attempt eight days later ended equally badly. To Cordonnier this was senseless slaughter, made worse by the fact that he had overflown the area and formulated a plan by which the formidable Bulgarian defences could be bypassed. Sarrail saw this as a challenge to his authority, and relieved Cordonnier of his post. His replacement, Leblois, took over as the weather deteriorated markedly: lashing rain and a snow-line edging down the mountains, betokening the coming winter.

The battering-ram approach did pay slow dividends. Bulgarian resolve began to show signs of cracking, and in mid-November its army ceded Kenali, another stepping-stone on the way to Monastir. However, worsening conditions created enormous logistical problems for the Allies. Neither army was in peak condition, but when 17 November provided a bright, clear weather window, the Allies were determined to make the most of it. The town's defenders had no answer and were forced to evacuate, employing scorched-earth tactics to ensure the new occupants would inherit nothing of value. By 19 November Monastir had fallen, with great fanfare on the part of the victors. But the state of the men and the prevailing conditions meant pursuit of the retreating Bulgars was not feasible. Operations were closed down for the winter, and the fillip Monastir had given the Allies was soon offset by the fall of Bucharest.

Left: British labour battalions drain the marshes on the Salonika Front.

Opposite above: French soldiers finally captured Monastir in December 1916, thus ending the three-month offensive. Casualty figures were high and included thousands evacuated through sickness or disease.

Opposite right: The sinking of the RMS *Franconia* was captured on camera from a ship coming to its rescue.

Opposite below right: An officer in a British submarine surveys the horizon through a periscope.

Opposite below left: Allied troops wind their way through a valley on their way to attack the town of Monastir. The three-month long Monastir Offensive began in September and aimed to assist the Romanian Army while pinning down the Bulgarian troops.

BRITISH AND SERBIAN PUSH IN MACEDONIA.

NEW BRITISH DASH NORTH | THE GREEK CRISIS. | FRESH FRENCH GAIN. | RAILWAYMEN | FIRE AT SOLDIERS' | WITH THE

PURSUIT FROM MONASTIR.

FRENCH 2 MILES TO NORTH.

DESPATCH FROM THE TOWN.

PRILEP THE NEXT STEP.

3rd YEAR of the WAR : 110th DAY.

On the **Macedonian** front the Serbians, French, and Russians are not resting on their laurels after the capture of Monastir, but are pushing rapidly forward. They are now over 2 miles north of the city. Our Athens Correspondent says that there may be a race for Prilep, 25 miles north-east of Monastir and close to the immensely strong Babuna Pass, and that the Allies will have the help of a fire motor road constructed by the enemy.

Our special correspondent in Macedonia, Mr. G. Ward Price, telegraphs from Monastir an account of the entry of the Allied Army.

Admiral du Fournet, commanding the Allied fleets, has taken vigorous measures against spying at **Athens** by ordering the enemy Ministers to leave Greece by tomorrow.

HOW ALLIES ENTERED.

TROOPS FLOWER-DECKED BY POPULACE.

From G. WARD PRICE,

Monastir, Sunday, Noon.

The Allies are in Monastir at last—here in the heart of the town. Down the streets, which are black vistas of closed iron shutters, come the French cavalry, which were the first to enter. They are now maintaining a strict patrol. Their horses' necks are hung with wreaths of flowers, for the inhabitants, after peeping timidly out from behind their barred windows for a while, have at length ventured out and are offering posies and garlands to the French and Russian soldiers who come constantly marching in.

Even to me these signs of welcome have been proffered, for I have had the fortune to be the first English-

Salonika bound Franconia torpedoed

RMS *Franconia* was launched on 23 July 1910 at the Swan, Hunter & Wigham Richardson shipyard in Newcastle upon Tyne. After several years service in the North Atlantic, she was taken into service as a troop transport in early 1915. On 4 October 1916, while heading for Salonika, she was torpedoed and sunk by the German U-boat UB-47 195 miles east of Malta. She was not carrying any troops but out of her 314 crew members, 12 died.

Brusilov and the Eastern Front

As the Somme offensive wore on, its enormous cost set against the fluctuating objectives of breakthrough and attrition, it was the Eastern Front that provided the Allies with their most substantial credit in the annual accounts. At the beginning of the year, the front extended more than 500 miles, from the Baltic Sea to the border of Rumania – a country whose neutral status would soon be abandoned. Early in 1916 Russian troops mounted a successful attack against the Turks, giving a bloody nose to an army exulting in its Gallipoli triumph. But a spring assault in Lithuania, which might have relieved the pressure on the French at Verdun, was roundly rebuffed by German forces. These were but a

foretaste of a grand summer offensive, undertaken in accordance with the Chantilly agreement to squeeze the Central Powers in both west and east. It was led by General Alexei Brusilov, who had just assumed command of the southwestern sector of the front, having emerged from earlier battles in Galicia and the Carpathians with much credit. He actively sought a spearhead role in the forthcoming attack, despite the fact that his fellow commanders to the north, Evert and Kuropatkin, enjoyed a significant numerical advantage over the enemy, while he had parity at best. On the other hand, Brusilov faced Habsburg soldiers, not Germans.

Below: **German soldiers take a break from the fighting on the Eastern Front.**

Opposite below left: **Kaiser Wilhelm (left) meets his top Generals Paul von Hindenburg (right) and Erich Ludendorff (middle). In summer 1916 von Hindenburg took over the** role of Chief of Staff from Erich von Falkenhayn and Ludendorff assumed the position of his deputy as Quartermaster General. **The pair made up the Third Supreme Command and were effectively military dictators superseding the Chancellor and the Emperor.**

Opposite above left: **Russian soldiers undertake a dangerous mission to cut the wires in front of a German trench.**

Opposite above right: **A group of German prisoners captured by the French.**

The Russian Army punched an enormous hole in the Austrian line, taking 400,000 prisoners.

RUSSIANS ROLLING BACK THE AUSTRIAN ARMY.

USTRIAN FRONT BROKEN | BRITISH SHIP'S DASH. | GEN. JOFFRE IN | OUR HEAVY GUNS | GREECE CLIMBING | THE HAMPSHIRE
FOR 100 MILES. | | LONDON. | ACTIVE. | DOWN. | ON FIRE.

Austrian army in disarray

The situation worsened from the Allies' perspective when Austria assaulted the Italian army in the Trentino in May. Brusilov responded on 4 June, launching an offensive that ranked among the most resounding successes of the war – at least, in its opening phase. It was success born of meticulous planning. One of the most important lessons that had to be learned in breaking the impasse – a lesson that applied on both major fronts – was for artillery and infantry to operate in close co-ordination. That was evident in Brusilov's attack, which also had the key element of surprise. To that end saps were surreptitiously dug, putting the Russians within 100 yards of the enemy line. The decision to attack over a wide, 300-mile front was deliberate, Brusilov intending to leave his rival commanders guessing as to where to station their reserve strength. There was no drawn-out bombardment to put the Austrians on the alert; instead, a brief barrage before the first of Brusilov's four armies attacked, swiftly followed by the other three. The Austrian enemy was soon in disarray, unsure which gap to plug. In the end, none was filled adequately as contradictory orders muddied the waters further. The Russian army punched an enormous hole in the Austrian line, taking thousands of square miles of territory and 400,000 prisoners. The lack of organisation of the Austrian troops and indifferent quality of their generals notwithstanding, it still ranked as an impressive return.

A GAS ATTACK BY THE RUSSIANS.—This vivid picture from the Russian front shows their trenches in a dense pine wood from which they are sending out gas clouds before attacking the enemy.

German reinforcements

Germany could not and did not sit idly by. Reinforcements were rushed from west to east, enough strength not merely to apply the brakes but to hit back with a vengeance. They were helped by Evert and Kuropatkin's dithering. Both had shown their capacity for caution during the planning stage, vacillation that now played into Germany's hands. The decision to deploy troops southwards to try to capitalise on Brusilov's success, rather than mount separate attacks in accordance with the original plan, was misguided. German rail links were superior, hence its reinforcements were in place first. A feeble Russian attack in the northern sector came in late July; too little, too late. The prize, so tantalisingly within reach, was gone. Brusilov carried on the fight into September, but the chance for even greater glory had long since evaporated.

Along with compatriot Alexander Kerensky, Brusilov was the only commander to lend his name to an offensive. He had performed admirably, yet the scheme ultimately unravelled. Though it forced Germany into a hasty redeployment, the transfer of men was insufficient to prise open the door at the Somme. Nor could the recruitment of Rumania into the Allied fold on the back of it be counted as a great coup, as events would show.

By the end of the year, many of Russia's gains had been snatched away, with predictable consequences for morale. Russian troops had endured much, given their all, taken punishing losses – for what? Discontent reached epidemic proportions, affecting soldiers and civilians alike. Since Tsar Nicholas II had taken over as supreme commander in 1915, there was but one target for the ordinary Russian's sense of grievance. Brusilov concurred. "My armies," he wrote, "which in 1916 had accomplished miracles of bravery and wholehearted devotion to Russia and to their duty, saw all their feats of arms brought to nothing by what they considered a lack of intelligence and decision on the part of the supreme command."

Above: German soldiers experiment with a captured Russian cavalry gun.

By the end of the year, many of Russia's gains had been snatched away, with predictable consequences for morale.

Opposite: German troops housed in a relatively luxurious four metre-deep trench on the Eastern Front. One of the four soldiers wrote on the back of the photograph: "My present parlour is by Russian standards a salon, dug four metres deep into the earth, safe from bombs and grenades, but absolutely unprotected against mice, fleas, rats and lice. These beasts are, in fact, a real plague and have an insatiable hunger like everything else here in the Russian Jungle."

Below: A large group of Russians, with many wearing the traditional Cossack hat, are taken prisoner by German forces.

RUSSIAN MOVE IN GALICIA.

6 GUNS AND 1,000 PRISONERS.

The Russians have invaded north-east Galicia at a point south of Lutsk. An advance here might compel the retreat of the Austrian army defending Brody, which lies on the railway to Lemberg, and is 41 miles distant from it. This way is the Russians' shortest route to the Galician capital.

Russian Official. PETROGRAD, Tues. Aftn.

In street fighting during the advance in the village of Galichanie (on the northern border of Galicia) we captured two more guns and 77 Austrian and German prisoners. *Last night the gallant regiments under General Sakharoff broke through the wire entanglements of the enemy on the River Stonovka (in Galicia, 12 miles north of Brody, on the left flank of the Austrian General Böhm-Ermolli's army, which is defending Brody). In the region of Leshniov (in the same district) a furious battle is going on.*

In the region of Briaza and Fundul, Moldavia (South-West Bukovina), three enemy regiments attacked our cavalry. One of the gunners, Letchkin, who resisted the attack, continued to work his gun, in spite of the fact that his hand had been torn away by a bomb, until the gun was removed from the line. The enemy was repulsed.

Evening.

On the River Stonovka front the crossing of the river by our troops continues without interruption under the fire of the enemy. During to-day's advance we captured 1,000 prisoners, 4 guns, and 5 machine guns, which were turned against the enemy.—Wireless Press.

ENEMY ADMITS SUCCESS.

German Official. BERLIN, Tuesday.

Attacks by weak Russian detachments south-east of Riga and Russian patrols on the Dvina were repulsed.

Enemy attacks on the River Stonovka front, south of the Stonovka, and south of Beresteczko succeeded over a small front in penetrating our first line.

West of Burkanov a Russian aeroplane was shot down in an air fight.—Wireless Press.

Romania joins the Allies

The success of the Brusilov Offensive in summer 1916 was instrumental in adding a new partner to the Allies' fold. Rumania, the sole undeclared Balkan state, was encouraged to make common cause with the Entente, believing this was where the upper hand lay, and promised Austro-Hungarian territory might thus be secured at a reasonable price. "The war is lost!" was the anguished response of Kaiser Wilhelm on hearing the news that another half a million men were ranged against him; an overreaction, as events soon showed. Following the late-August declaration, the Rumanian army moved into neighbouring Transylvania, Hungarian ground coveted by the invaders for the ethnic links they shared. Over two million Rumanians were domiciled in this quarter of the Habsburg Empire, rendering the march a potential act of liberation as well as a cog in a collegiate enterprise.

The first in a series of autumn battles took place, exposing the Rumanian army's deficiencies. There was a mismatch, both in the fighting capabilities of the men and in the leadership of the generals. The Rumanian hierarchy had no figures to match the likes of Mackensen and Falkenhayn. The latter may have fallen from grace in the German command structure, cast aside in favour of the Hindenburg-Ludendorff duumvirate, but he and Mackensen were too wily for their counterparts in this short, decisive campaign. Rumania was more hindrance than help to Russia, and once the Brusilov Offensive ran out of steam, it proved relatively easy for the Central Powers' forces to deal with the very limited Rumanian threat. Its position was hardly helped by the lack of activity from the Allies based at Salonika. During pre-entry negotiations, Rumania had stipulated that the Macedonian force should go on the offensive in order to keep Bulgaria – its hostile southern neighbour – fully occupied. When that failed to materialise, it meant Rumanians were battling on two fronts; difficult enough for a first-class army, virtually impossible for theirs.

Early gains were soon wiped out, after which the enemy made rapid inroads into Rumanian territory. Victory culminated in the occupation of the capital, Bucharest, in early December. Militarily, the defeat of a recent recruit and minor ally was not a devastating blow to the Allies. Of more significance was the fact that it gave the victors access to valuable resources, especially oil and grain, which would help the German war machine to keep running and mitigate the effects of the blockade.

Above: **A stark image of dead bodies strewn along the side of a Romanian road. After joining the Allies in mid-1916, the Romanian Army was completely overwhelmed and Bucharest was lost to German forces in early December.**

Left: Russian Jews watch German forces advance into Russian territory on the Eastern Front.

Below: A group of Russian prisoners of war includes a 15-year-old boy (centre left), who claimed he volunteered in order to avoid starvation after his father joined the army and his mother left their home.

Below: German troops pose before a mortar in position near Predeal in Transylvania, Romania.

Opposite below right: Picture map showing the mountainous country in which the Rumanians are resisting German attacks.

Sir Douglas Haig

Among the most controversial figures in British military history, Douglas Haig still divides opinion a century on from the campaigns with which his name is most closely associated. Advocates highlight the single-mindedness and strength of purpose of a leader who played a significant role in turning the war in the Allies' favour in 1918. Critics point to reckless offensives that were shockingly wasteful of human life. Positions taken in assessing Haig's contribution tend to be as entrenched and immovable as the Western Front itself. Was he the heroic architect of a famous victory over the Central Powers? Or prime candidate for the asinine role in the oft-quoted assessment that British troops were "lions led by donkeys"?

Born in Edinburgh on 19 June 1861, Haig was a career soldier from the moment he left Oxford and entered Sandhurst. In his climb through the ranks he served with the 7th Hussars before studying at the Staff College at Camberley, where he was a contemporary of another distinguished World War One leader, Sir Edmund Allenby. Haig saw action in Sudan in the Boer conflict before being posted to India, where he was appointed Inspector-General of Cavalry. By 1906 he was back at the War Office, where his duties included drafting training manuals. He also played a key role in establishing the Territorial Army, replacing a reservist system that was in need of overhaul. He was made General Officer Commanding at Aldershot, spiritual home of the British Army, and from there he prepared Ist Corps for action as part of the British Expeditionary Force, which mobilised when war was declared on 4 August.

Haig was promoted to full general after the first Battle of Ypres ended in November 1914, and a month later was chosen to command the newly formed First Army. In December 1915 Haig replaced Sir John French as Commander-in-Chief of the BEF, and in an effort to break the stalemate that had set in along the Western Front embarked on a series of offensives that incurred a high casualty toll. The former cavalry officer had to adapt to new-style trench warfare. Some said the fact that he persisted with frontal assaults at the Somme and Passchendaele showed that he did not adapt quickly enough; and that he was slow to recognise the importance of new technology. Long after the guns of World War One fell silent Haig was of the view that "aeroplanes and tanks are only accessories to a man on a horse". Others argue that his methods did ultimately wear down the

Passchendaele duly ran its course, fulfilling Lloyd George's grim prediction that no good would come of it.

enemy and pave the way to victory. Haig was righteous and uncompromising, his bulldog tenacity undoubtedly one of his great strengths. He maintained an unswerving belief in the application of pressure as the key to achieving a breakthrough. As losses mounted and some – Lloyd George among them – questioned the wisdom of such a strategy, Haig's clarion call was for a redoubling of effort. To apply the brake and allow the enemy time to recover was the real folly. That unyielding attitude led him to state that casualties totalling 120,000 in the first month of the Somme offensive "cannot be regarded as sufficient to justify any anxiety as to our ability to continue the offensive". With such comments admirable tenacity spilled over into reckless disregard from the critics' stance.

Germany's spring offensive of 1918 brought a response from Haig that showed his steely resolve. "There is no other course open to us but to fight it out. Every position must be held to the last man; there must be no retirement. With our backs to the wall, and believing in the justice of our cause, each one of us must fight to the end." Marshal Foch was made supreme commander of Allied forces as the war reached its critical point, but Haig's army was prominent in the battles that brought the conflict to an end.

The granting of a peerage, plus the sum of £100,000, was indicative of how the Establishment viewed Haig's achievements. He retired in 1921, devoting the last years of his life to improving the lot of ex-servicemen through the Royal British Legion, which he helped set up. Following his death on 28 January 1928, aged 66, a *Times* eulogy referred to the Somme campaign, pointing out that the heavy human cost was sometimes accorded undue prominence over the gains: namely, helping relieve Verdun and delivering a damaging blow to the German spirit. "In the judgment of history," it concluded, "it may be that the country will recognise the wisdom and discount the cost."

Over 80 years on, that judgment remains in the balance.

Left: (l to r) Albert Thomas, the French Minister of Munitions; Sir Douglas Haig; General Joffre and David Lloyd George at the 4th Army Headquarters at Méaulte on 12 September 1916.

Below right: Haig was a very adept horseman and a talented polo player. He represented England on a tour of the USA and became Chairman of the Hurlingham Polo Committee in 1914.

Oppsite inset: A poster encouraging votes for Lloyd-George in 1916.

Opposite below left: Herbert Asquith watches soldiers adjusting fuses near the frontline. The Prime Minister's son Raymond was killed in action in September 1916 during the Battle of Flers-Courcelette.

Opposite below right: David Lloyd George acknowledges the cheers from British troops as he emerges from a captured German dug-out at Fricourt.

Haig maintained an unswerving belief in the application of pressure as the key to achieving a breakthrough.

David Lloyd George

David Lloyd George, a peacetime Chancellor of the Exchequer, recognised at an early stage that "this is an engineers' war"; that industrial output at home was key to success in the field. Providing the army with the ammunition to fight and handling dilution of labour as men donned khaki in increasing numbers were major challenges following his appointment as head of the new Munitions Ministry in May 1915. A year later, he became War Minister, at a time when there was growing discontent regarding Asquith's leadership. The latter was widely thought to possess neither the vigour nor the vision necessary to steer the country to victory. Lloyd George, by contrast, believed he was the best man to take the tiller at a time of national crisis.

Matters came to a head in late 1916 over plans to form a leaner War Committee that would drive things forward more expeditiously. Asquith, still recovering from the loss of a son on the Somme, already suspected Lloyd George was angling to unseat him when it was proposed that that he should be excluded from this reconstituted Committee. The Prime Minister eventually accepted that it could function without him as long as he retained "supreme and effective control of war policy". But on 4 December The Times gave a damning assessment of the reorganisation; damning to Asquith's chances of surviving as premier. The change, ran the editorial, had been provoked by Asquith's uninspiring leadership. It spoke of "cumbrous methods of directing the war", and insisted "matters cannot possibly go on as at present". It was humiliating for Asquith, who suspected Lloyd George's hand had been guiding the leader writer's pen. He wrote to the latter, seeking to clarify the position. "Unless the impression is at once corrected that I am being relegated to the position of an irresponsible spectator of the war, I cannot possibly go on." He saw one chance to re-establish his authority: dissolution and the formation of a new government. Lacking support, he resigned. Conservative leader Andrew Bonar Law was invited to form an administration, but he wanted both Asquith and Lloyd George in any new government. The former, having held the top job for eight years, could not bring himself to accept a lesser role. Bonar Law stood aside, allowing Lloyd George to take control on 7 December 1916. From now on the Cabinet and War Committee were indistinguishable, and there was but one man in charge of both.

The new prime minister had deep reservations about Haig's ability to direct operations on the Western Front. Those misgivings were manifest in his backing for the Nivelle Offensive, and, when that failed, in his advocacy of a British-backed assault on the Italian front. But lack of faith in his commander-in-chief did not stir him to intervene as Third Ypres played out with the kind of catastrophic losses he had expressly wanted to avoid. Though power rested with the civilian government, he shied away from reining in a seasoned military campaigner. From the inception of Haig's summer offensive there had been a proviso: a halt would be called if success was not immediately forthcoming. The Nivelle fiasco undoubtedly weakened the politician's position and strengthened the commander's. Passchendaele duly ran its course, fulfilling Lloyd George's grim prediction that no good would come of it and severely draining Britain's fighting strength. He fulminated on the subject of how "the futile massacres of August piled up the ghastly hecatombs of slaughter on the Ypres front without achieving any appreciable results", yet stayed his hand whenever the opportunity to overrule his military chief presented itself.

Soldiers from a battalion of the Durham Light Infantry raise their steel helmets on their rifles. Most of these men came from Sunderland and this photograph was probably taken for distribution in their local area.

December 1916

1 The Battle of the Argeş began along the line of the Argeş River in Romania between Austro-German forces of the Central Powers and Romanian forces.

The Greek Government refused the Entente demands of 19 Nov.

2 Russian premier Alexander Trepov announced that the Allies acknowledged Russia's right to Constantinople and the Dardanelles.

3 German submarines entered Funchal Harbour in Madeira, sank three ships and bombarded the town.

4 Admiral Sir John Jellicoe was appointed as First Sea Lord, replacing Admiral Sir Henry Jackson.

5 Prime Minister Herbert Asquith resigned.

6 German forces captured Bucharest in Romania.

7 David Lloyd George replaced Asquith as British Prime Minister.

8 The Allied naval blockade of Greece began.

9 The new British War Cabinet was formed replacing the War Committee which had held its last meeting earlier in the month.

11 The two month long Battle of Cerna Bend between Bulgarian forces and French and Serbian troops ended in a tactical victory for the Entente powers.

12 German, Austro-Hungarian, Bulgarian and Turkish Governments all delivered a Peace Note to their respective United States embassies stating they are ready to negotiate for peace.

13 British forces in Mesopotamia began operations to recapture Kut-al-Amara.

14 Allied powers sent an ultimatum to Greece demanding the removal of all forces from Thessaly.

15 The Greek Government accepted the Allied Ultimatum.

16 The United Kingdom recognized the Sherif of Mecca as King of Hejaz.

17 The Greek Government issued a warrant for the arrest of Eleftherios Venizelos on a charge of high treason.

18 The longest battle on the Western Front, the Battle of Verdun ended with huge losses but no tactical or strategic advantage had been gained by either side.

US President Woodrow Wilson issued a Circular Note, asking all belligerents to state their war objectives, as a first step towards peace.

19 The British Government instituted National Service.

The British Government formally recognised the Venizelos Government of Greece.

20 Count Heinrich Karl Clam-Martinic replaced Ernst von Koerber as Prime Minister of Austria.

21 British forces occupied El Arish in their advance across the Sinai.

22 The British Government formed new Ministries of Food, Pensions and Shipping.

23 The Battle of Magdhaba took place in the Sinai peninsula during the Defence of Egypt section of the Sinai and Palestine Campaign. After a day long battle, Turkish troops surrendered to the British.

25 King George V sent a message to the troops on the third Christmas Day of the war.

26 An Anglo-French conference met in London to discuss the German and US Peace Notes as well as the campaign in Salonika and the division of forces on the Western Front.

27 The German colony of Togoland was divided into British and French administrative zones.

29 Two relatives of Tsar Nicolas II, Grand Duke Purishkevich and Prince Felix Yusupov poisoned the confidant of the Tsarina, Father Grigori Yefimovich Novykh (Rasputin) at Yusupov's home in Petrograd. After this attempt at murder failed, the pair shot Rasputin and dropped his body through the ice of the River Neva.

30 The Bulgarian Government accepted President Wilson's proposals for peace negotiations.

Right: Soldiers home on Christmas leave buy their turkeys at a stall near Victoria Station.

Below left: British troops negotiate with a French market trader for some mistletoe for their billet.

Bottom: Christmas dinner for these men is bread, jam and tea in a shell hole at Beaumont Hamel, next to the graveside of one of their comrades.

Below right: A corrugated iron shed and brazier provides shelter and warmth for one lucky British Tommy.

Opposite above left: Christmas cards illustrated by the artistic members of various battalions are sent to families back home.

Opposite middle left: British soldiers raise a glass for King and country.

Opposite above right: This official photograph of a warm, dry, well-fed, smiling "Tommy Atkins"— the generic name for a British soldier — created an impression far removed from reality.

Opposite below: A cheery group, complete with a pet dog, are home on leave from France.

TUESDAY, DECEMBER 26, 1916.

THE THIRD CHRISTMAS OF THE WAR IN PICTURES.

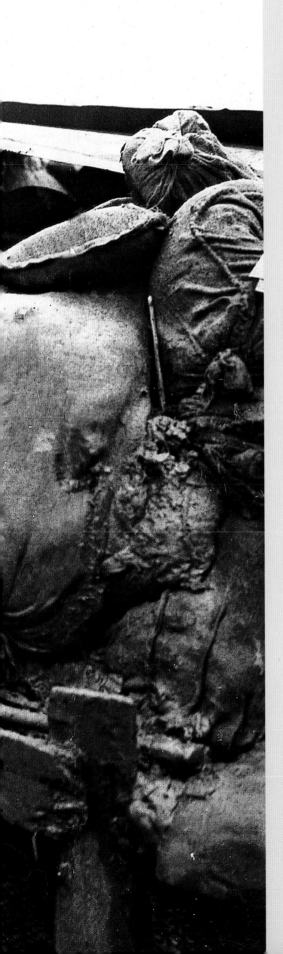

Chapter Four

1917

A World War

1917 in brief

The beginning of the new year saw Woodrow Wilson, recently elected for a second presidential term, still fighting to keep the USA out of the war. Wilson invited the belligerents to state the terms on which hostilities could end. The Central Powers offered no reply. The Allies' response, issued on 10 January 1917, stated that the aggressors, whose conduct had been "a constant challenge to humanity and civilization", had to evacuate all territories that had been invaded and pay substantial reparations. Despite the Entente Powers' reaffirmation of a commitment to "peace on those principles of liberty, justice and inviolable fidelity to international obligations", Wilson's decision was far from clear cut. He was wary of hegemony in any form, and although the Central Powers had violated sovereign territory, Britain and France were themselves great imperialist powers. Altruism would play no part in the President's decision making. Wilson wanted whatever was in America's best interest and knew that it might be necessary to commit to war in order to shape the peace.

America joins the Entente

Even after Germany launched its plan of unrestricted submarine warfare on 1 February 1917, Wilson would not be drawn into the war. America severed diplomatic relations with the Reich, but for the next two months the country pursued a policy of "armed neutrality". In March, three US cargo ships were sunk and the pressures increased. But for many Americans the final straw was an attempt by Germany to capitalise on long-standing grievances held by Mexico towards their country. Germany's Foreign Secretary, Arthur Zimmerman, sent a telegram to Mexico offering support for action to reclaim territory lost to America in the previous century, including Arizona and Texas. The telegram was intercepted by the Allies and its contents revealed. There was a backlash across America and those previously wedded to an isolationist stance became pro-war in large numbers.

Wilson went to Congress to seek approval for a declaration of war on 2 April; the decision was ratified four days later. Even then Wilson studiously avoided the term "ally". The USA had thrown in her lot with the Entente Powers but would not be a signatory to the Pact of London, the agreement which bound the Allies to act in concert and not to conclude separate peace deals.

The formal declaration of war on 6 April was more a psychological than a military watershed. It would be some considerable time before the USA would be able to make a telling contribution to the fighting, something which Germany's high command was gambling on. Hindenburg and Ludendorff, sceptical about the chances of victory on the Western Front, put their faith in the U-boats. On land they would play a defensive game; at sea the German submarines, now unrestricted in their choice of targets, would crush Britain while America was still gearing up for war.

The Siegfried Line

Germany's plan involved a withdrawal on the Western Front. In September 1916 work had begun on a new defensive line, one which would shorten the front by some thirty miles and provide, correspondingly, a welcome reduction in demand for resources. German forces withdrew to the Siegfried Line – or Hindenburg Line as the Allies would call it – in the early months of 1917. One thousand square miles of land – territory which had been fought over so bitterly and with so much bloodshed – was conceded virtually at a stroke. As they withdrew, the Germans executed a comprehensive scorched-earth policy. The ground ceded to the Allies would have no useful resource, not even a drop of water, as all available supplies were poisoned.

Long before the Allies became aware of the German withdrawal they had met to plan their own strategy for 1917. Initially it was to be more of the same: concerted offensives on all fronts to stretch the enemy forces to the limit. That carried the prospect of another Somme, however, the spectre of which haunted Lloyd George. In the event a change in France's command structure dramatically altered the Allies' thinking, much to the British Prime Minister's relief. General Robert Nivelle replaced Joffre as Commander-in-Chief of the French Army in December 1916. Nivelle had distinguished himself at the Battle of the Marne and Verdun and his stock was so high that he had little difficulty in carrying the political leaders with him, not least because he told them exactly what they wanted to hear. Nivelle's plan was for an Anglo-French spring offensive on the Aisne. Saturation bombardments would be followed by a "creeping barrage", behind which the infantry would advance. A decisive breakthrough would be achieved within days. Haig was among the dissenting voices to this scheme but Lloyd George's approval meant his hands were tied.

Spring Offensive

By the time the offensive got under way, on 9 April, it had already been undermined by Germany's withdrawal to the Hindenburg Line. Undaunted, Nivelle pressed on. There was early encouragement as the British attacked Arras and the Canadian Corps took Vimy Ridge, but when the main thrust came it proved to be yet another false dawn. The French army sustained over 100,000 casualties in the attack in Champagne. To make matters worse the strict time limit that had been imposed to achieve victory fell by the wayside. On 15 May Nivelle paid the price, replaced by General Pétain. This alone was not enough for the French infantry, however. After more failed promises and more mass slaughter they had had enough and there was mutiny on a mass scale. Had the German Army been aware of the situation an easy victory might have been had.

Pétain responded with a mixture of carrot and stick. The offensive was called off and conditions on the front line were improved. On the other hand anarchy could not go unpunished and 23 mutineers faced a firing squad "pour encourager les autres".

Privation, hardship and mass slaughter for no discernible gain would provoke dissent in the ranks of all the major combatants. Everywhere the consensus required to prosecute the war seemed in danger of breaking down and all leaders recognised that the morale of both troops and civilians needed careful monitoring. In Russia, dissent spilled over into full-blown revolution: the winter of 1916-17 saw both Russia's Army and her people at breaking point. Poorly fed, ill-equipped and badly led, the troops refused to fight. The civilian population was faced with dwindling food supplies and soaring prices. On 8 March workers in Petrograd went on strike and took to the streets. Unlike 1905, when a similar uprising had been brutally put down, the troops' sympathies lay with the protestors. The Duma announced that it no longer recognised the Tsar, who abdicated on 15 March.

A moderate provisional government was established but the seeds of a second revolution were already sown. Exiled revolutionaries, including Lenin, returned to Russia determined to take advantage of the fact that the country was in a state of flux. Germany was only too pleased to assist his passage, quick to realise the value of internecine strife in the enemy camp. And it was Russia's involvement in the war which became the key issue. The provisional government believed that the war still had to be won; the Bolshevik revolutionaries wanted an immediate end to a conflict which was seen as a product of capitalism and imperialism.

Bolsheviks seize Power

Russia's allies and enemies waited. The House of Commons sent a message of "heartfelt congratulations" to the Duma. It was hoped that with a new democratic structure Russia would prosecute the war with "renewed steadfastness". In June 1917 she tried to do just that, with disastrous consequences. A failed offensive in Galicia left Russian soldiers believing they were no better off under a post-Tsarist regime. There was desertion on a mass scale. On 7 November – 26 October in Russia, which was still operating on the Julian calendar – the Bolsheviks seized power with minimal resistance.

The events in Russia in 1917 were not only the consequence of disaffection with war but also served to feed it. By the summer of 1917 there was also great discontent in the ranks of the Italian army. In August Italy launched its eleventh unsuccessful offensive against Austro-Hungarian forces across the Isonzo river. General Cadorna's army had sustained huge losses in these campaigns in the north-east of the country, but the twelfth was to prove even more devastating. The disintegration of the Russian Army meant that German troops were able to be deployed to aid their allies. Ludendorff masterminded the twelfth battle of the Isonzo, in which the Central Powers aimed to break through the Italian line near Caporetto.

The offensive began on 24 October 1917 with a heavy artillery bombardment, mainly of gas shells against which the standard issue Italian masks were largely ineffective. Even so, General Otto von Below, who led the attack, could hardly have imagined the ease with which his infantry were able to advance. The Italian Army was soon on the retreat. In freezing conditions ten regiments chose surrender instead. Crumbling morale had once again provoked mutinous action. Italian machinery for dealing with indiscipline was the severest of all, yet here was further proof that the military and political leaders could no longer take unquestioning loyalty for granted.

The Central powers did not escape their share of rebelliousness. The Allies' blockade meant shortages and hardship both in Austria-Hungary and Germany. There was civil unrest but for now this did not spread to the armed forces on any significant scale. To forestall that eventuality, Ludendorff instigated a programme in which the troops were invited to restate their love for the Fatherland and their unswerving desire for victory.

The Battle of Passchendaele

After the disastrous Nivelle spring offensive, the French were in no position to instigate a fresh attack on the Western Front. But Haig, his authority restored, was determined to do just that. His plan was to break through the German line at Ypres and push through to the Belgian coast, cutting off the enemy's right flank. This would also put the Allies within striking distance of the German submarine bases at Ostend and Zeebrugge. The Entente Powers were deeply concerned by Germany's U-boat policy and any action which could harm that operation was an attractive proposition. Lloyd George was still concerned about the ghastly prospect of another Somme. Pétain was also sceptical. He favoured a defensive operation until America could mobilise in numbers. With the cracks in the French Army still not healed and America a long way from battle-readiness, Haig saw the chance of a glorious victory for the British Expeditionary Force. He got his wish and plans for the third Battle of Ypres – or Passchendaele, as it would come to be known – got under way.

The first target was Messines Ridge, a key vantage point to the south of Ypres which had been held by the Germans for two years. General Sir Herbert Plumer led the successful attack on the ridge on 7 June. Preparations for the main assault could now proceed unhindered and unobserved. Six weeks passed between the taking of the Messines Ridge and the launch of the main offensive, a delay which the Germans put to good use. The bombardment, when it came, churned up ground whose drainage system had long since collapsed. To make matters worse, the rains were early and heavy, and in the advance the British soldiers had to contend with thick mud and water-filled craters as well as enemy fire. The Germans had already abandoned the idea of entrenched positions in such conditions, choosing instead to defend with machine guns housed in pillboxes. It would be another month before the weather improved and the Allies gained a sight of Passchendaele Ridge, which had been among the first-day objectives. In October the rains returned but Haig remained unshakeable, seduced by the desire to capture Passchendaele and the belief that the German Army was about to crack. Passchendaele did finally fall, on 6 November, though at enormous cost. More than 250,000 casualties had been sustained in an advance of just five miles. The German Army had not been vanquished, while Zeebrugge and Ostend continue to service the submarines that had been inflicting such grievous losses on Allied shipping.

Four hundred tanks attack Cambrai

To keep up the momentum gained by taking Passchendaele the Allies launched one final offensive on the Western Front in 1917. The Battle of Cambrai, which began on 20 November, was notable for the number of tanks deployed. Over 400 spearheaded the attack, the first time tanks had been seen on a battlefield in such numbers. Encouraging early gains were made, but direct hits and mechanical breakdowns meant that tank numbers were depleted following the initial breakthrough. The German Army countered and the inevitable stalemate was soon restored.

A year beset by difficulties for the Allies ended on a somewhat brighter note when news came through that General Allenby's Egyptian Expeditionary Force had captured Beersheba and Gaza before marching into Jerusalem on 9 December. But on the main fronts there was little to celebrate: the Nivelle fiasco and Passchendaele in the west, Caporetto in Italy and complete collapse in the east following the Russian Revolution. The total war waged by German U-boats, which had been devastating in the early months, had been mitigated somewhat by the use of the convoy system, whereby merchant ships travelled together, under the protection of warships. Rationing was introduced into Britain at the end of 1917, a measure to which even the King and Queen succumbed. However, Germany's attempt to bring Britain to her knees had failed. 1918 held out the prospect of the American Expeditionary Force led by General John Pershing becoming a key player on the Western Front, as recruits and conscripts completed their training and became ready for frontline duty. Germany had won the battle in the east but it was she who was living on borrowed time.

Below: **British troops march to the front past their French allies.**

NO ONE MUST BUY MORE THAN 14 DAYS' FOOD.

| GRAVE FOOD WARNING. | MR. LLOYD GEORGE TO RUSSIA. | THE HOUR IN IRELAND. | GERMAN MYSTERY WOMAN. | GERMAN LINE STIFFENS |

Food stocks low

Germany felt the blockade pinch first. Its government struggled to find workable measures that mitigated the effects of having its import lifeline largely severed. All the major foodstuffs were rationed. Substitutes appeared, usually unappetising and, more worryingly, lacking in nutritional value. The impact this was having on the population was not lost on the military leadership, and in 1917 the plan was to give the enemy a taste of their own medicine. One enemy was surrounded by water, a prime candidate for applying a U-boat ligature. The attempt to starve Britain into submission did not materialise, though care and creativity were needed to put food on the table. As was the case in Germany, where goods were in short supply, substitutes had to be found. Margarine replaced butter, horsemeat deputised for choicer cuts and even dandelion roots were used as a makeshift coffee. Compared with unpalatable ersatz goods, Britain had far the better of the deal. It came at a price, however. Potatoes, bread, cheese, eggs, bacon and sugar all went up by at least 50 per cent in the first two years of war. For those on fixed incomes it meant real hardship, while the better off were fortunate if they completed their shopping without having to queue. Wheat stocks gave particular cause for concern in 1917, prompting an "Eat less bread" campaign endorsed by the royal household. A state-subsidised "ninepenny loaf" ensured there was at least one affordable staple, even if it was not the pure white variety most wanted. The government also encouraged meatless days, and for people to grow their own produce in order to ease the pressure on imports. Millions of acres of land were requisitioned to bolster production, the newly formed Women's Land Army providing much of the labour. Voluntary rationing gave way to a compulsory system for certain foodstuffs in 1918, but this was more to do with efficient, equitable distribution than pressing need.

WEEKLY ALLOWANCE FOR ALL

Bread	-	-	4lb.
Meat	-	-	2½lb.
Sugar	-	-	¾lb.

The Food Controller puts the Nation on its honour not to consume more than the above quantities.

It is for the Women of Great Britain to see that these Orders are strictly carried out, and thus defeat the German plan for starving us out by a submarine blockade.

The following is the text of Lord Devonport's instructions:—

MINISTRY OF FOOD, Grosvenor House.

The necessity for some curtailment of the Nation's Food Consumption is urgent. An amount sufficient for each individual requires, in consequence, to be stated.

The quantity indicated as being sufficient has been arrived at on no haphazard basis but after full examination of the actual position of stocks immediately available or visible. Only by the adoption of and working to such an average apportionment will it be possible to maintain an adequate margin to meet not only the actual situation but contingencies which have to be allowed for. The main factors taken into reckoning are exigencies as affecting freight and transport and the necessity to curtail the nation's normal consumption so as to adjust it to the needs of the situation. The urgency of the position allows of no delay in informing the Country of what is demanded of it. The Public require and desire to have the need explained to them, and only by whole-hearted co-operation on the part of all can the object in view be achieved.

The three most important staples of daily consumption are Bread, Meat, and Sugar, and forethought for the sustenance of the population requires a decision as to whether compulsion is necessary to ensure an equitable distribution and conservation of available supplies. Compulsory rationing to a fixed quantity per head involves a very elaborate machinery which in itself absorbs labour, and for that reason alone ought to be avoided unless absolutely necessary. Therefore, having carefully weighed the advantages and disadvantages, I have come to the conclusion that a voluntary system is preferable until further experience is gained, and to rely meanwhile on the Nation's instinct of self-discipline. The allowance indicated is based on the average weekly consumption of each of these commodities which should be permitted to each person. After consideration of available stocks and probable means of future supplies, the situation requires that Heads of Families should endeavour to limit themselves to the weekly purchase for each person comprising the household of the following quantities per head per week:—

THE WASTE OF WASTE FOOD.

To the Editor of *The Daily Mail.*

Sir,—Will you permit me to draw your attention to a point where your unique power may achieve something in connection with the economy campaign?

There is great and recurrent waste in all the private houses of this country owing to the fact that all the valuable food refuse is mingled with the waste paper, coal ashes, and general domestic dust. Will you use your influence with all local boards, asking them to issue an order to their collectors to separate food refuse from general waste? Let the boards also issue instructions by order to all their ratepayers to place in two distinct boxes (1) that which can be used for pig-feeding, and (2) that which is useless for such a purpose. I feel sure that by such means an immense aggregate supply of waste food may be collected and utilised in the nearest available pig-geries.

I think that if attention be directed to such a small matter and its importance be once realised, it may be a most useful step in the education of people in this country on the value of detail economy. HERBERT C. LEE.
Conservative Club, St. James's-street, S.W.

Unrest amongst the Allies

The third winter of war saw all participants weighing the heavy cost of carrying on the fight. Austria and Russia had had enough by the beginning of 1917 and were both seeking an exit strategy. Germany held enough sway over its chief ally to prevent Habsburg peace overtures from amounting to anything, but France and Britain could only look on as their eastern partner was riven by internal strife. German morale, too, was severely dented, the mood for an end to hostilities growing with each passing day of the "turnip winter". There was even a vaguely worded German peace note delivered on 12 December 1916, though in truth the chances of either side accepting what the other was prepared to offer at that point were nil. Both had taken body blows but were far from staring into the abyss, hence unprepared to entertain major concessions. Hindenburg and Ludendorff did recognise that even with an entire nation geared to the war effort, there was a large question mark over how long that effort could be sustained. It was against this backdrop that the high-risk decision to remove the leash from its U-boat fleet was taken. Might a policy of unrestricted submarine warfare bring Britain to heel before America – who would in all probability be provoked into joining the Allies – could mobilise?

The Entente powers separated by the English Channel were not immune from discontent and war weariness, but it was not at a critical level. Verdun and the Somme had left their mark, though, and there was a demand for more efficient, less profligate prosecution of the war. In both countries there were changes at the top. Lloyd George took the prime ministerial reins from Asquith in December 1916, his work at the munitions ministry, and more recently as secretary of state for war, making him the all-party choice to lead the country. He had charisma and the common touch, qualities that could also be seen in Robert Nivelle, hero of Verdun, who replaced Joffre as commander-in-chief of the French army in the same month that Lloyd George took up residence in Downing Street.

Opposite: **Roll call of the Seaforth Highlanders.**

Opposite inset: The "potato squad" at Eton carry their tools to the potato field they have renamed Mesopotamia. The schoolboys have been encouraged to contribute to the country's food supply.

Above: British soldiers carry stove pipes during the harsh winter of 1916-17. It was one of the coldest in living memory; bread was too frozen to be cut, boiled water soon turned to ice and cases of frostbite were common.

Below: The trenches were frequently flooded, adding to the risk of trench foot. At times men would take off their boots in an attempt to warm them up, only to find their feet had swollen so much they couldn't put them back on again.

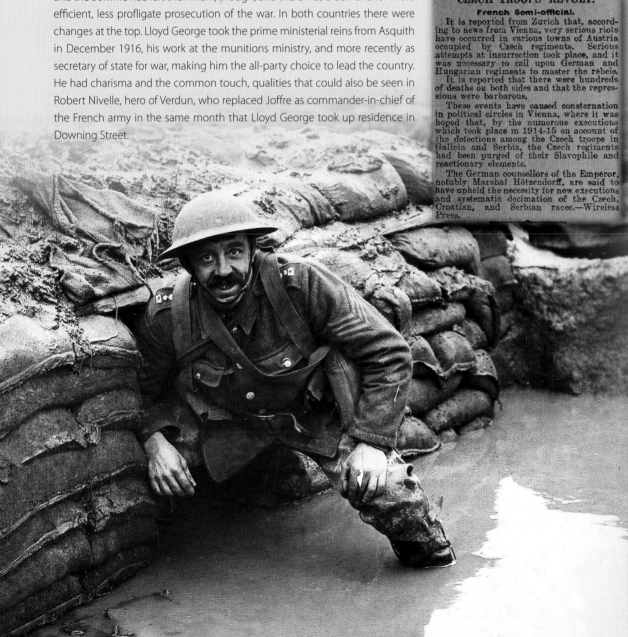

CZECH TROOPS REVOLT.
French Semi-official.

It is reported from Zurich that, according to news from Vienna, very serious riots have occurred in various towns of Austria occupied by Czech regiments. Serious attempts at insurrection took place, and it was necessary to call upon German and Hungarian regiments to master the rebels.

It is reported that there were hundreds of deaths on both sides and that the repressions were barbarous.

These events have caused consternation in political circles in Vienna, where it was hoped that, by the numerous executions which took place in 1914-15 on account of the defections among the Czech troops in Galicia and Serbia, the Czech regiments had been purged of their Slavophile and reactionary elements.

The German counsellors of the Emperor, notably Marshal Hötzendorff, are said to have upheld the necessity for new executions and systematic decimation of the Czech, Croatian, and Serbian races.—Wireless Press.

GERMANY STILL FIGHTS TO WIN.
WHY SHE RISKS WAR WITH THE STATES.
By LOVAT FRASER.

We shall not fully appreciate the present situation unless we begin by recognising that *Germany is still fighting to win.*

My personal surmise is that the German Government did not deliberately seek to bring about a rupture of their diplomatic relations with the United States. They simply took that risk because they had what they conceived to be a larger end in view.

The Germans perceive most clearly that after the failure of their insolent peace manœuvres they can only hope to win the war by encompassing the overthrow of Great Britain. They have the most intense faith in their swarms of new submarines, not altogether without reason. They believe their latest submarine campaign will starve this country out within six months. If they can accomplish their purpose, they are meanwhile not inclined to trouble very much about the United States.

The German policy of sea warfare inaugurated at the beginning of this month is desperate and criminal, but not in the least mad. It is plainly the outcome of long and deep calculation. The widely prevalent theory that Germany has sought to force war on the United States merely in order to enable herself to yield to the whole world in arms does not bear examination. *The Germans still think they can snatch some sort of victory.*

No Government in their senses who wanted to win would deliberately try to range another 90 millions of people against themselves. The German authorities have evidently been guided by two main considerations. They have persuaded themselves, on the evidence of the last two and a half years, that in any case the United States probably will not fight. They have possibly become further convinced that even if President Wilson took the extreme step of declaring war he can do nothing effective in the field for the next six months. The Germans are staking all their chances on *victory in Europe within six months.* They think that in the meantime anything that the United States may do does not matter.

As to the first consideration, it must be remembered that the arrogant Prussians do not understand the true American spirit in the very least and entertain a profound contempt for the United States. Their attitude of mind is sufficiently revealed by von Papen's insulting reference to the "idiotic Yankees." They have completely misconceived the character of the President's unexampled patience. They have overlooked the effect of those swift waves of emotion which sometimes sweep like a tornado across the United States from ocean to ocean. Just as they misunderstood Great Britain in 1914, so they have thought, after repeated experiments, that the United States Government would endure any insult.

I repeat that the Germans are neither mad nor blind. They have only made another miscalculation.

SOMME BATTLES IN THE SNOW.

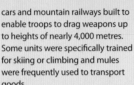

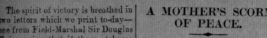

Above left: A tangle of barbed wire is almost buried beneath the snow. As the new year commenced the Allies planned a renewed offensive, combined with fresh initiatives on both the Eastern Front and Italy.

Above right: A group of captured Germans is gathered together and guarded on the battlefield. At the British prisoner of war camps the men worked in a variety of jobs including agriculture and road repairs. They were paid at a set rate, some of which was retained for their keep while the rest was given to the prisoner.

Middle right: The Italian Alpini, Italy's elite mountain troops, were given specific areas of the Alps to defend. Underground shelters were blown into the mountainside and cable cars and mountain railways built to enable troops to drag weapons up to heights of nearly 4,000 metres. Some units were specifically trained for skiing or climbing and mules were frequently used to transport goods.

Below right: Despite the devastation in this ruined church the crucifix remains unharmed.

Below left: A French "poilu" receives a letter while on duty on the front line. This informal name for a French front line infantryman during the conflict originated from the time of Napoleon Bonaparte and literally meant "the hairy one" – a reference to the beards and moustaches worn by recruits who were often from agricultural backgrounds.

"PULL TOGETHER AND TRIUMPH IS CERTAIN."

SIR D. HAIG TO THOSE AT HOME.

STILL GREATER EFFORTS NEEDED.

The spirit of victory is breathed in two letters which we print to-day—one from Field-Marshal Sir Douglas Haig saying that if those at home and the men in the trenches pull together, our triumph is certain, and another written by a French mother who simply but eloquently protests that peace now would mean that the rising generation would have to fight the battle all over again.

It is stated that the Allies' reply to the United States Note may indicate the only preliminaries on which we would be prepared to negotiate peace.

SIR D. HAIG'S MESSAGE.

THE BEST PRESENT WE CAN GIVE THE ARMY.

Field-Marshal Sir Douglas Haig has written to Mr. Ben Tillett:

GENERAL HEADQUARTERS, BRITISH ARMIES IN FRANCE,
December 22, 1916.

Dear Mr. Tillett,—Thank you very much for your letter and good wishes. You can tell Labour at home that the best of all Christmas presents that they can make to their comrades in the field is the assurance that so far as in them lies nothing during the coming year shall hinder the regular, constant, and increasing output of munitions and material.

The workers have done splendidly in the past. We look for even greater efforts in the future. If the men and women workers at home and the troops in the trenches pull together the triumph of our cause is certain. With every good wish.

Believe me, yours very truly,
D. HAIG.

OUR REPLY TO THE U.S.

THE ONLY PRELIMINARIES TO PEACE NEGOTIATION.

The reply of the Allies to President Wilson's Note will be published perhaps a couple of days after it is in the hands of the President, says Reuter.

It seems likely that in again going over the ground for the responsibility of the war the Allies on this occasion will also emphasise the only possible terms of peace. It will thus be in contrast to the reply to the German Note, which was purposely negative in character, rehearsing the conditions of peace that would not be acceptable.

A MOTHER'S SCORN OF PEACE.

NEW WAR IF WE GAVE WAY NOW.

FROM OUR OWN CORRESPONDENT.

PARIS, Tuesday.
M. Gustave Hervé in La Victoire prints the following letter written him by the wife of a working man—perhaps a country labourer:—

December 23, 1916.
Sir,—I don't know if I shall dare send you this letter, but if you do get it please read it, though you don't know me. It's about your articles on this peace. But, of course, sir, we mustn't make peace. You say that if the working men that are at the front or the women that are left behind were to be asked they'd be quite pleased at it. That shows that you're writing for people that haven't got any children.

Sir, I've lost a brother of twenty-five and my husband was called up at the beginning of the war, and he's at the front, where the fighting is; and since he's been gone we're not often able to keep very warm, and we've not always got enough to eat when we're hungry. But, sir, we don't want peace, though it would mean that we should have more money again; we've got children, and though we're only working people we don't want them to have to fight in ten or fifteen years; and that's what would be sure to happen.

And there's my husband, and he's had enough of this war, but he'll go on fighting as long as we've got to, so as to give those Germans a good thrashing and make them have the kind of peace that we won't have to worry about the children. And it isn't only my husband that feels like that, sir, he says all the others are just the same. Of course there's grumbling sometimes, and people aren't quite satisfied with things, but, sir, you mustn't think that we want peace because of that; indeed we don't.

When we saw in the papers that they were talking about peace my next-door neighbour, who has three children, she said to me, "Those dirty Huns, they are trying to have us." And after that we didn't so much as mention it again, we thought it was so stupid. And then there come people who have got education who seem to be taking it seriously. Sir, they haven't got any children or else they don't love them, because they would sooner their children had to fight than them.

Sir, you needn't worry, the soldiers who've got children, and the women who are left behind and who are working to take the father's place, they'll hold out as long as is wanted, a year more or even two, so that the little children won't have to see this sort of thing later on.

I am, dear sir, yours very respectfully,
Mrs. H——.

M. Hervé adds

Below: Canadian-American Lieutenant-Colonel Peter Nissen developed the design for the so-called Nissen huts in 1916, when he served with the 29th Company of Royal Engineers on the Western Front. It was rapidly put into production with at least 100,000 huts constructed during the war.

Bottom: The structure was very quick to erect – the record being 1 hour 27 minutes, although on average it took six men four hours. They were economical in their use of materials and extremely portable as the curved sections could be stacked together.

THE NISSEN HUT.

TOMMY'S NEW HOME AT THE FRONT.

By FILSON YOUNG.

WITH THE BRITISH ARMY IN THE FIELD, Saturday.

At about the same time as the tanks made their memorable début on the battlefield, another creature, almost equally primeval of aspect, began to appear in the conquered areas. No one ever saw it on the move or met it on the roads; it just appeared. Overnight you would see a blank space of ground; in the morning it would be occupied by an immense creature of the tortoise species, settled down solidly and permanently on the earth, and emitting green smoke from a right-angled stem at one end, where its mouth might be, as though it were smoking a morning pipe.

And when such a pioneer found that the situation was good and the land habitable it would apparently pass the word; for by twos and threes, by tens and hundreds, its fellow-monsters would appear, so that in a week or two you would find a valley covered with them that had been nothing but pulverised earth before.

The name of this creature is the Nissen hut. It is the solution of one of the many problems that every war presents. The problem here was to devise a cheap, portable dwelling-place wherein men could live warm and dry; cheap enough to be purchasable by tens of thousands; portable enough to be carried on any road; big enough to house two dozen men; simple enough to be erected by anybody and on any ground; and weatherproof enough to give adequate protection from summer heat and winter cold.

All these conditions are fulfilled by the Nissen hut, the invention of a Canadian Engineer officer who sat down and thought it out on an idle day in May 1916. He did his preliminary thinking so well that the third hut he built is of the pattern now being used, of which there are at least 20,000 in the country to-day and which are the homes of some half-million of British Tommies.

NO WALLS.

One peculiarity of the Nissen hut is that it has no walls. It consists of a roof, ends, and a floor. The roof is simply an arch of corrugated iron, so there are no eaves or gables to fit. Thus the greatest amount of standing space is enclosed with the least amount of material. You can order a Nissen hut as you would order a garden chair, and it will arrive neatly packed, with instructions how it is to be put up. Anyone can put it up, but four men can do it easily in four hours. The only tool required—a spanner—is supplied with it. The whole can be packed on an Army wagon, and its weight is two tons; but no single part or package is heavier than can be unloaded by two men. All the parts are interchangeable. The whole thing rests on three longitudinal sills 27 feet long. On these you lay the panels of floor-boarding. There are twelve of them; you can put them down in any order you like—they are all the same. The roof is in 48 pieces—all the same. You arrange them in three 9-foot sheets, with a 6-inch overlap—that is, one corrugation of overlap. You go on fitting them together anyhow, in any order, and when they are all used you find that the roof is complete.

The lining, of half-inch matchboard, is fastened to ribs of T-iron that follow the semi-circular shape of the roof. There are five ribs made of three segments each. These segments are nested in bundles of five; you use them in any order you like—they are all the same. There

January 1917

1 The Cunard troopship *Ivernia* was torpedoed and sunk by German submarine *U-47* off the Greek coast in the Mediterranean Sea.

General Sir Douglas Haig was promoted to Field Marshal.

3 German forces captured Focsani in Romania.

4 The Russian battleship *Peresvet* sank off Port Said, Egypt, after hitting a mine laid by German U-boats.

5 A conference was held in Rome between representatives from the British, French and Italian Governments.

6 The last Russian and Romanian forces evacuated Dobrudja in Romania.

7 The Allied Conference in Rome closed.

9 The day long Battle of Rafa completed the recapture of the Sinai Peninsula when Ottoman forces were driven back by British troops during the Sinai and Palestine Campaign.

The Royal Navy battleship HMS *Cornwall* was sunk by German submarine *U-32* in the Mediterranean.

Prince Nikolai Dmitriyevitch Golitsyn replaced Alexander Trepov as Prime Minister of Russia.

10 The Allied powers replied to US President Wilson's Peace Note of December 1916 outlining their peace objectives.

11 Germany and Turkey signed a Settlement Treaty in Berlin.

German and Austro-Hungarian Governments issued a Note repudiating responsibility for continuance of the War.

14 A provisional Council of State was set up in Warsaw, Poland.

The Japanese battle cruiser *Tsukuba* was sunk while in port at Yokosuka after an internal explosion.

16 The German Foreign Secretary Arthur Zimmermann sent a telegram to his ambassador in Mexico, instructing him to propose

an alliance against the United States with the Mexican government. Zimmermann believed that a war between Mexico and the United States would prevent American involvement in the European war.

17 An Inter-Allied conference convened at Petrograd to discuss war policy, finance and cooperation.

19 The Zimmermann telegram was intercepted and deciphered by the British.

A massive explosion in East London occurred when a large quantity of TNT exploded at a munitions factory in Silvertown.

20 General Reginald Hoskins succeeded General Jan Smuts in command of British forces during the East African Campaign.

22 US President Wilson addressed the US Senate and appealed for a settlement of the conflict in Europe on the basis of "peace without victory".

23 Royal Navy destroyer HMS *Simoom* was blown up by gunfire from German destroyers during action off the Schouwen Bank near Zeebrugge.

24 The Greek Government formally apologised to Allied Governments for refusing the Entente demands in December 1916.

25 German destroyers shelled Southwold and Wangford on the Suffolk coast in England.

A British attack on the Turkish salient at Hai met initial success but was beaten back by a Turkish counterattack.

26 British and Indian troops recaptured the trenches lost on 25 January at Hai.

27 The British steamer SS *Artist* was torpedoed and sunk by the German submarine *U-55* west of The Smalls near Newport in Wales.

31 The German Government announced that it would resume unrestricted naval warfare from the 1st February.

Casualties of war

Providing medical care to combat units dates back to the formation of Britain's first standing army in the 17th Century. The development of the service was somewhat haphazard – during the Crimean War it was derided as being unfit for purpose – but the establishment of the Royal Army Medical Corps in 1898 placed it on a sounder footing. It numbered around 140,000 officers and men at its peak in World War One, by which time the triage system was in operation. The wounded were assessed and, if the injuries were superficial, treated on the spot at forward Aid Posts or Dressing Stations with a view to enabling the patient to return to duty quickly. Those with more serious wounds might be removed by field ambulance to a Casualty Clearing Station, and thence to a Base Hospital well behind the line if that was deemed appropriate. Repatriation was an option, and some soldiers struggling with the rigours of frontline service positively hankered after a "Blighty touch" – an injury that might see them shipped home to convalesce.

Those who lay stricken on the battlefield owed much to the stretcher-bearers, who themselves risked life and limb in trying to render assistance. Transport to the Casualty Clearing Station might be by horse-drawn wagon or motorised vehicle; in either case travelling across uneven ground must have added greatly to the discomfort they were already experiencing. Those who could reach a treatment centre unaided did so – the "walking wounded". Casualty Clearing Stations were often located where there was easy access to the railway network, and many were invalided home minus a limb, for amputations were carried out at these treatment centres. Grim practicality meant cemeteries are often to be found where the stations were sited.

Initial assessments inevitably saw some placed in a third category: those whose wounds were so severe that the use of scarce resources could not be justified. The priority was to give attention not to those in greatest need but to those who would most benefit. Difficult decisions about likely outcomes had to be made, often in pressure-cooker circumstances.

Below: Refreshments are provided for the walking wounded. During the conflict the British Red Cross and the Order of St John supported the Royal Army Medical Corps, forming a Joint War Committee.

Opposite top right: Once the wounded were brought clear of the battlefield, medical staff could triage them and arrange medical care according to the severity of their injuries.

Opposite centre inset: Nissen huts were used to create hospitals to treat the wounded.

Opposite middle right: This group of British soldiers nursed their colleagues who contracted typhus in the Gardelegen prison camp in Germany. The disease was spread by lice, which were rife in the cramped, unsanitary conditions that prevailed in many German camps.

Opposite left: A wounded man is lifted from an ambulance wagon at a farmhouse hospital station. Over half of the injuries during the conflict were caused by shells or trench mortars but as the war progressed the number of gas casualties significantly increased.

Opposite bottom: Red Cross ambulances on hand to support the medical services. At the beginning of the conflict there were around 9,000 medical staff mobilised from the Royal Army Medical Corps but by the time peace was declared they numbered nearly 133,000. Nearly 7,000 medical staff were killed during the course of the war.

Some hankered after a "Blighty touch" – an injury that might see them shipped home to convalesce.

Disease in the broiling heat

Bombs and bullets were by no means the only concern. Even when the shells weren't flying, men might fall victim to a range of illnesses. Trench foot and fever affected many on the Western Front, while in the broiling heat of the Mediterranean, Middle East and Africa, diseases such as dysentery, typhus, typhoid and malaria were a constant threat. Diarrhoea laid many low, and venereal disease, too, was rife. The challenges facing the medical personnel were great, but they were better equipped than their 19th century counterparts. Recent advances in the understanding of blood groups meant transfusions were available, while improvements in the treatment of wounds helped stave off infection. The use of mobile X-ray units was also a boon in the diagnostic process. Double Nobel Prize-winning scientist Marie Curie played a key role in establishing these units, and even learned to drive to help the war effort personally. By the end of the conflict over a million men had benefited from X-ray assessment, which identified bullets and shrapnel lodged in the body, and shattered bones requiring treatment.

Marie Curie played a key role in establishing mobile X-ray units and even learned to drive to help the war effort personally.

February 1917

1 Germany began a policy of unrestricted submarine warfare.

3 President Wilson severed diplomatic relations between the United States and Germany.

In the Bay of Biscay, the German submarine *U-53* torpedoed and sank the US liner *Housatonic* which was carrying a cargo of wheat. The crew was later picked up by a British steamer.

4 Mehmed Talat Pasha replaced Said Halim Pasha as Grand Vizier of the Ottoman Empire.

5 A British armoured force won an engagement against the Senussi at the Siwa Oasis.

6 The Turks evacuated the south bank of the Tigris east of the Hai-Tigris junction near Kut.

7 The British passenger steamer SS *California* was torpedoed by the German submarine *U-85* as she returned from New York to Glasgow.

8 The British destroyer HMS *Ghurka* was on patrol off Dungeness when she struck a mine laid by *UC47* and sank.

10 A meeting took place in London between the British Government and members of the International Zionist Movement about a Jewish homeland in Palestine.

12 The American schooner *Lyman M. Law* was sunk in the Mediterranean Sea off the coast of Cagliari, Sardinia by the German submarine *U-35*. The ship was on a journey from Maine to Palermo in Italy when the Germans ordered the crew off the schooner before a bomb was detonated, setting fire to the 1,300-ton wooden vessel prior to its sinking.

13 Scandinavian Governments published a joint protest against German submarine warfare.

14 The British Government gave a pledge to the House of Commons that restoration of Alsace and Lorraine to France was an aim of the war.

16 Japan and Great Britain agreed that Japan should receive all German concessions in China and German Pacific islands north of the equator. Britain would receive German Pacific islands south of the equator.

17 An Australian War Government was formed.

18 The British steamer *Asturian* was damaged by gunfire from a German U-boat whilst en route from Liverpool to Alexandria.

20 Japan and Russia agreed that Japan should receive all German concessions in China.

23 The Second Battle of Kut was fought between Indian and British troops and Ottoman forces at Kut. The battle was part of the British advance to Baghdad which began in December 1916.

24 British and Indian troops recaptured Kut al Amara.

The Zimmermann Telegram was passed to the US by Britain, detailing the alleged German proposal of an alliance with Mexico against the US.

25 The Cunard ocean liner RMS *Laconia* was torpedoed and sunk by the German U-boat *U-50* while returning from the United States to England.

The Germans began to retreat from front line positions on the Ancre as part of the withdrawal to the Hindenburg Line.

26 President Wilson addressed Congress requesting powers to arm US merchant ships following the unprovoked sinking of the American liner *Housatonic* and the schooner *Lyman M. Law*.

27 The German Chancellor justified the country's policy of unrestricted submarine warfare and proclaimed it to be a great success.

28 The American press published the German proposals for an alliance with Mexico against the United States.

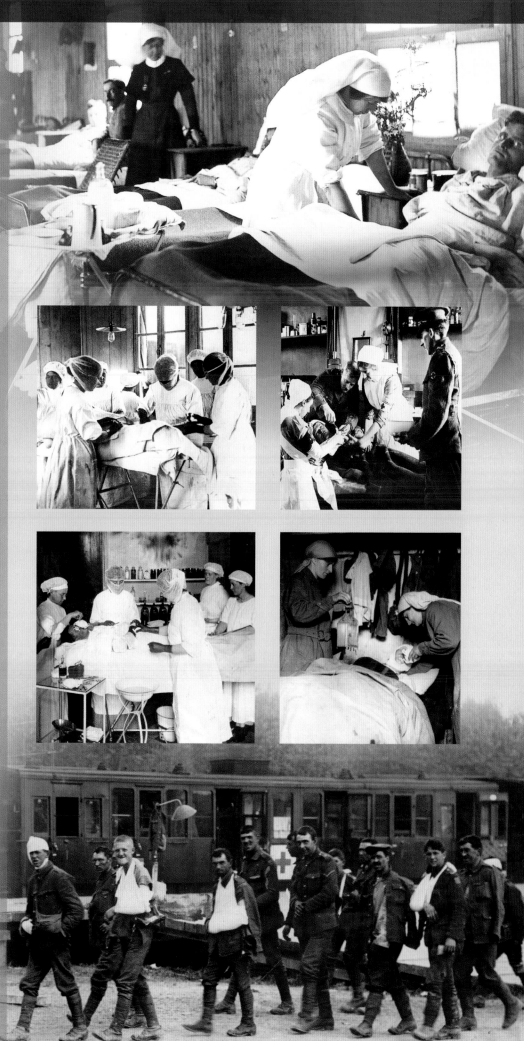

Opposite top: **Voluntary Aid Detachments provided volunteers to assist the nursing profession. Although not as skilled, they provided invaluable support often giving the critical bedside care needed.**

Opposite above right: **During the time of major offensives medical staff often needed to operate through the night as the casualty rates dramatically increased.**

Opposite below right: **Mairi Chisholm (left) and Elsie Knocker, nicknamed the "Madonnas of Pervyse" by the press, nurse a wounded Belgian soldier.**

Opposite above left and opposite below left: **The RAMC initially turned down women doctors who then sought other pathways to contribute. The Scottish Women's Hospital established a 200-bed hospital in Royaumont Abbey, France where female doctors were able to operate on their patients.**

Top: **The Joint War Committee was the first to provide motor ambulances for the Red Cross, speeding up the transportation of the wounded. Many thousands of civilians at home supported the fundraising.**

Above left: **The Red Cross flag flies above an advanced dressing station.**

Above middle and right: **A wounded Anzac has the benefit of travelling in a new Red Cross motor ambulance (above right) but many horse drawn vehicles were still used (above middle).**

Opposite below and below: **The walking wounded assemble ready to board a Red Cross train.**

Women in action

While millions of women "did their bit" at home, there were those keen to get nearer to the action. Nursing was the chief occupation of those who served overseas, but women also drove ambulances and acted as stretcher-bearers.

Perhaps the most famous among those who provided medical care close to where the shrapnel was flying were the redoubtable Elsie Knocker and Mairi Chisholm. The former had nursing and midwifery training, but the friendship was forged on a shared passion for motorcycles. At the outbreak of war the duo thought their skills might be put to good use as dispatch riders, but jumped at the chance to join the Flying Ambulance Corps being set up by Scottish doctor Hector Munro. Thirty-year-old Elsie and Mairi – just 18 at the time – were soon on their way to Flanders, initially based in a field hospital some 20 miles behind the front line. Mortality was high, and made worse by the time delay in transporting casualties from the battlefield. The bumpy terrain also did little to help their chances. Knocker and Chisholm realised that survival rates would improve dramatically if treatment could be given more speedily, and to that end established their own first-aid post in a cellar in the bombed-out village of Pervyse, a short distance from Ypres and perilously close to the front-line trenches. There they remained for over three years, saving countless lives. The precepts of their humanitarian work meant that all soldiers were treated equally. Chisholm recalled taking cocoa to a Belgian sentry, losing her way in the darkness and happening upon a German soldier. She promptly offered him refreshment. The luck of the "Angels of Pervyse" finally ran out in 1918, when they were debilitated in a gas attack. It was not fatal, and both lived to enjoy their celebrity status; they were said to be the most photographed women of the conflict. They were also much decorated, honours including the Military Medal, awarded after rescuing a downed pilot in no-man's-land; and the Order of Leopold, conferred on them by the Belgium's King Albert I in recognition of their selfless service to that country.

For Flora Sandes it wasn't enough merely to treat the wounded. This middle-class clergyman's daughter from Suffolk was the only Western woman to see front-line action in World War One. Flora was a natural adventurer, tomboyish, and with quixotic notions about soldiering. Although she was approaching her 40th birthday when war broke out, Flora volunteered to go to Serbia within days of the declaration. Initially, she worked in military hospitals, but as Serbia's position worsened she entered the ranks, something unthinkable in her native land though not so unusual in that Balkan state. Her courage earned her admiration and the Karageorge – a decoration rarely awarded – for distinguishing herself in battle. Badly wounded in November 1916, she not only returned to action but was given a commission, staying on long after the war was over.

But when it comes to women donning battle fatigues and taking up arms, no group can match Russia's "Battalion of Death". There had been female combatants before in the Russian Army, but in spring 1917 all-women units were formed at a time when morale in the ranks was at rock bottom. Leading from the front was Maria Bochkareva, a Siberian peasant driven by a fierce patriotic fervour – Russia's Joan of Arc, according to one contemporary commentator. In commanding 1st Russian Women's Battalion of Death, it was said she was no different from any other military leader, though "four times stricter". Following one enemy encounter, a battalion member said: "Bochkareva was everywhere among us, calling upon us to die like Russian soldiers. We saw a bunch of Germans right ahead of us. Then suddenly they were in our midst. They threw down their rifles, terribly frightened. "Good God! Women!" they exclaimed." From the perspective of Russia's newly installed Provisional Government, Bochkareva and her ilk were meant to inspire male soldiers whose spirits were flagging, or else shame them into redoubling their efforts for the summer 1917 offensive. An American correspondent who tracked the Battalion of Death in July described them thus: "There are women of all types: peasants, intellectuals, doctors, stenographers, telephone girls and others. Whilst we were travelling from Petrograd, crowds on the station platforms made fun of us asking: "Why do girls want to fight?" "Because you men are cowards," retorted the women." The correspondent concluded: "It had never occurred to me before that women ought to go to war, but I am convinced now that in any country under such conditions women ought to step into the breach, guns in hand."

This page: Mairi Chisholm (right) and Elsie Knocker drive their motor ambulance through the ruins of Pervyse. They were both awarded the Military Medal in 1917.

Opposite top left: Young women guards and clerks were employed to work on the London Underground to cover for the men fighting on the front line.

Opposite top right: A female glazier arrives at a house in Wood Green carrying the glass on her back.

Opposite middle left: Two members of the auxiliary forces on the way to the Meeting of Women Workers at the Albert Hall in March 1917, also attended by the Queen. Among the subjects discussed was a call for National Service for women.

Opposite middle right: Mrs Butcher from Birmingham became the first woman licensed to drive a taxi in Britain.

Opposite below left: Nearly one hundred women were employed at this paper mill at Purfleet near the Thames.

Opposite below right: Army nurses leave Buckingham Palace after receiving decorations from the King.

20,000 WOMEN WANTED.

WOMEN TAXI-DRIVERS.

LICENCES TO BE ISSUED IN LONDON.

Women taxicab-drivers are to be seen in London at last.

The Home Secretary, replying yesterday in the House of Commons to Sir Henry Norman, said: In view of the opinion of the Army Council that it has become necessary to call up certain drivers hitherto exempted by the tribunals, the Commissioner of Police, who is the licensing authority, proposes, with my approval, to license qualified women to be drivers of public carriages.

The proposal that women should drive taxicabs in London has been made many times but has always been vetoed by the police and previous Home Secretaries, chiefly on the ground that women were not equal to the strain. With a shortage of men drivers some of those who still plied have behaved with insolence, knowing that the public was at their mercy.

It is understood that if a woman applies at Scotland Yard now she will be given a licence provided she can pass the usual tests. These will not be relaxed in her favour. A woman must possess the engineering qualifications demanded of men and must fulfil physical requirements. They must also have a perfect "knowledge of London," the one test in which men fail and which cab companies have urged should be made less exacting.

GERMAN WAR WOMEN.

A MILLION AMAZONS.

By FREDERIC WILLIAM WILE,
Late Berlin Correspondent of "The Daily Mail."

War has worked many wonders in Germany as in England but none more revolutionary than the recognition which women have won for themselves as indispensable members of industrial society. It is barely 20 years since the Prussian Statute-books barred women, *along with children and lunatics*, from the right even to attend political meetings!

Women began filling men's jobs in Germany considerably earlier than their unimagined talents were discovered in war-time Britain. They mounted the conductors' platforms of the tramway-cars, for instance, almost simultaneously with the mobilisation order on July 31, 1914.

At first these *Kriegsfrauen* (war women) were only the wives of men called up, who took up the work more in the keep-the-home-fires-burning spirit than out of utilitarian motives. Germanic women, of course, were not strangers to manual labour of arduous sort. In Austria-Hungary nearly half of the nation's women were professional wage-earners. In Germany they did scavenger work for years before the war, and it did not outrage the susceptibilities of German "gentlemen" to see a woman harnessed to a dog, pulling carts and vans. Indeed, when I first arrived in Berlin, now nearly sixteen years ago, an animated discussion was raging round a "scientific" pamphlet entitled "*Ist das Weib ein Mensch?*" (Is woman a human being?)

EVERY TRADE INVADED.

To-day a report just issued by the German women's trade unions proclaims boldly that without women neither Germany's munitions nor food could possibly have "held out." There is not a trade, however strenuous its physical exactions, that German women have not invaded wholesale and effectively. They are making steel and building warships. They are supplanting men on the farms and doing the work of navvies. The iron industry is full of them. In blast-furnaces, with its soul-breaking demands on the strongest men, three German women are accomplishing the work of two men—sometimes one woman does all any man did. In a Silesian foundry forty women are earning their living as stokers.

At Krupps, who employ tens of thousands

WOMEN'S PLUCK IN THE LABOUR FIELD.—EXCLU

Scorced earth retreat

The decision of Germany's war leaders to put their eggs in the basket of an unshackled untersee fleet meant they were content to take a defensive posture in the ground war. A fresh Allied attack on the Western Front was anticipated, and with this in mind the German army began withdrawing to a new position in February 1917, preparations for which had been ongoing throughout the bitter winter. There was no small irony in the fact that Operation Alberich yielded a large tract of land between Arras and Soissons when so much blood had been spilt to gain meagre yardage, yet the move was based on sound reasoning. Shortening the line by around 30 miles produced an instant return in terms of resources freed up, while the new position, based on elastic defence-in-depth, presented a formidable barrier for any renewed Allied offensive. As a parting gesture, the Germans implemented a scorched-earth policy, ensuring that the new occupants would inherit nothing of value, merely denuded acreage. Booby-traps and poisoned wells presented a further hazard. Newly promoted French commander Robert Nivelle, to whom Haig would have to defer in the forthcoming offensive, was jubilant. "Had I been able to command the German armies, I couldn't have given them orders more favourable to my plan."

GERMANS ABANDONING BAPAUME RIDGE.

SH FORCE NEW HUN RETREAT | ON THE ENEMY'S | BEYOND BAGHDAD. | 'POOLED' BREWERIES | MR. LLOYD GEORGE AND LANCASHIRE. | OUR PRIS GERM

Opposite above and middle: The inhabitants of villages formerly under German occupation gather on the streets to welcome a contingent of British soldiers. "Vive Tommie!" was the common cry. In many places able-bodied men had been transported elsewhere to work while women, children and the elderly were left with very few rations.

Opposite below: Little remained of the village of La Barque.

Opposite far left: Map of the German retreat, published on 19 March, with a photograph of Sir Douglas Haig inset, showing the approximate battle line from Ransart to Noyon as officially reported.

Above left: A pine forest in Lorraine is interlaced with barbed wire fortifications.

Above right: Even the churches weren't saved from the wave of destruction.

Below: An Anzac patrol in the Rue de Peronne, Bapaume. They entered the town on 19 March while the buildings were still ablaze.

Germans implemented a scorched-earth policy, ensuring that the new occupants would inherit nothing of value.

ANOTHER BIG ALLIED ADVANCE.

[TISH] ADVANCE 8 MILES. | **PERONNE A SHELL** | **DOVER PATROL** | **CZAR'S PALACE FOR** | **LEAKY BLOCKADI**

BRITISH ADVANCE 8 MILES.

40 MORE VILLAGES TAKEN.

OUR CAVALRY ENGAGED WITH UHLANS.

ARRAS-BAPAUME ROAD CROSSED.

FRENCH MARCH TOWARDS ST. QUENTIN.

3rd YEAR OF WAR : 229th DAY.

The British and French armies made another great advance yesterday between Arras and the Aisne, the cavalry having many encounters with Uhlans. Our troops gained as much as 8 miles, and 40 more villages fell into our hands.

Between Arras and Bapaume the enemy has fallen back altogether from 10 to 15 miles. Our infantry

From SIR DOUGLAS HAIG.

FRANCE, Monday Night.

The pursuit of the enemy was continued to-day, our cavalry and advanced guards driving back the enemy's rearguards.

The ground gained extends to a depth of from two to eight miles, and 40 more villages have fallen into our hands.

The enemy raided our trenches early this morning in the neighbourhood of Loos and north-east of Ypres. A few of our men are missing.

Our aeroplanes did much valuable work yesterday in co-operation with our infantry. The enemy's troops were engaged successfully with machine guns, and bombs were dropped on a number of places behind his lines.

In air fights one German machine was destroyed and one driven down damaged. Two of our aeroplanes are missing.

FRENCH NON-STOP ADVANCE.

GERMAN CONVOY CAPTURED.

FRENCH OFFICIAL.

Monday Night.—During the day our troops advanced beyond Ham (12 miles south-west of St. Quentin) on the Somme, and Chauny (7 miles south-west of La

The map indicates approximately the battle line from the sea to Verdun. The area between the dotted line and the black line from Arras to Noyon shows the extent of the German retreat in that region.

are 7 miles east of Bapaume itself. South of Péronne they have reached Epénancourt, 5 miles east of Chaulnes.

Fère) on the Oise. We hold a large number of localities between these two towns.

Our cavalry is operating several miles to the north of Ham and has captured a convoy which was retiring in the dir...

HAIG'S GREAT ADVANCE.

PERONNE AND | SIR DOUGLAS HAIG'S | **PETROGRAD JOY.** | power otherwise than from the hands of the people | **TURKS IN FULL**

Nicht ärgern, nur wundern!

PERONNE A SHELL.

WANTON RUIN.

From W. BEACH THOMAS.

WAR CORRESPONDENTS' HEADQUARTERS,
FRANCE, Monday.

I have just returned from Péronne after crossing the Somme most precariously on piles.

The town is the most thorough example seen or imagined of the deliberate brutality of German destructiveness. The front of every house worth the name has been blown in by mines laid and exploded over a series of days. The town has been largely spared by French and British guns, and the Germans knew when they left on Saturday night that their own guns would be out of range, yet I could find only one house with an unbroken façade.

These naked ruins are mostly rubbish heaps. Within, after long and deliberate search, I could discover nothing in furniture, metal, crockery, or any other sort, valuable enough to be worth collection by a penny tinker or a rag-and-bone merchant. What was not removed was hammered to pieces.

In the course of my wanderings I met the first man to enter the town, a young officer from a Midland battalion who cut through 20ft. of German wire soon after sunrise on Sunday morning and penetrated with five men into the square. He found an absurd dummy figure of Britannia.

Beyond the town the tracks of the German transport were visible on the fresh rime. One prisoner was taken in a dugout, a magnificent-looking soldier from the Danish frontier who disapproved of the war in all its bearings.

The dug-outs and few buildings on Mount St. Quentin are destroyed with equal thoroughness, all except one where the half-consumed fuse of a mine was discovered.

Opposite page: In Bapaume a mine exploded shortly before Allied troops entered the town. The German scorched earth policy and their treatment of French civilians was soon reported in neutral countries, damaging the prestige of the German Empire.

Above left: The Allies were able to reach Peronne by using a pontoon and rafts to cross a river and canal. Infantry from the 1/8th Royal Warwickshire Regiment entered the town only to be met with familiar scenes of devastation.

Below: Allied troops in pursuit of the retreating enemy.

Above right: German soldiers left a note on Peronne's town hall, which had served as their headquarters. It read: "Don't be angry, just be amazed". The town hall had housed a precious museum that lost 98 per cent of its collection during the enemy action.

HINDENBURG'S "CHOSEN BATTLEFIELD."

ADVANCE AGAIN. | ARTILLERY DUMB. | EMPIRE WAR CABINET. | THE GOLDEN HOUR IN IRELAND. | AFTER WAR TRADE CREDIT BANKS TO HELP | OLD

THE MARK OF THE BEAST.

By W. BEACH THOMAS,
Our Special Correspondent with the British Army

War Correspondents' Headquarters, France, Tuesday.

I should like to put on record, in more deliberate detail than was possible in hurried telegrams written at the end of long and laborious journeys, the naked facts of the German evacuation of French towns and villages.

I saw from a point within reach of the pellets the very last shells fired at Bapaume, have traversed many blasted villages, and have spent almost leisurely hours in Péronne—fondly called by the French La Pucelle—which has lost under German treatment every touch of her maidenly grace and beauty. With such opportunities it is not difficult to tell how much of the ruin has been wrought by shell-fire, how much by mine or fire or army house-breakers. Calculated brutality, scientific evisceration, cannot cloke themselves under the guise of acts of war.

My object for the moment is solely to report facts, and to smooth out some of the rumpled contradictions that necessarily result from partial messages and hurried emphasis. The facts are these: As soon as the inhabitants were driven off and sent behind this great fortified line of which the German papers boast, all that was worth having was carted off and all the rest destroyed. The manner of destruction varied with the thing to be destroyed. In Péronne are many fine trees planted for ornament. The German military authorities, probably from lack of labour, could not cart them away, could not even spend time in felling them.

So instructions were given to hack every tree, as a hedge-layer cuts hedge-stakes, just deep enough to ensure the death of the tree. So the German left "his mark," a V-shaped convict's mark, cut half-way through each trunk of the avenue. Fruit trees are more carefully severed than ornamental trees, and especial care has been taken to destroy completely the espaliers and prettily trained fruit trees in which French gardeners take special and peculiar delight. I do not know why, but the sight of these little fruit trees with their throats cut filled me with more trenchant rage against the German mind than all the rest of the havoc. Probably a list of trees and other things that the inhabitants of the Bapaume and Péronne districts will need after the war is already filed in the Commercial Department at Berlin.

Opposite above and below right: Troops find any means to cross the waters just outside Peronne.

Opposite below left: The sign says "No road this way". The German destroyed roads and railways to make the Allied advance as difficult as possible.

Top: Local residents queue for basic provisions in the town of Noyon. Everyday life in occupied France was controlled by the authorities so German soldiers were allowed to "requisition" anything they wanted from citizens be it food, livestock, food, machinery or household possessions. Civilians were often short of food shortages leading to malnutrition, illness and disease.

Middle: The remains of the town hall in Bapaume.

Bottom: On 20 March 1917 a torpedo hit the British hospital ship *Asturias*, just off the coast of Devon. Fortunately she had just dropped the injured troops at Avonmouth before returning to her base in Southampton. However, most of the remaining crew and hospital staff were still aboard when the torpedo ripped through the engine room and thirty-five people were killed.

March 1917

1 The British hospital ship *Glenart Castle* was damaged by a mine whilst en route from Le Havre to Southampton.

Arz von Straussenberg replaced Conrad von Hötzendorf as Commander-in-Chief of the Austro-Hungarian army.

2 A Russian offensive reached and occupied Hamadan in western Persia.

4 The Armed Ship Bill was filibustered and defeated in the US Senate.

5 US President Woodrow Wilson was inaugurated for a second term. President Wilson's Democratic Party controlled the House of Representatives while the Republicans dominated the Senate.

6 On the Western Front the British line extended south of the Somme to the neighbourhood of Reims – twice the length of a year before.

7 British and Indian forces crossed the Diyala in pursuit of the Ottoman forces towards Baghdad.

8 Police fired into crowds as protestors and striking workers took to the streets in Petrograd.

10 British troops captured Irles near the Ancre on the Western Front.

11 After a two year campaign, British and Indian forces captured and occupied Baghdad.

12 The Russian Revolution began and a Provisional Government was formed.

President Wilson ordered the arming of American merchant vessels in the war zone.

13 The Russian Premier Prince Golitsyn and Minister for War General Byelyayev were removed from office by the Revolutionary Party.

14 German forces began their withdrawal from the Somme sector to the Hindenburg Line.

15 Tsar Nicholas II abdicated in favour of his brother Michael.

Prince Georgy Yevgenyevich Lvov replaced Prince Golitsyn as Prime Minister of Russia.

16 Nicholas' brother refused the throne until a Constitutional Assembly was formed to invite him formally.

A mutiny broke out in the Russian Baltic fleet after the sailors received word of the Revolution in Petrograd.

17 On the Western Front the British occupied Bapaume and nearby villages; French forces advanced to reoccupy Roye.

A public disagreement with members of his cabinet over war policy precipitated the resignation of French Prime Minister Aristide Briand. He was succeeded by Alexandre Felix Joseph Ribot.

18 German destroyers fired on Ramsgate and Broadstairs on the Kent coast of England.

British troops occupied Péronne in the area evacuated by the Germans while the French occupied Noyon.

19 The French battleship *Danton* was torpedoed and sunk by a German U-boat off the coast of Sardinia while en route to aid a blockade.

20 The first meeting of the British Imperial War Conference was held to co-ordinate governance of the British Empire during the war and prepare for the post-war situation.

21 The British hospital ship *Asturias* was attacked and torpedoed by a German submarine on her way to Southampton after landing her wounded at Avonmouth.

22 The Provisional Government in Russia was recognised by Britain, France, Italy, USA, Romania and Switzerland.

25 Forming part of the Samarrah Offensive, the Battle of Jebel Hamlin saw a British-led force attempt to encircle 15,000 Turkish troops retreating from Persia.

26 The First Battle of Gaza was fought during the first attempt by the Egyptian Expeditionary Force to invade the southern region of the Ottoman Empire territory of Palestine during the Sinai and Palestine Campaign. Fighting took place in and around the town of Gaza on the Mediterranean coast but the attempt to capture the city failed.

27 The Petrograd Soviet (workers' council) issued a proclamation in favour of self-determination and peace.

28 The British steamer *Cannizaro* was torpedoed and sunk by German submarine *U-24* on its way from New York to Hull.

30 The Russian Provisional Government acknowledged the independence of Poland.

31 The United States formally took possession of the Danish West Indies. Renamed the Virgin Islands, America purchased the islands from Denmark because of their strategic location in relation to the Panama Canal.

Nivelle's spring offensive

General Nivelle's stock was high going into 1917. His plan to punch a war-winning hole in the German line in the Champagne region was presented with such persuasive gusto that the generals and politicians who harboured misgivings – and there were many – felt unable to demur. Even Lloyd George was won over, at a time when the new British prime minister was highly sceptical of further frontal assaults in France and Flanders. Perhaps this French commander could produce results rather less wastefully than his British counterparts. The Coalition leader was prepared to let him try. It helped, of course, that France was to bear the brunt in the planned offensive on the Aisne. British troops were designated a supporting role, diverting attention and tying up enemy reserves with an attack at Arras. That was launched on 9 April, a week before the main attack further south. The Allied plans had already needed amending following Germany's spring withdrawal to the Hindenburg Line, an ill omen as events transpired. Initial gains of up to five miles were encouraging. Canadian Corps, under the direction of General Sir Julian Byng, mounted a successful attack on Vimy Ridge, and the objective of drawing German forces away from the main battle zone was achieved. But as the battle dragged on into May there were diminishing returns and the casualty count grew at an alarming rate. That might have been tolerable had it been accompanied by positive tidings from the Aisne. It was not.

The Nivelle Offensive began at 6.00 am on the morning of 16 April, following a week-long hurricane bombardment. More than one million men lined up to attack between Soissons and Reims, an operation whose scale dwarfed that which its author had undertaken at Verdun. The infantry set off into no-man's-land behind a creeping barrage with the assurances of a largely unhindered passage through the enemy line ringing in their ears. "The stamp of violence, of brutality and of rapidity must characterise your offensive," he exhorted. His confidence had been transmitted to the poilus; wholly misplaced as events played out. In the first place, the terrain was in the defenders' favour: the heights at Chemin des Dames rose

some 600 feet. Then there was Germany's deep defence, which left the front line relatively lightly fortified but had plenty of firepower and reserve strength further back. They also took full advantage of the protection offered by the reverse slopes. Finally, there were security breaches that told German commanders what to expect, and when. Far from the 48-hour, war-winning thrust Nivelle had promised, it was a disaster waiting to happen. The poilus were scythed down like corn by German machine-gunners on a day that bore comparison to 1 July 1916 at the Somme. Field hospitals were swamped as Nivelle's estimates of casualties proved pitifully wide of the mark. The tanks deployed to support the attack had negligible impact, and the few footholds established fell prey to effective counterattack. When the battle overran Nivelle's 48-hour threshold for success, he blamed others, not himself. Part of the ridge was eventually captured, far less than Nivelle had promised at far too high a price. The offensive was finally abandoned on 9 May, and six days later the discredited Nivelle's brief time as Haig's superior came to an abrupt end.

"The rupture of the front is possible in 24 to 48 hours, on condition it is made with a single stroke and by a sudden attack."   GENERAL ROBERT NIVELLE

"To Haig and myself the plan seemed to have in it many fallacies. A breach in the enemy defences on the scale contemplated couldn't possibly be effected within 48 hours."

SIR WILLIAM ROBERTSON, CHIEF OF THE IMPERIAL GENERAL STAFF

Top: The 5th Australian Brigade band marched triumphantly into Bapaume, regardless of the smoking embers around them.

Above: Following his successes at Verdun, General Nivelle was promoted to commander-in-chief of the French armies on the Western Front in December 1916.

Left: Whenever possible field telephones were used during the conflict to provide instant communication between battalions and the troops. They relied on landlines that were hazardous to lay with troops constantly exposed to enemy shelling.

Below: As part of the Nivelle Offensive the British agreed to make a diversionary attack in the Arras sector to draw German troops away from the Aisne region, enabling the French to launch a surprise assault.

Opposite top: Troops load heavy Howitzers on the front line near Monchy. These weapons were ideal for firing over obstacles as they had a high trajectory and a steep line of descent .

Opposite upper middle: A member of the cycling corps continues to mend a puncture despite the shellfire around him. These men

provided an invaluable line of communication, especially in conditions where animals and motor vehicles were liable to struggle. The Haldane Reforms had created fourteen battalions of cyclists by the time war was declared.

Opposite lower middle: Four divisions of the Canadian Corps opened the Battle of Arras; their aim to capture the German-held Vimy Ridge to prevent the enemy from firing down on British troops who were to advance below.

Opposite bottom: As commanders survey the battlefields, flooded shell holes can be seen.

MORE FORTRESSES STORMED.

HAIG DEFIES THE WEATHER.

FINE GAINS ALL ALONG THE BATTLE FRONT.

April 1917

1 French troops drove German forces back to Vauxaillon, north-east of Soissons on the Western Front.

2 President Woodrow Wilson delivered a war address to Congress asking for a Declaration of War against Germany.

3 The torpedo gunboat HMS *Jason* was sunk by a mine near Coll Island off the west coast of Scotland.

4 The US Senate voted in favour of a Declaration of War.

5 German forces finished their withdrawal to the Hindenburg Line.

6 The United States of America came out of neutrality and declared war on Germany.

7 Cuba and Panama declared war on Germany.

8 Austria-Hungary severed diplomatic relations with the USA.

9 The Battle of Arras began when British, Canadian, New Zealand and Australian troops attacked German defences near the French city of Arras on the Western Front.

The Battle of Vimy Ridge formed part of the opening phase of the Battle of Arras fought mainly between Canadian and German forces as a diversionary attack for the French Nivelle Offensive.

10 The British hospital ship HMS *Salta* hit a mine laid by the German submarine *UC-26* off the coast at le Havre.

Bulgaria severed diplomatic relations with the USA.

11 In a flanking operation during the Arras offensive Australian troops attacked the village of Bullecourt and pushed German troops out of their fortified positions and into the reserve trenches.

12 Canadian forces completed their capture of Vimy Ridge near Arras.

13 Bolivia severed diplomatic relations with Germany.

14 A British attack made gains east of Monchy-le-Preux as the first phase of the British offensive at Arras came to an end.

15 German forces penetrated the Australian front line and occupied the village of Lagnicourt but counter-attacks from Australian battalions restored the front line.

16 The Second Battle of the Aisne, also known as the Nivelle Offensive, began when French forces attacked the Germans along the front from Soissons to Rheims.

17 Three weeks after the failure of the first offensive, the Second Battle of Gaza began when British forces attacked Ottoman forces during the Sinai and Palestine Campaign.

18 The French advance continued east and north-east of Soissons.

19 The Second Battle of Gaza ended when Ottoman forces resisted the British attack leaving the city firmly in Turkish control.

20 During a German destroyer attack on Dover, HMS *Swift* and HMS *Broke* engaged a force of six enemy destroyers and fended them off although both ships were damaged.

22 The Battle of Istabulat took place in Mesopotamia.

23 The Second Battle of the Scarpe began when the British launched an assault towards Vis-en-Artois on the Western Front.

24 British and Indian forces captured Samarra in Mesopotamia.

25 Afonso Augusto da Costa succeeded António José de Almeida as Prime Minister of Portugal.

26 A second German naval raid took place on Ramsgate on the Kent coast of England.

27 Guatemala severed diplomatic relations with Germany.

28 British and Canadian troops launched an attack towards Arleux and captured the village.

29 General Philippe Petain was appointed French Chief of General Staff. He replaced General Robert Nivelle, whose failed offensive earlier in the month had provoked widespread mutinies in the French Army.

Acq
The Labyrinth
Aubigny
Neuvireuil
Oppy
Bailleul
Fresnes
Ecurie
Roclincourt
Gavrelle
Marœuil
Anzin
Le Point du Jour
Ste Catherine
St Nicolas
St Laurent
Athies
Fampoux
Plouvain
Duisans
ARRAS
Rœux
R. SCARPE
Hamblain
Dainville
Blangy
Feuchy
Pelves
Tilloy les Mofflaines
Achicourt
Warlus
Monchy
Boiry
Beaurains
Remy
Agny
Wailly
Guémappe
Neuville
Wancourt
Vis
Héninel
Rivière
Ficheux
St Martin
Chérisy
Mercatel
Hénin
Bailleulval
Blairville
Fontaine
Bailleulmont
Boisleux
Boiry
La Herlie
Ransart
Hendecourt
Boyelles
Croisilles
SCALE OF MILES
Railways
Roads
Loos
Grenay
Lens
Lievin
Henin-Lietard
Avion
Vimy
VIMY RIDGE
Souchez
Carency
Givenchy
Thelus
Willerval
Arleux
Izel
DOUAI-4m.
Vitry en Artois
ARRAS
Croisilles
Quéant
Ecoust
BAPAUME 4m.
Vaux
Courcelles

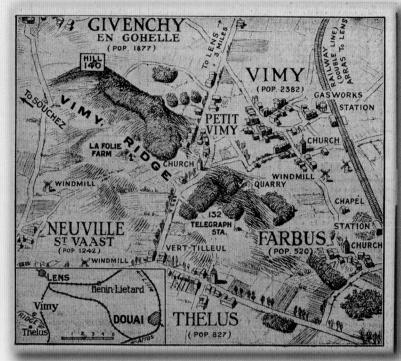

Above: The slopes of Vimy Ridge are pitted with shell craters. The British reinforced the Canadian artillery with twenty-four additional artillery brigades giving a fighting force of heavy guns every twenty yards and field guns every 10 yards.

Below: Canadian troops successfully captured about 4,000 German soldiers at Vimy.

Opposite left: Map of the front showing the Allies' progress between Givenchy and Henin.

"Canada will be proud that the taking of the coveted Vimy Ridge has fallen to the lot of her troops."   THE KING TO SIR DOUGLAS HAIG

Above: A picture map published on 11 April showing the topographical features of the Vimy Ridge which dominates the Plain of Douai. Throughout the war the Ridge was regarded by both sides as being of significant strategical importance.

AND "OVER THE TOP" THEY GO.—"Time's up; over you go!" The Canadians went up the Vimy Ridge, the backbone of the Hun retreat area, and carried it "early in the morning."   [*Official Photograph.*]

BEYOND THE VIMY RIDGE.

HARD FIGHTING.

GERMAN LINE TURNED EAST OF ARRAS.

RETIRING TOWARDS DOUAI.

11,000 PRISONERS AND OVER 100 GUNS.

The British Army, continuing its glorious advance, is beyond the Vimy Ridge, so magnificently stormed by the Canadians on Monday, and has turned the German line east of Arras, whence the enemy is retiring towards the Reserve Hindenburg line in front of Douai.

Over 11,000 prisoners and more than 100 guns have now been taken. A feature of the attack was our adoption of the Germans' own liquid fire, which was used with terrible effect.

From FIELD-MARSHAL SIR DOUGLAS HAIG.

Tuesday Morning.

During the night there was severe fighting at the northern end of the Vimy Ridge [north of Arras], where the enemy had retained a holding. He was ejected, and an attempted counter-attack failed to materialise. The eastern slope of the ridge has been cleared of the enemy and counter-attacks repulsed.

Our troops advanced and seized the village of Fampoux [3 miles east of Arras] and neighbouring defences north and south of the [river] Scarpe.

The number of prisoners taken yesterday exceeds 9,000, and over 40 guns have been captured.

In the neighbourhood of St. Quentin the enemy has been driven from the high ground between Le Verguier and Hargicourt [north-east of the town].

Fighting continues throughout the whole battle front.

After an intense bombardment the enemy made a strong attack last night on a narrow front south-east of Ypres and succeeded in reaching our support line. He was immediately ejected from our trenches, leaving several dead.

Tuesday Night.

Battle for Vimy Ridge

Vimy Ridge was among the most formidable strongholds on the entire Western Front. Germany had seized control of these heights overlooking Arras in the early weeks of the war, and repeated attempts to unseat them had been bloodily expensive. The Canadian Corps was charged with taking this key vantage point as part of the diversionary offensive supporting Nivelle's grand scheme, bidding to become the first Allied troops to set foot on the ridge since the French army's fleeting gains there in spring 1915. Meticulous planning went into the assault on the four-mile-long ridge. Models of the terrain were constructed to prepare for the 9 April assault, and extensive tunnelling operations brought the troops into forward positions unmolested. Such preparations would have counted for little without the artillery firestorm that pounded the enemy line in the days before the battle commenced. The effectiveness of both the preliminary and the creeping barrage, along with the determination of the Canadian infantry, brought about the single greatest coup of the spring 1917 Allied offensive; indeed, one of the most spectacular successes of the entire war. The Corps took over 10,000 casualties, including 3,500 killed, so the triumph, as ever, was heavily diluted.

The taking of Vimy Ridge was imbued with a significance beyond that which attended the capture of a strategically important, enemy-held position. For the first time, all four Canadian divisions had been deployed as an entity, bestowing a sense of national pride on the operation. As Brigadier-General Alexander Ross put it when recalling the three-day struggle for mastery of the heights: "In those few minutes I witnessed the birth of a nation."

Above: **Prior to the attack on Arras the Royal Engineers spent six months constructing a network of tunnels so the troops could arrive safely and in secret. By the time the operation began there were 12 miles of tunnels, including railways and tramways, that could hide 24,000 men. They were equipped with lighting, toilets, kitchens and even a medical centre with a full operating theatre.**

Below: **Limbers pass through the ruins of Athies during the battle.**

Opposite above: **The Allies were able to use creeping barrages with great effect, sending the gunners ahead of the troops to lay a network of high explosives and shrapnel shells. This forced the Germans to remain in their trenches and meant the Allies did not have to contend with machine gun fire.**

Opposite middle: **Tanks were on hand and deployed during an attempt by Australian troops to break through at Bullecourt. However, the tanks suffered from mechanical problems and were so slow that they failed to get past the wire defences.**

Opposite below right: **When the first day of the battle dawned at Vimy it was snowing heavily in the direction of the German trenches, making it more difficult for the occupants to see what was happening.**

Opposite below left: **An officer keeps watch as troops advance over the open ground at Vimy, digging themselves in whenever the enemy shells begin to explode in the distance.**

CANADIANS TO THE FORE.

TANKS CARRY A HILL.

GARRISON SURRENDERS.

FRANCE, Monday.

The battle which began before daylight this morning on a front extending roughly from opposite Lens to St. Quentin [45 miles] is raging with unabated vigour.

Along most of the front the advance of the infantry was not strenuously opposed and the battle developed strictly in accordance with programme, but near Arras the Germans offered determined resistance and a large pocket of the enemy was reported to be still holding out at midday although entirely surrounded. The famous Harp, a redoubt but little less formidable than the Labyrinth, was captured, with practically a whole battalion.

Several tanks were reported climbing Telegraph Hill at 7.30 this morning, and as this little eminence commands the Harp I think we may reasonably associate the presence of these ugly brutes with the surrender of the position.

Along the railway running through to the Scarpe Valley [east of Arras] our troops have made good progress, and upon the Lens branch of the line they have gained and taken the Bois de la Maison Blanche.

In Blangy, the suburb of Arras through which the German front line has run since the winter of 1914, several strong points have offered a vigorous resistance, but our bombing parties are gradually reducing these.

I hear that the Canadians have fought their way well forward upon the Vimy slopes, but the resistance here is stiffening.

HEAVY GUN PREPONDERANCE.

One of the most striking features of the great battle is the immense preponderance of heavy artillery which we have over the enemy. It is impossible to believe that anything can live long under such a concentration of guns as we can bring to bear anywhere along the whole front of the offensive. A pretty good proof of this is the thoroughness with which the dense wire defences have been torn and shredded, and it is only when the entanglements dip into gullies so that it is difficult to see them that they have escaped destruction.—Reuter.

THE FIERCEST FIGH

HAIG'S TERRIFIC BATTLE.

DESPERATE GERMAN ATTACKS.

robbed of the dash and obstinacy that marked the fresh troops, especially those newest to fighting.

Among the prisoners taken south of Gavrelle was a bearded man who had never been out of Germany till the eve

HUN LI

ATTEMP

w are give
r Office re

GERMAN

of the Crou
ras battlef
on French t
he second g
rough the
l heaviest b
ing masses
against our
yesterday
tle increas
Soon
troops,
ke forwar
9-mile fro
are rece

SHA

HIND

TING OF THE WAR.

TO CLAIM A 'VICTORY.'

TO CHEER UP GERMANY.

SEAPLANES BOMB HUN DESTROYERS.

ENEMY SHIP PROBABLY SUNK

U.S. & IRELAND

THE GOLDEN HOUR FOR SETTLEMENT.

Opposite above: Jubilant British soldiers march away from battle after the successful start to the Arras campaign.

Opposite middle: Canadians advancing over the crest of Vimy Ridge.

Opposite below: Despite the heavy shellfire the 29th Canadian Infantry battalion trudges across no-man's land towards the German lines.

Above left: Troops leave the safety of the trenches to launch the attack.

Above right: Canadian artillerymen from the 17th battery use a captured 4.2-inch Howitzer against the enemy. On 9 April over 80 per cent of German heavy guns were neutralized by counter battery fire.

Right: At an advanced dressing station the stretcher cases are prepared for hospital treatment further behind the lines while the bodies of fallen soldiers lie respectfully covered.

HAIG'S FIERCE ONSLAUGHT.

ARLEUX AND STRONG TRENCH SYSTEM STORMED.

976 PRISONERS.

GUNS SMASH COUNTER-ATTACKS.

1,001st DAY OF THE WAR.

On Saturday, the eve of the 1,000th day of the war, Haig began the third stage of the Battle of Arras, the bloodiest conflict of all.

Arleux, north-east of Arras, was captured on Saturday, with two miles of trenches to north and south of it, and yesterday our brave troops stormed a mile of the German trench system a little farther south. The prisoners number 976.

It is a struggle, however, in which gains of ground seem to matter less than the number of Huns killed, and again Hindenburg's reserves were sent forward to the slaughter in fierce but futile counter-attacks.

At some periods the hand-to-hand fighting was such that the artillery on either side had to cease fire.

One of the war correspondents says that the battle is one of exhaustion. If we consume the German reserves the rest follows. But the decision is not in sight yet, and the scale of the fighting is the surest evidence of the need for every man.

From W. BEACH THOMAS.

WAR CORRESPONDENTS' HEADQUARTERS, FRANCE, Sunday.

From the eastern slope of Vimy Ridge I saw yesterday the whole field of our attack, especially at its centre and focus, the villages of Arleux and Oppy, west of the plain and at the edge of the "cockpit of Europe." It was pencilled out in minute distinctness even to its fauna or present population—I mean the invading Germans, whom I saw near and far, some labouring up a slope as prisoners, some running in groups from trench line to trench line, some gathering at the corner of a wood. Some, away to the right, came forward, wave after wave, in far separate lines, and away in the distance horse transport was bringing up ammunition for the guns, whose flashes here and there were clearly visible to well-placed observers.

Seldom was a landscape so laid out for a view of war. The great fighting plain of Europe was spread out to our view when Vimy fell, and there the fight has begun. But the general view is nothing when the enemy is in sight, and when my companion and I came away we had both

Above left: Allied troops assemble outside one of the fortifications on the Hindenburg Line.

Below: Horse-drawn ambulances arrive at an advanced dressing station near Vimy. Despite the Canadians' success in capturing the ridge over 3,500 Allied troops were killed and another 7,000 wounded.

Above right: Soldiers load the ammunition wagons at Wytschaete. Once full these would be pulled to the front line by teams of horses.

Opposite above left: British troops at Thelus watch the shellfire in the distance. By the end of the offensive the Allies had gained very little ground and suffered 150,000 casualties.

Opposite above right: The men from a Canadian battalion establish a signalling station to communicate with Allied aircraft.

Opposite middle: The strict time limit that had been imposed to achieve victory quickly fell by the wayside.

This page: Arras was frequently bombarded during the war and by 1917 very little remained of the Gothic Town Hall (above and below) or the Cathedral (above right). Restoration work began after the war, replicating the original architecture as closely as possible.

Opposite above: Sir Sam Hughes and his party view the effects of German shellfire on the town.

Opposite middle left: A family home in Arras is exposed after the external wall was destroyed by shelling.

Opposite middle and bottom right: The Grand Place, Arras, before and after it was destroyed in the fighting. Under the town are some of the tunnels dug to hide the Allied troops just before they attacked. Most were dug by the New Zealand Tunnelling Corps who were able to break through nearly 100 yards of limestone a day. Cavers rediscovered this labyrinth in the 1990s and evidence of the tunnellers' underground existence can be found with graffiti and portraits etched into the stone.

Opposite bottom left: The German army removed the statue of General Faidherbe, a French colonial administrator, from this plinth in Bapaume and replaced it with a dummy anti-aircraft weapon, made from a stovepipe. After the town's liberation scores of men wrote their names on the pedestal, including this Anzac soldier.

WILSON DECLARES WAR ON THE KAISER.

UR GREAT NEW ALLY.

AR RESOLUTION IN U.S. CONGRESS.

THE NAVY NEEDS YOU! DON'T **READ** AMERICAN HISTORY— **MAKE IT!**

U·S·NAVY RECRUITING STATION 48 North Queen St., Lancaster

HISTORIC SCENE. ALLIED AMBASSADORS ON THE FLOOR OF THE HOUSE.

THE GERMAN AMERICANS.

THE KAISER'S BIG CONFERENCE.

EMPEROR CARL, BETHMANN AND HINDENBURG.

STORY OF AN "OFFER."

FRENCH STORM 8 MILES OF FRON

STRONG POSITIONS WRESTED FROM LARGE HUN FORCES.

4 VILLAGES AND SEVERAL HEIGHTS.

FRESH BRITISH GAINS.

OUR LIGHTNING INFANTRY.

DAILY MAIL FEBRUARY 2, 1917
Germany defies US

Germany has sent a Note to the United States which in effect declares a hunger war on that country and on the world. A Washington report says that President Wilson may, in reply, warn Germany against unrestricted submarine warfare and threaten a breach in relations if Berlin is unheeding.

The Note announces that German submarines will observe no restraints, and forbids neutral shipping to enter the waters round Great Britain, France and Italy, and the Eastern Mediterranean. It imposes on United States trade these conditions:

1. Only one steamer a week between the United States and Britain.
2. That vessel must run to and from Falmouth.
3. It must be painted in a particular way and lighted at night.
4. The United States Government must guarantee that it carries no contraband, and must warn other ships not to enter the "barred zone"

All previous promises given by Germany to President Wilson are repudiated. The German demand is a violation of the sovereignty of all neutrals, as the above regulations are not permitted by international law and interfere with neutral rights at sea.

The Note says that the German Government is actuated by "the highest sense to serve humanity," and hopes that the people and Government of the United States will "appreciate the new state of affairs from the right standpoint of impartiality."

This page: On 30 August 1917 two million people crowded onto Fifth Avenue in New York to witness the departure parade of the 27th Division, part of the Army National Guard. Led by Major General John F O'Ryan, the parade represented every branch of the army service. Among those reviewing the troops were Colonel Roosevelt, Governor Whitman and Major General J Franklin Bell.

Inset: The Conscription Act was quickly passed in June and soon extended to men between the ages of 18 and 45. By the end of the war 24 million had enlisted with 3 million inducted to fight.

Opposite below middle: President Woodrow Wilson kept America out of the conflict but when Germany launched a policy of unrestricted submarine warfare in February 1917 and then tried to woo Mexico into joining the Central Powers, Wilson finally went to Congress asking for permission to go to war. It was granted and war was declared on 6 April 1917.

Opposite below left: An early recruit for the US Army was Marshall Field III (right), soon dubbed the "golden private", as he was joint heir to his grandfather's $80 million fortune. He joined the 1st Illinois Cavalry and served with the 122nd Field Artillery in France. After enlisting as a private he eventually rose to the rank of Captain.

Opposite below right: Applicants for the Royal Flying Corps are enrolled at the recruiting offices on Fifth Avenue in New York. By 1917 Britain, America and Canada had combined their training, setting up camps first in Canada and then in the States. The recruitment office in New York aimed to sign up British citizens but also attracted around 300 Americans.

Opposite above right: Major General Pershing was appointed commander of the American Expeditionary Force and insisted on thorough training before his troops were sent to the frontline. At Fort Sheridan in Illinois trench mock-ups were used and Allied tactics and techniques practised for six months before the troops travelled to Europe. They then received two months further training before heading for the front.

America enters the war

Woodrow Wilson was re-elected to the White House in November 1916, a narrow victory secured in part by the course he had steered in keeping America out of the internecine struggle engulfing the old world. Millions of Americans had ancestral roots in each of the rival camps, providing a natural counterbalance in public opinion. Condemnation of German militarism cut little ice with Irish Americans whose forebears had suffered at the hands of an English oppressor. As the conflict entered its third year, the desire to remain on the sidelines took precedence over allegiances forged through lineage. America was content to reap the economic bonanza of providing matériel, food and lines of credit – to the Allies' advantage – without having to spill a drop of American blood. That position was about to change.

Tensions rose when American lives were lost in the sinking of the Sussex in the English Channel in March 1916, less than a year after the Lusitania had been torpedoed off the Irish coast. German U-boats did show a measure of restraint after the incident, enough to mollify Wilson if not his Republican predecessor Theodore Roosevelt, one of the more strident anti-isolationists. But it was pragmatism, not altruism, driving German policy. It had too few submarines to inflict war-winning damage on the enemy, and thus adhered to "cruiser rules" in keeping with international law and, in the eyes of world opinion, common humanity. Suspect ships would not be sunk until proper investigations had been conducted and all on board had disembarked. At the same time U-boat construction was redoubled, and by late 1916 Germany was in a position to play its trump card again. The country was feeling the brutal effects of Britain's naval blockade, facing a "turnip winter" that showed the effectiveness of choking off imports. With every meagre, unappetising mouthful German morale sank further. The High Command thought it time to give Britain a large dose of the same medicine by unshackling the submarines and hitting the transatlantic supply line, especially as another year drew to a close with no prospect of breaking the deadlock on the Western Front. German Chancellor Bethmann Hollweg was left to weigh projections showing how much tonnage could be prevented from reaching British shores against the risk of provoking America. Could Britain really be brought to its knees before America mobilised? Was it time to risk all in pursuit of a great victory for the Fatherland? If so, the Fatherland might have to carry an even greater share of the burden, for its Austrian ally was faltering. The octogenarian Franz Josef died in November 1916, and the new emperor, Karl, wanted to sue for peace with the Habsburg dynasty teetering on the brink. Bethmann Hollweg decided to explore that avenue.

Peace soundings failed

Meanwhile, Wilson sought to mediate, inviting the belligerents to state their terms. Hopes of an early end to hostilities faded as Germany refused to give assurances over Belgium, top of a lengthy list of concessions that might have been acceptable to a defeated nation; not to one still contesting the war. Germany held out its own olive branch on 12 December, one so vague that it was quickly dismissed. Peace soundings had failed, predictably so since both sides believed outright victory was theirs for the taking and thus were in no mood to give much ground.

Wilson sought to mediate, inviting the belligerents to state their terms.

America severs diplomatic relations

Germany's position hardened at the start of 1917. With the introduction of unrestricted submarine warfare in Allied waters from the beginning of February, the Chancellor said of the Entente: "They want to hear only of a peace which they dictate." Such intransigence meant the conflict would continue. "We have been challenged to fight to the end. We accept the challenge." Hindenburg was equally pugnacious in his defence of the new policy. If giving U-boats licence to target all shipping provided the means to injure Germany's enemies most grievously, then now was the time for it to begin.

The torpedo threat soon became stark reality. America severed diplomatic relations with Germany and adopted a stance of armed neutrality that lasted only a matter of weeks. On 2 April Wilson went before Congress to put the case for sending in troops. "The present German warfare against commerce," he said, "is warfare against mankind. It is a war against all nations." In his speech he referred to a spy network abroad in the country, agents seeking to agitate and destabilise working on behalf of the Imperial Government. This was the final straw, a development that even the presidential peacemaker could not ignore.

The enemy within had been responsible for numerous acts of sabotage on American soil. A New Jersey depot full of ammunition bound for Allied guns was blown up in July 1916, the explosion heard over 50 miles away. But it was political dynamite written in ink that caused a much greater shock wave among the American people. In January 1917 German foreign minister Arthur Zimmerman sent a coded telegram to the envoy in Mexico. It contained a proposal to be put before the Mexican government: in the event of an American declaration of war, if

Mexico opened hostilities with its northern neighbour, support would be given for the country's long-standing territorial claims in Arizona, Texas and New Mexico. There was also an invitation for Japan to join the alliance, breaking the treaty obligation that brought that country into the war on Britain's side in August 1914.

This missive was intercepted and decoded by British intelligence, its explosive contents revealed to the US authorities in late February. When it became public knowledge, American opinion was swayed decisively and political resistance to the idea of becoming a belligerent dwindled. A country that had absorbed maritime atrocities was incensed at a scheme to incite unrest on its doorstep. This was an outrageous attempt to undermine the tenets of the century-old Monroe Doctrine, which warned Europe's imperial powers that their days of meddling in the Americas were over. "The theory of comfortable isolation is rudely shaken," as one correspondent put it. An incandescent Roosevelt said of the White House incumbent: "If he does not go to war with Germany, I shall skin him alive!" President Wilson was safe from bodily harm since his forbearance was exhausted. He cited the Zimmerman telegram in his rallying call to arms, unimpeachable proof that Germany could not be trusted. "That it means to stir up enemies against us at our very doors the intercepted note to the German minister at Mexico City is eloquent evidence," he said, adding: "In such a government, following such methods, we can never have a friend". Four days later, 6 April 1917, Congress overwhelmingly accepted Wilson's plea that "right is more precious than peace", and the global war had a new, powerful combatant.

Below: Members of the 8th Infantry march through Canal Street destined for the station and then their training camp.

Opposite top: American sailors in London watch the Changing the Guard. By June 1917 14,000 troops, or "doughboys" as they came to be known, had arrived in Europe although did not join the frontline until October.

Opposite above: American nurses drilling before leaving for France. There were over 20,000 women serving in the Army Nurses Corps and nearly half of these were deployed overseas. The first units arrived in Europe before the troops so hospitals could be established. They worked in many bases including field hospitals, mobile units and transport ships.

Opposite middle left: Prior to the outbreak of war the American Red Cross had 17,000 members. Volunteers flooded to help and by 1918 its membership had increased to 20 million adults and 11 million juniors. In excess of $400 million was donated to help provide funds and materials.

Opposite middle right: In common with their British counterparts American women soon found they were filling the roles of men leaving for the front. Miss Lucille Patterson, a well-known artist, paints advertisements on a building in 42nd Street in New York.

Opposite below left: Liberty Bonds were issued to support the cost of the conflict. These poster bond drives were so successful they raised two thirds of the cost of the war. Wilson knew it was essential to secure the support of the American people and the Division of Pictorial Publicity was launched. Over 300 artists, cartoonists and designers used the national symbols of Uncle Sam, the American flag and the Statue of Liberty to engender a sense of patriotism and commitment.

Opposite below middle: An American soldier receives his new equipment.

Opposite below right: Miss Loretta Walsh became the first female active-duty (non-nursing) Naval recruit when she enlisted on 17 March 1917, and was appointed as the first female petty officer four days later as Chief Yeoman. Eventually 13,000 women were recruited as "yeomanettes" receiving the same rights and pay as men.

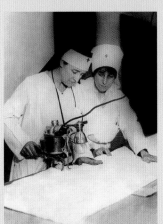

PRESIDENT WILSON'S ADDRESS.

HISTORIC SPEECH: FULL REPORT.

WASHINGTON, Tuesday.

PRESIDENT WILSON said: I called Congress in Extraordinary Session because there are serious, very serious, choices of policy to be made, and made immediately, which it was neither right constitutionally nor permissible I should assume the responsibility of making.

On February 3 I officially laid before you the extraordinary announcement of the German Government that it was its purpose to put aside all restraints of law, of humanity, and use its submarines to sink every vessel that sought to approach either the ports of Britain or the western coasts of Europe or any of the ports controlled by the enemies of Germany in the Mediterranean. That had seemed to be their object earlier in the war, but since April 1916 the German Government had somewhat restrained the commanders of its under-sea craft in conformity with its promise then given us that passenger boats should not be sunk and due warning would be given to all other vessels which its submarines might seek to destroy when no resistance was offered or escape attempted, and care would be taken that their crews were given at least a fair chance to save their lives in their open boats. The precautions then were meagre and haphazard enough, as was proved in distressing instance after instance in the progress of the cruel and unmanly business, but a certain degree of restraint was observed.

The new policy swept every restriction aside. Vessels of every kind, whatever their flag, character, cargo, destination or errand, have been ruthlessly sent to the bottom without warning, without thought of help or mercy for those on board, vessels of friendly neutrals along with those of belligerents. Even hospital ships, ships carrying relief to the sorely bereaved and stricken people of Belgium, though provided with a safe-conduct by the German Government itself, and distinguished by unmistakable marks, were sunk with the same reckless lack of compassion.

THE LAW OF THE SEA.

The principle of international law had its origin in an attempt to set up some law which would be respected and observed upon the seas, where no nation had the right of dominion, where lay the free highways of the world. By painful stage after stage has that law been built up, with meagre enough results indeed, but always with a clear view at least of what the heart and conscience of mankind desired.

This minimum the German Government swept aside under the plea of retaliation and necessity and because it had no weapons which it could use at sea except these, which it is impossible to employ as it is employing them without throwing to the winds all scruples of humanity or respect for the understandings supposed to underlie the intercourse of the world. I am not now thinking of the loss of property involved, immense and serious as it is, but only of the *wanton and wholesale destruction of the lives of non-combatant men, women, and children* engaged in pursuits which have always, even in the darkest periods of modern history, been deemed innocent and legitimate. Property can be paid for; the lives of peaceful and innocent people cannot be.

The present German warfare against commerce is warfare against mankind. It is a war against all nations.

THE U.S. DECLARATION.

I advise that Congress declare that the recent course of the Imperial German Government to be in fact nothing less than war against the Government and people of the United States; that it formally accepts the status of a belligerent which is thus thrust upon it; and that it take immediate steps not only to put the country in a more thorough state of defence but also to exert all its power and to employ its resources to bring the Government of the German Empire to terms and end the war.

Top left: German prisoners of war work in the market garden at Evesham. They were paid a standard rate of 4d an hour.

Above left: Members of the City of London National Guard Volunteer Corps dig trenches on the site of the old General Post Office under the shadow of St Paul's. This training exercise for home defence included many city gentlemen.

Top right: The Imperial War Cabinet first met at 10 Downing Street in March 1917. It aimed to co-ordinate the government of the British Empire during the war and to prepare for events after the conflict was over. Lloyd George, elected Prime Minister in December 1916, realised that the dominions had made a considerable contribution to the war effort and therefore needed greater consultation. Front row (l to r) Viscount Walter Long (Secretary of State for the Colonies), Sir Robert Borden (Canadian Prime Minister), General Jan Smuts (South Africa), Lloyd George, Sir James Meston (Lieutenant-Governor of the United Provinces of Agra and Oudh), Bill Massey (New Zealand Prime Minister), Hon Robert Rogers (Canada), Sir George Perley (Canada), Arthur Balfour (Foreign Secretary), Arthur Henderson (Minister without Portfolio) and Sir Maurice Hankey (Secretary of the Imperial War Cabinet). Back row (l to r) Andrew Bonar Law (Chancellor of the Exchequer), John Douglas Hazen (Canadian Minister of Marine), Sir Joseph Ward (New Zealand), Sir Austen Chamberlain (Secretary of State for India), Sir Edward Carson (First Lord of the Admiralty), Sir Ganga Singh, Maharajah of Bikaner (India) and Lord Curzon (Leader of the House of Lords).

Right: As the war progressed men who had originally been exempt from conscription, as they were deemed to be in reserve occupations, began to receive their call-up papers.

"CONSCIENCE" MEN.

PRINCETOWN FARCE.

"WORK-SHIES" WITH MOTOR-BICYCLES.

The irritation of members of the House of Commons over the preferential treatment given to "conscientious" objectors was manifest again yesterday.

Answering various questioners, Mr. Brace, for the Home Office, said the "conscientious" objectors have no right to commandeer football fields. Discipline at Princetown is improving.

Mr. Shirley Benn: Are not these the men who went before their local tribunals claiming to be "conscientious" objectors but were found to be only faked "conscientious" objectors who were not exempt from military service? (Cheers.)

"SOME ARE SHIRKERS"

Mr. Brace: I think the facts are as stated, but they were afterwards held by a central tribunal to be "conscientious" objectors, and hence they came under this scheme.

Mr. Butcher: Is there any chance of these shirkers being brought under military service?

Mr. Brace: Well, that is a matter of policy for the Government.

Mr. Outhwaite (indignantly): Does the right hon. gentleman accept the description of these men as shirkers?

Mr. Brace (emphatically): It is quite true as regards some of them. (Cheers and laughter.)

Mr. Brace also said the Committee were meeting that day to consider the facilities now given "conscientious" objectors for getting leave and free railway travel. On March 20 instructions were given that "conscientious" objectors were to be put on the Food Controller's rations for civilians. Complaints have been received that extra supplies are bought in Princetown, and the committee are in consultation with the Food Controller on this matter.

Above: Millions of dollars in gold in the form of 28-pound bars are stacked in the Mint at Philadelphia waiting to be coined into money. During the war millions of pounds worth of gold went from Britain to the United States.

Below and opposite above: The Dartmoor conscientious objectors These men were housed at Dartmoor Prison where they were given relative freedom but required to work throughout the war. Once conscription was introduced a clause allowed "conscientious objection to bearing arms". This freed men from military service for reasons including religion, political objections and pacifism. Some would still help in the munitions factories or become stretcher bearers at the trenches but "absolutists" refused to do anything connected with the conflict. Out of 16,000 recorded conscientious objectors, about a quarter were Quakers.

The Pacifists

That the government allowed for exemption from the Military Service Bill on conscience grounds did not sit well with some MPs. The pacifist stance of the Society of Friends prompted much debate, but it was clear that any allowance could not be confined to a single denomination. That made it a "slackers' charter" to some, one Member describing the concessions as reducing the legislation to "a rotten, mutilated piece of compulsion". The hard-liners were little assuaged by assurances that those seeking exemption would be engaged in valuable war work. That compromise in turn brought disdain from one Quaker MP, who said even non-combatant service was unacceptable if it was forced labour.

The brief of tribunals established to hear exemption applications was not to convince the applicants of their error, it was said, but to gauge their sincerity. That meant some probing questions, and in some cases sharp verbal jousting. One man said taking a life would consign him to an existence of unabated misery. What if the Germans landed and threatened a member of his family? He had no answer for such a hypothetical situation, yet his application was granted. The chairman of the Nairn County Tribunal was far from indulgent when he enquired of the man before him: "Do you read the Bible? You are told in the Bible that you are to fight the Devil… and if the German Emperor is not worse than the Devil, I am a Dutchman. We give you no exemption."

The Bishop of Lincoln weighed in to the debate in a letter to *The Times*, saying he was no apologist for "cowards or shirkers", but pointing out that "the will or capacity to take an enemy's life is not the only element in good citizenship". He cautioned against a country "in its military zeal slipping into the old vices of intolerance and persecution". That brought a sharp riposte from fellow clergyman A W Gough, vicar of Brompton, who pulled no punches in his estimation of conscientious objectors. "We have no use for them. They render nothing to Caesar. And we do not think they render anything to God. And the prospect of their being with us in increased number – screened from war risks and glorified by bishops and coteries – can only be made tolerable if the State be relieved of the indignity of their citizenship."

Colonel Sir Henry Knollys also took a jaundiced view of Conscientious Objectors, for different reasons. Principle, he opined, could not always be invoked in defence of a position taken. What of a pickpocket, he said by

way of illustrating his point, who pleaded a belief that wealth was unevenly distributed? His imaginary felon might argue: "My conscientious opinion is that I am bound to contribute to redressing an injustice, hence I relieved this gentleman of his purse and watch."

The newspaper that published all three contributions to the debate outlined its own position in a leader on 8 April 1916. While conceding that conscience was "a sacred thing", the editorial distinguished "between liberty to hold opinions as individuals and liberty to act upon them as members of a community". It cited the words of John Stuart Mill, a staunch defender of personal freedoms who nevertheless accepted that very distinction. Mill's assertion that "everyone who receives the protection of society owes a return for the benefit" was quoted, and it was also stated – in support of Knollys' contention – that society often ignores conscience-driven claims, such as might be expressed by anarchists. The same applied in civil matters, the raising of tax, for example. "Objection to taking life may be and is allowed as a valid plea," the piece concluded. "But objection to ambulance or hospital work or digging trenches justly exposes the holder to contempt." Those seeking exemption who found themselves on the receiving end of public opprobrium could scarcely complain when others expressed their own views, and that could not be deemed persecution.

ABDICATION OF THE CZAR.

Russia in revolt

All war leaders knew that the means to fight was of little use without the will to do so. Morale was vital to maintaining an effective fighting force. In manpower if not organisation, Russia's strength was enormous, matched by the scale of that country's sacrifice. No combatant suffered greater casualties. By the beginning of 1917, those losses added to a drip-effect erosion of the Russian people's desire to continue – not just with the war but with the dynastic Romanov rule dating back 300 years. The mood was for systemic change, born in the heat of battle but gestating over many decades.

Socialist revolutionaries had dreamed of sweeping away tsarist autocracy when Nicholas II's grandfather sat upon the imperial throne. Alexander II acknowledged the need for reform, releasing over 20 million from bondage when he ended serfdom in 1861. For the peasant class that effectively meant the freedom to remain poor, for they were denied the land they believed was their due. Most accepted their lot fatalistically, leading those who tried to foment rebellion to a stark conclusion: that the disadvantaged masses were too apathetic to mobilise, and that the bounteous gifts of revolution would have to be imposed upon them.

Every liberalising move was a step too far for landowning conservatives, not far or fast enough for those wanting root-and-branch change. Great disparity and a sense of injustice bred dissent, and with the vested interests including the Orthodox Church, direct action was inevitable. Alexander II –

the "Liberator" – was among the many assassination victims. His successor, Alexander III, was a man with somewhat less reforming zeal, and he too faced an attempt on his life in 1887. This time it was the plotters who fared worse. Among those executed was the brother of teenage Vladimir Ilyich Ulyanov, whose revolutionary mission now had a personal element. Better known as Lenin, he was leading a political party based on Marxist philosophy by the turn of the century. His was not the only left-wing group to be formed. Some favoured campaigning to change the system, others advocated more precipitate means. In 1903 Lenin's own socialist camp suffered a schism over how best to bring about the proletarian revolution. Lenin favoured a hard-line approach, a movement led by a cadre of dedicated activists. That number included Joseph Stalin, a Georgian who had studied at a seminary before becoming radicalised and adopting his "Man of Steel" surname. The faction Lenin headed and Stalin supported took its name from the Russian word for majority: Bolshevik. The minority Mensheviks, who argued for broadening the level of support, included Leon Trotsky. These and other radical groups did not escape the watchful eye of the secret police.

Nicholas II acceded to the throne in 1894, aged 26, facing the same problem as his immediate forebears: how to advance to keep pace with other industrial powerhouses, while looking backwards for the model of imperial authority. The Tsar believed in absolute rule invested in him through God. He considered himself the nation's patriarch and had an unshakeable faith in his own judgment, for mortal decisions had the seal of divine approval. In

exercising that judgment he was warmly encouraged by his consort, Alexandra, a German-born princess who was a favourite granddaughter of Queen Victoria. Their standing with the Russian people was dented when a crush during their coronation festivities claimed hundreds of lives, yet the royal couple continued with their plans to attend a gala ball. More troubled times lay ahead.

Nicholas and Alexandra had four daughters before a male heir, Alexei, was born in 1904. There was uncertainty as to whether the Tsarevich would survive to gain his birthright for he was a haemophiliac, a little-understood congenital condition where everyday bumps and bruises might have fatal consequences. Health scares over the child played a part in loosening the Romanov grip on the levers of power, for it cemented Grigori Rasputin's place in the royal court. An illiterate Siberian peasant with a dubious past, Rasputin was well known to the police, but after being introduced to the Tsar and Tsarina he quickly became untouchable. His entreé into the inner circle of the imperial household was based on claims to have special powers. On more than one occasion Nicholas and Alexandra believed he had saved Alexei's life, placing great faith in him as a sage and healer. The Tsarina, a religious zealot, fell under the spell of this miracle-worker, and rumours even circulated of an improper relationship. Rasputin's influence was viewed with alarm, even by staunch monarchists. The left was also agitating. Loyalty to the crown was at issue, and in 1905 discontent reached flashpoint on the streets of St Petersburg.

Russia was reeling from military defeat to Japan, seen by many as a symptom of the malaise infecting the country. Even if the war had gone well, there were activists who were not about to be swayed by the outcome. Matters were too far gone for victory to arouse patriotic fervour and a show of national unity. Defeat merely made an unsettled populace even readier to voice its protest. Those who took to the streets on 22 January 1905 were petitioning for greater rights and improved working conditions. Many carried pictures of the Tsar, content for him to remain in place if reforms were implemented. What began as a peaceful demonstration outside St Petersburg's Winter Palace turned ugly as troops opened fire. Estimates of the number killed on "Bloody Sunday" vary from one hundred to thousands. Nicholas was not present to witness the bloodbath, but felt the backlash as a wave of unrest swept the land. His uncle became the latest assassination victim; the crew of the battleship *Potemkin* mutinied at Odessa when presented with tainted food; there were widespread strikes; railways fell into rebel hands, paralysing the transport system; workers councils – soviets – were formed. The Tsar was advised to make concessions. He responded by issuing the October Manifesto, granting various freedoms and assenting to the establishment of Russia's first elected legislative body, the Duma. Moderates were satisfied, while the more extreme factions remained unconvinced. The latter were vindicated as the October Manifesto was much diluted by the time it was enacted, and the Duma revealed to be a toothless sop to those seeking democratic reform. The Tsar dissolved the assembly as it suited, the first after just 73 days when it had the temerity to suggest handing land to the peasants. Only when voting rights had been skewed to favour the election of the property-owning class – assured conservative loyalists – did it run for a full term. Many dissidents were arrested or exiled, and ultimate power remained at the imperial centre.

GREAT EVENTS IN RUSSIA.

COMPLETE OVERTHROW OF GERMAN INFLUENCE.

THE PEOPLE AND THE ARMY AT ONE WITH THE ALLIES.

DUMA'S PROVISIONAL GOVERNMENT.

REGENT APPOINTED.

The Czar has abdicated. This is the news that comes from Russia after three days' silence.

His brother the Grand Duke Michael Alexandrovitch is regent for the young Czarevitch, with a provisional Government of the Duma, Army, and people in power—a Government that is at one with the Allies and is determined to win the war.

A benign revolution has taken place in Russia to rid her of the pro-German and reactionary elements which made use of the horrible Rasputin, as explained in Mr. Hamilton Fyfe's long despatch in *The Daily Mail* of February 1.

The Duma or Parliament on Monday declared a Provisional Government. Prince Lvoff, a notable upholder of the Alliance, is the new Premier.

The Duma sent two warnings to the Czar, telling him delay meant death. No answer was received. The leading generals at the front sent the Czar similar messages.

Details of the abdication are not yet known.

The Army, including the Czar's own bodyguard, joined the Duma and the people.

Moscow and other cities have joined the National Government.

The first demonstrations on Sunday led to bloodshed, but by yesterday Petrograd was calm, and the officers have gone back to the front.

The new Government has sent all the armies on the various fronts orders to carry on face to the foe. That is being done.

Opposite below right: Lenin returned from his 20-year exile in April 1917 and published his *April Theses*, his directives for the Bolshevik party.

Opposite below left: Provisional Government forces open fire on Bolshevik protestors in Petrograd in July 1917. The Bolsheviks spent five days instigating spontaneous protests against the Provisional Government and made an unsuccessful attempt to turn these into a coup, forcing Lenin back into hiding.

Opposite above left: With their banners held high the soldiers of the Keksgolm Regiment stage a protest on the streets of Petrograd in October 1917.

Opposite above right: France's General Balfourier talks to English and Russian officers while flanked by those from Serbia and Japan.

This page: At Toulon bread and other supplies are handed out to Russian soldiers who are bound for the Western Front.

Another brutal winter

The Fourth Duma, still dominated by reactionaries but with a radical presence, had been in session for two years when the Sarajevo assassination occurred. War brought a brief window of national fervour, after which the Duma became increasingly critical of the way it was being prosecuted. And when Nicholas added supreme commander to his tsarist powers in 1915, it made him a target for disapproval if things went badly. A man who believed himself empowered through God was no more attracted to the idea of constitutional monarchy now than he had been during the crisis of 1905. As Russia entered her third wartime winter – brutal even by that country's standards – the situation on both the domestic and battle fronts was becoming desperate. There were bread queues and fuel shortages, sometimes down to inept management of available supplies. Taxes and prices rose. As ever, the peasant class suffered most. Strike action increased, as did desertion from the battle zone by war-weary troops. An Allied delegation arrived early in 1917 to discuss campaign plans for the year ahead, but British ambassador Sir George Buchanan read the danger signals and urged the Tsar to try to regain the trust of the people. He was waved away, along with the Duma leader, who warned that if no remedial action was taken, "the destruction of Russia and the dynasty is inevitable".

By then the royal couple had lost the services of their vaunted mystic. With Nicholas preoccupied by military strategy, the Tsarina had taken control of the affairs of state, and her faith in Rasputin meant she deferred to him on a range of policy issues. Senior loyalists had failed to remove Rasputin by appeal, so in December 1916 they took matters into their own hands. Court insider Prince Felix Yusupov was the knife-wielding chief conspirator; or more accurately the man who administered poison – which appeared to have no effect – then shot Rasputin before dumping his body in a frozen river. Removing an individual regarded as having a damaging influence on the monarchy was to the plotters an act of nobility and patriotism. Nicholas saw it as a flagrant challenge to his imperial authority and sent Yusupov into exile.

The end of Romanov rule

By early March there was open protest on the streets of Petrograd, the new name of the administrative capital since 1914, replacing German-sounding St Petersburg. The city's garrison was charged with dealing with the rioting hordes, a sea of red: the colour of revolution. En masse the troops joined the protesters, the latest error of judgment by the Tsar, and this time a fatal miscalculation. He might have believed he was God's instrument, but the enforcers of his and the Almighty's will had switched their allegiance. Nicholas had no better joy with the Duma, which refused the latest dissolution command. Within days he was gone. To the last he sought to protect the dynasty by handing power to his brother, Mikhail. That arrangement crumbled in a matter of hours. Three hundred years of Romanov rule was at an end.

There were bread queues and fuel shortages, sometimes down to inept management of available supplies.

RASPUTIN'S DEATH.

PALACE OCCUPANTS' "SHOTS IN SELF-DEFENCE."

From a Special Correspondent.

PETROGRAD, Thursday.

Further details about the death of the monk Gregory Rasputin (who exercised an evil influence in high Russian circles) largely tend to corroborate the accounts I have already quoted. It is surmised that six persons were present at supper at the palace here of Prince Youssoupoff on the fatal evening of Friday last, and the theory that more than one took part in killing Rasputin is borne out by the statement that three wounds were found in his body inflicted by bullets of different calibre.

Judging from the position of the trail of blood in the neighbourhood of the tragedy the victim was not killed by the first shot, but attempted to escape, till the third bullet laid him low. His assailants attached a weight to the body before throwing it from the Petrovsky Bridge into the Neva, but in falling the body struck projecting timbers and the shock detached the weight. The body was carried some distance by the current before being drawn under the ice.

Some papers report that the legal proceedings in connection with Rasputin's death will shortly be discontinued, because his assailants were acting in self-defence. The persons who were subjected to domiciliary detention were released on Tuesday morning.

Rasputin's body has been conveyed to the mortuary of the Chesdensk almshouse, five miles from Petrograd, in order to remove it beyond the range of public curiosity. The dead monk's flat in Gorokhovaya-street is being closely guarded. All the rooms and documents have been sealed.

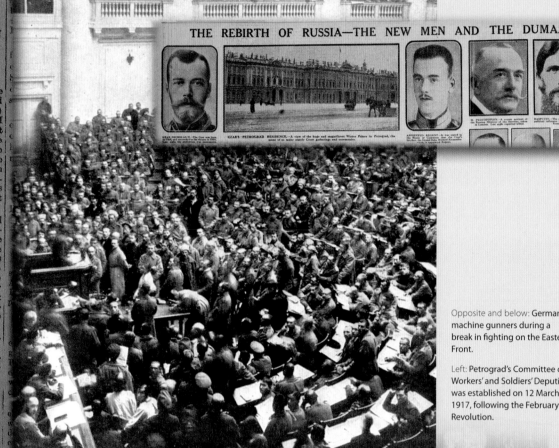

THE REBIRTH OF RUSSIA—THE NEW MEN AND THE DUMA.

Opposite and below: German machine gunners during a break in fighting on the Eastern Front.

Left: Petrograd's Committee of Workers' and Soldiers' Deputies was established on 12 March 1917, following the February Revolution.

BATTLE OF ARRAS RESUMED.

HAIG ATTACKS AGAIN.

OME GAINS BUT TERRIFIC RESISTANCE.

GERMAN LOSSES VERY HIGH.

OVER 1,500 PRISONERS

HINDENBURG'S TOWERS.

TREMENDOUS DEFENCE.

MASS OF LITTLE FORTS.

From W. BEACH THOMAS,
WAR CORRESPONDENTS' HEADQUARTERS,
FRANCE, Monday.

At dawn, after several days of bombardment of unusual precision and great banks atta...

had worked frantically, as if developing a new estate by substituting trenches for roads and machine-gun nests for villas. These were strewn everywhere in apparent disorder, but each was selected by virtue of some rise in the ground or command of an avenue of approach. T-shaped, Z-shaped, and E-shaped defences had been cut at night here, there, and everywhere, with cover for several machine guns and deep funk-holes for the gunner, whither he retired during our creeping barrage. Besides, there were villages and two wooded known as Sart and Vert, whose natu defences had been increased.

BRITISH AIRSHIP LOST.

DESCENT IN FLAMES SEEN IN THE STRAITS.

ADMIRALTY, Monday.
One of H.M. airships left on patrol from an east coast air station on Saturday morning and has not returned. Reports received ...ship was seen to descend in ...ts of Dover about noon ... An aeroplane or sea...

MR. BALFOUR MEETS MR. WILSON.

ALLIED CO-OPERATION WITH THE U.S.

From W. F. BULLOCK.
NEW YORK, Monday.
Everything, including the weather, is combining to render auspicious the first working day of the Balfour mission. Its arrival yesterday upon a perfect spring afternoon was a complete success.

This page: Troops in the trenches at St Quentin. General Pétain replaced Nivelle as Commander-in-Chief of the French forces on 15 May and decided to hold off from any major offensives until American troops were present on the front line.

Opposite top: The ruins of Pozières, with an abandoned German trench in the foreground. By May 1917 the French troops were tired, frustrated and disillusioned. Divisions began to mutiny, turning up for work drunk and without any weapons. These actions quickly spread to over fifty other divisions and about 30,000 men deserted their posts. Pétain quickly identified and punished the ringleaders but also improved the soldiers' living conditions and leave arrangements.

Opposite middle: The bell of Reims town hall lies abandoned but intact after the building was devastated by shellfire.

Opposite below: German explosives reduced the chateau at Caulaincourt to a pile of rubble.

May 1917

1 The Polish Council of State presented demands to the Central Powers regarding the creation of an independent Poland.

2 The first USA destroyer flotilla arrived at Queenstown in Cork, Ireland.

3 The Third Battle of the Scarpe and the Second Battle of Bullecourt began during the Arras Offensive.

4 French forces captured Craonne on the Chemin des Dames ridge.

5 A major military engagement was fought between the forces of the Central Powers and the Entente near Vardar as part of the Allied Spring Offensive, designed to break the stalemate on the Macedonian Front.

7 With support from Australian troops part of Bullecourt was seized by the British.

8 Germans recaptured Fresnoy on the Arras front.

9 French, Russian and Serbian troops launched a coordinated offensive in Macedonia, but Bulgarian and German defenders repulsed them.

10 Major General John J. Pershing was appointed to command the United States Expeditionary Force.

11 British and French war commissioners paraded down Fifth Avenue in America to celebrate the United States' entry into the war. The slogan "Show your colours" brought forth a patriotic flurry of Union Jacks, Tricolores and Stars and Stripes.

12 The Tenth Battle of the Isonzo began when once again Italian and Austro-Hungarian troops battled each other along the Isonzo River.

14 The German Zeppelin *L22* was destroyed in the North Sea by a British flying boat during a reconnaissance mission.

15 Fourteen British drifters were sunk in the Otranto Straits when British and Austrian naval forces clashed.

Philippe Pétain replaced Robert Nivelle as Commander-in-Chief of the French Army. He was tasked with turning back an imminent German offensive and quelling the mutinies in the French army.

17 Honduras severed diplomatic relations with Germany.

Following fierce German resistance the Second Battle of Bullecourt ended. Few of the initial objectives had been met.

18 The Compulsory Service Act became law in the United States. All American men aged 21-30 had to register for the draft.

19 The United States Government announced it would send a Division of the US Army to France.

20 Thanks to the actions of the French Commander-in-Chief, Philippe Pétain, a month of sporadic mutinies in the French army came to an end.

21 British troops captured the Siegfried line from Bullecourt to one mile east of Arras.

22 Brigadier-General Nash succeeded Sir Eric Geddes as Director-General of Transportation.

Count István Tisza resigned as Prime Minister of Hungary.

24 The British Royal Navy introduced a newly created convoy system, whereby all merchant ships crossing the Atlantic Ocean would travel in groups under the protection of the British navy.

25 Heavy casualties were sustained in a German aeroplane raid on Folkestone, Kent on the south-east coast of England.

26 *HMS Dover Castle* was torpedoed and sunk by the German submarine *UC-67* in the Mediterranean en route from Malta to Gibraltar.

28 An Anglo-French conference in London discussed the deposition of King Constantine of Greece and considered the occupation of Athens and Thessaly.

29 The French liner SS *Yarra* was torpedoed and sunk by the German submarine *UC-74* near Kreta in Greece.

30 The South African military commander General Jacob van Deventer succeeded Major General Reginald Hoskins in command of British forces in East Africa.

Right: Exhausted troops grasp the opportunity to get some sleep in this German dug-out on the Vimy Ridge.

Middle: By 1917 Britain and France had lost over half a million horses. As the conflict progressed, military leaders realised the mighty force of the cavalry charge was no longer a viable weapon when faced with deep trenches, barbed wire and deadly machine gun fire. However, horses were still invaluable for transporting materials to and from the frontline over the difficult terrain.

Below: British troops catch the motorbus back to their billets after the intense fighting at Monchy. Their trenching tools are hung on the backboard.

Opposite above: Canadian troops look cheerful after their triumph at Vimy Ridge.

Opposite below left: A shell bursts dangerously close to an advanced dressing station.

Opposite below right: Americans from the Foreign Legion on duty in a frontline trench. By joining this famous unit men from the United States were able to fight from the beginning of the war and took part in some of the fiercest battles.

DAILY MAIL JUNE 8, 1917
Haig strikes

We attacked at 3.10 a.m. the German positions on the Messines-Wytschaete Ridge [south of Ypres] on a front of over 9 miles. We have everywhere captured our first objectives, and further progress is reported to be satisfactory along the whole front of attack.

The Battle of Messines Ridge, as the sequel to the Battle of Vimy Ridge, will be almost the greatest battle in our history, if we keep what we have won. At the moment that I write our skied observers see German divisions in mass gathering for attack, but whatever may happen in the future it remains that we took what we meant to take exactly as we meant to take it and at the precise minute we meant to take it.

Left: The all too familiar landscape of the Western Front.

Below: Scottish troops load their equipment into the last of a long line of wagons.

Oppositeabove: German prisoners try to talk to their Canadian captors after the assault on Arieux. The distinctive coal scuttle shape of the German "Stahlhelm" steel helmet can be clearly seen .

Opposite below: British troops on the streets of Arras on 7 June 1917. Barbed wire entanglements line the centre of the road and some men begin to run to avoid shellfire.

June 1917

1 Zeebrugge, Ostend and Bruges were heavily bombed by the Royal Naval Air Service.

2 After some of its vessels were sunk by German submarines, Brazil revoked its neutrality and seized all German ships in Brazilian ports.

3 Italy proclaimed its Protectorate over independent Albania.

The Independent Labour Party and the Socialist Party met in Leeds to advocate a peace settlement. Among the attendees were future British Prime Minister Ramsay MacDonald and philosopher Bertrand Russell.

4 General Aleksei Brusilov succeeded Mikhail Alexeiev as Russian Commander-in-Chief.

5 German aeroplanes bombed the port of Sheerness and other Naval establishments on the Thames Estuary during daylight hours.

7 The Battle of Messines launched an Allied offensive near the village of Messines in Flanders. The battle began when a number of enormous underground mines were detonated under the Messines Ridge.

8 The Tenth Battle of the Isonzo was called off by Chief-of-Staff Luigi Cadorna with only minor territorial gains for the Italians.

9 The Russian Provisional Government refused a German proposal for unlimited armistice.

10 The Battle of Mount Ortigara began between Italian and Austro-Hungarian troops to gain possession of Mount Ortigara, on the Asiago Plateau.

11 Allied Governments delivered an ultimatum to Greece demanding the abdication of King Constantine I.

12 King Constantine I of Greece abdicated his throne in the face of pressure from Britain and France and internal opponents – including Greek Prime Minister Eleftherios Venizelos – who favoured Greece's entrance into the war on the side of the Allies.

13 US Major General John J. Pershing arrived in France.

German Gotha aircraft launched a major heavy bomber raid on London in daylight.

14 The German Zeppelin L43 was shot down by a British fighter aircraft during a reconnaissance mission in the North Sea.

The British Admiralty approved plans for the convoying of merchant ships.

15 The Espionage Act was passed in the United States. The act prohibited any attempt to interfere with military operations, to support US enemies during wartime, to promote insubordination in the military, or to interfere with military recruitment.

All Irish veterans of the Easter Rebellion still in custody were freed by the British government.

17 The German airship L48 was intercepted and destroyed by British fighters over the sea near Great Yarmouth.

18 Austrian Premier Count Heinrich Clam-Martinitz resigned.

19 General Arthur Currie was appointed to command the Canadian Corps.

20 The British Sloop HMS Salvia, operating as a Q-ship, was sunk by German submarine U-94 off the west coast of Ireland.

23 The P&O liner SS Mongolia struck a mine and sank off the coast of Bombay.

25 The first contingent of United States troops arrived at the port of Saint Nazaire in France.

An Austrian counterattack in Trentino recaptured Monte Ortigara.

27 Greece severed diplomatic relations with Germany, Austria-Hungary and Turkey and a state of war was declared.

28 General Edward Allenby succeeded Sir Archibald Murray in command of the Egyptian Expeditionary Force.

29 The Russian Summer Offensive began along a broad front in Galicia.

30 The British steamer SS Ilston was torpedoed and sunk by the German submarine UB-23 on a voyage from Swansea to France with a cargo of railway material.

HEAVIEST AIR FIGHTING OF THE WAR.

War in the air

Aeronautical technology moved on apace during the 1914-18 period, and with it the role of aircraft as an instrument of war altered radically. Compared with the giant, gas-filled airships with their large payloads, most of the heavier-than-air machines in service at the outbreak of hostilities were puny indeed. Typically around 25 feet long, with fabric stretched over wooden frames, these early aircraft were powered by small rotary or in-line engines that might propel a two-man crew through the air at 70mph. Nor were there many of them. The Royal Flying Corps had fewer than 50 machines at its disposal when the events in Sarajevo sparked the global conflict. Barely a decade on from the Wright brothers' breakthrough, the main military application of these flimsy, rudimentary craft was thought to be reconnaissance and observation – the new sky-riding cavalry scouts. Already the prewar opinion of French general Ferdinand Foch that aviation was fine as a sporting pursuit but offered nothing to the battlefield had been disproved. Reconnaissance aircraft were often defenceless apart from any small arms carried by the crew, but adding firepower was a logical step: there was a clear advantage in gathering intelligence on enemy positions while preventing rival aircraft from doing likewise.

Devastating Gotha bombers

The combination of height and gravity made aircraft an attractive proposition for dropping ordnance. Indeed, the first true bomber raid occurred in 1911, when tensions between Italy and Turkey boiled over. Initially, the available hardware couldn't meet military aspiration, small payload being the main drawback. Some early bombers were no more sophisticated than a crewman dropping explosives from the open cockpit by hand. The French Voisin that attacked Germany's Zeppelin sheds in autumn 1914 carried just 60kg of bombs, though all nations soon developed more powerful machines that increased that figure substantially. By 1917 the latest model of Germany's renowned Gotha bomber had almost ten times the carrying capacity of the Voisin, as London and other parts of east England discovered. The Handley Page, Britain's first dedicated bomber, more than matched the Gotha. This Rolls-Royce-powered giant with a 100-foot wingspan could deliver its 750kg payload a long way from home, thanks to its 650-mile range.

THE BIRTH OF A HUN AIR RAID: MACHINES READY FOR THE STARTING SIGNAL.—A squadron of dual-engined raiding planes drawn up at an aerodrome ready to start in formation on a bombing expedition to England.   [Berlin "War Pictures."

Reconnaissance aircraft

The notion of the fighter aircraft took longer to germinate. In the early days of the war the chief preoccupation was how to improve ground-to-air communication so that information could be transmitted from cockpit to commander as quickly as possible. Dropping weighted messages was among the methods employed until wireless telegraphy was adopted. Much thought was given to camera design and how they were mounted to give the best image quality of enemy positions. Early aerial reports helped the Germans prevail at the Battle of Tannenberg, while on the Western Front French pilots gave notice that the enemy had swept east of Paris, information that helped the Allies halt the German advance at the Marne.

The fact that that the aeroplane's role was "to see, not to fight", as one German officer put it, influenced design. Stability was the main requirement; speed and manoeuvrability were not key considerations for scouting and spotting missions where accurate observations and clear photographs were needed. Thus reconnaissance aircraft were highly vulnerable to ground fire. "I would not mind quite so much if I were in a machine that was fast and that could climb a little more willingly," said one pilot of his unnerving experience in the face of anti-aircraft shelling.

Opposite above left: British bombs destined for the Germans at Ostend. The first ones dropped from aircraft were very basic in design and only a limited number could be carried.

Opposite above middle: German officers make the final preparations before a Zeppelin raid.

Opposite above right: Initially, bombs were released by hand over the side of the aircraft and aimed in the general direction of the target, without any real accuracy.

Opposite below left: A group of German airmen proudly bearing their Iron Cross medals. The award was first introduced during the Napoleonic Wars, and was then re-authorized by Kaiser Wilhelm II in 1914. It was divided into three grades with the highest reserved for senior generals.

Opposite below inset: The German flying ace Baron von Richthofen's Jagdgeschwader 1 squadron is ready for action. He formed the unit in June 1917 and it soon

became known as "The Flying Circus" partly due to its brightly coloured planes and also the unit's method of moving from one area to another setting up tents to create temporary airfields.

Above: A French pilot uses a machine gun during a nosedive. Initial attempts to mount machine guns in the cockpit included "pusher" type aircraft, which had the engine and propeller sited behind the pilot and facing backwards. This allowed the gun to be fired forward without any obstruction from the propellor.

Below: A British perspective on the bombing exchanges published on 17 September. The map graphically shows how London was well within reach of German planes, while Allied raids on enemy aerodromes, railways, ammunition dumps and docks are also indicated.

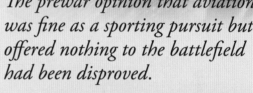

The prewar opinion that aviation was fine as a sporting pursuit but offered nothing to the battlefield had been disproved.

25 HUN PLANES DOWN.

BRITISH LOSE EIGHT.

From SIR DOUGLAS HAIG.

Sunday.

There was great activity in the air yesterday and a number of large enemy formations were engaged by our machines and dispersed. In the course of the fighting 7 hostile aeroplanes were brought down and 9 others driven down damaged. Eight of our machines are missing.

TOTAL CASUALTIES IN HUN AIR RAIDS ON LONDON AND SOUTH-EAST COAST DURING THE LAST 4 MONTHS — KILLED 492, INJURED 1117, TOTAL 1,609

LT.-GEN. SIR DAVID HENDERSON. Director of Army Aeronautics. [Official Sketch.]

MAJOR-GEN. HUGH M. TRENCHARD, C.B., D.S.O., commanding our Flying Corps in the Field. [Official Sketch.]

LIEUT.-COL. THOMSEN. Chief of the General Staff of the German Air Forces.

BIG AIR BATTLE.

20 HUNS DOWN AND 15 OF OURS.

ENEMY TRAINS HIT.

LITTLE GAIN NEAR ARRAS.

From Field-Marshal SIR D. HAIG.

Monday Morning.

In a small local operation between MONCHY-LE-PREUX and the SCARPE [eastward of Arras] we captured a few prisoners and improved our position during the night.

Our troops also carried out a successful raid north of YPRES, capturing 18 prisoners and a machine gun.

Monday Evening.

An attack made by the enemy during the day upon our new positions between MONCHY-LE-PREUX and the SCARPE River was completely repulsed.

Hostile artillery has been active on both banks of the Scarpe.

There was great activity in the air yesterday and during the night. Bombs were dropped with effect at a number of points behind the enemy's lines, causing several fires, and in one case a large explosion. Three enemy trains were also hit by our bombs.

The enemy fought hard to protect the points attacked, and in the course of the fighting 10 German aeroplanes were brought down and 10 others were driven down out of control.

Fifteen of our machines are missing.

RED CROSS AEROPLANE IN FLIGHT.—At 80 miles an hour no discomfort from vibration was felt by the "wounded." A height of only 500 feet is maintained so that the Red Cross may be plainly seen.   ["Daily Mail."

THE WAR WILL BE WON IN THE AIR.

Admirable in every respect, vigorous, true to life, specially timely in view of Lord Rothermere's declaration in favour of reprisals, and splendidly fresh is the story of "An Airman's Outings" (Blackwood, 5s. net), by "Contact," a flying man of renown.

None is more convinced than he that the war will be won in the air:

Towards the end of the war hostilities in the air will become as decisive as hostilities on land or sea . . . By the end of 1918 aircraft numbered in tens of thousands and with extraordinary capacity for speed, climb, and attack will make life a burden to ground troops, compromise lines of communication, cause repeated havoc to factories and strongholds, and promote loss of balance among whatever civilian populations come within range of their activity.

Those pundits who once disbelieved in air warfare are having its importance impressed on them in very painful wise, so that they will hardly question "Contact's" verdict. In another passage, precious for the very superior people who will hear nothing of bombing the Hun at home, he remarks that the damage done by aircraft at the front is "as much moral as material since nothing unnerves war-weary men more than to realise that they are never safe from aircraft."

*   *   *   *   *

Top: Troops guard the debris from two Gothas brought down over London in December 1917.

Right: Manfred von Richthofen, commanding officer of the Flying Circus, was often referred to as the Red Baron due to the colour of his aircraft. He was credited with 80 air combat victories during the war but was finally shot down on 21 April 1918.

Below left: Officers take charge of a German scout aeroplane brought down in April 1918.

Below right: A searchlight tower and a crow's nest form part of the air defences for Paris. In recent years it has been revealed that a "dummy Paris" was secretly built 15 miles north of the city centre to fool German bombers into believing they were targeting the centre of the capital. Replicas of the city's famous landmarks were erected with intricate lighting systems designed by electrical engineer Fernando Jacopozzi, the man who first illuminated the Eiffel Tower.

Opposite above: A German plane bears the iron cross symbol of the Deutsche Luftstreitkräfte (German Air Force). This military organisation was part of the German Army rather than a separate force but was dissolved in 1920 and all planes destroyed under the conditions of the Treaty of Versailles.

Opposite below: The British flying ace Billy Bishop in the cockpit.

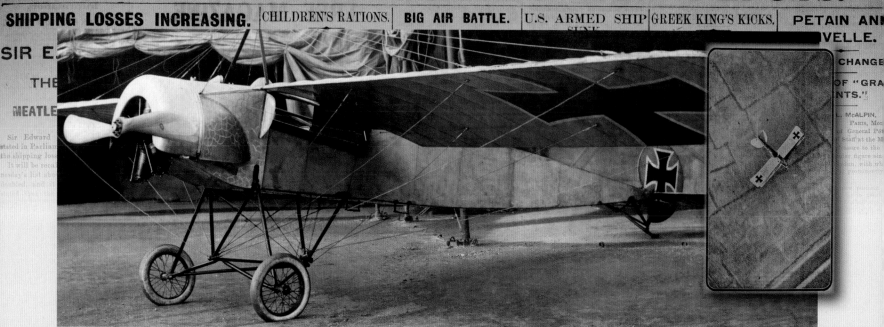

GREAT AIR ATTACK ON HUN DEPOTS.

SHIPPING LOSSES INCREASING. | CHILDREN'S RATIONS. | BIG AIR BATTLE. | U.S. ARMED SHIP | GREEK KING'S KICKS. | PETAIN AN

The "Fokker Scourge"

For self-protection and to give pilots the means to attack, machine guns were required. Some aircraft had rear-mounted propellers – "pushers" – and the field was clear to position a forward-facing gun in the cockpit. Front-mounted propellers offered superior performance, but also raised the prospect of a bullet striking a propeller blade. One answer was to mount the gun on the wing, which kept the bullets clear of the propeller but made reloading a cumbersome if not dangerous procedure. Another approach was to fire through a propeller fitted with deflectors to parry the bullets that struck it. The latter arrangement, first used by French ace Roland Garros early in 1915, was best in terms of siting the gun, but having bullets ricocheting off the piece of hardware keeping the plane airborne was clearly less than perfect. Max Immelman, one of Germany's most celebrated airmen, is thought to have plunged to his death in 1916 after a technical mishap saw his propeller disabled by his own gunfire. The ingenious solution to the problem came from Dutch designer Anthony Fokker. Working on behalf of the Germans, Fokker developed interrupter gear that synchronised machine-gun fire with propeller rotation. His Eindecker monoplane – the first to deploy the new system – temporarily gave Germany the edge in a seesawing development battle. The "Fokker Scourge", as it was called, would not last.

> *At the bleakest times Britain's Royal Flying Corps was losing men and machines at such an alarming rate that it was called the Suicide Club.*

Pilot's code of honour

With all bullets negotiating the propeller arc, the aircraft was now an even more potent weapon. It was but a small step for the rival air forces to form fighter squadrons and join battle in the skies above the Western Front, mirroring the attritional combat taking place on the ground beneath. Whatever the trenchbound Tommies may have thought, aerial jousting was no soft option. Gone were the days when enemy pilots gave each other a cheery wave and went about their business. The code of honour and mutual respect persisted, but this was no less a life and death struggle. At the bleakest times Britain's Royal Flying Corps was losing men and machines at such an alarming rate that it was called the Suicide Club. The Corps' nadir came in "Bloody April" 1917, when German Jasta squadrons inflicted heavy losses as their latest Albatros aircraft enjoyed a period of superiority. Of the 22,000 British pilots who saw service in World War One, over half joined the casualty list. At one stage the average survival time for a new RFC pilot was less than two weeks, his plight made worse than his French and German counterparts in that parachutes were deemed superfluous. They added unnecessary weight and bulk, and might have encouraged pilots to bail out prematurely. If disaster befell them it seemed they were expected to follow the naval precedent and go down with their vessel. Many pilots did not even make it to battle stations, some 8,000 perishing during training.

Survival was down to good aircraft, providence and skill. The first two were beyond the airman's control, but dexterity in handling the plane and shrewd tactical awareness skewed the odds significantly. Pilots learned to use sun, cloud and altitude to advantage, and although lone-wolf operations retained a romantic appeal, it quickly became clear that operating as a unit was more effective. From the dogfights that played out above the pockmarked battlefields a new breed of hero was brought to the public's attention.

CANADIAN AIRMAN RECEIVES V.C., D.S.O., AND M.C.—Captain W. A. Bishop, R.F.C., who has brought down over 40 Hun machines, decorated by the King yesterday.

OUR AIRMEN PAYING BACK THE HUNS.

| DUS RAIDS IN | FRENCH ATTACK. | MORE PIGS AND | 12 BIG SHIPS SUNK. | HUN BOOTY IN |
| RMANY. | DEEP INTO HUN LINES. | POTATOES. | BRITISH LOSS LAST WEEK. | RUSSIA. |

OVER 400 PRISONERS.

ORKS AND FACTORIES.

From GENERAL PETAIN.

Wednesday Night.

In Lorraine north of Bures and east of

BEST WAY TO INCREASE FOOD.

USE FOR TOWN WASTE.

Admiralty return of last week's British shipping losses:

'HUNDREDS OF GUNS.'

The Germans have replied to the offer of Lenin and Trotsky, sent by wireless, to sign peace on the German terms that their dispatch cannot be regarded as authentic as it lacks the original signatures. The Russians have replied that a confirmatory

"FORCED DOWN."—A Hun 'plane photographed just as it struck the ground when forced down by French airmen.

Opposite above: A German plane is photographed minutes after French airmen force it to the ground.

Below left: Troops on the Western Front watch for enemy aircraft overhead.

Below middle: A cavalryman aims a Hotchkiss gun at an enemy airman. These machine guns, predominantly used by the French and the Americans, were very sturdy and reliable, weighed 24kg and had a range of over two miles.

Below right: This Lewis anti-aircraft gun is fixed on a cartwheel that revolves on its axis set into a socket on the ground. These guns were popular weapons for anti-aircraft defence as they were light, air-cooled and had their own 97-round drum magazines.

Top: An early German Fokker plane designed by the Dutch engineer Anthony Fokker. When the war began he set up a factory in Germany to supply the German Army and as the war progressed developed a synchronization gear so machine gun bullets could be fired between the propeller blades.

Above left and middle: Life expectancy for pilots was low but many of the accidents occured during training rather than in combat situations.

Above right: Members of the Royal Flying Corps in India receive and record an airman's message from the sky.

Left: This German scouting aeroplane was used by the British, hence the markings. In February 1918 it was on display in Cairo.

Right: A German seaplane ready for take-off.

Below left: Lieutenant D Dening from the 42nd Kite Balloon Section secures his parachute harness. Kite balloons were positioned a few miles behind the frontline and tethered to the ground by cable with a telephone line attached. The structures could rise to a height of 5,000 feet and report enemy movement to colleagues below. It was a hazardous job and the crew members were highly trained.

AMERICAN TROOPS IN FRANCE.

TERS.	DURHAMS' MODEL ATTACK.	BIG SHIPS DOWN.	80,000 MORE MEN.	EIGHT
AT A	WONDERFUL BIG GUN.	21 AGAINST 27.	ARMY FOR THE LAND.	MACHINE-GU

DURHAMS' MODEL ATTACK.

WONDERFUL BIG GUN.

From W. BEACH THOMAS.

WAR CORRESPONDENTS' HEADQUARTERS, FRANCE, Wednesday.

Some troops from Durham, who with others have received a whole-hearted letter of congratulation, have put to their

BIG SHIPS DOWN.

21 AGAINST 27.

P. & O. LINER SUNK OFF BOMBAY.

British Ships Sunk.   Unsuccessfully   All Ships U.K. Ports.

80,000 MORE MEN.

ARMY FOR THE LAND.

House of Lords, Wednesday.

From one source or another 70,000 to 80,000 additional men have been secured for the land to aid farmers in the great task of increasing the home supply of wheat and bringing 3,000,000 addi-

EIGHT

MACHINE-GU

PONTOON H

The following aw Cross for conspicu nou_ced in a supp Gazette:—

Lt. Robert Grierson (killed).

He led his compa

Opposite above left and this page below left: Parisians turn out in force to welcome US troops as they parade through the capital in July 1917. These men were often nicknamed "Sammies" in a reference to Uncle Sam.

Opposite above right: The first batch of US soldiers arrives in France.

Opposite below left and this page top: Londoners give the Americans a warm reception as they march through the city towards Buckingham Palace.

Opposite below right: American soldiers stop for dinner at a training camp in France. After rigorous training in the States, they received an additional induction before heading for the frontline.

Right: The companion lion outside Portsmouth's Town Hall wears "Old Glory".

Bottom left: US troops joined the Allies on the frontline just as the Spring Offensive was coming to an end, bringing their much-needed fresh troops to fight alongside the weary men already stationed there.

Bottom right: Arrows indicate Allied progress near Lens in the last week of June.

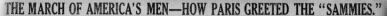

THE MARCH OF AMERICA'S MEN—HOW PARIS GREETED THE "SAMMIES."

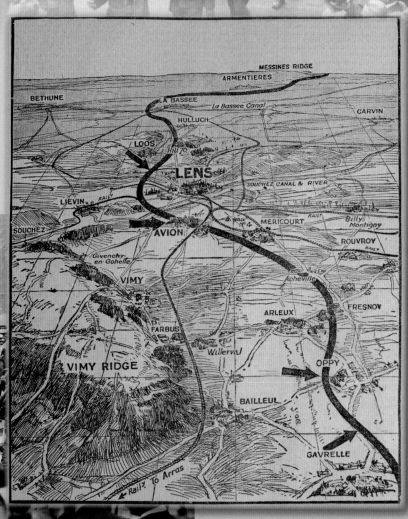

Planes raid London

Improvements in Britain's air defence system largely neutralised the Zeppelin threat as the conflict wore on, exposing the inherent weaknesses of these lumbering giants. Sporadic airship raids continued into 1918, though for the last 18 months of war German aeroplanes presented the greater aerial menace. On 25 May 1917 the inhabitants of Folkestone bore the brunt of the first sortie by Gotha IV bombers, an attack mounted in broad daylight that resulted in almost 100 fatalities. The capital witnessed a midday raid on 13 June, the first time enemy aircraft had targeted London without the cloak of darkness. Eighteen children were killed in a direct hit on Upper North Street School in Poplar, most of them under the age of six. Fifteen were buried in a mass grave. Elsewhere, a police constable sacrificed himself in trying to protect a group of warehouse workers. An engineer received a telegram calling him home, where he learned that his infant daughter was dead and his mother seriously injured. She later succumbed. A bootmaker lost his wife and four of his seven children. There was further loss of life when bombs struck a train and a brass foundry. The death toll reached 162, making this the single worst bombing attack of the war. Not one of the Gothas was downed.

By autumn 1917 more effective air defences – including the deployment of Sopwith Camels and extensive use of barrage balloons – forced the German bombers to abandon daylight raids and return to night-time operations. One such rocked the capital once again on the evening of 28 January 1918, claiming over 60 lives. It was not a Gotha but one of the R-class Giant bombers that wreaked the most havoc. A massive bomb exploded near the Odhams printing works, not far from the Strand. The building was set ablaze, killing 38.

Increasing German losses brought a temporary suspension to such operations, and thereafter the country's aerial firepower was primarily devoted to supporting the last-ditch bid for victory on the Western Front. There was one final large-scale air assault on the night of 19 May, a month after the Royal Flying Corps and Royal Navy Air Service merged to form the Royal Air Force. It added 49 to the overall death toll, though British fighters and anti-aircraft gunners accounted for six enemy aircraft. In all, 1,413 people were killed in German bombing raids, a tiny figure in comparison with the carnage across the Channel but highly significant in marking both a turning point and signpost in the conduct of war: that civilians far from the theatre of operations were reachable and considered a justifiable target.

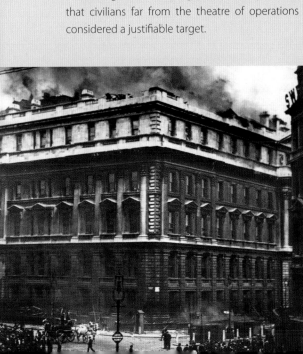

Opposite top left: Shrapnel-proof helmets were issued to London special constables for use during air raids.

Opposite top right: In July 1917 policemen began to patrol the streets carrying notices displaying the message "Police Notice-Take Cover" if an air raid was expected. They blew whistles as they walked and afterwards Boy Scouts toured the area blasting on bugles to give the all clear.

Opposite middle left: The shaded part on the map shows the area covered in recent months by the German aeroplane raiders. The mileage from Zeebrugge is shown by semi-circular lines and the towns which were bombed from May to September are indicated.

Opposite middle right: 210 Well Hall Road in Eltham was hit in August, killing all four inhabitants.

Opposite below left and below middle: The Central Telegraph Office in London was bombed during a daylight raid. Thanks to an air raid warning system nobody was hurt but it brought down the roof and temporarily suspended the telegraph system.

Opposite below right: Damage is caused to the Sphinx on the Thames Embankment after an air raid in September.

Top left: A family reads a notice offering the use of a cellar during air raids.

Top right: Pedestrians watch for signs of German planes during a raid on London.

Above left: The Little Theatre in the Adelphi, London was hit but eventually rebuilt after the war.

Above middle and right: A memorial for the eighteen children killed in a school in Poplar was built from local donations and unveiled in June 1919.

Below: Over 600 wreaths were presented at the Poplar school children's funeral service led by the Bishop of London.

Below left: Mothers and their children injured during the raids.

WOMEN'S WORK IN THE AEROPLANE FACTORIES

COVERING THE WINGS OF AEROPLANES.—The most important part of an aeroplane is the engine, the construction of which calls for the utmost accuracy. Women are now entrusted with much of this work, and are undertaking processes which are often carried out to an accuracy of half-a-thousandth of an inch. They are also employed in sewing work in connection with the wings, the painting or "doping," and the milling. Above, girls are seen at work covering aeroplane wings with fine linen.

WOMEN'S WORK ON AEROPLANES.—Since Lord Derby made an appeal for 6,000 women to help to make aeroplanes for our flying services, a very large number of women workers have entered various aeroplane factories and are doing extraordinarily good work. A busy scene in an engine fitting shop.

ENLARGEMENTS of Official War Pictures on the Western Front.—Cut the picture you wish to have enlarged from a newspaper and post with remittance, giving the date on which it appeared, to War Picture Dept., "Daily Mail," Carmelite House, London, E.C. 4.   Size : 8 by 6 inches, 1/6 ; 12 by 10 inches, 2/6 ; 15 by 12 inches, 3/6.

13 WOMEN KILLED.

SOLDIERS' WIVES IN EXPLOSION.

By an explosion and fire in the Ajax Chemical Company's factory at Barking on Thursday evening, 13 women and girls lost their lives and a few others were injured.

The following are the killed, all the addresses being East Ham except where otherwise stated :—

Mrs. Gurry, 52, Talbot-rd.
Mrs. England, 10, Washington-rd., Upton Park.
Mrs. Stevens, 98, Napier-rd.
Mrs. King, Arthur-rd.
Mrs. Abbott, 5, Caulfield-rd.
Mrs. Maskell, same address.
Mrs. E. Smith, 7, Bartle-avenue.
Miss Clarke, Parkhurst-rd., Manor Park.
Miss Rainbow, Hardwick-st., Barking.
Mrs. Foley, 50, Hockley-rd.
Mrs. Webb, Talbot-rd.
Miss Knight, 112, Walton-rd., Manor Park.
Miss Alice Cole, 12, Howard's-rd., Barking.

Two injured women, Mrs. Florence Wales and Mrs. Sarah Stephens, are still in the hospital.

The works stand in flat, open country, hard by Barking Creek. Large allotment fields divide them from a row of houses, a quarter of a mile away. The building involved was one of brick and concrete, two stories high and about 60ft. by 30ft. in dimension. A narrow roadway separates it from the other buildings of the works.

It was divided into four "shops," as the workrooms are called, two on each floor. Between 30 and 40 women and girls were employed in it, with three lads to fetch and carry. Their work was delicate and they wore rubber shoes to avoid the danger of explosion.

About six o'clock, just as the women were getting ready to leave for the day, a dull explosion occurred in one of the upper rooms. A bluish, suffocating smoke arose and it was followed instantly by a fierce blaze, which shot outwards through the open windows. Women in the yard screamed in alarm, and Mr. Cox, an official of the works, ran into the burning building. Two girls and a boy jumped from windows, one of the girls injuring herself so badly by the fall that she had to be taken to the emergency hospital. Women from the upper floor escaped by a fire ladder; those on the ground floor were all out in a minute or two.

GIRL ENGINEERS.

We work automatic machines, but we are [not] thought worthy of being trained to do highly [skil]led work or to design," complained a girl [en]gineer" the other day. It was the truth. [The] engineering workshops have been flooded [wit]h women who do simple operations under the [sup]ervision of skilled men. Many of them are [inte]llectually superior to their supervisors.

[I]n the early days of the war, when quick [ada]ptation was a first consideration, this was [und]erstandable, but conditions have altered. [The] war machine is now running smoothly, and [we] ought to consider if we cannot utilise the [lab]our of women to greater advantage. If a [littl]e foresight had been exercised three years [ago], and girls of fifteen or sixteen had been ap[pre]nticed to the highly skilled sections of the [engin]eering industry, a great and increasing num[ber] of men would have been liberated for the [arm]y. Instead, however, we have thousands of [you]ng men in their teens and early twenties in [mu]nition works who cannot be spared.

[T]he Government advertise for women who are [will]ing to be trained at certain centres as fit[ters], electricians; and draughtswomen, but [ever]yone knows that these recruits will be "one-[job]" artisans. They will be specialists in the [nar]rowest sense. Specialisation is necessary [now]adays, but the successful specialist is he, or [she,] whose specialised and expert skill has [spru]ng out of a wide knowledge of a craft.

[It] would be a national calamity if women [wer]e to be driven out of engineering after the [war.] There is a general recognition among [thin]king people that they have come to stay. [The]y have proved a great asset, and in the days [of s]tress to come the nation that will soonest [reco]ver from the effects of the war will be that [one] which to the fullest extent utilises its re[sour]ces.

GENERAL OFFICES.

Opposite above: **Women working in an aeroplane factory cover wings with fine linen and apply varnish to the different sections (opposite below right).**

Opposite below left: **Winston Churchill addresses munitions workers in Glasgow after becoming Minister of Munitions in July 1917. He re-joined the British Army after the Dardanelles Campaign and commanded a battalion of the Royal Scots Fusiliers on the Western Front. Lloyd George subsequently called him back to the Cabinet to oversee the production of arms.**

Top right: **In France women were employed in shell factories to replace absent men.**

Top left: **Members of the Elsie Inglis unit of the Scottish Women's Hospitals Organisation leave Buckingham Palace after an inspection by the King and Queen.**

Above right: **Members of the Land Army set off for work in Lincolnshire.**

Left: **A woman operates the cinema lantern in the North London Picture Palace.**

Below: **A man works his seam of peat in Somerset. During the conflict a mixture of peat and coke was recommended as a substitute for coal for use in kitchens.**

July 1917

1   Russian troops, under the command of General Brusilov, began an offensive against Austro-Hungarian and German forces in Galicia, pushing toward Lemberg.

2   British and German representatives signed an agreement at the Hague for the exchange of combatant and civilian prisoners of war.

3   The British steamer *SS City Of Cambridge* was sunk by the German submarine *UC-67*, 10 miles northwest of Jijelli on a voyage from Alexandria to London.

4   A concerted German submarine attack on United States transport vessels was defeated.

6   The Battle of Aqaba was fought for the Jordanian port of Aqaba. The attacking forces of the Arab Revolt, led by Auda ibu Tayi and T. E. Lawrence (Lawrence of Arabia), were victorious over the Turkish defenders.

7   In a sustained German air raid 22 Gotha bombers attacked London and Margate in Kent.

8   US President Woodrow Wilson ordered an embargo on the exportation of food, fuel and war supplies.

9   The British battleship HMS *Vanguard* suffered an internal explosion and sank whilst at anchor at Scapa Flow.

10 After intense bombardment German forces gained ground near the mouth of the Yser and destroyed parts of two British battalions.

12 Austen Chamberlain resigned as Secretary of State for India following inquiries into the failure of various British campaigns in Mesopotamia including the loss of the British garrison at Kut.

14 German Chancellor Theobald von Bethmann Hollweg resigned and was replaced by Georg Michaelis.

15 The Constitutional Democratic Party (Kadets) walked out of the Russian Provisional Government, threatening the Mensheviks and the Socialist Revolutionaries with the breakup of the governing coalition.

16 Militant soldiers, sailors and factory workers began spontaneous demonstrations in Petrograd.

T.E. Lawrence and the Arabs liberated Aqaba in Jordan after crossing the Nefu desert, and opened the route north for the Arab Army.

17 King George V issued a Royal Proclamation changing the name of his family from the German *Saxe-Coburg-Gotha* to the English *Windsor* due to anti-German sentiment in Britain.

18 The uprising in Petrograd collapsed. The government arrested several Bolshevik leaders and Lenin went into hiding.

19 The German Reichstag passed a resolution regarding their war aims.

20 The Corfu Declaration was signed on the island of Corfu by the Yugoslav Committee of exiled politicians from Croatia, Montenegro, Serbia and Slovenia. The agreement called for the unification of a Kingdom of Yugoslavia.

21 Alyeksandr Fyodorovich Kerensky replaced Prince Georgy Yevgenyevich Lvov as Prime Minister of Russia.

22 Siam declared a state of war with Germany and Austria-Hungary.

23 The British armed merchant cruiser HMS *Otway* was torpedoed and sunk off the Hebrides by German submarine *UC-49*.

24 German and Austro-Hungarian forces captured Stanislau and Tarnopol in Galicia.

25 An Inter-Allied conference met in Paris to discuss the Balkan situation with regard to a possible Russian collapse.

    The exotic dancer Mata Hari (Margaretha Geertruida Zelle) was sentenced to death by a French court for spying on Germany's behalf.

27 British troops occupied a section of the abandoned German front line at Ypres.

28 The British Tank Corps was established, replacing its predecessor the Heavy Branch of the Machine Gun Corps.

30 German and Austro-Hungarian forces recaptured Zeleszczyki in Galicia.

31 The Battle of Passchendaele (the Third Battle of Ypres) began along the Western Front for control of the ridges south and east of the Belgian city of Ypres in West Flanders.

Haig plans Third Battle of Ypres

Ypres witnessed its first bloody battle in autumn 1914 as both armies fought to gain the upper hand during the "race to the sea". Germany launched a second month-long offensive at the Ypres salient the following spring, when chemical weapons so nearly broke the stalemate. It left Allied troops disadvantaged, facing an enemy occupying the surrounding high ground. As plans were drawn up for the 1917 campaign, Sir Douglas Haig became wedded to the idea of a grand undertaking focused on that same patch of ravaged Flanders terrain.

The appalling losses suffered at the Somme led some to doubt the wisdom of yet another large-scale assault on the Western Front. David Lloyd George, who replaced Asquith as prime minister in December 1916, was firmly in that camp. He favoured taking the fight to the enemy on the Italian front, striking at Germany's junior partner, Austria. Though that idea received little support, Lloyd George was adamant that there should be no great Haig-led offensive on the Western Front in 1917.

A change at the top in France's command structure seemed to give the British premier exactly what he wanted. General Robert Nivelle – hero of Verdun – replaced Joffre as commander-in-chief of the French army and he bullishly outlined his idea for a spring breakthrough at Chemin des Dames, in the Champagne region. It would be achieved in 48 hours, said Nivelle; honeyed words to the ears of those desperate to avoid a rerun of the Somme catastrophe. It was such cheering news that no one scrutinised the small print to determine how exactly the Verdun success was to be replicated on a much larger scale. Lloyd George was among the cheerleaders. He warmly endorsed a plan that had British troops playing the support role – they would occupy German reserves by attacking at Arras – and which held the added attraction of making Haig subordinate to his French counterpart. It did nothing to defrost the mutual antipathy that existed between the head of the coalition government and Britain's senior army commander. Haig had little choice but to occupy the back seat and watch a disaster unfold that would breathe new life into his own design.

Nivelle Offensive fails

The Nivelle Offensive was stillborn. Its author's hopes for a massive bombardment followed by a rapid infantry advance behind a creeping barrage died with Germany's early-year retreat to the well fortified Hindenburg Line. The ground Nivelle planned to occupy was given gratis, yet still the plan went ahead. By now there were doubters, but Nivelle's stock was still high – high enough for him to flaunt a resignation letter under the government's nose if his undertaking was not implemented. Not for long, though. A security breach alerted the Germans to what was afoot, and an ineffectual bombardment put paid to what was already a long-odds bet. Nivelle's campaign ground on for almost a month, the disappointment made all the more bitter by the persuasive optimism with which it had been sold. It was a failure too far for the French ranks. Dissenting voices spilled over into widespread mutinous action. Pétain replaced the discredited Nivelle and took charge of a desperate fire-fighting situation. He restored order with a combination of carrot and stick: conditions were improved, while a few dozen executions were carried out to discourage further dissent. Most importantly, a moratorium was put on profligate offensives that shed much blood and achieved little.

Haig's authority was restored, and his own Flanders initiative now took centre stage. Lloyd George, chastened by his backing for the failed Nivelle scheme, felt he had to defer to his military strategists. He harboured reservations about Haig's plan, but it was the only one on the table, the default option. Besides, backing the enterprise came with an insurance policy: the plug could be pulled if it threatened to go the way of the Somme.

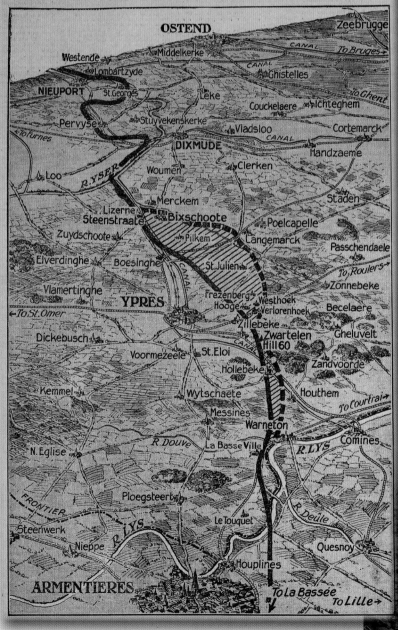

MAP OF THE NEW ALLIED ADVANCE

Left: **Men from the Durham Light Infantry dig trenches during the Third Battle of Ypres. After three months of fighting the village of Passchendaele was finally captured but at the cost of over 300,000 Allied casualties.**

Opposite: **The bodies of dead German artillerymen lay abandoned after the Battle of Pilckem Ridge.**

GREATEST BRITISH BATTLE BEGUN.

HAIG STRIKES.

SINES RIDGE STORMED.

MILES OF DEFENCES TAKEN.

ER 5,000 PRISONERS.

IC MINES AND NEW "ENGINES."

m FIELD-MARSHAL SIR DOUGLAS HAIG.

Thursday Morning.

acked at 3.10 a.m. the German positions on the MESSINES-
E RIDGE [south of Ypres] on a front of over 9 miles.

ve everywhere captured our first objectives, and further pro-
rted to be satisfactory along the whole front of attack.

Thursday Night.

erations south of YPRES have been continued methodically
the day, and have been attended by complete success.

ESSINES-WYTSCHAETE RIDGE, which for over two and a half
ominated our positions in the YPRES SALIENT, was stormed by
his morning.

attack we captured the villages of MESSINES and WYTSCHAETE
emy's defence systems, including many strongly organised
efended localities on a front of over nine miles from south of
Brook to north of MONT SORREL

n the day our troops

senses than the human tissue has endured
in history.

I must postpone to a later telegram any
account of how they fared after the first
triumphant rush over the enemy's first
system. Prisoners were trooping back as
I left our part of the front, though the
battle was less than two hours old. The
men said that the suddenness and fury of
our fire left them aghast. They could
only surrender as quickly as might be and
hope to get out alive. Some of these
troops against us are said to have recently come from the Russian front, and
we are pitted against some of the pick of
the Bavarian and Prussian troops, with
reserves heavily massed behind them.

Later.

The Battle of Messines Ridge, as the
sequel to the Battle of Vimy Ridge, will
be almost the greatest battle in our history, if we keep what we have won. At
the moment that I write our skied observers see German divisions in mass
gathering for the attack, but whatever
may happen in the future it remains that
we took what we meant to take exactly as
we meant to take it and at the precise
minute when we meant to take it.

When the Anzac troops went to storm
the crown of this famous ridge the enemy
stopped them not at all; till they waited
for was the advance of their own barrage,
and some of the more ardent spirits would
not wait

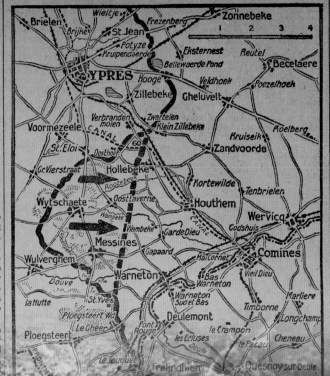

MR. LLOYD GEORGE C
TO LISTEN.

Mr. Lloyd George, who was
Walton Heath on Wednesday
called at three o'clock yesterda
in anticipation of the explosion
the battle opened and of the ex
which he had been notified.

He and others heard clear
mendous shock. Sleepers in
were awakened by it, and even
some heard shortly after 3 a.m
judged to be heavy guns acros
nel, till the account of the fi
ponderous mine told them wh
was.

450 TONS OF EXPLOS

FRANCE, T

The total quantity of the cha
off in the mine explosions was
tons. It is the most fitting a
ceivable to the Kaiser's bomba
collapse of our offensive.

The spectacle this morning i
The whole geography of the
been churned and blown and f
of recognition, and how many
lie amid the hecatomb the Reco
alone can tell.—Reuter's Specia

LORD NORTHCLI
MISSION.

QUESTIONS IN THE

Lord Northcliffe's mission
as the subject of a question i
Commons yesterday, Mr. Sa

Battle for Messines Ridge

Haig envisioned an offensive that drove through the German line to the Belgian ports of Ostend and Zeebrugge, home of the submarine menace threatening to starve Britain into submission. He took his cue from First Sea Lord Sir John Jellicoe, who warned that merchant shipping losses had left Britain on the brink of collapse. The situation worsened following Germany's decision to allow its U-boats free rein on the high seas in February. America's entry into the war two months later was of little immediate value, and if the U-boat threat wasn't dealt with, it was said, Britain might not survive long enough to greet her new ally in the field. Matters were exacerbated by the deepening crisis in Russia, which held out the unpalatable prospect of large numbers of German troops being freed to move from east to west.

Haig's adventurous plan involved a coastal attack and amphibious landing, both in concert with the hole he planned to punch in the enemy line at Ypres. Phase one yielded encouraging results. General Plumer's 2nd Army took Messines Ridge, a key German-held vantage point to the south of Ypres. The advance followed the detonation of 19 huge mines beneath the Germans' feet on 7 June, a spectacular conclusion to an exhaustive tunnelling operation. Those who survived a blast that reverberated across the Channel – said to be the largest man-made explosion on record – were so unnerved that Allied infantry had control of the ridge within hours. All objectives were met by the time the first part of the operation ended a week later.

AFTER THE BATTLEFIELD UPHEAVALS AT MESSINES

A GREAT MINE CRATER ON THE MESSINES RIDGE.—This official photograph issued   Mr. Beach Thomas wrote :—"The air shock as the earth shock, and where the earth end

BATTLE MINE HEARD IN LONDON.

MR. LLOYD GEORGE CALLED TO LISTEN.

Mr. Lloyd George, who was staying at Walton Heath on Wednesday night, was called at three o'clock yesterday morning in anticipation of the explosion with which the battle opened and of the exact hour of which he had been notified.

He and others heard clearly the tremendous shock. Sleepers in the district were awakened by it, and even in London some heard shortly after 3 a.m. what they judged to be heavy guns across the Channel, till the account of the firing of the ponderous mine told them what it really was.

450 TONS OF EXPLOSIVES.

FRANCE, Thursday.

The total quantity of the charges touched off in the mine explosions was nearly 450 tons. It is the most fitting answer conceivable to the Kaiser's bombast about the collapse of our offensive.

The spectacle this morning is incredible. The whole geography of the district has been churned and blown and furrowed out of recognition, and how many stark Huns lie amid the hecatomb the Recording Angel alone can tell.—Reuter's Special.

Rain and mud at Passchendaele

The main attack, spearheaded by General Gough's 5th Army, was launched on 31 July. It was directed at an enemy that had not been idle in the six-week hiatus. Defences that were already formidable were further strengthened under the guidance of Colonel Fritz von Lossberg, Germany's foremost expert in that field. Had the second attack followed hard on the heels of the first, as originally discussed, Gough would not have had to face a defensive line that was now dauntingly deep. The scale of the task quickly became clear after the battle was launched. Among the immediate targets was another ridge, the site of a village whose name would become shorthand for the Third Battle of Ypres: Passchendaele.

Haig knew the weather would be an important factor in determining the outcome. The low-lying ground surrounding the 200-foot ridge was prone to flooding, and the damage done to the drainage system by the artillery bombardment made the need for clear skies all the greater. Instead Haig got rain, five inches falling in the first month alone. Aerial reconnaissance was hampered. A landscape of cloying mud and vast water-filled craters was not just an impediment – especially in regard to tank deployment – it was also a death trap. One false step could see soldier and beast alike swallowed up, with little hope of rescue.

"I remember trying to help a lad in this copse about a hundred yards from our jumping-off trench. There was no hope of getting to him, he was struggling in this huge sea of mud. Then I saw a small sapling and we tried to bend it over to him. We were seasoned soldiers by then, but the look on the lad's face was really pathetic – he was only a mere boy. It pricked my conscience, I felt I should try and do something more for him, but I couldn't do a thing. Had I bent it a little more I should have gone in with him, and had anyone else gone near this sea of mud they should have gone in with him too, as so many had."
Sergeant Cyril Lee, London Regiment

The blast reverberated across the Channel – said to be the largest man-made explosion on record.

Opposite above: British soldiers marching through France buy oranges from a local girl.

Opposite right: From Wytschaete to Walton Heath – Lloyd George rose at 3 am on 7 June to hear the great mines explode in Flanders. It took 12 minutes for the sound to travel the distance.

Opposite below: Allied bombardment before an attack.

Below: Troops dig out drainage channels in an attempt to clear away some of the surface water. The land drains had been destroyed by shelling and the constant rain created treacherous conditions making it very difficult for troops and tanks to cross the terrain.

Above: Men from a Midland regiment leaving by train after a spell in the rain sodden trenches at Flanders.

FIRST FRUITS OF MESSINES SUCCESS.

HAIG ADVANCES AGAIN. | CHANNEL DRIFTER BEATS SEAPLANES | OUR WAR AIMS. | STRANDED PACIFISTS. | GREECE'S CROPS. | BERLIN TO-DAY.

VICTORIOUS ULSTERMEN AFTER MESSINES.

Opposite top left: The padre has a few comforting words for a wounded man brought in on a light railway.

Opposite top right: Troops lean on the parapet of their trench to watch the shell-burst in the distance.

Opposite middle left: The early French Saint-Chamond tanks were limited in their performance as they were under-powered and their caterpillar tracks were too short for the vehicle's length and weight. This made them prone to ditching in trenches.

Opposite below left: A French nurse brings flowers to a soldier's grave in France.

Opposite middle right: Three men of the Irish Guards wear suits of German body armour found in Flanders.

Opposite below right: Some of the 7,000 German prisoners captured following the Battle at Messines Ridge. Haig called the victory "Final and conclusive proof of the approaching defeat of the German armies".

Opposite bottom: An ambulance and guns move forward.

Above: The scene at an Anzac field dressing station during the Battle of Messines.

Left: Allied troops take over a German observation post.

TERRIFIC GERMAN COUNTER-ATTACK.

G LOSES SOME GROUND.

TUBBORN FIGHTING.

GERMANS HARD HIT.

MANY DIVISIONS BROKEN.

OUR GUARDS' RUSH.

ridge; we are at the bottom of the valley beyond, along the Steenbeek River, and we overlook all the German trenches as just now the enemy overlooked ours. The victory is complete in itself thereabouts.

18 BIG BRITISH SHIPS SUNK.

WHY GERMANY TALKS PEACE—

PREMIE

HEN

NO ME
GER

THE PA

AN EYE ON

Above: As a light railway with the railway workers aboard travels down, a trench party moves up. The railways were mainly used to transport ammunition and trench materials.

Below: Men lie on stretchers at a field dressing station. Although conditions were usually very basic the medical care given was frequently a life-saver for many soldiers.

Above right: A map showing the German dominion, now stretching 3,250 miles from Ostend to north west of Baghdad, a distance greater than that from New York to San Francisco, comprising 1,300,000 square miles of territory and a population of 170 million.

Opposite above: Irish Guardsmen on the march. They were sent to France eight days after war was declared and fought on the Western Front throughout the entire war.

Opposite below left: A gas sentry from the York and Lancaster battalion stands on duty in a heavily sandbagged lookout station. The warning sign indicates there is no imminent threat of a gas attack. The Germans used mustard gas for the first time during the Third Battle of Ypres. It caused blistering to skin, sore eyes and internal and external bleeding and remained active on the ground for several weeks.

Opposite below right: A wiring party loads up a horse ready to move to the front. It was a very dangerous task as their job was to sabotage the enemy's wire defences as well as maintaining their own, frequently exposing them to enemy fire.

Battle of Pilckem Ridge

Those who favoured a holding operation until American forces arrived in strength in 1918 received grim news from First Sea Lord Admiral Jellicoe, who said shipping losses were such that Britain would not be able to carry the fight far into the new year. That bombshell swung the argument for a large-scale summer offensive Haig's way, and he received qualified approval days before the operation commenced. The commander-in-chief entrusted General Gough and his 5th Army with the opening phase of the Third Battle of Ypres, launched at 3.50 am on 31 July 1917. He attacked with the French 1st Army on his left, Plumer's 2nd Army to the right. As well as maintaining pressure on the enemy, Haig wanted to secure the Belgian coast, thereby neutralising the U-boat threat that prompted Jellicoe's warning. The enterprise was to be aided by an amphibious landing. Passchendaele Ridge and the Roulers-Thourout railway were key objectives, and even the commander-in-chief thought Gough's assessment of when they would be taken was overambitious. For once it was Haig favouring piecemeal caution, though as the general on the ground, Gough was given a wide degree of latitude. In any event, the immediate targets when the operation got underway included Pilckem Ridge and Gheluvelt Plateau. As if on cue, the heavens opened, a foreboding of the atrocious weather to come at a time when the drainage system on this low-lying ground had been smashed to smithereens. Yet there was early encouragement as the Allies established a firm grip on Pilckem Ridge, robbing the Germans of an important vantage point overlooking the Ypres salient. They also made some headway into Gheluvelt Plateau, breaching the enemy's first defensive line. Gough failed to place enough emphasis on capturing the latter ground, the importance of which Haig recognised but did not communicate with sufficient vigour. At the end of day one Gough had averaged around half of the 6,000-yard advance he had envisaged, some 18 square miles gained for the loss of fewer than 30,000 men. Such respectable returns were not to be repeated. The Germans had the defensive expertise of Fritz von Lossberg to call upon, while the attacking army faced a quagmire that put paid to any hope of British tanks making an effective contribution to the battle.

This page: The wreck of an artillery limber and its dead mules lie beside the road at Pilckem while two pack-horses continue their journey.

Opposite: A sketch of the whole territory from the sea in the north to a point below Lens in the south.

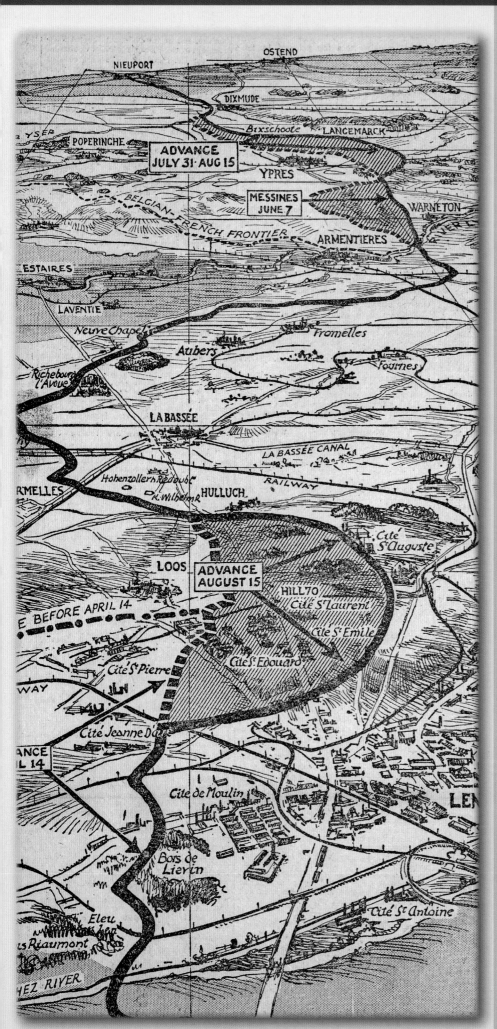

August 1917

1   The Vatican published a Peace Note from Pope Benedict XV suggesting an initiative on which a peace might be based.

2   General Lavr Kornilov succeeded General Brusilov as Russian Commander-in-Chief.

Artillery shelling continued at Ypres, but infantry advances were suspended due to torrential rain.

3   Austrian-German forces recaptured Czernowitz in Bukovina on the Eastern Front.

4   Liberia declared war on Germany.

5   Richard von Kühlmann was appointed Secretary of State for Foreign Affairs in Germany.

6   The Battle of Mărăşeşti began when German troops launched an attack against Russian and Romanian forces.

7   The British steamer SS *Iran* was sunk in the Azores by the German submarine *U-155* whilst on a voyage from Calcutta to London.

9   Count Móric Esterházy resigned as Premier of Austria.

10 The British Labour Party decided to send representatives to a consultative conference in Stockholm.

British forces attacked on the Gheluvelt Plateau but achieved only small gains in the offensive at Ypres.

11 Arthur Henderson resigned from the War Cabinet when his idea for an international conference on the war was voted down.

12 German Gotha bombers attacked Southend and Margate in a bombing raid which resulted in dozens of casualties.

14 The new Chinese President Feng Kuo-chang (Féng Guózhāng) declared war on Germany and Austria-Hungary.

15 The Battle of Hill 70 began between the Canadian Corps and the German Sixth Army along the Western Front on the outskirts of Lens in the Nord-Pas-de-Calais region of France.

17 The second Allied general attack in the Ypres Offensive, the Battle of Langemarck began. Both German and British forces were severely hampered by adverse weather conditions.

18 Italian forces battled against the Austro-Hungarians along the Isonzo River again in the Eleventh Battle of the Isonzo.

20 The Second Offensive Battle of Verdun took place on the banks of the River Meuse when British troops launched an assault on the Verdun battlefields.

21 Sándor Wekerle was appointed Prime Minister of Hungary for the third time in his career.

24 Italian forces occupied the summit of Monte Santo and continued their advance towards the Bainsizza Plateau during the Eleventh Battle of the Isonzo.

25 The Battle of Hill 70 came to an end. The localised battle had included extensive use of poison gas on both sides and ultimately the goals of the Canadian Corps were only partially accomplished.

26 British forces captured enemy positions east of Hargicourt. French forces launched an attack on the front at Verdun and captured Le Mort Homme.

27 The United States replied to the Papal Peace Note. President Wilson rejected a peace based on the Pope's proposals and implied that there was no chance of peace until the German people overthrew their government.

28 The Moscow State Conference closed after 3 days. It had been convened by the Provisional Government to mobilize all the counterrevolutionary forces in Russia

29 The British steamer SS *Treloske* was sunk by the German submarine *U-93* on a voyage from Barry to La Spezia with a cargo of coal.

31 Louis Malvy resigned as French Minister of the Interior after he was blamed for not suppressing pacifist agitators.

THE KING AMONG HIS SOLDIERS AT THE FRONT.

The King in Flanders

In July 1917, with plans for the next phase of the Ypres offensive well advanced, King George V and Queen Mary toured the Western Front. Over a two-week period the royal couple made morale-boosting visits to numerous sites of interest, often with separate schedules in order to cover more ground. The King's itinerary took in Wytschaete-Messines Ridge, scene of a great victory the previous month following the detonation of 19 huge mines. Queen Mary saw Royal Flying Corps planes and British Expeditionary Force tanks at close quarters, and visited a casualty clearing station. As they made their way back to England, historic changes were taking place affecting the reigning monarch and his heirs. On 17 July the House of Windsor came into being, King George adopting this not just for dynastic lineage purposes but also as a surname. Anti-German sentiment prompted the change, consigning the House of Saxe-Coburg-Gotha to the history books.

Above: King George V on a morale-boosting visit during the Ypres offensive.

On 17 July the House of Windsor came into being, consigning the House of Saxe-Coburg-Gotha to the history books.

Capture of Westhoek

On 10 August – by which time Passchedaele itself was to have been securely in Allied hands – Gough pressed on with an attack on Westhoek Ridge, which lay a couple of miles east of Ypres and formed part of the plateau Haig was desperate to control. He had cautioned that Gough should bide his time and wait for more favourable weather, which would help the artillery to provide effective support. His general ploughed on regardless. Both Westhoek itself and nearby Glencorse Wood had been first-day targets, further indication of the speed with which Gough's plan had gone awry. This fresh attempt was a valiant but ultimately unsustainable effort, for those who reached their goal came under ferocious counterattack and were forced to withdraw. German artillery, ranged on the plateau's reverse slopes, did their deadly work. The attack was called off, and Gough drew breath for six days before taking the fight to the enemy once again.

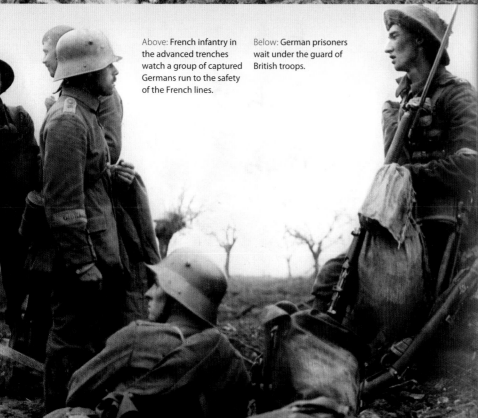

Above: **French infantry in the advanced trenches watch a group of captured Germans run to the safety of the French lines.**

Below: **German prisoners wait under the guard of British troops.**

The Battle of Langemarck

Conditions were scarcely any better on 16 August, when Gough renewed the offensive, this time on a broad front. As had been the case on the first day, it was in the north where the Allies enjoyed most success, notably with the capture of Langemarck. Even here there were setbacks, appalling casualties inflicted by machine-gun emplacements robust enough to escape the shelling. A latticework of concrete pillboxes presented a difficult obstacle to troops wrestling with glutinous terrain and poor visibility. At least there was something tangible to show for those losses, albeit a village that was little more than a shattered ruin. The same could not be said in the central and southern sectors, where the high casualty figures were not mitigated by territorial gain. Overall, the operation added 15,000 men to the toll, with Langemarck the greatest prize. Had it been Gheluvelt Plateau, Haig would have been well satisfied, but that remained stubbornly in German hands.

Above: A young German officer walks towards Allied lines after being captured by Canadians during the Battle of Hill 70. It had been hoped that this localised conflict would draw German troops away from the main offensive but the tactic was only partially successful.

Left: Officials practice the use of an aeroplane to transport the injured.

Below: A shell bursts near an 8-inch Howitzer during the Battle of Langemarck. Troops immediately seek shelter behind tree trunks to avoid the flying splinters.

Opposite above and below left: Members of the Chinese Labour Corps work alongside British forces. China had been a neutral country throughout the conflict, preventing Chinese men from taking part in any fighting, but on 14 August 1917 China finally declared war on Germany.

Opposite above right: Tommies clean their rifles after trench duty.

Opposite below: A soldier shields himself as a shell bursts nearby. The barren landscape meant troops were constantly exposed to enemy fire once they left the safety of the trenches.

YPRES ADVANCE AMID BITTER FIGHTING.

BRITISH ATTACK AT YPRES.

SUBSTANTIAL GAINS AND A FIERCE DEFENCE.

FRENCH SMASH VERDUN EFFORTS.

In bitter figh[t]
Ypres our troops
tions on a front
very heavy losse[s]
says we, too hav[e]

After repellin[g]
Tuesday night th[e]
was quieter yest[er]
approach 7,000.

The Italians ha[ve]
on the Bainsizz[a]
Gorizia, and on t[he]
admit losses of
taken by our All[ies]
13,000.

GAINS ON

CUT-OFF HUN

From SIR

Wednesday Night.

Successful operations were undertaken by our troops this morning east
and north-east of
of a series of stro[ng]
farms lying a fe[w]
front of our positi[on]
MENIN road [sou[th]
between the YPRE[S]
LANGEMARCK [nor[th]

Bitter fighting
points. The en[emy]
repeated count[er]
suffered heavy l[osses]
and machine[gun]

ITALIAN BATTLE RAGING.

13,000 PRISONERS.

GAINS ALL ALONG LINE.

FROM OUR OWN CORRESPONDENT.
MILAN, Wednesday.
For four days the Isonzo-Carso battle
has continued with increasing violence
without a single pause, nor is there yet
sign
been
Gene[ral]
ught a
s of r[
he me[n]
n resi[st]
he 3rd
Aosta,
ny Cor[ps]
z, who
brave
cial im[
red the[
la. C[
pared
ate de[
sion
The
mns a[
hours'
parti[
the
the effect[

Accord[ing]
mation w[
ading t[
threa[t]
nvested
s and
rific fir[e]

ORTH

hile
ly o[
ring
and have been used hard
guns worked so continuously that, as we
know, a German relief was carried out.

FIELD HOSPITALS BOMBED.

NEW FRIGHTFULNESS.

DELIBERATE AIM.

*The Huns have adopted a new form of
frightfulness—bombing raids at night on
British and French field hospitals. The*

15 BIG SHIPS DOWN.

Week Ended	British Ships Sunk. Over 1,600 tons.	British Ships Sunk. Under 1,600 tons.	All Ships U.K. Ports Arrivals.	Sailings.
Aug. 19 ...	**15**	**3**	2,838	2,764
„ 12 ...	14	2	2,776	2,666
„ 5 ...	21	2	2,673	2,796
July 29 ...	18	3	2,747	2,776
„ 22 ...	21	3	2,791	2,791
„ 15 ...	14	4	2,828	2,920
„ 8 ...	14	3	2,836	2,798
„ 1 ...	15	5	2,745	2,846
June 24 ...	21	7	2,876	2,923
„ 17 ...	27	5	2,897	2,993
„ 10 ...	22	10	2,767	2,822
„ 3 ...	15	3	2,693	2,642

INTERNED OFFICERS.

PARTY COMING HOME FROM SWITZERLAND.

FROM OUR OWN CORRESPONDENT.
VEVEY, Monday.
The following is a list of officers interned
in the Château d'Oex district who have
passed the Swiss medical examination for
repatriation to England under the provisions of the recent Hague agreement. The
names of the officers residing in the region
ble :—
Guards;
Doughty
Robert-
ordons), C.
Innis-
.A.), C.
rwen
Knight
rks), A.
r (Royal
ters), C.
al Innis-
Turner
skilling

anadian
.C.), J.
. Earle
d (60th

High-
lso been
d in the
ssed the
ring re-
examin-
at the
by the
r fresh
mbled at

IGA.

TTLE.

he Ger-
marches
avalry
south as fa[r]

3 GO

11 K
AN

10 R.

FI[

Fr

Ten ene[my]
Kentish [
10.15 a.m.
gaged by
R.N.A.S. [
aircraft gu[ns]
penetrate [

A small [
Margate, [
The remai[n]
south as fa[r]

Two of [
brought d[own]
and our ow[n]

The late[st]
bombs wer[e]
planes at [
gate.

No casu[alties]
at Dover [
killed and[
a number [

One of [
having fa[

In am[
port issue[d]
[p]lanes o[
by naval[

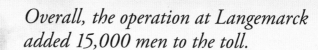
*Overall, the operation at Langemarck
added 15,000 men to the toll.*

VIOLENT GERMAN ONSLAUGHTS AT YPRES.

Y HUN ATTACKS.

NCED TROOPS FORCED BACK.

IN WINS AGAIN.

G GAINS AT VERDUN.

in progress in Fla
rdun, and the whole
line.

Germans yesterd
s in violent counte
forced back our a
they gained grour
e Hun losses we
as been slightly a
St. Julien.

d fighting continu
d the tunnelled sl

roops, after a pau
rs, have delivere
ul blow on the V
all and more th
front of over
304 and ri

ITALIANS PRESS ON.

PRISONERS NOW 20,500.

FROM OUR OWN CORRESPONDENT.

MILAN, Friday.

All the correspondents telegraphing from the enemy's headquarters to the Austrian, German, and Swiss papers agree in stating that this is the longest, greatest, and fiercest battle ever fought on the Isonzo front. They particularly emphasise the terrible power of the artillery.

The *Munich Latest News* says the re

NEW AGITATION IN RUSSIA.

KERENSKY'S DANGER.

MOSCOW TEST.

FROM OUR OWN CORRESPONDENT.

PETROGRAD, Thursday.

At last the Moscow Conference is fixed for Sunday in the great theatre

MAROONED TANK.

ALL-DAY FIGHT WITH FORT.

From W. BEACH THOMAS,

WAR CORRESPONDENTS' HEADQUARTERS, FRANCE, Friday.

How the tanks won a battle to their own cheek north of St. Julien is now old history, though the experiences of their crows, some among the most dramatic in the war, are as yet untold.

One of the best of these I heard yes-

8 SOLDIERS DROWNED

LIVING CHAIN RESCUES.

During a bathing parade in Blyth Bay, Northumberland, yesterday, when several hundred soldiers were in the water, a number got into difficulties and eight or nine are believed to have been drowned.

The men reported missing are: Second-Lieutenant Kenneth Brown, Sergeant Riley, Privates Beaven, Noy, Southern, Blunn, Shale, and Forley. The body of another man, Private Childs, has been recovered.

TITLES FOR

THE KING
LIS

DAMES AND
THE EM

The first lists of a
King in the new Or
the Order of the Bri
new Order of t
nour—both open a
men—are issued to
The two first class
British Empire
e Knight (Sir) and
me. The Queen a
list of Dames, fo
mple of disinteres
manhood of the na
n this new Order
rvices recognised by
m in their own na
r husbands. The
nd Cross and I
Dame before
ourse, they allow
Is may be ra
though her kn
Bed of

£15 FOR FIRST U.S. PRISONER.

From Our Own Correspondent.

PARIS, Monday.

The French military authorities have informed the American Commander-in-Chief, General Pershing, that the Kaiser has promised a reward of £15 and three weeks' leave to the first German who captures an American. The information is furnished by German prisoners, who state that the offer has been made in general orders.

Opposite above left: A German officer with his head held high, surrenders to Allied troops. During the Third Battle of Ypres the Allies captured over 24,000 prisoners.

Opposite above right: Two US soldiers man a listening post. It was a huge undertaking to transport so many Americans to France so cruise ships were pressed into service along with loaned Allied vessels. US engineers arriving in France built 82 new ship berths, nearly 1,000 miles of standard gauge railway track and set up over 100,000 miles of telegraph and telephone lines to aid their passage to the frontline.

Opposite below: Staff cars, mule limbers, lorries, an ambulance, infantrymen and their officers crowd the roads at Fricourt in August 1917.

Right: Members of the cavalry make their way through the ruins of a French village.

Below: Troops from the 124th Battery, Royal Garrison Artillery manhandle a 9.2-inch Howitzer over muddy ground.

HAIG'S ADVANCE ON THE MENIN ROAD.

POWERFUL POSITIONS STORMED.

HEAVY ENEMY LOSSES.

NAMES OF TROOPS THAT WON.

From FIELD-MARSHAL SIR DOUGLAS HAIG.

Thursday Morning.-

Battle of the Menin Road Ridge

Following further fruitless attacks in the second half of August, Haig finally lost patience with Gough. The next large-scale attack was scheduled for 20 September, by which time operational command had passed to General Plumer. He knew the Ypres sector better than any and had masterminded the successful Messines attack. He was also known for meticulous planning and a cautious approach that endeared him to his men. Three weeks' preparation went into the new assault, which centred on the Menin Road, a notoriously dangerous avenue that ran in a southeasterly direction out of Ypres. Strongpoints on Gheluvelt Plateau were the target, with Gough's 5th Army taking the supporting role to Plumer's left.

To neutralise the threat of well protected German defensive positions Plumer ordered a bombardment that exceeded the preliminary to the opening-day barrage. Sound ranging and flash spotting were used to locate battery positions in the run-up to zero hour, and these were to come under a storm of shellfire as the infantry advanced. Unfortunately, far fewer German guns were knocked out than had been hoped for. The weather again played its part, hampering observation. Mobility of German batteries was another factor; it was hard to lock on to a shifting target. Some enemy guns were kept deliberately silent during the preliminary exchanges to avoid attention. Even so, the main thrust of the attack was successful. The bill was steep, though: in securing some six square miles – one-third of the ground taken on 31 July – the Allies' casualty toll topped 20,000. On a strict pro rata assessment, more ground was taken on the first day, at lower cost. That Plumer's reputation was enhanced while Gough's was damaged lay in the fact that the former set and achieved more modest goals. Better to downplay expectation and meet targets than fall short of optimistic forecasts. Equally significantly, Plumer had made inroads into Gheluvelt Plateau, identified by Haig from the outset as the key to the entire campaign. On that score Gough underachieved in comparison with his fellow general.

PICTURE MAP OF THE MENIN ROAD BATTLE

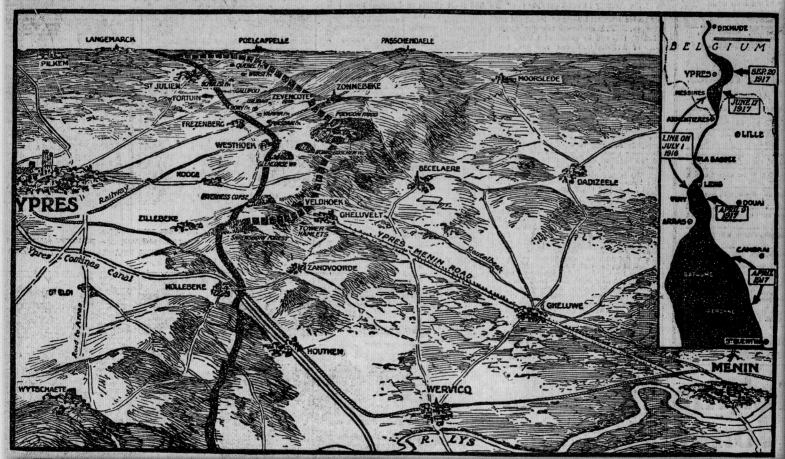

Opposite above: The devastated landscape surrounding the Menin Ridge after the area is captured. Fortunately, the weather improved for this offensive and an intense programme of road repairs made it easier to move men and ammunition forward.

Opposite below: German prisoners are marched away from the area. Over 3,000 were captured during the six-day battle at Menin Ridge.

Top: The thick dotted line marks the Allies' advance and shows the important tactical positions of Glencorse Wood and Inverness Copse wholly behind the new line.

Above left: Packhorses, cavalry and motor machine guns march to their rendezvous on a road constructed by German troops.

Above right: Four tanks were employed but one got stuck and the infantry advance was so rapid, the other three were not able to keep up and so were used to carry ammunition up to the front.

Right: Wounded soldiers are carried off the battlefield as shells burst in the distance.

Left: Stretcher-bearers make their way to the frontline. Advancing troops were not allowed to help injured comrades so the wounded had to wait until they were found. In muddy conditions it would frequently need six men to carry one injured soldier to safety.

Below: A fellow soldier tends these Canadian graves.

Bottom: Allies investigate the remains of a German pillbox. These defensive concrete fortifications were often reinforced with iron girders and were generally used to house machine guns and artillery.

Opposite top and middle: Proud German soldiers of the Ypres campaign.

Opposite left: The latest news of the advance, published on 27 November.

Opposite below right: The harsh and harrowing conditions of Flanders.

Opposite bottom: Water-filled shell craters in Polygon Wood. Although the weather had improved, the treacherous conditions created by earlier fighting remained.

Battle of Polygon Wood

Six days after the Menin Road battle, Plumer struck out for Polygon Wood, the next of Haig's targets. Heavy German artillery fire in the intervening period, and a counterattack on 25 September – the eve of Plumer's latest push – provided ample evidence that this would be no walkover, this was no enemy on the brink of capitulation. Events bore that out. A recurring theme of the Passchendaele offensive as a whole was the difficulty in aligning the infantry advance with the creeping barrage, the curtain of shells behind which the men moved forward. Ground conditions were such that the troops often lost the connection with their gunners, and thick mist on the morning of the 26th exacerbated the problem in the drive to capture Polygon Wood. Even so, 5 Australian Division took the high ground in the centre of the wood, and by mid-morning all the main objectives had been secured. The rest of the day was spent rebuffing enemy counters, successful in nearly all cases. Haig was well satisfied with the day's work and already planning the next phase. His optimism should have carried a cautionary footnote that the Polygon Wood attack had made 1,200 yards on an 8,000-yard front. At that rate of progress it would take four such set pieces to envelop Passchendaele, which had been one of the immediate targets when the offensive opened up. The addition of 15,000 to the casualty list was another salutary factor on the debit side. The Third Battle of Ypres was fast becoming the kind of protracted, Somme-like operation Lloyd George had said should be avoided at all cost.

ADVANCE OF A MILE.

TOWER HAMLETS SPUR ALL TAKEN.

ZONNEBEKE STORMED.

FIERCE HUN RESISTANCE.

From FIELD-MARSHAL SIR DOUGLAS HAIG.

Wednesday Night.

Our attack this morning was delivered on a total front of nearly 6 miles, from south of TOWER HAMLETS to east of ST. JULIEN. Our operations were entirely successful. Later in the day the enemy delivered a series of heavy counter-attacks along our new front, resulting in hard fighting which is still continuing at certain points.

South of the YPRES-MENIN ROAD the attack carried out by English troops successfully completed the capture of the TOWER HAMLETS SPUR and gained possession of the strong German field works on its eastern slopes which formed our objectives. A powerful counter-attack from the direction of GHELUVELT was repulsed.

On the right of our main attack north of the YPRES-MENIN ROAD our troops met with obstinate resistance, and heavy fighting took place in the area across which the enemy counter-attacked yesterday. After a severe struggle lasting throughout the greater part of the day English and Scottish battalions drove the enemy from his positions and accom-

Our advance yesterday was between the Tower Hamlets and Zonnebeke.

The Daily Mail Bird's Eye Map of the Front, No. 1, is printed in Colours and is on a large scale. It is the best means of following the battle and can be had from any newsagent or bookseller for 7d., or 8d. post free from the Map Publisher, Carmelite House, E.C. 4.

plished the task allotted to them of securing the flank of our principal attack. In their advance our troops relieved two companies of Argyll and Sutherland Highlanders who had held out with great gallantry during the night in a forward position in which they had been isolated by the enemy's attack yesterday morning.

September 1917

1 German forces attacked the northernmost end of the Russian front during the Riga offensive.

2 German troops attacked and crossed the Dvina bridgehead on the Eastern Front.

German Admiral Alfred von Tirpitz and other conservatives founded the Fatherland Party to oppose peace initiatives.

3 German bombers raided the Chatham naval station in Kent resulting in over 200 casualties.

4 German submarines shelled Scarborough on the Yorkshire coast of England.

5 German forces captured the strategic port of Riga as Russian troops retreated and evacuated the city.

6 Sun Yat-sen became the Generalissimo of the Military Government of Nationalist China.

7 The Harland and Wolff built ocean liner SS Minnehaha sank after being torpedoed by German submarine U-48 off the Fastnet Rock.

8 General Lavr Kornilov headed a revolt against the Russian Provisional Government and organised a march on Petrograd.

9 French Prime Minister Alexandre Felix Joseph Ribot resigned after losing the support of the Socialists.

10 Alexander Kerensky assumed the dictatorship of Russia and issued a proclamation declaring Lavr Kornilov a traitor.

11 The first party of British POWs were repatriated through Switzerland and reached England.

12 The Eleventh Battle of the Isonzo ended when the Italian attack was halted. Italian troops had captured five mountain peaks before the offensive petered out and the Austro-Hungarians eventually held their positions.

Paul Painlevé replaced Alexandre Ribot as Prime Minister of France.

14 General Lavr Kornilov was arrested at Mogilëv, accused of plotting the overthrow of the Provisional Government.

15 The Provisional Government proclaimed a Russian Republic under Alexander Kerensky.

17 The British steamer SS Queen Amelia was first stopped by gunfire from the German submarine U-95 and finally sunk by a torpedo from UB-62.

20 The third general British attack of the Ypres Offensive, the Battle of the Menin Road Ridge, took place in the Ypres Salient in Flanders on the Western Front.

21 Count Bernstorff's (German Ambassador in London) correspondence with Berlin concerning German intrigues was published.

22 German forces stormed Jacobstadt on the banks of the Dvina river, forcing the retreat of Russian troops.

23 German flying ace and rival of the famous Red Baron Manfred von Richthofen, Werner Voss was shot down and killed by British fighter pilots near Frezenberg in Belgium.

25 British Prime Minister David Lloyd George committed to an extension of the British line in France at the Anglo-French Conference in Boulogne.

The Battle of the Menin Road Ridge ended in an Allied victory as British troops had successfully held their lines against German counter-attacks.

26 The Battle of Polygon Wood was a successful joint Australian and British attack when their forces advanced against the Germans and occupied all of the Polygon Wood.

28 The Battle of Ramadi was fought between the British and the Ottomans as part of the Mesopotamian Campaign.

29 The British operation at Ramadi concluded after the Ottoman garrison was quickly outflanked and captured.

TERRORS OF THE FLANDERS QUAGMIRE.

IN A SWAMP.

' 11 HOURS' MARCH
TCH DARKNESS.

NT ACHIEVEMENT.

RUSH A REDOUBT.

"LOCAL FIGHTING."

NO REAL CHANGE.
GUNS STILL ACTIVE.

From SIR DOUGLAS HAIG.

Wednesday Morning.

The enemy delivered several counter-attacks yesterday evening in the neighbourhood of the YPRES-STADEN RAILWAY. All these were repulsed, but to the south of the railway on a front of about 2,000 yards our advanced troops were forced back a short distance.

Other counter-attacks made by the enemy north-east of Broonseinde during

14 BIG SHIPS SUNK.

A SLIGHT INCREASE.

The Admiralty return of last week's merchant shipping losses is :

Week Ended	British Ships Sunk. Over 1,600 tons.	Under 1,600 tons.	All Ships U.K. Ports. Arrivals.	Sailings.
Oct. 7 ...	14	2	2,519	2,632
Sept. 30 ...	11	2	2,680	2,742
,, 23 ...	13	2	2,775	2,691
,, 16 ...	8	20	2,695	2,737
,, 9 ...	12	6	2,744	2,668
,, 2 ...	20	3	2,384	2,432
Aug. 26 ...	18	4	2,629	2,680
,, 19 ...	14	4	2,838	2,784
,, 12 ...	14		2,776	2,666

BOLO.

DAILY BULLETINS BY HIS COUNSEL.

Though the French Commission which is to make inquiries in England in connection with the Bolo Pasha case has not yet arrived, valuable help is expected from Paris in the discovery of our British Bolos.

Bolo Pasha, a Frenchman, is charged with communicating with the enemy. He is alleged to have received over £300,000 through the Deutsche Bank for the purpose of peace propaganda in

100,000 U.S. AIRMEN.

DR. PAGE ON AMERICA'S GREAT EFFORT.

Dr. Page, the United States Ambassador, at Leeds yesterday said there was a grim and unalterable determination in the United States to victory, and there would be no change of that mood and no weariness or slackening of effort until the task was done. Under the scheme of conscription 10,000,000 men between 20 and 30 years old were registered in one day. To these must be added the State militia and the small but admirable Regular Army, already greatly

MUT
G
ADM

AG

REPR

Above: Stretcher-bearers rescue a wounded soldier. Their challenge was to negotiate the mud without jogging the stretcher, which would cause additional pain and shock to the injured.

Left: Troops mark out the ground ready to construct a new road. By the time the Canadians finally took Passchendaele on 6 November the area around it was little more than a mass of rubble.

Opposite above: Troops and mules cross safely using a "corduroy road". These temporary tracks, designed to produce a safe crossing place on an impassable road, were built with planks or logs laid perpendicular to the direction of the road. The name came from its similarity in appearance to the fabric corduroy.

Opposite below: Horses and limbers are caked in mud as they transport ammunition to the frontline.

The Third Battle of Ypres was fast becoming the kind of protracted, Somme-like operation Lloyd George had said should be avoided at all cost.

DAILY MAIL OCTOBER 15, 1917

Swamp of death and pain

Every inch we gained in Friday's battle is worth a mile as common distance is reckoned. Some troops went forward 1,700 yards or even more, fighting all the way; and when their relic came back some part of that heroic journey no enemy dared follow them, so foul and cruel was their track.

They left behind them a Golgotha, a no man's land, a dead man's land. Five or six miles separate our troops from any place where you can step firm, where you can find any break in the swamp. It is a nightmare journey to traverse it, in spite of the ceaseless labour of pioneers.

Our soldiers coming out of this swamp of death and pain maintain incredible serenity. If we could advance so far in such conditions we could go anywhere in fine weather. We were nowhere beaten by the enemy, though more defensive wire was left round shell-holes and pill-boxes and fewer machine gunners knocked out than in any recent attack. We were beaten by the rain that began to fall in torrents at midnight before the attack, so they all say and feel, and so it was.

One of them, still full of humour, said he considered Friday an unlucky day for him. "You see," he argued, "I was first hit in the shoulder by a machine-gun bullet, and as I stumbled was hit in the foot, and as I lay another hit me in the foot and another hit me in the side. Decidedly Friday is an unlucky day." It was a terrible day for wounded men, and alternate advance and retreat now always leave a wide, indeterminable no man's land from which escape to the mercy of either side is hard. But the best is being done, and the immortal heroism of the stretcher-bearers was backed by both the daring and skilful work of doctors at advance dressing stations and ambulance drivers a little farther back.

The trouble was how to find people or places. Wounded men, runners, contact officers, and even whole platoons had amazing journeys among shells and bullets searching for dressing-station headquarters, objective or what not, and, as we know, even Germans on the pure defensive had similar trouble and their units were inextricably confused. It was all due, as one of them said, to the sump, or morass.

All that can be said of the battle is that we are a little higher up the slope than we were and a little further along the crest road to Passchendaele. How we succeeded in capturing over 700 prisoners is one of the marvels of the day. A marvel, too, is the pile of German machine guns. They are some small concrete proof of the superhuman efforts of our infantry. If the world has supermen they were the men who waded forward up to their hips astride the Ravelbeck and stormed concrete and iron with flesh and blood. They were at least the peers of the men who fought "upon their stumps" at Chevy Chase.

To-day the artillery fire has died down, the sun is bright, though the cold west wind threatens showers.

Verbrandemis
Manyelaare
Schaap Baillie
Mortierhoek
ROULERS
Draeibank
Koekhuyt
Westroosebeke
Oostnieuwkerke
De Ruiter
Bischoote
Wydendrel
Poelcappelle
Colliemolenhoek
Lizerne
Steenstaate
Spriel
Kalve
Langemarck
Goudberg
Vierkanenhoek
Den-Aep
Hetsas
Margermierie
Zilverterg
Kersselaere
Passchendaele
Wallemolen
Duivelhoeksken
Pilken
Stroombeek
Koekuythoek
Farm
Boesinghe
Gravenstafel
Moorslede
Nieuwendulen
Tuimelaarehoek
Farm
St Julien
Zevencote
St Pierre
Zaanhof
Fortuin
Elverdinghe
Hannebeek
Brodseinde
Waterdamhoek
CANAL
Wiel
Zonnebeke
Slypscappelle
Brijke
Frezenberg
Westhoek
YPRES
St Jean
Verlorenhoek
Strooyboomhoek
3 Towers
Polygon Wood
Brielen
Potyze
Ekoternest
Potteryebrug
Reutel
Noordhofwyk
Kruipenduerde
Becelaere
Dadizeele
Nonne boschen
Molenhoek
Hooge
Veldhoek
Peazelhoek
Vufwegen
Kruistraate
Zillebeke
Gheluvelt
Zuidhoek
Terhand
Kezelberg
Rl. to Comines
Vieux Chien
Reutelbeek
Dickebusch
Zwartelen
Koelberg
Pannemolen
Verbranden
Hill 60
Klein Zillebeke
Vormezeele
Zandvoorde
Kruyseek
Gheluwe
Comerenhoek
Mille Kruis
Plas
St. Eloi
CANAL
Klytmolen
MENIN
Gr. Vierstraate
Hollebeke
Kasteelhoek
America
YPRES to LILLE
Kortewilde
Tenbrielen
WERVICQ
Houthem

Battle of Broodseinde

Buoyed by the success of the Menin Road operation, Haig mapped out follow-up attacks that would lead, piece by piece, to Passchendaele Ridge. Ostend and Zeebrugge were firmly back on the agenda. To meet that target before autumn turned to winter would have required the German line to collapse like a pack of cards. That was far from the case. Haig set his sights on the next target, Broodseinde, contemplating that his beloved cavalry might soon be pressed into service. Anzac troops were to the fore when the attack was launched on the morning of 4 October. Many never made it beyond the start line, cut down in a German shell-storm. It transpired that the enemy had been planning an assault of their own at the selfsame moment, and this was the prelude. That coincidence cut both ways, for the Germans had more men in the forward zone than usual in readiness for their attack, men who were caught in the Allied bombardment. Surviving Anzac troops went on to take possession of the ridge at Broodseinde as once again the advantage of setting limited objectives was demonstrated. "Great happenings are possible in the very near future," Anzac commander General Monash recorded. "Our success was complete and unqualified." Most of Gheluvelt Plateau was now in Allied hands, and they were edging ever closer to Passchendaele itself.

Opposite below: Men from the 8th East Yorkshires move up to the frontline during the Battle of Broodseinde.

Top: The Zion Mule Corps was founded in March 1915 and fought at Gallipoli under the command of Lieutenant-Colonel John Henry Patterson DSO. It consisted entirely of Jewish soldiers who had their own emblem and flag. In August 1917 a Jewish regiment was raised at Fort Edward in Nova Scotia as the 38th Battalion of the Royal Fusiliers. Men were invited to apply and came from as far afield as Britain, Russia, Canada and Palestine.

Middle: A British soldier contemplates the state of battle from a captured German pill-box. Troops now had a new type of phosphorus bomb to throw into these defensive buildings, which produced both fumes and an incendiary action to force the inhabitants out.

Below: The trees uprooted by shelling were used for road-making, bridges and strengthening dugouts.

Battle of Poelcapelle

"A general attack was launched at 5.20 am today…The results were very successful." Haig's diary entry for 9 October 1917 revealed a triumph of hope over cold, hard facts. The bid to take Poelcapelle was badly hampered from the start. Appalling weather rendered logistics a nightmare; moving supplies for the men, and ammunition to feed the guns, was desperately difficult. Conditions also impeded observation vital to effective artillery fire, with unfortunate consequences. The shelling that did take place failed to provide a platform for the infantry, many of whom had had an onerous trek to the start line before a shot was fired. Some units went into battle under strength. By contrast, the enemy they faced were in better fettle: many freshly arrived at the front, supported by reinforced artillery in that sector. German pillbox-ensconced gunners cut down hordes of the British and Australian attackers, some of whom had to try to pass through uncut wire to add to their woes. The assault on Poelcapelle delivered marginal gains on the fringes but failed completely in its central purpose. Scarcely a yard was gained.

The assault on Poelcapelle delivered marginal gains on the fringes but failed completely in its central purpose.

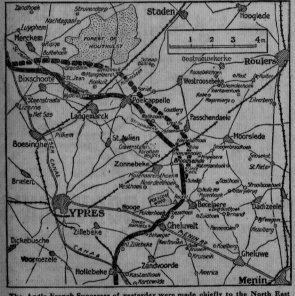

MILE MORE OF THE RIDGE

GAINS ALL THE WAY.

POELCAPELLE TAKEN AND THE GREAT FOREST REACHED.

NAMES OF 3 LANCS. REGIMENTS.

SPLENDID FRENCH SHARE.

From FIELD-MARSHAL SIR DOUGLAS HAIG.

Tuesday Night.

Heavy rain fell continuously during the afternoon and evening yesterday, causing the ground to become sodden and very difficult for the passage of troops. Notwithstanding the stormy weather and the waterlogged condition of the ground, our troops succeeded in launching an attack at 5.20 a.m. to-day, in conjunction with the French on our left, with very successful results.

The front of attack extended from a point south-east of BROODSEINDE to ST. JANSBEEK (1 mile north-east of Bixschoote). On the extreme right **Australian troops** moved forward over the crest of the ridge east and north-east of BROODSEINDE, securing all their objectives.

On the right centre a third-line Territorial division, comprising the **Manchester, East Lancashire, and Lancashire Fusilier Regiments,** advanced one mile northwards along the ridge in the direction of

The Anglo-French Successes of yesterday were made chiefly to the North East of Ypres, where the Forest of Houthulst was reached and Poelcapelle all taken. The dotted line in above map shows the new advance.

The Flanders battlefield is shown with great clearness in *The Daily Mail* Giant Bird's Eye Map of the Front, No. 1, printed in colours. The map costs 7d. at any newsagents' or booksellers', or can be got from the Map Publisher, Carmelite House, E.C. 4, for 8d. post free.

PASSCHENDAELE, capturing all its objectives under the most trying and difficult circumstances with great determination and gallantry.

In the centre, between the main ridge and POELCAPELLE, a considerable advance was made, which includes the capture of many fortified farms and concreted redoubts. In the left centre we have completed the capture of POELCAPELLE.

On the extreme left of the British attack **English, Welsh, and**

From W. BEACH THOMAS.

WAR CORRESPONDENTS' HEADQUARTERS, FRANCE, Wednesday.

The Battle of Poelcappelle will be always famous for the personal and particular grit and determination of the Lancashire troops forming the third-line Territorial division mentioned in last night's communiqué. The troops of a neighbour county did as well, fought as hard, and won as full a success, but were saved some of the preliminary hardships which a party of the Lancashire and Manchester men endured.

They set out on a good stiff march with plenty of time, as was reckoned, to arrange matters for the coming charge and to rest and eat on the way. Nothing indicated the superhuman trial they were to endure. An occasional high-velocity shell rattled the fallen rafters and dust of a murdered village they traversed, and a little shrapnel from the anti-aircraft guns clattered on the road. Our guns were firing spasmodically, but not in great volume. Rain was falling, but the road was not bad going. They marched in steel helmets and gasbags, on the alert, and they whistled and sang scraps of song. The prospects of their first big fight stirred all ranks to excitement as they threaded the press and tumult of war.

Day fell when they crossed the Yser Canal and darkness fell almost tropically. They now marched over a country absolutely formless and featureless. Miles of it stretched in front of them. The only light was the reflection of the gun flashes from the clouds and the perpetual alarm lights from the distant German lines. Their march from this point was a nightmare. Half a mile an hour was almost a gallop, for the night was pitch dark, lights could not be shown, and the country, already battered into shapelessness, was slimy with the day's rain and deep with the rain of days caught in the blue sticky clay of the saucer ridge that encloses Ypres.

Opposite page: After a fine, dry September, when important gains were made, the weather soon deteriorated again creating these swampy conditions in Poelcapelle.

Above: Men from the Argyll and Sutherland Highlanders in their quarters near the Broodseinde battleground.

Below: German soldiers attempted to flood this fortification before retreating.

October 1917

2 The armoured cruiser *HMS Drake* was torpedoed and sunk by the German submarine *U-79* in Rathlin Sound.

The British Government ordered an embargo on trade with neutral nations Denmark, the Netherlands, Norway and Sweden to prevent supplies reaching the Germans.

3 The US Congress passed the War Revenue Act which increased income taxes in order to raise more money for the war effort.

4 The Battle of Broodseinde was fought in Flanders at the east end of the Gheluvelt Plateau between the British and German armies. The battle was the most successful Allied attack of the Battle of Passchendaele.

5 The Peruvian Government in Lima voted to sever diplomatic relations with Germany.

6 US Major General John J. Pershing was promoted to General of the National Army of the United States.

7 In Montevideo Uruguay severed diplomatic relations with Germany.

8 Leon Trotsky became President of the Petrograd Soviet Presidium.

9 The third phase of the Ypres Offensive began with British and French troops taking Poelcapelle. The battle marked the end of a series of successful British attacks during September and early Oct.

11 German forces began offensive operations against the Baltic islands.

12 The First Battle of Passchendaele took place in the Ypres Salient area of the Western Front, during the Third Battle of Ypres. The British launched their latest assaults near the village of Passchendaele but the attempted breakthrough to Passchendaele Ridge failed.

15 A French firing squad executed the Dutch-born dancer Mata Hari as a German spy at Vincennes outside of Paris.

16 The 10,000 ton British tanker *San Nazario* was torpedoed by German submarine *U-53* whilst en route from Plymouth to Tampico.

17 British destroyers HMS *Strongbow* and HMS *Mary Rose* were attacked by German cruisers *Brummer* and *Bremse* in the North Sea whilst escorting a convoy of 12 merchant ships from Norway. The German cruisers went on to sink nine of the twelve ships in the convoy.

18 German forces captured Moon Island and Dago Island during their attack on the Baltic Islands.

19 A fleet of 11 German Zeppelins carried out an air raid over Southern and Central England. Three of the airships were shot down over France and Germany on their return trip.

Nils Edén replaced Carl Johan Gustaf Swartz as Prime Minister of Sweden.

21 A Turkish attack on the Arab stronghold at Petra was repelled.

23 An offensive operation on Chemin des Dames ridge was led by General Philippe Pétain when French forces attacked the Germans at the town of Malmaison.

24 The Twelfth Battle of the Isonzo (also known as the Battle of Caporetto) began as Austro-German forces crossed the Isonzo River at Caporetto and launched another attack on Italian lines near the town of Kobarid.

25 Italian Prime Minister Paolo Boselli resigned.

26 A further attack during the Third Battle of Ypres, the Second Battle of Passchendaele took place in the Ypres Salient area in and around the Belgian town of Passchendaele. Canadian divisions continued the advance which had started during the First Battle of Passchendaele.

28 Austro-Hungarian forces advanced in Italy to reach Udine and recapture Gorizia.

29 Vittorio Emanuele Orlando became the 23rd Prime Minister of Italy following the resignation of Paolo Boselli earlier in the month.

30 Reinforced with the addition of two British divisions, a second offensive was launched in torrential rains to capture Passchendaele. The Allies initially held the town in the face of repeated German shelling and counterattacks.

31 Allied forces under General Edmund Allenby initiated an attack on Turkish positions at Beersheba in Palestine and launched the Third Battle of Gaza.

DEADLY BATTLE FOR PASSCHENDAELE.

PASSCHENDAELE BATTLE.

ERE FIGHTING ON SLOPES.

NUMEROUS FORTS STORMED.

ONET, BOMB, AND PISTOL.

WNPOUR STOPS ATTACK.

rom FIELD-MARSHAL SIR DOUGLAS HAIG.

Friday Night.

ithstanding heavy rain which fell during the night our troops in forming up for the attack which was launched at 5.25 morning.

ress was made along the entire fron outers railway on the south to our junction with the Fren itheen mile of Houthurst Fores has lived a large number of dogou

them before, and his men were tuned up to the highest pitch.

Our men on the main ridge rushed on to their first objective line and, after some pause, to their second, using bayonet and bomb all the way, and the distance was a mile. Neither they nor anyone else have perhaps ever fought hand-to-hand continuously over so long a stretch, and the number of Germans killed is immense.

Tho troops on the left had worse going and even more resistance. In Augustus Wood alongside a beek an officer alone captured a pill-box, but was wounded as he shot with his pistol the last of the garrison to resist. The wood was full of isolated machine guns hidden behind boxes and fallen trees. The machine-gun posts, concrete and other, on the Bellevue Spur across the stream, especially below Meetcheele village, were as thick as junipers on a Hertfordshire common, and all through the battle a constant

NEW AIR CHIEF.

OTHER WORK FOR SIR D. HENDERSON.

GEN. BRANCKER FOR ABROAD.

War Office, Friday Night.

Lieutenant-General Sir David Henderson, D.S.O., having been deputed to undertake special work, has been lent for such service and has thereby vacated his seat on the Army Council.

The Secretary of State for War has appointed Major-General J. M. Salmond as his successor as Director-General of Military Aeronautics, with a seat on the Army Council.

Major-General Brancker, at present Deputy Director of Military Aeronautics, has been appointed to a command abroad, and for the present his place will not be

GEN. SALMOND.

HUN 'MUTINY' SEQUEL

ADMIRAL CAPELLE SACRIFICED.

TIRPITZ' CAMPAIGN.

FROM OUR OWN CORRESPONDENT.

Ams

A telegram from here says that the learns from Berlin t Capelle, the Minister dered his resignation.

A Cologne telegr Cologne Gazette's Be learns that " Admira claration concerning man Navy did not act the Chancellor's view Natural indignation and Herr Dittmann ances caused Admir sight of the limits c Chancellor's view. stances people ar Capelle crisis."

SIR JOHN SIMON

JOINING THE ARMY IN FRANCE.

Sir John Simon, K.C., M.P., has been given a commission in the Army and has joined the forces in France.

BY OUR SPECIAL C

To induce Holland mous shipments o cement to Belgium, w German military pur declined to permit t Dutch commercial ca parts of the world.

The embargo is r will be maintained u ernment yields. Tho has resorted to co sure with reluctance the ordinary method persuasion were ove tain quarters in L

All our attack along the ridge northeastwards towards Passchendaele went well, though the full advance was not maintained. The Australians won their chief objective over a narrow front on the ridge. It is said that some of the third-line Territorials would not be refused and went on into the outskirts of Passchendaele itself, now about 1,000 yards in front of our line.

SHELL-HOLE HEADQUARTERS.

North of this the line begins to sag. The Ravelbeek here is what the Stroombeek is farther north, and the details of the fighting are very much the same in essentials. Men laboured to help one another out of the slush, while German snipers were busy in front and from the flanks. Bellevue Farm and Yetta House were rookeries of machine guns, and concrete blockhouses were scattered thick as houses in Surrey suburbs. Battalion commanders could establish headquarters only in shell-holes, and all communication was slow and laborious to the pitch of madness. Yet the impossible was done. English troops waded the Ravelbeek swamps and established a line on the firm higher ground on the far side. It was a minor and yet a triumphant achievement. No troops could have shown more hardihood and endurance. Stretcher-bearers who could not walk up were seen crawling up on all fours. Every man was as caked with mud from head to heels as completely as if you had taken a plaster cast of him.

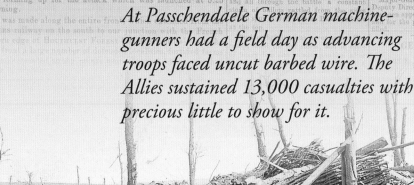

At Passchendaele German machine-gunners had a field day as advancing troops faced uncut barbed wire. The Allies sustained 13,000 casualties with precious little to show for it.

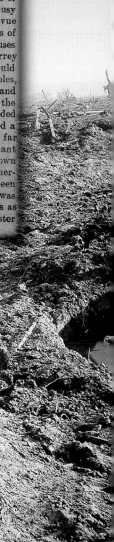

First Battle of Passchendaele

Haig's chief concern was to maintain pressure on an enemy he believed close to collapse. That single-minded approach seemed to shunt potential obstacles that might derail the campaign into the sidings. Not least among those was deteriorating weather. September had been kind; it was a lot to ask the same of October. Moving men over cloying slime and rain-filled craters was bad enough; transporting guns and shells required herculean effort. Then there was the decreasing amount of time between each phase. Plumer had had three weeks to plan his 20 September attack, a luxury that would not now be afforded him. Lloyd George, who had countenanced the Flanders offensive as long as it was not another Somme, might have intervened but did not. He took a jaundiced view of what had been achieved thus far and what might be accomplished by the end of the fighting season, yet he was not minded to intervene.

The 9 October assault on Poelcapelle, which went badly and yielded virtually nothing, deterred neither Plumer nor Haig. A mere three days later they would strike for Passchendaele. That brief window did not allow many more guns to be brought up, which had consequences for any creeping barrage. The Anzacs asked to carry out the task in tandem with this questionable artillery support were hardly in peak fighting condition. The auguries were not good, particularly when considering that Plumer was attempting to advance further than he had in any of his earlier efforts, when circumstances were more favourable. The infantry paid the price as the ill omens produced an inevitable outcome. German machine-gunners had a field day as advancing troops faced uncut barbed wire. The Allies sustained 13,000 casualties with precious little to show for it. To a sceptical British prime minister, it was the perfect opportunity to overrule the commander-in-chief. And yet, four days later, Lloyd George sent Haig a congratulatory telegram, keeping his deep reservations out of the public domain.

PASSCHENDAELE DESOLATION.

OUR INCOMPARABLE INFANTRY

SWAMP OF DEATH & PAIN.

HUNS' NEW RED CROSS CRIME.

Opposite: **The corpses of German soldiers lying at the entrance of a fortified stronghold were found by advancing Allied troops once the battle was over.**

Below: **One regiment marches up to the front while another rests. Morale among the troops at this time was low. The constant rain and mud meant soldiers were rarely dry and constantly struggled to manoeuvre around the feared water-filled shell holes where men could easily get sucked under and drown.**

Above: **Soldiers are transported to the frontline at Polderhoek for yet another "last push".**

Second Battle of Passchendaele

The failure of the first attempt to take Passchedaele gave Haig pause for thought. There was no question of abandoning the venture, but he recognised the need for increased preparation time, allowing fresh troops and sufficient artillery to be brought up. After a fortnight's stay, the next push began on 26 October, led by General Currie's newly arrived Canadian Corps. The target was less than a mile distant, yet Currie envisaged a three-phase advance; this was a prize that would be landed yard by yard. The Canadians took their second bite on 30 October, putting them on the fringes of Passchendaele village. A week later, on 6 November, both the village – what was left of it – and a section of the ridge was under Allied control. A jubilant Haig made a diary note marking the event. "The whole position had been most methodically fortified. Yet our troops succeeded in capturing all their objectives early in the day with small loss – under 700 men!" adding, "Today was a very important success."

In praising a great victory, it helped that the aims were amended to accord with what had been accomplished. Under the original plan Passchendaele was to have been gobbled up immediately as part of a sweeping thrust towards the Belgian coast. Now, Haig declared himself satisfied with occupation of a ruined village and precarious foothold on the ridge where it lay. The commander-in-chief's thoughts were already turning to Cambrai and another set-piece attack before the year was out. One soldier on the ground at Passchendaele described the spoils of the three-and-a-half month campaign that had seen over a quarter of a million killed or wounded. "Dante would never have condemned lost souls to wander in so terrible a purgatory." If that was a poetic description of the barren wasteland that was now theirs, what of the military implications for the Allies? The answer was, not too encouraging, as even Haig himself conceded after the dust had settled. He had possession of an exposed salient, ground that was difficult to defend. Any concerted action on the part of a revitalised, reinforced enemy was almost bound to succeed.

"Dante would never have condemned lost souls to wander in so terrible a purgatory."

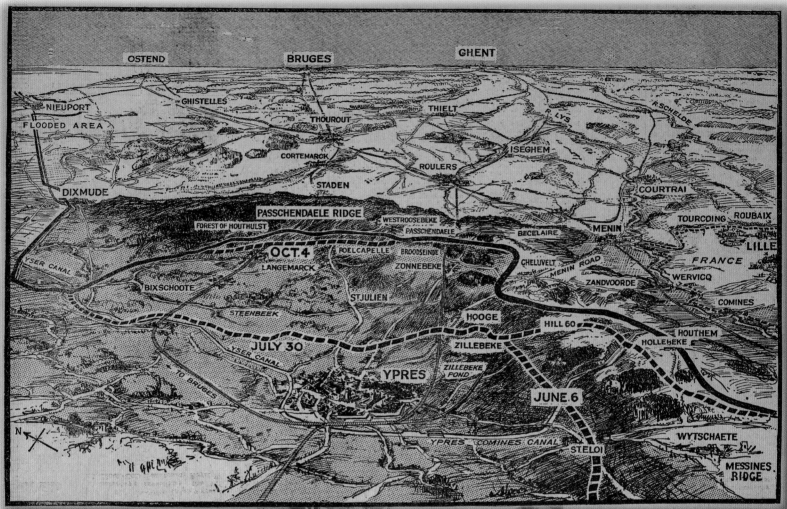

Opposite above: A Canadian stretcher party negotiates the water-filled shell holes.

Opposite below: Men of the 16th Canadian machine Gun Company hold the line at Passchendaele. The Canadians had relieved the weary II Anzac Corps and successfully took the village of Passchendaele.

Above: A map showing the progress made by 20 October. The positions of Allied forces on 6 June, 30 July and 4 October are indicated by dotted lines.

Right: British troops return to billets to rest in a small French town. Soldiers were housed wherever possible with some French villagers offering spare rooms to the welcome troops.

Below: A panoramic view of the devastation of the battlefield of Passchendaele in November 1917.

NEW FLANDERS BATTLE.

HAIG AGAIN ROBBED BY RAIN.

MORE OF THE RIDGE AND 800 PRISONERS.

From SIR DOUGLAS HAIG.
Friday Night.

Operations with limited objectives were undertaken by the British and French Armies early this morning on the YPRES battle front. After a fine day yesterday, with a drying wind, which gave promise of improved fighting conditions, the weather changed suddenly during the night. Heavy rain has fallen almost without break since a very early hour this morning.

Notwithstanding the great difficulties with which the Allied troops had to contend, considerable progress has been made and valuable positions have been won on the greater part of the fronts attacked. The main operation was carried out by **English** and **Canadian** regiments on our front north of the YPRES-ROULERS Railway. **Canadian** battalions moved forward along the main ridge in the direction of PASSCHENDAELE and, passing beyond their objectives, established themselves on the rising ground immediately south of the village. Other **Canadian** battalions, with troops of an **English Naval Brigade** and battalions of **London Territorials**, made further progress in the face of strong opposition along the spurs between the main ridge and our positions east of POELCAPPELLE, capturing a number of strong points and fortified farms.

East and north-east of POELCAPPELLE heavy fighting took place in which **West Lancashire** and **North Country** troops made progress at certain points. Subsidiary attacks were made simultaneously by English troops in the neighbourhood of the MENIN ROAD and by the French north of BIXSCHOOTE. Fierce fighting has taken place all day on both sides of the MENIN ROAD and east of POLDERHOEK in which our troops have made progress and taken a considerable number of prisoners.

North of BIXSCHOOTE **French troops**, attacking with great gallantry, crossed the flood of the ST. JANSBEEK and captured their objectives beyond with a number of prisoners.

Over 800 prisoners have been captured by the Allies in the course of these operations.

BATTLE IN SWAMP.

BRITISH WADE TO THEIR GOAL.

From W. BEACH THOMAS.
WITH THE BRITISH ARMY, Friday.

At 7.30 this morning our troops were seen hauling prisoners out of Polderhoek Château, at 7.40 greencoats were filing out of a pill-box on Meetscheele Spur. Such was the first news of the fresh Flanders battle this morning.

One could scarcely believe the possibility of the good news, so hopeless seemed the conditions when at midnight a bright hunter's moon was obscured by clouds and a dense clinging rain restored the drying ground to a gleaming marsh. Only the energy and stamina of our artillery drivers had made any battle possible.

Night after night without rest they have played their part of obscure heroism and driven their teams without flinching through noisy but invisible shells; for in these days of aiming by map the Germans double and treble their fire when darkness falls, shooting blind with the fury of a blinded Cyclops.

The rain was a disaster, but both airmen and infantry, following the example

Yesterday's British-French attack was on a 12-mile front, extending from south-west of Houthulst Forest to south of the Ypres-Menin road.

Along with the Somme, Passchendaele has become a byword for the horror of trench warfare, extravagant generals making miserly gains on the back of reckless expenditure of human life.

Below: Sappers were able to rapidly construct new bridges to replace those left in ruins by the German Army.

November 1917

2 The Balfour Declaration was sent from Britain's Foreign Secretary, Arthur Balfour, to Walter Rothschild, a leader of the British Jewish community, for transmission to the Zionist Federation of Great Britain and Ireland. The letter supported plans for a Jewish national home in Palestine.

4 British troops arrived in Italy.

5 Under the command of General Sir Stanley Maude British troops made headway against the Turks at Tikrit in the Mesopotamian Campaign.

6 Turkish forces withdrew from Tikrit as British troops occupied the town.

The Canadian Corps captured Passchendaele and the ridge beyond, effectively ending the three month long Third Battle of Ypres.

7 After months of fighting British Battalions finally captured Gaza from the Turks.

The "October" Revolution began with an armed insurrection in Petrograd as the Bolsheviks began to takeover Government buildings.

8 Following the Bolshevik coup in Petrograd, the Winter Palace was taken and Vladimir Ilyich Lenin succeeded Alexander Kerensky as Russian Prime Minister.

Armando Diaz replaced Luigi Cadorna as Commander-in-Chief of the Italian Army.

9 The text of the Balfour Declaration was published in the Press.

10 After the village of Passchendaele had been taken by Canadian Divisions on 6, the final action of the battle saw an attack designed to straighten out the line. Even after this final assault, the Germans still held the northern end of the Passchendaele Ridge.

11 Otto Ritter von Dandl replaced Georg von Hertling as President of the Council of Ministers of Bavaria.

13 Paul Painlevé resigned as Prime Minister of France and was succeeded by French statesman Georges Clemenceau.

14 The battle of Junction Station, which had begun the previous day, saw the British defeat a Turkish attempt to defend the line of the railway to Jerusalem.

15 Alexander Kerensky fled from Petrograd as the Bolsheviks took power.

16 After several days of fierce fighting the Bolsheviks seized control in Moscow.

17 The Second Battle of Heligoland Bight took place in the North Sea. The inconclusive naval engagement was fought between British and German squadrons when a force of cruisers was sent to attack German minesweepers which were attempting to sweep a channel through British minefields in the Heligoland Bight.

18 General Sir Stanley Maude died of cholera and was replaced by Lieutenant General William Marshall who halted operations in Mesopotamia for the winter.

20 The Battle of Cambrai was launched with the use of massed tanks supported by heavy artillery bombardment. Six divisions of British infantry attacked the German Second Army, led by General Georg Von Marwitz.

21 The French ambassador received a note informing him that the Bolshevik government, under the leadership of Lenin and Trotsky, intended to begin pourparlers of peace.

22 A German counterattack at Cambrai captured the village of Fontaine.

24 The Battle of Nebi Samwil ended. The battle, which had begun on 17, was the first British attempt to capture Jerusalem during their 1917 invasion of Palestine. It was fought between the British Empire's Egyptian Expeditionary Force and troops from the Ottoman Empire.

25 German troops, under the command of Colonel von Lettow-Vorbeck, crossed the Rovuma River into Portuguese East Africa at Ngomano and defeated Portuguese troops.

27 Russian and German delegates met to discuss an armistice.

28 In the Mwiti Valley in German East Africa, German forces under Captain Theodor Tafel surrendered to the British.

29 An Inter-Allied Conference opened in Paris.

30 The Germans launched a counter-attack on the Cambrai front and regained much of the territory lost. British forces then recaptured Vacquerie.

"Passchendaele was only a step in the long struggle but it was a definite step towards victory." GENERAL SIR HERBERT PLUMER

Third Battle of Ypres: the reckoning

The offensive ended with territorial gains along a seven-mile front – some 20 square miles in all. Some of it was advantageous high ground, so there was a strategic dividend. On the debit side of the ledger, those gains had been achieved at a cost of some 250,000 casualties – roughly equal to the losses inflicted on the enemy. The U-boat bases survived intact. And Passchendaele itself stood upon a precarious salient, which Haig recognised would be "difficult and costly to hold". That was borne out early in the new year, when possession of the hard-won ground changed hands once again, rather more quickly than the three long months it had taken the Allies to capture it.

A grim and futile fight

Along with the Somme, Passchendaele has become a byword for the horror of trench warfare, extravagant generals making miserly gains on the back of reckless expenditure of human life. This was the battle, fought upon a shell-blasted morass, that moved one staff officer to comment: "Good God! Did we really send men to fight in this?" It put Haig squarely in the dock, with Lloyd George as chief accuser, and eventual victory did not temper the former prime minister's views when he came to write his memoirs. Passchendaele, he wrote, ranked alongside "the most gigantic, tenacious, grim, futile, and bloody fights ever waged", adding that it would not have been sanctioned had the War Cabinet been in possession of the full facts. The newly installed Pétain, he claimed, had been against a major British offensive, but his advice – known to Haig – was kept from the political leadership. Lloyd George further asserted that Haig's generals were not fully behind the operation. Almost two decades on from the events, Plumer clarified his own position, stating that as the weather worsened he did recommend calling a halt to the offensive, only to be informed by Haig that there were "other considerations" necessitating its continuation – a reference Plumer later took to be the state of the French army, whose collapse had been a closely guarded secret.

The position of Britain's ally became the subject of much debate. Had Pétain pleaded with Haig to conduct a pressure-relieving offensive, then Passchendaele had a justification beyond mere territorial gain. In 1927 Haig wrote: "The problem for us was how to prevent the Germans from attacking the French, who were then incapable of offering an effective resistance. The mere suggestion of a pause in our attacks in the north at once brought Pétain in his train to see me, and beg me to put in another effort against Passchendaele without any delay. Knowing as I did what the state of the French Army was in 1917 (for Pétain told me more than once about his awful anxieties) I felt thankful when the winter came and the French army was still in the field."

In fact there was no direct appeal. The defensively minded Pétain had more than half an eye on the transatlantic army that was mobilising and was content to play a waiting game. Lloyd George said Haig's report to Cabinet in October 1917 made no mention of French entreaties to carry on, something he would surely have included in vindication of a costly offensive that had failed to reach its objective. The idea of winning the war before the year was out, before American boots were on the ground, appealed to Haig. In trying to achieve that end perhaps he assumed he was also assisting a beleaguered partner; that Pétain would not be averse to a British attack while he was applying balm to his ailing troops.

Writing in 1934 – six years after Haig's death – Plumer, far from agreeing with Lloyd George's contention that Passchendaele was a futile undertaking, used a sporting metaphor to express his view: "When one of two great boxers has knocked out his opponent, say in the 12th round, how much of that result is due to the heavy blows they exchanged in previous rounds?" He hammered home the point: "Passchendaele was only a step in the long struggle but it was a definite step towards victory."

Plumer, then, articulated Haig's own ubiquitous secondary aim, a reliable stand-by in the absence of a grand breakthrough: wearing down the enemy, consuming his resources, breaking his will. Ludendorff said Passchendaele strained the German army severely. The fact that Haig regarded Western Front action as "one great and continuous engagement" rather than a series of separate battles – Passchendaele thus rendered part of a vast four-year-long endeavour – showed him in a favourable light. At a stroke it gave him a 100 per cent success rate: one battle, one victory. Just as Lloyd George sought to distance himself from a battle he had the power to halt but did not, so Haig chose an interpretation that defused the charge that Passchendaele was an exercise in obtuse bungling. Perhaps both were guilty of presenting partial, self-serving accounts.

Left: **Troops undertake trench maintenance during a lull in the fighting. Ladders were fixed to the sides of the banks to allow soldiers to scale them quickly when launching an attack.**

Battle of Malmaison

Under Pétain the morale of the French army improved markedly in the second half of 1917. Nivelle's successor was even able to mount limited offensives while the events at Ypres played out. In August the French attacked at Verdun, reclaiming territory lost in 1916. Then, as their Western Front partner closed in on its Flanders objective in late October, Pétain's forces were also on the attack in Chemin des Dames. The Battle of Malmaison was a resounding success. The chief aim had been to reduce a salient in this sector, but the French exceeded all expectations. They made excellent use of the artillery at their disposal, and with a gun every six yards the bombardment was highly concentrated. It was also a good day for their tanks, over 70 taking to the battlefield and most surviving intact. The encounter ended with all French objectives met, and the Germans discouraged enough to withdraw completely from the ridge at Chemin des Dames.

Notwithstanding those few bright spots in France's campaigning year, during the autumn its leaders exhorted Britain to take a greater share of the burden in the line. Consenting to that request would have had implications for the Ypres offensive: manpower constraints meant Britain could not extend the length of front for which it was responsible and at the same time focus its efforts on Flanders. It was another opportunity for the politicians to rein in the military, an invitation to shut down the Passchendaele offensive under the banner of assisting the country's chief ally. That invitation was declined, and the Third Battle of Ypres was allowed to run to its conclusion on Haig's timetable.

Below: The Battle of Malmaison, was a huge success with the French capturing the fort and taking 13,000 prisoners. Two thousand guns and 120,000 shells a day had been used with the usual devastating effects on the landscape.

Above right: Germany looks for peace and to close her account with the Allies while holding a big balance in her favour.

Opposite: French soldiers man their guns in captured German positions.

CROWN PRINCE RETIRES
WITHDRAWAL BEFORE PETAIN.
FORCED FROM THE CHEMIN-DES-DAMES.

From GENERAL PETAIN.

Friday Night.

The results of the victory of LA MALMAISON have not been long delayed. The enemy, threatened on his right by the pressure of our infantry and overwhelmed by our artillery, which bombarded from newly captured positions without cessation his organisations to the south of the Ailette, was compelled to abandon the CHEMIN-DES-DAMES, to which he has clung for six months, on a front of about 13 miles, from as far as FROIDMONT FARM up to the east of CRAONNE.

Our troops, pouring down from the slopes north of the CHEMIN-DES-

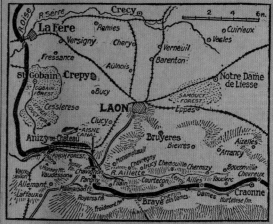

Ten days ago the French captured Malmaison Fort and forced the Germans across the Oise-Aisne Canal. Now the enemy has had to abandon the strongly fortified Chemin-des-Dames.

DAMES, have occupied the German positions to a depth of more than half a mile at certain points.

The villages of COURTECON, CERNY-EN-LAONNOIS, AILLES, and CHEVREUX are in our hands.

Our patrols, keeping contact with the enemy, have reached the Ailette, between BRAYE-EN-LAONNAIS and CERNY.

GERMAN OFFICIAL (Afternoon).—At the Oise-Aisne Canal and along the ridge of the Chemin-des-Dames there was a considerable increase in the fighting activity. After several hours of drum-fire strong French forces attacked near Braye. Their assaults collapsed with heavy losses before our lines.

Evening.—Unnoticed and undisturbed by the enemy, we systematically withdrew our lines from the hilly front of the Chemin-des-Dames during last night.—Admiralty, per Wireless.

The Germans were discouraged enough to withdraw completely from the ridge at Chemin des Dames.

PETAIN SECURES HIS GAINS.

OVER 70 GUNS CAPTURED.

BRITISH REPEL TWO MORE ASSAULTS.

GERMAN CLAIMS ON ISONZO.

"SOME THOUSANDS OF PRISONERS."

Five of the fronts are now very active —the British, French, Italian, and Russian, and also the Allied line in the Balkans.

Pétain's men are securing their great gains of Tuesday south-west of Laon. That the Germans suffered very heavily at their hands is indicated by the fact that ... far they have made no counter-attack but have only shelled the new French line on the crest of the ridge commanding the Laon railways. Our Allies' captures now exceed 8,000 prisoners and more than 70 guns.

On the Flanders front two more Hun attacks on our positions in the Houthulst Forest are recorded, without effecting any material change. During artillery fighting a big explosion was caused behind the German lines.

The Austro-German offensive against the Italians to the north of the Bainsizza plateau, the opening of which our Milan correspondent reported in yesterday's *Daily Mail*, has resulted, according to yesterday's German report, in the cap-

From GENERAL PETAIN,
Wednesday Afternoon.

The night has been calm generally on the whole of the battle front north of the AISNE. The enemy has attempted no infantry counter-attack and has confined himself to bombarding our new lines, especially in the region of VAUDESSON.

Our troops are organising themselves on the conquered ground.

The number of prisoners counted up to the present is 8,000, of which 160 are officers. They belong to 8 different divisions, including two of the Guards. The staff of three regiments, including their three colonels, are among the prisoners.

Two enemy divisions which had been placed in reserve behind the front were engaged in yesterday's fighting and were severely handled.

The enemy last night delivered a violent attack north-east of HILL 344 (north of Verdun). After a desperate fight we repelled the enemy.

CAPTURES YESTERDAY.

Wednesday Night.

North of the Aisne the German guns showed special activity in the sector of La Royère-Les Bovettes and in the region

Haig has repelled two more attacks on the south of Houthulst Forest (Map No. 1). The Austro-Germans claim the capture of Italian trenches between Mount Rombon and a point south of Tolmino (Map No. 2). Petain has secured his gains on the crest where a dent is shown in the line (Map No. 3).

ture of the foremost Italian trenches and of "some thousands" of prisoners.

of Malmaison Fort. On our new front, which extends from Monkey Hill, which we occupy entirely, to Chavignon

HEAVY FIGHTING WEST OF CAMBRAI.

'S VICTORY.   spired everybody at the outset. I met this morning, as usual, columns of infantry going up to the fight or return- ing for a rest, whistling and singing.   BRITISH WAR MISSION.   GREAT STAND BY ITALIANS.   RUSSIA AND TRUCE.   8-COURS

LORD READING'S SUCCESS.   HUN GENERAL'S JOURNEY.   RIOT O

Tanks attack en masse at Cambrai

The Allied "victory", of sorts, at Passchendaele, did not bring to an end the year's action on the Western Front. Even as that battle petered out, Haig was giving consent to an offensive that offered the Tank Corps the opportunity to show its worth in the field. Under fire from his political masters, the commander-in-chief needed a good-news story, and the tank might help end the year on an upbeat note. Rain-lashed, shell-blasted Ypres had not been amenable to this weapon of war still in its infancy. Perhaps further to the southeast, in the relatively quiet sector around Cambrai where the ground did not resemble a lunar landscape, the tank would fare better? And this time it would not be a piecemeal affair: hundreds would descend upon the Hindenburg Line to give the vaunted German defence a stern examination.

General Tudor's surprise attack

The Cambrai battle plan was the brainchild not of Tank Corps staff but artillery commander Brigadier-General Hugh Tudor. His idea was for a surprise attack with no pre-registration of guns and an infantry advance behind a large number of barbed-wire-flattening tanks. This was put before General Sir Julian Byng, whose 3rd Army held the sector. At the same time, the Tank Corps' chief of staff Lieutenant-Colonel John Fuller had his own idea for an offensive around St Quentin, and was drawing up plans as to how tanks could be deployed to best advantage. The two schemes were amalgamated, but after the experience of the Third Battle of Ypres, Haig demanded rapid results or the attack would be halted.

Under a cloak of secrecy around 470 tanks were transported to the battle zone. Fuller had overseen training exercises that laid down precisely how tanks and infantry should progress towards the enemy line. The hardware was the Mk IV tank, which came in "male" and "female" varieties. Both were fitted with Lewis guns, but the former was beefed up with the addition of six-pounders, which meant it weighed in slightly the heavier at 32 tons. Half of the eight-strong crew manned the weapons, the rest responsible for getting the metal behemoths from A to B. Turning was no simple task: it required two gearsmen to work in tandem, selecting the ratio for each track independently. On good ground these lumbering giants might make speeds approaching 4mph; considerably less if the terrain was difficult. Those difficulties included negotiating 14-foot-wide trenches, constructed with the tank threat in mind. To cross that barrier tanks carried fascines – thick bundles of brushwood that could be dropped into any gulf too steep and wide to drive over. Once deposited there was no going back, hence it was desirable for as many tanks as possible to make use of the same fascine. All well and good in one of Fuller's drills; perhaps not so easy in the heat of battle.

For all their armour plating, tanks were certainly not impervious to enemy fire, and their slow rate of progress made them an easy target. With high levels of vibration, stultifying heat and carbon monoxide leakage, the crews had to tolerate considerable discomfort. Conditions also impinged on tank fire accuracy when it was on the move. Gunners might do better when the vehicle was stationary, but that was hardly desirable. Mechanical breakdown – a frequent problem – was another handicap. Germany's engineers did eventually produce their own tank, the A7V, but the teething issues and drawbacks that bedevilled this new technology meant there was no great rush to the drawing board when the first British tank was seen advancing across no-man's-land in 1916.

Below: A British tank is grounded on the German Second line about one mile north of Ribecourt. By the end of the first day of Cambrai 71 tanks had mechanical damage, 43 were ditched and 65 were destroyed.

BATTLE FOR CAMBRAI.

VILLAGE TAKEN & LOST.

LAST HINDENBURG LINE ENTERED.

PRISONERS NEARLY 9000.

From FIELD-MARSHAL SIR DOUGLAS HAIG.
Thursday Morning.

Yesterday evening our troops, moving forward north of CANTAING, attacked and captured the village of FONTAINE-NOTRE-DAME [two miles from the western outskirts of Cambrai], together with a number of pri-soners.

Thursday Night.
On the southern battle front the day has been spent in consolidating the large area over which our troops have advanced during the last two days. This has been successfully carried out, except at FONTAINE-NOTRE-DAME, which the enemy has retaken by a counter-attack.

Much credit is due to the transportation services for the rapidity with which the concentration for the operations of the last few days was

Advances over six-mile front

On the eve of battle Tank Corps commander Brigadier-General Hugh Elles issued an order relishing the opportunity before them, the chance "to operate on good going in the van of the battle". At 6.20 am the next morning, 20 November, a 1,000-gun bombardment opened up on General von Marwitz's 2nd Army. The early stages went entirely the Allies' way, with advances of over four miles on a six-mile front. Two enemy trench lines were breached, the Germans resorting to blowing up bridges in a desperate attempt to prevent a rout. Significant gains had been made at a cost of, by Western Front standards, moderate casualty figures of just 4,000. Back in Blighty church bells tolled in celebration – prematurely, as events transpired.

> *The early stages went entirely the Allies' way, with advances of over four miles on a six-mile front.*

The tank had played a full part in the stunning early success, though as one Corps member recalled, it was by no means all plain sailing:

We found ourselves in dire peril. A tank close on our right received a direct hit and burst into flames. I only saw one man roll out of the side door. The tank on our left also had a direct hit. I did not see anyone get out of that tank… I saw the German field gunners well in the fore loading their gun and I knew this lot was for us. There was a terrific roar and "Hotspur" shuddered from stem to stern. I saw our left caterpillar track fly into the air. Our left nose was blown off. The tank was filled with smoke and I thought we were on fire. But not so. If that last shell had landed two feet nearer to where the officer and I sat we would most certainly both have been killed and the tank smashed up.

Lance Corporal Alfred Brisco, 8th Tank Battalion

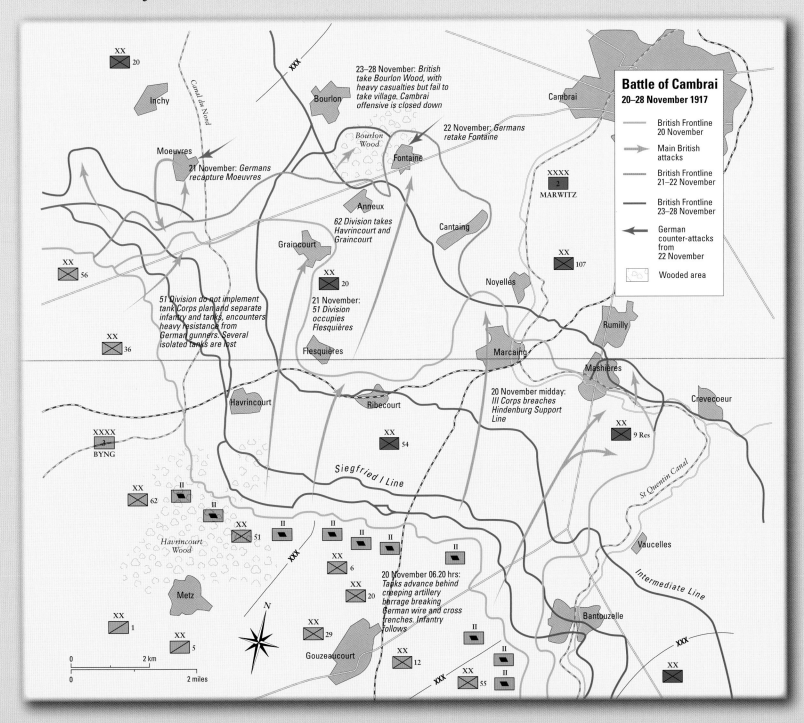

German counter attacks

A familiar pattern then emerged with a failure to capitalise on early gains. In some ways the advance fell victim to its own success as communication lines were stretched and the reserve strength was inadequate for the rate of progress. In particular the failure to take Flesquières on the first day – where tank and infantry became separated – was seen as a missed opportunity. The attack was further hampered by the need to reinforce the Italian front in response to the latest German-Austrian attack which came just when manpower was most needed to press home the advantage. The surprise element had gone, the tank force much depleted. There was but a brief window before the German line was strengthened. Haig could have stuck to his 48-hour threshold, but instead demanded that the vital high ground of Bourlon Wood be taken forthwith. That target receded into the distance during fierce fighting over the following days, and on 30 November the German counter began in earnest. Von Richthofen's Flying Circus was also on the scene, giving Germany the edge in the aerial struggle. Thoughts of advance dwindled as the Allies withdrew to a defendable line for the winter, harried by the shock tactics of the new breed of German stormtroopers. Most of the ground taken had been surrendered by the time the battle ran its course on 7 December. In terms of territory and casualty numbers, honours were shared.

Cambrai signalled the death knell for week-long bombardments that revealed the attackers' hand and all too often failed in their destructive intent. Shorter bursts of artillery fire, making full use of the gunners' ability to fire off the map without the need for ranging shots, was found to be far more effective. Advances in sound detection to pinpoint the position of enemy guns were equally important to maintaining the element of surprise.

What of the tank's contribution? Its ability to override barbed wire up to 100 yards wide in places was amply demonstrated. Some German soldiers had fled or surrendered in the face of the advancing metal monster. On the other hand, half of Fuller's "moving fortresses" had fallen victim to enemy fire,

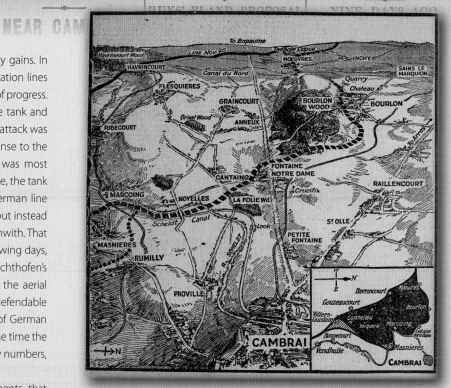

mechanical gremlins or the terrain. German engineers cannibalised those they could lay hands on and sent them into battle in the new year while developing their own A7V. Cambrai was thus a signpost rather than a destination; the tank of 1917 had limitations as well as promise. All the indications were that in the next round of campaigning it would come further into its own, especially when used in close co-ordination with artillery and infantry. If that was the future of warfare, the past was also in evidence at Cambrai in the shape of Haig's revered lance and sabre-bearing cavalry, waiting to exploit a major breakthrough that never came.

Below: **Highland Territorials cross a German communication trench during the attack on Flesquières. The troops and tanks became separated allowing enemy forces to strike back.**

Above: **A map reflecting the Central Powers' perspective indicates the advance since 20 November. The thick broken line shows the front on 2 December.**

Cambrai signalled the death knell for week-long bombardments that revealed the attackers' hand.

Top left: A tank is grounded trying to cross the difficult terrain.

Above left: The deserted town of Ribecourt immediately after its capture.

Above right: Men of the 11th Leicester Regiment in a captured German Second line trench at Ribecourt.

Right: A mixture of "male" and "female" tanks were used – males carrying small artillery pieces and females armed with machine guns.

Below: An ammunition column stretches as far as the eye can see while a heavy gun manned by Anzac artillerymen is in position on the left.

OUR BOY FIGHTERS IN THE AIR—
England's "best aviator" killed

A proud son of Nottinghamshire, Albert Ball joined the Sherwood Foresters at the outbreak of war, turning 18 as hostilities ensued. He was mechanically minded and drawn to the fledgling Royal Flying Corps, to which he transferred on completing his pilot training. It was a busy time for Ball, who combined soldiering duties with learning to fly at Hendon, where he proved himself an eager rather than exceptional pilot. The latter adjective was soon being appended to his name as this combative, unassuming character began racking up victories that would make him one of most celebrated airmen of the war. Ball was fearless in the face of overwhelming odds; indeed he preferred to plough his own furrow than be part of a mass attack. On one occasion he took on six enemy aircraft single-handed, ever prepared to take his own plane within yards of his quarry before letting rip with his machine gun. A favoured tactic was to strike from below, strafing the underside of enemy aircraft. He did not glory in his successes. Ball was a man of deep religious conviction, his deadly trade a matter of duty and service. "I hate this game," he wrote, "but it is the only thing one must do just now. Won't it be lovely when all this beastly killing is over and we can just enjoy ourselves and not hurt anyone?"

Ball demonstrated that spirit on one occasion when he and an opponent faced each other, their ammunition spent. They smiled and waved before going their separate ways. For all his combat successes this much decorated hero no doubt looked forward to a peace settlement, when he could devote more time to gardening and playing the violin. But his date with destiny arrived long before the armistice was signed.

In April 1917 he was posted to France with 56 Squadron, which was showing off the capabilities of the new SE5 fighter. In his brief time with that unit the tally of enemy planes he had accounted for rose to 44. Ball took off for the final time on 7 May 1917, leading an 11-strong team into yet another aerial battle. This time he tangled with Germany's crack Jasta 11 squadron, usually commanded by Manfred von Richthofen – the famous Red Baron – but on this occasion led by his brother Lothar. Ball pursued Richthofen into dense cloud, eyewitnesses reporting that when he emerged into clear air he was flying upside down, his propeller not rotating. He crashed near the village of Annoeullin in northern France, dying in the arms of a young woman who went to render assistance.

Posthumous VC

Lothar von Richthofen had also been brought down in the fight but survived, proud to claim such a notable scalp. It remains a mystery as to whether enemy fire did for Albert Ball or whether mechanical failure and disorientation may have precipitated the fatal crash. What is certain is that at 20 he had already achieved legendary status. He was awarded a posthumous VC, while France bestowed the Legion d'honneur. His home city had already made him a Freeman, almost unheard of in one so young. RFC commander Sir Hugh Trenchard said that Captain Ball "was the most daring, skilful and successful pilot the Royal Flying Corps has ever had". One who served alongside him said: "England has lost her best aviator." Germany paid its own tribute, sending word that he had been buried with full honours. It was they who marked his grave with the inscription: "Fallen in air combat for his Fatherland".

Germany paid its own tribute, sending word that Ball had been buried with full honours.

British Empire's top ace

William Avery Bishop is a legendary figure in his native Canada, a man whose name adorns an airport and about whom a stage musical has been written, to name but two of many tributes. Credited with 72 victories, he stands atop the list of World War One aces hailing from Britain and her dominions.

Born in Owen Sound, Ontario, on 8 February 1894, Billy, as he was commonly known, preferred outdoor pursuits to scholarship. He was a fine horseman and a deadeye shot, but his academic ability and lack of application proved a handicap during his cadetship at the Royal Military College. There were serious doubts as to whether he would stay the course. Those evaporated once war was declared, and in June 1915 he crossed the Atlantic as a 2nd lieutenant in the Canadian Mounted Rifles. For Billy, flying in clear air held much more appeal than wading through cloying mud, and he soon landed an observer's role with the Royal Flying Corps. One of his reconnaissance sorties ended with a crash landing that put him in hospital with leg injuries, but he was undeterred in his ambition to become a pilot. He was not the most naturally gifted airman; he was dogged, though, and his marksmanship made up for any deficiency in his flying ability.

By March 1917 he was back in France, a fully-fledged pilot, flying Nieuports with 60 Squadron. Before the month was out he had claimed his first combat successes. The first was a hairy experience, for he followed his stricken quarry earthwards, only for his own engine to cut out. He just managed to limp to safety. "Bloody April" was costly for the Allies but a profitable month for Bishop. He preferred to fly solo, sometimes stalking his prey as he manoeuvred into prime attacking position, sometimes adopting a more direct approach, backing his flying and gunnery skills. He also began toying with the idea of attacking an enemy airfield, perhaps involving Albert Ball in the scheme, the British ace whom Bishop held in highest regard. Ball's death on 7 May meant that his plan would revert to a lone-wolf operation.

The attack took place in the early hours of 2 June 1917. He was back at base before 6.00 am, having left his imprint on Estourmel airfield. He described how he knocked out one plane before it had barely left the ground. Another crashed on take-off, harried by Bishop's looming presence. Two enemy aircraft did manage to get airborne. "I climbed and engaged one at 1,000 feet, finishing my drum, and he crashed 300 yards from the aerodrome," he recorded. Bishop spent the last of his ammunition on the fourth, then headed for home, his plane showing distinct signs that some of the ground fire had found its mark.

Billy Bishop was awarded the Victoria Cross for this action, and by the time he went to Buckingham Palace for the investiture ceremony he also had the Military Cross and Distinguished Service Order to collect. It is said King George V noted that presenting all three simultaneously was a first.

A period of well earned home leave in autumn 1917 enabled Bishop to tie the knot with his fiancée, Margaret. In a letter to her he confided that the business in which he was engaged and at which he was so clinically proficient on occasion got to him. "Sometimes all of this awful fighting makes you wonder if you have a right to call yourself human. My honey, I am so sick of it all, the killing, the war. All I want is home and you."

Duty called, however, and Bishop responded as he took command of 85 Squadron in spring 1918. He took his victory tally to 67, and ended his combat career by adding five to the total shortly before being grounded, deemed too valuable a property to expose to further risk. He was promoted to lieutenant colonel – later air marshal – and played a key role in establishing the Royal Canadian Air Force, though the armistice came before the RCAF was up and running. After the war Bishop ventured into civil aviation, teaming up with compatriot and fellow ace William Barker in an enterprise that did not flourish. He also worked in the oil industry, from which he retired in 1952, four years before his death, aged 62.

Opposite above right: Nottinghamshire-born Ball joined the Sherwood Foresters at the outbreak of war when he was just 18.

Opposite above left: Ball's parents, sister and a friend joined him at Buckingham Palace on 18 November 1916. He had just been invested with the DSO and Bar and the Military Cross by King George V.

Opposite below left: Ball in the cockpit of his Caudron G3.

Opposite below middle: Albert Ball was buried in Annoeullin in northern France. After the war ended his grave was found and a new cross was erected by Number 207 Squadron. Ball's father asked that Albert's body remain in Annoeullin and erected his own headstone. Later he purchased the field where his son died and established a memorial there.

Opposite below left: It remains a mystery as to whether enemy fire or mechanical failure and disorientation caused Ball's fatal crash.

Above right: When Billy Bishop joined his first patrol the average life expectancy for a fighter pilot was 11 days.

Below: Bishop's Nieuport 17 aircraft had a 110-horse-power engine and a Lewis gun capable of firing a projectile at over 2,800 feet per second.

Bishop preferred to fly solo, sometimes stalking his prey as he manoeuvred into prime attacking position.

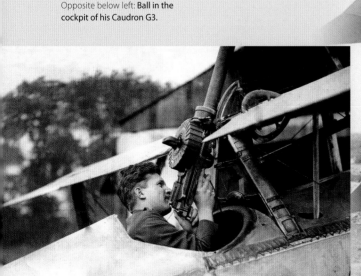

RUSSIANS MUTINY IN BATTLE.

MUTINY IN BRUSILOFF'S ARMY.

DEBATES DURING GERMAN ATTACK.

REGIMENTS RETIRE OR DEFY ORDERS.

The agitation carried on by the Russian extremists, many of whom are in German pay, has created a serious position in Galicia.

General Brusiloff reports in a most remarkable communiqué that when the Germans launched their offensive on Thursday east of Lemberg a Russian regiment retired without orders, and that others, after discussion in the midst of the conflict whether they would obey a command to support the section attacked, refused.

The result was that the enemy was able to "develop his success" and, according to Berlin, to carry three zones of defence, apparently meaning three trench systems. The enemy claims that up to Thursday afternoon "a few thousand" prisoners had been taken.

In Southern Galicia on Tuesday a Russian regiment "began to leave" a captured village, but later Russian native cavalry from the Caucasus impetuously attacked, carrying with them the regiment which had retired, and restored the position.

ATTEMPT TO KILL KERENSKY.

ASSASSIN'S BULLET MISSES.

PETROGRAD, Thursday.

An attempt has been made on the life of M. Kerensky, the Russian War Minister, in the town of Polotsk (east of Dvinsk). A shot was fired but missed.

PETROGRAD ITSELF AGAIN.

PARTISAN TRUCE.

From ALEXANDER M. THOMPSON.
PETROGRAD, Thursday, 6 p.m.

The rainstorm is spent, the sun shines again, and the insurrection has vanished as suddenly and almost as completely as the clouds. Looking back to Tuesday, the change seems magical. The bridges are reopened, the tramway-cars are running, shopkeepers are timidly taking down their shutters, and the everlasting babel of street debaters is resumed with, if possible, increased verbosity.

M. Pechekhonoff, the Socialist Food Minister, with whom I had a long talk this morning, expresses the conviction that trouble for the present is ended. The revolution naturally will not reach rock bottom immediately perhaps, and may in the course of settlement touch one or more extremes, but all the Ministers agree that despite economic, industrial, and financial difficulties the situation has distinctly improved in the last month.

In his own department of food supply the chief trouble is transport. There is a shortage undoubtedly of meat, butter, and other articles owing to consumption

Above: **Members of the German army assess the Russian machine guns and mortars captured at Riga on 3 September 1917.**

Left: **A Russian soldier assaults his retreating comrade at Ternopil. A combination of the Provisional Government's policies and Bolshevik agitators caused riots and mutinies on the frontline.**

Below: **Russian troops flee from the fighting at Ternopil in total disarray. It was the first day of the ill-fated Kerensky Offensive, destined to collapse two weeks later.**

Opposite below middle: **Bolshevik militias take aim at rival Mensheviks on the Nevsky Prospect during the October Revolution.**

Opposite below right: **Lenin reads an edition of *Pravda* (inset) at his office in the Kremlin. The paper closed down in 1914 but was able to reopen after the overthrow of Tsar Nicholas II in February 1917. It became the official voice of the Soviet Communists and was used to promote the party's propaganda. By the end of the year it was selling nearly 100,000 copies daily.**

Bolsheviks seize power

Russia's new Provisional Government, formed from the Duma in March, immediately introduced a raft of reforms. Justice Minister Alexander Kerensky expanded civil liberties and issued plans for a fairer electoral system, measures that might once have helped the Tsar survive as sovereign in a constitutional monarchy. The new administration also faced two pressing questions: what to do about the royal family, and about the prosecution of the war. On the first matter, opinion ranged from leniency to holding a trial to unconfined bloodlust. The family was put under house arrest, initially in relatively comfortable surroundings. King George V, the Tsar's cousin, baulked at the idea of a haven in Britain. Perhaps they might be allowed to live out their days in Crimea, as Nicholas hoped? As for continuing the war, Britain was sanguine about the internal events that had overtaken its ally. Lloyd George opined: "We believe that the revolution is the greatest service the Russian people have yet made to the cause for which the Allied peoples have been fighting." That seemed a reasonable statement, particularly as the Provisional Government articulated its intention to maintain its alliance obligations. But the picture was clouded by the existence of a separate revolutionary body with a strong power base at work in the very same building: the Petrograd Soviet. The two groups eyed each other warily. Soviet spokesmen made much capital from the fact that the newly installed prime minister was Prince Georgy Lvov. Had the Tsar simply been replaced by a government leader steeped in privilege? It was an uneasy stand-off. Not uneasy enough for Germany, though. The smooth transfer of power and renewed war aims was not what the Fatherland wanted. Its interests were served by an inward-looking Russia riven by strife; and it identified the very person to fan the flames of unrest in Lenin, the Bolshevik leader who for years had been agitating from beyond his country's borders.

Lenin: power to the Soviets

Lenin had no time for Germany, or any of the capitalist-imperialist belligerents. But they were in tune regarding welcoming war, if for rather different reasons. Lenin believed this internecine struggle would sweep away the old order, ushering in a golden age of democratic centralism where workers, not financiers, would reap the benefits of their labours. Bread, land and peace was his popular slogan. "All power to the soviets." He was contemptuous of the Provisional Government, decried as a militant republic taking the place of a militant monarchy. The new administration was made up of "capitalists who want to continue the imperialist war and adhere to the robber treaties of the tsarist monarchy". It was music to the ears of Germany's leadership, which had arranged for this "plague bacillus" – Churchill's metaphor – to be spirited into his homeland by sealed train. He found Kerensky, now Minister of War, rallying the troops and making plans for a summer offensive in Galicia. But it was the peace message of the Bolsheviks – amply represented in the new government – that captured the prevailing mood. Where once the army simply wanted more effective and efficient management of the war effort, there was now general antipathy.

"The revolution is the greatest service the Russian people have yet made to the cause for which the Allied peoples have been fighting." LLOYD GEORGE

THE DAILY MAIL, FRIDAY, JULY 20, 1917.

GERMAN ATTACK IN FORCE ON RUSSIA.

RY BY AIR.   SPAIN'S HOUR.   *LATE WAR NEWS.*   BRITISH ATTACKED NEAR COAST.   GERMAN OFF

NS FOR AEROPLANE   SPEECH OF GERMAN CHANCELLOR.   "RUSSIAN FRONT

ODUCTION   HUNS THROWN BACK.

KORNILOFF MARCHING ON PETROGRAD.

NTER-REVOLUTION IN | RAIDS AND PATROL | GERMAN-SWEDISH PLOT | RUSSIAN ARMY CHAOS. | LT. M

RUSSIAN ARMY CHAOS.

KORNILOFF'S WARNING.

ANARCHY & FAMINE.

The Russian Commander-in-Chief, General Korniloff, has given the Moscow National Conference some hard facts about the disorganisation and indiscipline in the Army; the enormous fall in the production of guns, shells, and aeroplanes; and the muddle on the railways.

General Korniloff demanded the adoption of stern measures, which he outlined, in order to restore the fighting strength of the Army. He was fully supported by General Kaledin, speaking for the Cossacks.

From ALEXANDER M. THOMPSON.

Monday.

Moscow's beautiful gold and red theatre has doubtless seen many brilliant assemblies and exciting dramas, but none to eclipse to-day's. All that Russia has of distinction in science, art, letters, arms, and politics was gathered on the deep stage and the six tiers under the superb crystal chandelier. To-day, for the first time, the opposing forces were sharply defined in an electric atmosphere, the hostility of the masses and the sullen nitrous oxide of the Left awaiting contact with the sulphurous fire-damp of the Right.

The entrance of General Korniloff, the Commander-in-Chief, marked the cleavage at the outset. The whole of the Right rose, frantically cheering, while the Left sat with folded arms, looking glum. Kerensky, entering with his quick, sharp, characteristic step, roused both sides, but when in jerky, verbal snaps, like the crack of a whip, he called the audience to applaud the Army in the person of General Korniloff, himself leading by clapping his hands, the morose Left remained motionless, despite protests from the indignant Right.

Kornilov's bid for power

Kerensky's offensive was launched in July under General Brusilov. Early encouragement soon dissipated under the weight of a German-backed counter. Despondency in the Russian ranks increased still further, as did the desertion rate. Kerensky found himself with an uphill battle. This moderate socialist was elevated to the office of prime minister, but his immovability on the issue of war put him at odds with the majority. People took to the streets once again, Lenin and the Bolsheviks offering the masses what they wanted. However, the army was not quite ready to turn on a government in its infancy. Lenin was again forced into hiding, many of his supporters rounded up. There was blood on the streets. German collusion in Lenin's return was splashed across the front pages. The Bolsheviks then had a slice of great good fortune, for Kerensky laid aside his differences with the radicals to deal with a new danger. It came from Brusilov's replacement as commander-in-chief, General Kornilov, who believed martial discipline was required to deal with the escalating disorder. He aimed to march on Petrograd and quash the rabble-rousers, which appealed to Kerensky until he had qualms that the Provisional Government itself might be next in Kornilov's sights. He needed unity and a show of strength to counter the threat, and that meant a truce with the Bolsheviks and their legion of worker-soldiers, the Red Guards. Kornilov's bid for power came to nothing, but it left the Bolsheviks with a powerful, armed militia in the city. They also controlled the workers' and soldiers' councils. Lenin saw his moment. "History will not forgive us if we don't seize power now," he wrote.

KORNILOFF'S STAFF SURRENDERS.

ALEXEIEFF JOINS KERENSKY.

RUSSIANS ATTACK RIGA - GERMANS.

General Korniloff's advance is at a standstill, his staff has surrendered, and General Alexeieff, who has joined M. Kerensky, the Premier and Commander-in-Chief, as his Chief of Staff, is in telephonic negotiation with General Korniloff himself and has refused a request for terms. His unconditional surrender is expected very soon.

With the disappearance of M. Chernoff from the post of Minister of Agriculture in M. Kerensky's Cabinet there seems to be a prospect of the strongest men among the Constitutional Democrats joining the Ministry, a step they have up to now refused to take because of M. Chernoff's programme of land expropriation.

Amid all the disturbance a surprising fact is that the Russians are advancing again east of Riga and have, after fierce fighting, recovered a number of positions. The Germans yesterday admitted that their cavalry posts north of the Dvina River have fallen back.

inclined to form a Socialist Government. It has been decided that M. Chernoff (champion of land expropriation) will resign, and that M. Peshekhanoff will become Minister of Agriculture. The duty of carrying on the military campaign will be left to General Alexeieff, but M. Kerensky will have the last word on questions of policy, and he will be responsible for seeing that there are no further adventures of a mutinous type. His name will assure as far as possible in these chaotic times some feeling of security. M. Nekrasoff remains Assistant Premier. This arrangement is a temporary one, and will last till matters shape themselves.

M. Savinkoff, the Military Governor-General of Petrograd, has issued a number of proclamations to the inhabitants. All street meetings and demonstrations are prohibited, and strict registration is ordered of all arrivals and departures of residents at private houses and hotels.

The city has remained calm all day. The energy of the Government, once it began to act, has given satisfaction to all thinking elements.

The bread ration, which was to have been reduced to half a pound, is to continue at its present weight of three-quarters of a pound per day, as stocks have increased during the week. This is most welcome news to the inhabitants of Petrograd.

GENERAL ALEXEIEFF

M. KERENSKY'S CHIEF OF STAFF.

From Our Own Correspondent.

PETROGRAD, Wednesday, 1.30 p.m.

KORNILOFF'S TERMS

Above left: General Lavr Kornilov, appointed commander-in-chief in July, reviews the troops on the frontline.

Top right: The Russian Parliament in Petrograd is seized by revolutionary soldiers.

Above right: General Alexei Brusilov was appointed commander-in-chief in May 1917 and although sympathetic to the revolutionaries

was intent on winning the war, which did not sit well with the politicians. He was replaced by General Kornilov after the failed Kerensky Offensive.

Opposite left: The rather cautious and indecisive Russian General Nikolai Ruzsky played a key part in persuading the Tsar to abdicate but after the February Revolution was dismissed from command. He joined the other Tsarist Generals at

the Caucasus but was executed by the Bolsheviks after the October Revolution.

Opposite middle: Prime Minister of the Provisional Government Alexander Kerensky (left) visits troops at the front.

Opposite right: Russian troops waiting for the signal to advance at Ternopil.

FALL OF RIGA: RUSSIAN FLIGHT.

CAPTURED | sailed with demands for the refusal of | LINER MINED. | MOONLIGHT RAIDS. | THE NEW MEAT PF

LAST NIGHT'S VISIT.

BUTCHERS PUZZLE

RIGA CAPTURED.

RUSSIAN MUTINY DURING NEW GERMAN ADVANCE.

HASTY FLIGHT NORTH.

VILLAGES BLAZING BEHIND.

Last night's German report announces the capture of Riga.

The Russian Army became demoralised during the new German advance, which began on Saturday with the crossing of the Dvina. Russians mutinied or deserted, and " in view of the threatening situation" the abandonment of the Riga region was ordered. Russian columns are hastily going north-east (Petrograd is about 350 miles away), burning the villages behind them.

ORDER TO RETREAT.

RUSSIAN OFFICIAL.

Monday.

On the left bank of the River Dvina, to the west of Riga, our troops towards Sunday morning retired to the line of Bilderlingshof (on the coast), Medem, and Dalen (south-east of Riga).

In the direction of Uxkull, 18 miles south-east of Riga, on the north bank of the Dvina, in the course of Saturday-Sunday the Germans conducted stubborn attacks chiefly on the front of Shtal-Melmuger, Skripto, Lausin, and the confluence of the River Oger (east of Ux-

HOW KERENSKY IS HAMPERED.

From ALEXANDER M. THOMPSON.

PETROGRAD, Saturday, 8 p.m.

On the eve of departure from a country whose problems and troubles I have so earnestly and anxiously studied in recent weeks, I asked myself whether the conditions have improved since my arrival, and I fear the answer is not a cheering one.

Outwardly there are signs of betterment. Street meetings have been suppressed; the busy German agents buzz-

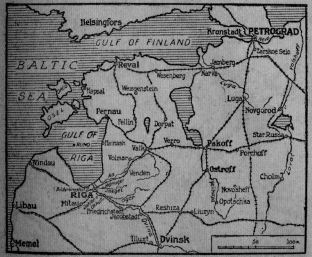

The map shows the line of the Russian flight from the Riga region.

German advance captures Riga

In April 1917, with Russia destabilised by the first of two revolutions it would experience that year, General Oskar von Hutier assumed command of Germany's 8th Army. It was a key appointment, for von Hutier would soon drive a nail into the coffin of Russia's waning resistance as a fighting force. He was an arch-exponent of the new infiltration tactics adopted by both sides: using fast-moving storm troops to puncture the enemy line, bypassing strongpoints. When used in tandem with the more effective artillery techniques now being applied, the results could be spectacular, as the Russian army found to its cost in an attack at Riga on 1 September. The surprise element was maintained – there was no drawn-out shelling to signal intent – but when the battle began the German gunners did pin down Russian reserves. Instead of pounding away at the enemy line, the barrage targeted strategic positions. Negating the opposition's ability to strike provided better returns than vain attempts at wholesale destruction. Colonel Georg Bruchmuller orchestrated the artillery attack, another forward-thinking officer who embraced new methods when the old ones were shown to be fruitless. The fall of Riga was followed by a sweep of the Baltic islands, the whole enterprise causing severe consternation in Petrograd. It left in shreds the Provisional Government's hopes that Russia should maintain its contribution to the Entente cause. The army was in full-scale retreat, Kerensky's time was almost up and the Bolsheviks were waiting in the wings. As for von Hutier, he was transferred to the western theatre before the year was out in readiness for Germany's great assault in the new year.

Lenin: "History will not forgive us if we don't seize power now."

THE ALLIES WARN RUSSIA.

EACE PLAN. | **PARIS CONFERENCE.** | **HAIG GAINS.** | **RAILWAY MIRACLES.** | **STRIKE OF 50,000 AIR WORKERS.**

A MEETING FOR WORK. | WEST OF BOURLON. | ARMY THAT "GETS A

Kerensky flees

On 7 November it was announced that power had passed to the Soviet. Kerensky fled Petrograd to see what military support could be mustered, leaving the Bolsheviks the straightforward task of marching on a lightly defended Winter Palace and rounding up the remaining Provisional Government members. Eight months after the end of autocratic rule, control of Russia had changed hands once again, and once again with little blood spilt. Much brutality would follow, however. The disparate anti-Bolsheviks formed the so-called White Army of opposition, but in the ensuing civil war ultimately proved no match for the Trotsky-led Red tide, even with the backing of Western governments.

Lenin moved swiftly to reorganise the country into a Communist state. Assets were nationalised, the Orthodox Church's power weakened. "Citizen" became the universal form of address in the new classless society, or "Comrade" for party members. It mattered little that the Bolsheviks were roundly beaten by the rival Socialist Revolutionaries in the November 1917 election. A "bourgeois parliamentary system" was a retrograde step, said Lenin. "Elections prove nothing." The assembly was quickly dissolved, with echoes of the tsar's roughshod treatment of the Duma. Russia was turned into a one-party state, its Red Army and secret police – the feared Cheka – ready to suppress any counter-revolutionary movement.

Lenin was also now free to make good on his peace promise. Weeks passed following the December 1917 armistice, Russia stalling in the hope that a workers' revolution would spread to Germany. When that didn't materialise, Germany tired of the delaying tactics and turned bellicose once more. In February the Central Powers agreed separate terms with Ukraine, hoping its grain would mitigate the punishing effects of the Allied blockade. Lenin accepted the need for peace at any price, and the Treaty of Brest-Litovsk, concluded 3 March 1918, formally took Russia out of the war. The cost was indeed high: the loss of Finland, the Baltic states, Poland and territory in the Caucasus, as well as the abandonment of all claim to Ukraine. At a stroke almost half of Russia's industrial base was relinquished, along with a third of her population.

With the Bolshevik takeover, the royal family's position worsened. Extremists carried them off to their final prison, in Ekaterinburg, where they endured ritual humiliation and ill treatment. The ordeal ended in the early hours of 17 July 1918. News of White Army movement in the area brought a death sentence, endorsed by Lenin and carried out by members of the Cheka. Nicholas, Alexandra and their five children were herded into the building's basement, along with a few faithful retainers. All were shot. Bejewelled garments acted as bulletproof vests, but it was a mere stay of execution. Bayonets were used to ensure that the White Army would not be able to rally around royalty. For decades there was speculation that Anastasia, the youngest daughter, may have survived, but DNA analysis of exhumed remains has proved conclusively that all seven members of Russia's last ruling family met their grisly end at the same time.

"We cannot, will not and must not continue a war begun by tsars and capitalists in alliance with monarchs and capitalists. We will not and we must not continue to be at war with workers and peasants like ourselves."

Leon Trotsky

Below left: Russian soldiers hold a meeting in the trenches. Army discipline was breaking down and the revolutionary influences were taking effect.

Below middle: Lenin addresses the Vsevobuch troops on Red Square in Moscow. The Vsevobuch system of Universal Military Training was established by the Bolsheviks to fight the remnants of the opposition to Soviet rule.

Below right: Russian officers are taken prisoner by their own men.

Above: Lenin moved swiftly to reorganise the country into a Communist state.

Opposite top row: The four daughters of Tsar Nicholas II and the Tsarina Alexandra. (l to r) Grand Duchesses Anastasia, Olga, Maria and Tatiana. After the Tsar's abdication they spent much of their time in exile in Tobolsk. However, in April 1918 they were moved to Yekaterinburg where they were finally executed by a firing squad on 17 July 1918.

Opposite middle row far left and left: The Tsar with his youngest child Tsarevich Alexei.

Opposite middle row right: After his abdication Tsar Nicholas II wanted to go into exile in Britain. The British government initially agreed to offer him asylum but the King overruled this decision after political advice suggested the Tsar's presence might incite an uprising.

Opposite middle row far right: Tsar Nicholas II (left) bore an uncanny resemblance to his cousin King George V. Both were grandsons of Queen Victoria.

Opposite bottom: Russian soldiers throw down their weapons and come out of the trenches to surrender.

RUSSO-GERMAN PACT SIGNED.

| EM'S WELCOME | MAN-POWER PLANS. | DESPERATE FIGHTING IN | WAR-BUYING UNITY. | VLADIVOSTOK. | RUSSIA |
| | SIR A. GEDDES' STATEMENT. | ITALY. | PURCHASES IN U.S.A. | JAPANESE DENY LANDING | |

Italian disaster at Caporetto

Under the command of General Luigi Cadorna, the Italian army targeted the port of Trieste, the pursuit of which required crossing the Isonzo river and defeating an enemy that commanded the high ground. By the end of 1916, this had been the scene of nine indecisive battles, the Italian army bearing the greater brunt of the casualty toll. Meanwhile, the Austrian attack on the Trentino in May that year might have reaped greater dividends had its leaders not been forced to redeploy troops to meet a fresh Russian assault. Italian pleas for the Brusilov Offensive to begin as a matter of urgency were answered, providing timely relief.

The dawning of the new year saw the rival camps both in crisis. New Austrian leader Karl I was desperate to bring peace to his creaking empire. Ludendorff, equally desperate to breathe life into the corpse to which the Fatherland was shackled, recognised the need for German troops to shore up an Austrian army that had come off second best in the 11th Isonzo clash, which took place in August 1917. Russia's implosion freed up resources, and ahead of the latest Isonzo round in October eight German divisions led by General Otto von Below gave added bite to the attack. For this was not simply a defensive measure to prop up a faltering partner. In committing German forces, Ludendorff demanded a fruit-bearing offensive. It was launched on the morning of 24 October.

A German-reinforced attack was Italy's nightmare scenario, and came at the worst possible time. The will to fight was fast ebbing away, the last vestiges of Italian resolve crumbling in a hail of gas shells, against which the troops had little protection. War-weary, disillusioned, poorly fed and ill served by brutish, incompetent generals, the Italian infantry wilted in the face of a reinvigorated enemy that crossed the river and breached their line. The very sight of the German pickelhaube was enough to instill panic and prompt hundreds of thousands to desert. A young Erwin Rommel – the distinguished Desert Fox of the century's next global conflagration – accepted the surrender of thousands of Italian troops, who gave up without a fight. Cadorna and the rump of his disintegrating army had no choice but to retreat, leaving the enemy in possession of Caporetto, the town that gave the 12th Battle of Isonzo its popular name.

Monumental defeat

Withdrawing over 60 miles to the River Piave afforded Cadorna the opportunity to establish a solid defensive base. Venice lay within 15 miles, and he rallied his men once more. If it was a choice between death and submission, he exhorted, then here they would die. They were helped by the rapid Austro-German advance that left the pursuers overextended, and by the arrival of British and French reinforcements. Now that the senior partners on both sides had thrown their weight behind their junior allies, a measure of stasis was restored. Italy had held, just. Yet there was no disguising the monumental scale of a defeat in which fractional gains accumulated over more than two years of fighting, and at appalling cost, were swept away.

A young Erwin Rommel accepted the surrender of thousands of Italian troops, who gave up without a fight.

Below: **The thick black line curving from the middle of the range of Julian Alps at the top of the map through Tolmino and the Bainsizza Plateau and down to the Carso Plateau shows the Italian front as it was in mid October. On the left of the map the thicker black line just behind the river Tagliamento marks the new front to** which Cadorna had brought his armies by the start of November.

Opposite above: **Italian troops man their first-line trench running along the southern bank of the River Piave. The defensive lines set up by the river protected the Venetian plains, and Venice itself, from attack.**

Opposite below: **Italian troops retreat along the Udine-Codroipo Road in north-east Italy after their defeat by Austro-Hungarian and German forces at Caporetto in the Isonzo Valley, November 1917. The retreat was famously described in Hemingway's novel *A Farewell to Arms*.**

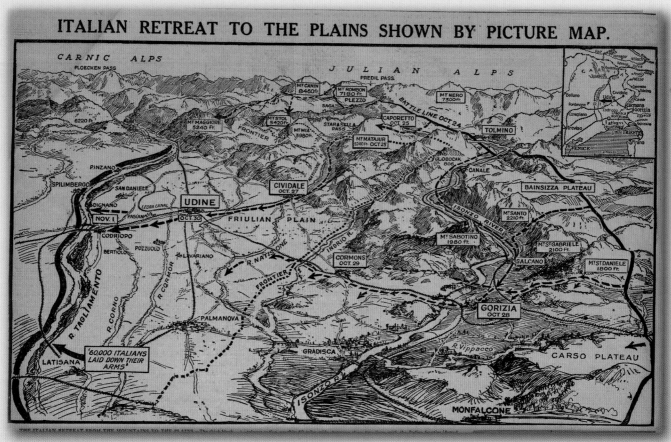

ITALIAN RETREAT TO THE PLAINS SHOWN BY PICTURE MAP.

FULL STORY OF THE ITALIAN RETREAT.

ment for many years to come of the great war, for it will be worth no one's while to move them. It was not till the enemy was already engaged with the Italian rearguard on the Torre River, only three or four miles east of Udine, that the outflanked Italians on the Carso withdrew. Had their retirement been de-

CROWN PRINCE RETIRES

WITHDRAWAL BEFORE PETAIN.

KERENSKY TO U.S. INTERVIEWER.

RUSSIA AND THE WAR.

CURIOUS STATEMENTS.

New York, Friday.
"Russia is worn out by the strain

SINN

VALERA'S

TO-MORROW

ME

Since the foll graphed, we ha feeling of mor Dublin last nig some country dis Fein meetings Newbridge and military centr been proclaimed

This may c last night that t

FROM OUR IR

DESPERATE FIGHTING IN ITALY.

AUSTRIAN MOUNTAIN GAINS.

RACE AGAINST SNOW.

Fighting of extreme desperation is proceeding in the mountains between the Brenta and the Piave. By throwing very large forces repeatedly against the Italian positions the Austrians have succeeded in gaining a peak close to the Brenta Valley and also some ground farther east near the Piave.

About a foot of snow has fallen, and this may have prompted the enemy to speed up his advance, which is designed to reach the plain and to force the French, British, and Italians to retire from the Piave area, which might also involve the loss of Venice.

Lawrence and the Arab Revolt

The bitter experience of Gallipoli and Kut provided further evidence that to defeat Turkey it would be hugely beneficial to make common cause with the Arab population. The Arabs were a subjugated people with a desire for autonomy; a desire that could stir them to insurrectionary action given suitable prompting, direction and reward. Britain was prepared to play on that mood of disaffection, to foment rebellion in order to achieve her military aims. An Arab Bureau was established in Cairo with a view to providing support for the uprising. Turkey was about to face twin-pronged attacks in the region, and an Oxford scholar was to find the great purpose he believed was his destiny.

The rallying figure on the Arab side was Sherif Hussein of Mecca. Providing the link between the British Army and the disparate band of tribesmen was Thomas Edward Lawrence, a student of history who had immersed himself in the culture of the Middle East. Lawrence had been engaged in archaeological work before joining the intelligence service, but when the Arab Revolt began in June 1916 he was not content to play the role of passive liaison officer. This was his chance to be a pivotal figure in a grand scheme, and he wanted to be more than a mere facilitator in the insurgency.

Lawrence shared the Arab vision for a people free from the Ottoman yoke and masters of their own destiny, the very promise made them as reward for their co-operation in the fight against Germany's ally. He soon suspected that his political masters were dissembling, that after paying the price the Arabs would not receive the promised goods. The division of the territorial cake would come later; first there was a war to be won.

As the struggle began Lawrence struck up a close relationship with Sherif Hussein's son Emir Feisal, the man tasked with carrying the plan forward. Lawrence took to wearing Arab garb, bringing him greater acceptance as well comfort. He would be photographed and painted many times in headdress and flowing robes, an image that helped cast him as a romantic hero. It was a double-edged sword, for though he had a desire to make his mark, in later life he would struggle to break free from the "Lawrence of Arabia" legend.

> *Lawrence shared the Arab vision for a people free from the Ottoman yoke and masters of their own destiny*

Left: Lawrence enlisted in October 1914 and was immediately posted to the intelligence service based in Cairo. By 1916 he had been promoted to Major, was an advisor to Emir Faisal, son of Sherif Hussein of Mecca, and had the confidence of General Sir Edmund Allenby, commander-in chief of the Egyptian Expeditionary Force.

Below: Turkish prisoners are held under guard in the desert.

BAGHDAD CAPTURED YESTERDAY.

OF BAGHDAD | DARDANELLES. | FOOD AND SHIP | MR. GERARD LANDS AT HAVANA.

FRENCH NEWSPAPER COMMENT. | U.S. VESSELS T SHOOT.

FALL OF BAGHDAD

BRITISH ENTRY YESTERDAY.

SIR STANLEY MAUDE'S SWIFT MOVES.

TURKS BEATEN AT ALL POINTS.

From LIEUT.-GENERAL SIR STANLEY MAUDE,
COMMANDING-IN-CHIEF, Mesopotamia.

Sunday, March 11.

The British forces occupied Baghdad early this morning.

3rd YEAR OF WAR · 221st DAY.

No further details have yet been received from Sir Stanley Maude about the entry into Baghdad, the ancient city of the Khalifs and of Harun-al-Raschid, who figures in the "Arabian Nights." It is of historic and picturesque significance and retrieves the disaster of Kut last April, but it has to be borne in mind that the war will be won in the West.

Baghdad was the intended terminus of the German railway to the East.

An official report of the swift

SWIFT STROKES.

SUCCESS DESPITE BLINDING DUSTSTORMS.

WAR OFFICE, Sunday Night.

In continuation of the announcement [see below] that our forces were engaged with the enemy on the line of the Diala on Thursday night, our troops succeeded, in spite of bright moonlight, in effecting a surprise crossing of the Diala and in establishing a strong post on the right [west] bank of that river.

Meanwhile on Thursday morning, the Tigris having been bridged at some distance down-stream from the confluence of the Diala, a strong British detachment

strokes delivered a few miles south and south-west of the city, which led to its fall, is printed in the next column. It shows the same methodic process that was employed for the capture of the Turkish fortresses round Kut, 100 miles to the south-east, only 16 days ago.

marched up the right [west] bank and found the enemy holding a position about six miles south-west of Baghdad.

The enemy was driven from this position to another two miles in rear.

During Friday night the passage of the Diala was forced and our troops advanced some 4 miles towards Baghdad.

During Friday our forces on the right

The shaded sections of the map indicate the territory now under British and Russian influence, though the actual battle line of the Allies is not yet continuous. The unfinished parts of the Berlin-Baghdad Railway are dotted.

Below left: King Feisal leads his army into Wejh.

Below right and newspaper inset: After Ottoman forces evacuated the town, General Maude led his victorious troops into Baghdad on 11 March 1917.

Top middle: General Sir Stanley Maude was appointed the new commander of the British Army in Mesopotamia following the end of the siege of Kut in April 1916. He spent the rest of the year rebuilding the army and planning new transport links.

Rest of page: Conditions for those men fighting in Mesopotamia were very different from those on the Western Front. Temperatures of 120°F were common and the flies, mosquitoes and vermin led to very high levels of disease and sickness. Hospitals could be as much as a two-week boat ride away and troops were often badly equipped and inadequately trained.

Jerusalem taken

Throughout 1917 Arab and Allied forces largely prospered at Turkey's expense. The Mesopotamia campaign was restarted under a new commander, Sir Stanley Maude, whose re-equipped army was soon on the march. Kut was retaken in February, and this time the drive to Baghdad was unimpeded. Turkey was on the back foot, though Russia's implosion released significant resources from that front for deployment further south. General Sir Edmund Allenby, who took over command of the Egyptian Expeditionary Force in July, knew time was of the essence. Allenby's predecessor, Sir Archibald Murray, had paid the price for failing on two occasions to take Gaza in the spring. His replacement – an iron-willed general known as "The Bull" would not make the same mistake.

There was an immediate fillip with a victorious Arab attack on Aqaba, news of which so impressed Allenby that he authorised increased funding for such operations. Meanwhile, Lawrence recognised that Feisal's "irregulars" were best suited to guerrilla warfare. Though Mecca had fallen quickly, Turkey had a numerical superiority that the insurgents negated by stretching and separating its resources. The Hejaz railway – the vital artery on the western side of the Arab Peninsula – was dynamited, leaving Turkish-held Medina isolated. In targeting the infrastructure that sustained Turkey's fighting force, the Arabs caused maximum disruption for minimum loss. These tactics were a boon to British operations in Palestine, for Turkish troops that might have opposed the Allies in that quarter were removed from the equation.

Allenby's Christmas present

In autumn 1917 Allenby routed the Turks at Beersheba after deceiving them into believing he would attack at Gaza. The Australian cavalry charge showed that here, at least, horses could still be used to good effect in the battlefield. With Turkey's main defensive line broken, Allenby had Jerusalem in his sights. On 11 December he strolled into the city, Lawrence among the throng that greeted his arrival. The "Christmas gift to the nation", as Lloyd George called the capture of Jerusalem, had been delivered with impeccable timing.

JERUSALEM CUT OFF.

TURKS SURRENDER THE CITY.

GENERAL ALLENBY'S TRIUMPH.

CEREMONIAL ENTRY TO-DAY.

Mr. Bonar Law read the following statement in Parliament yesterday:—
General Allenby reports that on Saturday he attacked the enemy's positions south and west of Jerusalem. Welsh and Home Counties troops advancing from the direction of BETHLEHEM drove back the enemy and, passing Jerusalem on the east, established themselves on the JERUSALEM-JERICHO road.

At the same time London Infantry and dismounted Yeomanry attacked strong enemy positions west and north-west and established themselves astride the JERUSALEM-SHECHEM road [north of Jerusalem]. The Holy City, being thus isolated, was surrendered to General Allenby. (Cheers.)

British political officers, together with

THE KING'S JOY.

PLEASURE THAT HOLY PLACES ARE INTACT.

From the King to General Allenby:

The news of the occupation of Jerusalem will be received throughout my Empire with the greatest satisfaction, and I heartily congratulate you and all ranks on this success.

Such an achievement is a fitting sequel to the hard marching and fighting of the troops, as well as to the organisation by which the difficulties of supply, transport, and water have been overcome.

I rejoice to think that by skilful dispositions you have preserved intact the Holy Places.   GEORGE R.I.

General Allenby enters Jerusalem to-day. On the Baghdad front the Turk has just suffered another blow in the loss of positions in the rear of his defences in the Jebel Hamrin.

the British Governor, accompanied by French, Italian, and Mahommedan representatives, are on their way to safeguard the city and Holy Places.

HUNS' TANK TERROR.

VIVID GERMAN ACCOUNT.

Far left and opposite above right: Gurkha Rifle battalions in the front line trenches in Palestine. Over 200,000 Gurkhas served with the British Army during the war and the 2nd/3rd Gurkha Rifles took part in the conquest of Baghdad.

Left: A British gun is hauled through the streets of the ancient city of Caliphs, while a crowd looks on.

Opposite above left: The Union Flag is hoisted over the Town Hall of Jaffa after the town surrendered to the New Zealand Mounted Rifles.

Opposite middle: The Turkish Army on the march in Palestine.

Opposite below: British troops rest in the valley of the river Wadi Ghuzze, five miles south of Gaza.

Opposite inset: The line showing the advance of General Allenby's forces on 18 November.

ALLENBY ENTERS JERUSALEM.

FRIENDLY RECEPTION.

HOLY PLACES PROTECTED.

From GENERAL ALLENBY.

JERUSALEM, Tuesday, 2 p.m.

I entered this city officially at noon to-day with a few of my staff, the Commanders of the French and Italian detachments, and the military attachés of France, Italy, and United States of America.

The procession was all on foot. At the Jaffa Gate I was received by guards representing England, Scotland, Ireland, Wales, Australia, New Zealand, India, France, and Italy.

The population received me well.

Guards have been placed over the holy places. My military governor is in touch with the acting custos of the Latins and Greek representative. The governor has detailed an officer to supervise the Christian holy places.

The Mosque of Omar and the area around it has been placed under Moslem control, and a military cordon composed of Indian Mahommedan officers and soldiers has been established round the Mosque. Orders have been issued that no non-Moslem is to pass this cordon without the permission of the military governor and the Moslems in charge of the Mosque.

VICTORY IN MESOPOTAMIA.

SEVERAL THOUSAND TURKS CUT OFF.

COMMANDER AND STAFF PRISONERS.

After a lull of five months in Mesopotamia during the great heat Sir Stanley Maude resumed the offensive on Thursday, and in a few hours captured on the Euphrates, west of Baghdad, a large part of the Turkish force which has faced his left flank for some time.

The Germans have boasted that they would recapture Baghdad by this route.

From GENERAL SIR STANLEY MAUDE,
COMMANDER-IN-CHIEF, MESOPOTAMIA FORCE.

After an advance on Thursday night we attacked the enemy's advanced position at MUSHAID, 4 miles east of RAMADIE [which is on the Euphrates, 60 miles west of Baghdad], early on Friday morning.

MUSHAID RIDGE was occupied with little difficulty, and our column, continuing the advance, manoeuvred away from the river, attacking the Turkish main positions about RAMADIE from the south-east, while our cavalry moved wide round to the west of RAMADIE.

A severe battle ensued, lasting throughout Friday, but by night-fall our troops had carried the enemy's main positions and were encircling RAMADIE from east, south-east, and south at a distance of under 2 miles from the town. Our cavalry completed the land cordon to the west of RAMADIE, while the Euphrates runs along the north side of the town. The enemy during the night attempted to break through westwards, but was headed back by our cavalry.

Our troops resumed the attack vigorously on Saturday at daybreak, with the result that by 9 a.m. the enemy was surrendering everywhere.

Included in our capture are guns, arms, ammunition, stores and equipment, also much other booty, and several thousand prisoners, Ahmed Bey, the Turkish commander, and his staff being among the latter. The enemy were taken entirely by surprise, and practically the whole garrison at RAMADIE fell into our hands.

Our troops displayed great gallantry, determination, and endurance under most difficult conditions.

During Thursday night another column moved out north-east of BAGHDAD and after a sharp skirmish with a Turkish cavalry detachment inflicted casualties, capturing 4 prisoners and 300 Turkish supply camels.

Military discipline

Whether volunteers, conscripts or regulars, soldiers faced the same stringent punishments for a range of misdemeanours, from having incomplete kit to desertion. The range of sanctions available for front-line transgressions was limited; thus for offences that might carry a period of incarceration during peacetime there was "Field Punishment No.1". This saw the transgressor bound in cruciform position, to a wheel or similar, and left exposed to the elements. He might have to endure the biting cold of the Western Front in winter, or the broiling heat of the desert.

When news of such harsh practices reached the home shores there was widespread anger. Field Marshal Sir Douglas Haig, among others, gave the top-brass perspective, insisting that without such codes "a far larger percentage of those men whose moral fibre requires bracing by the daily fear of adequate punishment would give way at moments of supreme stress, and recourse to the death penalty would have to become more frequent". In short, physical punishments kept the men up to the mark and prevented them from wilting under pressure.

This defence failed to quieten the loud dissenting voices at home. More prescriptive instructions were introduced regarding how Field Punishment No.1 should be carried out. Offenders were to be bound in such a way as to allow more freedom of movement, and in particular they were not to be spread-eagled. People had been incensed at the thought of Tommies doing their bit for king and country and being crucified for their pains.

Shell shock victim executed

With the introduction of a more "benign" disciplinary regimen, the row died down, only to reignite over the issue of offences that carried a death sentence. Some 3,000 capital sentences were passed on British and Commonwealth servicemen by courts martial during the course of the war, of which over 300 were carried out. Desertion was the chief capital crime, but concerns that shell shock was the root cause of the aberrant behaviour provoked much comment, including some heated exchanges on the floor of the House of Commons. One such occurred in November 1917, when a Labour MP sought an inquiry into the execution of a 21-year-old private in the Royal Scots Fusiliers who had deserted. It was stated that he had already been invalided home suffering from shell shock, and that his "crime" occurred when his nerves were shattered. The request for an inquiry was denied, the responding minister affirming his faith in the courts martial process. That brought forth a volley of angry questions. "Is the War Office prepared to allow a scandal like this to go

without inquiry, when a mere boy overcome with nervousness was executed?""Do you think you are strengthening the army by sending soldiers suffering from shell shock back to the front?""How is it that young lads of tender years who have failed in their duty are shot and that generals are promoted?" Each case, they were told, was investigated by a commanding officer just as anxious as they were about the lives of his men. Care was taken to ensure that shell shock was not a factor, and that the accused was entirely responsible for his actions.

Some traumatised by the horrors and din of war chose self-inflicted wounding, a more tangible sign of incapacity than shredded nerves. Doctors were warned to be vigilant about injuries that might not have been sustained in the heat of battle. The medics were under pressure not to assign a mental-infirmity label to too many soldiers. On one occasion when a doctor attested that one-third of a unit were unfit for duty because of shell shock, he was swiftly relieved of his post. The prevailing view was that while exploding shells could have a temporary deleterious effect on a soldier's mental wellbeing, if the condition persisted it was a sign of a character defect or weakness of constitution. The problem lay with the man, not the extreme situation. It followed that discipline was vital, and the ultimate sanction sometimes warranted, both to punish and deter.

Relatives of those who lost their lives in such circumstances campaigned for years to have the taint of wrongdoing removed. A stain on the character of men such as Private Harry Farr, who suffered a severe nervous disorder requiring five months' hospitalisation, yet he was still court-martialled after breaking down and refusing to go to the front line in September 1916. Today the diagnosis would doubtless be Post-traumatic Stress Disorder or similar. With the Battle of the Somme raging it was deemed "misbehaving before the enemy in such a way as to show cowardice". Farr was 25 when he faced the firing squad on 18 October.

Private Charles Kirman fought at Mons and the Somme, sustaining a number of injuries before he could finally take no more and went awol in September 1917. He later handed himself in, but still forfeited his life.

Private Herbert Burden lied about his age so that he could join up. He was just 17 when he faced a firing squad in July 1915, found guilty of deserting his post. The court heard Burden's unit had been ordered to the front when he took himself off to comfort a bereaved friend. Private Burden has been immortalised as the model for the Shot at Dawn monument, a blindfolded figure bound to a stake awaiting his fate. It was unveiled at the National Memorial Arboretum, Staffordshire, in 2001. Five years later, in 2006, the British Government pardoned those executed for cowardice and desertion, belated official acknowledgment that many had paid the ultimate price for no greater crime than mental disintegration.

Opposite above: Over 300 British soldiers lost their lives to the firing squad, on the orders of their own officers. On most occasions relatives were not given the real reason for their death – just that they had died somewhere in battle.

Opposite below: German troops execute an English soldier captured at Cambrai. He was accused of complaining about his food and inciting a mutiny. The photograph was obtained by a corporal of the Tyneside Scottish while a prisoner of war and was smuggled out of the country.

Top: Georges Clemenceau (left) on the battlefield with French officers near Le Mort Homme. He became Prime Minister of France in November 1917 and his frequent visits to the front raised the spiritis of the demoralised troops. Their respect for this man who was not afraid to go close to the German frontline earned him the title "Le Père de la Victoire" (Father of Victory).

Above right: French commanders General Joffre (left) and General Foch (right) meet with Field Marshal Sir Douglas Haig, commander of the British Expeditionary Force.

Below: An American general (centre) is shown around the battlefield by British generals as German prisoners are escorted away in the background.

Desertion was the chief capital crime, but concerns that shell shock was the root cause of the aberrant behaviour provoked much comment.

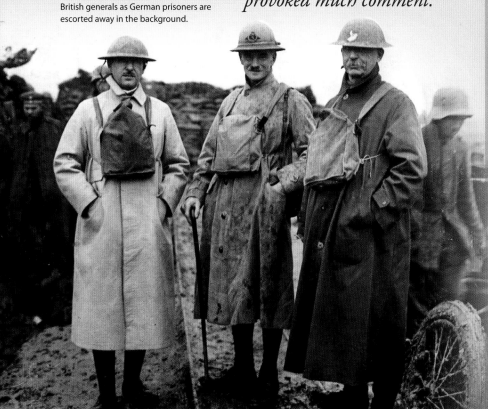

December 1917

1   The last resistance in German East Africa ended when General von Lettow-Vorbeck withdrew his troops across the Rovuma River into Portuguese territory.

2   The suspension of hostilities between Russian and German Armies began prior to the truces arranged between official negotiators.

3   The first session of the "Truce Delegates" took place at the Brest-Litovsk headquarters between Russia and the Central Powers.

4   The British withdrew from their initial gains at Cambrai and the offensive ended.

6   The Finnish Parliament declared independence from Russia under acting Head of State Pehr Evind Svinhufvud.

7   President Woodrow Wilson signed a declaration of war against Austria-Hungary.

8   British troops launched a final advance against the Ottoman Empire and entered the city of Jerusalem.

9   The Ottoman Army retreated and Jerusalem was taken by British forces in Palestine. The fall of the city marked the climax of an offensive against the Turks which had begun in October with the capture of Beersheba.

10 Panama declared war on Austria-Hungary.

11 General Edmund Allenby formally entered the Old City of Jerusalem. It was the first time that Jerusalem was in Christian hands since the Crusades.

12 A convoy of British ships was attacked by four German battleships. The destroyer HMS *Partridge* was torpedoed and sunk.

14 General Maurice Sarrail was recalled from Salonika by French Prime Minister Georges Clemenceau.

15 An armistice between Russia and the Central Powers was signed on the Eastern Front at Brest-Litovsk.

16 Sir Edmund Allenby was made GCMG (Knight Grand Cross of the Most Distinguished Order of Saint Michael and Saint George).

17 The armistice agreed upon between the new Russian Government and the Central Powers came into effect.

18 The United States passed the Eighteenth Amendment, also known as the Temperance Amendment, prohibiting the manufacture, sale or transportation of intoxicating liquors.

19 Two United States submarines, USS *F-1* and USS *F-3*, collided while manoeuvring in exercises off the coast of California. USS *F-1* sank within ten seconds of the impact.

20 The first of a succession of Soviet state security organizations, the Cheka was established in Russia by the Council of People's Commissars after a decree issued by Vladimir Lenin.

21 The Battle of Jaffa was fought over two days between the forces of the British Empire and the Ottoman and German Empires during the Sinai and Palestine Campaign. The conflict ended with an emphatic victory for the British.

22 A secret pact regarding the future of Poland was agreed between Germany and the Russian Bolshevik Government at Brest-Litovsk.

23 The Independent Republic of Moldavia was proclaimed at Kishinev.

26 The Defence of Jerusalem was one of three battles which made up the "Jerusalem Operations" along with the Battle of Nebi Samwil and the Battle of Jaffa. The engagement began when the Turkish Army launched a counter-attack against British infantry on the outskirts of the city.

27 Sir Rosslyn Wemyss was appointed First Sea Lord of Great Britain.

30 The final objectives were achieved at the climax of the Defence of Jerusalem when the whole front line was secured by British troops.

31 The British fleet messenger carrying troops and medical personnel, HMS *Osmanieh* was sunk after hitting a mine at the entrance to Alexandria Harbour.

Above left: The troops stationed at Neulette eagerly open this large Christmas postbag from Blighty.

Above right and far left: This young soldier delightedly holds his army Christmas pudding. The Army Christmas Pudding Fund collected donations to ensure every man fighting on the front during the festive period received his own pudding.

Left: A brigadier-general acts as a waiter to troops at the Tommy's Leave Club in the Hotel Moderne, Paris.

Below right: After two years in Russia and Persia these naval armoured-car men are finally on their way home for a holiday.

Below left: Wartime Christmas cards from the front usually conveyed very positive messages with no indication of the horrors of war.

Above left: Members of another American regiment wave their goodbyes to friends and relatives as their boat sets sail for France and their next training camp.

Above right: A French wireless operator stands outside a telegraph station near the firing line. The deep dug out is well protected by sandbags.

Left: A long queue for food stretches along a London street at the end of the year. Food supply was maintained in the early part of the war but once Germany introduced its policy of unrestricted submarine warfare, this affected merchant ships and the ability to import food was significantly reduced.

Below middle: Similar queues formed outside the Maypole Dairy Shop in Hulme, Manchester. The government used the Defence of the Realm Act to requisition over 2.5 million acres of land for farming during the conflict but as the situation grew worse some communities were suffering from malnutrition and rationing was introduced in 1918.

Bottom left: At the Army Parcel Post Office mountains of Christmas gifts are gathered to send to the troops serving at the front. In a normal week 1,000 tons of parcels passed through this depot.

Bottom right: Captain Edward Tupper from the Seaman and Fireman's Union stands on top of HM *Landship* in Trafalgar Square and appeals to the crowd to buy War Bonds.

FOOD QUEUES.

To the Editor of *The Daily Mail.*

Sir,—Food queues have been stopped in Petrograd by allowing people only to buy at certain shops, and rationing the shops according to the number of their customers. This was one of the Bolshevik measures.

I see Lord Rhondda is now thinking about enforcing such a plan. Will he do it? Or must we have a Bolshevik Administration here to take the situation firmly in hand? HAMILTON FYFE.

COME AND BUY WAR BONDS AT THE TANK

Chapter Five

1918

Victory at a Price

1918 in brief

By the end of 1917 the German high command had little room for manoeuvre. It was clear that the U-boat threat had diminished and could not now be the instrument of victory. It was also clear that the condition of her army and civilians – and that of the other Central Powers – meant that war could not be waged for much longer. The Allied blockade was continuing to bite, and although it fell short of starving Germany into submission, it was causing suffering which would only be supportable in the short term. Hardship could be borne while there remained the prospect of a great military victory. Equally pressing was the fact that 1918 would bring American forces across the Atlantic in ever greater numbers. The Bolshevik Revolution provided a welcome fillip to Ludendorff and von Hindenburg for it brought an end to hostilities on the Eastern Front in December 1917. Although it would be another three months before a formal treaty between Germany and Russia was signed, at Brest-Litovsk on 3 March 1918, from the start of the year Germany's military leaders were able to plan their strategy with this in mind.

Storm Troopers deployed

In fact there was little to discuss. There had to be a deployment of troops from east to west, for it was in France and Belgium that Germany must play her final cards, and play them before US forces arrived in numbers. Operation Michael was conceived, a spring offensive around Arras which would shatter the Allied line and drive relentlessly northeastwards to the Channel coast. A new tactic would be employed. Instead of fixed objectives Ludendorff put his faith in a rapid infiltration of the enemy line by specially trained sturmtruppen or storm troops. Momentum was the key, and at all costs the Allies were to be given no breathing space to recover. It was a huge gamble. Up to one million men had had to remain in vanquished Russia and some of Germany's senior officers thought the plan far too ambitious. But it was a gamble virtually forced on Ludendorff. If he could drive a wedge between the British and French forces, victory might yet be salvaged from the jaws of defeat.

Allies welcome US

The Allies, by contrast, went into 1918 in a more defensive frame of mind. This was partly down to the reverses of the previous year. Lloyd George was wary of committing significant numbers of troops to Haig, whom he felt was too profligate with lives, too ready to embark on futile offensives. The Entente Powers also knew that time was on their side. And it wasn't only American troops that were eagerly awaited. The prosecution of the war had left Britain close to bankruptcy. The final bill would be £10 billion, of which some £7 billion was borrowed. By 1918 three-quarters of the country's national income was directed at the war effort; never before had the nation's resources been so overwhelmingly linked to a single undertaking. Such was the nature of total war. It meant that the financial backing of the US would be as welcome as her manpower and machinery.

Britain's situation remained a delicate one, however. In 1918 the number of days lost to strikes exceeded six million, an indication that the exhortation to show restraint in support of the war effort was wearing thin. In March the Defence of the Realm Act was amended to make it an offence for women to pass on sexually transmitted diseases to servicemen, the incidence of which was reaching epidemic proportions. The fact that this was made punishable by a heavy fine or imprisonment had more to do with the need to have men fit for active duty than any question of morality. As a hedge against future manpower needs, the 1918 Military Service Bill raised from 41 to 50 the age at which men were liable to be conscripted. Woodrow Wilson did not wait for American resources to play a part in winning the war. On 8 January 1918 he delivered an address to Congress in which he outlined his ideas for post-conflict Europe. The famous "Fourteen Points" speech envisioned a Europe of nations based on democracy and self-determination. States should be armed only insofar as to provide for domestic security. A League of Nations would oversee international relations and provide collective security. Wilson delivered the speech without consulting the Allies, and not all of his pronouncements would have been well received. Freedom of navigation on the seas, both in peace and in war, was a stipulation by which Britain, a great naval power, would have felt hamstrung. And the president's call for transparent pacts between governments was a far cry from the secret deals by which many of the minor combatants had been seduced to declare for one side or the other. However, Wilson knew he held a strong hand in January 1918 and was determined to be the prime mover in shaping the new world order.

Only 300,000 US troops had reached Europe by the time Operation Michael was launched, on 21 March. Meanwhile, trains had been transporting German troops from the east day and night for weeks. Although some used this huge logistical undertaking as an apposite moment to desert, Germany now had a numerical advantage on the Western Front for the first time since the opening months of the war. A last-ditch effort for victory posed a formidable threat.

The Allies suspected that an attack was imminent but did not know where or when. A heavy artillery bombardment, including the use of gas shells, announced the beginning of the offensive in the early hours of 21 March. The main point of attack was between Arras and St Quentin, with the British Third and Fifth Armies bearing the brunt. The shelling then switched to a creeping barrage and the infantry began their advance. Initial gains were spectacular as waves of fresh troops joined the attack in a rolling spearhead, a tactic which maintained the vital forward momentum. The German army swept across the Somme battlefield and quickly took Peronne, Bapaume and Albert. Disagreement between Haig and Pétain regarding the Allies' response served the German army well. The assault threatened to separate the French and British, which could have had catastrophic consequences.

Foch becomes Allies' Generalissimo

On 26 March Marshal Ferdinand Foch became the de facto Supreme Allied Commander on the Western Front and on his shoulders fell the immediate problem of co-ordinating the defences and staunching the potentially fatal haemorrhage. Foch quickly realized that Amiens would be a key German target and must be defended at all costs. He was helped by Ludendorff, who opted to advance on too wide a front instead of focusing his efforts on taking Amiens. With every day the Allied line was becoming better reinforced and stronger, while the German line was becoming overstretched and weaker. The advance petered out on 8 April.

Ludendorff tried to regain the lost momentum by switching the point of attack. A fresh offensive was launched to the north, around the River Lys. Attacking here had been considered as an alternative to Operation Michael; it now became the focal point of a secondary onslaught. Again there was an immediate breakthrough which offered the Germans encouragement. On 11 April Haig issued a Special Order of the Day, a rallying call to all the ranks. "There is no other course open to us but to fight it out. Every position must be held to the last man; there must be no retirement." Originally he ended his stirring appeal to his hard-pressed men with the words "But be of good cheer, the British Empire must win in the end", but thought better of this optimistic note and struck it through.

By the end of April the new German offensive had again fizzled out. Ludendorff was in a cleft stick, caught between the need to make a decisive breakthrough and the need to conserve his dwindling resources. On 7 May Germany was buoyed by the news that Rumania had signed the Treaty of Bucharest and posed no further threat. After Russia's withdrawal Rumania had felt dangerously isolated and saw the need for an early armistice. Germany exacted a heavy price from the defeated country but it signified little. The war was now in its endgame phase and that had to be played out on the Western Front.

On 27 May Ludendorff tried yet another initiative, against the French Sixth Army along the Chemin des Dames. The German army swept across the Aisne and reached the Marne; Paris, only some 50 miles away, was threatened and a partial evacuation of the capital took place. The city did come under artillery fire but the attack was halted on the on the outskirts. In three months of concerted effort the German army had made great territorial gains and inflicted considerable losses on the Allies, but as more and more American divisions poured into the theatre these were not as critical as the losses sustained by Ludendorff. In June alone the German army suffered over 200,000 casualties. That same month saw a further significant depletion in Ludendorff's manpower as a flu epidemic broke out among the ranks.

Ludendorff's final effort to achieve a breakthrough came on 15 July with an offensive around Reims. Three days later the French, supported by fresh American troops, countered. The Second Battle of the Marne, as it was called, was the turning point. From now until the end of hostilities Germany would be on the retreat. The Allies forced Ludendorff's army backwards relentlessly and the morale of the rival forces shifted accordingly, this time irrevocably.

On 8 August General Rawlinson led a combined Allied force in the Battle of Amiens, which caught the enemy off guard and quickly shattered any remaining hopes of victory. More than 2000 guns bombarded the German line and 400 tanks were deployed in support of the infantry. The recently formed RAF helped to give the Allies massive air supremacy. Also, the backroom staff had finally come up with their own solution to the problem of synchronizing machine-gun fire with the rotation of the propellers, something that Anthony Fokker had achieved for the Germans in 1915. Improvements in wireless telegraphy meant that reconnaissance aircraft could now relay information regarding enemy positions and batteries more efficiently. Although the attrition rate was high - on the first day of the Amiens offensive the RAF lost 45 planes to anti-aircraft fire – the contribution was significant.

"Black Day" for German Army

The ferocity of the Amiens offensive prompted Ludendorff to declare it "the black day of the German army". The coup de grace would be to breach the Hindenburg Line – which finally came on 29 September – but even before that happened both Ludendorff and the Kaiser knew the outcome was now inevitable and the war had to be brought to an end.

Everywhere the noose around the Central Powers was tightening. On 27 September Bulgaria sued for peace, the first of Germany's allies to fall. There was widespread resentment among the Bulgarians that they had been treated as second-class citizens by the Reich, not trusted allies. Scarce food resources were commandeered by the German army, leaving Bulgarian soldiers and civilians to go hungry. When the Allies launched a large-scale offensive from Salonika in mid-September Bulgaria's powers of resistance quickly ebbed away.

Defeat of the Ottoman Empire soon followed. Since taking Jerusalem in December 1917 General Allenby had been hampered by the redeployment of resources to the Western Front. In September 1918 he was ready to go on the attack once again. Allenby –"the Bull" – expertly tricked his opposite number, Liman von Sanders, into thinking the point of attack would be inland. In fact Allenby struck along the coast, near Megiddo. The Turkish army, which had suffered heavily from guerrilla raids organized by the Arabs, assisted by T E Lawrence, was particularly weak in this area and a swift breakthrough was achieved. Damascus, Beirut and Aleppo fell in quick succession and Turkey finally capitulated on 30 October.

Austria-Hungary sues for peace

Four days later Austria-Hungary submitted. The Dual Monarchy had been on the point of collapse for months, politically as well as militarily. Its disparate peoples had become increasingly unwilling to suffer further hardship for an empire to which they felt little allegiance. Following the Battle of the Piave in June 1918, in which the Austro-Hungarian army was rebuffed by the Italians, the commitment of the Hungarians, Croats, Czechs and Slavs was further eroded. Emperor Karl, the Imperial head of the Dual Monarchy since the death of Franz Joseph in November 1916, had already gone behind Germany's back in an attempt to secure a peace deal and save his country. Belatedly he offered autonomy to the main ethnic states over which he presided, but instead of binding the Austrian army together, the prospect of federal status served to further split the empire asunder. There was mass desertion as previously subject peoples sought to reach homelands which now had a new political identity. When the Italians launched their offensive on 24 October, Austrian resistance was virtually non-existent. On 3 November the Dual Monarchy accepted terms.

Even before Germany lost her chief ally the leadership knew it was time for the Reich to yield. On 4 October the new chancellor Prince Max of Baden sent a note to Washington hoping to secure an armistice based on Wilson's Fourteen Points, which was considered to be the least worst option. If Germany expected more favourable terms from America than Britain or France she was to be disappointed. The Reich had no bargaining chips and would have to accept whatever terms were imposed, a fact not lost on the US president. Wilson didn't apprise the British or French of the dialogue entered into between Washington and Berlin, exchanges which reached a conclusion with Germany's acceptance of US terms on 27 October.

Meanwhile Foch continued to turn the screw. General Pershing's American forces, supported by the French, were at the forefront of a huge offensive in the Meuse-Argonne region, which began on 26 September. The aim was to capture vital rail links that were Germany's main line of communication. Over the next five weeks the American army sustained over 100,000 casualties but on 1 November the final breakthrough of the war was achieved. Ludendorff had already fallen by then and it was only a matter of time before his country followed. On 3 November the German navy mutinied at Kiel and there was revolution on the streets of Berlin. On 8 November Marshal Foch received Germany's armistice delegation in a railway carriage in the forest of Compiegne. The defeated country was given seventy-two hours to agree to the terms laid down, which included democratization. The German delegation didn't need three days to deliberate. The following day the Kaiser abdicated, decamping to neutral Holland. The armistice was signed at 5.00 am on 11 November, to come into force six hours later. Some German soldiers fought to the last minute before laying down their weapons. While Foch acclaimed the Allied victory as "the greatest battle in history", von Hindenburg led his defeated troops home to a country in chaos. All the privation and hardship had failed to produce a glorious victory and mobs vented their anger by attacking the war-weary officers of the Reich.

The war had been won. It now fell to the victors to shape a peace in which principles and ideals would clash with self-interest.

Top left: "Piko Nei Te Matenga" – these words, meaning "when our heads are bowed with woe", are being sung by Maori soldiers at the grave of their leader Lieutenant Colonel G King, Commander of the New Zealand Pioneer Battalion. This Maori lament was usually reserved for high-ranking chiefs.

Top middle: Field Marshal Foch (left) was appointed Supreme Commander of the Allied forces in March 1918.

Top right: Two soldiers operate a Lewis gun on the front line.

Above left: German troops wear their original Pickelhaube helmets with the traditional spike. As the war progressed it was clear they offered little protection against shrapnel and shell fragments and the spike offered an obvious target so they were replaced by the Stalhelm steel helmet.

Above right: A child's pram with a stretcher placed on top is used to carry a wounded British soldier out of the battle zone.

Left: A group of Tommies huddle round a roadside fire in January 1918 as the war enters yet another year.

Top: **Fresh troops disembark at a French port in February 1918. By the spring American forces were joining their Allied counterparts on the frontline at the rate of 10,000 a day.**

Middle: **A comrade helps a stranded officer out of the mud.**

Below: **Two American marines in a communication trench are fully equipped with gas masks and steel helmets.**

January 1918

1 The Swedish steamer SS *Eriksholm* was sunk by the German submarine *UC-58* off the coast of Aberdeen whilst on a voyage from Methil to Göteborg with a cargo of coal.

2 The British Government formed the Air Ministry which had responsibility for managing the affairs of the Royal Air Force.

3 The Air Council took over management of Britain's air services from the Air Board with Lord Rothermere, the first Air Minister, as President.

4 The British hospital ship HMHS *Rewa* was torpedoed and sunk in the Bristol Channel as she was returning to Britain from Malta carrying wounded troops.

   The Russian Bolshevik and Swedish Governments formally recognised the independence of Finland.

5 British Prime Minister David Lloyd George outlined British War Aims in a speech to Trade Union delegates.

6 Germany and France recognized the independence of Finland.

8 Speaking to a joint session of Congress, President Wilson of the United States proposed a fourteen point program for world peace. These points were later taken as the basis for peace negotiations at the end of the war.

9 The British Beagle class destroyer HMS *Racoon* ran aground in bad weather and sank off the North coast of Ireland with the loss of all hands. The battleship was en route from Liverpool to Lough Swilly to take up anti-submarine and convoy duties in the Northern Approaches.

10 The British Government assured the Russian Bolshevik Government of their support in the creation of an independent Poland.

12 The British steamer HMS *Whorlton* was torpedoed and sunk by the *UB-30* in the English Channel with the loss of all hands.

14 German destroyers bombarded Great Yarmouth on the Norfolk coast of England.

   The former Prime Minister of France Joseph Caillaux was arrested on charges of high treason.

15 General strikes were held in Prague and Budapest as workers' peace movements gathered momentum.

18 The Russian Constituent Assembly convened in the Tauride Palace in Petrograd in order to write a constitution and form a government for post revolutionary Russia.

19 Following a 13 hour meeting the Russian Constituent Assembly was dissolved by the Bolshevik Government, an action that is generally reckoned as marking the onset of the Bolshevik dictatorship.

20 At the Battle of Imbros, a naval engagement outside the Dardanelles, the Turkish cruiser *Midilli* (formerly the German SMS *Breslau*) and British monitors HMS *Raglan* and HMS *M28* were sunk.

21 Sir Edward Carson resigned from the War Cabinet.

22 The Russian Bolshevik Government protested about inaccuracies in the reports of proceedings at Brest-Litovsk negotiations.

23 Negotiations between the Russian Bolshevik Government and the Central Powers were suspended at Brest-Litovsk.

24 The German Chancellor Georg von Hertling and Austrian Foreign Minister Count Ottokar Czernin made public their replies to statements on war aims made by US President Woodrow Wilson and British Prime Minister David Lloyd George

26 The Irish passenger steamer SS *Cork* was torpedoed by German submarine *U-103* whilst travelling from Dublin to Liverpool.

27 Lieutenant General Sir Launcelot Edward Kiggell resigned as Chief of the General Staff to the British Expeditionary Force .

28 Increasingly frustrated with the continuing Great War 100,000 workers took to the streets of Berlin, demanding an end to the war on all fronts.

30 Negotiations were resumed between the Russian Bolshevik Government and the Central Powers at Brest-Litovsk.

31 Martial Law was declared in Berlin due to the escalation of the workers' strikes.

PRESIDENT WILSON'S WORLD-PEACE TERMS.

President Wilson's Fourteen Points

On 8 January 1918 Woodrow Wilson, the US President, delivered an address to Congress. He outlined his ideas for a post-conflict Europe in his "Fourteen Points" speech, in which he envisioned a Europe made up of nations based on democracy and self-determination, which were armed only as much as was necessary for internal security. A "League of Nations" would provide collective security and oversee international relations. Wilson did not confer with the Allies before delivering his speech, and not all of it would have been well received had he done so. Complete freedom of navigation on the seas at all times (whether at peace or war), for instance, was a stipulation which would not have pleased Britain, a great naval power. In addition, Wilson's call for transparent pacts between governments was far removed from the secret deals by which many of the minor combatants had been persuaded to support one side or the other. But President Wilson knew that he held a strong hand in January 1918, and he was determined to be the prime mover in shaping the new world order.

Top: President Wilson delivers his Fourteen Points to Congress. He was awarded the Nobel Peace Prize the following year for this peace initiative to try to resolve the conflict.

Above far left: The USS *Pennsylvania*, a 31,400 ton ship, was one of the first oil burning battleships. Only coal powered vessels were able to join the Grand Fleet due to the lack of oil tankers for refuelling. *Pennsylvania* remained at her base in Yorktown but was valuable as a training ship.

Far left: A makeshift shelter for these US troops in the woods of the Argonne forests.

Bottom left: At a training camp in England, American airmen line up to receive letters from home.

Middle left: American soldiers wear German flamethrowers captured in enemy trenches.

Below: US troops move wounded comrades back from the front line to receive further medical assistance.

General John Pershing

The man who led the American Expeditionary Force had a lifespan that bridged the American Civil War and the dropping of the atomic bomb. Born in the Midwest town of Laclede in 1860, Pershing graduated from West Point aged 25 and saw his first action in the American Indian wars, where Geronimo numbered among the enemy. He served as a cavalry officer in the Spanish-American War of 1898, which erupted over US involvement in the Cuban War of Independence and spread to the Pacific. Pershing's commanding officer said he was "the coolest man under fire I ever saw" in a conflict won decisively by US forces. He next faced an insurrection in the Philippines, annexed by America after defeating the Spanish. Here he displayed diplomatic as well as military skills in quelling unrest among the indigenous population who resented swapping one imperial power for another. In 1905 White House incumbent Theodore Roosevelt promoted Pershing from captain to Brigadier-General, over the heads of hundreds of senior officers who might have expected such preferment.

By the time the guns opened up on the battlefields of World War One, Pershing's focus was on cross-border raids perpetrated by Mexican bandits. He commanded a task force that went into that country in pursuit of rebel leader Pancho Villa, showing professionalism in the face of a personal tragedy: the loss of his wife and three daughters in a fire at their home on San Francisco's Presidio military base. Pershing was now father to just one son.

He arrived on the Western Front in June 1917, ahead of the citizen army that was being raised in answer to Woodrow Wilson's call to arms. He bore the responsibility of overseeing a force that swelled to two million in just 18 months, antagonising his fellow Allied commanders by insisting that America should fight as an independent entity. He modified that position during Germany's 1918 Spring Offensive, placing his forces at Foch's disposal. A great champion of the offensive spirit, Pershing was keen for his men to be allowed to show their mettle, and during Germany's last-ditch bid for victory, British and French concerns about the effectiveness of his "Doughboys" were allayed. At Cantigny on the Somme, then at Chateau Thierry and Belleau Wood as the German army drove towards the Marne, Pershing's forces amply proved their worth. And when defence turned to attack, the newly formed Ist Army showed outstanding battling qualities in taking the San Mihiel salient. By the time the Meuse-Argonne offensive was launched, America's 2nd Army was also in the field. "Your achievement is scarcely to be equalled in America's history," the proud commander said of his troops. It was another feather, too, in the cap of their leader, "Black Jack". During the conflict he was promoted to full general; only George Washington, Ulysses Grant, William Sherman and Philip Sheridan had achieved that rank in the annals of US military history.

Following the Allied victory, Pershing was decorated by nine foreign nations, while his native land gave him a hero's welcome on his return home. Congress conferred upon him the title General of the Armies of the United States, the only serving officer to have held that rank, though Washington was accorded the same honour as part of the country's bicentennial celebrations in 1976. Pershing retired from active service in 1924, but was a frequent visitor to Europe in his work on behalf of America's battle monuments commission. He was an octogenarian when the Second World War broke out, yet still offered his services to his country. On his death in 1948, aged 87, thousands filed past the coffin of a true national hero before his burial with full honours at Washington's Arlington National Ceremony.

Pershing bore the responsibility of overseeing a force that swelled to two million in just 18 months.

Above right: **General Pershing, Major Summerall and officers stand to attention while the Adjutant of the 1st Division reads the citation to officers and men to be decorated with the Distinguished Service Cross.**

Above left: **Pershing pins the DSC on Lieutenant Colonel J M Cullison, a US Infantry commander. He was awarded the medal for his actions at Laversines, France, in July 1918.**

Middle: **An American engineer was killed and another was wounded after a bomb hidden in this cave exploded. It had been left by German troops before their retreat.**

Below: **Troops gather round a monument erected in memory of Sergeant Fred Harris, the first man of his battalion killed in the conflict**

LAST CHANCE FOR HOARDERS.

Above left and right: Food queues form outside shops on the King's Road, Chelsea, and Stamford Street at Blackfriars (above right). By January 1918 sugar was rationed and at the end of April meat, cheese, butter and margarine were added to the list. Everyone had to register with a butcher and a grocer and ration cards were issued.

Middle left: Lieutenant E Whitwell leads a recruiting campaign in Trentin, New Jersey.

Below: Troops relax in the sunshine on Batchworth Heath, Hertfordshire before leaving for the Front.

Middle right: This six-horned siren was used for air raid warnings in Paris.

Below right: The Mayor of Oldham purchases a war bond worth £100,000 on behalf of the town. Tank 141 "Egbert" was one of six Mark IV male tanks known as "tank banks" that toured the country to promote the sale of War Bonds and War Savings Certificates. The scheme eventually raised over £2 million.

Left: Food rationing explained graphically in the press.

WHAT YOUR FOOD COUPONS WILL BUY.

MEN / WOMEN

YOUR BREAD RATION.—From this pictorial table, to be issued by the Ministry of Food, you can see your daily bread ration.

Top: **British and French troops combine forces to cook a meal.**

Middle: **War widows wait to receive their husbands' gallantry medals during an investiture ceremony in Hyde Park, London.**

Below: **Troops march through Hatfield in Hertfordshire.**

February 1918

1   Governments of the Central Powers formally recognised the Ukraine republic.

3   The British Government announced the enlargement of powers of the Supreme War Council at Versailles.

4   General Mikhail Alexeiev moved towards Moscow with a force of Don Cossacks for action against the Bolsheviks.

5   The British liner SS *Tuscania* was torpedoed and sunk off the coast of Ireland by the German submarine *UB-77* while carrying American troops to Europe.

  The Russian Government announced the separation of the Russian Orthodox Church from the state.

6   The German Government sent an ultimatum to the Romanian Government demanding peace negotiations within four days.

8   The Royal Navy destroyer HMS *Boxer* sank after colliding with the merchant ship SS *St Patrick* in the English Channel.

9   A peace treaty was signed at Brest-Litovsk between the Central Powers and the Ukraine.

  Alexandru Averescu replaced Ion I. Constantin Brătianu as Prime Minister of Romania after Brătianu refused to negotiate with the Germans and resigned.

10   British Prime Minister David Lloyd George entrusted Lord Beaverbrook with the responsibility of establishing the new Ministry of Information in charge of propaganda.

11   US President Wilson addressed Congress to add extra aims to his fourteen point program for world peace.

  A staunch opponent of the Bolsheviks, Russian General Alexei Maximovich Kaledin committed suicide by shooting himself.

12   The British steamer HMS *Polo* was torpedoed and sunk without warning by German submarine *UB-57*.

14   The Gregorian calendar was adopted in Russia. The Council of People's Commissars had issued a decree that Wednesday 31 January 1918 was to be followed by Thursday 14 February 1918, thus dropping 13 days from the calendar.

15   A sustained German destroyer raid in the Straits of Dover resulted in the sinking of a British Admiralty trawler and several net drifters.

16   General Lionel Dunsterville led his "Dunsterforce" troops to Enzeli on a mission to gather information, train and command local forces, and prevent the spread of German propaganda.

18   The Armistice on the Russian front expired. German armies resumed hostilities and began to advance towards Dvinsk on the Eastern Front.

19   The Russian Bolshevik Government indicated a willingness to sign the peace treaty at Brest-Litovsk.

20   German troops continued their advance towards Petrograd, Moscow and Kiev.

21   British forces captured Jericho in Palestine, thus depriving the Turks of their advance base for the defence of Palestine.

22   Owing to the growing fear of German spies and domestic labour violence, the Montana Sedition Law restricting freedom of speech and assembly was passed in the United States.

23   An Inter-Allied Labour and Socialist Conference in London passed a resolution with regard to war aims.

24   Turkish forces recaptured Trebizond in Asia Minor.

25   German forces captured Pernau and Pskov as the advance against Russian troops continued.

26   British hospital ship *HMHS Glenart Castle* was sunk by German submarine *U-56* in the Bristol Channel whilst en route from Cardiff to Brest to pick up war survivors.

28   In the United States a new bill was introduced which was intended to protect war materials including arms, ammunition, clothing, food supplies, and other items used by the military.

Fighter ace suffers fate he most feared

Edward "Mick" Mannock was an unlikely air ace, a childhood illness having left him with impaired vision in one eye. The son of a serving soldier, he was born in County Cork in 1887 but spent part of his childhood in India, where his father was posted. By the time he was in his mid-teens Mannock was living in Kent, he and his mother left impoverished after his father deserted them. He took up employment in the engineering arm of the Post Office, and the period just before the outbreak of war saw him cable-laying in the Turkish capital. His citizenship was enough to see him incarcerated, the ill-treatment he suffered leaving him with a burning hatred of the German foe. Those feelings fed a desire to serve once he had been repatriated in 1915. His captors erred badly in believing he was so debilitated that he could pose no threat to the Central Powers.

Mannock's skills found an outlet in the Royal Engineers, but he was soon drawn to the Royal Flying Corps. Neatly sidestepping the eyesight test, he was ready to take to the skies in spring 1917. Already in his 30th year, Mannock was considerably older than many of his fellow recruits and not especially well liked among them. His cocksure manner and keenness to get at the enemy left him lacking in a few social graces. But it was bluffness that masked an understandable apprehension. "I have an idea that my nerves won't take very much of it," he wrote, and there was a shaky baptism when he first saw action. Mannock went on to prove himself a master of aerial combat and was soon promoted to captain. His skill, along with his readiness to lead by example, earned him the admiration of those he taught and those who served under him. He in turn showed a great duty of care to his men.

In early 1918 Mannock returned to France with 74 Squadron, whose training he had overseen. He was showing clear signs of combat stress: visibly shaking and often sick before sorties, tormented especially by the thought of a fiery death. His nerves were not salved by the news that his friend, mentor and fellow ace James McCudden met his end, not in battle but during a routine flight.

Mannock's deepest fear was realised on 26 July 1918, less than three weeks after McCudden's death. Under his wing that day was a novice from his new command, 85 Squadron, whom he was keen should claim his first victory. Mannock had 50 attested "kills" to his name; fewer than the top-scoring McCudden, but today it was more important for young Donald Inglis to break his duck. To his delight the junior pilot duly downed an enemy plane, whereupon Mannock, inexplicably, broke his own golden rule and tracked its descent. Strafed by ground fire, his aircraft also plunged earthwards, consumed in flames. He was in the habit of keeping a revolver in the cockpit for just such an eventuality; it is unclear whether he had the chance to choose a swift, self-inflicted death.

Already the recipient of the Military Cross and DSO, he was posthumously awarded the Victoria Cross, for his overall contribution to the war effort rather than any individual act of valour. He and McCudden, who received the same honour three months before his death, were two of just 19 pilots awarded the VC during World War One.

Left: Major Edward "Mick" Mannock, recipient of a posthumous Victoria Cross as well as the Distinguished Service Order and Two Bars and the Military Cross and Bar.

Top left: Major James McCudden received more gallantry medals than any other British airman during the conflict. The recipient of a VC, DSO and Bar, Military Cross and Bar, and the Military Medal, he was killed during a routine flight when an engine fault caused the plane to crash.

All above: On 28/29 January 1918 two Sopwith Camels, piloted by Captain George Hackwilll and Lieutenant Charles Banks, chased and gunned down a Gotha, sending it crashing to the ground near Wickford, Essex. All three members of the crew were killed. Afterwards mechanics and pilots used this opportunity to study the remains of the aircraft.

Who shot down the Red Baron?

As a young cavalry officer Manfred von Richthofen's war began with him kicking his heels behind the lines, awaiting the infantry breakthrough that would plunge him into the thick of the action. That prospect receded as trench warfare set in, and a frustrated Richthofen observed in the skies above the petrol-driven battlefield scouts that threatened to consign horses to the realms of military history. He secured a transfer that took him airborne, first in an observer's role, and by the end of 1915 as a pilot.

Richthofen was still a relative novice when selected to join a new élite fighter squad formed by Oswald Boelcke, the man who devised the air combat tactics drilled into every German pilot. These were the Jagdstaffeln or Jasta squadrons, and in September 1916 Richthofen took his place in the first of these crack outfits, Jasta 2, headed by Boelcke himself. He soon scored his first victory in his Albatros biplane, but within weeks was reminded that even the cream were vulnerable as Boelcke crashed to his death following a mid-air collision with one of his own. Richthofen would more than fill the void left by Boelcke and fellow German ace Max Immelman, who also perished that year. He was less a knight of the air than a ruthless predator, as his encounter with one of Britain's finest airmen in November 1916 showed. Richthofen took on Major Lanoe Hawker, using his superior machinery to gain advantage before closing in for the kill. As he added to his victory tally, so his collection of souvenirs retrieved from fallen victims grew. In Hawker's case it was a Lewis gun; on another occasion he turned an entire engine unit into an ornamental chandelier.

In January 1917 Richthofen was the recipient of the Pour le Mérite award, Germany's highest bravery decoration, popularly known as the Blue Max. The successes mounted for both him and his squadron, whose brightly painted aircraft earned it the "Flying Circus" soubriquet. In July 1917 the circus ringmaster had a narrow escape, managing to land his plane despite suffering a serious head wound in a dogfight. He was soon bandaged up and back in action, this time at the controls of a new Fokker triplane. It was a highly manoeuvrable aircraft, its wing design giving it a rate of climb that paid large dividends during enemy engagements. Britain would respond with excellent fighters of its own, such as the Sopwith Camel, but for a brief period Richthofen and the Fokker Dr.I made an unrivalled combination in the skies above the Western Front.

When he took off from Cappy for a routine patrol on 21 April 1918, Richthofen had just taken his victim tally to 80. It could not affect the outcome of Germany's Spring Offensive, but his exploits had a propaganda value far beyond any military significance. Germany's commanders knew that if the great Red Baron fell in battle it would be a damaging blow to morale. And that blow was struck as he chased down Lieutenant Wilfred May, of the RAF's 209 Squadron, over the Somme valley on the morning of 21 April. The pursuit attracted ground fire from the Australian force controlling that sector, both machine gun emplacements and individual rifle pot shots. It also brought 209 Squadron's Canadian leader Captain Roy Brown into the

Richthofen was less a knight of the air than a ruthless predator, as his encounter with one of Britain's finest airmen showed.

picture, and he too sprayed bullets in the direction of the scarlet triplane. Richthofen was dead before the aircraft hit the ground, one of the bullets having struck him on the right side and jagged its way through his chest cavity. But whose? The initial investigation concluded that the bullet's path indicated an aerial source, and Captain Brown was credited as the man who had brought down the Red Baron. But Brown claimed to have fired downwards and from the left, whereas the bullet that killed Richthofen hit the right side of the fuselage and passed through his body on an upward trajectory. The attitude of the plane at the critical moment is key. There are various scenarios in which a ground gunner could have fired a shot consistent with the physical evidence. It is almost impossible to reconcile Brown's account with that evidence, yet he went to his own grave in 1944 feted as the man who downed the ace of aces.

Top left: The "Red Baron" Manfred von Richthofen was regarded as the top flying ace of the conflict, with 80 official combat victories attributed to him.

Top middle: Richthofen talks with other German officers. In January 1917 he had taken over command of the fighter squadron Jasta 11 which included some of the most elite German pilots.

Top right: The Red Baron and his fellow squadron members pictured just before a flight.

Middle right: An aerodrome in Flanders used by Richthofen and his flying circus.

Above right: A French aircraft factory works day and night to manufacture planes.

Left: The Canadian pilot Captain Arthur Brown was credited with firing the shot that killed Richthofen but controversy still reigns with many claiming the fatal shot was fired by an Australian machine gunner on the ground.

March 1918

2   German forces captured Kiev in the Ukraine.

3   The Treaty of Brest-Litovsk was signed between Russia and the Central Powers. Russia recognised the independence of Ukraine, Georgia and Finland while handing over Poland and the Baltic States to Germany and Austria-Hungary.

4   German forces occupied Narva in Estonia

5   Representatives from Romania and the Central Powers, Bulgaria and Turkey signed a preliminary peace agreement at Buftea.

6   Shipping loss figures were released in Britain on the same day as the British steamer HMS *Kalgan* was torpedoed and sunk by the German submarine *U-53*.

7   Germany and Finland signed a peace agreement.

8   The first case of Spanish influenza was reported. The disease quickly spread and the resulting worldwide epidemic ended up killing more people than the war.

9   The Marxist revolutionary Georgy Vasilyevich Chicherin was appointed as the People's Commissariat for Foreign Affairs in Russia.

10   The British hospital ship HMHS *Guildford Castle* was torpedoed, but not sunk, by a German U-boat in the Bristol Channel while she was flying the Red Cross flag.

12   Lenin and the Russian Bolshevik Government left Petrograd for the new capital city of Moscow.

13   German forces occupied Odessa on the Black Sea.

14   The Congress of Soviets met at Moscow to ratify the Brest-Litovsk treaty of peace with the Central Powers.

15   Prince Lichnowsky's pamphlet, which had accused the Russian Government of failing to support him in efforts to avert the war, was published in the Swedish journal Politiken.

17   On Saint Patrick's Day cartoonist Clifford Berryman published a cartoon depicting Uncle Sam rolling up his sleeves and preparing to use a large club to deal with the many German propagandist snakes slithering in the grass around him.

18   The Entente Governments issued a Note which formally refused to recognise the German-Russian peace treaty.

The Dutch Government accepted the Allied terms for the use of Dutch shipping in United States and Entente ports, with reservations.

19   President Woodrow Wilson signed up to the Standard Time Act, setting federally mandated time zones across the nation and calling for daylight saving time (DST) to begin on 31 March.

21   The Second Battle of the Somme was launched as a series of attacks against British forces along the Western Front. The offensive was made up of four separate German attacks, codenamed Michael, Georgette, Gneisenau and Blücher-Yorck launched in that order.

22   In Operation Michael German forces continued to make gains in the northern sector, capturing Vracourt, Tergnier and the Oise Canal.

23   The Paris Gun, a German long-range artillery weapon, was used to bombard Paris from 120 km (75 miles) away.

German forces continued to press their advantage on the Somme as British troops pulled back.

24   In the First battle of Bapaume the towns of Peronne and Bapaume were captured by German forces as Operation Michael succeeded in forcing a retreat by the British Army.

25   In further action during Operation Michael, the town of Noyon was captured by German forces.

26   The Doullens Conference was held between French and British military leaders in order to better coordinate British and French military operations on the Western Front.

27   At the Battle of Rosières the Germans captured the strategically important communications centre of Montdidier.

28   Under the codename Operation Mars the Germans attacked the southern Arrras sector, but were defeated sustaining heavy losses.

29   A single shell from the Paris Gun hit the roof of the St-Gervais-et-St-Protais Church in Paris whilst a Good Friday service was in progress, collapsing the entire roof on to the congregation and resulting in a high number of casualties.

30   The First Battle of Villers-Bretonneux saw the renewal of a German assault on the French position on the south of the newly formed Somme salient whilst another attack was launched towards Amiens.

Top: Men from the 20th British Division and the 22nd French Division shelter in hastily dug rifle pits in the Nesle Sector in March 1918.

Upper and lower middle: Field guns on the battlefield at Arras stretch as far as the eye can see.

Below: Highland troops move up to the frontline to meet Germany's new offensive. By the end of March General Hubert Gough, commander of the Fifth Army, had been replaced by General Sir William Birdwood.

Opposite: American troops advance through a gap in the enemy's barbed wire.

Germany's final throw of the dice

1917 had hardly been a good year for the Allies. The Nivelle disaster, a French army in disarray, the loss of Russia's fighting strength, Passchendaele, Caporetto: all major setbacks that took the gloss off encouraging news from Cambrai – the early part of that battle, at least – and the Middle East. Entering the next campaigning season Haig also had deep concerns about manpower. But Germany's position was even more perilous. Turning the U-boats loose had not starved Britain into submission; indeed it was the Allied blockade that was biting deeper. With shortages of provisions came growing unrest on Germany's home front. Strikes broke out, there was disorder on the streets. Flexing military muscles rang hollow to people struggling to put food on the table. The mood was for an end to privation, and in July 1917 the Reichstag came out in favour of negotiating a peace without annexations or indemnities, perhaps fearing that volatile public sentiment might ignite into Russian-style conflagration. There was already left-wing extremism in the shape of the Spartacists, formed in 1915 by Rosa Luxemburg and Karl Liebnecht. Their uprising would not take place until after the guns had fallen silent, and unlike Russian Bolshevism would be ruthlessly nipped in the bud, but at the beginning of 1918 the communist threat was real enough. Politicians who had deferred to the military in allowing the economy to be geared to prosecuting the war began to assert themselves.

Operation Michael

For all the political posturing, however, it was Hindenburg and Ludendorff who remained the power brokers, and they were in no mood to concede. Their answer to a recalcitrant Reichstag was to orchestrate the removal of chancellor Bethmann Hollweg, replaced by the more compliant Georg Michaelis. The government purse strings loosened once again in pursuit of victory, while the founding of the new Fatherland Party in September 1917 provided a counterbalance to left-leaning dissent. The High Command was equally firm on the matter of Woodrow Wilson's 14-point plan for a peace settlement, set before Congress on 8 January 1918. Hindenburg and Ludendorff were unmoved by the president's urging for Germany "to accept a place of equality among the peoples of the world, the new world in which we now live, instead of a place of mastery." Why accept a deal that spoke of addressing "the wrong done to France by Prussia in 1871 in the matter of Alsace-Lorraine" while there remained a chance of outright victory? The High Command did recognise that, as American troops poured in, the window of opportunity to achieve such a victory was growing ever narrower. The resources released by the armistice with Russia – over 40 divisions – could be deployed in the west to tip the balance in Germany's favour. Pétain calculated that the enemy would be able to hold the front with half its available strength, allowing the rest to be concentrated in a powerful offensive. It was an uncomfortable thought. But for Germany the clock was running. Nothing more could be squeezed from wheels of industrial production already turning at maximum revs. No new German ally with almost unlimited manpower lay on the horizon. This was an advantage with strict time limits.

Ludendorff's Spring Offensive

Ludendorff's Spring Offensive – Kaiserschlacht, the great imperial battle – opened astride the Somme on 21 March. This was where General Gough's 5th Army rubbed shoulders with their French allies, offering the attacker the chance to divide the partners; to hammer home a deep wedge in the hope that those partners might be on differing wavelengths when it came to deciding how to respond. Launched with a hurricane bombardment in thick fog, Operation Michael yielded results that vindicated the latest approach to trench warfare: silent registration of guns, and the use of machine-gun and flamethrower-bearing shock troops as a spearhead. These fleet-footed, élite *stosstrupps* had a clear objective: targeting the enemy's weak points and paving the way for the main assault. Flexibility and surprise were key, and the British line, heavily outnumbered, was swamped. A war of movement returned as German troops advanced on a 50-mile front. The breach was serious enough to threaten Paris, enough to persuade the Allies that a unified command was necessary to co-ordinate the response. Foch duly became supreme commander on the Western Front, the resoluteness he displayed at the Allied leaders' conference at Doullens on 26 March sufficient to override Haig's apprehension over ceding command. Not another inch would be given, said Foch. The ground already lost, and the collapse of the 5th Army in particular, needed a scapegoat, however, and the hapless Gough, who had warned that he had insufficient strength for the length of front he had to hold, was the obvious candidate.

Péronne, Bapaume and Albert fell in quick succession and Amiens lay within Germany's grasp.

GREATEST BATTLE OF ALL.

ATTACK BY 600,000 GERMANS.

SOME PROGRESS AT CERTAIN POINTS.

THROWN BACK AT OTHERS.

VERY HEAVY ENEMY LOSSES.

From SIR DOUGLAS HAIG.

Friday Night.

This morning the enemy renewed his attacks in great strength along practically the whole battle front. Fierce fighting has taken place in our battle positions and is still continuing.

The enemy has made some progress at certain points. At others his troops have been thrown back by our counter-attacks.

Our losses have inevitably been considerable, but not out of proportion to the magnitude of the battle.

From reports received from all parts of the battle front the enemy's losses continue to be very heavy, and his advance has everywhere been made at a great sacrifice.

Our troops are fighting with the greatest gallantry. When all ranks and all units of every arm have behaved so well it is difficult at this stage of the battle to distinguish instances.

Exceptional gallantry has been shown, however, by troops of the 24th Division in the protracted defence of LE VERGUIER (north-west of St. Quentin) and by the 3rd Division, who maintained our positions in the neighbourhood of CROISILLES (south-east of Arras) and to the north of that village against repeated attacks. A very gallant fight was made by the 51st Division also in the neighbourhood of the BAPAUME-CAMBRAI ROAD against repeated attacks.

Identifications obtained in the course of the battle show that the enemy's opening attack was delivered by some 40 German divisions [possibly 600,000 men], supported by great numbers of German artillery, reinforced by Austrian batteries. Many other German divisions have since taken part in the fighting, and others are arriving in the battle area.

Further fighting of the most severe nature is anticipated.

Above: A French village is alive with troop movement in April 1918. By the following month there were over one million US soldiers stationed in France with half of these at the frontline.

Rest of page: At the start of the conflict the German army was one of the most efficient in the world. It already had a mass conscription scheme in place, with military service followed by a length of time as a reserve. In 1914 there were 700,000 serving troops but within a week 3.8 million reserves had been called up, all trained and ready to fight.

German men were keen to come forward to fight, believing they were defending the Fatherland. Constant propaganda was issued by various means, including the mobile cinemas sent to the frontline. These provided entertainment but also sent out positive messages to the troops and portrayed events in a pro-German light.

However, as the war dragged on, exhaustion and a sense of betrayal was rife amongst the troops. Many opted for desertion while others fought on, often physically and spiritually demoralised. Their senior generals refused to acknowledge the mood until a "black day" in August when German troops surrendered in their droves.

THE GERMAN BATTLE-CRY : "A Single Combat has been Opened between England and Germany to Decide our Future Position in the World and whether the Anglo-Saxons Shall Continue to Press Their Will Upon the World."

GERMAN OFFENSIVE.

50 MILES OF OUR FRONT ATTACKED.

IN OUR BATTLE LINE AT SOME POINTS.

ENEMY LOSSES EXCEPTIONALLY HEAVY.

NO OBJECTIVES ATTAINED.

From SIR DOUGLAS HAIG,

Thursday Night.

At about 8 a.m. this morning, after an intense bombardment of both high-explosive and gas shells on forward positions and back areas, a powerful infantry attack was launched by the enemy on a front of over 50 miles, extending from the RIVER OISE in the neighbourhood of LA FÈRE to the SENSÉE RIVER about CROISILLES [south-east of Arras].

Hostile artillery demonstrations have taken place on a wide front north of LA BASSÉE CANAL and in the YPRES sector.

The attack, which for some time past was known to be in course of preparation, has been pressed with the greatest vigour and determination throughout the day.

In the course of the fighting the enemy broke through our outpost positions and succeeded in penetrating into our battle positions in certain parts of the front.

The attacks were delivered in large masses and have been extremely costly to the hostile troops engaged, whose losses have been exceptionally heavy.

Severe fighting continues along the whole front.

Large numbers of hostile reinforcing troops have been observed during the day moving forward behind the enemy's lines. Several enemy divisions which have been specially trained for this great attack have already been identified, including units of the Guard.

Captured maps depicting the enemy's intentions show that on no part of the long front of attack has he attained his objectives.

Above: Weary British soldiers rest on a mud bank. During Operation Michael the Allies lost nearly 255,000 men.

Right: A number of Allied artillerymen ride away from a captured ammunition store at Omiecourt in March 1918. Before leaving they set the stores alight to prevent the Germans from using the shells.

Below: Highland troops man the support line.

BRITISH YIELD MORE GROUND.

Above: Troops and guns pass through a village in the battle zone.

Right: A band of Tommies in an army wagon move up to the front line.

Below: Soldiers temporarily relieved of frontline duty.

Opposite below: French and English troops rest their rifles and machine-guns while they wait for signs of German attack.

Opposite above: Troops move up to the front line. During the three-week Operation Georgette, Foch took over command of the Allied forces and on 14 April agreed to send French reserves to the Lys sector to reinforce the troops.

↑ 26582

Haig's clarion call

By the end of March the Allies had rallied and Operation Michael fizzled out, a victim of its own success as there were insufficient reserves to capitalise on the great forward surge, and artillery could not keep pace with the attack. The advancing army had made full use of supplies that fell into their possession, undernourished soldiers gorging themselves on treasure-trove Allied provisions. That hindered progress, as did the need for rest and recuperation. Foch, by contrast, had new strength at his disposal and employed it well. Ludendorff now prodded at the enemy line in Flanders, south of Ypres around the River Lys, still hoping to isolate the Channel ports from which American strength would disgorge. First in the firing line were raw Portuguese recruits, who suffered badly. On 11 April, 48 hours into this second phase of the onslaught, Haig issued his famous backs-to-the-wall Order of the Day, a clarion call befitting the desperate situation and high stakes.

Ludendorff's Lys offensive – Operation Georgette – also juddered to a standstill with the arrival of reinforcements, who faced an overstretched, exhausted foe; though not before Passchendaele, the most vulnerable part of the Ypres salient won at such enormous cost just a few months earlier, was returned to German hands. Messines Ridge, too, though Ypres itself stood firm.

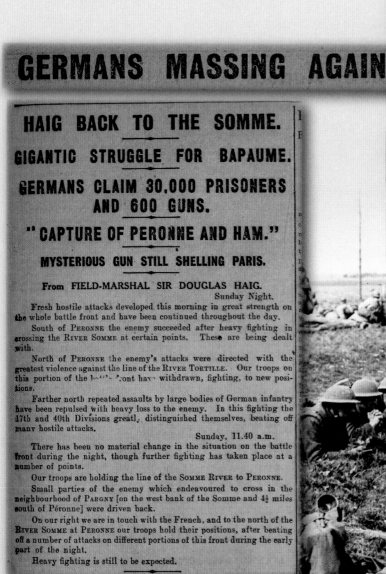

GERMAN ATTACKS: MAP OF THE WHOLE LINE.

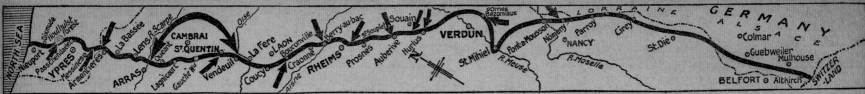

The above shows the whole battle line from the sea to the Alps. The thick bracketed arrows point to the section where the German push was made; the

whole of our 50 miles of front between the Scarpe and the Oise. The Germans entered our battle positions at some points. The other arrows indicate places

where minor attacks and raids took place before the bigger blow was delivered, notably near Verdun. The length of the whole of the Western front is about 590 miles.

The line holds but the crisis is not past

The British Army has made its valiant answer to Sir Douglas Haig's general order calling upon it to stand and fight – to the last man – for "the safety of our homes and the freedom of mankind."

For the past 48 hours, in the face of repeated attacks by masses of Germans and of a terrific bombardment, our devoted lads have held their ground firmly and unflinchingly. The line is still unbroken, and though the crisis is not yet by any means over, there is at least good hope that the men of 1918 will hold fast and win through like the heroes of 1914. There must still be considerable danger so long as there are signs of a powerful German concentration in another quarter, between Arras and Albert. But each hour gained in the north is of priceless importance.

During the last two days our troops have beaten off an attack at Festubert. They have held Bailleul, a point of supreme importance, as it threatens the communications of Ypres. They have recovered Neuve Eglise, on the flank of the Ypres defences, and they have kept it against repeated attacks. They have maintained their positions on the high ground. They still have the enemy below them in the intricate marsh and meadow land, where movement is not facilitated by the nature of the ground.

THE ALLIED LINE EAST OF AMIENS.

Top left: Battlefield camaraderie is strong as French poilus and British Tommies share their rations.

Top right: Howitzers in action at the corner of a wood near Domart.

Left: Allied troops return to their billets for a short rest.

Above left: The shaded area of this map, published 3 April, shows the area over which the Central Powers claim to have advanced since the opening of their offensive. The thick black

line indicates the Front before the battle began while the dotted line shows the Front line before the battle of the Somme in July 1916.

Above: How the Front progressed as the offensive intensified.

Opposite above: British troops move through a village in Picardy. As part of the Spring Offensive German commanders planned to take Ypres and force the Allied troops back to the Channel ports.

Opposite middle: In Picardy French villagers load up their possessions to escape the advancing German Army.

Opposite below: A Gotha aircraft crashes to the ground inside the British lines.

April 1918

1 The Royal Flying Corps and the Royal Naval Air Service were amalgamated to form the Royal Air Force – the first independent air force in the world.

2 Martial Law was declared in Canada following the anti-conscription Easter Riots that had occurred in Quebec City between 28 March and 1 April.

4 The Battle of the Avre constituted the final German attack towards Amiens which was fought between advancing German troops and defending Australian and British troops.

5 Operation Michael was halted when an attempt by the Germans to renew the offensive towards Amiens failed after British troops forced them out of the town.

9 Following the failure of Operation Michael, The Battle of the Lys began. The second of the series of attacks making up the German Spring Offensive, Operation Georgette was planned by General Erich Ludendorff with the objective of capturing Ypres and forcing the British troops back to the Channel ports.

10 The Battle of Messines 1918 began as German forces attacked north of Armentières and captured the town.

The British Government passed an extension to the Military Service Act of 1916 raising the upper age of conscription to 50. The law was also extended to Ireland, the Channel Islands and the Isle of Man.

11 The American steamer SS *Lakemoor* was sunk by German submarine *U-64* whilst en route from Newport to Glasgow.

12 During the German Operation Georgette offensive, Field Marshal Sir Douglas Haig issued his famous order that his men must carry on fighting, "With our backs to the wall", appealing to his forces to stand fast and fight to the last man.

13 The Battle of Bailleul began with British troops under the command of General Herbert Plumer.

14 General Ferdinand Foch was appointed Commander-in-Chief of Allied forces on the Western Front.

15 The Battle of Bailleul ended when the town of Bailleul was captured by German forces.

16 German forces progressed on the Lys River and reoccupied Passchendaele.

17 Frenchman Bolo Pasha, originally named Paul Bolo, was executed by firing squad after his conviction as a traitor and a German spy.

18 The Third Military Service Act came into force in Britain.

19 German forces entered the Crimea region.

20 British Secretary of State for War, Lord Derby resigned and was replaced by Lord Alfred Milner.

21 German flying ace Manfred von Richthofen (more commonly known as the Red Baron) was shot down and fatally wounded while flying over Morlancourt Ridge on the Somme front.

22 The British Royal Navy attempted to blockade, and thus neutralise, the key Belgian port of Zeebrugge by sinking obsolete British ships in the entrance to the harbour. The port was used by the German Navy as a base for their U-boats which posed a serious threat to Allied shipping.

23 Guatemala declared war on Germany.

24 The Second Battle of Villers-Bretonneux was launched against British lines in front of Amiens during the Battle of the Lys. It was the first tank-versus-tank battle in history.

25 At the Second Battle of the Kemmelberg the German Army attacked and captured the Kemmel Hill (Mont Kemmel).

27 Sir William Weir was announced as the Secretary of State for the Royal Air Force.

29 A final German attack captured the Scherpenberg, a hill to the northwest of the Kemmelberg and ended the Battle of the Lys.

30 British troops advanced east of Jordan at the Second Action of Es Salt in Palestine.

BATTLE AT MESSINES.

BRITISH BACK TO THE RIDGE.

GERMANS DRIVEN FROM THE VILLAGE.

DESPERATE FIGHT ON THE LYS.

From FIELD-MARSHAL SIR DOUGLAS HAIG.

Wednesday Night.

Following upon the bombardment already reported, the enemy this morning launched a fresh attack in strength against our positions between the LYS RIVER at ARMENTIERES and the YPRES-COMINES CANAL.

Heavy fighting has been taking place in this sector throughout the day, as well as on the whole front of yesterday's attack north of LA BASSEE CANAL.

North of ARMENTIERES the weight of the enemy's assaults has pressed our troops back to the line of the WYTSCHAETE-MESSINES RIDGE and PLOEGSTEERT [2¾ miles south of Messines]. Bodies of German infantry who had forced their way into MESSINES were driven out this morning by a counter-attack by our troops.

South of ARMENTIERES the enemy succeeded after a prolonged struggle in establishing himself on the left [north] bank of the LYS RIVER at certain points east of ESTAIRES and in the neighbourhood of BAC ST. MAUR.

This morning the enemy also crossed the LAWE at LESTREM [2 miles south-west of Estaires], but was counter-attacked by our troops and driven out of the village and back across the river.

Between ESTAIRES and GIVENCHY our positions have been maintained.

On other parts of the British front the day has again passed comparatively quietly.

Below: A sign indicates the dividing line between the British and Belgian sectors.

Opposite above: Household goods and chattels provide an effective barricade for these soldiers during street fighting in Bailleul.

Opposite middle and opposite elow: The cathedral and surrounding buildings in Reims were heavily shelled.

FRESH AMIENS BATTLE.

GERMANS CAPTURE VILLERS-BRETONNEUX.

DESPERATE FIGHT FOR HANGARD.

HOLDING NORTH OF BETHUNE.

From FIELD-MARSHAL SIR DOUGLAS HAIG.

Wednesday Night.

At about 6.30 a.m. this morning, after a violent bombardment, the enemy attacked on the whole British front south of the SOMME and against the French on our right, and was repulsed.

Later in the morning the attack on our positions in this sector was renewed in strength and, though repulsed with loss on the southern and northern portions of the front, made progress at VILLERS-BRETONNEUX [8¾ miles east of Amiens], where fighting has been severe throughout the day. The enemy has gained possession of the village and fighting is continuing.

Other attacks made by the enemy this morning on the north bank of the SOMME and north of ALBERT were repulsed. We secured a few prisoners.

OUR YPRES POSITIONS.

HEAVILY SHELLED.

FIGHTING 2 MILES TO THE SOUTH.

BATTLE FOR LOCRE.

HEAVY GERMAN LOSSES.

BERLIN REPORTS OUR LINE WITHDRAWN.

From FIELD-MARSHAL SIR DOUGLAS HAIG.

Sunday Night.

A hostile attack in the neighbourhood of LOCRE [between Kemmel Hill and Rouge Hill] was reported to be developing this afternoon. Otherwise infantry action to-day has been confined to local engagements on different parts of the battle fronts.

South of the SOMME a number of prisoners have been brought in by our patrols in the neighbourhood of VILLERS-BRETONNEUX [east of Amiens].

Artillery activity has continued on both sides. This afternoon hostile artillery heavily bombarded our positions in the YPRES sector.

THE YPRES BATTLEFIELD.

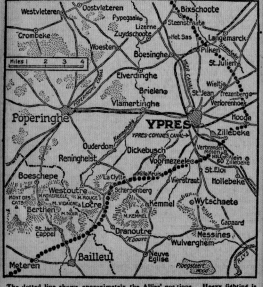

The dotted line shows approximately the Allies' positions. Heavy fighting is taking place at Voormezeele and Locre.

BATTLE FOR BETHUNE.

GERMANS REPULSED.

THEIR LOSSES EXTREMELY HEAVY.

FIERCE GIVENCHY FIGHTING.

ATTEMPTS ON KEMMEL FAIL.

From FIELD-MARSHAL SIR DOUGLAS HAIG.

Thursday Night.

There has been severe fighting again to-day on the greater part of the LYS battle front. From LA BASSEE CANAL at GIVENCHY to the LYS RIVER east of ST. VENANT [a front of 10 miles, to the north of Béthune] the bombardment reported this morning was followed by strong hostile attacks, all of which have been repulsed.

The losses inflicted on the attacking German infantry by our fire are again reported to have been extremely heavy, and over 200 prisoners have been taken by our troops.

The struggle has been particularly fierce in the neighbourhood of GIVENCHY, where the enemy has made determined efforts without success to retrieve his previous failures. The fighting in this locality has not yet ceased and the activity of the enemy's artillery is continuing on the whole of this front.

Later in the morning further attacks, accompanied by heavy shelling, developed against our positions south of KEMMEL [which is west of Wytschaete] and were repulsed.

Beyond considerable artillery activity in different sectors, particularly south and north of the SOMME, there is nothing further of special interest to report from the British front.

Passchendaele, won at such enormous cost just a few months earlier, was returned to German hands in April.

FALL OF WYTSCHAETE AND BAILLEUL.

GERMANS ON THE RIDGE.

ATTACK IN MIST.

BRITISH FIGHTING IN METEREN.

ENEMY SHELLING PASSCHENDAELE.

From FIELD-MARSHAL SIR DOUGLAS HAIG.

Tuesday Night.

Severe fighting has been taking place to-day on the front from METEREN to WYTSCHAETE [about 7½ miles]. At dawn this morning the enemy renewed his attacks in strength in the neighbourhood of WYTSCHAETE and SPANBROEKMOLEN. Supported by a heavy bombardment, his troops approached our positions under cover of the mist, and after a prolonged struggle gained possession of both localities.

At METEREN the enemy also succeeded during the morning in obtaining a footing in the village, where fighting is continuing. On other parts of the above front the enemy's attacks were repulsed.

This morning the enemy also delivered a strong local attack upon our positions opposite BOYELLES [6 miles south of Arras], and fighting is still taking place in this neighbourhood.

Hostile artillery has been more active to-day south of ALBERT and in the neighbourhood of LA BASSEE CANAL. Bodies of German infantry assembling in the vicinity of LOCON [7 miles north-west of La Bassée] were engaged and dispersed by our artillery.

There has been increased artillery activity on both sides in the PASSCHENDAELE sector [north-east of Ypres]. On the remainder of the British front the situation is unchanged.

HOLDING ON.

BIG BATTLE AT NEUVE EGLISE.

BRITISH KEEP THE VILLAGE.

ATTACKS NEAR BAILLEUL REPULSED.

GERMAN LOSSES AGAIN GREAT.

From FIELD-MARSHAL SIR DOUGLAS HAIG.

Sunday Night.

At the close of many hours of obstinate fighting during the night and again this morning about NEUVE EGLISE [midway between Messines and Bailleul] our troops remained in possession of the village. The enemy's attacks in this sector have been pressed with great determination and his losses have throughout been heavy. To-day the enemy has renewed his attempts to gain possession of the village and fighting continues.

The attack commenced by the enemy early this morning in the neighbourhood of BAILLEUL was repulsed by our troops, and another hostile attack which developed later in the morning in the neighbourhood of MERRIS [3½ miles south-west of Bailleul] was equally unsuccessful.

During the morning hostile infantry also attempted to attack northwest of MERVILLE [where the battle line bends south towards La Bassée], but was caught and dispersed by our artillery.

Hostile artillery has been more active to-day in the neighbourhood of ALBERT. On the remainder of the British front there is nothing of special interest to report.

Far left: A few of the 200 Royal Marines who leapt upon the Zeebrugge Mole to try to destroy the German gun positions. Many were equipped with flame-throwers.

Left: This bird's eye view captured by a German airman immediately after the raid, shows the block ships at low tide partially above water and effectively closing the canal.

Middle left: Time for kit inspection on a British transport.

Below left: HMS *Vindictive*, returns home battered by gunfire. The following month she was sunk in Ostend Harbour during an attempt to block another port. The operation was not totally successful but did stop larger vessels from getting through.

Below right: On 16 August 1920 HMS *Vindictive* was re-floated as part of the works to clear the waterway. She was subsequently broken up, although the bow section remains in Ostend Harbour as a memorial. One of its howitzers is now with the Imperial War Museum.

Inset map: The position of Zeebrugge and Ostend harbours on the Belgian coastline.

Opposite: The engine crew of the *Vindictive* who gallantly stayed at their posts during the raid.

Daring raid at Zeebrugge

George Nicholson Bradford joined the Royal Navy aged 15. He rose to lieutenant commander and saw action at Jutland, but it was the Zeebrugge raid on the night of 22-23 April 1918 that brought him the highest military honour – and cost him his life. The aim of the raid was to neutralise the threat from U-boats operating out of Bruges, an inland harbour connected to the port of Zeebrugge by canal. This was to be achieved by sinking three obsolete, cement-filled vessels at the mouth of the canal. It was a daring plan, for Zeebrugge was protected by a curved, mile-long mole, where German defences were formidable. During the planning stage, those taking part spoke of being members of the "Suicide Club". George led the assault unit aboard the ferry-boat Iris II, whose task was to disembark at the mole and engage the enemy. Two problems quickly arose. A change of wind direction meant the approaching ships lost their smokescreen cover and were exposed to enemy fire. The water was also so choppy that it proved difficult to steady the ship enough to deploy scaling ladders for the troops to use. One man was killed in the attempt. As leader of the storming party, George had no brief to secure the ship, yet unbidden he climbed a derrick and jumped onto the mole carrying a parapet anchor. No sooner had the vessel been made fast than he was cut down by enemy fire, falling into the turbulent waters between ship and mole. He died on his 31st birthday. George's body later washed up along the coast at Blankenberge, where he was buried by the Germans with full honours.

George's death marked the third Bradford son within a year to make the ultimate sacrifice. James, who was born between George and Roland, died from battle wounds sustained in May 1917, shortly after being awarded the Military Cross. The eldest of the four, Thomas, was an officer in the Durham Light Infantry, recipient of the DSO and the only member of the remarkable quartet to survive the conflict.

Eight VCs for Zeebrugge raiders

The Zeebrugge raid was hailed a great success but in fact disrupted German sorties from Bruges for only a short period. Nevertheless, the valour shown during this daring attack brought forth recommendations for high honours. Six were originally selected for the VC, some of those by ballot. Able Seaman Albert McKenzie, 19, claimed a number of enemy soldiers with his Lewis gun before it was shot to pieces in his hand. He recovered from wounds received during the raid, only to fall victim to influenza shortly before the Armistice was signed. Sergeant Norman Finch, 27, was a gunner on HMS Vindictive. The turret took a direct hit, killing several and wounding others – including Finch – but he returned to his station and continued firing until another shell disabled his weapon. Alfred Carpenter, acting captain of Vindictive, was against choosing one man for the VC above others and abstained from the ballot – which he won. Captain Edward Bamford, 30, was among those who reached the mole, and his courage under fire saw him chosen for the VC by the men he commanded. Lieutenant Percy Dean, 40, commanded the launch that rescued over 100 men from the blockships sunk in the harbour. The last of the six was Lieutenant Richard Sandford. He led one of the explosives-laden submarines that rammed the viaduct linking the mole to the mainland, thereby preventing German reinforcements from arriving on the scene. Sandford refused to use the gyro steering system, which would have allowed earlier evacuation of the floating bomb. Having lit the fuses, he was wounded as the crew rowed clear, and, like McKenzie, was unfortunate to survive the perilous operation only to be carried off by typhoid later that year. He was 27.

The commander of the Zeebrugge raid, Vice-Admiral Sir Roger Keyes, made representations for two who did not make it back to be awarded posthumous VCs, taking the total to eight. One was George Bradford, the other Lieutenant Commander Arthur Leyland Harrison, 32, who shrugged off a shrapnel wound to carry the fight to the enemy. He was killed just before the action was called off.

NAVAL FEAT AT ZEEBRUGGE.

OLD CRUISERS DASH IN.

BLOWN UP TO BOTTLE THE BASE.

MOLE SUBMARINED.

OUR MEN LAND AND FIGHT.

VOLUNTEERS FOR CERTAIN DEATH.

The Admiralty at midday yesterday issued a brief announcement of a British naval operation against Ostend and Zeebrugge, in the course of which five obsolete British cruisers and an old submarine were deliberately sunk to block the harbour exits. This first report was made in anticipation of the Germans wirelessing that they had sunk these cruisers by gunfire.

At 4 p.m. Sir Eric Geddes, First Lord of the Admiralty, gave the House of Commons the story, so far as it is known at present:

"I respond with great pleasure to the request to supplement the first communiqué issued to-day and give the House such further information as has so far come to hand concerning the extremely gallant and hazardous raid carried out last night. I would ask the House to appreciate the fact that most of the officers and men from whom we got the information have been fighting the greater part of the night, and some of them are not yet in. The raid was undertaken under the command of Vice-Admiral Roger Keyes, commanding at Dover. (Cheers.) French destroyers co-operated with the British forces. (Cheers.)

"There were six obsolete cruisers which took part in the attack—BRILLIANT,

THE KING'S MESSAGE.

SPLENDID GALLANTRY.

The King to Vice-Admiral, Dover:
I most heartily congratulate you and the forces under your command who carried out last night's operations with such marked success.

The splendid gallantry displayed by all under exceptionally hazardous circumstances fills me with pride and admiration. GEORGE, R.I.

plosives, were to be blown up, destroying and damaging the pile-work connection.

"At Ostend the operation was simpler. Two of the block-ships were to be grounded and blown up at the entrance to the port. The difficulties of the undertaking were considerably increased by mist and rain, with corresponding low visibility, and the consequent absence of effective aerial co-operation.

"The results so far as known are as follows: At Ostend the two block-ships were run ashore and abandoned after being blown up. It is too early yet to say whether their objective has been accomplished or not. It was misty, and, so far as those concerned could see in the darkness, they were slightly off their course.

May 1918

1 German forces occupied Sevastopol in the Crimea and established a military dictatorship in the Ukraine under Field Marshal Hermann von Eichhorn.

2 The Netherlands concluded an agreement with Germany regarding the export of sand and gravel.

4 The Second action of Es Salt ended. The battle had been fought by General Sir Edmund Allenby's Egyptian Expeditionary Force east of the Jordan River following the failure of the First Transjordan attack on Amman during the Sinai and Palestine Campaign.

5 Field Marshal Sir John French was appointed Lord Lieutenant of Ireland.

6 German and Turkish delegates arrived at Batum to negotiate peace with the Georgians and Armenians.

7 The Treaty of Bucharest was signed at Buftea between Romania and the Central Powers and Turkey. Under the terms of the agreement Romania ceded Dobrudja and the Carpathian passes and leased its oil fields to Germany for 99 years.

8 German forces captured Rostov in south Russia.

9 British Prime Minister David Lloyd George overwhelmingly won a censure motion brought by his predecessor, Herbert Asquith.

10 The British launched a second raid on Ostend. The Royal Navy warship HMS *Vindictive* was successfully scuttled in the harbour entrance to prevent German cruisers using the port.

11 Finland and Turkey signed a peace agreement in Berlin.

12 The flag of the Republic of Finland, with a crest in red and yellow depicting a lion, was raised for the first time, on Viapori.

13 The creation of the Independent Air Force was announced. The IAF was a strategic bombing force, part of the Royal Air Force, used to strike against German railways, aerodromes and industrial centres.

15 The Entente powers signed an agreement with Japan and China at Peking regarding German penetration in the Far East.

16 Three months after Montana had passed a similar law, The Sedition Act was passed by the United States Congress. The legislation extended the Espionage Act of 1917 to cover a broader range of offenses, notably speech and the expression of opinion that cast the government or the war effort in a negative light or interfered with the sale of government bonds.

17 A number of Sinn Fein leaders, including Éamon de Valera, were arrested and interned due to their campaign against conscription in Ireland.

18 Turkish forces occupied Alexandropol in Georgia.

19 The German Air Force launched an intense air raid on London inflicting a high number of casualties.

21 A naval engagement was fought between the American armed yacht USS *Christabel* and the German submarine UC-56 in the Atlantic Ocean off Spain.

23 Costa Rica declared war on Germany.

The British armed mercantile cruiser SS *Moldavia* was torpedoed and sunk in the English Channel by the German submarine UB-57 while carrying American troops from Halifax, Nova Scotia, to London.

24 General F C Poole landed at Murmansk, to organise the North Russian Expeditionary Force.

25 Following the arrests of the Sinn Fein leaders the British Government published accounts of the alleged Irish-German plot to start an armed insurrection in Ireland.

26 The Transcaucasian Federal Republic was dissolved. The Democratic Republic of Georgia proclaimed a National Government under the Menshevik politician, Noe Zhordania.

27 German forces attacked the French along the front between Soissons and Rheims in the Third Battle of the Aisne, crossing the river and splitting the French and British forces.

28 The first American offensive of the war, the Battle of Cantigny was fought and won near the village of Cantigny between American and French troops and the German army.

29 The Aisne offensive continued as the Germans captured Soissons and pushed the Allies back to the River Vesle.

30 The towns of Fere-en-Tardenois and Vezilly were taken by German forces as their advance continued on the Western Front.

31 Having fought King Albert I over the neutrality of their country, Gérard Cooreman resigned as Belgian Prime Minister after he had lost the support of his party. He was succeeded by Charles de Broqueville.

Operation Blücher

Ludendorff had one final card to play, this time against the French at Chemin des Dames in late May: Operation Blücher. The Allied line was again broken and German troops swept across the River Aisne and on towards the Marne. From here the heavy guns could reach the French capital. But with American support, the tide was stemmed once more. The Kaiser himself appeared in the field to urge a girding of the loins ahead of the second Marne battle. It failed. By mid-July Germany's race was run. The sweeping territorial gains had extended the German line significantly, creating worryingly large salients, all of which had to be manned by a shrinking army shorn of many crack troops. None of the occupied ground was of strategic value. The knockout blow had failed to materialise, and to make matters worse, the first victims of the influenza pandemic were struck down. Both sides had incurred heavy losses in Ludendorff's four-month-long gamble, but one was buoyed by the arrival of US boots on the ground, a quarter of a million by the month of mustard-keen, fresh-faced "doughboys". The other was deflated in the field, dispirited at home. Germany was a spent force, vulnerable to a counterattack and coup de grace.

SOISSONS LOST.

FIGHTING OUTSIDE RHEIMS.

ENEMY ADVANCES 6 MILES.

25,000 PRISONERS CLAIMED.

ALLIES FIGHTING STUBBORNLY.

Yesterday the Germans entered Soissons. They were also fighting a mile from Rheims.

On Tuesday night, when the Germans had crossed the Vesle, they brought up fresh reinforcements and forced the battle on both flanks towards Soissons and Rheims. The French retired fighting stubbornly on Soissons. The Germans succeeded in entering the town, and fierce fighting followed in the streets for several hours. In the end the French fell back, holding the roads on the outskirts.

The French, too, offered a fine defence on the heights south of the Vesle, but according to the latest report the Germans have succeeded in pushing their advance about six miles farther at its deepest point, making a total of 15 miles since the battle began on Monday.

The attack towards Rheims was even more stubbornly resisted. Unofficial reports say the Germans are almost half

round the town and firing on the defenders from three sides, but the latest official news is that the Franco-British troops still hold on the edge of the canal a mile north-west of the town proper.

The Germans claim 25,000 prisoners. They state that the weather is changing.

The reason why Sir Douglas Haig's reports do not refer to the Aisne battle may be that, as the French Staff did not record events in the recent Flanders fighting, where their troops were fewer than ours, so the British Commander-in-Chief is refraining in the present battle, where our troops are in the minority.

The Americans have crushed attempts to recover Cantigny, west of Montdidier, which they stormed on Tuesday. The Germans admit the loss of the village to "the enemy." It does not suit their book to say that the Americans have had a success because Germany has been told that the Americans do not count.

FRENCH OFFICIAL REPORT.

Wednesday Night.

The battle has been particularly violent on our left wing near Soissons. After desperate resistance and street fighting which stayed the enemy for many hours, our troops have been forced to evacuate the town, but they hold its approaches.

From the west to the south-east of Soissons, the battle is spreading over the plateaux bordered by Belleu, Septmonts, Ambrief, and Chacrise.

In the centre we gave ground under the pressure of the enemy near Loupeigne [11½ miles south-east of Soissons].

The Franco-British troops farther east successfully maintained their positions on the line Brouillet, Savigny, Thillois [roughly 2½ miles south of the Vesle].

The troops covering Rheims retired behind the Aisne Canal, north-west of the city.

Opposite top: British soldiers defend a canal in May 1918.

Opposite upper middle: Troops man a machine-gun post in a French barn.

Opposite lower middle: Both German and French wounded soldiers troop along a country lane while a convoy passes them in the opposite direction heading for the front line.

Opposite bottom: Belgian troops sandbag a local river.

Above right: France's premier, Georges Clemenceau, inspects a British division.

Above left: Soldiers negotiate a tree covered in wire, which has been felled across a canal to impede navigation of the waterway.

Left: A flock of sheep joins British troops marching near Verneuil.

June 1918

1   The Battle of Belleau Wood, fought between the United States Marine Corps and German forces, began near the Marne River in France during the German Spring Offensive.

2   German forces reached the River Marne at Château-Thierry whilst the US Marines held the frontline near the Paris-Metz Highway.

3   The British, French and Italian Governments declared their support for the national aspirations of Poles, Czecho-Slovaks and Yugo-Slavs at Versailles.

    The German submarine *U-151*, commanded by Heinrich von Nostitz und Jänckendorff, was responsible for the sinking of nine American ships off the coast of New York over two days.

4   American Major General Omar Bundy took command of the American sector of the front at Belleau Wood and continued to repel the incessant German assaults.

5   The British Independent Air Force was constituted under the command of Major-General Sir Hugh Trenchard with its headquarters situated near Nancy in France.

6   The Dutch hospital ship PSS *Koningin Regentes* was torpedoed and sunk by the German submarine *UB-107* on her way from Boston to Rotterdam.

    American troops captured Bouresches and the southern part of Belleau Wood.

7   British forces landed at Kern in northern Russia.

    A Czech-Slovak force in Russia occupied the key railway town of Omsk in Siberia.

8   The Russian Bolshevik Government ordered Allied forces out of northern Russia.

    The Georgian Government and Armenian Council signed a peace agreement with Turkey; Georgia also signed a treaty with Germany.

9   The German offensive Operation Gneisenau began. Also known as the Battle of the Matz the Germans launched an attack on the French sector between Noyan and Montdider.

10 The Austro-Hungarian dreadnought SMS *Szent István* was torpedoed by the Italian Motor Torpedo Boat *MAS-15*. The battleship capsized and sank several hours later near Premuda Island, Croatia.

11 French and American troops counterattacked on the Marne salient. The Americans captured Belleau Wood while the French captured Mery, Belloy and Fretoy.

13 The Battle of the Matz ended when the Germans halted their offensive.

15 The Battle of the Piave began in Italy with an Austro-Hungarian offensive along the River Piave from Lake Garda to the Adriatic.

16 Austro-Hungarian forces attacked Italians troops across the Piave River. In the Montello sector they established an effective bridgehead but elsewhere they were driven back to their original line.

18 The Russian battleship *Svobodnaya Rossiya* was scuttled by four torpedoes fired by the destroyer *Kerch* in Novorossiysk harbour to prevent her from being turned over to the Germans as required by the Treaty of Brest-Litovsk.

19 Italy's leading flying ace Francesco Baracca was killed whilst on a strafing mission on the Montello hill area in northern Italy.

21 Aleksandar Pavlov Malinov replaced Vasil Hristov Radoslavov as Prime Minister of Bulgaria.

22 Austro-Hungarian forces started their withdrawal across the River Piave.

23 The Austro-Hungarians were ordered to retreat by Charles I of Austria. The Allies recaptured all territory on the southern bank of the river ending the Battle of the Piave.

25 The first Crimean Regional Government was established under German protection with General Maciej Sulkiewicz as Prime Minister.

26 American troops forced the Germans out of Belleau Wood and brought to an end the German Aisne offensive.

27 The British hospital ship HMHS *Llandovery Castle* was torpedoed and sunk by the German submarine *U-86* off the coast of Ireland whilst on a voyage from Halifax to Liverpool.

29 The United States Government announced a view that all Slav races should be free of German and Austrian rule.

Top: The abbey at Mont des Cats was destroyed by bombing raids in May 1918. The building was home to an order of Trappist monks who were forced to evacuate the building.

Above: A roll call is held in a labour camp. The names of these Chinese men are inscribed on streamers attached to a rotating drum.

Below: Men of the Worcestershire Regiment are in optimistic mood as they march to the front at Acheux.

THRUST ON THE AISNE.

TRYING A NEW WAY TO PARIS.

GERMANS ADVANCE A LITTLE.

FRENCH SUCCESS NORTH OF COMPIEGNE.

The Germans yesterday continued their push westward near Soissons, where they are trying with considerable forces to envelop Villers-Cotterets Forest, an important advanced defence of Paris, and also to squeeze out the French who remain north of the Aisne. Their effort did not attain any great result, and their total gain here in two days has been about 2¼ miles on a narrow front.

The Germans are still 45 miles from Paris by the north and 39 by the east.

On the left of the battle-front, southeast of Montdidier, they attempted to deprive the French of their gains of Tuesday, but failed completely.

In the centre, north of Compiègne, the enemy, apparently exhausted by several

FRENCH UNDER AMERICANS

ARMY COMPLIMENT,

From HERBERT BAILEY.

WITH THE AMERICANS, Thursday.

The excellent relations existing between the French and American commands is shown by the fact that a regiment of Zouaves and a division of French artillery are now working under an American divisional command on this front. This is a new development of the war and marks a distinct advance in Franco-American relations.

I hear that a Russian prisoner has reported that Russian and French prisoners are compelled to work in the German first-line trenches close to Château-Thierry, while several German aeroplanes with

PARIS BATTLE CIRCLES.

The curved lines show distances from Paris. The Germans are at present attacking outside the 40-mile line to the south-west of Soissons.

From SIR DOUGLAS HAIG.

TUESDAY MORNING.

Continuous pressure was maintained by the enemy all day yesterday against the British troops engaged on the AISNE front, and severe fighting is still taking place on the whole front of the British sector. On our right the 21st Division, in touch with our Allies, held their battle positions throughout the day and successfully withstood the enemy's attempts to advance.

In the centre and on the left of the British sector troops of the 8th, 50th, and 25th Divisions, by a determined resistance, maintained their second-line positions against the enemy's assaults until a late hour. Towards the end of the day the weight of the enemy's attacks carried his troops across the AISNE, west of the British sector, and compelled the left of our line to fall back

The enemy is developing his attacks in great strength along the whole of the AISNE battle front

On the LYS front local fighting recommenced this morning in the area east of DICKEBUSCH LAKE [south of Ypres]. On the remainder of the British front a number of prisoners have been taken by our troops in successful raids at different points during the night, and artillery has been active on both sides.

TUESDAY EVENING.

Counter-attacks early this morning by French and British troops successfully re-established our line east of DICKEBUSCH LAKE [just south-west of Ypres, where the enemy retained about 800 yards of line on Monday]. Several prisoners were captured

In the enemy's attacks yesterday morning in this sector and to the south as far as LOCRE four German divisions are known to have been engaged. In the course of the fighting heavy losses have been inflicted on these divisions and the Allied line has been maintained at all points.

On the remainder of the British front there is nothing to report beyond artillery activity on both sides in different sectors.

FRENCH OFFICIAL REPORT.

TUESDAY AFTERNOON.

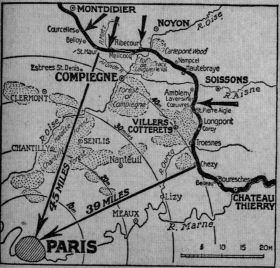

Top left: A British soldier tries to protect himself from shrapnel as shells explode nearby.

Upper middle left: A German officer acknowledges the camera while troops prepare to operate the Howitzer behind him.

Lower middle left: Colonel Robert R McCormick (right) and his officers led their troops to capture Cantigny from the Germans in May 1918. It was the first US offensive of the conflict and with French support the division successfully took the village in 45 minutes.

Bottom left: A German soldier lies dead next to his machine gun.

Above right: French engineers in Noyon inspect the street for signs of weapons. It was common practice for German troops to lay mines before withdrawal and it was vital for engineers to make the area safe before soldiers could enter.

July 1918

1   The US troop transport ship *USS Covington* was torpedoed by German submarine *U-86* off Brest, France.

3   Turkish Sultan Mohammed V of the Ottoman Empire died at the Yildiz Palace in Constantinople and was succeeded by his brother, Mohammed VI.

4   The Battle of Hamel took place. The successful attack was launched by the Australian Corps and American troops against German positions in and around the town of Hamel in northern France.

5   The Treaty of Bucharest, which had been signed between Romania and the Central Powers in May, was ratified by the Romanian Senate.

6   Wilhelm von Mirbach, the German ambassador to Russia, was assassinated in Moscow. He was succeeded by Karl Helfferich.

8   Ernest Hemingway was severely wounded when he carried a fellow worker to safety while working as a Red Cross ambulance driver on the Austro-Italian front. Hemingway was sent home and later received the Italian Silver Medal of Bravery for his heroism.

9   Paul von Hintze succeeded Richard von Kühlmann as Germany's Minister for Foreign Affairs.

10 The Russian Constitution was adopted by the Congress of Soviets.

11 Henry Ford's innovative new type of anti-submarine vessel, the first Eagle class patrol craft was launched in the United States.

    Prince Wilhelm of Urach was elected King of Lithuania with the regnal name Mindaugas II.

12 The Imperial Japanese Navy battleship *IJN Kawachi* sank in Tokuyama Bay after an ammunition magazine exploded.

13 Turkish forces attacked British positions on the Jordan River and began their final offensive to recover Jericho.

14 US Air Service pilot and son of former US President Theodore Roosevelt, Quentin Roosevelt was shot down and killed by a German Fokker plane over the River Marne in France.

15 The Second Battle of the Marne began and marked the final phase of the German Spring Offensive when German divisions attacked French troops.

16 Austro-Hungarian commander-in-chief Field Marshal Conrad von Hötzendorf was relieved of his command.

17 In the early hours of the morning, Tsar Nicholas II, his wife Alexandra, their children Alexei, Olga, Tatiana, Maria and Anastasia were executed together with other members of their household by the Bolsheviks in the town of Ekaterinburg.

18 A French led counterattack halted the German forward momentum during the Second Battle of the Marne and seized the initiative for the Allies on the Western Front.

19 The British troopship HMS *Justicia* was sunk after she was torpedoed by the German submarines *UB-64* and *UB-124* off the coast of Scotland whilst sailing from Belfast to New York.

20 The British destroyers HMS *Marne, Milbrook* and *Pigeon* attacked *UB-124* with depth charges and sank the German submarine with gunfire after she surfaced.

21 The Attack on Orleans took place when a German U-boat opened fire on the US town of Orleans, Massachusetts and several merchant ships nearby. A tugboat was sunk but the town only sustained minor damage in the naval and aerial action.

22 The Battle of Soissons between French and American troops and the German armies ended after four days with the Allies recapturing most of the ground lost to the German Spring Offensive in May 1918.

24 French and American troops advanced south of Ourcq towards Fere-en-Tardenois and along the Marne in the Forest of Fere.

25 Baron Max Hussarek von Heinlein replaced Ernst Seidler von Feuchtenegg as Prime Minister of Austria.

26 A coup d'état overthrew the Bolsheviks in Baku and launched the Battle of Baku between the Ottoman-Azerbaijani coalition forces and Bolshevik forces. The battle was fought as a conclusive part of the Caucasus Campaign.

28 Allied forces recaptured Fere-en-Tardenois as the northward advance continued from Marne.

30 General Field Marshal Hermann von Eichhorn was assassinated in Kiev by the Socialist-Revolutionary Boris Mikhailovich Donskoy.

AMERICANS CROSS MARNE.

BIG FIRES IN HUN LINES.

FRENCH TAKE 49 MORE GUNS.

OLD LINE REGAINED IN CHAMPAGNE.

Above and Opposite below left: American troops march through London. As they passed Buckingham Palace they were watched by the King and Queen and Princess Mary.

Below: Advisory notices warn Allied troops of potential dangers.

Bottom: A soldier inspects a portable wire entanglement. These posed a formidable obstruction but could also be moved from place to place with ease.

THE GREATEST FOURTH.

ALLIED HOMAGE TO THE U.S.A. TO-DAY.

1,019,000 AMERICANS OVER.

To-day is the greatest Fourth of July (anniversary of the American Declaration of Independence on July 4, 1776). It will be observed in Great Britain and France by elaborate national celebrations in honour of the United States, whose President fittingly announces that 1,019,000 American troops have been transported to Europe in the cause of freedom, over a quarter of the number having come in June alone.

Programmes for the day and special messages will be found in another column.

The French report artillery activity in the Argonne, between Rheims and Verdun, an area where it has been suggested the Germans might make their next attack.

The French have recaptured high ground between the Oise and the Aisne and have taken 457 prisoners.

The Germans have got back the little ground they lost to our troops north-west of Albert on Sunday.

The Italians have advanced nearly 2 miles to the north-east of Venice, between the two mouths of the Piave, and have made 1,900 Austrians prisoners.

On Monday our airmen over Zeebrugge wiped out in a few minutes 8 Hun machines, the whole of a squadron which attacked them. On Tuesday at the front our pilots brought down 22 machines against 4 of ours missing.

STRIKING MESSAGES.

ADMIRAL SIMS & GEN. BIDDLE.

From a number of well-known Americans now in England, including the Commanders-in-Chief of the United States Naval and Military Forces, "The Daily Mail" has received the following messages:—

Vice-Admiral W. S. Sims, Commander-in-Chief, American Naval Forces operating in European waters:

The four great milestones of human liberty are the British Magna Charta, the Italian Renaissance, the American Declaration of Independence, and the French Revolution.

It is from every point of view appropriate that Britain, Italy, France, and America should now be fighting together to attain the fifth great milestone—the defeat of the appalling German menace to human liberty on both land and sea.

The mission of the Allied Navies to-day is not only to support the armies in the field but also to ensure the future safety of peaceful commerce on the high roads of the world—the High Seas.

I can assure the public that with our peoples' continued loyal support the Navies will completely attain their war aims.

Major-General John Biddle, N.A., Commanding U.S. Military Forces in United Kingdom:

On July 4 Americans for almost a cen-

MR. WILSON'S GREETING
TO AMERICANS OVER-SEAS.

Top left: A soldier brings a message to a company in reserve and awaits a reply from the officer in charge.

Middle left: The battered town of Albert was again taken by the Germans in March 1918 but successfully captured by Allied troops, remaining in their hands until the end of the conflict. The town had 7,000 inhabitants at the beginning of the war but only 120 remained by 1919.

Left and Below: Very little remained of the cathedral in Albert by the time British troops entered the town.

GREAT GERMAN ATTACK.

MARNE BATTLE.

ONLY 3 MILES ACROSS.

AMERICANS CAPTURE 1,000 HUNS.

COMPLETE CHECK EAST OF RHEIMS.

FRENCH OFFICIAL REPORT.

Monday Evening.

The German attack begun this morning shortly before 4.30 continued all day on both sides of RHEIMS with unabated violence. West of RHEIMS there were furious struggles in the region REUILLY—COURTHIEZY—VASSY [roughly a mile], south of the MARNE, which the enemy crossed at some points between FOSSOY and DORMANS.

A vigorous counter-attack by American troops drove back to the north bank enemy elements which had reached the southern bank west of Fossoy.

Between DORMANS and RHEIMS Franco-Italian troops are resisting with tenacity on the line CHATILLON-SUR-MARNE—CUCHERY—MARFAUX—BOUILLY [generally speaking, 3 miles south of the enemy's starting point]. East of RHEIMS the enemy attack, which extended from SILLERY to the MAIN DE MASSIGES, met an impregnable defence.

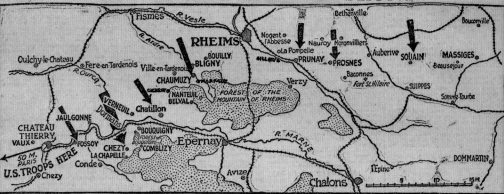

THE 50-MILE BATTLE FRONT.

The arrows show where the Germans are attacking and where they have crossed the Marne.
Note where the U.S.A. troops are engaged, marked in the bottom left corner.

U.S. TROOPS HIT BACK.

SIDE BY SIDE WITH FRENCH.

GROUND RETAKEN.

From HERBERT BAILEY.
WITH THE AMERICANS, Tuesday,
5.40 p.m.

At the moment of telegraphing a weighty counter-attack against the Germans in the region of St. Agnan, in which American and French troops are fighting side by side, is in progress.

Early this afternoon St. Agnan, all of Hill 223 to the west, and La Chapelle-Monthodon had been retaken, and the attack was still progressing in a northerly direction. On the right, too, the French troops have been fighting excellently, and it is evident that the enemy is in considerable difficulties in this area.

Certainly the original plans of the enemy in the region of Château-Thierry have been shattered.

The enemy attempted again to raid the American positions at Vaux this morning but was repulsed. On the other side of Château-Thierry there has been heavy artillery fire.

BATTLE NEAR RHEIMS.

FRESH BRITISH GAIN.

VITAL GERMAN POINT.

COUNTER-ATTACKS CRUSHED.

FRENCH OFFICIAL REPORT

WEDNESDAY EVENING.—Between the OURCQ and the MARNE our attacks were renewed this morning and continued with success during the day. On our left we hold the village of ARMENTIERES and CHATELET WOOD, beyond which we progressed as far as BRECY which we occupy.

In the centre the Franco-American troops made at certain points an advance of about 2 miles. Desperate fighting took place in the region of EPIEDS and TRUGNY. EPIEDS, which was recaptured by the Germans at the end of yesterday, was retaken in a counter-attack by the Americans. North of these two villages we carried our line beyond COURPOIL.

On our right we are making progress in the Forest of FERE, north of CHARTEVES and JAULGONNE.

Farther east we extended our bridgehead at TRELOUP and captured the southern corner of RIS FOREST. In this sector we have captured 5 6in. guns, about 50 machine guns, and considerable material.

Between the M——E and RHEIMS there were intermittent artillery actions. In yesterday's fighting, during which our troops captured RHEIMS WOOD, to the south of COURMAS, we took several hundred prisoners.

North of MONTDIDIER, the total number of prisoners taken by us on Tuesday in the Mailly-Raineval-Anhviliers region is 1,850, including 52 officers, among whom are 4 battalion commanders. The material captured includes 4 guns, 45 trench guns, and 300 machine guns.

THE WESTERN FRONT: REIMS, VERDUN AND THE ARGONNE

THE LONDON GEOGRAPHICAL INSTITUTE

Opposite above left, middle left and below right: The city of Reims and the Cathédrale Notre Dame de Reims were systematically destroyed during the conflict. The German Army initially occupied the city in 1914 but withdrew to the higher ground, from where they regularly attacked with artillery shells. The cathedral was the victim of over 300 direct hits but after the war was restored under the guidance of architect Henri Deneux, eventually re-opening in 1937.

Opposite below left: Allied troops continued to defend the city despite constant pressure from the enemy.

Opposite above right: German soldiers carry a fallen comrade under the watchful eye of an Allied guard.

Left: Brown stars mark the forts protecting Reims and Verdun.

Below right: The Allies hold the whole southern bank of the River Marne, 22 July.

Bottom: German prisoners of war held in France, are armed with only scythes and rakes as they are escorted to the fields to work the land.

GERMANS SLOW BUT NEARER.

GAINS SOUTH-WEST OF RHEIMS.

FRENCH & ITALIANS FIGHTING FOOT BY FOOT

HEAPS OF HUN DEAD.

The Germans yesterday again strove their hardest to capture Rheims by encircling the great wooded height to the south, but they were met everywhere with great stubbornness by the French and Italians and did not advance more than a mile and a half.

They have extended their footing south of the Marne towards the east and are 6 miles from Epernay. Their losses were again very heavy. East of Rheims there is no change.

FRENCH OFFICIAL REPORT.
Wednesday Evening.

The battle continued to-day with sustained violence on the whole front west of Rheims. Despite his efforts, the enemy did not increase his advance. By heroic resistance and incessant counter-attacks we headed him off after fluctuating struggles.

South of the MARNE fighting is in progress on the wooded slopes north of ST. AGNAN and LA CHAPELLE-MONTHODON. In very sharp fighting north of COMBLIZY and FESTIGNY we held the enemy on the southern edge of BOUQUIGNY and CHATAIGNIERS Woods [the latter just north of Festigny]. East of OEUILLY [on the Marne] the Germans regained a footing in MONVOISIN. Between the MARNE and RHEIMS the struggle continued north of REUIL in ROI WOOD [which is north-east of Montvoisin] which the Germans entered and which we are defending foot by foot.

Violent fighting in COURTON WOOD. The enemy is held west of NANTEUIL. The Germans repeatedly but vainly tried to reach POURCY. A brilliant Italian counter-attack west of Pourcy drove the enemy back into the ARDRE VALLEY.

The number of enemy dead in front of the lines proves their heavy losses.

No change from VRIGNY to RHEIMS. South-east of RHEIMS we broke an attack between BEAUMONT and SILLERY [south-east of Beaumont]. Our positions remain intact on the whole Champagne front.

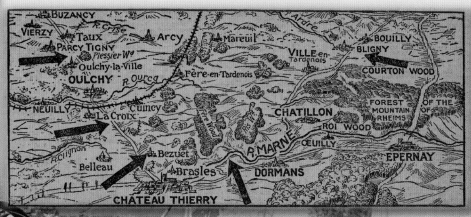

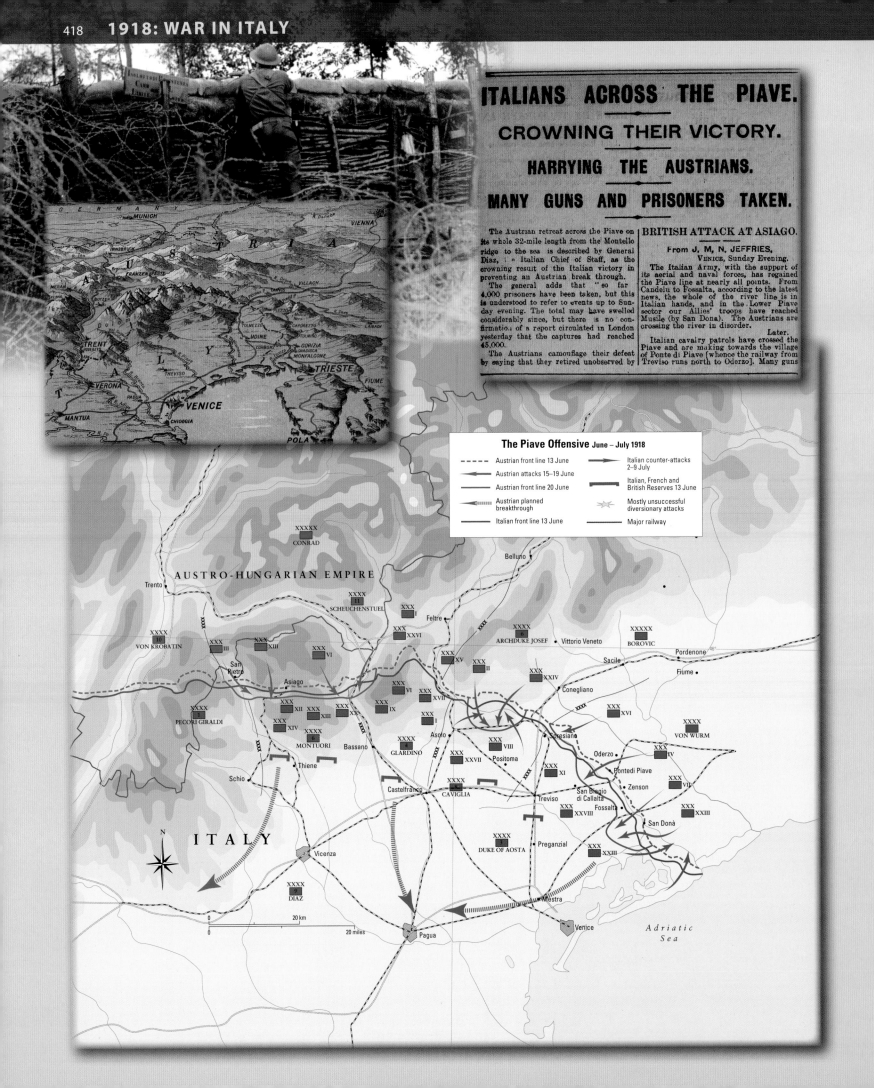

ITALIANS ACROSS THE PIAVE.

CROWNING THEIR VICTORY.

HARRYING THE AUSTRIANS.

MANY GUNS AND PRISONERS TAKEN.

The Austrian retreat across the Piave on its whole 32-mile length from the Montello ridge to the sea is described by General Diaz, the Italian Chief of Staff, as the crowning result of the Italian victory in preventing an Austrian break through.

The general adds that "so far 4,000 prisoners have been taken, but this is understood to refer to events up to Sunday evening. The total may have swelled considerably since, but there is no confirmation of a report circulated in London yesterday that the captures had reached 45,000.

The Austrians camouflage their defeat by saying that they retired unobserved by

BRITISH ATTACK AT ASIAGO.

From J. M. N. JEFFRIES,

VENICE, Sunday Evening.

The Italian Army, with the support of its aerial and naval forces, has regained the Piave line at nearly all points. From Candelu to Fossalta, according to the latest news, the whole of the river line is in Italian hands, and in the Lower Piave sector our Allies' troops have reached Musile (by San Dona). The Austrians are crossing the river in disorder.

Later.

Italian cavalry patrols have crossed the Piave and are making towards the village of Ponte di Piave [whence the railway from Treviso runs north to Oderzo]. Many guns

The Piave Offensive June – July 1918

- – – – – Austrian front line 13 June
- ← Austrian attacks 15–19 June
- —— Austrian front line 20 June
- ⊢⊣⊢⊣ Austrian planned breakthrough
- —— Italian front line 13 June
- ⟶ Italian counter-attacks 2–9 July
- ▬▬ Italian, French and British Reserves 13 June
- ✴ Mostly unsuccessful diversionary attacks
- ══ Major railway

Italy turns the tide

With British and French support, the Italian army had just managed to avert disaster following the rout at Caporetto in autumn 1917. The German-backed Austrian surge was halted at the Piave river, the attacking force overstretched just as the retiring army was bolstered. Cadorna was held responsible for Caporetto, his successor, General Armando Diaz, presiding over an improved picture in which the mood of defeatism dissipated. That was in no small part down to the more benevolent approach of the new commander, who raised morale by increasing soldiers' rations and leave, while drawing a line under costly offensives. Effectively, he replicated the measures Pétain adopted when the French army was on its knees in the wake of the failed Nivelle campaign. This was the setting as the so-called "White War" moved into 1918; a front on which the rivals' specialist mountain fighters – the Italian Alpini corps and Austro-Hungarian Kaiserschützen – vied to deliver a telling blow; a front where thousands who managed to avoid an enemy bullet were killed in avalanches.

Austrian onslaught

The Austrians made their final bid for glory in June 1918, attempting to do what their senior partner had been essaying since March: to strike decisively before American strength completely negated the advantage derived from Russia's withdrawal. Emperor Karl I's covert efforts to negotiate a separate peace had recently been made public by the French, leaving him with little choice now but to stay the course. The Austrian onslaught was timed to coincide with Operation Gneisenau, the latest phase of Germany's Spring Offensive on the Western Front. Before the Battle of the Piave, which opened on 15 June, the Austrian commander Conrad von Hoetzendorff gave a stirring address to his men. "For months, resisting victoriously amidst the glaciers and the snows, accomplishing faithfully your duty in the tempests of winter, you have looked down upon the sunny plain of Italy. The time to go down into it has come … You will prove to the world that nobody can resist your heroism."

Rousing words, along with a small numerical advantage, could not mask the fact that the Austrian army was in anything but peak fighting condition. Shortages of food and equipment and ebbing morale were problem enough, compounded by the decision to divide the available manpower prior to going on the attack. Conrad himself took charge of the advance on the Asiago Plateau, leaving General Boroevic to push across the Piave river. The latter established bridgeheads beyond the river before being beaten back by the Italian counter. This natural feature, negotiating which must have been a psychological boost when on the front foot, represented a tricky obstacle when beating a retreat, especially as it was swollen and some of the pontoon bridges had been destroyed. The Austrians took heavy losses. Conrad's attack assumed a similar shape: profitable gains in some parts, followed by a riposte that left the assaulting troops fighting a desperate rearguard. By 22 June the Austrian bolt had been shot, to no effect. The desertion rate spiralled over the summer months .

Italians sweep through Vittorio Veneto

Military defeat and imperial dismemberment swiftly ensued. Karl belatedly sought to address the fragmentation happening before his eyes by offering a degree of autonomy to the member states in a federal arrangement. It was too little, too late. With the war in its death throes, the Czechoslovaks, Yugoslavs and Hungarians began the drive for independence and a severing of old Habsburg ties. In the last week of October, the endgame was played out on the battleground of the Italian front. Having shown circumspect caution over the summer, General Diaz was required by his political masters to press home the initiative with a view to securing the best possible bargaining chips at the peace table. The rump of the Austrian army held out briefly before succumbing to an Allied advance across the Piave and in the mountain region. This time there was no German assistance stiffening the defensive line. Resistance evaporated, and on 30 October, a year after Austria threatened to overrun Venice, its race was run as the Italians swept through Vittorio Veneto. The humiliation of Caporetto was avenged as the final nail was driven into the coffin of the Habsburg Empire. An armistice was concluded on 3 November, hostilities formally coming to an end the following day.

Opposite above left: **Major Everson of the US army pictured at the Piave Front.**

Opposite: **Maps detail the action at the River Piave and its location between Italy and Austria-Hungary.**

Above left: **General Armando Diaz replaced General Cadorna as chief of general staff in November 1917. His success at Vittorio Veneto brought him much public praise and he was rewarded with the title "Ducca della Vittoria" (Duke of Victory) after the war.**

Above right: **An infantryman waits by an outpost at Piave.**

Below: **Italian anti-aircraft gunners brought down an Austrian bomber on the Piave front, capturing the pilot and lieutenant observer. It was carrying eight hundredweight of explosives.**

"You will prove to the world that nobody can resist your heroism."

Austrian commander Conrad von Hoetzendorff

8 August 1918: Germany's "black day"

Ludendorff launched the fifth and final phase of his spring assault on 15 July 1918: Friedensturm, the Peace Offensive. Diminishing returns had set in since the early success of "Michael"; this last attack quickly juddered to a halt, and gave its architect no bargaining power for making peace. If there was a crumb of comfort for Ludendorff as his army was halted in the Second Battle of the Marne, it was the belief that the Allies were themselves in no state of readiness to mount a major offensive. How wrong he was. Even before Friedensturm had begun, the riposte was underway. On 4 July Australian troops took Hamel, and on the 18th French forces, with American support, drove into the Marne salient, from which the routed Germans soon withdrew. These were a prelude to a massive counterstrike east of Amiens, the important rail junction that had remained in Allied hands – just. Guns, ammunition and men were clandestinely transported to the target area, with some sleight-of-hand tricks to throw the enemy off the scent. A crack Canadian force was moved to Flanders in the full knowledge that its presence would be monitored and taken as a sign of an imminent attack. Conspicuous air and tank activity suggested the hammer would fall far north of Amiens, the deception supported by a trail of false messages. Everything was done to maintain the element of surprise, including wrapping tank wheels in straw and using the engine noise of Handley Page bombers to drown out the sound of a mass attack in the making. The RAF helped prevent enemy air reconnaissance from getting wind of what was afoot. A special directive was issued to the men of General Rawlinson's 4th Army, who were in the forefront of the operation: "Keep your mouth shut!"

Notwithstanding all the efforts to maintain utmost secrecy, reports of a build-up of enemy forces at Amiens did reach the German High Command's ears. An attack was so inconceivable that the information was disregarded. Then, shortly before the day of the attack, German raiders took a number of POWs. How much did they know, and had they told their captors? The plan was too far advanced to contemplate cancelling an offensive, possibly needlessly.

2,000 guns at 4.20 am

The system of preparing the artillery without prior registration had been further refined since the Battle of Cambrai, another vital factor in the Allies' plan to deliver a heavy, unexpected blow on a 14-mile front. It began at 4.20 am on the morning of 8 August, when 2,000 guns burst into life. Over 400 tanks began their advance alongside the infantry behind a creeping barrage. The curtain of shellfire fell 200 yards into no-man's-land and moved forward in 100-yard lifts. It was precision choreography. Co-ordinating tank and manpower movement had also been rationalised since Cambrai, and there was new armoured hardware available: the Mark V, which could be driven by one man instead of four, and the lighter "Whippet" tank, which offered greater speed and manoeuvrability.

Below and opposite top: **The 5th Australian Infantry Brigade, complete with tanks, advances towards the German lines near Lamotte-en-Santerre. They had already passed the German first and second lines and successfully captured the village on 8 August.**

Opposite above left: **Hindenburg (left), Emperor Wilhelm II and Ludendorff (right). The Kaiser's power gradually diminished throughout the conflict as these two men effectively ran a military dictatorship between them.**

Opposite bottom right: **In Albert two British soldiers drag a wounded man to safety while German troops continue shooting in the streets.**

Opposite bottom left: **Troops are finally able to patrol the streets of Albert after the British 18th (Eastern) Division entered the town on 22 August.**

Australian and Canadian infantry to the fore

Misty conditions helped the Allied cause and created confusion in the defensive ranks. Communications cables were laid as the advance proceeded, giving important feedback to the gunners, whose counter-battery fire was excellent. Knocking out German gun emplacements meant that the infantry advanced up to seven miles on day one largely unmolested, a rarity indeed for the Western Front. Cavalry divisions were pressed into service to exploit the widespread gains. German soldiers, whose will to carry on was exhausted, surrendered in droves. Only in the aerial battle did Germany share the honours. Richthofen's Flying Circus had lost its famed leader but remained a formidable adversary for the RAF. But that was a sideshow to the great ground battle, and this was a spectacular success for what was a multinational Allied effort. To the south there was General Marie Debeney's French 1st Army, which had been placed under British control. There was also an American contingent. But at the end of the second day Rawlinson reserved special praise for the Australian and Canadian infantry, who were "probably the decisive factor".

There was much discussion about how to build on the early success. Foch, ever keen to remain on the front foot, favoured pursuing the enemy across the Somme, for surely his will was broken. Had he but known it, there were indeed defeatist cries from German soldiers, berating those hastily brought in to stem the tide. Did they want to prolong the war? Did they not understand that if the Allies reached the Rhine it would all be over? Meanwhile, Rawlinson and Sir Arthur Currie – commander of the Canadian Corps – voiced their concerns about advancing over the old Somme battlefields, where defences would be strong and casualties high. Germany had indeed poured reinforcements into

the area, while by 11 August only one-tenth of the tanks that had begun the battle were still serviceable. Any further action might have been so costly as to negate what had been a well conceived and executed operation. That, in turn, would have brought opprobrium from Lloyd George and the War Cabinet. Haig received a note from his political masters warning against incurring unacceptable losses rather than offering congratulations on a stunning success. He harrumphed at the meddling of those who would waste no time in taking the plaudits, and equally quickly wash their hands of any misfortune. But in the end he paid heed to his generals and closed down the operation. Hard lessons had been learned since the Somme bloodbath: the new paradigm was for an advance to be curtailed as soon as it stalled. The objectives had been met. Better to switch the point of attack, to hit a more vulnerable part of the German line using fresh manpower. With that in mind, the next phase of the operation to exert a terminal stranglehold on Ludendorff's army began within a matter of days, denying the German army the breathing space it so badly needed. Foch widened the front southward, while on 21 August the British 3rd Army attacked at Bapaume. Over the next 100 days the noose would be inexorably tightened, but it was 8 August – the "black day of the German army", as Ludendorff called it – where the ligature was applied.

"Everything I had feared and of which I had so often given warning had here, in one place, become a reality. Our war machine was no longer efficient... The 8th of August put the decline of our fighting power beyond all doubt."
Erich Ludendorff

August 1918

1 The Allied Expeditionary Force captured the port of Archangel in northern Russia.

2 The Japanese Government decided to land troops at Vladivostok.

3 The hospital ship SS Warilda was sunk by the German submarine *UC-49* whilst carrying wounded from Le Havre to Southampton, despite being clearly marked by red crosses.

4 British forces arrived at the city of Baku on the Caspian Sea.

5 German airships launched an unsuccessful attack on East Anglia in England; the raid resulted in the loss of Zeppelin *L 70*.

6 General Ferdinand Foch was declared Marshal of France.

7 The French armed cruiser Dupetit-Thouars was sunk by the German submarine *U-62* 400 miles west of Brest.

8 The Battle of Amiens, also known as the Third Battle of Picardy, began. The battle was the opening phase of the Hundred Days Offensive – the final period of the War, during which the Allies launched a series of offensives against the Central Powers on the Western Front. Allied forces made one of the greatest advances of the war on the first day.

10 French forces attacked and recaptured Montdidier, Picardy.

11 The Allied offensive at Amiens continued to advance, though not with the same spectacular results as were achieved on 8 August.

12 The Battle of Amiens ended in a decisive Allied victory. Amiens was one of the first major battles involving armoured warfare, marking the end of trench warfare on the Western Front.

13 The British Government formally recognised the Czecho-Slovaks as an Allied nation.

15 Part of the Hundred Days Offensive, the Battle of Montdidier ended.

16 Japanese General K Otani, commanding the Allied expedition, arrived at Vladivostok.

17 The Second Battle of Noyon began as French forces renewed their offensive on the Somme.

18 British forces in Flanders began a successful offensive operation in the Action of Outtersteene Ridge.

19 Merville was recaptured by British troops on the Lys Front.

21 The Battle of Albert was the first phase of a fresh offensive launched by British forces during the Second Battles of the Somme.

22 The town of Albert was recaptured by British troops.

24 The British merchant ship SS *Flavia* was torpedoed without warning and sunk by the German submarine *U-107* near County Donegal, Ireland whilst travelling from Montreal to Avonmouth.

26 The British launched a fresh offensive as the Battle of the Scarpe began during the Second Battle of Arras.

27 Stiff resistance from the Germans and their heavily defended positions, coupled with very bad weather limited Allied gains during the Battle of the Scarpe.

28 Canadian Divisions seized part of the German Fresnes-Rouvroy defence system after three days of intense fighting.

29 The town of Bapaume was recaptured during the Battle of Albert as the British advanced on the Somme.

30 Russian political revolutionary Fanya (Dora) Kaplan attempted to assassinate Vladimir Lenin as he left a meeting in Moscow, seriously wounding him.

31 Australian troops crossed the Somme River during the night and breached the German lines at Mont Saint-Quentin and Péronne at the beginning of the Battle of Mont St Quentin on the Western Front.

Top: Stretcher bearers carry a wounded British soldier to safety while another takes the opportunity to catch up on some sleep in one of the trenches.

Middle: A shell hit the Basilica of Notre-Dame de Brebières in January 1915, causing the "Golden Virgin" statue of Mary and baby Jesus to topple to a horizontal position. Several superstitions arose including the belief among Germans that whoever made it fall would lose the war, while the Allies believed the war would end the day it hit the ground. Eventually British troops destroyed the tower in April 1918 to prevent Germans from using it as an observation post.

Below: Jubilant scenes in a British seaport town after American troops have disembarked.

Opposite maps: The Allied advances at Amiens and their proximity to other major towns can be clearly seen.

Opposite below right: A German machine gun lies abandoned in an enemy trench.

THE WESTERN FRONT: ARRAS TO SOISSONS

SCENE OF THE 9-MILE PUSH.

GREAT ADVANCE.

BRITISH AND FRENCH UNDER HAIG.

100 GUNS, 7,000 PRISONERS

WHOLE AMIENS LINE FORWARD.

9 MILES AT ONE POINT.

CAVALRY CAPTURE VILLAGES.

The Allies won a great success yesterday on the whole line from Albert almost to Montdidier and especially east of Amiens.

Sir Douglas Haig launched the attack in mist at dawn. He directed the 4th British Army under General Rawlinson, and the 1st French Army under General Debeney (not Anthoine, as at first believed).

Our barrage was terrific, but lasted a bare four minutes. Infantry, tanks, and aeroplanes then attacked, taking the enemy by complete surprise. Prisoners were coming back within a few minutes. Our wounded were not numerous.

The weather cleared, and by 3 p.m. we had gained all our objectives on the main 12½ miles Amiens front. The cavalry did gloriously, riding down Germans and capturing villages. By then over 100 guns and 7,000 prisoners were counted. Our average advance is 4—5 miles. At the deepest point, Framerville, it is 9 miles.

FOCH STRIKES.

FROM CHAMPAGNE TO MEUSE.

FRENCH AND YANKS.

SEVEN MILES GAINED.

PERSHING'S 5,000 PRISONERS ALREADY.

From GENERAL PERSHING.

Thursday, 9 p.m.

This morning north-west of VERDUN the 1st Army attacked the enemy on a front of 20 miles and penetrated his lines to an average depth of 7 miles.

Pennsylvania, Kansas, and Missouri troops serving in Major-General Liggett's Corps stormed VARENNES, MONTBLAINVILLE, VAUQUOIS, and CHEPPY after stubborn resistance. Troops of other corps, crossing the FORGES BROOK, captured the BOIS DE FORGES and wrested from the enemy the towns of MALANCOURT, BETHINCOURT, MONTFAUCON, CUISY, NANTILLOIS, SEPTSARGES, DANNEVOUX, GERCOURT, and DRILLANCOURT.

The prisoners thus far reported number over 5,000.

In late August the Allies pushed towards Albert. Bapaume and Péronne soon fell.

Left: Shells burst just south of Arras as the cavalry wait to move forward.

Middle: Troops use the protection of a wall during daylight patrols in Albert only days before the town was captured.

Below: A German soldier surrenders to soldiers from the 62nd Division during the Second Battle of the Marne. It was a significant victory for the Allies who captured over 29,000 German prisoners, nearly 800 guns and 3,000 machine guns.

Opposite above: General Foch played a significant part in preventing the German advance on Paris in 1918.

Opposite map: Foch planned a carefully co-ordinated series of attacks along the German line, each under the command of an Allied general.

Opposite below: Troops pass the saluting point in front of the French General Henri Berthelot. Foch appointed him as commander of the Fifth Army in July.

FOCH'S FOUR BLOWS—

Ferdinand Foch

Foch assumes overall command

The man who became the Allies' "Generalissimo" as the war reached its endgame was a son of Gascony, born in the Pyrenean town of Tarbes in 1851. Though he saw no action in the Franco-Prussian War after enlisting in 1870, he had found his vocation. Both a student and teacher of military history, and author of two influential books on the waging of war, Foch was in his sixties before he had the opportunity to put theory into practice on the battlefields of the Western Front.

Foch entered the military academy in 1871 and went on to gain a commission in the artillery regiment. In 1885 he commenced his studies at the prestigious École de Guerre, where he later returned as a lecturer of great repute. Foch believed in the importance of imposing one's will on the enemy, an arch-proponent of the offensive. The duty of a commander was to inspire such confidence that his army refused to accept defeat. In the early days of the war, following his promotion from XX Corps commander to lead the new 9th Army, Foch played a key role in halting a marauding enemy threatening to cross the Marne. It is here that he is said to have uttered the famous words that encapsulated his indomitable spirit: "My centre is giving way, my right is in retreat. Situation excellent. I shall attack."

In attempting to champion the offensive with Gallic élan as the Western Front settled into entrenched stalemate, Foch – like Haig – came in for his share of criticism. Operations in Champagne and Artois achieved too little at too high a price, some argued, and when Joffre fell from favour in late 1916, Foch was sidelined to apply his mind to Allied strategy – demotion in all but name. Within months he was on the rise once more, replacing Pétain as chief of staff following the latter's promotion in the wake of the disastrous Nivelle Offensive. On 26 March 1918, five days into Ludendorff's spring assault, Foch assumed overall command of Allied forces. In August, when Germany's final push had been rebuffed and the Allies began to tighten the screw, Foch was appointed to the rank of marshal. A year after the Armistice, King George V presented him with his British field marshal baton.

The great liberator

Foch was the principal military adviser to the Allied delegates at the Versailles conference, failing in his bid to achieve a frontier on the Rhine for his native land. His prediction that all that had been achieved was a 20-year ceasefire proved eerily prescient, but he did not live to see it come to pass. Foch retired from active service after the peace conference, remaining his country's most distinguished military figure until his death in 1929, aged 77. On hearing the news of his passing, former prime minister Paul Painlevé described him as a great liberator, deserving of a place in military history alongside Julius Caesar, Alexander the Great and Napoleon. He also recalled Foch's words in one of their last conversations: "I have made mistakes, but if I had not made them I should not have been able to do what I did in 1918." Britain paid its own tribute to a staunch ally, which included the commissioning of a statue, erected outside Victoria Station, the departure point for so many soldiers bound for France and Flanders. The inscription reads: "I am conscious of having served England as I served my own country".

American Heroes

Wild Bill Donovan and the "Fighting 69th"

William "Wild Bill" Donovan is best remembered as the father of America's intelligence service, established during the Second World War, but he also left his mark on the 1914-18 conflict. Born on 1 January 1883 of Irish Catholic stock, Donovan was raised in Buffalo, New York. He chose law school over the priesthood – an early aspiration – and joined the legendary "Fighting 69th" Irish Regiment of the National Guard long before America declared its combatant intentions. As battalion commander of a unit with a proud history dating back to the Civil War, he drilled his men with relentless intensity, determined to toughen them up for the rigours to come. A taskmaster who led from the front, he earned his "Wild Bill" nickname from those who sweated under his watchful eye.

Donovan was utterly fearless in the field, and it was for his bravery under fire during the Second Battle of the Marne in July 1918 that he was awarded the Medal of Honor. To that was added the Légion d'Honneur, Croix de Guerre and Order of Leopold, just some of the honours that made Donovan among the most decorated soldiers of the war. Tales of the Fighting 69th were irresistible to Hollywood, George Brent portraying Wild Bill in the 1940 film of that name. His postwar ambition initially lay with the post of Attorney General – he served as assistant during the Coolidge administration but was passed over for the top job. In 1932 he ran unsuccessfully for the governorship of New York, his designs on becoming America's first Irish-Catholic president in tatters. But as the country geared up for the second global conflict in a generation, Franklin Delano Roosevelt appointed Donovan to head the new intelligence service, later renamed the Office of Strategic Services – the famed OSS. A staff of one – Donovan himself – grew into an extensive worldwide network of agents; its director became the country's first spymaster. When the OSS was shut down in September 1945, he formulated plans for a peacetime intelligence service ("The greatest nation in the world cannot rely on physical strength alone"). Truman set up the CIA along the lines Donovan proposed, but sour relations between the two meant the latter had little chance of leading the new agency. Wild Bill Donovan died in February 1959, aged 76.

Below left: "Wild Bill" Donovan received the Medal of Honor for his bravery during the Second Battle of the Marne.

Below right: Another Medal of Honor recipient, Sergeant Alvin York received his award for single-handedly killing over 20 Germans and taking 132 prisoners during the Meuse-Argonne offensive.

Opposite left: Captain Eddie Rickenbacker was America's most successful fighter ace and credited with 26 victories. He belatedly received his Medal of Honor in 1931.

Opposite right: Soldiers of the 369th (15th New York) who won the Croix de Guerre for gallantry in action. They were the first African-American regiment to fight with the AEF and earned the nickname the "Harlem Hellfighters".

Sharpshooter Sergeant York

Alvin York, America's most decorated soldier of World War One, was an unlikely war hero. Hailing from Pall Mall in the Tennessee mountains, he was a devoutly religious pacifist who wrestled with the prospect of taking life and the call of patriotic duty. When the draft came his way, he sought conscientious objector status, which was refused. Following his induction into the army, York was assigned to 82nd Infantry Division, arriving in France in May 1918. He was soon displaying the deadeye marksmanship learned during an impoverished youth when hunting was a prime means of putting food on the table. Crucially, his superior officers convinced him that the cause they were fighting for was compatible with biblical teaching and York's Christian beliefs.

He wrote his name into the history books on 8 October, during the Meuse-Argonne offensive. Having lost over half his unit and inherited command, he attacked a machine-gun emplacement single-handedly, credited with killing over 20 and taking 132 prisoners. He received a ticker-tape parade on his return to New York, was received at the White House and had dozens of honours heaped upon him from various nations, including the Congressional Medal of Honor and Croix de Guerre. Pinning the latter medal on him, Marshal Foch hailed his achievement as "the greatest accomplishment by any private soldier of all the armies of Europe".

The self-effacing York was no fan of the limelight, resisting most offers to exploit his celebrity. "This uniform ain't for sale," he said, and when Hollywood came calling, keen to tell his story, he agreed only when the studio agreed to build a bible school. Gary Cooper gave an Oscar-winning performance playing Alvin in the 1941 film *Sergeant York*, but it's said the star found himself ticked off on set for infringing the no-smoking, no-drinking rule imposed by the real-life war hero. York gave innumerable talks describing his wartime experience, not for personal aggrandisement but to fund the construction of a school; he himself never made it beyond third grade. Alvin Cullum York died in 1964, aged 76.

"Captain Eddie" – ace of aces

Eddie Rickenbacker was the top American ace of the war. Born in Columbus, Ohio in 1890, he had little formal education but showed strength of purpose in rising to the top in three fields. The first was the automobile track, where he displayed a daredevil streak long before taking to the skies. Rickenbacker was one of the country's foremost racing drivers, a regular on the grid in the early days of the Indianapolis 500 following its inception in 1911.

He enlisted shortly after America entered the war, tweaking his actual surname – Reichenbacher – to remove the Germanic tinge of his ancestral roots. His sights were set on the fledgling air corps, hopes that were dashed as he was assigned to driving duties on Pershing's staff. At 26 he was deemed too old for pilot training. But with the help of Colonel – soon-to-be General – Billy Mitchell, a firm believer in the military potential of aircraft technology, Rickenbacker secured the transfer he had been angling for. He saw his first action in spring 1918 as part of 94th Squadron, registering the first of his 26 confirmed victories in April. Under his command 94th Squadron became the most successful unit in the American air force, and he believed that a leader should set an example. "I shall never ask any pilot to go on a mission that I won't go on," he wrote in his diary. On 25 September, shortly after assuming command, Rickenbacker's Spad took on seven enemy aircraft during a routine patrol, gallantry that brought him the Medal of Honor. He downed two that day, 22 enemy aircraft in all, plus a few observation balloons for good measure.

In peacetime he launched an automobile business before turning to civil aviation. He acquired Eastern Air Lines in 1938 and ran it profitably for a quarter of a century, the "Ace of Aces" surviving a couple of plane crashes along the way. "Captain Eddie", as he was popularly known, died in 1973, aged 82.

The lost battalion

On 26 September 1918 the Allies launched the massive Meuse-Argonne Offensive, with the rump of the German army fighting a fierce rearguard. Among those battling in the Argonne forest was a battalion of the US 77th Division, led by Harvard-educated lawyer Major Charles Whittlesey. The Allies were firmly on the front foot; it was merely a matter of time before the final capitulation, something Ludendorff had long accepted. But on 2 October, while renewing the offensive near Charlevaux, Whittlesey and his men of the 308th Infantry were about to find themselves in a desperate plight. The units on either side suddenly met stiff resistance and their advance stalled, leaving Whittlesey and his battalion isolated as it pressed on into a steep-sided ravine commanded by an enemy in possession of the high ground. The pursuer was now at the enemy's mercy. Retreat was impossible, the situation made worse by a worrying lack of supplies. As if that wasn't bad enough, they also had to contend with friendly fire as Allied gunners mistook their position. Whittlesey had two avenues of communication: runners and carrier pigeons. He deployed both, but could not be sure whether any man had managed to slip through the net. The battalion's last remaining bird was a favourite called Cher Ami – Dear Friend – which lived up to its name by reaching the Allied line despite taking a bullet. The men were at least safe from their own ordnance, though that was but one element in a dire predicament.

The attackers felt time was on their side and waited for the Americans to expend their meagre resources, deplete their ammunition. A supply drop fell behind enemy lines. So close were the opposing forces that it would take a slice of good fortune for an aircraft to hit the small pocket in which the unit was stranded. After four days Whittlesey was offered the chance to surrender, an invitation swiftly rejected. By the time relief arrived on 7 October, over 100 of the 550-strong force lay dead, with 200 wounded and dozens more missing. The entire battalion was cited for valour, Whittlesey awarded the Medal of Honor. Cher Ami was not overlooked: he received the Croix de Guerre.

There was a tragic postscript for the battalion commander – now Colonel Charles Whittlesey – a man of sensitive disposition who was deeply scarred by the experience. On Armistice Day 1921 he relived the nightmare yet again when he served as a pallbearer at the interment of the Unknown Soldier at Arlington National Cemetery. Two weeks later, Whittlesey boarded a ship bound for Cuba. In mid-ocean he threw himself overboard; the Lost Battalion had lost its leader three years after the guns fell silent.

Harlem Hellfighters

Like many of America's volunteer National Guardsmen, the men of New York's 15th Regiment were ready, willing and able to fight when the call came in 1917. But as the city's cosmopolitan "Rainbow Division" defence force left for Europe with cheers ringing in their ears following a grand send-off parade, the all-black 15th was seen as a pariah. Black, it was said, was not a colour of the rainbow. Even commander-in-chief General John Pershing regarded African-Americans as second-class soldiers, content to see them confined to support roles such as dock or kitchen work. Fraternisation with French civilians was expressly forbidden.

The French army, replete with black troops from its colonial outposts, had no such issue with integration. Indeed, the depletion of its manpower – both fallen in battle and lost through desertion – meant that fresh troops were warmly welcomed. And so the New York 15th became the 369th Infantry Regiment under French command. These men knew peacetime struggle, which served them well when it came to displaying battling qualities. Among the ranks were Privates Henry Johnson and Needham Roberts, the first US recipients of the Croix de Guerre, awarded for selfless bravery as the pair faced overwhelming odds during action on the night of 14 May.

The unit's commander was Colonel William Hayward, a white lawyer poles apart from those he led in the social pecking order at home. But in France he stood as one with men he was proud to say never took a backward step or had a man captured. The 369th – or "Harlem Hellfighters", as they came to be known – served at the front for 191 days. No American unit saw more action, none so highly decorated. They left a lasting cultural legacy, too, for the Hellfighters also boasted an unrivalled jazz band led by Lieutenant James Reese Europe. Morale-boosting concerts were mixed with front-line fighting, and by the time the Americans left for home, jazz was coursing through French veins.

Reports of the Harlem Hellfighters' achievements had filled many column inches, and in the New York victory parade of February 1919, those who had been so pointedly overlooked before leaving for France now basked in a tumultuous reception for the conquering heroes. For James Europe the future should have been bright as the Jazz Age dawned and his Hellfighters Band was in great demand. But having survived the war, one of the most influential musicians of the early 20th century was killed following a confrontation with a band member in May 1919. New York gave Jim Europe a funeral service the like of which had never been accorded to one of its black citizens prior to his burial in Arlington National Cemetery.

Heroes

Monash knighted in the field

On 12 August 1918, the day following the Amiens battle which had been an unalloyed triumph for the Allies, King George V visited the Australia Corps headquarters at Bertangles and knighted its commander, General John Monash. Not since Agincourt had such an honour been conferred in the battlefield. Monash had only recently taken over the leadership of Australia's 200,000-strong army, operating for the first time as a single unit. Ahead of the battle he roused his men with the prospect of a success "which will re-echo throughout the world and will live forever in the history of our homeland". The call was answered with numerous examples of valiant service, but this corps commander was more concerned with precise calculation than gung-ho bravery.

In the 1920s, Monash was widely regarded as the most popular living Australian.

nothing better than solving fiendishly difficult mathematical problems naturally had a cerebral approach to waging war. He was punctilious, a great organiser; a man who paid attention to microscopic detail in the battlefield, as he was required to do in his peacetime occupation. He saw action at Gallipoli and served in Egypt before cementing his reputation in France. Feeding endless lines of men into the Western Front mincing machine was anathema to him, thus he was devastated when required to send Anzacs into battle and almost certain doom at Passchendaele. He reviled the waste of human life, contemptuous of the sheer "inefficiency" of such practice.

Monash was born in Melbourne in 1865, the son of immigrant parents who had left Poland in search of a better life in Victoria. He was a brilliant scholar and gifted pianist who might have made a career in music. Instead he turned to civil engineering, and later to the courtroom; professions that suited his meticulousness and razor-sharp intellect. He was also a reserve soldier, one of several handicaps he had to overcome on the road to proving himself among the most capable wartime leaders. Regulars invariably looked askance at such "part-timers", and the fact that he was a son of German-born Jews was hardly a guarantor of advancement. Hailing from the dominion backwaters marked him out even further as an outsider. But a man who enjoyed

During the Allied offensive that led to Germany's capitulation, Monash's men liberated over 100 towns and villages.

Monash applied his considerable intellectual powers to methods that would reduce the losses incurred in attritional combat. He championed the use of dummy tanks to fool the enemy into believing they faced a greater force than was the case, putting another hobby – performing magic tricks – to good use. Infantry, he wrote, ought not to be sacrificial lambs but "to advance under the maximum possible protection of the maximum possible array of mechanical resources, in the form of guns, machine-guns, tanks, mortars and aeroplanes; to advance with as little impediment as possible; to be relieved as far as possible of the obligation to fight their way forward". His ideas bore fruit when on 4 July 1918 Australian troops, with American support, took the village of Hamel on the Somme. He faced down superiors who informed him at the last minute that General Pershing had not sanctioned the use of US troops. Americans did help win that Independence Day battle, Monash's sole disappointment that he missed his 90-minute target for success – by three minutes. During the Allied offensive that led to Germany's capitulation, his men liberated over 100 towns and villages.

Monash returned to civvy street after overseeing the repatriation of Aussie troops. In the 1920s he was widely regarded as the most popular living Australian, held in such high esteem that when the country faced economic difficulties and civil unrest some wanted him to take autocratic control in what amounted to a military coup. Monash, who had fought to preserve democracy, was horrified. His death at the age of 66 in 1931 brought thousands onto the streets to pay their respects, while his name lives on in any number of memorials and institutions, including Monash University in the city of his birth.

AUSTRALIAN GAIN.

SOMME CREST CARRIED.

From W. BEACH THOMAS.

With the British, Monday.

In a moonlight attack just after midnight Australians won the crown of the spacious high road which bisects the tapering land between the Ancre and the Somme, dominating the wide marshes of the Somme valley and the country to the south. Prisoners were taken almost on the site of the old prisoners' cage that I saw filled and refilled many times during the Battle of the Somme.

It was a skilful assault, very conservative of life, and met with complete success. Several times have the Australians done the same thing thereabouts, but the value of last night's advance close up to the crossroad joining Morlancourt and Sailly is that the highest point of the main road is now in our hands and the little villages along the sinuous banks of the Somme are dominated. The chalk down, becoming absolutely bare and barren, runs higher towards the north-east but is crossed there by no road worthy of the name.

The German retaliation was surprisingly small. The infantry, who suffered more heavily than the 140 prisoners would suggest, resigned themselves to defeat, and the artillery were more sparing of shells than usual, though their fire would have been called heavy according to the older standard of the war.

As an example of what artillery fire means now, over 12,000 shells, mostly gas, were the other day loosed against one of our brigade fronts within ten hours, though no action followed or preceded.

Almost at the hour when the Australians attacked, the enemy raided one of our outpost positions farther north and captured the machine gun with one of its crew. A counter-attack was set afoot so quickly that the considerable German patrol was surrounded, a good many killed, some taken prisoner, and the machine gun, with the captured member of its crew, retaken. The example is characteristic of our local control of No Man's Land. In most sectors Australians, New Zealanders, and Canadians are, perhaps, peculiarly successful in pegging out claims and keeping off land jumpers, and now No Man's Land is often uncharted and unsurveyed. Certainly many German officers have very little idea of its size or shape or how far it has been peacefully penetrated.

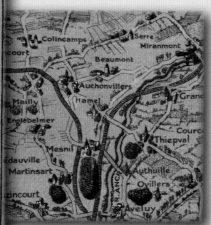

Above: General Sir John Monash, the Australian military leader, was regarded as one of the most effective Allied commanders of the conflict.

Opposite: The professional footballer Walter Tull was the first mixed race officer in the British Army. He was killed in action on 25 March 1918. Tull was cited for his "gallantry and coolness" during action at the Piave river in Italy.

Walter Tull:
hero of the terraces and the battlefield

2nd Lieutenant Walter Tull was killed in action on 25 March 1918, one of the many who sacrificed their lives and whose remains lie somewhere on the battlefields of Western Europe. What distinguishes Walter's story from countless others is his accomplishment in two fields of endeavour: professional sport and the military. He was not quite the first black footballer to play league football in Britain; but he was the first black officer in the nation's army, at a time when colour prejudice was enshrined in the very articles by which that institution operated.

Walter's father, Daniel Tull, swapped Barbados for Kent in the mid-1870s. He found work as carpenter and also a bride, Alice Palmer, whom he married in 1880. Walter arrived eight years later, the fourth of five children who survived infancy. The Tulls had lost a baby daughter, and tragedy struck again when Alice succumbed to cancer in 1895. Six-year-old Walter soon had a stepmother, Daniel marrying Alice's niece, Clara. Whether the incentive for the union was pragmatism, to provide a maternal figure for the children, it also expanded the family with the birth of a daughter. Clara, still only in her 20s, was left with six dependants when Daniel died in 1897. To relieve the overstrained family budget, Walter and his brother Edward were placed into the care of a Methodist orphanage in Bethnal Green. The two were extremely close, the fraternal bond doubly important to boys who had had more than their share of tragedy and disruption. That relationship also fractured when Edward was adopted by a Glaswegian couple in 1900. Living at opposite ends of the country, the brothers inevitably saw less of each other, but when Walter signed up for wartime service it was Edward whom he named next of kin.

> *A private valiantly tried to carry him to safety until heavy fire forced him to abandon his load.*

Before then, Walter enjoyed a brief career in professional football. He won the FA Amateur Cup in his short period on the books of Clapton FC, then in 1909 signed for a Spurs side about to have its first taste of top-flight competition. Two years later he moved to non-league Northampton Town, signed by a young Herbert Chapman, who would go on to great things with Huddersfield Town and Arsenal. Tull certainly experienced overt racism in his playing days – there was no recourse to law over such matters in Edwardian England. He bore it with equanimity, a quality he would need when he faced institutional prejudice in the armed forces.

Walter signed up to a footballing pals' battalion in December 1914, already a lance sergeant by the time he headed to France late the following year. In common with many, Walter's constitution was not always up to fulfilling his desire to do his duty. A nervous disorder required a period of convalescence, but by the end of 1916 he had not only returned to action but been recommended for a commission by his commanding officer. Army regulations of the day reveal the prevailing attitude to "coloured troops": those "belonging to savage tribes and barbarous races should not be employed in a war between civilised states". If that was the view with regard to the ranks, advancement was scarcely a matter for consideration. Non-whites were prohibited from holding positions of authority; those put forward had to be "of pure European descent", in the words of the rulebook. To the military hierarchy, the thought of a black officer commanding white soldiers was unconscionable. The exigencies of war brought a relaxation of stipulations that would have been set in stone

in peacetime, and Walter spent the early months of 1917 undertaking officer training in Scotland. He passed out in May as 2nd Lieutenant in the Special Reserve, the British Army's first black infantry officer.

In autumn 1917 Tull's 23rd Middlesex battalion was in action in Italy, part of the Allied reinforcement of an Italian line facing an enemy onslaught on the River Piave. Cited for "gallantry and coolness" in an operation mounted on New Year's Day, Walter had not only broken the mould in becoming the first black officer to lead white soldiers into battle, but had done so with distinction. He was back in France by the time Germany launched its Spring Offensive, and it was while fighting a desperate rearguard at the Somme that Walter Tull sustained a fatal head wound. A private valiantly tried to carry him to safety until heavy fire forced him to abandon his load. 2nd Lieutenant Walter Tull, 29, would be commemorated in a number of ways, but the spot where he fell is unknown.

In recent years the retelling of Walter's story has brought him widespread recognition. Visitors to Northampton Town's ground pass along Walter Tull Way, just one example of how his name lives on. But he does not have the military honour some believe is his due and ought not to be denied, even a century after his death. The letter Edward received informing him of his brother's demise spoke of a decoration in the offing, most probably for the episode in Italy at the beginning of the year. "He had been recommended for the Military Cross & had certainly earned it," the missive ran, even though it was a breach of rules to release such speculative information. Was it a slip on the part of 2nd Lieutenant Pickard, the officer who wrote to Edward? Or, as some have surmised, did he guess the honour would not be forthcoming? If the latter, perhaps Pickard wanted the family to be aware that Walter had merited the MC, even if political sensitivities meant the medal would not be awarded.

The final push

After the "black day" at Amiens, Ludendorff accepted that the war could not now be won. A defensive battle was the best that could be managed. His offer to resign was not accepted, leaving him prey to wild mood swings as the Allies relentlessly tightened their grip. Within weeks the ground Germany had claimed during the Spring Offensive was lost, though effective troop marshalling meant that the Hindenburg Line remained intact. It merely delayed the inevitable. In late August the Allies pushed towards Albert. Bapaume and Péronne soon fell, while plans were drawn up for a multi-pronged assault bearing some resemblance to Germany's own five separate attempts to seize the initiative earlier in the year. "Tout le monde à la bataille!" was the cry of Foch, the generalissimo. Germany's efforts in the spring had foundered. How would the Fatherland's dispirited army stand up to the test?

On 12 September, a fortnight before the final push began in earnest, General Pershing at last saw his wish for American soldiers to fight as a separate body realised. With French support, the newly formed US 1st Army executed a copybook attack on the San Mihiel salient, a 16-mile projection into the Allied line south of Verdun that the enemy had held since 1914. The first operation by an independent American force was a stunning success, completed in four days. But this was merely the overture. Pershing's doughboys now had to be moved en masse in readiness to play their part in the grand offensive, a logistical feat directed by staff officer and future US Army commander Colonel George C Marshall. The final act could now begin.

The Meuse-Argonne battle

The target for the Americans, in tandem with French forces, was the stretch of line west of Verdun, between the River Meuse and Argonne Forest. As they struck northward, British troops would mount an attack at Cambrai, with the Belgian army under King Albert also on the march in Flanders. This concerted effort was launched on 26 September in the Argonne, where the doughboys experienced tougher going than San Mihiel, on more difficult terrain. Every mile came at a considerable cost, yet Foch, impatient for swifter returns, was not satisfied with the gains of the first week. Pershing ordered his men forward, determined that America should play a pivotal role in the war-winning assault. In mid-October he passed command of the 1st Army to General Hunter Liggett, who found it no easier to break the last threads of German resistance. Pershing now had manpower enough to form a 2nd Army, determined to take Sedan before a settlement was reached. The Meuse-Argonne battle was still raging as the minutes leading up to the armistice ticked away.

WIDE GERMAN RETREAT.

BRITISH NEARING PERONNE.

FRENCH REACH THE SOMME.

LONDONERS CAPTURE CROISILLES.

The Germans are in full retreat on the southern half of the battle front, a line of about 30 miles.

The British are so close at their heels that the enemy has been forced to defend the crossings of the Somme south of Péronne, from which our troops are only 4 miles distant. The French on our right, too, have advanced very fast and line the bend of the Somme south of Péronne and have half-encircled Noyon, the present limit of the retreat. Our Allies have taken among great booty three trains loaded with munitions.

The Americans have taken over a new section north of Soissons, where Chavigny has been captured and important ground has been gained near Juvigny. On the Vesle, south-east of Soissons, they have foiled a strong enemy attempt to cross the river.

On the northern part of the battle front, east and south-east of Arras, Ludendorff has had to throw in fresh divisions, which have been resisting stubbornly, but our troops have nevertheless gained valuable positions and are close up to the powerfully fortified Hindenburg "switch" line, the penetration of which might cause the enemy to lose the Lens coalfield and Douai and would again menace Cambrai.

After a fierce struggle troops of the 1st British Army have made a most important gain of ground south-east of Monchy (4½ miles east of Arras), where they have pushed forward 1,000 yards on the road from Arras to Cambrai. Here they are on ground which has never been fought over.

The capture of Croisilles yesterday is in this section is particularly gratifying, as it follows desperate German efforts to hold it.

Hun counter-attacks south of Bapaume have recovered Flers and Delville Wood, but our advance towards Maurepas should soon loosen their hold on those places.

4 MILES TO PERONNE.

FIGHT FOR SOMME CROSSINGS.

BRITISH OFFICIAL REPORT.
Wednesday, 9 p.m.

South of the RIVER SOMME Australian troops are pressing the enemy vigorously and have reached the general line FRESNES-HERBECOURT [the latter 4 miles from Péronne]. The enemy is offering a stubborn resistance in front of the passages of the river at BRIE and PERONNE.

HUNS FIGHT HARDER

FRESH TROOPS THROWN IN.

From W. BEACH THOMAS.
WITH THE BRITISH, Wednesday.

Over beyond Arras, where the ash sappings grow through the paving-stones of the dismantled city, which echoed like an empty room to the clatter of rare bursts of high and heavy shrapnel; over beyond Monchy, now visible as an active volcano; beyond the woods of Sart and Vert, now like a winter hop-garden, the Canadians at noon to-day went out to hit their shifty enemy a third blow—Wednesday's blow, after Tuesday's and Monday's.

Just before that hour I found officers in a dug-out enjoying hugely the account of

THE BATTLE LINE.

The dotted line was the starting point of the present attack, which began on the 21st. The black line shows the gains made since. The Hindenburg "switch" line eastward of Arras runs irregularly from Drocourt to Queant.

Sections 2 and 3 of The Daily Mail Giant

Left: Australian troops prepare to go over the top at Mont St Quentin in September. General John Monash planned the attack on the peak. They successfully broke the German lines, taking the summit and the town of Péronne.

Opposite top: Only a single tree was left standing in the strech of woods at La Grande Tranchée de Calonne, Meuse.

Opposite upper middle: A small section of the bombs due to be dropped on German positions by an RAF squadron in one night.

Opposite lower middle: Fortified German dugouts captured by the US 103rd Infantry.

Opposite bottom right: A view of the wrecked bridge across the River Meuse and a pontoon bridge built by French troops at St-Mihiel. General Pershing commanded the attack on the town using his US forces, supported by 48,000 French troops.

Opposite main image: Tanks and infantry move forward in the final push.

Hindenburg Line breached

Elsewhere the news provided greater cheer. The attack mounted by the British 1st and 3rd Armies towards Cambrai on 27 September soon pierced a six-mile hole in the Hindenburg Line on a 12-mile front. A day later, the Belgians and General Plumer's 2nd Army attacked at Ypres, sweeping across the Passchendaele battleground where so much blood had been spilt the previous year. In a single day the Allies had command of ground that had been fought over for three long months. Still there was no respite for the Germans as General Rawlinson's 4th Army, with French support, breached the Hindenburg Line at St Quentin. Defences here were over three miles deep and included a canal with steep banks that formed a daunting natural obstacle. In overcoming this a psychological barrier was also crossed: the attackers buoyed as they soon found themselves in open country, the defenders' morale struck another savage blow. The besieged German army fought an unequal struggle, trying to plug ever increasing gaps with ever fewer reserves. In places – especially against the Americans in the Argonne – their fighting spirit held up. But there was despair and resignation too, encapsulated in signs daubed on the railway carriages taking them to the battlefield: "Slaughter cattle for Wilhelm & Sons". Many thought filing into the abattoir was a pointless gesture and laid down their weapons. Those who still appeared keen to fight were harangued for prolonging the agony. Many voted with their feet, deserting in droves or simply failing to return from leave. Soldiers painted a grim picture of the frontline situation, which undermined the efforts of the propagandists and heightened the pervading mood of pessimism at home. A sizeable proportion of those who remained at their posts were simply going through the motions, effectively participating in a Militärstreik – a covert withdrawal of their soldierly labour. One who witnessed the army's disintegration first hand was Adolf Hitler, an Iron Cross-winning dispatch runner for regimental HQ. His war ended when he was temporarily blinded in a mustard gas attack in Flanders in mid-October, though psychiatric treatment suggested that the wounds were more psychological than physical. The searing pain of defeat endured long after any impairment to his sight had healed.

The first operation by an independent American force was a stunning success, completed in four days.

Germany in a state of collapse

The evidence was all pointing in one direction. Germany was in a state of collapse both in the field and at home. The Allies themselves were surprised at the rate of progress, for plans had already been made regarding the strategy for 1919. Those were suddenly looking redundant as it became clear that the issue could be forced before the onset of winter. There was but one question for Germany's leaders now: what terms could be secured?

THE WESTERN FRONT: METZ, NANCY AND STRASSBURG

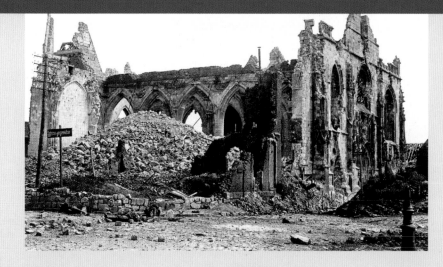

September 1918

1 Australian forces recaptured Péronne from the Germans on the Western Front.

2 The defensive line constructed by Germany between the French towns of Drocourt and Quéant, was taken by the Canadian Corps during the Hundred Days Offensive as the two day long Battle of the Drocourt-Quéant Line began.

3 The Second Battles of the Somme and Arras officially ended.

Fanya Kaplan was executed with a bullet to the back of her head in Moscow for the attempted murder of Lenin.

4 The Battle of Mont St. Quentin ended in a victory when Australian troops forced the Germans to withdraw.

5 North of Vladivostok, Japanese forces captured the strategically important port of Khabarovsk.

7 British and French troops pursued German forces as they retreated towards the Hindenburg Line.

8 A State Conference of anti-Bolshevik forces was convened in the city of Ufa in an attempt to form a unified anti-Bolshevik authority.

9 Charles Ruijs de Beerenbrouck was appointed as Prime Minister of the Netherlands replacing Pieter Cort van der Linden.

10 The Red Army's offensive against the Czechoslovak Legion came to an end when Trotsky's troops recaptured the city of Kazan.

11 Allied forces seized Ukhtinskaya on the Murmansk Front in North Russia.

12 The Battle of Saint-Mihiel began between the American Expeditionary Force and French troops against German defensive positions.

The Battle of the Hindenburg Line began with a series of Allied offensives. The Battle of Havrincourt between British and German troops was the first of these, ending with a British victory the same day.

14 British troops began to evacuate Baku on the Caspian Sea after Turkish forces launched an assault on the city.

15 Allied offensive operations began in Macedonia with the Battle of Dobro Pole which ended with a decisive victory over Bulgarian forces.

16 Built as a coastal defence ship for the Royal Norwegian Navy, HMS *Glatton* had to be torpedoed after a fire broke out in one of her magazines in order to prevent an explosion that would have devastated the port of Dover on the Kent coast.

18 The Battle of Épehy was fought by British troops under the command of General Henry Rawlinson against German outpost positions in front of the Hindenburg Line.

19 The Battle of Megiddo began on the Plain of Sharon between the Allied Egyptian Expeditionary Force and forces from the Ottoman Empire. The assault was the final Allied offensive of the Sinai and Palestine Campaign.

20 Allied troops advanced and captured Nazareth and Beisan in Palestine.

22 The Ottoman Army was attacked and began to retreat from the River Jordan and Amman.

23 Allied forces advanced across the Jordan to capture Es Salt in Palestine.

26 The Meuse-Argonne Offensive began early in the morning. After a six-hour-long bombardment on German defences during the previous night, American and French forces advanced against German positions in the Argonne Forest and along the River Meuse.

27 The Battle of Canal du Nord began as part of a number of closely sequenced Allied attacks at separate points along the Western Front during the Hundred Days Offensive. The battle took place in the Nord-Pas-de-Calais region of France, along an incomplete portion of the Canal du Nord.

28 The Fifth Battle of Ypres, also known as the Advance of Flanders and the Battle of the Peaks of Flanders, began a series of battles in northern France and southern Belgium from late to October 1918.

29 The continuing Battle of the Hindenburg Line moved into its next phase as the Battle of the St Quentin Canal began. The offensive involved British, Australian and American forces in a spearhead attack against German troops.

30 The Bulgarian Army surrendered and signed an Armistice with the Allied Powers: hostilities ceased at noon.

Opposite left: **A sign warns incoming troops of the danger of mines in the devastated town of Noyon. The town was captured on 29 August and engineers soon discovered the mines were connected to a power plant at Crisolles, eight miles away.**

Opposite middle left: **Allied troops crossed the Canal du Nord and finally broke through the Hindenburg Line at the end of September, immediately taking 36,000 prisoners.**

Opposite middle right: **A light tank makes its way over the top during the capture of Saint-Mihiel.**

Opposite right: **Australian troops work their way along a trench during the assault on Mont St Quentin.**

Opposite bottom: **The ridge north of Péronne ablaze in the wake of the German army's retreat.**

Top: **Péronne Cathedral was reduced to a shell by the time the Allies entered the town on 18 September.**

Middle: **Cavalry on the Menin Road, heading towards Gheluvelt.**

Bottom: **Australian troops warily pass a possible booby trap as they pursue the retreating German army.**

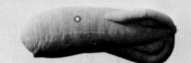

Top left: Fortifications left after the Germans abandoned their positions.

Above and left: By the time US troops reached the town of Thiaucourt, German soldiers had retreated after setting the buildings on fire.

Top right: French troops make their way through the ruins of a village.

Below: The 308th engineers construct a road while troops gather on the battlefield in the distance.

U.S. ARMY'S PUSH.

PERSHING ATTACKS NEAR METZ.

5 MILES GAINED.

8,000 PRISONERS TAKEN.

AMERICAN OFFICIAL REPORT.

Thursday Night.

This morning our troops operating in the St. Mihiel sector [south-east of Verdun and south-west of Metz] made considerable gains. Assisted by French units, they broke the enemy's resistance and advanced at some points to a depth of 5 miles.

We have counted 8,000 prisoners up to the present. The operation is still in progress.

FRENCH OFFICIAL REPORT.

Thursday Night.

The American Army attacked this morning in the St. Mihiel region. The operations are developing in the best conditions.

One of the great moments of the war came yesterday when General Pershing with the 1st American Army opened the attack, reported above, in co-operation with the French, on both sides of St. Mihiel, where the Germans in September 1914 drove a deep loop into the French front. This is the first large operation carried out by an independent American

From HERBERT BAILEY.
With the Americans, Thursday Morning.

The 1st American Army, under the personal command of General Pershing, for the first time went into action to-day in the St. Mihiel salient, between the Meuse and the Moselle.

Never before has there been such a large concentration of American troops for one operation

YANKS' VICTORY.

WHOLE ST. MIHIEL LOOP.

14 MILES ADVANCE.

OVER 13,000 PRISONERS.

AMERICAN OFFICIAL REPORT.

Friday Night.

In the St. Mihiel sector we have achieved further successes. The junction of our troops advancing from the south of the sector with those advancing from the west has given us possession of the whole salient to points 12 miles north-east of St. Mihiel and has resulted in the capture of many prisoners.

Forced back by our steady advance the enemy is retiring, and is destroying large quantities of material as he goes.

The number of prisoners has risen to 13,300.

Our line now includes Herbeuville, Thillot, Hattonville, St. Benoit, Xammes, Thiaucourt, and Vieville.

General Pershing, with the First American Army, has brilliantly completed the operation which he began on Thursday morning and has flattened out the deep loop in the Allied line at St. Mihiel, south-east of Verdun. He has taken more than 13,000 prisoners and 60 guns Allowing for other casualties, the Hun loss in this signally successful affair cannot be less than 20,000 men.

The Americans advanced rapidly from both the western and southern sides of the loop and their forces met yesterday. While they cut off the retreat of any troops near St. Mihiel, the French attacked in front of the town to hold the Germans there fast.

The Allied line now runs from Combres (south-east of Verdun) to Hattonville, and thence eastward almost straight to the Moselle, just south of Pagny. The depth of the loop flattened out is about 14 miles, as the advance began from a

From HERBERT BAILEY.

With the Americans, Thursday Night.

The day has gone well indeed for the Americans. They have fought with their customary ardour and distinction, and once more the Germans have found themselves completely outclassed as fighting men and in power of endurance.

From early morning the battle has been raging in sunshine and in rain, with interminable lanes of mud to impede progress. But the Americans have accepted all the disfavours of the weather with their usual humour, and the satisfaction of having once more achieved something that adds another proud page to their record in France is rich compensation for all the trials of a splendid day.

At noon to-day the Americans and the French who fought so well with them had reached the objectives assigned for the day. Montsec, that supreme, dominating height which overlooks Seicheprey, is still offering some resistance At various points the Germans have brought up reserves in motor-trucks.

But the Americans have again proved irresistible, and at 11.30 this morning

THE CAPTURED LOOP.

The dotted line and the arrow show the Yanks' advance.

Top: Cavalry and limbers pass along the Menin Road.

Insets above: The final Meuse-Argonne Offensive began on 26 September and lasted through to the end of the conflict. 1.2 million US soldiers led the campaign using 380 tanks and 840 planes. They finally cleared the Argonne Forest by the end of October while the British and French were also closing in on the Germans from other directions.

Below: The devasation left on the battlefields after troops withdraw.

Top left: Troops repair the Menin Road, the route that carried a constant stream of soldiers from the town of Ypres to the battlefields.

Top right: An exploding shell suddenly disturbs a British soldier who was quietly repairing his shirt outside a captured German hut.

Middle left: A party of young British officers cheerily embark on their well-earned home leave.

Middle right: This formidable iron mantrap was one of two found by American troops in the Alsace sector. The spring exerted a pressure of 300lbs.

Above: VAD drivers in France line up to receive their allowance of petrol.

Bottom: German Red Cross workers pick up the dead and wounded after an engagement near the Argonne Woods.

ENEMY IN FULL RETREAT.

Confident Predictions of French Experts.

PARIS, Tuesday.

M. Marcel Hutin writes in the *Echo de Paris*:—

The formidable battle for a decision now taking place on our front can only end in a complete victory which will make it impossible for Germany to continue the war.

Marshal Foch is not leaving it to the enemy to decide where he will fight the last battle, and this will be a Sedan on a big scale whence the enemy will retreat in haste to the other side of the Meuse.

But it is by no means certain that his withdrawal may not be turned into a disorderly retreat, or even a debacle.

Three British armies, under Generals Horne, Byng, and Rawlinson, in close liaison with our magnificent First Army,

Further progress has been made through the Forest of Mormal. Our troops took 1,000 prisoners at the capture of Le Quesnoy yesterday.

have resolutely been flung on the powerful German positions covering the roads of Avesnes, Maubeuge, and Hirson, and are following up their advance despite the desperate efforts of the Germans.

At the moment of writing this advance

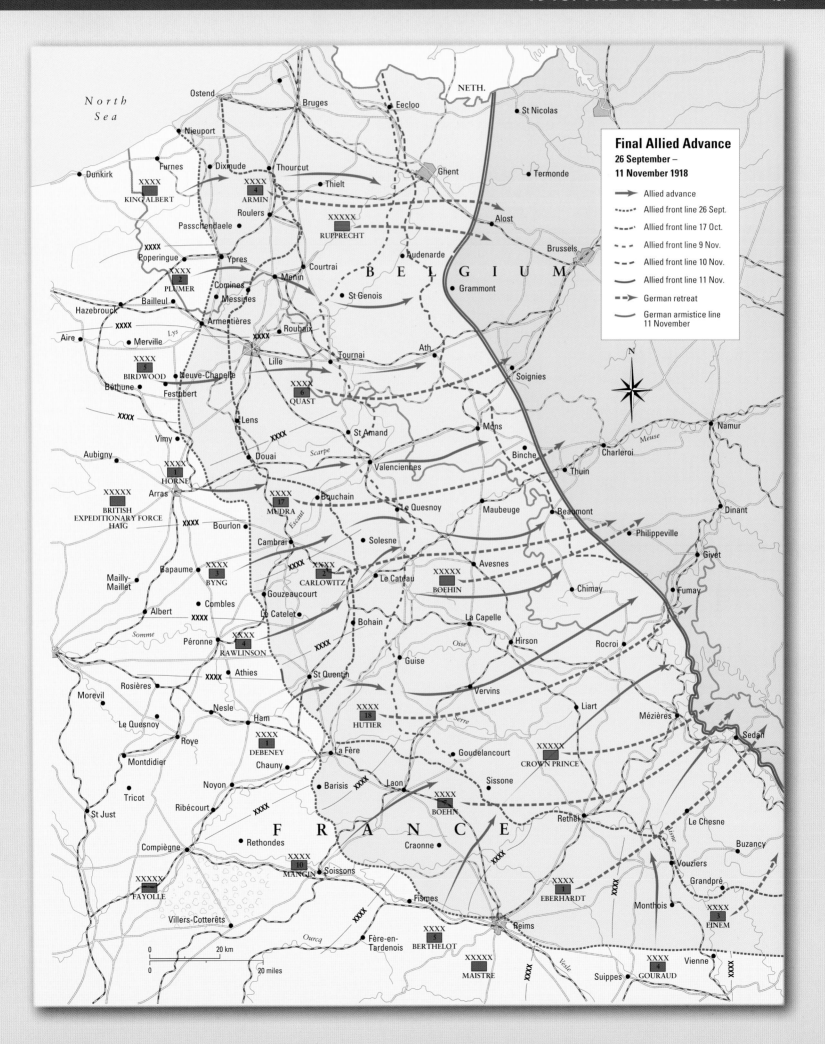

North Sea

NETH.

Ostend
Bruges
Eecloo
St Nicolas
Nieuport
Dunkirk
Furnes
Dixmude
Thourout
Ghent
Termonde
XXXX
KING ALBERT
XXXX
4
ARMIN
Thielt
Roulers
Passchendaele
XXXXX
RUPPRECHT
Alost
Brussels
Poperinge
XXXX
Ypres
Audenarde
BELGIUM
Courtrai
PLUMER
XXXX
2
Comines
Messines
Menin
Grammont
Bailleul
St Genois
Hazebrouck
Armentières
Roubaix
Ath
Soignies
Aire
Merville
Lys
Lille
Tournai
XXXX
XXXX
5
BIRDWOOD
Neuve-Chapelle
Béthune
Festubert
XXXX
6
QUAST
Lens
St Amand
Mons
Namur
Vimy
Meuse
XXXX
Douai
Scarpe
Valenciennes
Binche
Charleroi
Aubigny
XXXX
1
HORNE
Bouchain
XXXX
17
MUDRA
Le Quesnoy
Maubeuge
Beaumont
Dinant
Arras
XXXXX
BRITISH
EXPEDITIONARY FORCE
HAIG
Escaut
Solesne
Avesnes
Philippeville
Bourlon
Cambrai
XXXX
XXXX
3
BYNG
XXXX
XXXX
2
CARLOWITZ
Le Cateau
XXXXX
BOEHIN
Chimay
Givet
Bapaume
Mailly-
Maillet
Gouzeaucourt
Bohain
La Capelle
Hirson
Rocroi
Fumay
Albert
Combles
Le Catelet
Somme
Péronne
XXXX
4
RAWLINSON
Oise
Vervins
Mézières
Athies
XXXX
St Quentin
Sedan
Rosières
XXXX
18
HUTIER
Serre
Liart
Morevil
Nesle
Guise
Le Quesnoy
Ham
XXXX
1
DEBENEY
La Fère
Goudelancourt
XXXXX
CROWN PRINCE
Le Chesne
Roye
Montdidier
Chauny
Sissone
Rethel
Tricot
Noyon
Barisis
Laon
Aisne
Buzancy
St Just
Ribécourt
XXXX
FRANCE
Craonne
Vouziers
Compiègne
Rethondes
Grandpré
XXXX
10
MANGIN
Soissons
XXXX
1
EBERHARDT
XXXX
Monthois
XXXXX
FAYOLLE
Fismes
Reims
XXXX
3
EINEM
Villers-Cotterêts
Ourcq
Fère-en-
Tardenois
XXXX
5
BERTHELOT
Vesle
Vienne
XXXXX
MAISTRE
Suippes
XXXX
4
GOURAUD

Final Allied Advance
26 September –
11 November 1918

→ Allied advance
⋯ Allied front line 26 Sept.
Allied front line 17 Oct.
Allied front line 9 Nov.
Allied front line 10 Nov.
Allied front line 11 Nov.
⇢ German retreat
German armistice line
11 November

N

0   20 km
0   20 miles

Germany seeks terms

As the war of movement gathered pace in the final weeks of the conflict, so the political manoeuvres clicked into high gear. October began with the appointment of a new German chancellor, the liberal-minded, pro-reform Prince Max of Baden, who immediately sought an armistice along the lines of Woodrow Wilson's Fourteen Points. Ludendorff, now in a state of near total disintegration, had also concluded that this was the only viable option. In directing his appeal to the American president rather than the Entente governments, the chancellor hoped to obtain a less punitive peace settlement. Bypassing the politicians, Germany also made a direct appeal to the general populace in a leaflet drop. It spoke of evacuating Belgium and France, reaching an "honest understanding" over Alsace-Lorraine and a return to restricted submarine warfare. "Who is to blame," it ran, "if an armistice is not called now?" It was a desperate attempt to paint the new administration as the epitome of reasonableness, to condemn anyone refusing the olive branch.

America's stance hardens

Had the German offer been made at the beginning of the year, when the Fourteen Points were first laid down, Passchendaele still raw, Russia a spent force and transatlantic reinforcement a distant prospect, the Allied stance might have been different. Wilson's position had also shifted since his January declaration, from an Allied associate gearing up for battle to a fully-fledged belligerent with the casualty toll to prove it. During October a series of notes passed between Wilson and Berlin, in the middle of which Germany did its negotiating cause no favours as RMS *Leinster* became the latest U-boat casualty, torpedoed in the Irish Sea with the loss of 500 lives. Even before that event, the Allied stance was hardening. *Daily Mirror* cartoonist W K Haselden proffered the paper's editorial line – and widely held view of the chancellor's proposal – in his 8 October offering. It shows Germany, embodied in a pickelhaube-wearing soldier, attempting to gain entry into the house of peace. He beats fruitlessly on the door marked "Negotiation" before being directed to a side entrance: "Surrender". Pershing certainly favoured crushing the enemy completely and marching through the streets of Berlin. His reservations about anything less than an emphatic military victory were not without foundation, for there was indeed a strand of German thinking that maintained an armistice was the perfect means of acquiring breathing space; that any agreement could be rejected when the next cohort of German youth was battlefield-ready. Foch remained sanguine, confident that the terms dictated rendered armistice synonymous with surrender. Those stipulations included a refusal to negotiate with the military hierarchy that had been running the country. Constitutional reform was essential to forestall the possibility of a future leader wielding overweening power and threatening world peace. That meant the removal of the Kaiser, who had already noted the mounting unrest in Berlin and slipped away to Spa, putatively to be nearer the heart of battle. He was not about to give up the imperial throne quietly.

Bulgaria, Turkey and Austria surrender

The harshness of the Allies' demands reinvigorated Ludendorff, who was sabre-rattling once more in late October. It was he who fell on his sword, however, the very suggestion of renewing the fight the final misjudgment of a gifted strategist whose behaviour had become wildly erratic. Meanwhile, one by one Germany's allies gave up the struggle; Bulgaria before September was out, Turkey and Austria within days of each other as October turned into November. Then, on 3 November the German navy mutinied. The sailor ranks had been kicking their heels since the Battle of Jutland, and now, with all hope of victory gone, they were being called upon to put to sea in what was tantamount to a heroic sacrificial gesture. It was the tipping point. They tore down the fleet's imperial colours and sought proletarian fellowship with dock employees. Soviet-style workers councils sprang up. Revolution was in the air, and mob rule. It spread to all the major cities, including the Bavarian capital, Munich, from where King Ludwig III beat a rapid retreat as the centuries-old monarchy was swept away and replaced with a socialist republic. The Kaiser soon followed. Informed that he had lost all support, and with the country teetering on the brink of anarchy, the embittered Wilhelm II headed to neutral Holland and exile. The House of Hohenzollern was consigned to the history books, its last ruler having lost not only a war but the seat of a great empire.

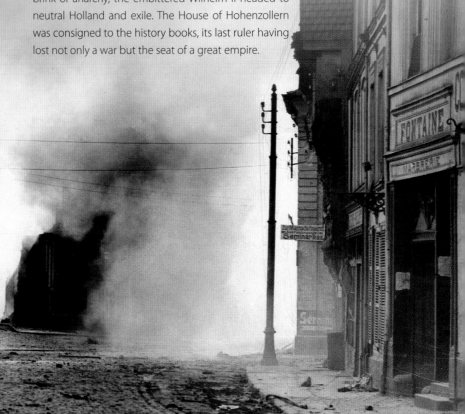

The streets were ablaze when Allied troops entered the town of Cambrai on 8 October. German soldiers had deliberately started a series of fires before evacuating and several buildings were reduced to burnt-out shells.

GERMANY ASKS AN ARMISTICE.

PEACE NOTE TO MR. WILSON

PROFESSED ACCEPTANCE OF HIS "POINTS."

M. CLEMENCEAU'S ANSWER.

NO PEACE WITH THE HOHENZOLLERNS.

"Who is to blame if an armistice is not called now?"

AIL, WEDNESDAY, OCTOBER 9, 1918.

PRESIDENT WILSON'S REPLY

BACK TO GERMANY FIRST.

TWO STRAIGHT QUESTIONS.

A TEST FOR THE HUNS.

WASHINGTON, Tuesday.

The following are the two documents given out by the Secretary of State to-day, the first the translation of the German Note, the second the reply from the Secretary of State.

The following is the Note from the German Chancellor transmitted through the Swiss Chargé d'Affaires:—

"The German Government requests the President of the United States of America to take steps for the restoration of peace, to notify all belligerents of this request, and to invite them to delegate plenipotentiaries for the purpose of taking measures to avoid further bloodshed.

"The German Government requests the President of the United States to bring about the immediate conclusion of a general armistice on land, on water, and in the air.

"MAX, Prince of Baden, Imperial Chancellor."

The following is the Note from the Secretary of State to the Swiss Chargé d'Affaires:—

The Department of State, October 8, 1918.

Sir: I have the honour to acknowledge, on behalf of the President, your Note of October 6, enclosing a communication from the German Government to the President; and I am instructed by the President to request you to make the following communication to the Imperial German Chancellor:—

Before making a reply to the request of the Imperial German Government, and in order that the reply shall be as candid and straightforward as the momentous interests involved require, the President of the United States deems it necessary to assure himself of the exact meaning of the Note of the Imperial Chancellor.

Does the Imperial Chancellor mean that the Imperial German Government accepts the terms laid down by the President in his address to the Congress of the United States on the 8th of January last and in subsequent addresses, and that its object in entering into discussions would be only to agree upon the practical details of their application?

The President feels bound to say with regard to the suggestion of an armistice that he would not feel at liberty to propose a cessation of arms to the Governments with which the Government of the United States is associated against the Central Powers so long as the armies of those Powers are upon their soil.

The good faith of any discussion would manifestly depend upon the consent of the Central Powers immediately to withdraw their forces everywhere from invaded territory.

The President also feels that he is justified in asking whether the Imperial Chancellor is speaking merely for the constituted authorities of the Empire who have so far conducted the war. He deems the answer to these questions vital from every point of view.

Accept, sir, the renewed assurances of my high consideration.

ROBERT LANSING.

It is officially announced that no answer to the Austrian peace proposals is contemplated for the present.—Reuter.

October 1918

1   T.E. Lawrence entered Damascus after it was occupied by British and Arab forces.

2   The Bombardment of Durazzo was fought in the Adriatic Sea when a large Allied fleet attacked the naval base at Durazzo on the Albanian coast. The fleet destroyed the Austro-Hungarian shore defences and several ships and submarines.

3   The Battle of the Beaurevoir Line began with simultaneous attacks by Australian troops on the third (Beaurevoir) line, the last defensive system of the Hindenburg Line.

Max von Baden was appointed to take office as the new German chancellor, after conflict within the German military and Government leadership caused his predecessor, Georg von Hertling, to resign.

4   German and Austro-Hungarian peace proposal was sent to US President Woodrow Wilson requesting an armistice based on his Fourteen Points.

5   Australians captured the village of Montbrehain and broke through the Hindenburg Line to conclude the Battle of the Beaurevoir Line.

6   The armed merchant cruiser HMS *Otranto* collided with fellow troopship, HMS *Kashmir*, in the rough seas off the west coast of Islay whilst ferrying American Marines to the Western Front.

8   President Woodrow Wilson replied to German and Austro-Hungarian notes and demanded the evacuation of occupied territories as a first condition of any armistice.

The Second battle of Cambrai began when Allied troops entered the city.

9   Prince Friedrich Karl of Hesse was elected as King of Finland; he later renounced the throne in December 1918.

10 The Irish mail boat SS *Leinster* was torpedoed and sunk by the German submarine *UB-123* in the Irish Sea while bound for Holyhead.

12 The German Government indicated that it would accept President Woodrow Wilson's conditions regarding the armistice.

The British Government recognised the Polish National Army as autonomous and allied.

13 French forces recaptured Laon and La Fère and continued their advance on the Western Front.

14 The Battle of Courtrai, also known as the Second Battle of Belgium or the Battle of Roulers, began. The assault was one of a series of offensives in northern France and southern Belgium.

President Wilson added military conditions for any armistice talks with Germany and stated he would deal only with a democratic government.

15 Allied forces made further progress in Flanders as they advanced towards Courtrai and captured Menin.

16 Charles I of Austria issued the Manifesto, promising a federal structure for the Austrian part of Austria-Hungary.

17 Hungary responded to the Manifesto and declared complete independence from the Habsburg Empire.

Allied forces liberated Lille, Douai and Ostend. As multiple offensives continued along the Western Front, British and American troops launched attacks at the Battle of the Selle.

19 Belgian forces recaptured Zeebrugge and Bruges in Flanders and went on to complete the capture of all of the Belgian coast.

20 Germany accepted President Wilson's conditions for armistice talks.

23 President Wilson replied to Germany and agreed to submit the matter to the Allied Governments.

24 Italian forces with some British, French, American and Czech contingents attacked the Austro-Hungarians along the River Piave at the Battle of Vittorio Veneto.

25 The Battle of the Selle ended when German troops were repulsed and pushed back by the Belgian Army.

26 British forces captured Aleppo in Syria.

27 The Austrian Government asked Italy for an armistice and submitted a Note to President Wilson asking for an immediate armistice without awaiting the result of other negotiations.

29 German sailors aboard the High Seas Fleet mutinied at Wilhelmshaven in the North Sea when they refused to weigh anchor or engage the British Fleet.

30 The Armistice of Mudros was signed and ended the hostilities between the Ottoman Empire and the Allies. It was signed on board HMS *Agamemnon* in Mudros harbour on the Greek island of Lemnos.

31 Hostilities between the Allied Powers and Turkey ceased at noon.

CAPTURE OF OSTEND
ADMIRAL KEYES LANDS.
BRITISH TAKE LILLE.
CITY LEFT UNDEVASTATED.
DOUAI ENTERED.

DAILY MAIL   OCTOBER 18, 1918

Capture of Ostend

Yesterday was the Allies' greatest day

The British landed at and took Ostend, captured Lille, entered Douai, and reached the outskirts of Tourcoing. The Belgians are on the edge of Bruges and the French are at Thielt, 16 miles only from Ghent.

British, Americans, and French between Le Cateau and the Oise advanced 2 miles towards the Hun line of retreat from the south and took 3,000 prisoners.

Lille's ecstasy

The Germans left Lille at 4 o'clock this morning. Our airmen saw people in the streets waving flags, and an hour after it was reported that our patrols were in the streets. The first people to enter were received with such ecstasy that it was impossible to move and escape without the help of the civic authorities. Cars were laden with flowers and gigantic bouquets; women and children crushed forward to embrace the English who entered, and cheers for England resounded down all the streets.

The German retreat is apparently general along the coast, but the enemy is holding hard for the moment in Courtrai and north of it, where our troops are fighting hard.

AUSTRIA OUT OF THE WAR.

ARMISTICE SIGNED.

ITALIANS LAND AT TRIESTE.

NEW GERMAN FRONT OPEN TO ALLIES.

BERLIN WITHIN EIGHTY MINUTES BY AIR.

10, Downing-street, Whitehall, Sunday, 6.10 p.m.

A telephone message has been received from the Prime Minister in Paris to say that the news has just come in that AUSTRIA-HUNGARY, the last of Germany's props, has gone out of the war.

An armistice was signed by General Diaz this afternoon and is to come into operation to-morrow at 3 o'clock.

The terms of the armistice will be published on Tuesday.

AUSTRIAN OFFICIAL REPORT.

VIENNA, Sunday.

In the Italian theatre of war our troops have ceased hostilities on the basis of an armistice which has been concluded. The publication of the conditions will be issued separately.—CHIEF OF THE GENERAL STAFF. —Admiralty, per Wireless Press.

Renter's Agency was informed last night that the terms arranged with the Austrian Commander-in-Chief virtually amount to unconditional surrender.

TURKEY SURRENDERS.

FLEET TO SAIL TO CONSTANTINOPLE

REVOLUTION IN VIENNA AND BUDAPEST.

AUSTRIA'S WHITE FLAG.

GERMANY FIGHTING ALONE.

Turkey has surrendered. An Allied fleet is to proceed to Constantinople and the Black Sea.

On the day that the armistice was signed, Wednesday, our Army captured the last 7,000 Turks in Mesopotamia and are marching to Mosul.

Austria has sent a white flag party to General Diaz to negotiate an armistice. The Italians, meanwhile, are advancing at a great pace, and have scooped up 50,000 prisoners and 300 guns. The whole line is now bending.

Revolutions have begun in Vienna and Budapest. The soldiers have seized control and are shouting, "Down with the Hapsburgs."

The Czecho-Slovaks have occupied railways on the enemy's line of retreat, and have cut the lines from Berlin to Vienna and Budapest.

British, French, and Americans attacked yesterday on the Scheldt front and gained their objectives. Our men took 1,000 prisoners.

BULGARIA SURRENDERS.

ALLIES TO ENTER.

OUR DANUBE FRONT.

CAPTURE OF USKUB.

HERTLING RESIGNS: KAISER'S SOP TO PEOPLE.

GREAT FLANDERS SUCCESS.

Bulgaria has surrendered unconditionally. Her forces laid down their arms at noon yesterday, after the French had taken Uskub.

By an armistice signed at the same hour—a purely military convention—her army demobilises, the Allies take control of her railways and Danube front and transport, and may, if they think fit, prosecute the war against the Austrians on the one hand and Turkey on the other.

This creates a Danube front for the Allies, with enormous possibilities. If Austria is compelled to face a new danger on the east she may have to weaken her Italian front or withdraw her aid to the Germans in the west.

There is no definite news of Turkey.

The Kaiser has accepted Count Hertling's resignation in a letter professing that he (the Kaiser) desires that the people shall co-operate more in governing Germany.

Features of the war news are a big advance towards Roubaix and Tourcoing, in Flanders; fighting close round and even in Cambrai, a deeper penetration of the Siegfried line north of St. Quentin, a hurried Hun retreat over the Chemin-des-Dames, and, amid fierce resistance, important French gains in Champagne. In the Argonne the Americans have held their positions against heavy attacks.

THE BALKAN STATES

Opposite top: Once the Allies entered Ostend they discovered abandoned gun positions and concrete dugouts all along the sea front. In some the Germans had left messages such as "My compliments to you!"

Opposite middle: A sailor surrounded by children in Ostend studies the column of barbed wire defences running the length of the promenade.

Opposite below: Flags fly high above the town as the citizens of Ostend celebrate their release from German invaders.

Top: Allied troops advance towards Cambrai.

Middle: Total devastation greeted the Canadian troops who were the first to enter Cambrai.

Above: British troops and Belgian firemen work together to quell the flames in Tournai.

Above left: Allied troops scale the banks of the St Quentin canal.

Top right: Excited children in Lille welcome Allied soldiers after General Sir William Birdwood and his men liberated the town. German troops destroyed over 2,200 buildings and occupied the town during the war.

Middle right: American machine gunners advance up a hill in the Saint Mihiel Salient.

Bottom far right: A view of Cambrai taken from a German aeroplane.

Right: General Pershing (left) decorates Brigadier General Douglas MacArthur with the Distinguished Service Cross. MacArthur went on to play a prominent part in World War II as commander of US forces in the Pacific.

Below: Men from the Machine Gun Corps make a dash for their outposts.

Opposite top: British infantry advance under the shelter of a canal bank in the Cambrai area.

GERMAN ARMISTICE DELEGATES.

REPORTED EN ROUTE TO THE FRONT.

MR. WILSON'S NOTE.

FULL COMPENSATION FOR ALL.

The German armistice delegates, according to a Reuter telegram, so far not confirmed officially, left Berlin yesterday afternoon for the western front. They are Gen. von Grüdell, Gen. von Winterfeld, former Military Attaché in Paris; Admiral von Hintze, former Foreign Minister; and Councillor Meurer, a legal official of the Admiralty.

It they want to know the Allies' armistice terms they have got to send a white flag party to Foch.

President Wilson's reply to the last German Note asking for the Allied armistice terms has been received in Berlin. It contains the Allies' observations, which state that they accept Mr. Wilson's 14 points with two modifications:

1. The Allies reserve complete freedom on the question of freedom of the seas.
2. They will require Germany to make compensation "for all damage done to the civilian population of the Allies and to their property by the aggression of Germany by land, by sea, and from the air."

This necessarily includes replacement of all property damaged in the field and of shipping and cargoes destroyed by the U-boats.

MR. WILSON'S REPLY.

Mr. Lansing's reply on Mr. Wilson's behalf to Germany states:

WASHINGTON, Tuesday.

The President is now in receipt of a memorandum of observations by the Allied Governments, as follows:

"The Allied Governments have given careful consideration to the correspondence which has passed between the President of the United States and the German Government. Subject to the qualifications which follow, they declare their willingness to make peace with the Government of Germany on the terms of peace laid down in the President's address to Congress of January 8, 1918 [the 14 points speech], and the principles of settlement enunciated in his subsequent addresses.

FREEDOM OF THE SEAS.

"They must point out, however, that Clause 2, relating to what is usually described as the Freedom of the Seas, is open to various interpretations, some of which they could not accept. They must, therefore, reserve to themselves complete freedom on this subject when they enter the Peace Conference.

COMPENSATION FOR ALL.

"Further, in the conditions of peace laid down in his Address to Congress of January

Left: US troops enjoy a cheerful hour in a captured German canteen. The invaders did not have time to remove their lager beer so the American troops took full advantage.

Above: Canadian troops on the streets of Cambrai.

Below: Cheers of victory from Allied troops in the St Quentin area.

Over 2,500 deaths were recorded between the time that pen was put to paper and the appointed hour for the end of hostilities.

November 1918

1   The Battle of Valenciennes was launched by the British Army to advance to the French-Belgian border and the city of Valenciennes. The offensive lasted two days and resulted in the recapture of the city.

2   British cargo ships SS *Surada* and SS *Murcia* were both sunk by the German submarine *UC-74* near Port Said.

3   The Allied Governments agreed to German proposals for an armistice based on President Wilson's fourteen point program of 8 January 1918.

Austria-Hungary signed an armistice with the Allies.

4   The Battle of the Sambre began, and continued the advance by British and French troops in the direction of Valenciennes. The offensive included the Second Battle of Guise.

25-year-old English poet Wilfred Owen was killed in action during the crossing of the Sambre-Oise Canal in France.

6   American forces captured the city of Sedan in France.

7   The monarchy under King Ludwig III of Bavaria was abolished in favour of a republic. Socialist politician Kurt Eisner was proclaimed as head of the Bavarian Government.

8   At Compiègne in France, representatives of the German Government were presented with armistice terms by Marshal Ferdinand Foch. The terms included German evacuation of all occupied territory, an Allied occupation of Germany west of the Rhine River, surrender of weaponry including all submarines and battleships, and indefinite continuation of the naval blockade.

9   The Kaiser's Imperial Government collapsed as a German republic was proclaimed with Friedrich Ebert heading the new provisional government. Kaiser Wilhelm II abdicated and was advised to leave the country amid concerns for his safety after his generals warned him they might not be able to protect him from the volatile situation in Germany.

10 Kaiser Wilhelm II, now private citizen Wilhelm Hohenzollern, crossed the border by train and went into exile in the Netherlands which had remained neutral throughout the war.

11 At 5:00 am, in a railway car at Compiègne the Germans signed the Armistice which became effective at 11 am – the eleventh hour of the eleventh day of the eleventh month. Fighting continued all along the Western Front until precisely 11 o'clock.

12 The reign of Emperor Charles I of Austria ended following his Proclamation of 11 November acknowledging the decision taken by German- Austria to form a separate State.

13 The Occupation of Constantinople began when British, French and Italian troops started to occupy the capital city of the Ottoman Empire following the Armistice of Mudros.

14 Tomás Garrigue Masaryk was elected President of the Czechoslovak republic by the National Assembly in Prague.

15 SMS *Königsberg* arrived in Scapa Flow carrying Rear Admiral Hugo Meurer for a meeting with Admiral David Beatty, the commander of the Grand Fleet, to negotiate the place of internment of the German fleet.

16 The Polish President Józef Piłsudski declared Poland an Independent and Sovereign State.

18 The Republic of Latvia was proclaimed an independent state in the Second Riga Theatre and the Democratic Republic of Latvia was established.

20 The first contingent of German submarines surrendered to the Royal Navy at Harwich. Over 100 U-boats would be surrendered during the following months.

21 At the Capitulation of Rosyth, the German High Seas Fleet surrendered to British authorities for internment at Scapa Flow.

23 The Yugoslav National council voted for the formation of a common state to include Serbia and Montenegro.

24 The Yugoslav National Council expressed its concern regarding Italian regional territorial claims on South Slavic territory in the former Austro-Hungarian Empire.

25 German forces commanded by General von Lettow-Vorbeck surrendered to the British at Abercorn in German East Africa.

26 Entente squadrons arrived at Odessa and Sevastopol and took over the remainder of the Russian Black Sea Fleet from the Germans.

27 King George V visited Paris where he received an enthusiastic reception.

28 Kaiser Wilhelm II officially signed the Abdication Proclamation renouncing his claims to the throne of Prussia and to the German Imperial throne.

30 Kaiser Wilhelm II's Abdication Proclamation was formally published in Berlin.

Above and opposite: **Canadian troops patrol Cambrai.**

Below: **A lone soldier advances cautiously in Peronne Square shortly after the German army's withdrawal.**

German monarchy collapses

On 8 November, Germany's peace delegation met with Foch in a railway carriage in the forest at Compiègne, north of Paris. The Allied demands were every bit as draconian as the delegation's leader, Matthias Erzberger, feared. The territorial losses and financial reparations alone were daggers to national pride and future prosperity, and the list did not end there. Erzberger's pleas for the blockade to be lifted and for the wherewithal to quash the insurgency fell on deaf ears. It was a take-it-or-leave-it deal. There would be no ceasefire – another Erzberger request – until it was signed, and if Germany did not agree within 72 hours, the war would take its course. During those three days the crises at the front and on home soil would persist. Erzberger did not have the authority to sign the armistice, and as he made arrangements to take soundings from Berlin – now in the grip of a general strike – Germany proclaimed itself a republic. There was great rejoicing by red flag-waving hordes, who greeted the formal end of monarchy with the kind of wild abandon that might have been reserved for news of outright military victory. Prince Max ceded the chancellorship to Social Democratic Party leader Friedrich Ebert, but the streets were full of people demanding a Russian-style antidote to the failures of imperialism. On 9 November the forces of Bolshevism were not merely at the door of the Reichstag but in the chamber itself, threatening to topple the new Social Democrat administration before it conducted its first business. The collapse of the monarchy had created a vacuum, with no certainty as to what new authority would fill the void.

The guns fall silent

Two days later, the guns fell silent. The Armistice was signed shortly after 5.00 am, to take effect at 11 o'clock that morning. In some parts of the line the rival forces marked time, in others the fighting went to the deadline and even beyond. Communication was one factor: word simply hadn't got through. But some stuck rigidly to the schedule; attacks planned for the morning of the 11th went ahead with all the zeal of military timetabling. Over 2,500 deaths were recorded between the time that pen was put to paper and the appointed hour for the end of hostilities. Canadian infantryman Private George Price is believed to be the last soldier of the British army to be killed in action. He was fatally wounded shortly before the ceasefire as Canadian troops advanced on Mons. The scene of the war's first great battle was the resting place for one of its final victims. Not the last, though. Twenty-three-year-old Henry Gunther was killed at 10.59 as he attacked a machine-gun post in a Lorraine village, the last American soldier to die on the battleground. Those he bore down upon shouted and gestured at him to stop before opening fire. Gunther, it transpired, had been demoted and was determined to regain his stripes before the war was over. His sergeant's rank was restored posthumously.

FOCH STATES THE TERMS.

YES OR NO BY 11 a.m. MONDAY.

LONDON: MONDAY, NOVEMBER, 11, 1918.

GERMANY SURRENDERS.

The Prime Minister made the following announcement to-day:—

The Armistice was signed at Five o'clock this morning, and hostilities are to cease on all Fronts at 11 a.m. to-day.

Left and right: Marshal Foch, Admiral Sir Rosslyn Wemyss, the First Sea Lord and British representative, and General Weygand, a French military commander, leave Foch's railway carriage in the forest of Compiègne, 40 miles north east of Paris.

Middle: Cinematographing the last shot fired before the Armistice on 11 November 1918.

HUNS CRYING OVER THE TERMS.

"LIKE THOSE OF ROME TO CARTHAGE."

HUN SOLDIERS MURDER OFFICERS IN BRUSSELS.

SPANISH MINISTER CALLS FOR KING ALBERT.

PRINCE RUPPRECHT SEEKS NEUTRAL SANCTUARY.

A COHERENT statement as to what is happening in Germany and Austro-Hungary can hardly be formed from the stream of reports pouring into London to-day from many sources, some reliable

The Prussian Diet.

THE LIGHTS O' LONDON RETURNING.

Some Districts "All Clear" by Week End.

Now that restrictions are removed, the people of London are calling insistently for more light.

A tour to-day of the City and various parts of the West End was made to-day by an *Evening News* representative to see if there was justification for the assertion that the local authorities were not taking sufficiently active measures.

The evidence went to show that before long there would be a return to pre-war conditions. The end of the week should see all clear.

In the City of London the acting City engineer, Mr. W. H. Noble, stated that very considerable progress had been made with the work, and it would be completed at an early date.

The gas and electric lighting companies are co-operating in the removal of the screening material.

In Holborn men were hard at work, two at a time, on tall movable scaffoldings, with solution and scrapers, getting off the darkening paint.

One of them stated that the job was a slow one, for the paint had become case-hardened, and it took him all he knew to clean off a big lamp in a couple of hours.

MAIN STREETS FIRST.

At the Holborn Borough Council offices

THE GENERAL ELECTION—

Second Week of December.

COALITION MASS MEETING AT ALBERT HALL.

Everything is ready for the general election, which will probably take place in the second week of December.

Complete agreement as to the Coalition programme to be put before the country has been reached, and it will be stated by the Prime Minister at a mass meeting to be held at the Albert Hall. He will be supported by Mr. Bonar Law, Mr. George Barnes, and other prominent Coalition leaders.

In many respects Mr. Lloyd George's speech will be the greatest one he has ever delivered. He will not only outline the terms which the Allied nations will demand at the Peace Conference and the reconstruction measure which are to be adopted in this country, but he will show that many of his old political views have been transformed under the influence of the terrific events of the last four years.

ASQUITH TO-NIGHT.

In the new House of Commons the Opposition will be formed by the Asquithians,

THE END OF THE WAR.

Top left: French, British and American troops lead a group of revellers in Paris.

Top middle: Crowds in Trafalgar Square celebrate the end of the conflict.

Top right: American naval and military men cheer as they ride through the streets.

Upper middle left and upper middle: The Canadian Field Artillery enters the main square in Mons on 11 November. Troops vowed to enter the town before the war officially ended.

Above: The first military bridge is opened on 23 November, crossing the Scheldt at Tournai.

Lower middle left: At last the Italian flag flies from the cathedral of San Giusto in Trieste Harbour. The town had come under Habsburg rule in 1382 and Italian leaders were determined to take the city away from Austro-Hungarian rule and return it to Italy.

Lower middle: Under the terms of the armistice concluded with Turkey (on 30 October 1918), the Dardanelles and the Bosporus were opened to Allied warships and the vanquished nation's forts subject to military occupation.

Bottom left: The band of a Highland Regiment pipes its way through the village they have just captured.

DAILY MAIL NOVEMBER 11, 1918

Kaiser in flight

The Kaiser has abdicated and fled to Holland with the Crown Prince, and apparently also Hindenburg and the General Staff. If they went in uniform they must be interned.

He signed the abdication following a revolution in Berlin, where the Social Democrats under Ebert have hoisted the red flag on the palace and are forming a Government. Most of the army seems to have gone over to the 'Red' workers.

The courier with the armistice terms from Foch arrived at Spa, the German headquarters, only yesterday morning. Further emissaries have arrived there from Berlin and have wirelessed to the envoys at French headquarters that 'a delay of some hours' is probable. It is not clear who will sign.

Our cavalry are racing along the Brussels road. The infantry are outside Mons. Maubeuge they took on Saturday, and east of it they have captured many trains, as, farther south, have the French, who are well beyond Hirson and Mezières. France is nearly freed.

1,561st day of the war

Three weeks ago the Kaiser, aged 59 and a monarch for 30 years, called on his people to rally round him. Shortly after, he left German soil for his headquarters at Spa, in Belgium, 20 miles south of the Dutch frontier. He has not since set foot on German territory so far as is known.

Following the revolt in the Fleet and Army at home and the Republic in Bavaria, soldiers' and workmen's councils were formed in the chief cities and in many of the smaller German States.

Finally, revolution broke out in Berlin on Friday. By Saturday authority there was in the hands of the Socialists. Most of the garrison, including Guardsmen and a number of Guards and other officers, joined the revolutionaries. There was little fighting except at the cockchafers (or cadets') barracks, where some firing took place.

A large crowd proceeded to the Reichstag, where Friedrich Ebert announced that he had been charged by Prince Max of Baden to take over the Chancellorship. He is a harness maker of Heidelberg, one of the group of Socialists who supported the war so long as it was successful.

He is introducing general suffrage for men and women, who are to elect a Constituent Assembly. This will decide the form of the future Government and the position in it of the former German States. He has appealed for unity and the preservation of the food machinery. Associated with him is Scheidemann, another German Socialist leader, hitherto generally subservient to the Government. The banks have closed temporarily, to prevent a run.

It must be remembered that most of the information now available comes from the Socialists, who control the wires and the wireless.

Armistice envoys

Meantime, on Friday morning the German envoys reached Marshal Foch's headquarters and sent back a courier with the Allies' terms to German Army, which was exploding its dumps near the road he had to follow. He got to Spa only at 10.15 a.m. yesterday. More emissaries were sent thither from Berlin, and new delays seem likely.

Whose signature is valid if the armistice terms are accepted is not clear. Herr Ebert has announced that, so far as the Army is concerned, all orders must be countersigned by himself or a representative. The enemy is given till 11 this morning to say 'yes' or 'no.'

The Kaiser clung to his position almost to the last and clearly refused to abdicate till news of the revolution in Berlin arrived. Then, 'shivering and trembling,' he gave way. The Crown Prince renounced the succession, and together the two fled, accompanied, it is reported from Holland, by Hindenburg and all the staff. They did not wait to learn Foch's terms. They passed over the very ground in Belgium first violated by German troops late on August 3, 1914.

The Kaiser was in uniform and the staff was armed. Under international law they should be interned by the Dutch Government.

HOW THE KAISER ESCAPED.

RUSH INTO HOLLAND BY MOTOR CAR.

SHOTS FIRED AT HIS TRAIN.

ACCORDING to an Eysden message, shots were fired at the ex-Kaiser's train, and the Imperial fugitive thereupon made his escape across the Dutch frontier by motor-car. He is reported to have arrived at Middachten Castle.

The King of Wurtemberg has abdicated and left "for an unknown destination," and the King of Saxony and the Grand Duke of Oldenburg have been dethroned.

Everywhere throughout Germany the revolutionaries are apparently in full control. Sharp fighting is said to have taken place in Berlin, and at Kiel the revolutionaries have been joined by the battleships Posen, Ostfriesland, Nassau, and Oldenburg.

GERMAN ARMADA OURS.

SURRENDER INTACT TO THE ROYAL NAVY.

HISTORIC SCENE IN THE FORTH.

ADMIRAL BEATTY'S SIGNAL.

"THE GERMAN FLAG WILL BE HAULED DOWN AT SUNSET."

Years ago the ex-Kaiser said: "Our future lies upon the water." He built a fleet second in power only to our own. Yesterday all the latest ships of that fleet, intact, were shepherded in surrender into the Firth of Forth by the Royal Navy. When it had anchored, Admiral Sir David Beatty signalled:

The German flag is to be hauled down at sunset and will not be hoisted again without permission.

In the evening the whole British Fleet, and the American and French ships with it, offered thanks to God for the victory of Justice.

Top: Crown Prince Wilhelm (holding a stick) is pictured among his group of supporters. He abdicated on 9 November and went into exile where he was interned on the island of Wieringen in the Netherlands for five years. He was later allowed to return to Germany as long as he agreed to stay out of politics.

Above left: The ceasefire has been announced and these weapons near Mons are abandoned.

Above right: Crowds celebrate in London. The Armistice was signed at 5.10 am but it was agreed the ceasefire would begin at 11.00 am to allow the news to travel across the Western Front. Due to increasing technology people at home knew by 5.40 am but soldiers on the frontline carried on fighting, unaware of what had happened.

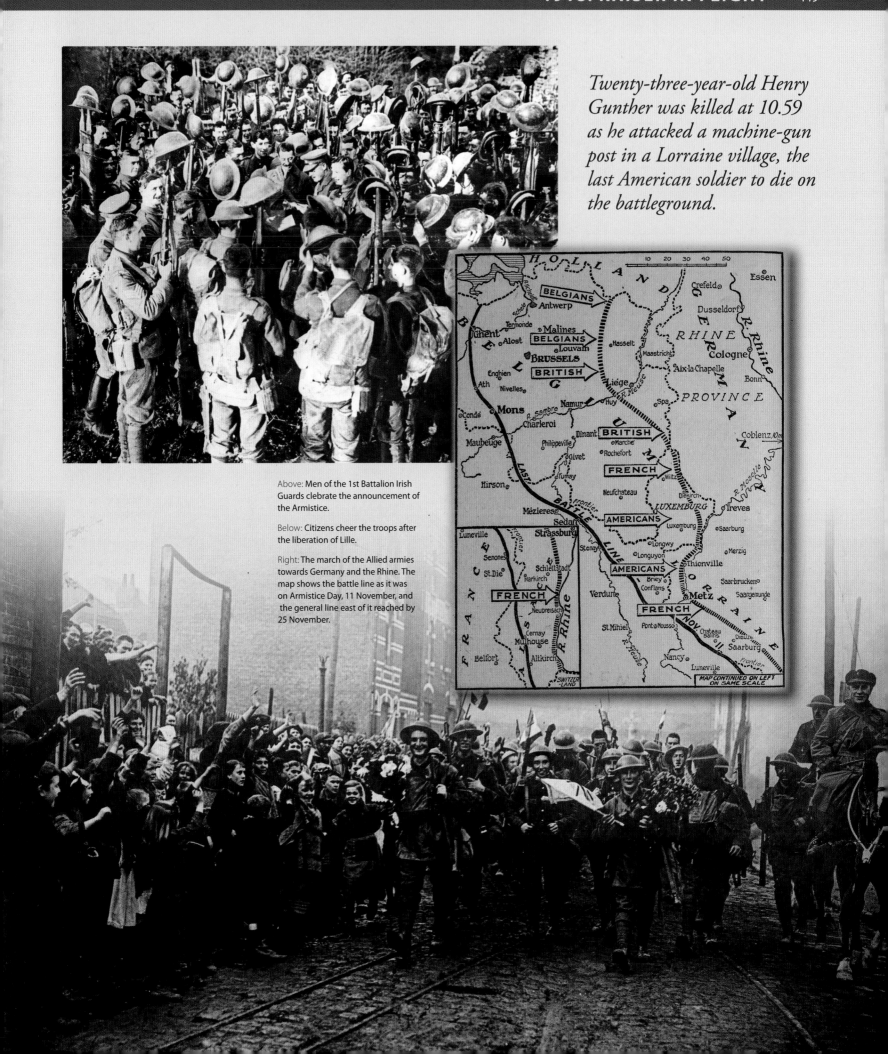

Twenty-three-year-old Henry Gunther was killed at 10.59 as he attacked a machine-gun post in a Lorraine village, the last American soldier to die on the battleground.

Above: Men of the 1st Battalion Irish Guards clebrate the announcement of the Armistice.

Below: Citizens cheer the troops after the liberation of Lille.

Right: The march of the Allied armies towards Germany and the Rhine. The map shows the battle line as it was on Armistice Day, 11 November, and the general line east of it reached by 25 November.

The Aftermath

December 1918
The Kingdom of the Serbs, Croats and Slovenes was established. The new kingdom included the previously independent kingdoms of Serbia and Montenegro and the South Slav territories in areas formerly subject to the Austro-Hungarian Empire.

January 1919
The Paris Peace Conference was convened at Versailles just outside Paris. The purpose of the meeting was to establish the terms of the peace after the War. Nearly thirty nations participated but the representatives of Great Britain, France, the United States and Italy were known as the "Big Four."

The Paris Peace Conference approved the proposal to create the League of Nations on 25 January.

February 1919
The German National Assembly met in Weimar to draw up a new constitution. The new President Friedrich Ebert addressed the opening session on 7 February.

April 1919
The Italian Prime Minister and head of the Italian delegation Vittorio Emanuele Orlando walked out of the Peace Conference after disagreements with US President Woodrow Wilson.

21 June 1919
The German High Seas Fleet was scuttled in Scapa Flow on the orders of German Admiral Ludwig von Reuter.

28 June 1919
The Treaty of Versailles was signed exactly five years after the assassination of Archduke Franz Ferdinand. The treaty formally ended the war between the Allied Powers and Germany. The final conditions were determined by the leaders of the "Big Three" nations, British Prime Minister David Lloyd George, French Prime Minister Georges Clemenceau and American President Woodrow Wilson, although Italian Prime Minister Vittorio Orlando returned to sign the treaty.

July 1919
The Cenotaph was unveiled ready for the London Victory Parade on 19 July. Designed by Sir Edwin Lutyens, the original Cenotaph was a temporary structure made from wood and plaster.

August 1919
German President Friedrich Ebert signed the new constitution for the Weimar Republic. The government was to consist of two houses of Parliament (the Reichstag) and a president elected by the people.

September 1919
The Treaty of St Germain was signed between the Allied Powers and Austria at Saint-Germain-en-Laye, near Paris on 10 September. The treaty formally dissolved the Austro-Hungarian Empire and recognised the independence of Hungary, Poland, Yugoslavia and Czechoslovakia.

November 1919
A banquet in honour of the President of the French Republic was hosted by King George V at Buckingham Palace on the evening of 10 November. The first Armistice Day service was held in the grounds of Buckingham Palace on the morning of 11 November.

January 1920
The League of Nations formally came into existence on 10 January. The first council meeting was held six days later on 16 January.

March 1920
The United States Senate failed to ratify the Treaty of Versailles and American involvement in the League of Nations.

April 1920
The League of Nations held a conference at San Remo in Italy to discuss the British mandate over Mesopotamia and Palestine. The international meeting was attended by four of the principal Allied Powers who were represented by the prime ministers of Britain, France and Italy and by Japan's Ambassador K Matsui.

June 1920
The Treaty of Trianon regulated the status of an independent Hungarian state and defined its borders. It was signed on 4 June at the Trianon Palace at Versailles between the Allies and the Kingdom of Hungary.

July 1920
The youngest son of former Kaiser Wilhelm II, Prince Joachim committed suicide by gunshot in Potsdam outside Berlin.

August 1920
The Treaty of Sèvres was a pact signed between the Allies and representatives of the Ottoman Empire on 10 August. The treaty abolished the Ottoman Empire and obliged Turkey to renounce all rights over Arab Asia and North Africa. The treaty was not recognized by the Turkish national movement.

November 1920
Sir Edwin Lutyens' Cenotaph design was built in Portland Stone from December 1919 and was finished in time for a parade to pass by it on 11 November 1920 to mark the interment of the British Unknown Warrior at Westminster Abbey. The United Kingdom and France simultaneously conducted services on Armistice Day 1920 . In Britain, the Tomb of the Unknown Warrior was created at Westminster Abbey, while in France La tombe du Soldat Inconnu was placed in the Arc de Triomphe.

November 1920
The Treaty of Rapallo (1920) was signed on 12 November between Italy and the Kingdom of the Serbs, Croats and Slovenes. Under the terms of the treaty Italy waived its claims to Dalmatia but annexed the port of Zadar and established the Free State of Fiume.

Republican politician Warren Gamaliel Harding was elected the 29th President of the United States.

December 1920
Outgoing President Woodrow Wilson received the 1919 Nobel Peace Prize in recognition of his Fourteen Points peace program and his work in achieving inclusion of the Covenant of the League of Nations in the 1919 Treaty of Versailles. The ailing President was not present at the ceremony, but sent a message which was read by Albert G. Schmedeman, the Minister to Norway, who accepted the prize on his behalf.

May 1921
Germany finally agreed to pay the war reparations demanded by the Allies in the Treaty of Versailles.

July 1921
British Prime Minister David Lloyd George and French Premier Aristide Briand endorsed President Harding's plan for a disarmament conference.

October 13 1921
The Treaty of Kars was concluded between Bolshevik Russia and Turkey to establish contemporary borders between Turkey and the South Caucasus states.

February 1922
The Washington Naval Treaty was negotiated between November 1921 and February 1922. The pact was signed by France, Italy, Japan, the United Kingdom and the United States in order to prevent an arms race by limiting naval construction.

April–May 1922
The Genoa Conference was held in Italy in 1922 from 10 April to 19 May. Representatives of 34 countries had gathered to discuss global economic problems in the wake of the Great War.

April 1922
The Treaty of Rapallo was signed between Germany and Bolshevik Russia. Negotiated by Germany's Walther Rathenau and Russia's Georgy Chicherin, the treaty re-established normal relations between the two nations and allowed for economic collaboration.

September 1922
The Treaty of Kars, which had been signed in October 1921, was ratified in Yerevan, Armenia on 11 September.

October 1922
Following the March on Rome when the National Fascist Party came to power, Benito Mussolini was sworn in as Prime Minister of Italy at the age of 39.

January 1923
After Germany fell behind on its war reparation payments, French and Belgian troops occupied the Ruhr industrial region inside Germany. German workers responded with strikes, sabotage and street demonstrations.

July 1923
The Treaty of Lausanne officially ended the state of war that had existed between Turkey on one side and Britain, France, Italy, Japan, Greece, Romania, and the Kingdom of Serbs, Croats and Slovenes on the other. The treaty was signed at Lausanne, Switzerland on 24 July and superseded the failed Treaty of Sèvres.

August 1923
US President Warren G Harding died suddenly in San Francisco on 2 August. He was succeeded by Vice President Calvin Coolidge who was sworn in whilst on holiday in Vermont.

Chapter Six

Germany's Postwar Turmoil

The Paris Peace Conference that formalised the end of war, where armistice terms were fleshed out and enshrined in treaty, began in January 1919. Even as Germany waited to see how high the settlement bill would be, the forces of left and right began to vie for the vanquished nation's soul. The country was ravaged, and domestic crisis had a polarising effect on the political scene. There was radicalism on both wings, violent collision inevitable. Friedrich Ebert, the Social Democrat leader who had been handed the reins of power, made a pact of mutual support with Wilhelm Groener, Ludendorff's successor as army commander. The military would back the interim government in suppressing any attempt to overthrow the new republic, and the immediate priority was to clamp down hard on the Bolshevik activists.

The Communist bid for power was launched early in the new year, Karl Liebnecht and Rosa Luxemburg attempting to emulate the achievement of Russia's Bolshevik leaders following the fall of the Tsar. Their Spartacist rebellion spluttered to a halt in a matter of days, undone by a lack of popular support and armed intervention by Groener's loyalist troops, supported by the paramilitary Freikorps. Led by former army officers, this volunteer force was dedicated to the defence of the Fatherland, in particular from the threat of a Red revolution. The Spartacists' co-leaders were captured and murdered just as the national temperature was being taken at the ballot box. The general election of 19 January left Ebert at the head of a coalition government cobbled together from left and centre. The politicians decamped to Weimar – which gave the new republic its name – to thrash out a constitution. Moderation, not radicalism, was the message from the electorate. Even in Bavaria, which had been ahead of the national curve in declaring its socialist credentials, voters came out heavily against the extreme left. The Communists ignored the poll and declared Bavaria a Socialist Republic, sparking a bloody civil war in spring 1919, much of it played out on the streets of Munich. The national government prevailed, again with heavy Freikorps backing. Rebel leader Kurt Eisner suffered the same fate as Liebnecht and Luxemburg.

Quashing this anti-democratic, Bolshevik rump had far-reaching consequences. Eisner, along with most of the insurgent hierarchy, was Jewish, adding fuel to existing anti-Semitic prejudices among right-wingers. In some minds Bolshevism and Judaism became interchangeable. Adolf Hitler, who was in Munich at the time of the rebellion, was one who saw the spread of socialism as part of a wider Jewish conspiracy. Crushing the Bavarian uprising also helped promote the right-wing agenda. Those who acted as a bulwark against Communist infiltration gained a platform they had not previously enjoyed. In other words, the far right gained an important foothold simply by dint of being a counterweight to its polar opposite on the political map.

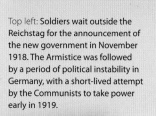

Top right: German pilots surrendered their planes to the Allies at the end of the war.

Upper middle right: The aerodrome at Beckendorf, near Cologne, was used by several of the Allies' squadrons in 1919.

Lower middle right: French troops march into Frankfurt for a brief period of occupation between 6 April and 17 May 1919.

Bottom right: French soldiers mount a machine gun on a cafe table in Frankfurt as a precaution against disorder in the town.

Above: British soldiers shop at a market in Bonn during their brief period of occupation of Germany after the war.

Below: Thousands of German helmets lie in a scrap merchant's yard in Wandsworth, London, ready for the smelting works.

Bottom left: A fully armed German sentry patrols the barbed wire barricade outside the station at Frankfurt in March 1920. In a minor uprising workers tried to enter the barracks but were fired upon, resulting in several casualties.

Top left: Soldiers wait outside the Reichstag for the announcement of the new government in November 1918. The Armistice was followed by a period of political instability in Germany, with a short-lived attempt by the Communists to take power early in 1919.

Upper middle left: Soldiers surrender their barracks to members of the Workmens' Soldiers Council. The banner says "Brothers, don't shoot".

Lower middle left: Armed revolutionary soldiers prepare for a "motor raid" through the streets of Berlin, December 1918.

Bottom left: Defeated German soldiers are marched through Belgium back to their own country.

The "November criminals"

Hitler was initially suspected of being party to the Bavarian plot. He persuaded the authorities of his vehement opposition to Eisner and his ilk by informing on those he knew to be sympathisers. The passion with which he articulated his contempt for the revolutionaries and what they stood for brought him a new job, lecturing soldiers on political theory. He had a ready-made audience to expound his views at a time when nationalist sentiment was stirred by the swingeing impositions of the Treaty of Versailles. Germany had not been defeated in the field, so the argument ran, and victory would have been attainable if only the Fatherland not been betrayed from within, stabbed in the back by supine politicians, left-wing agitators, striking workers, profiteers and Jews – the "November criminals". It was an attractive message to those struggling to come to terms with their country's military humbling and seething with resentment at the bitter pill the country had been forced to swallow at Versailles.

In September 1919, three months after the peace treaty had been ratified, Hitler joined the German Workers' Party, a group he had been asked to investigate on suspicion that it had seditious intent. In fact he found a band of like-minded individuals and quickly established himself as its most eloquent spokesman and effective propagandist. It was rebranded the National Socialist German Workers' Party – Nazi Party for short – on the way to becoming the most prominent right-wing group in Bavaria's political scene.

Political and economic crisis deepens

The turmoil went on. In March 1920 Wolfgang Kapp became the latest figure to try and topple a government reviled for its perceived collusion in a war-ending treaty that weighed heavily on the state. The man attempting to seize power was a co-founder of the nationalist Fatherland Party, formed in 1917 when the Reichstag's resolve was weakening and the mood was for a negotiated peace. The Freikorps-backed Kapp Putsch was serious enough for the government to flee Berlin, but evaporated in the face of a general strike, civil servants showing their unwillingness to co-operate with those staging the coup. Kapp left the country, one of the lucky ones in a period that witnessed over 300 political assassinations. The victims included the Compiègne delegation leader Matthias Erzberger. Even as he put pen to paper Erzberger had recognised that he was probably signing his death warrant, a sentence carried out by right-wing fanatics in August 1921. Far from clamping down on these murderous activities, the judiciary invariably treated those brought to book with leniency, revealing the judges' own sympathies.

The political and economic crisis deepened in 1922 over crippling reparations demands. Germany defaulted, which gave France, with armed support from Belgium, all the excuse it needed to extend its occupation of the Rhineland, beyond the demilitarised zone laid down in Paris. This was ground France had coveted, and been denied, in the division of spoils. To the French in particular, adherence to the Versailles agreement was a point of principle; any slackening would be the thin end the wedge, an invitation to Germany to ignore its other treaty obligations. Britain and America were more circumspect. Economist John Maynard Keynes, who had been a member of the British delegation in Paris, was among those who saw the folly of bleeding the country dry. Another member of the British delegation, Harold Nicolson, put it thus: "We arrived determined that a peace of justice and wisdom should be negotiated; we left conscious that the treaties imposed upon our enemies were neither just nor wise."

Right: The "Big Four" at Versailles. (seated l to r) Vittorio Orlando, Prime Minister of Italy; David LLoyd George, Prime Minister of Britain; Georges Clemenceau, Prime Minister of France, and Woodrow Wilson, President of the United States.

> *"We arrived determined that a peace of justice and wisdom should be negotiated; we left conscious that the treaties imposed upon our enemies were neither just nor wise."*

Hitler's bid for power

German resentment at the invasion was crystallised in a show of passive resistance. Industrial production in the Ruhr plummeted, while support for striking workers placed an even greater burden on the government. Plans were also made to undermine the occupying force by printing even more Reichsmarks, a policy the treasury had already adopted in the struggle to keep the country afloat. An economy already on its knees now fell prey to hyperinflation, where a wheelbarrow-load of cash might buy a few staples. The value of savings was wiped out. To Germany's woes was added a worthless currency. In September 1923 new chancellor Gustav Stresemann called a halt to the resistance movement and agreed to meet the reparations payments. A new currency, the Rentenmark, was temporarily introduced, a limited issue to deal with telephone-number banknotes not worth the paper they were printed on. The occupying force withdrew, though under the terms of the phased withdrawal from the demilitarised zone, troops remained in the Rhineland throughout the 1920s. The financial burden on Germany was also eventually eased under the 1924 Dawes Plan, belated recognition that Germany could tolerate only so much. By the time those revisions to the payment schedule were made Adolf Hitler had made his first bid for power.

With a cadre of his Brown Shirt supporters, Hitler descended on Munich's Bürgerbräukeller on 8 November 1923, interrupting a meeting calling for the restoration of the Bavarian monarchy. He had in mind a bolder revolutionary design. The next day, inspired by Mussolini's march on Rome a year earlier, he planned a similar assault on Berlin. The Beer Hall Putsch, as it came to be known, was peremptorily cut short by the Bavarian authorities. Hitler was arrested and handed a five-year jail term, heavily commuted. Months of incarceration gave him the opportunity to commit his doctrine of hatred to paper in *Mein Kampf*, in which he blamed Germany's ills on the Jews and set out his ideas for racial purity, Aryan supremacy and a 1,000-year Reich.

PEACE SIGNED.

VERSAILLES, Saturday.

The German Plenipotentiaries signed the Peace Treaty at 3.12 this afternoon.—Reuter.

LATES

ONLY 35
BREVITA

Treaty of Versailles

On 28 June 1919, six months of intense politicking came to an end in the Palace of Versailles' Hall of Mirrors, where the signing ceremony took place on the treaty meant to draw a line under the old enmities and usher in a brighter future. It was a brave hope. The very location had symbolical import, for it was here that the new German empire was proclaimed following the humbling of France in 1871. French prime minister Georges Clemenceau, who had vivid memories of that defeat at the hands of France's neighbour, revelled in the day of reckoning. Six months earlier he had embarked on the negotiating process with the aim of emasculating Germany and protecting his country from the kind of Prussian militarism that had taken place twice in the past half century. His was but one among many competing agendas that would lead to a compromise – some would say botched – peace deal that rang the curtain down on the Great War.

Delegates from over 30 countries descended on Paris in January, but three men would dominate proceedings: American president Woodrow Wilson, British prime minister David Lloyd George and Clemenceau. They had to contend with the collapse of four great European powers. As well as dealing with Germany, they had to wrestle with the fall-out from the fragmentation of the Austro-Hungarian and Ottoman empires. There was also post-tsarist Russia to consider, and the possibility of Bolshevism migrating westward. Even as they convened fighting continued in the east. The politicians thus faced a fluid situation where new states were already emerging. As they pored over maps and their pencils hovered, they did so in the knowledge that their decisions were bound to leave swathes of people on the wrong side of the divide, whose allegiance lay elsewhere. It was in many ways a poisoned chalice, a recipe for disaffection.

League of Nations

There was a balance to be struck between imposing punitive measures on the vanquished, while not exacting too heavy a price, one that might rebound upon the victors. Wilson certainly believed there should be scope for redemption. The establishment of a League of Nations was the most important aspect of the conference to the American president, central to his vision for a new world order that would break with the old ways in which nations settled their differences. Self-determination was a core tenet. Clemenceau, whose unyielding manner earned him the nickname "The Tiger", cast a jaundiced eye on this idealistic vision and the messianic zeal of its author. "God himself was content with 10 Commandments," he said, a contemptuous assessment of Wilson's 14-point blueprint for a better future. Lloyd George's chief concern was for a stable Europe, one that would never again require Britain to send men in such numbers to fight on Continental soil.

The return of Alsace Lorraine to France was a straightforward matter, but Clemenceau wanted to bolster his country's security and targeted the Rhineland as a buffer between the neighbouring states. Wilson vetoed occupation of German-populated territory and Clemenceau settled for a Rhineland demilitarised for 15 years. The Saar coalfields, also on Clemenceau's shopping list, were ceded to France, with sovereignty to be decided by plebiscite.

Carving up the world map

In the year of the Somme bloodbath France and Britain had carved up the Ottoman-ruled Middle East in the Sykes-Picot agreement. Britain was keen to stake a claim to Mesopotamia – the future Iraq – for its strategic value and its oil riches. Lloyd George got his wish, leaving Arab leader Prince Feisal sorely embittered. The latter's interpreter at the talks, T E Lawrence, wrote: "…when we achieved and the new world dawned, the old men came out again and took our victory to remake in the likeness of the former world they knew."

The horse-trading continued. Italian prime minister Vittorio Orlando walked out temporarily when Wilson blocked his attempts to appropriate part of the Adriatic. The Japanese delegation, thwarted in its attempt to secure a racial equality clause in the League's Covenant, also threatened to withdraw if their designs on Chinese Shantung – German territory they had fought for – were not met. This time Wilson relented.

Below: **President Wilson doffs his cap as he arrives at the Trianon Palace Hotel in Versailles.**

Top left: The assembled leaders of the newly formed League of Nations. The organisation began with 42 founder member states. During its lifetime another 21 countries joined the group, although others withdrew. The League was replaced by the United Nations in 1946.

Top right: The British Empire delegation met at the apartment where Lloyd George was staying in the Rue Nitot in Paris.

Above left: A bugler sounds the fall-in to a company stationed in an Austrian village in February, 1919.

Above middle: The German Foreign Minister and leader of the country's peace delegation, Count von Brockdorff-Rantzau, arrives at the Trianon Palace Hotel to learn the price of his country's defeat.

"…when we achieved and the new world dawned, the old men came out again and took our victory to remake in the likeness of the former world they knew."

Above: Georges Clemenceau leaves the hotel after the conclusion of the talks.

Below: Soldiers stand guard outside the Palace of Versailles as the Treaty is signed.

Bottom right: Delegates study their papers as they work out the terms of the Treaty.

Bottom left: Large crowds gather outside the Palace of Versailles waiting for news.

Top left: Georges Clemenceau (left), one of the main architects of the Versailles settlement, was intent on treating Germany harshly after the destruction inflicted on France.

Top middle: The War Council gathers on the steps of the Palace.

Top right: Woodrow Wilson meets King George V at Buckingham Palace during a visit to London.

Above left: The Peace Treaty is signed in the Hall of Mirrors at the Palace of Versailles.

Above right: Germany's representatives listen to Clemenceau's speech.

Middle left: The delegations from Canada and New Zealand arrive in Paris.

Middle right: General Pershing visits men from the US military who were building the Stade Pershing

in Vincennes, France, in June 1919. The multi-purpose sports stadium could hold nearly 30,000 spectators. That year it hosted the Inter-Allied Games and was then presented to France as a gift from the United States.

Below left: At Tilbury, the 2nd Battalion of the Grenadier Guards arrives home from the war. The troops were met by the massed bands of the Brigade of Guards.

Below right: British soldiers queue to register their votes in the General Election, held on 14 December 1918. Unsurprisingly, Lloyd George was returned to office, having led the country to victory. This was the first general election in which some women and all men over the age of 21 could vote.

Bottom: A crowded transport ship is on its way home from Egypt in May 1919.

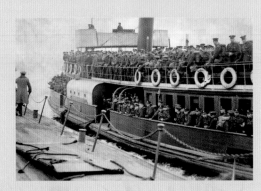

Germany's forfeit

Germany lost around one-eighth of its prewar territory – all of its overseas land was forfeit – and some 10 per cent of its population. There was particular resentment over the emergence of the new Poland, which was granted access to the sea along a corridor to Danzig. Germany's armed forces were reduced to skeleton strength. There was also the matter of a financial settlement. Reparations amounting to £1 billion had been handed over by the time payments were suspended in 1932. The economist John Maynard Keynes, who was a member of the British delegation, thought the financial penalty too severe, a view not shared by all historians. The German delegation that came to Paris in May was in defiant mood, the so-called "war guilt clause" further antagonising the representatives of the vanquished state. It needed a change of government in Berlin before the architects of the treaty learned that Germany would comply.

President Wilson's hopes for a new world order, embodied in his jealously guarded League of Nations, did not make it through the Senate. The League would have to begin its work without American participation. As he left Paris, Wilson knew he had been party to an imperfect settlement. "As no one is satisfied," he said, "it makes me hope we have made a just peace, but it is all in the lap of the gods."

Over the following year, separate treaties were concluded with Germany's former allies, Austria, Bulgaria, Hungary and Turkey. Reparations, disarmament and loss of territory were again common themes in The Treaty of Saint-Germain-en-Laye, which dealt with Austria in September 1919; the Treaty of Neuilly (Bulgaria, November 1919); and the Treaty of Trianon (Hungary, June 1920). The Covenant of the League of Nations was enshrined in all three. Recognition of the kingdom of Serbs, Croats and Slovenes – the future Yugoslavia – was also included, a deliberate attempt to secure protection for minorities in these ethnically diverse states.

Treaty of Sèvres

The last of the treaties, signed at Sèvres on 10 August 1920, confirmed the loss of Turkey's Arab territory in accordance with the clandestine discussions that took place between Britain and France in 1916. Syria and Lebanon became French mandates, Mesopotamia and Palestine came under British control. The Hijaz, now Saudi Arabia, became an independent state under Sherif Hussein of Mecca. Greece gained a sizeable chunk of Turkey's European land, and Italy also profited at the country's expense. An independent Armenia was established. Such terms were anathema to the military commander Mustafa Kemal, who opposed the conciliatory stance adopted by the ruling sultanate. Kemal proclaimed a new nationalist government based in Ankara, and as president vowed to overturn the treaty's impositions and restore Turkey to its former strength. After reclaiming Armenia, he waged war against Greece, at the conclusion of which, in October 1922, he became head of a modern, reforming republic ready to take its place in the western world. Lloyd George acquiesced, and a new treaty was signed in Lausanne in July 1923, releasing Turkey from the obligations of the Sèvres agreement and ending the postwar round of agreements that had begun four years earlier.

"As no one is satisfied. It makes me hope we have made a just peace, but it is all in the lap of the gods." President Wilson

Below: Allied leaders pictured during the postwar peace talks. (l to r) Marshal Foch; Georges Clemenceau (French Prime Minister); David Lloyd George (British Prime Minister); Baron Sidney Sonnino (Italian Foreign Secretary), and Vittorio Orlando (Italian Prime Minister).

Europe After World War I

Iceland
(Danish)

*Norwegian
Sea*

N

Faeroes
(Danish)

FINLAND

Helsinki
Petrograd
Oslo
Stockholm
Tallinn
ESTONIA

*North
Sea*

Riga
LATVIA

Glasgow   Edinburgh
DENMARK
LITHUANIA
Copenhagen
Kaunas
USSR

UNITED
Danzig
(free city under
League of Nations)
Königsberg

Dublin
IRELAND
Liverpool
KINGDOM
Amsterdam
Hamburg
East
Prussia

Birmingham
NETHERLANDS
Berlin
Warsaw
Brest Litovsk

Bristol
London
GERMANY
POLAND
Kiev

Brussels
Calais
BELGIUM
Cracow
Lvov

Rhine
LUX.
Frankfurt
Prague

SAAR
(autonomous under
League of Nations)
CZECHOSLOVAKIA

ATLANTIC
Paris
Vienna

OCEAN
Orléans
AUSTRIA
HUNGARY
Budapest
ROMANIA

Bern
SWITZ.
F R A N C E
Lyon
Trieste
Bucharest
Bordeaux
Milan
Venice
Belgrade
Danube

Genoa
Zara
YUGOSLAVIA
BULGARIA

MONACO
SAN
MARINO
*Adriatic
Sea*
ANDORRA
Marseille
Sofia

PORTUGAL
ALBANIA

Corsica
Rome
I T A L Y
GREECE
*Aegean
Sea*

Barcelona
Lisbon
Madrid
SPAIN
Naples

Balearic Is.
Sardinia

Alicante
M e d i t e r r a n e a n
Athens

Cádiz
Gibraltar
(British)
Almeria
Sicily
(Italian
occupied)

Tangier
(International zone)
Algiers
A l g e r i a
Tunis
Tunisia
Malta
S e a

Top left: **The 1st Battalion of the Scots Guard parade along Oxford Street on their return from Germany in March 1919. They were met at St Pancras Station by the massed bands of the Brigade of Guards and marched to Knightsbridge Barracks past the cheering crowds.**

Top right: **The first Armistice Day commemoration was held on 11 November 1919. As crowds gathered in London these passengers watch from a bus at Bank.**

Above left: **The Armistice Silence is observed at Piccadilly Circus.**

Above right: **Germans leaving London to return to their homeland.**

Below: **This US contingent were some of the 15,000 troops who took part in the Victory Parade through London on 19 July 1919. It was part of a four-day celebration which included thanksgivingservices and festivals.**

Top: **The first permanent war memorial was erected in Cirencester Street, West London.**

Above: **General Pershing receives a hero's welcome when he visits London after the war.**

Index

Above: Photographs taken before and after the war showing the Rue de Lille, or Rijseltraat, the principal street of Ypres, looking towards the famous Cloth Hall.

Below: The Third Battle of Ypres, resulted in nearly half a million casualties to all sides, and only a few miles of ground won by Allied forces. During the course of the war the town was all but obliterated by the artillery fire.